Markus Schuler

Frederick Leven

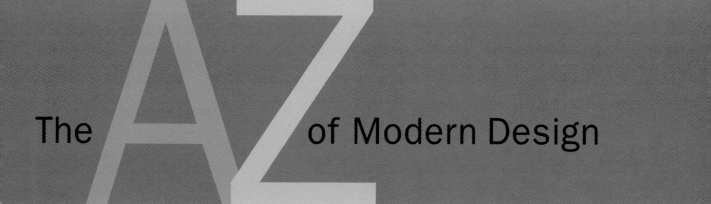

The AZ of Modern Design

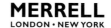

MERRELL

LONDON · NEW YORK

ABOUT THIS BOOK

The A–Z of Modern Design is an authoritative, accessible and easy-to-use guide to modern design that provides detailed commentaries, illuminating analyses and essential background information on more than 300 influential designers and manufacturers, both past and present, from all over the world. The products featured range from furniture, household items, lighting, glassware, metalware and ceramics to automobiles and computers, as well as other mechanical and electrical appliances. The entries are organized alphabetically and include several features for ease of reference:

A simple **colour-coded system** of entries – individual designers and design studios in green, manufacturers in red – ensures quick access to information. Details of location and areas of expertise or interest and, where applicable, website addresses appear at the top of each entry.

Easy-to-follow **sidebars** in each entry provide company histories, designer biographies and chronological listings of products.

Names in **bold type** in the text refer to entries on other designers, studios or manufacturers.

Arrows ▶ lead the reader to **illustrations** of products in other entries, offering easy access to additional information.

About the Authors

Bernd Polster is a writer specializing in design and cultural history. He regularly contributes to the *Financial Times Deutschland* and the *Frankfurter Rundschau* and is editor of the *Designlexicon* series.

Claudia Neumann is a journalist and the author of *Design Calendar* and *Designlexicon Italy*. She is also co-founder of a PR agency that specializes in design, visual arts and architecture.

Markus Schuler writes about product and graphic design and fashion. He also works as a PR consultant.

Frederick Leven has contributed to several books on design. He currently works at the StadtMuseum Bonn.

INTRODUCTION

by Bernd Polster

The *Blow Up* series of household items that was designed for the manufacturer **Alessi** by the Brazilian brothers **Fernando and Humberto Campana** consists of a range of objects made from thin metal rods welded together to give the impression of having been combined in a purely accidental or random fashion, like pick-up sticks, one on top of another. The series includes items as diverse as a table, a basket, a mat and an umbrella stand. The stainless steel from which the individual pieces are fashioned is reminiscent of offcuts from the factory floor. Indeed, among the defining features of the Campanas' work is the use of waste products and recycled and industrial materials. In this case, the brothers' ingenuity has produced particularly unusual and striking sculptural objects that not only have a practical function but are regarded by many as works of art, evocative of archaic cult objects. The Campanas are renowned for rule-breaking, for their disregard of the boundaries between disciplines and cultures and for consistently nudging 'design' into the realm of 'art'. This impulse to redefine or even obliterate traditional frontiers is illuminating for the issues it raises concerning the very nature of the design process, the meaning of the term 'design' and the status of the designer in modern society.

The tremendous surge of popular interest in design in recent years (particularly since the 1980s, when design began to permeate almost every sphere of everyday life) has perhaps tended to obscure the fact that it is a young discipline. The modern concept of 'design', in so far as it refers generally to the creation of objects with a practical function as well as aesthetic characteristics, arose out of a particular set of social and economic circumstances that developed in the West from the late eighteenth century onwards. First in Britain, and somewhat later in Continental Europe and the United States, the Industrial Revolution initiated a shift from craft to mass production and with it a separation of the design process from the actual manufacture of an object.

Aside from the impact of the Industrial Revolution, an equally important factor in the development of design was the rise of what may be termed autonomous art. In the early twentieth century, following the example of the Arts and Crafts Movement in nineteenth-century England, groups of artists in German-speaking countries in particular began to establish workshops for applied art. Many of the members of these groups in, for example, Dresden, Munich and Vienna were strongly identified with the artistic avant garde that arose around the same time. It was from this creative *mélange* that the first designers, or 'creators of form', emerged. (The words 'design' and 'designers' were not used widely until the second half of the twentieth century.) This was a time of tremendous innovation and change, an age when dominant ideologies were being challenged. The climate was ideal for the nurturing of a generation of highly talented and creative designers, and it produced such outstanding figures as **Josef Hoffmann**, **Charles Rennie Mackintosh**, Henry van de Velde and **Frank Lloyd Wright**. The question of industrial manufacture was, however, largely ignored in their work.

In 1907 the Deutscher Werkbund was founded by a group of industrialists, architects and designers. It sought to improve the quality of products by encouraging closer collaboration between designers and manufacturers in the hitherto alien worlds of art and industry. The bold experiment led to a heated debate – one that remains unresolved to this day – between representatives of artistic freedom and advocates of mass production. At one end of the spectrum is the free-spirited Bohemianism symbolized by such personalities as **Eileen Gray** and **Ron Arad**; at the other end is the more restrained approach typically adopted by designers employed by such large companies as **Nokia** and **Sony**. The indeterminate middle ground is populated by designers of every conceivable type. It is doubtless this category that, in the final analysis, comes to define 'the designer' as a species.

Despite the opposition that clearly exists between, on the one hand, the creation of works of art and, on the other, the functional and profit-orientated design of everyday objects, the two nevertheless have a great deal in

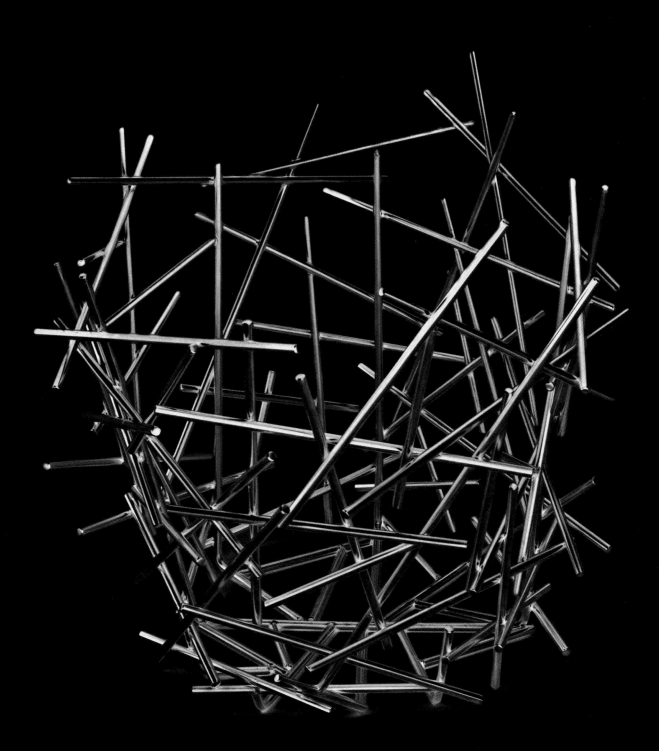

Blow Up fruit basket by Fernando and
Humberto Campana for Alessi, 2004

common, not least the need for innovation. Specialists are required for this task, and it was for this reason that the industrial 'creators of form' were from the very beginning experts in disregarding traditional boundaries: not only did they transcend the boundaries of conventional perception and of recognized professions, but they also ignored the borders between countries. And here there was also a parallel with the world of industry, which at precisely the same time was experiencing its first wave of globalization. **Thonet**, a German furniture manufacturer with a global distribution network, is a prime example of this development.

Following the end of the First World War the Dutch avant-garde artistic movement De Stijl and the Bauhaus school of art, architecture and design in Weimar, Germany (established in 1919 by the architect **Walter Gropius**) radicalized the new concept of design and gave it a distinctly international dimension. With such students, teachers and lecturers as the Hungarian **Marcel Breuer**, the Russian Vasily Kandinsky and the Dutchman Theo van Doesburg, the Bauhaus was in every respect a multicultural project, much like its reincarnation three decades later as the Hochschule für Gestaltung in Ulm, which was profoundly influenced by the Swiss designer **Max Bill**, the Dutchman **Hans Gugelot** and the Argentinian Tomás Maldonado. Another three decades on, the Milan-based Memphis design group, which helped Post-modernism achieve a breakthrough (partly by encouraging similar rebellions in Germany, Britain and other countries), was also highly cosmopolitan. Its protagonists included such designers as **Andrea Branzi** and **Michele De Lucchi** from Italy, **Michael Graves** from the United States, Hans Hollein and **Ettore Sottsass** from Austria, **George J. Sowden** from Britain and **Masanori Umeda** from Japan.

In the United States Henry **Ford** launched the *Model T* automobile in 1908. Five years later, in order to keep the cost of its cars as low as possible, the Ford Motor Company introduced the moving assembly line. By the 1920s, however, consumers were beginning to favour style over cheaper, standardized products. The profession of 'industrial designer' emerged to meet the demands of mass consumption. The design pioneers of the New World – among them Norman Bel Geddes, **Henry Dreyfuss**, **Raymond Loewy** and **Walter Dorwin Teague** – tended to come from theatre design or advertising backgrounds. They saw themselves as an extension of corporate America. They were thus the antithesis of Europe's radical and in large part politically motivated Modernists, although this is not to suggest that they were not influenced by European design. The world of design was affected by immigration as much as American society itself was, as reflected in the institutions that became synonymous with the avant garde in design in the United States: the Cranbrook Academy in Bloomfield Hills, Michigan, where **Harry Bertoia**, **Charles Eames**, Florence **Knoll** and **Eero Saarinen** either studied or taught, and the Museum of Modern Art (MoMA) in New York, which embraced the tenets of Modernism and functionalism as exemplified by the work of the Bauhaus émigrés. The term 'International Style' was coined. New York's status at this time as the design capital of the world was linked closely to its being a melting pot of cultures – just as its successors, Milan and London, are today.

Raymond Loewy, one of the most successful early American industrial designers, was a French immigrant. He was the first to personify the charismatic and cosmopolitan all-rounder, as represented today by **Philippe Starck** or **Karim Rashid**. Loewy perfected the commercial form of the design studio and was the first to establish branches abroad. In these times of globalization, this practice has now become the norm, particularly for Anglo-American studios such as **Ideo** and Pentagram. Loewy exported not only his unique way of working but also the name of the profession. In 1950 the Swedish designer **Sigvard Bernadotte** founded one of Europe's first studios for industrial design in Copenhagen. Even the lecturers at the Hochschule für Gestaltung in Ulm began to wonder whether they might perhaps be 'designers'. At the **Braun** company, the German manufacturer of electrical and audio-visual equipment with a clean, functionalist appearance, however, they still talked about *Produktgestaltung* ('product shaping').

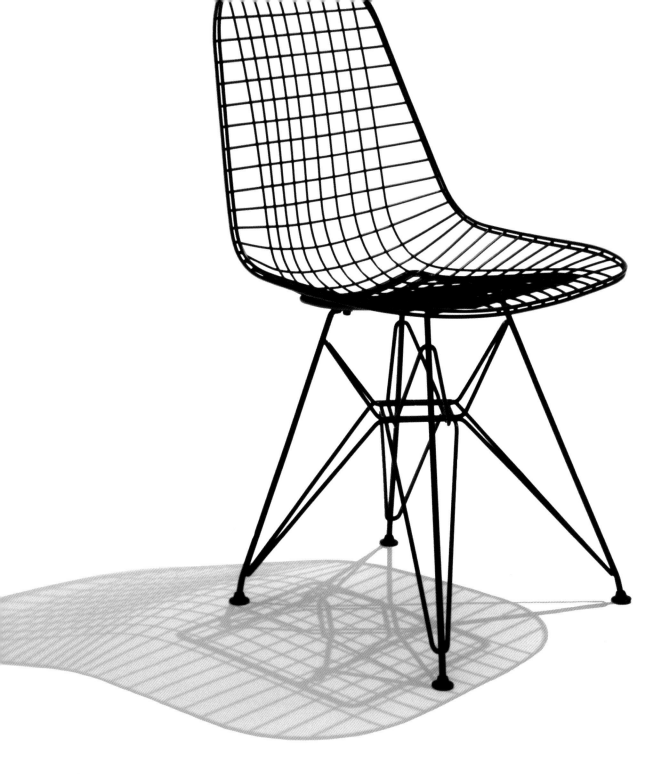

DKR wire chair by Charles and Ray Eames
for Herman Miller, 1951

Ultimately, the successful export of the concept of 'design' was a three-way transaction among the United States, Scandinavia and Italy. In 1954 the *Design in Scandinavia* exhibition opened in the United States and toured North America for the following three years. Possibly the most ambitious design campaign of all time, it inspired a series of similar exhibitions and created a huge boom in the sale of Scandinavian products. Up to this point it would not have occurred to **Arne Jacobsen**, **Bruno Mathsson** or **Tapio Wirkkala** to consider themselves 'designers'; they were architects, artists, craftsmen, 'creators of form'. It was only with the newly invented expression 'Scandinavian Design', and the consequent increase in commissions, that this perception began to change. Older terms gradually disappeared. Thus, in Denmark people began to speak only of *Dansk design*, and in Finland, Helsinki's tradition-rich Museum of Applied Art became known as the Design Museum. 'Design', an international loan word (derived originally from the French *dessin* and the Italian *disegno*, both meaning 'drawing'), was finally introduced into the Western world in the 1950s, a development that was consistent with the trend towards international marketing and the policies of design councils, which had been founded in a number of countries including Britain and West Germany in order to promote 'good design'.

Italy, where the supposedly 'Nordic' aesthetics had first been discovered (*Design in Scandinavia* consisted in large part of products that had been awarded prizes in Milan), followed the Scandinavian model and became a new design Mecca. It was from there that not only such apparently irreconcilable concepts as 'design classics' and 'Anti-Design' originated, but also the impetus for the final stage in the globalization of design. This took the innocuous form of a whistling bird on the spout of a kettle, a product by the American designer Michael Graves. Alessi launched the kettle in the mid-1980s under the name *Bird*. It was the first 'designer object' to be sold in large numbers, and it heralded a new strategy that transformed the upmarket manufacturer of metalware from Milan into the world's very first 'designer brand'. Alessi put its faith in author design, a philosophy that was subsequently to spread throughout the world. In the 1950s there was only one Raymond Loewy; today there are dozens. The concept of the star designer has extended as far as the automobile industry. Whereas for decades designers used to work in anonymous seclusion, nowadays the leading figures are very much in the limelight and are in great demand. Such prominent personalities as Chris Bird or Murat Günak change 'sides' in much the same way as Premier League football players. 'Design' has become an international buzzword, infused with glamorous significance.

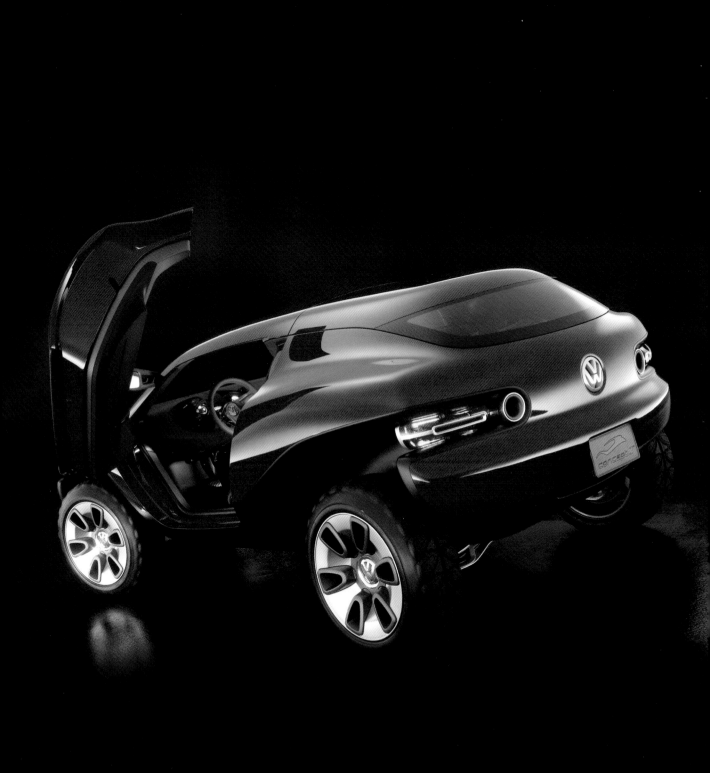

Concept T off-road coupé (concept)
by Volkswagen, 2004

FEATURED DESIGNERS

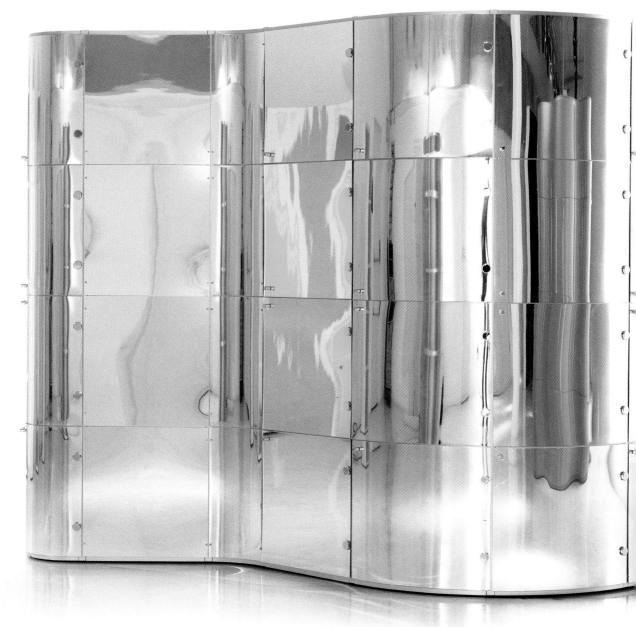

Paesaggi Italiani storage system
by Massimo Morozzi for Edra, 2003

FEATURED MANUFACTURERS

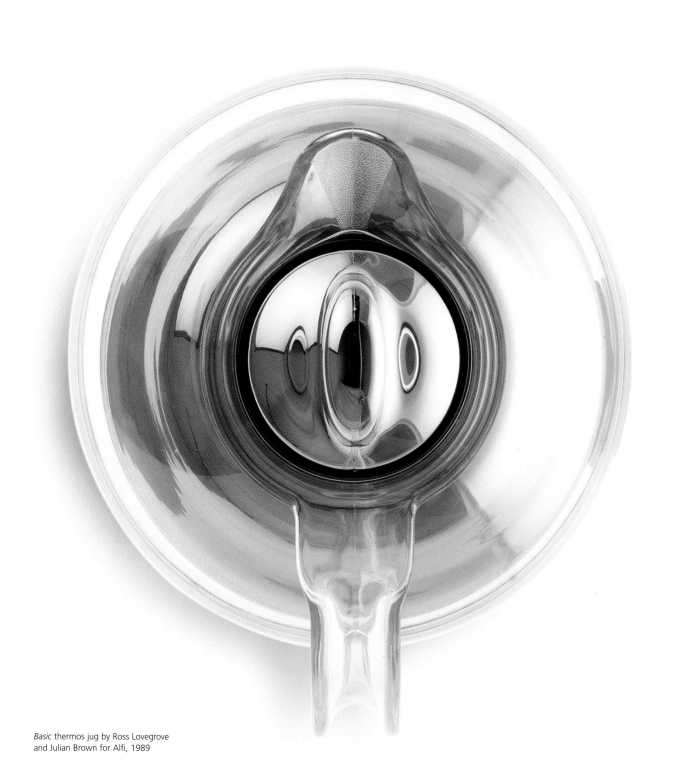

Basic thermos jug by Ross Lovegrove
and Julian Brown for Alfi, 1989

Alvar Aalto, *42* armchair, 1932

In the early 1920s the architect Alvar Aalto visited a Latvian furniture company that manufactured laminated wooden seats for trams. Aalto, who was interested in curved lines, gradually began to experiment with this pliable material. Over a period of many years he created a series of chairs, among them his C-shaped cantilever armchair, perhaps one of his most comfortable models, which he varied over and over again.

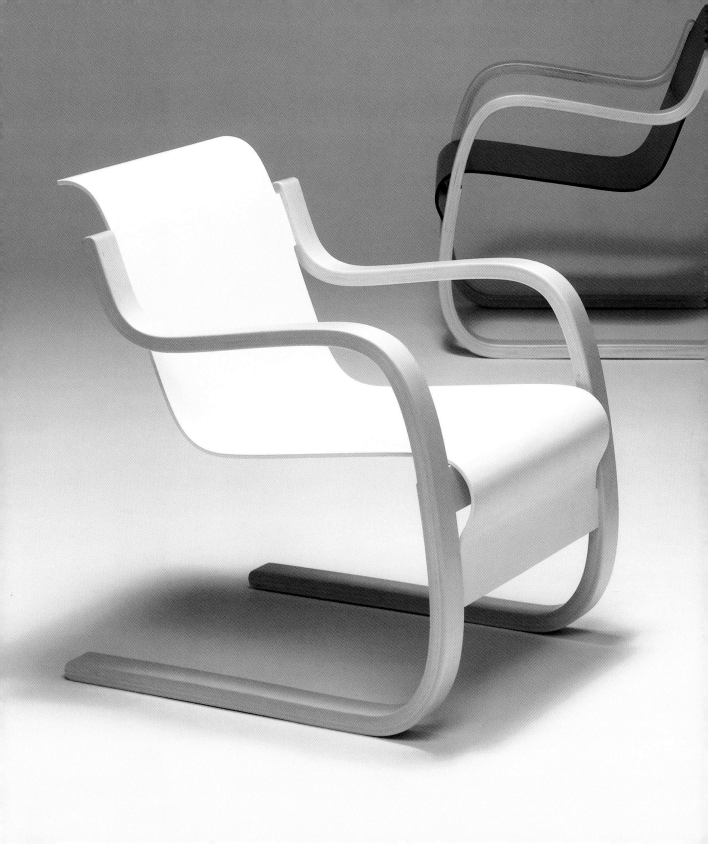

Alvar **Aalto**

Finland I Architect and furniture and glass designer I www.alvaraalto.fi I www.artek.fi

Alvar Aalto is regarded as one of the giants of twentieth-century architecture and design. From the mid-1920s he worked closely with his wife, architect Aino Aalto (formerly Aino Marsio). Around the same time, he began experimenting with laminated wood, a versatile material that he later used to produce chairs for a sanatorium in Paimio. Model *41* (also known as the *Paimio* chair) was revolutionary for its day, particularly in its striking combination of a bentwood frame and an S-shaped seat. The design of this piece was influenced by ▶**Marcel Breuer**'s *Wassily* chair. Whereas Breuer used tubular steel in his chair, Aalto's genius lay in his reintroduction of wood as a design medium and in his promotion of it as an inspiring, user-friendly material. The *42* armchair (▶p. 17), the wooden equivalent of **Ludwig Mies van der Rohe**'s cantilever chair, was something of a sensation. It was followed by the *43* cantilever chaise longue, with its curvilinear silhouette, and by the *406* chaise longue, a commercially successful variation of the same design principle. The *60* stool, with its L-shaped legs, designed for the lecture room at the Viipuri Library, is a surprisingly simple and stable solution to the problem of joining vertical legs to a horizontal seat.

One of the hallmarks of Aalto's furniture was his use of irregularly bent lines, a feature he incorporated repeatedly into his work, using a wide range of materials. These lines became a symbol of the move towards a softer, more natural and humanistic functionalism, all of which came finally to be encapsulated in the term 'Made in Scandinavia'. The large, undulating wooden panels of Aalto's Finnish Pavilion were presented at the *New York World's Fair* in 1939 and gave the new style a public forum. Glass, a medium capable of taking on almost any conceivable form, was in keeping with Aalto's organic vocabulary. The *Savoy* vase (originally called *Eskimo Woman's Leather Trousers*), today manufactured under the name *Aalto* by **Iittala**, achieved considerable fame. Integral to Aalto's overall architectural vision was his use of artificial lighting: he designed a large number of lamps, although very few of them went into serial production.

1898 Born in Kuortane, near Jyväskylä

1921 Graduates in architecture from Helsinki University of Technology

1923 Begins practising as an architect in Jyväskylä, later in Turku (1927) and Helsinki (1933)

1924 Marries architect Aino Marsio (died 1949)

1927 Begins experimenting with wooden furniture; Viipuri Library (to 1935)

1929 Paimio Tuberculosis Sanatorium (to 1933)

1935 Establishes furniture manufacturer Artek

1937 Finnish Pavilion for *Exposition Internationale des Arts et Techniques dans la Vie Moderne*, Paris

1938 Exhibits at Museum of Modern Art (MoMA), New York

1939 Finnish Pavilion for *New York World's Fair*

1952 Marries architect Elissa Mäkiniemi (died 1994)

1976 Dies in Helsinki

1998 Exhibition held at MoMA, New York

Products

1929 Stackable chair in birch wood

1931 *40* armchair in tubular steel and moulded plywood; *41* armchair (also *Paimio*) in moulded plywood

1932 *42* armchair, first wooden cantilever chair (▶ p. 17)

1933 *Flower of Riihimäki* vase; *60* stool and *65* chair with L-shaped legs

1936 *Savoy* vase and glass series (now *Aalto*); *43* chaise longue; *901* tea trolley; *100* screen

1938 *406* chaise longue (final version 1947)

1939 *Aalto-Flower* bowl collection

1947 *612* chair with Y-shaped legs

1954 *X 600* stool; *A 331* ceiling lamp

1959 *A 810* standard lamp

Products at Artek and **Herman Miller**

18

1 *Savoy* vase (now *Aalto*), 1936
2 *A 331* ceiling lamp, 1954
3 Bowl (*Savoy* glass series), 1936
4 *901* tea trolley, 1936
5 *41* armchair (also *Paimio*), 1931
6 *100* screen, 1936
7 *43* chaise longue, 1936
8 *60* stool, 1933

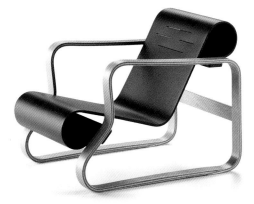

5

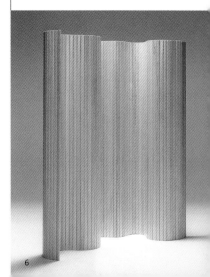

6

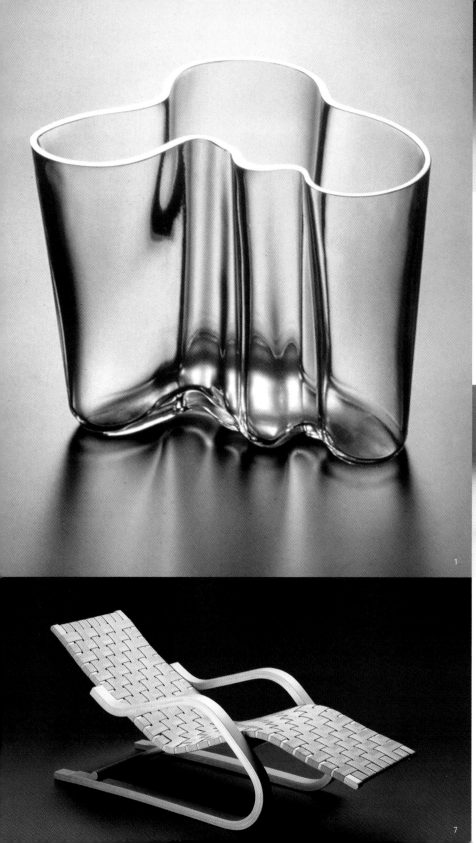

1

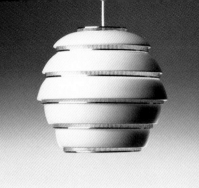

2

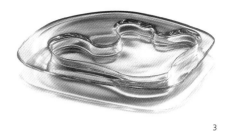

3

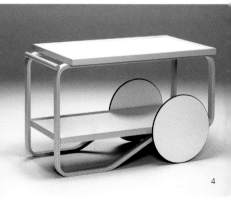

4

7

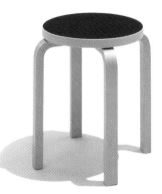

8

Eero **Aarnio**

Finland | Furniture designer | www.eero-aarnio.com | www.adelta.de

"Design a plastic chair" was the commission Eero Aarnio received at the beginning of the 1960s from Asko, Finland's biggest furniture company. Aarnio's response to this brief was to create an object that heralded an entirely new generation of chairs. *Ball*, an imposing fibreglass sphere resting on an iron base, looked as futuristic as a space capsule – a zone of peace and tranquility protected from the outside world. He followed up this initial success with a series of plastic furniture, sculptures for living, with such striking names as *Serpentine*, *Bubble* and *Tomato*. Aarnio's early designs brought together the experimental currents of the 1960s, such as the uninhibited use of plastic and shocking colour, and the iconoclastic disregard for hitherto valid design conventions. This playfully experimental approach was also reflected in his designs for children's furniture. The consistent use of organic shapes in Aarnio's chairs led to the complete fusion of the seat, frame and legs. In addition, plastic furniture was in keeping with the trend towards a more flexible style of living. *Pastille*, a modern reinterpretation of the rocking chair, is another of Aarnio's *tours de force*. For the second time in his career he had developed a completely new type of chair.

Although Aarnio's polished industrial style was tantamount to an attack on successful Scandinavian design in the 1950s, his rounded forms were nevertheless a continuation of that tradition. Overnight, his furniture designs became icons of a new consumer culture. However, the oil crisis in the early 1970s made it quite clear that the future did not lie entirely with polyester and polyethylene. In 1979 the production of *Ball* was discontinued (although it was resumed for a brief period in the 1980s). As in the days before his spectacular successes, Aarnio turned to natural materials. It was only towards the end of the twentieth century, when the 1960s lifestyle became popular again, that his work enjoyed a revival. The production of his early designs has been resumed, and new furniture has been added to his range. This innovative Finnish designer is once again working with plastic and experimenting with new manufacturing processes.

20

1 *Ball* chair, 1963

2 *Copacabana* table, 1991

3 *Pony* seat, 1973

4 *Bubble* hanging chair, 1968

5 *Pastille* chair, 1967

6 *Parabel* table, 1994

7 *Formula* chair, 1998

8 *Focus* chair, 2002

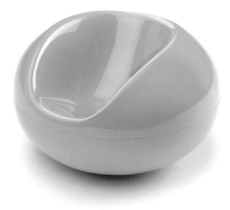

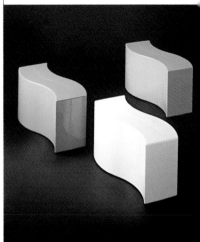

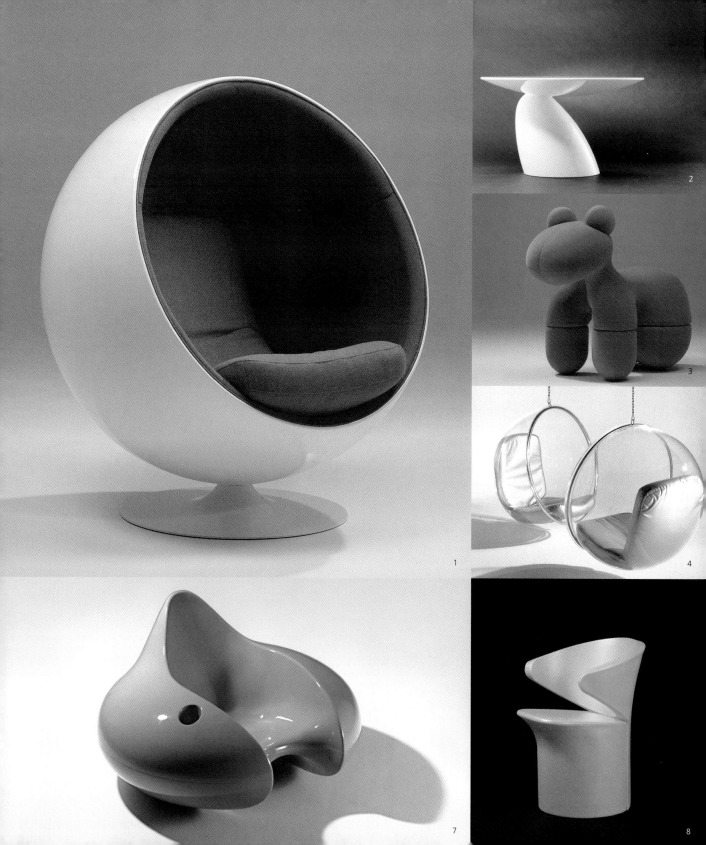

1

2

3

4

7

8

Agape

Italy I Agape Srl, Mantua I Manufacturer of bathroom fittings I **www.agapedesign.it**

Agape, from the Greek for 'divine love', is the word that the Italian brothers Emanuele and Giampaolo Benedini felt appropriate to describe the company they founded in the early 1970s. Their aim was to create a poetic vision of the bathroom, a space that, at that time, was regarded simply as a room for getting wet. For Agape, however, the bathroom is a place where each individual element has a distinct meaning in the contexts of comfort and architecture. Aesthetically pleasing washbasins made from traditional ceramics are an important part of the range, to which the company has recently added basins of marble, glass and even wood, as in the *Woodline* series by Benedini Associati. Agape has thus introduced materials into the bathroom that had hitherto been confined to living spaces. The company's accessories and small pieces of furniture, such as *Barralibera*, the versatile storage system by Marco Ferreri, also blur the distinction between the bathroom and living areas. Agape has a reputation for its excellent technical resources and for its incorporation of motifs from culture and nature. It has collaborated with such leading Italian and international designers as **Enzo Mari**, Fabio Bortolani, Giuseppe Pasquali, **Angelo Mangiarotti**, **Vico Magistretti** and **Konstantin Grcic**. In 2002 Grcic presented *Mach*, a range of minimalist bathroom accessories.

22

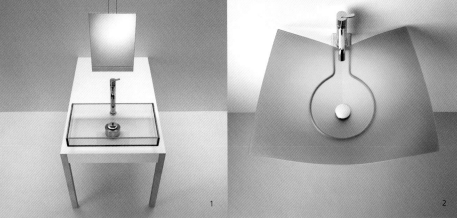

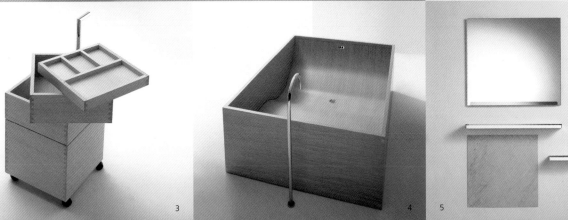

Werner **Aisslinger**

Germany | Furniture designer | www.aisslinger.de

In 1997 Werner Aisslinger's *Juli* chair was selected for the permanent collection of the Museum of Modern Art (MoMA) in New York; it was the first German chair to have been included for more than thirty years, and its selection caused something of a sensation. With its tulip form, the height-adjustable swivel chair resembles an offspring of **Arne Jacobsen**'s *Swan*. *Juli* is, however, created from a modern material – polyurethane foam, as used in the automobile industry. Aisslinger is famous for his bold use of unusual materials: his *Soft Cell* furniture collection was developed from a gel conventionally used in operating theatres. Other projects are equally daring: *Loftcube*, for example, is a portable living unit suitable for large cities. Aisslinger showcased the prototype by placing it on various rooftops overlooking Berlin. This innovative designer currently has a number of pieces of furniture in the collections of such prestigious Italian manufacturers as **Zanotta**, **Magis** and **Porro**.

Modular systems are a speciality of Aisslinger. His very first system, the *Endless Shelf*, produced by ▸ Porro, became a commercial success. He has also created a number of similar storage systems for ▸ **Interlübke**. Aisslinger's distinctive, functional style can be seen in several of Germany's pedestrian precincts in the showrooms he has designed for the mobile telephone company e-Plus.

1964 Born in Nördlingen

1989 Works for **Ron Arad** and **Jasper Morrison** in London

1991 Works for **Michele De Lucchi** in Milan

1993 Graduates from Hochschule der Künste, Berlin; opens office in Berlin

1994 Teaches design at Hochschule der Künste, Berlin

1996 Receives Bundespreis Produktdesign for *Endless Shelf* shelf system

1997 *Juli* chair selected for permanent collection of MoMA, New York

1998 Appointed professor at Hochschule für Gestaltung, Karlsruhe

1999 Presents *Soft Cell* furniture collection (seating with gel upholstery; studio project); *Soft Cell* selected for permanent collection of Vitra Design Museum, Weil am Rhein; designs flagship store with virtual showroom for **Mercedes-Benz** in Frankfurt

2003 Designs prototype of *Loftcube*, a modular, portable living unit

Products

1994 *Endless Shelf* modular shelf system for ▸ **Porro** (with plastic panels, 1997)

1996 *Juli* chair for **Cappellini**; showroom system for e-Plus

2000 *Soft* chaise longue for ▸ **Zanotta**

2001 *Plus Unit* drawer system for **Magis**

2002 *Case* container trolley and *Cube* cabinet system for ▸ **Interlübke**

2003 *Nic Chair* for Magis; *Gel Chair* for Cappellini

1 Chair (*Soft Cell* collection), 1999
2 *Case* container trolley, 2002
3 *Plus Unit* drawer system, 2001
4 *Juli* chair, 1996
5 *Loftcube* living unit, 2003

23

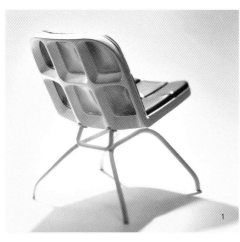

1

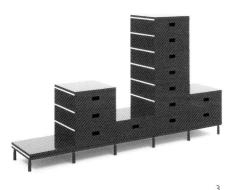

2

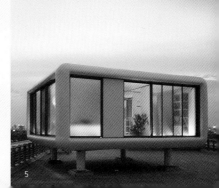

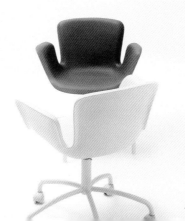

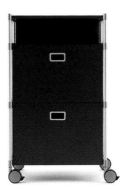

3
4
5

Franco **Albini**

Italy | Architect and furniture designer

Hailed by his friend and colleague **Alessandro Mendini** as "the great master of modern architecture in Italy", Franco Albini was a notable architect and exhibition designer, a dedicated Rationalist whose work owed much to the principles of the Bauhaus. He was also one of the protagonists of modern Italian furniture design. His designs are distinguished by their minimalism and functionalism as well as by an emphasis on the elements of construction. An early example is a transparent radio from the late 1930s, the components of which have simply been pressed between two rectangular panes of glass. The design was, however, too radical for its time and did not go into production.

Despite their precision and elegance, Albini's designs never seem anaemic or brittle. This is also true of his shelf systems, which he started designing in the late 1930s. These took the form of glass shelves in wooden or metal frames, suspended from chains, which gave them a dual function as shelves and space dividers. Albini later developed variants of this system, including the versatile *LB 7* shelving unit, which was designed to be wedged between floor and ceiling.

Following the Second World War, Albini took an active part in debates on the social role of architecture and design. He was editor of the magazine *Casabella*, a member of the Congrès Internationaux d'Architecture Moderne (CIAM) and a professor of architecture in both Venice and Turin. During this time he also continued to design furniture that bridged the gap between industrial manufacture and craftsmanship. An example is the angular *Luisa* chair for the Poggi company. With its careful construction and meticulous attention to detail, it more closely resembles miniature architecture than a piece of furniture. The *Margherita* wicker armchair (for Bonacina), the expressive *Fiorenza* armchair (for ▶ **Arflex**) and, in particular, the glass-topped desk revived (as *Albini*) by **Knoll**, all show his skilful use of form and material. In the 1960s Albini's designs included door handles for Olivari and lamps for Arteluce. One of his most ambitious projects at the beginning of the decade (in conjunction with Franca Helg and Bob Noorda) was the design of stations on Line 1 of the Milan underground and their signage systems.

1 *LB 7* shelf, 1950
2 *PS 16* rocking chaise longue, 1956
3 *PL 19* armchair, 1954
4 *TL 2* table, 1950
5 *Albini Desk*, 1958
6 *Cicognino* occasional table, 1954
7 *MB 66* sideboard, 1966
8 *Luisa* armchair, 1954

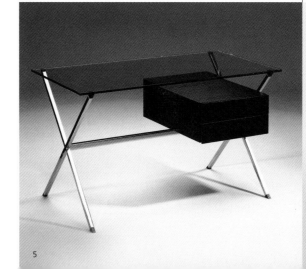

5

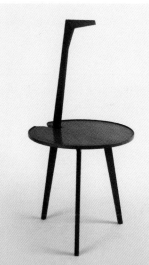

6

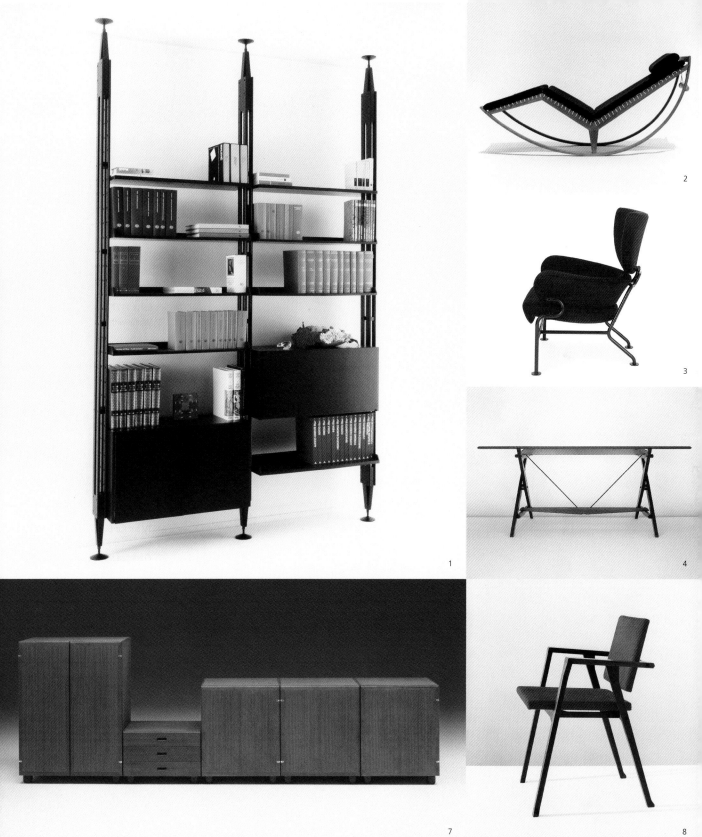

1

2

3

4

7

8

Alessi

Italy | Alessi SpA, Crusinallo | Manufacturer of kitchen and household items | **www.alessi.com**

Alessi *is* design: the prestigious northern Italian manufacturer has continued to represent this simple equation ever since 1990, the date of the launch of **Philippe Starck**'s influential *Juicy Salif* spider-legged lemon press. In the 1980s the company's owner, Alberto Alessi, initiated a gentle revolution in the kitchen by redefining this hitherto purely functional space as the welcoming, even cultural centre of the home. Alessi presented the *Tea & Coffee Piazza* project (tea and coffee services in the form of Post-modern pieces of 'miniature architecture'), designed by leading international architects, including the Alessi consultants **Alessandro Mendini, Aldo Rossi, Michael Graves**, Robert Venturi and Charles Jencks. At the Milan International Furniture Fair in 2003 the company displayed its *Tea & Coffee Towers* project, featuring designs by such creative talents as Zaha Hadid, Toyo Ito, David Chipperfield, Greg Lynn and ▶**Jean Nouvel**.

The company was founded at the beginning of the 1920s as a metal workshop. From the 1950s to the 1970s it continued to have a strong reputation for its excellent metalwork, and it supplied breadbaskets, sugar bowls and fruit dishes – still considered modern classics – to international hotels, restaurants and airlines. Alessi now has a wide range of products, and the legendary label is famous for its impeccably designed, high-quality stainless steel products, including espresso coffee makers by ▶Aldo Rossi and ▶**Richard Sapper**, cookware by ▶**Massimo Morozzi** and cutlery by **Ettore Sottsass** and **Achille Castiglioni**. The subsidiary brand Officina Alessi concentrates on the manufacture of innovative products in limited editions. Household articles in wood, designed by ▶**Andrea Branzi** and others, are sold under the *Twergi* label, which was introduced at the end of the 1980s. The *Family Follows Fiction* collection brings together typically playful plastic accessories, such as the bulbous *Mary Biscuit* biscuit boxes by **Stefano Giovannoni** and Mendini's *Anna G.* corkscrew. Alessi has also recently moved into new areas. The *Il Bagno Alessi* bathroom series was launched in 2002 and, a season later, the *Telefono Alessi* in conjunction with Siemens, both by Giovannoni. Alberto Alessi is a great promoter of young talent: many projects involving young designers are developed in his Alessi Study Centre in Milan.

26

1 *Anna G.* corkscrew, 1994
2 *Caccia* cutlery, 1938
3 *Mary Biscuit* biscuit box, 1995
4 *SG 67* hand-held vacuum cleaner, 2004
5 *826* breadbasket, 1951
6 *JM 24* wine cooler, 2004
7 *5070* oil and vinegar set, 1978
8 *Fruit Mama* fruit bowl, 1993

1921	Established by Giovanni Alessi Anghini as foundry and metal workshop
1932	Carlo Alessi joins company
1938	Experiments with steel
1977	Collaborates with **Alessandro Mendini**
1983	Launches *Officina Alessi* product line
1990	Opens Alessi Study Centre in Milan
1991	Launches *Family Follows Fiction* project
2002	Begins product development for bathrooms, clocks, watches and telecommunications

Products

1938	*Caccia* cutlery by Luigi Caccia Dominioni and Pier Giacomo Castiglioni
1945	*Bombé* coffee service by Carlo Alessi
1951	*826* breadbasket by Ufficio Tecnico Alessi
1952	*370* fruit basket by Ufficio Tecnico Alessi
1965	Wall clock by ▶ **Achille Castiglioni**
1970	*7690 Spirale* ashtray by Achille Castiglioni
1978	*9090* espresso maker by ▶ **Richard Sapper**; *5070* oil and vinegar set by **Ettore Sottsass**
1979	*Boston* bar accessories by ▶ Ettore Sottsass
1984	*Bird* kettle by ▶ **Michael Graves**; *La Conica* espresso maker by ▶ **Aldo Rossi**
1985	*Pasta Set* cooking pot by ▶ **Massimo Morozzi**
1988	*La Cupola* espresso maker by ▶ Aldo Rossi
1990	*Juicy Salif* lemon squeezer by **Philippe Starck**
1993	*Fruit Mama* fruit bowl and *Merdolino* toilet brush by ▶ **Stefano Giovannoni**
1994	*Anna G.* corkscrew by Alessandro Mendini
1995	*Mary Biscuit* biscuit box by Stefano Giovannoni
1997	*Cobán* espresso machine by ▶ Richard Sapper
2000	*Babyboop* bowl by **Ron Arad**; *Solferino* fruit basket by ▶ **Andrea Branzi**
2002	*Il Bagno Alessi* bathroom series by ▶ Stefano Giovannoni
2003	*Mami* tableware and kitchen accessories collection by ▶ Stefano Giovannoni; *Strelka* cutlery by ▶ **Marc Newson**; *Oval* tray by ▶ **Josef Hoffmann** (re-edition); *Tea & Coffee Towers* service by ▶ **Jean Nouvel** and others; *Alessandro M.* corkscrew by ▶ Alessandro Mendini
2004	*JM 24* wine cooler by **Jasper Morrison**; *SG 66* kitchen scales and *SG 67* hand-held vacuum cleaner by ▶Stefano Giovannoni; *Blow Up* fruit basket by **Fernando and Humberto Campana** (▶p. 7)

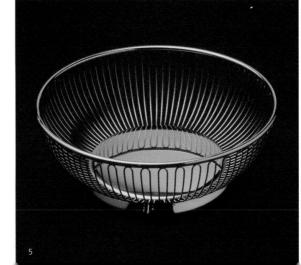

5

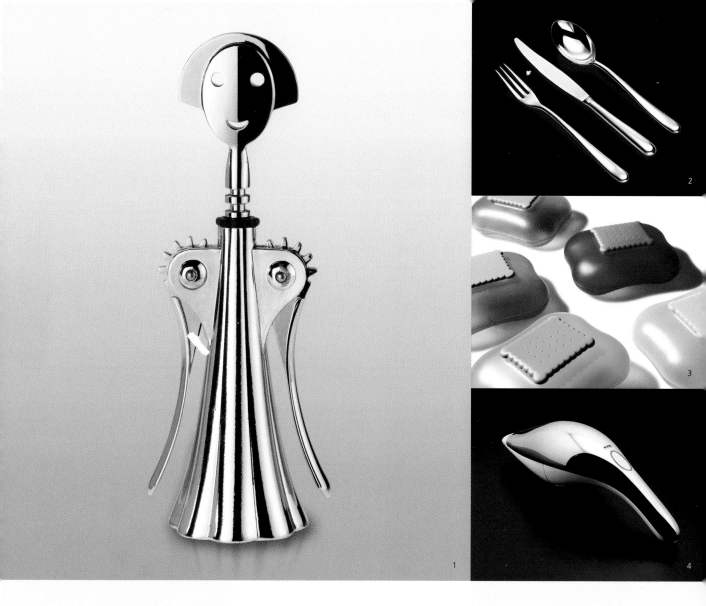

1

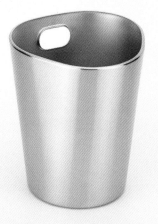

2

3

4

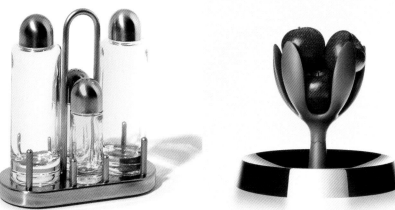

6

7

8

Alfa Romeo

Italy I Alfa Romeo (Fiat Auto SpA), Turin I Automobile manufacturer I **www.alfaromeo.com**

The only great Italian marque to be founded in Milan rather than in Turin boasts a unique history of automobile models and racing. Before the First World War, Alfa Romeo celebrated great racing triumphs, and the construction of engines for racing cars was for a long time the driving force behind its automobile production. From the 1930s prominent coachbuilders took up the challenge of designing car bodies that would clothe speed in suitably curvilinear forms. Italy's gradual emergence as a prosperous country at the end of the Second World War brought with it the advent of mass production. The elegant *Giulietta* series, which came on to the market in the mid-1950s, and for which both **Bertone** and **Pininfarina** designed models, paved the way. They extended the idea of 'Bel Design' that was emerging from Milan – as applied by Marcello Nizzoli to **Olivetti**'s typewriters, by Piaggio to the *Vespa* motor scooter and by **Fiat** to the *500* small car – to include larger products. Sports cars such as the *Giulietta Spider* by Pininfarina or the *Giulietta Sprint* coupé by ▶Bertone were perfect sculptures with harmonious proportions that are still admired. In succeeding years the marque was highly successful on the international market with such models as the *Spider Duetto* and the *Giulia Berlina*, both of which today enjoy cult status. Like many other successful models, the *Alfasud*, with a body designed by ▶**Giorgetto Giugiaro**'s company Italdesign, became something of a legend. A special production plant was built exclusively for this car.

Alfa Romeo went through a troubled period during the oil crisis of the 1970s and was eventually taken over by Fiat. However, its dashing image was revived in the 1980s with, for example, the stylish *164* saloon and the wedge-shaped *RZ* roadster by Zagato. Towards the end of the 1990s the introduction of the *156* strengthened the company's reputation for style and performance. This saloon is still impressive, with its smooth lines and a sense of unity that had never before been achieved so completely. This design approach was continued in the Alfa 'Style Centre' in Arese with such models as the *166* and the *156 Sportwagon*, an interpretation of the estate in typical Alfa fashion. The *Alfa Brera* by ▶Giugiaro, which its designers regard quite simply as "the most beautiful car in the world", has an even greater emotional appeal.

28

1 *166* saloon, 1998

2 *Kamal* off-road vehicle (concept), 2003

3 *GT Coupé*, 2003

4 *156 Sportwagon* estate, 2000

5 *Giulietta Spider*, 1956

6 *Alfasud Sprint Veloce* coupé, 1974

7 *Giulia Berlina* saloon, 1962

1909	Società Anonima Lombarda Fabbrica Automobili (ALFA) established in Portello near Milan
1915	Nicola Romeo joins company
1932	Company reorganization takes place
1938	Opens factory in Pomigliano d'Arco
1963	Opens factory in Arese
1967	Constructs *Alfasud* factory; Dustin Hoffman drives an Alfa *Spider* in the film *The Graduate*
1987	**Fiat** takes over company
2001	Receives European Car of the Year Award for *147* compact car

Products

1910	*24 HP* saloon
1950	*1900* saloon and coupé by **Bertone**
1954	*Giulietta Sprint* coupé by ▶Bertone
1956	*Giulietta Spider* by **Pininfarina**
1962	*Giulia Berlina* saloon; *Giulia Sprint GT* coupé by Bertone
1966	*1600 Spider* (*Spider Duetto*) by Pininfarina
1969	*GT 1300 Junior Zagato* coupé
1970	*Montreal* coupé by Bertone
1972	*Alfasud* compact car by ▶ **Giorgetto Giugiaro**
1974	*Alfetta* saloon and *Alfasud Sprint Veloce* coupé by Giorgetto Giugiaro
1987	*164* saloon by Pininfarina
1990	*SZ* coupé and *RZ* roadster by Zagato
1992	*155* saloon
1995	*Spider* and *GTV* coupé by ▶ Pininfarina
1997	*156* saloon
1998	*166* saloon by Pininfarina
2000	*156 Sportwagon* estate and *147* compact car
2003	*Alfa Brera* coupé (concept) by ▶ Giorgetto Giugiaro; *GT Coupé* by Bertone; *Kamal* off-road vehicle (concept)

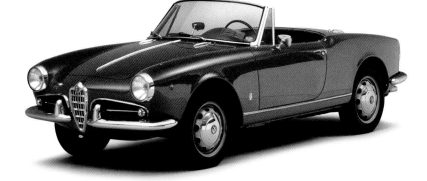

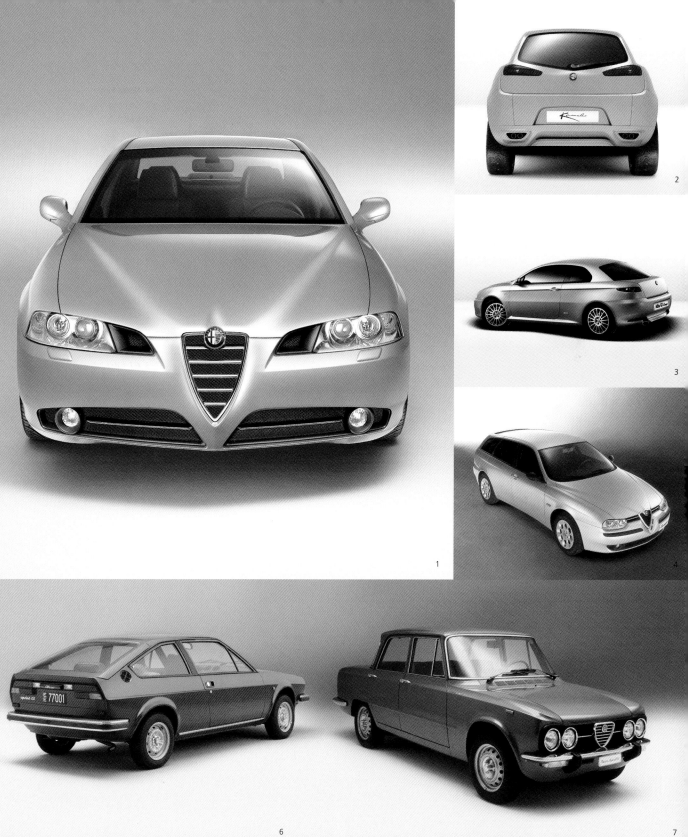

1

2

3

4

6

7

Alfi

Germany | Alfi GmbH, Wertheim | Manufacturer of household items | **www.alfi.de**

Most of the thermos jugs produced by the well-established Swabian firm Alfi are still made in the traditional way, using a metal casing with a special finish and a glass vacuum cylinder. The concept was devised originally by a Scottish professor of physics and then developed in Germany into the ingenious product that transformed picnics and tea or coffee breaks, keeping drinks hot or cold as required. *Juwel*, the company's most successful jug, was a line commissioned for the dining cars of a railway company in the United States. *Achat*, by Tassilo von Grolman, is a modern classic from the 1980s: the grooved, cone-shaped jug contrasts with the bulbous contours of many previous models. Alfi was perfectly attuned to the mood of an entire generation when it began to use translucent plastic in its designs, a trend that put the company on a par with such giants as **Dyson**, **Authentics** and **Apple**. Playful shapes in the manner of the *La Ola* jug gave the family firm (today part of **WMF**) the youthful image it had been looking for. **Ross Lovegrove** and **Philippe Starck** are among the star designers that have worked for Alfi. Lovegrove's *Basic* thermos jug (designed with Julian Brown; ▸ p. 15) marked the change towards the use of named designers. At the end of the 1990s the product range was extended to include kitchen accessories and, in 2000, the fashionable *DINK* cutlery.

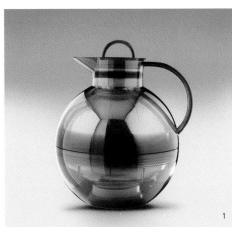

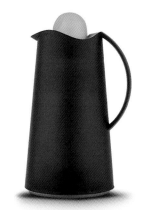

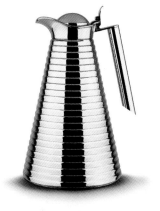

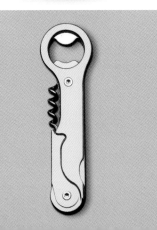

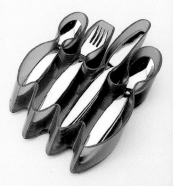

Alias

Italy | Alias SpA, Grumello del Monte | Furniture manufacturer | **www.aliasdesign.it**

The Italian company Alias presented three new products at the Milan International Furniture Fair in 2003: the elegant *Segesta* chair, made of technopolymer, by **Alfredo Häberli**; the *Frametable* folding table in aluminium by **Alberto Meda**; and a trendy little table by Tamar Ben David. These designs have one thing in common: like the entire collection, they are characterized by their simplicity and transparency. All Alias tables, chairs and shelves are highly original. Founded at the end of the 1970s, the company has always defined itself as the sum of its designers, much like a publishing company that gathers together different authors without imposing limits on their self-expression. *Spaghetti*, its very first chair, with a seat of tightly stretched rubber threads, was developed by Giandomenico Belotti and became a classic. Mario Botta sought to create an architectural effect with the *Prima*, *Seconda*, *Quarta* and *Quinta* chairs. Meda relied on technological innovation in his extremely light chairs in the *Frame* collection, among them the *Longframe* chaise longue. Other designers working for Alias include Carlo Forcolini, **Vico Magistretti**, Paolo Rizzatto, **Jasper Morrison** and Riccardo Blumer, who was awarded the Compasso d'Oro, the Oscar of the design world, for his particularly light *Laleggera* chair.

31

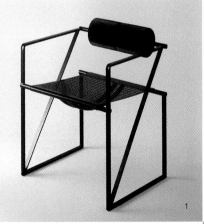

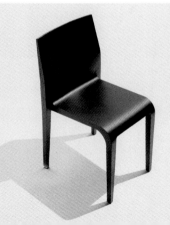

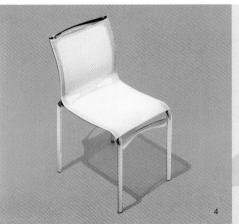

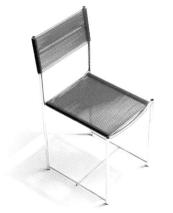

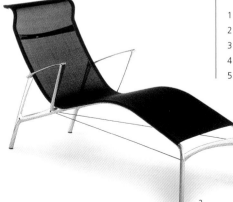

Apple

USA | Apple Computer, Inc., Cupertino, California | Computer and software manufacturer | **www.apple.com**

Steve Jobs and Steve Wozniak came from the hippy and hacker subculture of the 1970s. Frustrated by the primitive computers of that time, they decided to build their own. In 1976 *Apple I* was born. The company's logo – an apple with a bite out of it, a graphic emblem of the computer revolution – came from the accompanying advertising campaign. A year later *Apple II* was introduced, the *Model T* of the computer industry, ending dependence on the computer giant **IBM** and ushering in the democratization of the computer. The Californian underdogs' answer to IBM's 'PC' was the *Macintosh*, a quantum leap in the history of home and office computers. This all-rounder, soon referred to affectionately as the 'Mac', could be operated by non-professional users thanks to its graphic operating system. With its high processing speed and efficient software, it was a godsend to the creative professions. The external appearance of the light-coloured computers designed by Hartmut Esslinger's **Frogdesign** made them a visually appealing alternative to the more staid and conventional IBM models. However, the very fact that Apple's computers were so technologically distinct from IBM's PCs eventually worked against them.

From the end of the 1980s, Apple lost more and more of its technological edge, and its aura of the superior outsider began to fade. The company went into the red. A successful new start was made in 1997 with the return of Jobs, who had left the company in 1985. In 1998, under his management, the *iMac* was created, designed by a team of in-house designers headed by Jonathan Ive. The computer's bold design, in transparent, candy-coloured plastic, successfully transferred the lollipop look to a sophisticated and highly expensive piece of equipment. Previously disappointed customers – still mainly from the creative professions – flocked back to Apple. Follow-up models were also successful. The company's aesthetics oscillate between Post-modern fun and a rigour reminiscent of early **Braun** designs. Apple led the way once again with the *iPod* MP3 player, creating a pocket-sized digital jukebox that stores and plays music downloaded from the Internet.

1976 Established by Steve Jobs and Steve Wozniak

1977 Floats on stock market

1981 Opens production plant in Ireland; production for European market begins

1982 Collaborates with **Frogdesign** (until 1985)

1984 Television commercial launches *Macintosh* computer

1985 Jobs leaves company

1997 Jobs rejoins company; Apple acquires Next Software; co-operates with Microsoft; launches *Think Different* advertising campaign

1998 Jonathan Ive becomes chief designer

2002 Receives Red Dot Design Award, Design Team of the Year

2004 Launches iTunes Internet music store

Products

1976 Apple *I* computer

1977 Apple *II* computer

1981 Apple *III* computer

1983 *LISA*, first computer with a mouse

1984 *Macintosh* model series by **Frogdesign**

1987 *Macintosh II* model series

1989 *Macintosh Portable* laptop computer

1994 *Power PC* model series

1997 *Power Macintosh G3* computer

1998 *iMac* computer; *PowerBook G3* laptop computer

1999 *G3* computer with four handles; *iBook* laptop computer; *Power Macintosh G4* computer

2000 *Macintosh G4 Cube* computer

2001 *PowerBook G4 Titanium* laptop computer

2002 *OS X* operating system; *iPod* MP3 player

2003 *Power Macintosh G5* computer in aluminium

32

1 *iPod* MP3 player, 2002

2 *Power Macintosh G3* computer, 1997

3 *Power Macintosh G5* computer, 2003

4 *Macintosh* computer, 1984

5 *iBook* laptop computer, 1999

6 *iMac* computer, 1998

7 *iMac G4* computer with *OS X* operating system, 2002

8 *PowerBook G4 Titanium* laptop computer, 2001

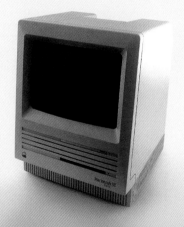

4

5

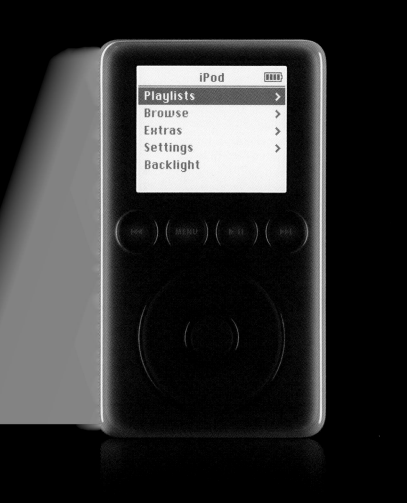

1

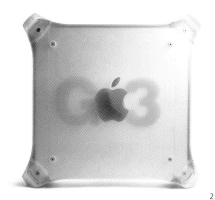

2

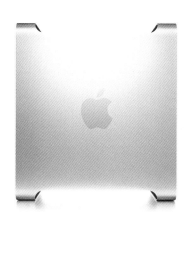

3

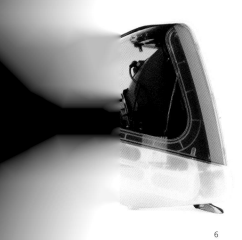

6

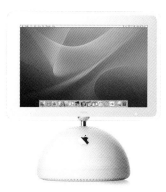

7

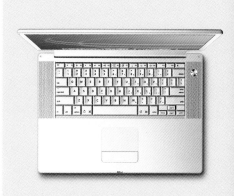

8

Arabia

Finland | Arabia, Iittala Oy A/B, Helsinki | Ceramics and glassware manufacturer | **www.arabia.fi**

Arabia was founded in the 1870s as a subsidiary of the Swedish porcelain manufacturer Rörstrand. In the twentieth century the Finnish company grew to become one of the largest ceramics manufacturers in Europe. The aesthetic quality of its products was enhanced at the beginning of the 1930s when Kurt Ekholm became artistic director. The young Swede set up studios in the middle of the factory, creating the beginnings of the present-day design department. He contributed greatly to the company's more modern profile with a number of functional designs, including the *Sinivalko* dinnerware service.

After the Second World War **Kaj Franck** was recruited by Ekholm, marking the beginning of Arabia's most innovative phase. Franck's basic idea was the mass production of versatile yet beautiful objects of everyday use. The *Koti* (Home) service, developed in the 1940s for the Finnish welfare agency, pointed the way. These design ideas proved both forward-looking and economical. The famous *Kilta* (today *Teema*) tableware conquered the market in Finland. The simple, tasteful Arabia products had a decisive influence in determining the image of Scandinavian product design. However, economic and design problems in the 1970s and 1980s led to a wave of mergers. Ironically, Arabia swallowed Rörstrand, the former parent company, and was then itself integrated into the **Hackman** empire, eventually becoming a division of **Iittala**.

The factory, which also sells a large number of charming figurines based on the Moomin characters created by Tove Jansson, employs in-house designers and is thus once again following its old successful strategy. In the late 1990s some of Arabia's products, such as the *24h* service by Franck's pupil Heikki Orvola, won several coveted prizes. The company works increasingly with leading international designers, including **James Irvine**, **Alberto Meda** and Richard Meier.

1873 Established as subsidiary of Rörstrand
1916 Company becomes Finnish after several changes of ownership
1929 Builds largest kiln in the world
1932 Kurt Ekholm, artistic director (until 1948), sets up studios for artists and establishes museum
1945 **Kaj Franck** joins as chief designer (artistic director from 1950 to 1961)
1983 Acquires Rörstrand
1988 Introduces *Pro Arte* collection
1990 **Hackman** group takes over Arabia and **Iittala** (Iittala established as international brand in 2002)

Products
1900 *Fennia* ceramics
1936 *Sinivalko* service by Kurt Ekholm
1938 *Myrna* service by Olga Osol (still in production today)
1952 *Kilta* service by ▶ Kaj Franck (discontinued 1974, reissued as *Teema*, 1981)
1956 *Hors d'œuvre* bowls by Kaj Franck
1958 *Liekki* tableware by Ulla Procopé
1994 *Storybirds* jugs by Kati Tuominen-Niittylä
1996 *Carambola* vases by Heikki Orvola
1997 *24h* service by Heikki Orvola; *Ego* service by Stefan Lindfors
1998 *Tilda* bowls by Pia Törnell
2000 *Fire* candlestick by Nathalie Lahdenmäki; *Rollo* salt and pepper shakers by Tony Alfström
2001 *Air* kitchenware collection by ▶ **Harri Koskinen**; *Earth* plant pots by ▶ **James Irvine**; *Water* jug by **Alberto Meda**
2002 *ABC* bowls by Pekka Harni; *Space* service by Richard Meier

34

1 *Kilta* service, 1952 (reissued as *Teema*, 1981)
2 *Carambola* vases, 1996
3 *Hors d'œuvre* bowls, 1956
4 Cup (*Ego* service), 1997
5 *24h* service, 1997
6 *Tilda* bowls, 1998
7 *Water* jug, 2001
8 *Storybirds* jugs, 1994

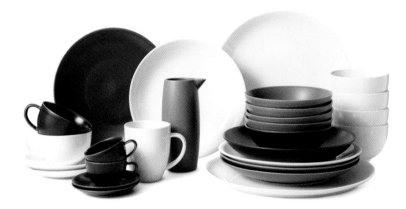

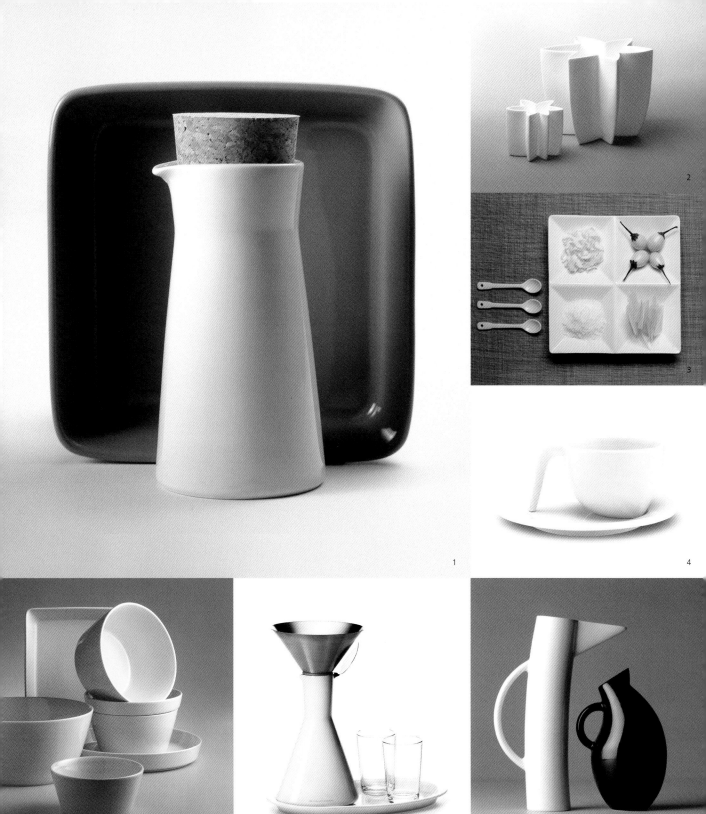

1

2

3

4

6

7

8

Ron **Arad**

England | Furniture and product designer | **www.ronarad.com**

'An endless, winding metal strip' perhaps best describes the highly sculptural work of the Anglo-Israeli designer Rod Arad. The most famous example of his distinctive sheet-metal furniture is the *Bookworm* shelf. But Arad is also an aficionado of transforming sheets of metal into exquisite headrests and expressive, bulbous armrests, as in the *Big Easy* armchair; or into chairs that almost appear drunk, as in his *Fantastic Plastic Elastic* (for **Kartell**); or, yet again, by twisting and turning the material, creating such chair structures as *Swan* for **Magis**. *After Spring/Before Summer*, a bow-like, chrome-plated steel chaise longue, represents the essence of Arad's design principles. Now a prominent, well-established figure in the design world, Arad has gradually progressed from the use of metal to that of plastic, and from the production of unique, one-off specimens to mass-produced articles.

The son of a painter and a photographer, Arad was born in Tel Aviv. Following his art studies in Jerusalem, he was attracted to London, where he studied at the Architectural Association under the architect Peter Cook. This unusual education may explain why the one-off, unique object was for many years so central to Arad's work. His designs are created with a welding torch in a Covent Garden studio called One Off, which he shares with Caroline Thorman. He creates raw objects that are influenced by the idea of recycling, as in the *Roverchair*, a tubular steel frame to which an old leather seat from a Rover car is attached. Arad's evolution as a designer of mass-produced items began with the *Well Tempered Chair,* manufactured by **Vitra,** with its typically expressive steel curves and rivets inspired by industrial aesthetics. The *Victoria & Albert* collection (for ▶**Moroso**) is another example of Arad's approach to mass production. The avant-garde experimenter has thus developed into a much sought-after designer who moulds everyday objects into expressive forms. The change of favoured material from metal to plastic – far more economical, in terms of both manufacture and cost – was encouraged by Kartell and has made Arad's designs affordable to a greater number of consumers who enjoy his exuberance and are happy that some of his ideas are now being recycled.

1951 Born in Tel Aviv, Israel

1971 Studies at Jerusalem Academy of Art

1973 Moves to London

1974 Studies at Architectural Association with Peter Cook

1981 Establishes One Off with Caroline Thorman and Dennis Groves

1989 Establishes Ron Arad Associates; designs foyer of Tel Aviv Opera House

1994 Establishes Ron Arad Studio in Como, Italy; appointed professor of product design at Hochschule, Vienna

1997 Appointed professor of furniture and product design at Royal College of Art, London

2003 Named Designer of the Year, *Architektur & Wohnen* magazine

Products

1981 *Roverchair* for One Off

1983 Concrete stereo system

1987 *Well Tempered Chair* for **Vitra**

1989 *Big Easy* armchair and sofa for **Moroso**

1990 *Spring* furniture collection for Moroso

1992 *After Spring/Before Summer* chaise longue; *Zigo* armchair for ▶ **Driade**

1993 *Empty Chair* for Tel Aviv Opera House

1994 *Bookworm* shelf for ▶ **Kartell**; *Schizzo* chair for Vitra; *Europa* steel sofa for Draenert

1997 *Tom Vac* chair for Vitra; *Uncut* armchair; *CD* shelf for **Alessi**

1998 *FPE* chair for ▶ **Kartell**; *Reinventing the Wheel* shelving for Hidden

2000 *Victoria & Albert* furniture collection for ▶ **Moroso**

2002 *Bad Tempered Chair* for Vitra

2003 *None Rota* armchair for **Cappellini**

2004 *RA 07* bottle cooler for Alessi; *S.O.S.* shelving unit for **Magis**

36

1 *Bookworm* shelf, 1994

2 *None Rota* armchair, 2003

3 *Big Easy* armchair, 1989

4 *Well Tempered Chair*, 1987

5 *S.O.S.* shelving unit, 2004

6 *After Spring/Before Summer* chaise longue, 1992

7 *Tom Vac* chair, 1997

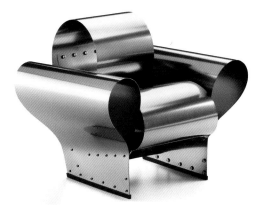

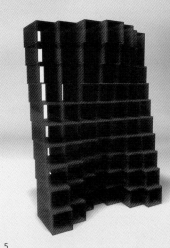

4   5

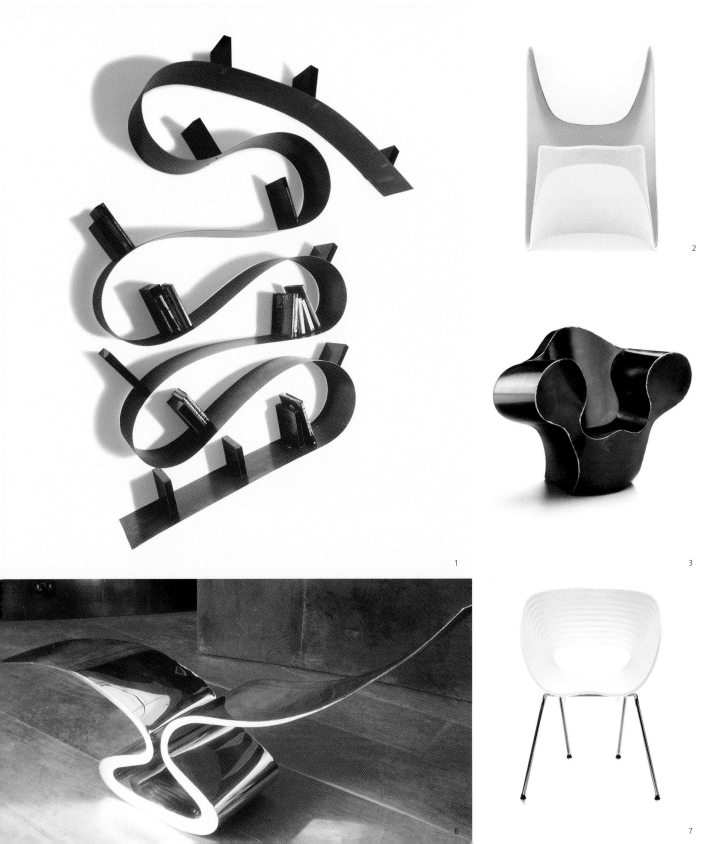

1

2

3

6

7

Arflex

Italy | Arflex International SpA, Giussano | Furniture manufacturer | **www.arflex.com**

Four foam rubber sections, a few elastic straps, and one of the most influential pieces of furniture in post-war Italy was complete. The *Lady* armchair was developed in 1951 by the young designer ▶ **Marco Zanuso** for the manufacturer Arflex, which had been founded two years previously. At the Milan Triennale the chair was cut open so that visitors could view its innovative interior. *Lady* won the gold medal and also became a pioneer of the organic style of the 1950s. Above all, however, it emerged as the symbol of a new vision of modern design that drew its inspiration from industry and technology.

When it was founded in 1949, Arflex was without doubt the most modern furniture company in Italy. Unlike numerous other firms in the country that had a tradition of crafts-manship, Arflex was a product of modern industry. The tyre manufacturer Pirelli had developed a new kind of material, a foam rubber called *gommapiuma*, which it planned to adapt for use, in conjunction with an elastic fabric, in the manufacture of furniture. Arflex became Pirelli's partner and worked with creative designers in order to enable the company to venture into completely new terrain in furniture design. From the outset, industrial production was the driving force behind the company. *Lady* and other designs by ▶ Marco Zanuso, such as the *Woodline*, *Martingala* and *Antropus* chairs or *Sleep-o-matic,* the practical sofa bed, were all great successes. Arflex also worked with **Franco Albini** and Erberto Carboni. The former created the modern, comfortable *Fiorenza* armchair, the latter the organic *Delfino* armchair. The collaboration with architect ▶ **Cini Boeri** in the 1960s was particularly significant: the polyurethane foam *Bobo* chair had for the first time absolutely no internal supporting frame, and from 1971 Boeri's *Serpentone* seating system wound its way through contemporary living rooms. Both were milestones in the history of furniture. In the course of time, **Burkhard Vogtherr** and **Hannes Wettstein** joined the ranks of collabrating architects and designers. Wettstein designed *Moods*, a range of geometric upholstered furniture, as well as the *Master* collection, which included a table of supreme purist elegance, and the distinctive *Spline* series of chairs.

1 *Delfino* armchair, 1954
2 *Martingala* armchair, 1954
3 *Bobo* chair, 1967
4 *Antropus* chair, 1949
5 *Fiorenza* armchair, 1952
6 Table (*Master* collection), 2000
7 *Virgola* armchair, 1991

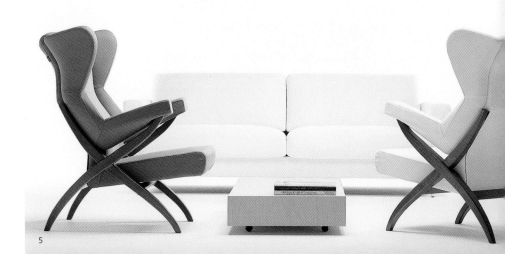

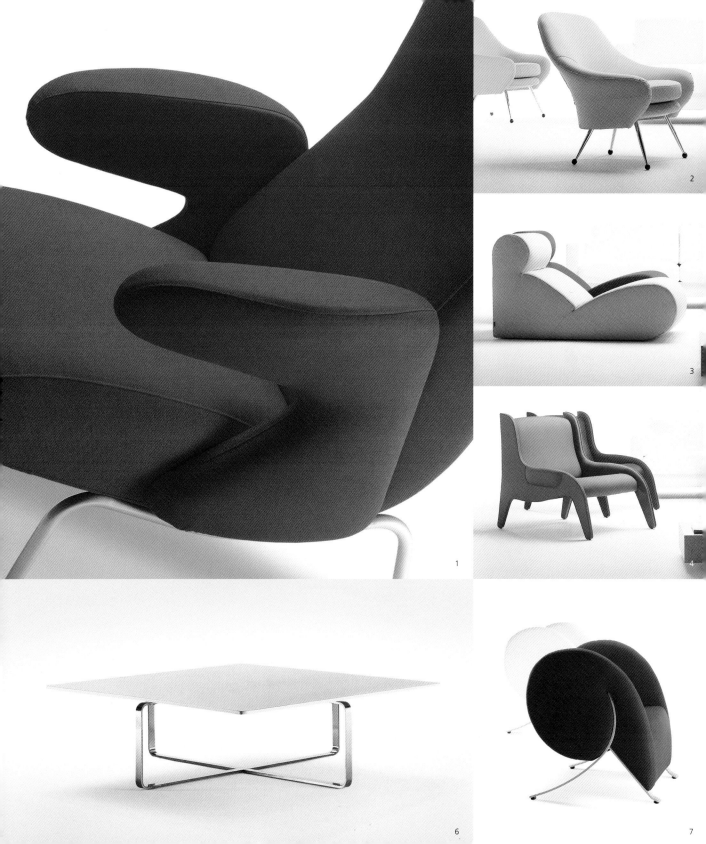

1

2

3

4

6

7

Artemide

Italy | Artemide SpA, Milan | Lamp manufacturer | **www.artemide.com**

There are many classic designs in the catalogue of Artemide, the Italian lamp manufacturer, but one lamp is more famous than all the others – *Tizio* by ►**Richard Sapper**. Highly functional, timelessly elegant, and innovative in technology and design, this table sculpture remains a bestseller more than thirty years after it was introduced. The *Tolomeo* desk lamp by ►**Michele De Lucchi** and Giancarlo Fassina closely rivals this success. There is hardly a design studio or architect's office that does not boast this mobile aluminium stand with its hat-shaped shade. Numerous later models by other manufacturers have been based on this simple, archetypal form. In every decade since the founding of Artemide in 1959 by the architect **Sergio Mazza** and the design enthusiast and aeronautical engineer Ernesto Gismondi (who has developed numerous lamps and was a patron of the avant-garde Memphis design group), the company has created products that were innovative for their time, many of which are still in production.

The 1960s, for example, saw the introduction of **Vico Magistretti**'s appealing *Eclisse* table lamp (with its adjustable reflector humorously simulating a half moon, full moon and new moon) and his elegant *Mezzachimera* standard lamp. The decade also witnessed *Boalum*, the Pop-style light tube by Livio Castiglioni and Gianfranco Frattini. Around this time, and before Gismondi halted production, Artemide was creating iconic chairs in plastic: they ranged from the elegant *Selene* by Magistretti to *Toga,* the voluminous throne-like Pop chair by ►Sergio Mazza. Today the company, which is active throughout the world, continues to set store by its collaboration with leading international designers, including **Antonio Citterio**, **Rodolfo Dordoni**, Norman Foster (of **Foster and Partners**), **James Irvine** and **Hannes Wettstein**, among others. The recent *e-light* series of desk lamps by Gismondi, inspired by the design of the ►**Apple** *iMac*, indicates that Artemide is still very much abreast of the times.

40

1 *Tolomeo* desk lamp, 1987
2 *Megaron* standard lamp, 1978
3 *Jian* wall lamp, 2003
4 *Boalum* lamp, 1969
5 *Selene* chair, 1969
6 *Eclisse* table lamp, 1965
7 *Sextans* standard lamp, 2003
8 *e-light* desk lamp, 1997

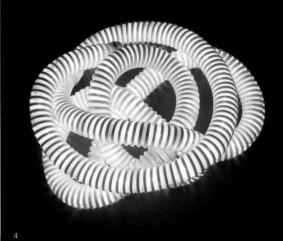

4

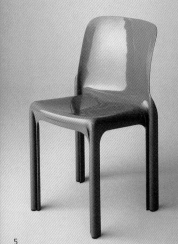

5

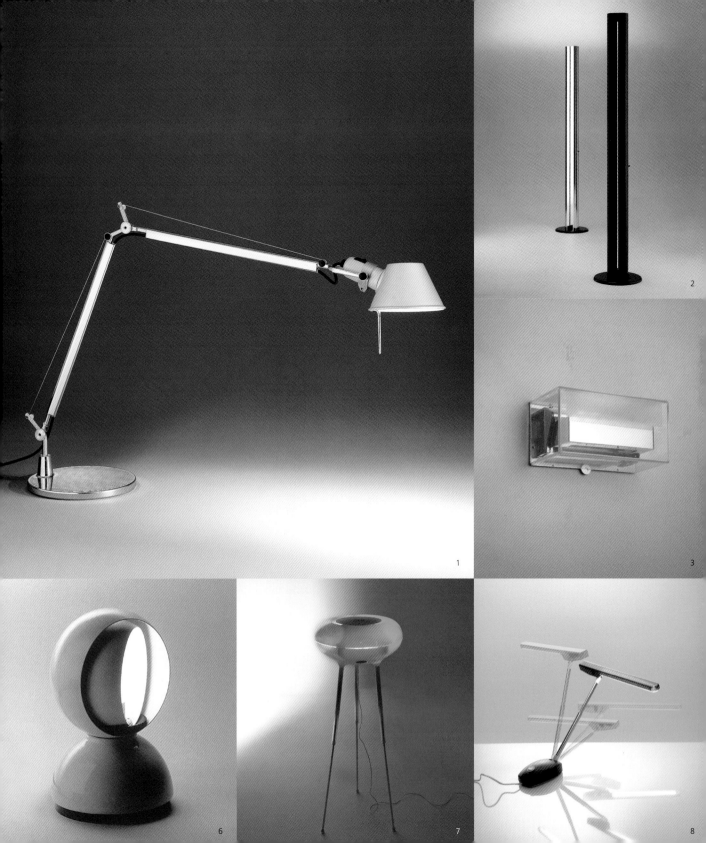

1

2

3

6

7

8

Artifort

The Netherlands | Artifort, Maastricht | Furniture manufacturer | **www.artifort.com**

Thanks to the disciplined playfulness of its products, Artifort has established itself as one of the relatively small number of design-conscious manufacturers. For more than forty years this Dutch company has exhibited admirable consistency in both its low-key profile and its product line, despite having derived much of its organic expressiveness from the Pop era. Its designs are amorphous, colourful and entirely independent of short-lived trends. The French elegance of ▸ **Pierre Paulin** fits harmoniously into the product range. This is one designer who has never succumbed to the temptation to achieve superficial effects, even in his more daring designs, such as the *Mushroom* or *Ribbon* chairs. Also noteworthy are the structured geometric works by the Dutch designer René Holten and the *Apollo* chair by the French designer Patrick Norguet. The *C 683* sofa by Kho Liang Le and the *Chaise Longue* by Geoffrey Harcourt are classics from the late 1960s and early 1970s. In the context of these Artifort products, even the minimalist designer ▸ **Jasper Morrison** felt inspired to produce something unexpected: the *Vega* chair, with its cartoon-like playfulness. Its name alone reveals the fusion of Pop exuberance and Artifort's ascetic Dutch puritanism, as evident in the restrained design of the chair's metal frame.

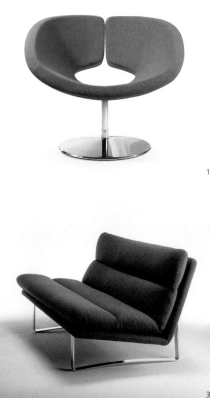

1

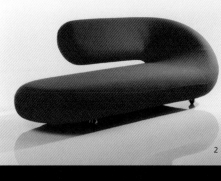

2

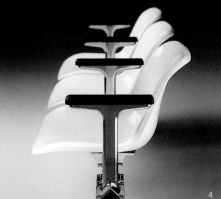

3

4

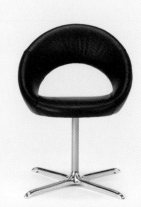

5

Asplund

Sweden | Asplund, Stockholm | Furniture and carpet manufacturer | **www.asplund.org**

In the early 1990s the brothers Christian and Thomas Asplund, one a bank employee, the other an art dealer, opened a furniture gallery with the aim of producing their own experimental furniture. They followed a clear principle from the outset: a limited series is preferable to aesthetic compromise. Many of Asplund's products are outstandingly simple, as in *Marc*, a carpet with a geometric honeycomb pattern reminiscent of paving; the *Unit* sideboard; and *Air*, a bench with a regular pattern of holes. At the same time, however, these designs also hint at something beyond the world of everyday objects. This is especially true of the carpets that were created by such prominent guest designers as **Marc Newson** and **James Irvine** and have now become hallmarks of the company. **Thomas Sandell**'s light and airy bench is likewise another example of a highly functional object that also works on a different, strictly visual level.

The contributions of leading non-Swedish designers such as Newson, **Tom Dixon** and **Alfredo Häberli** have extended the creative subtlety and sophistication that are characteristic of Asplund's products. The company has gradually evolved into one of the more distinctive of Stockholm's new design firms. Although it has not compromised its initial principles, it is quite happy to accept larger production numbers.

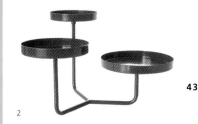
2

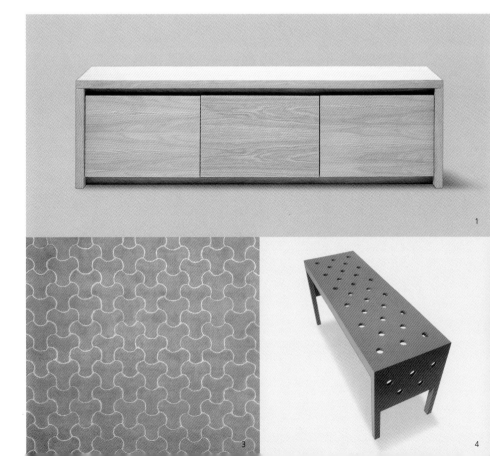

1

3   4   5

43

Aston Martin

England | Aston Martin Lagonda Ltd, Gaydon | Automobile manufacturer | **www.astonmartin.com**

Since 1914 the British car manufacturer Aston Martin has produced elegant, fast cars with an iconic shark-mouth grille. With more than 1500 sports cars sold in the year 2002, the company is highly successful, and manages to maintain an impressive balance between the cultivation of tradition and the spirit of innovation. The name of the most famous Aston Martin model, the *DB5*, which Sean Connery (alias James Bond) drove in the 1964 film *Goldfinger*, includes the initials of the industrialist David Brown, who bought the company in 1947. The *DBSV8* of 1969 by William Towns, which incorporated the characteristic grille, was the last model in the *DB* series, marking the end of an era for the accomplished car manufacturer. After the forward-looking *Lagonda*, with its extreme, wedge-shaped body, introduced an avant-garde note into the history of automobile design in the mid-1970s, the company (which now belongs to Ford) adopted a more traditional approach to form. Although new top models such as the *V12 Vanquish*, which was again put into the service of Agent 007, are more robust than their predecessors, they still sport the famous shark-mouth grille created by Frank Feeley.

1914	Bamford & Martin established by Lionel Martin and Robert Bamford in London
1926	Aston Martin Motors established in Feltham
1947	Industrialist David Brown (DB) takes over company
1959	*DBR1* wins Le Mans 24-hour race
1994	**Ford** takes over company

Products

1948	*DB* sports car
1950	*DB2* sports car
1958	*DB4* sports car
1963	*DB5* sports car
1965	*DB6* sports car
1969	*DBSV8* sports car
1977	*Lagonda* executive saloon
1988	*Virage* sports car
1992	*DB7 Vantage* sports car
2001	*V8 Vantage Le Mans* sports car
2002	*V12 Vanquish* sports car by Ian McCallum
2004	*DB9* coupé; *V12 Zagato* roadster

1 *DB2/4 Mk II* sports car, 1954
2 *V12 Vanquish* sports car, 2002
3 *DB5* sports car, 1963
4 *DBR1* racing car, 1957

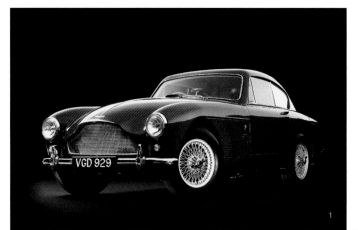

1

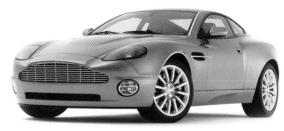

2

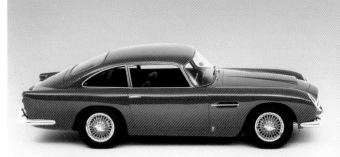

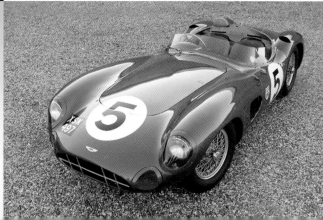

3

44

Antonia **Astori**

Italy | Furniture and exhibition designer | www.antoniaastori.it

Antonia Astori is not only one of Italy's few successful female designers but also a prominent businesswoman. At the end of the 1960s she was among the founders of **Driade**, the legendary, avant-garde furniture company for which, over a period of some thirty years, she has designed ingenious, perfectly constructed shelving and storage systems that clearly reflect her concept of 'room architecture'.

Astori's systems are complex, room-related inventions. *Oikos* (for ▸ Driade), from the 1970s, has a simple square as its basic element and is as suitable for living-rooms, studies and bedrooms as it is for kitchens and bathrooms. After having been on the market for a quarter of a century, the system has emerged as one of the classics of its genre, thanks to its clear geometry, high degree of formal precision and minimalist elegance. Other successful system designs include *Kaos* from the 1980s and *Pantos* from the 1990s, both of which have similar outlines to *Oikos*. Astori has created numerous other pieces of furniture for Driade and has thus contributed greatly to the firm's overall visual identity. This highly successful and much sought-after designer also designs exhibitions, booths at trade fairs, business premises and showrooms for companies throughout the world.

45

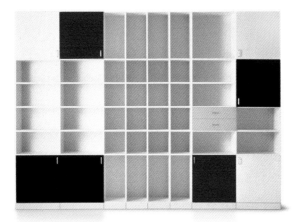

1

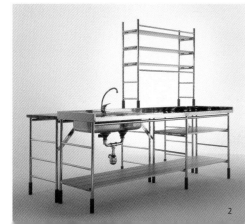

2

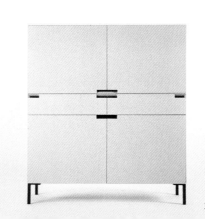

3

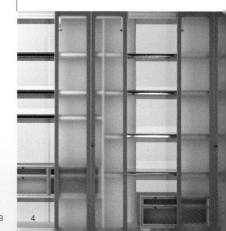

4

Audi

Germany | Audi AG, Ingolstadt | Automobile manufacturer | **www.audi.com**

Without informing **Volkswagen**, the parent company, Audi's head of development, Ludwig Kraus, designed a car in the late 1960s that was not only considerably larger than previous Audis but was equipped with a body optimized through wind-tunnel testing. As it turned out, the Audi *100* appealed greatly to the Volkswagen board, and, following its introduction, Audi rose like a phoenix from the ashes. A smaller car, the Audi *50*, followed some years later and was for a long time the bread-and-butter model of the Ingolstadt-based company (it was also adapted as the *Polo* by Volkswagen). The *Quattro,* introduced in the early 1980s, was equipped with a spoiler inspired by racing cars and with other sporty attributes such as ventilation slits, a coupé back and a box-like wedge form typical of the period. It was a complete contrast to Audi's other, somewhat conventional models. Although in the 1980s Audi was not noted for its unusual designs, these were undoubtedly the first steps towards the company's aesthetic emancipation. A later example of the change in focus came with the new Audi *80*, with its windows flush with the body above the high bonnet, recessed external door handles, a relatively small roof section and a very compact, smooth and polished-looking silhouette.

"The criticism that all cars look the same is as old as the hills. But there is a trend that challenges this view", noted Peter Schreyer, head of Audi design from 1994 to 2002. He made sure that design issues were at the very top of the agenda. Successors to the Audi *80* and Audi *100*, the *A4* and *A6* became the company's new flagship models. When the *A6* was presented in 1994, there was a certain stylistic affinity with its predecessor, but the overall impression of the car had changed completely. High tail lamps and soft curves were among the features that created a new, trend-setting look. The bodywork was characterized by its rounded, flowing form. With its domed roof, arch-shaped rear section and rounded front, this executive car established a new stylistic paradigm, displacing the traditional wedge shape of the saloon. It was therefore only a question of time before the estate version of the *A4*, the *A4 Avant*, won the renowned Bundespreis Produktdesign. Audi's *TT* sports car and the compact *A2* have also become design icons.

46

1 *LeMans* sports car (concept), 2003

2 *Quattro* coupé, 1982

3 *A3* compact car, 1996
   (2003 model shown)

4 *A8 W12* saloon, 2004

5 *100 S* coupé, 1969

6 *TT Coupé* sports car, 1998

7 *A2* compact car, 2000

1909	Audi established by August Horch, formerly of car manufacturer Horch, in Zwickau
1928	Car manufacturer DKW buys Audi
1932	Audi, DKW, Horch and Wanderer create the Auto Union, with head office in Chemnitz; new logo is four rings
1958	**Mercedes-Benz** takes over Auto Union
1959	Opens factory in Ingolstadt
1964	**Volkswagen** buys shares in Auto Union (becomes a fully owned VW subsidiary in 1966)
1969	Auto Union merges with NSU
1976	Hartmut Warkuss becomes chief designer (moves to Volkswagen in 1993)
1993	Audi AG becomes an independent marque with its own management
1994	Peter Schreyer becomes chief designer
1996	Receives Bundespreis Produktdesign for *A4 Avant* estate (1998 for *A3*)
1998	Takes over Cosworth and Lamborghini
2002	Walter de' Silva moves from **Alfa Romeo** to Audi; Peter Schreyer moves to Volkswagen

Products

1912	C *'Alpensieger'* open saloon
1925	M saloon
1928	R *Imperator* executive saloon
1933	*Front* saloon
1967	NSU *Ro 80* saloon by ►Claus Luthe
1968	*100* saloon
1969	*100 S* coupé
1972	*80* saloon by **Giorgetto Giugiaro**
1974	*50* small car by **Bertone**
1982	*Quattro* coupé
1986	*80* saloon (new generation)
1994	*A4* and *A6* saloons
1996	*A3* compact car
1998	*TT Coupé* sports car
2000	*A2* compact car with aluminium body
2003	*LeMans* sports car (concept)
2004	*A8 W12* and new *A6* saloons
2005	*Q7* hybrid car (concept)

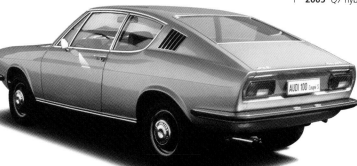

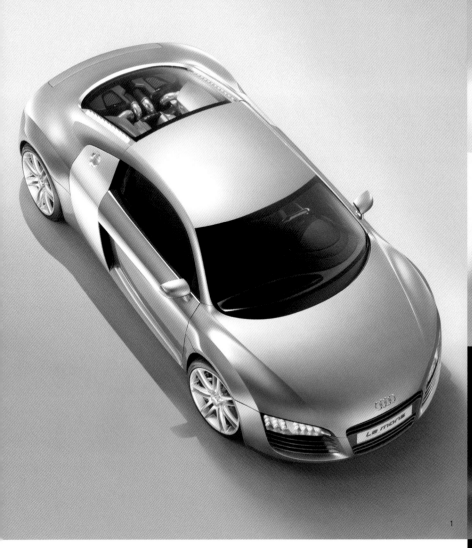

1

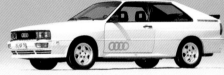

2

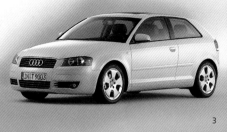

3

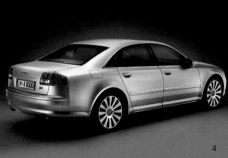

4

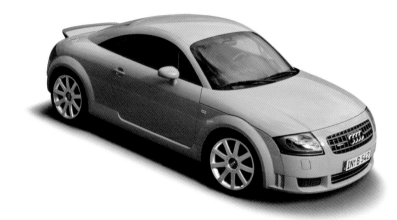

6

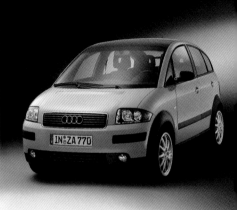

7

Authentics

Germany I Authentics GmbH, Gütersloh I Manufacturer of household items I **www.authentics.de**

The name Authentics encapsulates this manufacturer's design vision. Plastic is not regarded as a substitute material but as a viable, original and beautiful substance in its own right – a view that is shared by the Italian company **Kartell**. The founder of Authentics, Hansjerg Maier-Aichen, followed an Italian business principle and from the outset engaged numerous international designers, among them **Shin and Tomoko Azumi** from London and **Konstantin Grcic** from Munich.

It was at the end of the 1980s that Maier-Aichen first developed the idea of using translucent plastic in his products. In a very short time a surprisingly comprehensive array of practical articles for everyday use was created, ranging from a hand brush to a toothbrush beaker and a pocket calculator. The *Can* waste bin and its little brother, *Mini-Can*, were bestsellers. The Authentics brand became well known around the world for its transparent products, and soon other companies – **Apple**, **Dyson** and **Koziol**, to mention a few – began to pick up on the trend. In the late 1990s Authentics ventured into new territory and started producing glass objects and even furniture. The company experienced a slump in sales and unsuccessfully sued other manufacturers for copying its designs. Maier-Aichen left the business; Grcic, however, is still very much in charge of the distinctive look of the brand.

48

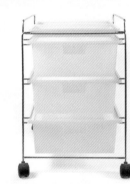

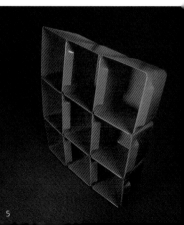

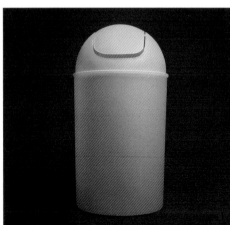

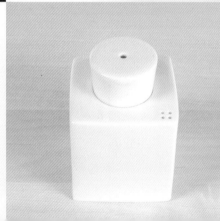

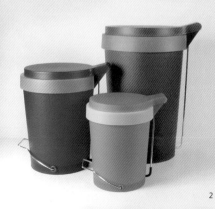

Shin and Tomoko **Azumi**

England | Furniture and product design studio | **www.azumi.co.uk**

The Japanese designers Shin and Tomoko Azumi develop products that clearly reflect their pleasure in devising ingenious solutions to design problems. Like Edward Barber and Jay Osgerby of **Barber Osgerby**, the Azumis both studied at the Royal College of Art in London. They opened their studio in the same city in the mid-1990s. They design household objects, lamps and furniture for such companies as Mathmos, Guzzini, **Lapalma**, E&Y, Habitat and Hitch Mylius. Their work defies neat categorization but nevertheless exhibits astounding simplicity, an innovative approach and an obvious desire to translate emotion into material form. Despite its formal balance and harmony, the doll-like *Snowman* salt and pepper set, designed for **Authentics**, is witty and has an appealingly human aura about it. The *Wire Frame* furniture series, designed for Meshman, adopts an intelligently executed minimalist approach. The bench from this series can be used as a chaise longue, or several can be stacked together and transformed into a shelf system – a typical example of the multi-functionalism that the Azumis love to create in their designs. From the porcelain service for **Muji** and jewellery for the German company Biegel to spatial installations, the work of the Azumis is proof that versatile all-rounders have not faded away entirely.

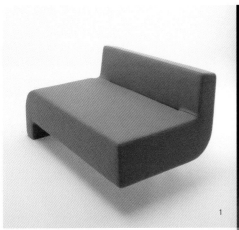

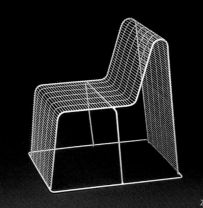

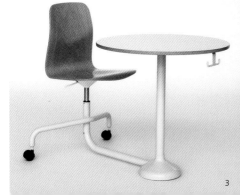

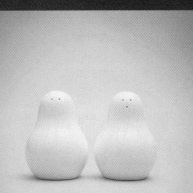

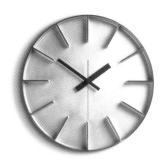

49

Braun, *ABW41* wall clock, 1981

In the same year that the Memphis design group challenged established design assumptions in Milan, Braun provided a further example of how aesthetic restraint and functionality can be combined. Its in-house designer Dietrich Lubs created something approaching the archetypal clock with his design of the simple but elegant *ABW41*. The clock's layered yet extremely flat surface is not only aesthetically pleasing but enhances legibility.

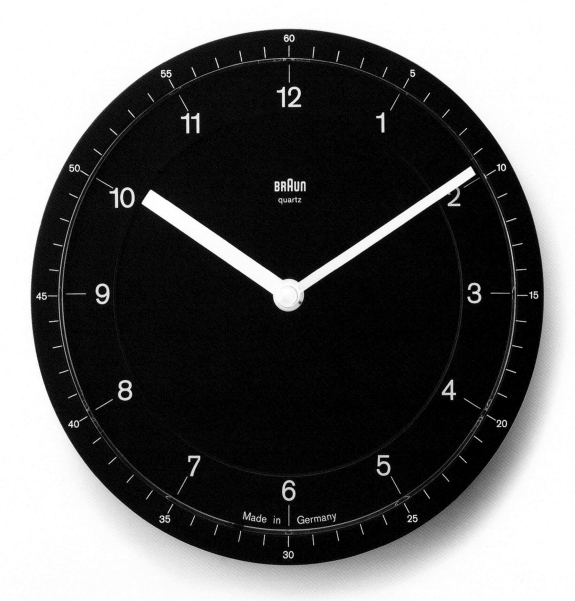

B&B Italia

Italy | B&B Italia SpA, Novedrate | Furniture manufacturer | **www.bebitalia.it**

B&B Italia is one of the most successful of Italy's numerous design-orientated furniture manufacturers. It was founded as C&B Italia in the mid-1960s by Piero Busnelli and Cesare **Cassina** and was renamed when Cassina left the firm in the early 1970s. From its inception, the company was a leader with a strong corporate identity that embraced all aspects of its operations; it also recognized the value of engaging such notable graphic designers as Bob Noorda, Pierluigi Cerri and Oliviero Toscani. The philosophy of the young company was based on the conviction that new ideas can be profitable. The wide range of styles offered by B&B Italia and its more traditional product line Maxalto includes not only practical pieces but also designs that are unique, elegant, comfortable and experimental. In the late 1960s an unusual object appeared in furniture stores. When the compressed packaging was opened, an amorphous piece of polyurethane furniture emerged and, as if by magic, assumed a rounded form inspired by the human body. Although ▶ **Gaetano Pesce**'s *Up* chair was an unconventional piece of Pop seating, its development was the result of intensive research in the company's laboratory. The firm's own large research centre was established in 1968, and it is from there that the designers still work today to perfect quality standards and develop innovative materials. This centre, in which 3 per cent of the company's turnover is invested annually, is the core of B&B Italia.

For four decades the company has produced countless innovative designs, many of which have become bestsellers. From ▶ **Mario Bellini**'s exciting *Le Bambole* series of upholstered furniture and **Vico Magistretti**'s *Tema* table, both from the early 1970s, to **Antoni Citterio**'s sofas, including *Sity* and *Diesis* from the 1980s, and the more recent *Charles*, *George*, *Mart* and *Marcel* collections – all stand for classic Italian elegance. The list of creations by notable international designers – Afra and Tobia Scarpa, Paolo Nava, **James Irvine**, **Richard Sapper**, Vincent van Duysen and **Uwe Fischer**, to name but a few – grows longer and longer. With more recent projects, such as the *Metropolitan* seating collection by ▶ **Jeffrey Bernett** and ▶ **Patricia Urquiola**'s spectacular *Lens* table series with transparent surfaces, B&B Italia has become one of the few international trendsetters.

52

1 *Mart* armchair, 2003
2 *Soft Wall* partition, 2001
3 *George* sofa, 2002
4 *Breakfast* bed, 2002
5 *Diesis* sofa, 1980
6 *Athos* table, 2001
7 *Metropolitan* chair, 2003

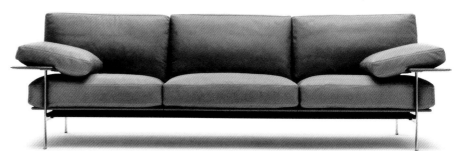

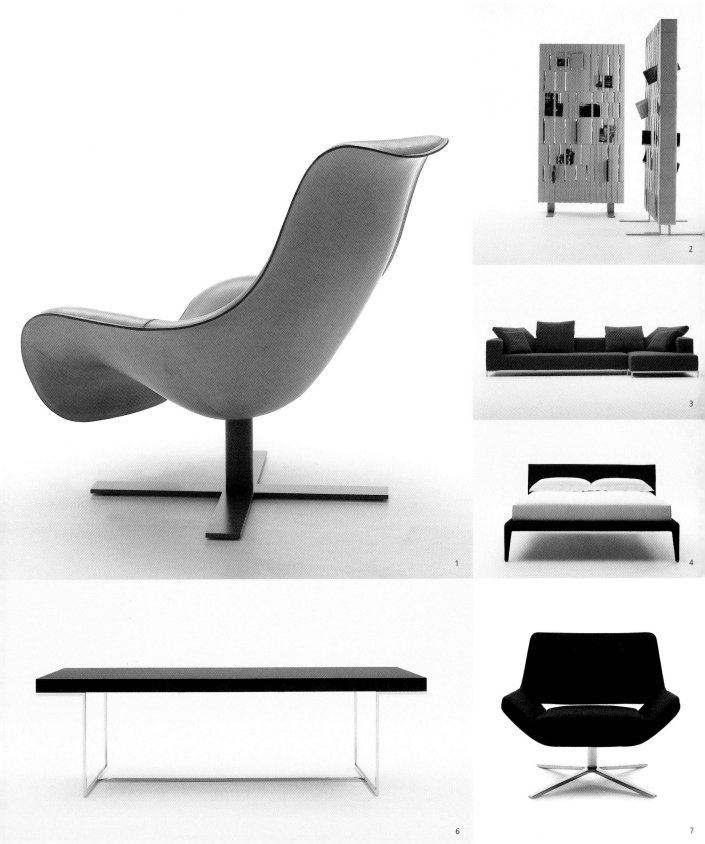

1

2

3

4

6

7

BD Ediciones

Spain | BD Ediciones de Diseño SA, Barcelona | Furniture manufacturer | **www.bdbarcelona.com**

The *Varius* chair is elegant, practical, timeless and a bestseller. It thus combines qualities that many designers attempt to emulate, albeit often unsuccessfully. The piece is delicate yet solid, and is considered a pioneering creation in modern Spanish design. The chair was designed by ▶ **Óscar Tusquets Blanca** and is manufactured by BD Ediciones. The company has always featured both classic and modern designs in its product range, and this chair successfully combines both styles in one product. This dual-product strategy has also been pursued by companies in other countries, including **Cassina** in Italy, **ClassiCon** and **Thonet** in Germany, **Ecart** in France, **Isokon Plus** in the United Kingdom and **Källemo** in Sweden.

BD Ediciones has been adding re-editions to its range since the mid-1970s. These include works by the eminent Scottish designer **Charles Rennie Mackintosh** and also by his contemporary, the ingenious Antoni Gaudí from Catalonia. The *Calvet* chair, designed by Gaudí around 1900, is a good example of Iberian Art Nouveau, but on a small scale. Gaudí's interesting ornamental fixtures are reminiscent of wilting plant forms that appear to fade and disintegrate. Salvadore Dalí's designs are also exceptional and unique. Apart from the famous lip-shaped sofa, Dalí contributed several other pieces of furniture and lamps. Each design represents the fusion of an article of practical, everyday use and a magical object. The 1930s *Bracelli* standard lamp, with its bent stem, gives the impression of a fragile and delicate creature to which the Surrealist painter has attached a crutch for support.

Some of the most renowned modern Spanish designers, such as Pete Sans, Lluís Clotet and Pepe Cortés, have extended the product range with numerous pieces of furniture and lamps, partly in collaboration with Tusquets Blanca. One of the more recent contributions by a modern designer is Tusquets Blanca's *Suma* metal shelf system, a tubular construction that can also be used as an airy partition. The polyethylene *bd.love* bench by the British designer **Ross Lovegrove**, with its curving seat, is part of a series of furniture designed for transit lounges. This unusual, boat-shaped bench recalls Dalí's classic lip-shaped sofa from the 1970s. The Swiss designer ▶ **Alfredo Häberli** has also contributed to the BD Ediciones catalogue with a design reminiscent of Spanish bar furniture. His *Happy Hour* series is a successful variation on the ever-popular theme of steel tubes used in a light and unobtrusive way.

54

1 *Suma* shelf system, 2000

2 *Coqueta* armchair, 1987

3 *Catalano* bench, 1974

4 *Burguesa* table, 1980

5 Bench (*bd.love* street furniture collection), 2002

6 *Bracelli* standard lamp, 1937 (reissued 1977)

7 *Gaudí* fixtures, 1902 (until 1910; reissued 1977)

8 *Calvet* chair, 1902 (reissued 1977)

9 *Olvidada* standard lamp, 1976

1972	Established by Pep Bonet, Cristian Cirici, Lluís Clotet, Mireia Riera and **Óscar Tusquets Blanca**
1990	Receives European Community Design Prize

Products

1973	*Hialina* shelf system by Óscar Tusquets Blanca and Lluís Clotet
1974	*Catalano* bench by Óscar Tusquets Blanca and Lluís Clotet
1976	*Olvidada* standard lamp by Pepe Cortés
1977	Begins re-edition of designs by Antoni Gaudí (incl. *Calvet* chair and *Gaudí* fixtures), Salvador Dalí (*Bracelli* standard lamp) and **Charles Rennie Mackintosh**
1980	*Burguesa* table by Óscar Tusquets Blanca and Anna Bohigas
1983	*Varius* chair (reissued 2003)
1985	*Bib Luz Doble* hanging lamp
1986	*Talaya* shelving; *Metalástica* chair
	Last four by ▶ Óscar Tusquets Blanca
	Duplex barstool by ▶ **Javier Mariscal**
1987	*Castor* ceiling lamp by Lluís Clotet; *Coqueta* armchair by Pete Sans
1993	*Urbana* rubbish bin by Cristian Cirici; *Big Banc* bench by Pete Sans
1996	*Perforano* bench by Óscar Tusquets Blanca and Lluís Clotet
2000	*Suma* shelf system by Óscar Tusquets Blanca
2001	*Happy Hour* furniture collection by ▶ **Alfredo Häberli**
2002	*bd.love* street furniture collection by ▶ **Ross Lovegrove**; *Chester* bench by Óscar Tusquets Blanca; *Mariscal* decanter by Javier Mariscal
2003	*Puff* ottoman by **Matthew Hilton**

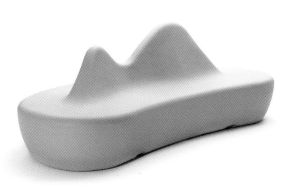

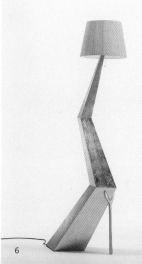

5

6

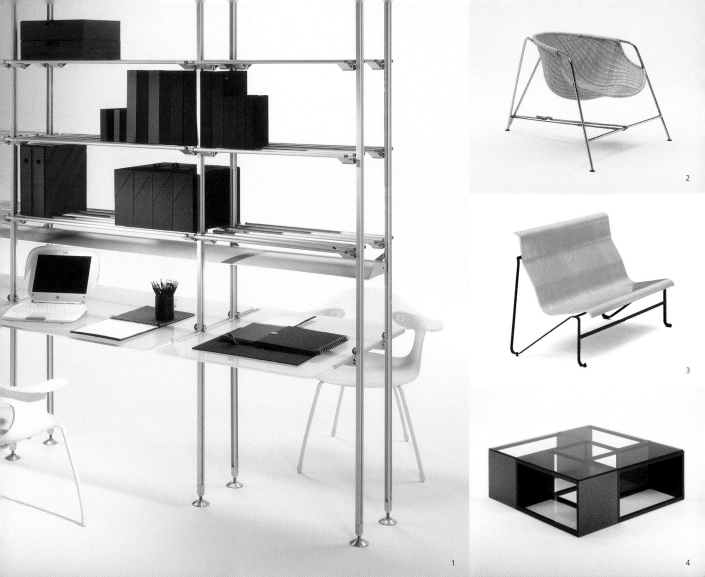

1

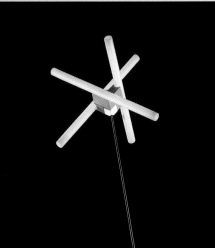

2

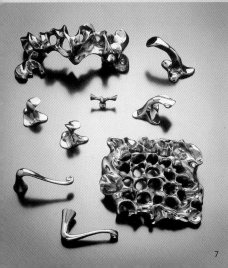

3

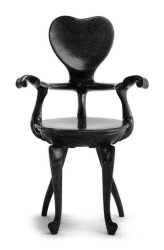

4

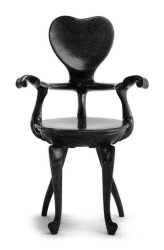

7

8

9

Baleri Italia

Italy | Baleri Italia SpA, Albano San Alessandro | Furniture and lamp manufacturer | **www.baleri-italia.it**

Baleri consistently puts its faith in international design and, in this respect, is typically Italian. The company is regarded as a trendsetting brand that collaborates with star designers from both home and abroad, among them **Philippe Starck**, **Hannes Wettstein**, Hans Hollein, Riccardo Dalisi, **Angelo Mangiarotti** and **Alessandro Mendini**. Enrico Baleri, who co-founded the firm with Marilisa Decimo during a highly experimental and creative phase in the mid-1980s, has produced numerous designs himself, however, including a variation on a **Ludwig Mies van der Rohe** chair.

Starck's elegant *Richard III* armchair – a radical, ironic piece of furniture that even today still polarizes opinion (thus demonstrating that 'taste' is, and always has been, highly subjective) – was a design milestone in the 1980s. The entire Baleri collection of chairs, tables, sofas and easy chairs is fundamentally minimalist, yet it also succeeds in being bold and innovative. Individual designers are given free rein to express themselves through their creations. In the mid-1990s the colourful egg seats that formed part of the *Tato, Tatino* and *Tatone* series of seating elements became style icons. Designed by **Denis Santachiara** (whose distinctive sense of humour is well known) in co-operation with Enrico Baleri, these spherical elements, scattered casually like marbles or balls of wool, are reminiscent of the *Sacco* seat-bag by Gatti, Paolini and Teodoro (for ▸**Zanotta**) in shape, ironic appeal and conceptual simplicity. In the 1990s Baleri himself also created the *Molly* armchair and the lens-shaped *Lunella* seat. The *Cartoons* screen by Luigi Baroli from 1992 is a reference to **Alvar Aalto**'s undulating designs and was promptly included in the permanent collection of the Museum of Modern Art (MoMA) in New York. This productive decade also saw the creation of the *Capri* armchair by Hannes Wettstein, an almost anthropomorphic object with a 'toe' peeping out from under its massive body. The chair is suitable for both the living-room and the office. In contrast, Wettstein's elegant *Juliette* chair, from 1987, is a completely different design concept, and encloses its occupant in a comfortable, semi-circular support.

1984	Established by Enrico Baleri and Marilisa Baleri Decimo
1994	Enrico Baleri and Marilisa Baleri Decimo launch Gloria lighting company
2001	*Cartoons* screen selected for permanent collection of MoMA, New York

Products

1977	*Mac Gee* shelving
1982	*President M.* table
1984	*Café Chair*
1985	*Richard III* armchair
	All by **Philippe Starck**
1986	*Bristol* sofa by Enrico Baleri
1987	*Juliette* chair by **Hannes Wettstein**
1991	*Mimi* chair by Enrico Baleri; *Capri* armchair by Hannes Wettstein
1992	*Cartoons* screen by Luigi Baroli
1993	*Molly* armchair by Enrico Baleri
1994	*Bill* sofa by Hannes Wettstein
1995	*Mama* rocking armchair by ▸**Denis Santachiara**
1996	*Ypsilon* shelf by **Angelo Mangiarotti**
1997	*Tato, Tatino* and *Tatone* seats by Enrico Baleri and Denis Santachiara
1998	*T-Table* and *Ad Lovis* table lamp by ▸Angelo Mangiarotti
1999	*Lunella* seat by Enrico Baleri
2001	*Lisa* stackable chair by ▸**King-Miranda Associati**
2002	*Giò* sofa by Luigi Baroli; *Ottavio* table and *Mimi* chair by Enrico Baleri
2003	*Mies* chair by Enrico Baleri
2004	*Giò* furniture collection by Luigi Baroli

56

1 *Capri* armchair, 1991
2 *Ottavio* table, 2002
3 *Richard III* armchair, 1985
4 *Tato, Tatino* and *Tatone* seats, 1997
5 *Ad Lovis* table lamp, 1998
6 *Juliette* chair, 1987
7 *Cartoons* screen, 1992

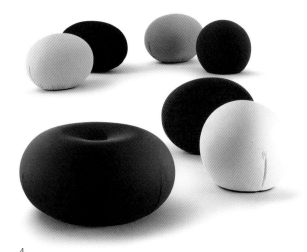

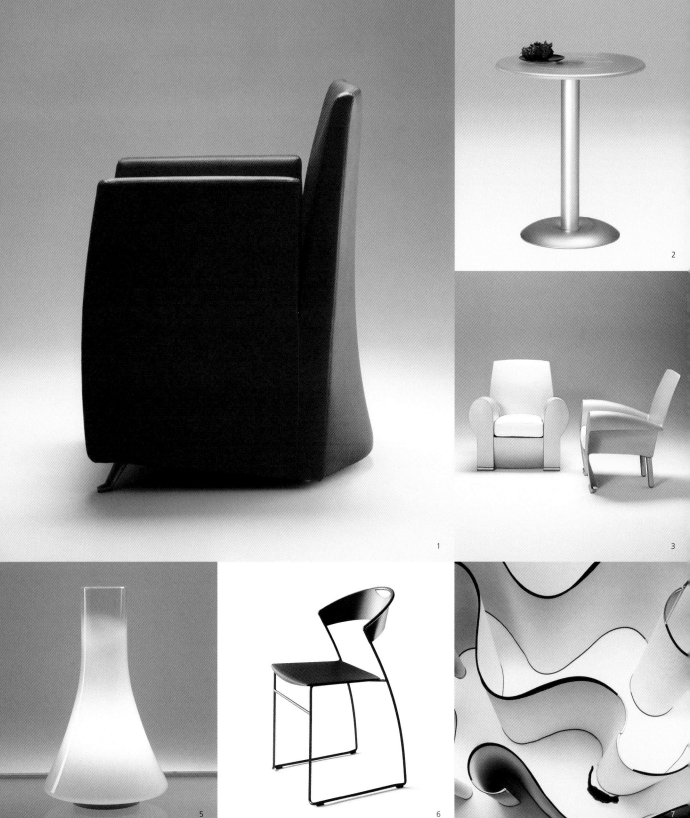

1

2

3

5

6

7

Bang & Olufsen

Denmark I Bang & Olufsen A/S, Struer I Manufacturer of audio-visual equipment I **www.bang-olufsen.com**

Although the company had made a name for itself before the Second World War, it was not until the beginning of the 1960s that Bang & Olufsen, Denmark's most famous radio manufacturer, found its own individual style. With the help of **Sigvard Bernadotte** and his partner, the industrial designer Acton Bjørn, and their former employee **Jacob Jensen**, the company abandoned the somewhat staid radio sets of the 1950s. Its new, slimline radio sets, with their geometrically arranged controls, were reminiscent of products by the German manufacturer **Braun**; by contrast, the elegant wooden casings were a Danish feature. Bang & Olufsen was transformed into an international brand with cult status, and its strict and rigorously applied approach became virtually synonymous with Danish industrial design, despite the fact that the company did not have its own design department.

Straight lines, sharp edges, immaculate surfaces and sparing use of graphics – Jacob Jensen was responsible for the introduction of this sleek minimalism. A recurring detail was the control knob (or slide control, as on the *Beomaster 1200* receiver), which exuded mathematical precision and elegance. It was this combination that tranformed Bang & Olufsen sets into something approaching fetish objects, even if the antiseptic casing did not always conceal state-of-the art technology. The *Beogram 4000* by ▸Jacob Jensen, however, was a true technological sensation. Although its highly polished surface appeared to eschew any suggestion of anything mechanical, it was the world's first record player with an electronically controlled tangential tracking arm.

An upmarket, medium-sized company with 3000 employees, Bang & Olufsen today commands a loyal following among well-heeled hi-fi enthusiasts. Following a change of management at the beginning of the 1990s, the company succeeded in reinventing itself. As well as manufacturing audio systems, it also supplies sound studios for country houses and penthouses around the world, and earns a good profit from its custom-built systems. Under the English in-house designer David Lewis, the company retained its proven recipe for success: extravagant understatement combined with sophisticated control technology, as in the *Beocenter 2*, a complete audio system with a control unit in the form of a discus, or the *Beosound 9000* CD player, with its rapid pick-up. The product range also includes telephone handsets and plasma TV sets in hi-tech chic. Bang & Olufsen does not simply produce equipment, it creates audio-visual architecture.

58

1 *Beocenter 2* control unit, 2003
2 *Beocom 4* cordless telephone, 2003
3 *Beovision 5* plasma TV set, 2003
4 *Beolab 5* speaker system, 2004
5 *Beomaster 1200* receiver, 1969
6 *Beosound 9000* CD player, 1996
7 *Beosystem 6500* music system, 1990

1925	Established by engineers Peter Bang and Svend Olufsen
1931	First Danish sound film recorded with B&O equipment
1948	Launches first tape recorder, followed by TV sets and telephones
1963	Begins collaborating with designers, notably **Jacob Jensen**
1966	Receives ID Prize for *Beolit 500* portable radio (twelve further prizes by 1994)
1978	*Bang & Olufsen: Design for Sound* by Jacob Jensen exhibition held at MoMA, New York
1990	**Philips** buys 25% share of company
1997	Repurchases Philips shares; collaborates with **Ericsson**

Products

1934	*Hyperbo 5 RG* audio cabinet with tubular steel frame
1939	*Beolit 39* Bakelite radio
1964	*Beolit 500* portable radio by ▸**Sigvard Bernadotte**
1967	*Beolab 5000* stereo system; *Beovox 2500* loudspeaker
1969	*Beomaster 1200* receiver
1971	*Beolit 400* portable radio
1972	*Beogram 4000* record player
1976	*Beomaster 1900* receiver
	Last six by ▸Jacob Jensen
1986	*Beovision MX 2000* TV set by David Lewis
1989	*Beocenter 9000* music system by Jacob Jensen
1990	*Beosystem 6500* music system by Jacob Jensen
1991	*Beocenter 8500* music system
1996	*Beosound 9000* CD player
1997	*Beocenter AV5* CD player
2003	*Beovision 5* plasma TV set; *Beocenter 2* audio-video system; *Beocom 4* cordless telephone
2004	*Beolab 5* speaker system
	Last seven by David Lewis

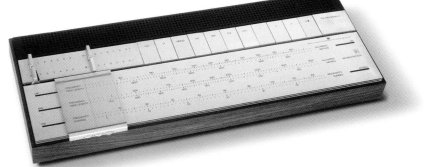

5

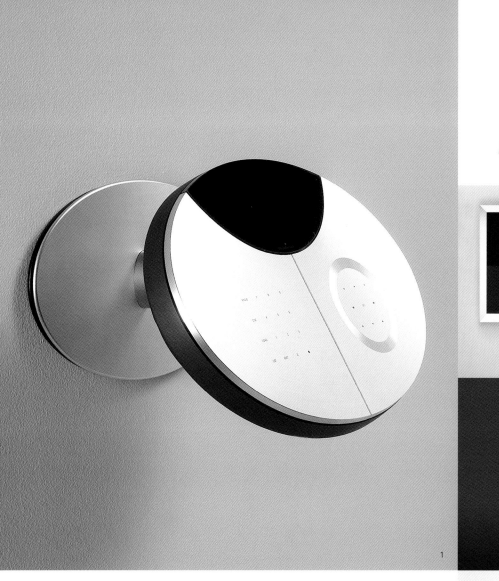

1

2

3

4

6

7

Barber Osgerby

England | Furniture and product design studio | www.universaldesignstudio.com

The two British designers Edward Barber and Jay Osgerby met during their studies at the Royal College of Art in London. Soon after their graduation they opened a design studio and made contact with several significant people in the profession, including manufacturers. The two minimalists, exponents of the simplicity that was rediscovered in the 1990s, came to the notice of the indefatigable talent scout Giulio **Cappellini**, and a year later his upmarket company presented the very restrained *Loop* chaise longue, its upholstery structured by carefully positioned darts in the fabric. In *Loop* and in also the *Flight* stool, Barber Osgerby forged a new, independent path through a historically overworked genre through the use of simple shapes. Anything sharp or pointed is anathema: stools, tables and entire room modules, such as a bathroom concept for **Dornbracht**, are composed of soft, curved forms. The open structure of the *Hula* stool, which has a rocking movement depending on how you sit on it, is tantamount to an expressive outburst from these designers. As well as developing products for leading manufacturers, Barber Osgerby is also involved with a significant aid project for South Africa.

1996	Design studio established by Edward Barber and Jay Osgerby in London
1998	Receives ICFF Editors Award for Best New Designer, New York
2001	Establishes Universal Design Studio to develop architectural and interior design projects with Stella McCartney, Paul Smith and Damien Hirst, among others

Products

1996   *Loop* coffee table for **Isokon Plus** (also at **Cappellini**)
1998   *Flight* stool for Isokon Plus
1999   *Loop* chaise longue for Cappellini
2000   *Home Dining Table* and *Home Coffee Table* for Isokon Plus; *Hula* rocking stool
2001   *Shell* table
2002   *Stencil* screen
        Last three for Cappellini
2003   *Portsmouth* bench and *Hang Up* coat stand for Isokon Plus; *Bespoke* tile for Stella McCartney showroom

1   *Stencil* screen, 2002
2   *Hula* rocking stool, 2000
3   *Loop* coffee table, 1996
4   *Loop* chaise longue, 1999

60

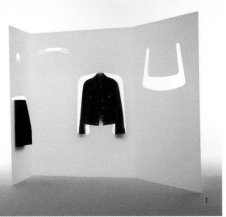

1

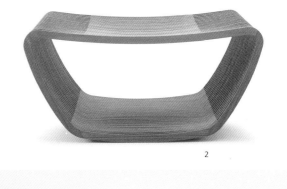

2

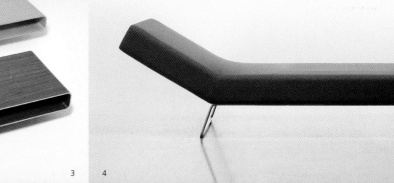

3   4

BEGA

Germany I BEGA Gantenbrink-Leuchten KG, Menden I Lamp manufacturer I **www.bega.com**

BEGA's range of products includes more than 2000 items, from fitted floor and ceiling lamps to wall lamps, pillar and bollard lamps, spotlights, underwater floodlights, light steles and mast-mounted lamps. The history of the company, which specializes in outdoor lighting, is a typical German economic miracle story. In the mid-1940s the goldsmith and sculptor Heinrich Gantenbrink began to manufacture traditional wrought-iron lanterns. The turning point came in the 1960s, when BEGA introduced the 'light brick', which signalled the move towards a more functional approach to design and led to a rapid increase in turnover. The company won its first design award, and numerous others followed. The reduction of traditional forms to simple, geometric elements was a radical new departure. For the first time, lamp designs were largely neutral in relation to their environment. It was therefore the light itself rather than the lamp that became the central focus. Today BEGA sells its products around the world, but the company has remained faithful to its basic principle of unmitigated functionality. At the same time, new lighting technologies and architectural projects have expanded its range of activities considerably, as is evident in commissions for the Reichstag in Berlin and the Guggenheim Museum in Bilbao.

1945 Heinrich Gantenbrink produces handcrafted wrought-iron lanterns
1949 First factory opens; company name established as BEGA
1950 Manufactures lighting for billboard advertisements
1961 Introduces trademark *Lichtbaustein* (light brick)
1992 BEGA luminaires used at Barcelona Olympic Games
1994 Receives Bundespreis Produktdesign for pole-top luminaires *8821*, *8822* and *8823*

Products
1951 *8650* lantern
1960 *3759* house-number luminaire
1961 *3659* and *4959* light bricks
1967 *3564* light grid
1970 *2166* light brick
1971 *9982* underwater luminaire
1978 *9639* bollard
1983 *8337* spotlight
1987 *9906* street lamp
1989 *8710* in-ground luminaire
1991 *8081* pole-top luminaire
1993 *8444* bollard
1997 *8210* pole-top luminaire
1999 *8212* bollard
2001 *2125* recessed lamp
2004 *3275* wall and ceiling lamp

1 *3275* wall and ceiling lamp, 2004
2 *8337* spotlight, 1983
3 *8212* bollard, 1999
4 *2125* recessed lamp, 2001
5 *8081* pole-top luminaire, 1991

61

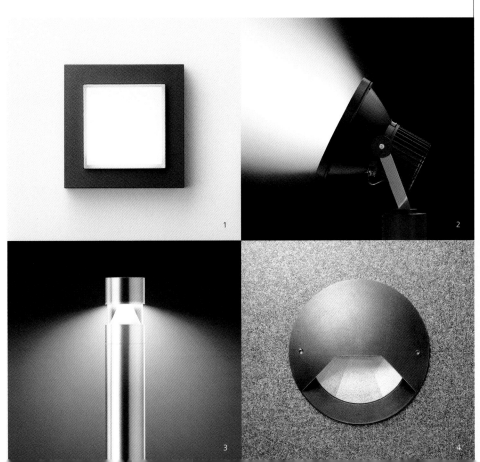

Mario **Bellini**

Italy | Architect and product and furniture designer | **www.bellini.it**

In the late 1990s the Italian designer and architect Mario Bellini created the *Bellini* chair for the American company ▸ **Heller**. Made from plastic, it was an inexpensive, groundbreaking design. It has been part of the company's repertoire ever since and is proof that a product of unusual design can be offered at a reasonable price.

Bellini is a passionate designer, but he has also remained faithful to architecture and, in his role as editor-in-chief of the renowned *Domus* magazine, to architectural and design theory. In the 1960s he achieved early fame with his innovative appliances for ▸ **Brionvega**, including, for example, the mysterious *Black ST 201* (redesigned as *Cuboglass*) television set, which has been included in the permanent collection of the Museum of Modern Art (MoMA) in New York. After the set has been switched on, the picture emerges gradually on screen, lending the technology an element of mystery and suspense.

From the 1960s to the 1980s, Bellini's designs exerted a strong influence on ▸ **Olivetti**. His *Divisumma 18* calculator was a handy, light object. Its sensitive technology was encased completely in a thin, tangerine-coloured rubber skin, which made using it a highly tactile experience. Bellini also designed the *Logos* series of calculators and the *Praxis 35* typewriter for Olivetti. These projects were followed by an industrial lamp, the *Eclipse* spotlight (for **Erco**). For the Japanese company ▸ **Yamaha**, Bellini designed such products as the *TC 800* cassette recorder in the 1970s.

In the field of furniture, Bellini's *Cab* chair (for ▸ **Cassina**) became an icon. For this design, he simply pulled leather upholstery over a skeletal steel frame and fixed it with a zip fastener. He created numerous other seating elements for Cassina and **B&B Italia**, including the *Le Bambole* series. This highly productive designer has always taken context into account in his work. Apart from their practical functions, his objects also have a sensual dimension, a feature evident in products as diverse as the **Vitra** office furniture, sofas for Natuzzi, lamps for **Artemide**, porcelain for **Rosenthal** and cars for **Renault**.

1935 Born in Milan

1959 Graduates in architecture from Politecnico, Milan; starts working in design office of La Rinascente department store (until 1961)

1962 Opens own architecture and design studio in Milan; receives Compasso d'Oro (also 1964, 1970, 1979, 1984)

1963 Hired as consultant for **Olivetti**

1978 Hired as consultant for **Renault**

1986 Appointed editor-in-chief of *Domus* magazine (until 1991)

Products

1965 *Programma 101* computer for Olivetti

1968 *GA 45 Pop* record player for Minerva

1971 *Lettera 25* typewriter for Olivetti

1972 *Le Bambole* sofa for **B&B Italia**

1973 *Divisumma 18*, *Logos 50* and *Logos 60* calculators for ▸ Olivetti

1974 *Area* lamp collection for **Artemide**

1975 *TC 800* cassette recorder for ▸ **Yamaha**; *Monitor 15* TV set for ▸ **Brionvega**

1976 *La Basilica* and *La Rotonda* tables for ▸ **Cassina**

1977 *Cab* chair for ▸ Cassina

1980 *Praxis 35* typewriter for Olivetti

1985 *Persona* office chair for **Vitra** (with Dieter Thiel); *Cupola* coffee service for **Rosenthal**

1986 *Eclipse* spotlight system for **Erco**

1992 *Cuboglass* TV set for ▸ Brionvega

1996 *Memo II* office system for Vitra

1998 *Bellini* chair for **Heller**

1999 *Ypsilon* office chair for Vitra; *Tavollini* stool for Heller

2001 *ArcoBellini* chair for ▸ Heller (with Claudio Bellini)

2002 *Breakfast* bed for ▸ B&B Italia

2003 *Doge* TV set for Brionvega; *MB 1* armchair for ▸ Heller

1 *Eclipse* spotlight system, 1986
2 *Praxis 35* typewriter, 1980
3 *Le Bambole* sofa, 1972
4 *Cupola* coffee service, 1985
5 *Logos 50* calculator (mock-up), 1973
6 *Bellini* chair, 1998
7 *Area* standard lamp, 1974
8 *Ypsilon* office chair, 1999

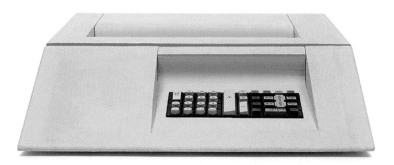

5

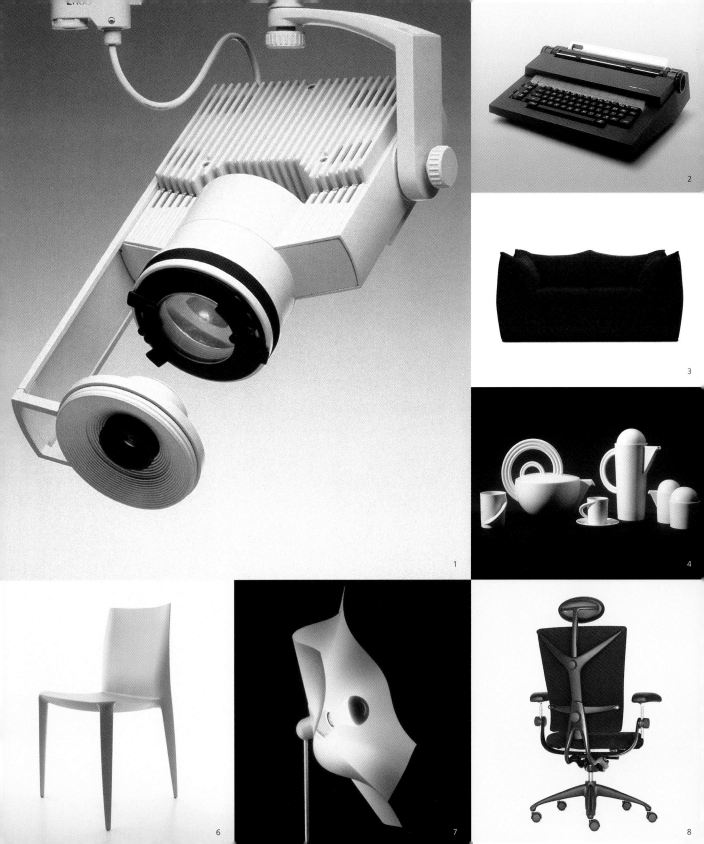

1

2

3

4

6

7

8

Belux

Switzerland | Belux AG, Birsfelden | Lamp manufacturer | **www.belux.ch**

Ron Arad, Andrea Branzi, Antonio Citterio, Danny Lane, **Michele de Lucchi**, Glen Oliver Löw, **King-Miranda Associati**, Borek Sipek, **Ettore Sottsass, Matteo Thun**, Benjamin Thut (son of the founder of **Thut Möbel**), **Burkhard Vogtherr, Hannes Wettstein** – the list of designers who have collaborated with the Swiss lamp manufacturer Belux is impressive. The resulting products are technically sophisticated yet beautifully simple in appearance.

The company (today part of **Vitra**) was founded in 1970 and acquired its distinctive profile in the design-obsessed 1980s. It all began with the *Snodo* and *Ball* lamps and *Metro*, the first low-voltage cable-track lighting system, all designed by ▶Hannes Wettstein. In the mid-1980s Belux organized an international design competition. Although it did not win the competition, the *Lifto* table lamp by Benjamin Thut went into mass production and subsequently received several awards. Intelligent lighting solutions became a feature of the company, as evident in the *Contacto* plug-in lighting system by Jürgen Medebach, Wettstein's *CYOS* (Create Your Own System) spotlight system, the *Meter by Meter* lighting system by Matteo Thun and the *Fokus* hanging lamp by Schwarz Späth, which enables large table surfaces to be illuminated glare-free. Belux's hallmark is brilliant simplicity.

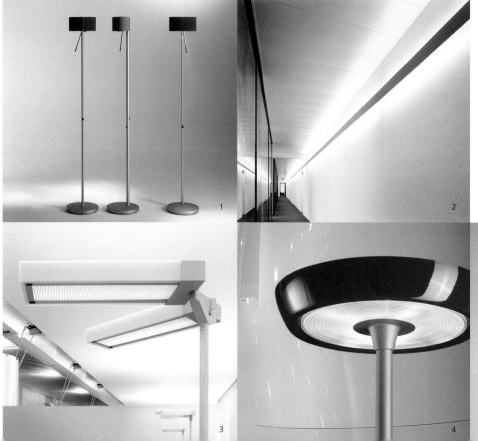
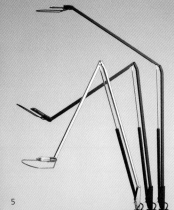

Sebastian **Bergne**

England/Italy | Industrial, furniture and lamp designer | www.sebastianbergne.com

The reductionist designs of Sebastian Bergne, which include furniture, lamps and table accessories, are among the most elegant to have emerged in the last few years. The concept 'less is more' captures the essence of these pieces, the quality of which is achieved only through true insight into the nature of form. Bergne, who was born in Tehran and opened a studio in London after completing his studies at the Royal College of Art, represents the multiculturalism of the English capital city and a new conceptualism. His *Lampshade 1* transforms the common lightbulb into a mysterious object and functions both as a reflector and as a shade that focuses the light. *Nipotino*, *Zia* and *Zio* (for **Luceplan**) are table lamps in the literal sense of the term: here the table-top also acts as a lampshade – an idea so simple that it takes a genius to conceptualize it. *Kult*, a series of table accessories designed for ▶**WMF**, includes small, carefully thought-out table sculptures of the highest precision that make a strong impression on account of their formal restraint. The same is true of the *Slot* armchair, with its slender bent frame. Bergne has also created elegant packaging designs, as in the small, rhomboid jewellery boxes he has produced for De Beers.

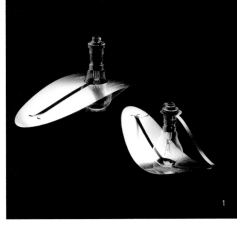

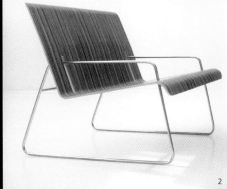

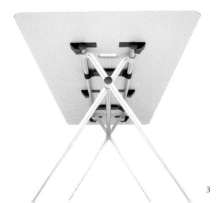

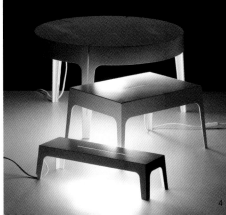

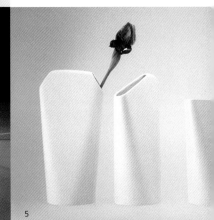

65

Sigvard **Bernadotte**

Sweden | Silversmith and product and furniture designer

It is not without a certain irony that a Swedish prince was one of the first people to put the socialist motto "beauty for all" into practice. Among the best-known designs by Sigvard Bernadotte are office items and practical kitchen utensils. A set of *Margrethe* plastic bowls can probably be found in the majority of Scandinavian homes. Bernadotte won international recognition for his approach to design, which combined functionality with a human element. This approach is evident even in complex pieces of technical equipment, such as a desk calculator, a videophone (for **Ericsson**) and portable radios (for **Bang & Olufsen**), some of which were completely new design solutions. Even from the very start of his career, Bernadotte's versatility was astounding. In the 1920s and 1930s he worked as a silversmith, textile artist, bookbinder and stage-set painter; he also collaborated with large film studios, first at Ufa (in Germany), then in Hollywood. At the beginning of the 1950s, inspired by the 'American way of design', he established the first studio for industrial design in Scandinavia (and one of the first in Europe), together with the Danish architect Acton Bjørn. Among his early associates was the young **Jacob Jensen**. From the mid-1960s the pioneering Bernadotte worked from his own studio in Stockholm.

1907	Born in Stockholm
1926	Attends University of Uppsala; later studies art in Stockholm and Munich
1930	Begins working in silver for **Georg Jensen**
1933	Works as assistant director at Ufa in Germany, later at MGM in USA
1950	Establishes Bernadotte & Bjørn industrial design studio with Acton Bjørn in Copenhagen, Denmark
1953	Publishes book *Industrial Design*
1956	Starts working for Bing & Grøndahl and **Rosenthal**
1961	Becomes president of International Council of Societies of Industrial Design (ICSID)
1964	Establishes own design studio in Stockholm
1998	Retrospective held at Nationalmuseum, Stockholm
2002	Dies

Products

1939	*Bernadotte* cutlery for Georg Jensen
1950	*Margrethe* plastic bowls for Rosti (with **Jacob Jensen**)
1952	Desk calculator for Facit
1957	*T1* typewriter for Facit
1959	*Agavox* dictaphone
1960	Desk calculator for Odhner
1962	*Zauberstab* mixer for Esge
1964	*Beolit 500* portable radio for **Bang & Olufsen**
1966	Cutlery service for SAS
1970	*GM* forklift
1971	Videophone for **Ericsson**

1 *Margrethe* plastic bowls, 1950
2 *Zauberstab* mixer, 1962
3 *Bernadotte* cutlery, 1939
4 *Beolit 500* portable radio, 1964
5 Desk calculator, 1960

66

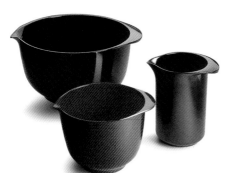

1

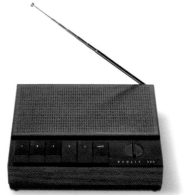

2

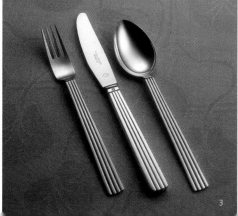

3

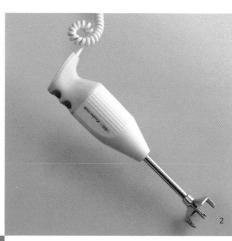

4

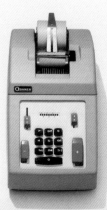

5

Jeffrey **Bernett**

USA | Furniture and product designer

The career path of the furniture and product designer Jeffrey Bernett has taken him from the Midwest of the United States to the design capitals of Europe. Bernett's disarmingly simple creations are an integral part of several notable European collections, including those of **B&B Italia** and **Cappellini**.

Bernett experienced the 'European way of design' mainly as a result of his visits to the Milan International Furniture Fair. He completed his studies in Dorset, England, before establishing Studio B in Manhattan in the middle of the 1990s. There, he creates furniture, lamps and accessories that bear his unmistakable imprint. More structured than the designs of **Pierre Paulin**, but more organic than the geometric furniture of **Maarten van Severen**, Bernett's objects have a cool, Modernist look that is always combined with an elegant finishing touch. His *Landscape* chaise longue (for B&B Italia), with its gentle curves, is an excellent example of his urban Modernism, which is also expressed in smaller objects, such as an ashtray designed for **Ligne Roset**.

1964 Born in Champaign, Illinois
1993 Studies furniture design at Parnham College, Dorset, England
1995 Establishes Studio B in New York
1996 Presents first furniture collection at International Contemporary Furniture Fair (ICFF), New York
2000 Receives ICFF Editors Award for Best New Designer, with Urburbia for Dune
2002 Named Young Designer of the Year, International Furniture Fair, Cologne

Products

1998 Vase and lamp for *Progetto Oggetto* collection for **Cappellini**
1999 Ashtray for **Ligne Roset**; *Monza* chair for Cappellini
2000 *Tulip* armchair for **B&B Italia**
2001 *Landscape* chaise longue for B&B Italia; washbasin for **Boffi**; *Urban* folding table for Cappellini; Murano glass collection for Covo
2002 Aeroplane seating for Northwest Airlines; lamp collection for Ligne Roset
2003 *Metropolitan* seating collection for ► B&B Italia; *Sascha* easy chair, footstool and daybed for **Swedese**

1 *Landscape* chaise longue, 2001
2 *Tulip* armchair, 2000
3 Washbasin, 2001
4 *Metropolitan* armchair, 2003

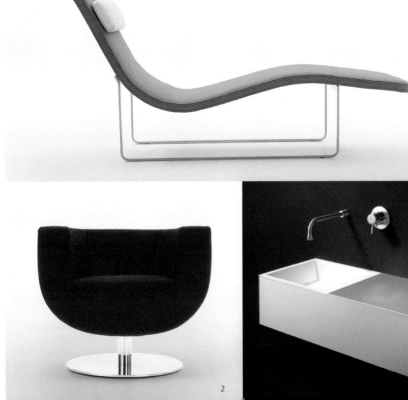

1

67

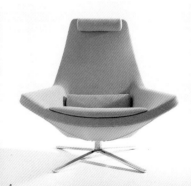

2   3   4

Harry **Bertoia**

Italy/USA | Artist, silversmith and furniture designer | **www.bertoiaharry.com** | **www.knoll.com**

Whether chrome-plated, painted or coated in coloured vinyl, the metal-wire basketwork of Harry Bertoia's *Diamond* range of chairs and armchairs (produced by **Knoll**) served as a model to generations of ambitious young designers. Bertoia was discovered in the mid-1930s by Eliel Saarinen, the father of **Eero Saarinen,** and was engaged by the Cranbrook Academy of Art in Michigan, where he taught metalworking. His work can be divided into two categories that correspond to the twofold nature of his talents: on the one hand, objects perfect for everyday use; and on the other, imaginative art and jewellery. Early in his carreer he discovered his unique style, which is reflected in the jazzy lines of his coffee and tea service from the beginning of the 1940s.

Like **Charles and Ray Eames**, in whose California studio he worked for several years, Bertoia was one of the modern American inventors of forms, and produced a variety of organic designs. His idea of separating the back and seat of plywood chairs and giving them a skeleton-like frame of tubular steel is a principle that has been copied throughout the world, although Bertoia has never been acknowledged as its author. His enduring legacy remains his creations in wire mesh.

68

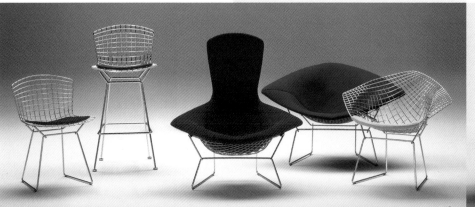

1

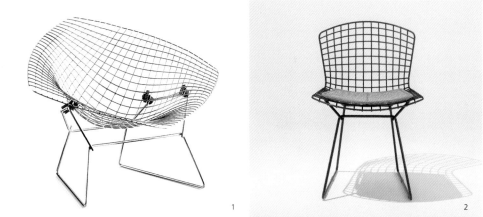

3

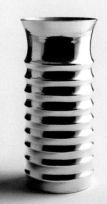

4

Bertone

Italy | Automobile designer and manufacturer | **www.bertone.it**

Giovanni Bertone opened a workshop for automobile body parts near Turin in northern Italy in 1912; his son Nuccio joined him in the 1930s. Elegant luxury cars, such as the majestic **Lancia** *Aprilia* convertible and the aerodynamic **Fiat** *1500*, were a speciality of that time. The company initially struggled to survive after the Second World War, but the stylish **Alfa Romeo** *Giulietta Sprint*, designed in 1954, heralded a golden era. This car had originally been designed for limited production, but was built unchanged for thirteen years. Bertone succeeded in creating highly desirable cult models with, for example, the Fiat *850 Spider* in the mid-1960s and the low, sporty ▶ Fiat *X1/9* in the early 1970s, a period when the name of Bertone – along with **Pininfarina** and **Giorgetto Giugiaro**, the other two legendary Italian coachbuilders – was virtually synonymous with automobile design. Bertone was associated with sports cars with a distinctive wedge shape. The lines of the Lamborghini *Countach* and the rally model Lancia *Stratos*, with its pointed front and compact tail, were typical of Bertone's designs. Successful mass-produced models created by the company include the convertible versions of the **Opel** *Kadett*, Opel *Astra* and Fiat *Punto*. The ▶ Alfa Romeo *GT Coupé*, introduced in 2003, is a clear indication that the characteristic wedge shape has the potential to be endlessly reinterpreted.

1912	Automobile body workshop established by Giovanni Bertone
1934	Son Nuccio Bertone joins company
1951	Franco Scaglione becomes chief designer
1959	**Giorgetto Giugiaro** becomes chief designer
1960	Car production begins
1965	Marcello Gandini becomes chief designer

Products

1921	**Fiat** *501* racing car
1939	Fiat *2800* convertible
1954	**Alfa Romeo** *Giulietta Sprint*
1958	NSU *Prinz* coupé
1962	**BMW** *3200 CS* coupé
1966	Lamborghini *Miura*
1971	**Lancia** *Stratos* sports car
1972	▶ Fiat *X1/9*; Lamborghini *Countach*
1982	▶ **Citroën** *BX* saloon
1985	**Volvo** *780 Coupé*
1994	Fiat *Punto* convertible
1999	BMW *C1* motorcycle
2000	Opel *Astra* convertible
2003	▶ Alfa Romeo *GT Coupé*

1 Lancia *Stratos* sports car, 1971
2 Lamborghini *Countach*, 1972
3 Alfa Romeo *Giulietta Sprint*, 1954
4 Volvo *780 Coupé*, 1985

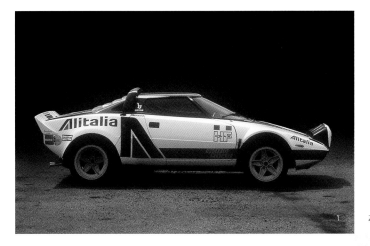

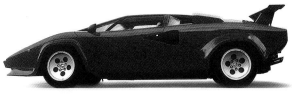

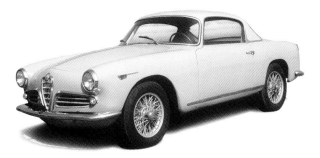

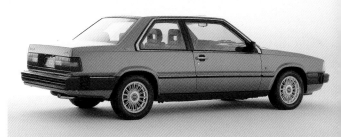

1   2

3   4

Max **Bill**

Switzerland I Architect, graphic artist and furniture and product designer I **www.bill-stiftung.ch**

Max Bill began his studies at the Bauhaus academy in Dessau when he was only eighteen years old, and was influenced greatly by the experience. On his return to his native Switzerland he made a name for himself with his 'concrete art' – stone and metal sculptures. He became famous in Germany after the Second World War for organizing the touring exhibition *Die Gute Form* (Good form), a title that became the design credo of the post-war period. Bill's consistent commitment to the spartan simplicity of Modernist aesthetics made him one of the most influential figures of that time. Together with Inge Scholl and Otl Aicher, he founded the Hochschule für Gestaltung in Ulm. Charged with updating the Bauhaus approach of the 1920s for the 1950s, Bill remained rector at Ulm until the middle of the decade and was also commissioned to design new buildings for the school.

The simple wall clocks and watches that Bill designed for Junghans attracted much attention. His furniture designs included a three-legged table. Bill's work reflects the spirit of his mentors László Moholy-Nagy, Piet Mondrian and **Walter Gropius**. The *Ulm Stool*, in particular, is characteristic of his style – a wooden stool as a portable, angular, minimalist object. Bill was something of a fanatical reductionist, although he himself warned others against an over-restrictive interpretation of functionalism.

1908 Born in Winterthur
1924 Begins silversmith apprenticeship
1927 Studies at Bauhaus, Dessau
1930 Joins Schweizerischer Werkbund (SWB); logo for Wohnbedarf
1933 Produces first sculptures
1938 Joins Congrès Internationaux d'Architecture Moderne (CIAM)
1944 Teaches theory of form at Kunstgewerbeschule, Zurich
1951 Co-founds Hochschule für Gestaltung, Ulm
1967 Appointed professor at Hochschule für Bildende Künste, Hamburg
1979 Receives Order of Merit of the Federal Republic of Germany; granted honorary doctorate from Universität Stuttgart
1985 Becomes chairman of Bauhaus Archive, Berlin
1994 Dies in Berlin

Products
1950 Three-legged table for Wohnbedarf
1954 Doorknob for Hochschule für Gestaltung, Ulm (with Ernst Moeckl); *Ulm Stool* (with **Hans Gugelot** and Paul Hilbinger; re-edition at **Zanotta**)
1956 Four wall clocks
1957 Kitchen clock
1962 Four wristwatches (re-edition 1993) All clocks/watches for Junghans

1 Wall clock, 1956
2 *Ulm Stool*, 1954
3 Kitchen clock, 1957
4 Wall clock, 1956

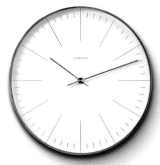

1

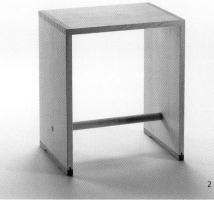

2

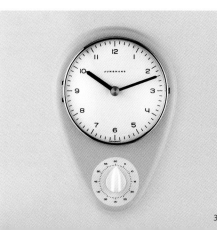

3

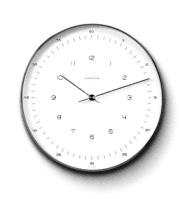

4

Biomega

Denmark | Biomega A/S, Copenhagen | Bicycle manufacturer | **www.biomega.dk**

"If anything could persuade us to get rid of our cars, it is the bicycles by Biomega", claimed the lifestyle magazine *Wallpaper**, in an attempt to encourage a change in modes of transport. In the late 1990s Jens Martin Skibsted and Elias Grove Nielsen joined forces to develop the ultimate urban vehicle and to transform the image of the bicycle as radically as **Bang & Olufsen** had changed the image of hi-fi systems. As a result of the boom in the sales of mountain bikes, the industry had already experienced something of a shake-up, but the two Danish entrepreneurs nevertheless entered the somewhat dowdy world of bicycle manufacture with a new and unusual concept. Their principle was "no model without technological innovation" – thus the *Copenhagen* trekking bike, for example, is driven by a shaft rather than a chain.

Biomega's designs are often inspired by the automobile industry. The *MN01 Extravaganza* model by **Marc Newson** was the first bicycle to be manufactured from two aluminium sections, but without a visible seam. Biomega's approach to design combines hi-tech with a penchant for organic forms, and is very much in the tradition of classic Scandinavian design by **Arne Jacobsen** and **Sigvard Bernadotte**. One of the most unusual designs is the *BioLove* mountain bike by **Ross Lovegrove**, the frame of which is made partly from bamboo.

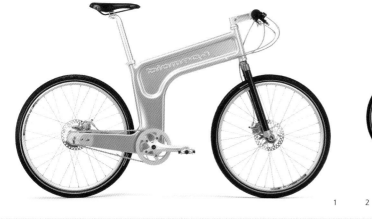

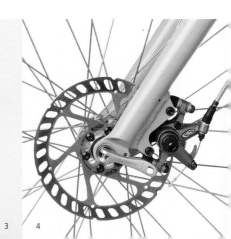

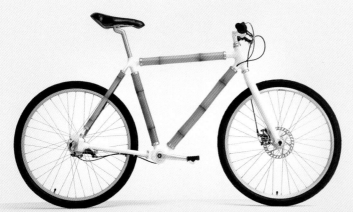

1   2

71

3   4

BMW

Germany | BMW Automobile AG, Munich | Automobile manufacturer | **www.bmw.com**

The year 1972 marked a turning point for the Bavarian car manufacturer BMW. Munich was host to the Olympic Games, and the company opened its new headquarters in the city. At the same time, the *520* saloon, an ideal combination of panache and comfort, was making significant inroads into the executive class. Paul Bracq was responsible for the design of the *5 Series* and the *Turbo* concept from the same year, both of which were highly influential. The *5 Series* succeeded in combining perfectly almost all the elements that were typical of BMW, including double headlights, the kidney-shaped grille and the so-called Hofmeister kink (named after its designer) at the rear side-window. The company had started out manufacturing aeroplane engines during the First World War. After taking over an automobile works in Eisenach, it initially produced models manufactured under licence. In the early 1930s, however, it began to produce models in its own right in Thuringia.

In the mid-1950s – by which time car production had moved to Munich – BMW revived the traditions of its magnificent past with the *507* roadster: light but also muscular, it was designed by Albrecht Graf Goertz, who lived in the United States. Its antithesis was the *Isetta*, a bulbous three-wheeled minicar that was created by the Italian motorcycle manufacturer Iso. This unique vehicle undoubtedly became the most successful microcar of the post-war period. In the early 1960s Wilhelm Hofmeister gave the BMW *1500* saloon not only its conspicuous 'waistline' but also its distinctive kink at the rear supporting column.

In the 1980s BMW presented several designs by ▶**Claus Luthe**, including the new *3 Series* convertible and the *750i* saloon. These models, together with the *Z1* roadster by Harm Lagaay (which had doors that retracted vertically), established BMW alongside **Mercedes-Benz** and later **Audi** as a major manufacturer of high-quality, high-specification cars in the luxury class. Controversial vehicles such as the *Z4* and *Z8* roadsters and the *7 Series*, which underwent a complete makeover at the design studio in California under Chris Bangle, were something of a sensation. Combining traditional elements with expressiveness and sharp edges, these cars presented an image that was unpopular with some people, but they nevertheless defined a new paradigm in automobile body design.

72

1   *6 Series* coupé (detail), 2003
2   *X Coupé* (concept), 2002
3   *Z8* roadster, 1999
4   *507* roadster, 1956
5   *1500* saloon, 1962
6   *5 Series*, from 1972

1916	Established as aircraft engine manufacturer in Munich
1923	Begins motorcycle production
1928	Takes over automotive works at Eisenach (licensed production)
1933	Develops first private car and 'double-kidney' radiator grille
1945	Loses Eisenach factory
1951	Moves car production to Munich
1962	Wilhelm Hofmeister becomes chief designer
1976	**Claus Luthe** becomes chief designer
1990	Establishes BMW–Rolls-Royce
1992	Chris Bangle becomes chief designer
1994	Takes over Britain's Rover group, including Mini, MG and Land Rover
2000	Sells Rover but keeps Mini
2004	Adrian van Hooydonk becomes chief designer

Products

1923	*R 32* motorcycle
1933	*303* saloon
1936	*328* sports car (racing version, 1940)
1951	*501* and *502* executive saloons
1955	*Isetta* bubble car (under licence)
1956	*507* roadster by Albrecht Graf Goertz
1962	*1500* saloon
1965	*2000 CS* coupé
1966	*02 Series*
1971	*02 Touring*
1972	*5 Series* (new series in 1981, 1988, 1995, 2005)
1975	*3 Series* (new series in 1982, 1990, 1998, 2005)
1977	*7 Series* (new series in 1986, 1994, 2006)
1978	*M1* sports car by **Giorgetto Giugiaro**
1987	*Z1* roadster
1989	*850i* coupé by Claus Luthe
1995	*Z3* roadster
1999	*Z8* roadster
2002	*X Coupé* (concept)
2003	*Z4* roadster; *6 Series* coupé
2004	*1 Series*

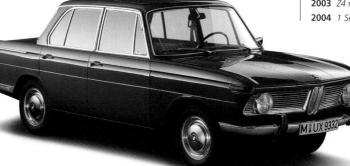

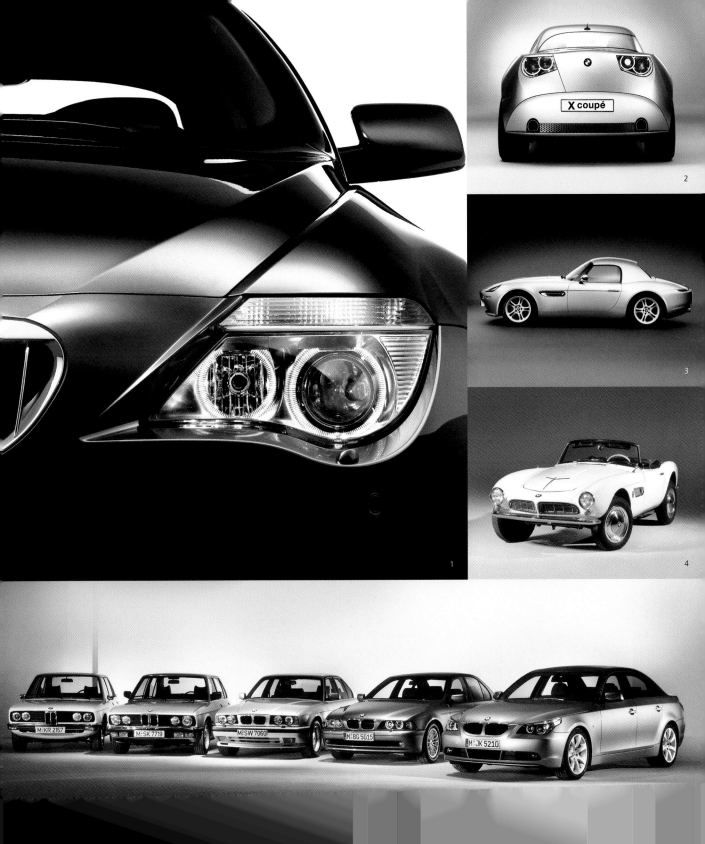

1

2

X coupé

3

4

Cini **Boeri**

Italy | Architect and furniture and lamp designer

The Milanese architect and designer Cini Boeri has created some highly original furniture, particularly for **Arflex**. Her famous *Serpentone* masterpiece from the early 1970s – a long stream of foam rubber winding through an entire room, producing a snake-like seating system – reflected the trend towards a more improvised and informal style of living. Also from the same era is the casual *Strips* chair, with its easily removable covers, and *Bobo*, a polyurethane foam chair without any firm internal structure. The Arflex range can be adapted to varying requirements and is designed to provide relaxation with an accent on wit and humour. An additional feature of Boeri's work are modular systems that can be easily expanded or modified. Her comfortable *Borgogna* reclining armchair, another intelligently devised piece of furniture dating from the 1960s, is mounted on castors and was an early form of the 'home office': writing implements and a telephone can be accommodated in the armrests, and a lamp can also be attached. The small *Cubotto* unit, from 1967, is a practical and charming mobile bar.

Boeri's productive career began at the studio of **Marco Zanuso** in the 1950s, and for five decades she has been committed to the concept of "the human dimension in living" (also the title of one of her publications). People's everyday needs are a major concern: all her products and buildings are designed to make life easier and better. As an expert in production processes, she is able to create furniture that is not only beautiful but also relatively inexpensive. Among her many commissions are lamps for **Artemide**, Arteluce and Stilnovo, door handles for Fusital, prefabricated houses, and numerous showrooms for **Knoll** in Milan, Arflex in Tokyo and **Venini** in Frankfurt. Furniture has always played an important role in Boeri's work: in the 1970s and 1980s she designed a timeless and elegant series of upholstered furniture for Knoll; for **Rosenthal** she created a comprehensive range of office furniture; and for the Italian company Fiam she devised the *Ghost* chair, made of transparent glass.

1924	Born in Milan
1951	Graduates in architecture from Politecnico, Milan
1952	Works at studio of **Marco Zanuso** (until 1963)
1963	Opens studio with Laura Griziotti in Milan
1979	Receives Compasso d'Oro for *Strips* sofa
1981	Showroom for **Arflex** in Tokyo
1983	Prefabricated house for Misawa Homes, Tokyo
1997	Office building for EDS, Rome

Products

1963	*Borgogna* armchair for Arflex
1967	*Bobo* chair and *Cubotto* mobile bar for Arflex
1969	*Gradual* sofa system for **Knoll**
1970	*Lunario* table for Knoll
1971	*Serpentone* seating system for Arflex
1972	*Strips* armchair and sofa for Arflex
1976	*Brigadier* sofa for Knoll
1979	*Double Face* storage system for Arflex
1980	*Folio* chair for **Rosenthal**
1981	*Steps* container collection for Estel
1982	*Tre B* door handle for Fusital
1984	*Chiara* table lamp for **Venini**
1986	*Brontes* table lamp for **Artemide**
1987	*Ghost* glass chair and *Voyeur* glass partition for Fiam
1988	*Ypsilon* table and sideboard system for Rosenthal; *Palo Alto* table for Arflex
1989	*Amado* sofa for Arflex
1997	*Jolly* and *Bar* tables for Meta
1999	*Me* office furniture system for Rosenthal; *Piatto* and *Fiore* tables for Meta
2001	*Meter* sofa for **Molteni & C**

1 *Me* office furniture system, 1999
2 *Ghost* glass chair, 1987
3 *Steps* container, 1981
4 *Bobo* chair, 1967
5 *Serpentone* seat, 1971
6 *Serpentone* seating system, 1971
7 *Strips* sofa, 1972
8 *Amado* sofa, 1989

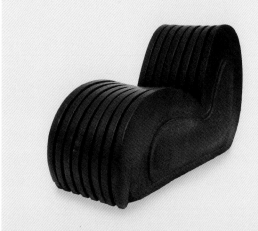

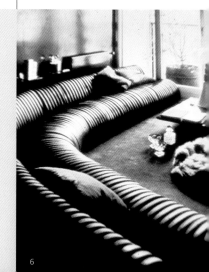

5

6

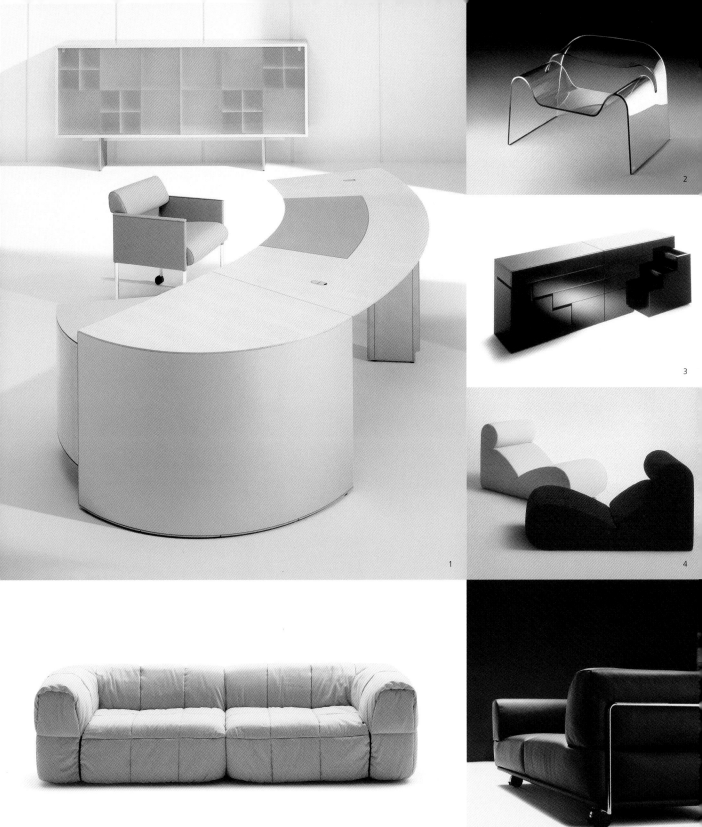

1

2

3

4

7

8

Boffi

Italy I Boffi SpA, Lentate sul Seveso I Kitchen and bathroom manufacturer I **www.boffi.com**

Boffi stands for luxury. The Italian company is one of the most internationally successful kitchen and bathroom manufacturers. Its history goes back to the 1930s, when the Boffi family established a carpentry workshop near Milan. The first kitchen factory was opened after the Second World War by the brothers Dino, Pier Ugo and Paolo. Since then, Boffi has consistently put its faith in good design, technical innovation and a willingness to experiment. The *C Cucina* kitchen (the C stood for *colori*) from the 1950s was unique in its use of colour and is today regarded as a classic. The designer **Joe Colombo**, who was also enthusiastic about new technologies, developed a container kitchen on castors for Boffi at the beginning of the 1960s – a radical new departure. *E 15*, the archetype of the modular kitchen, soon followed. In the 1970s, with Luigi Massoni's *Dogu* kitchen, wood and the traditions of craftsmanship returned to the Boffi kitchen. In the following decade, **Antonio Citterio** and Paolo Nava consciously sought to evoke an association with the aesthetic of the commercial kitchen with their *Factory* design. Later, designers such as **Piero Lissoni** and Marc Sadler contributed remarkable new products. Boffi's strength, however, lays in the fact that its early designs remain on the market. The company diversified into manufacturing luxury bathrooms with the *Boffi Bagno* product line.

1934 Established as carpentry workshop
1947 Builds first factory
1972 Participates in *Italy: The New Domestic Landscape* exhibition at MoMA, New York
1980 Presents first bathroom line
1990 Roberto Gavazzi joins company as partner
1995 Receives Compasso d'Oro for overall performance

Products
1954 *T 12* and *C Cucina* kitchens
1963 *Carrellone Mini-Kitchen* monobloc kitchen by **Joe Colombo**
1972 *Xila* kitchen by Luigi Massoni
1974 *Dogu* kitchen by Luigi Massoni
1980 *Factory* kitchen by **Antonio Citterio** and Paolo Nava (redesign 1999); *Punto* and *Xila Bagno* bathroom series by Luigi Massoni
1984 *Grand Chef* kitchen by Design Tanzi
1989 *Esprit* kitchen
1992 *Latina* kitchen
1995 *B 95* and *Works* kitchens
1997 *WK 6* kitchen
      Last five by **Piero Lissoni**
1998 *Alukit* bathroom series by Marc Sadler
2000 *Fort* bathtub and *Pipé* shower by **Marcel Wanders**
2001 *Mood* bathtub by ▶ **Claesson Koivisto Rune**; washbasin by ▶ **Jeffrey Bernett**; *Case system 5.0* kitchen
2003 *Case system 2.3* kitchen
2004 *Float* bathroom series
      Last three by Piero Lissoni

1 *Float* washbasin, 2004
2 *Xila* kitchen, 1972
3 *WK 6* kitchen, 1997
4 *Works* kitchen, 1995

76

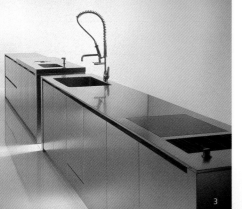
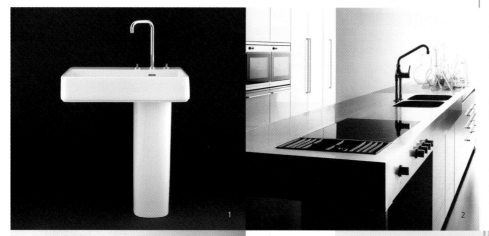

Jonas **Bohlin**

Sweden | Artist and furniture and interior designer | www.scandinaviandesign.com/jonasbohlin

At the beginning of the 1980s Jonas Bohlin presented a chair made of concrete and iron at the Stockholm Furniture Fair. The reaction was largely one of confusion, but there was also a sense of liberation. The controversial chair, which was soon produced in a limited edition by **Källemo**, marked a turning point in Scandinavian design, decisively bringing the postwar period to an end. Bohlin, who loves to be provocative, exhibits great poetic qualities in his work. His creations are like design aphorisms, however mundane the objects themselves may be: *Carpet on Carpet* (for **Asplund**), a woollen white rug decorated with a rectangle and fringe drawn in childlike scribble; or the *Nonting* chaise longue (for ▶ Källemo), a zoomorphic form with two tubular legs. In a variation of the gentle alienation effect produced by his designs, Bohlin has also transformed tutus and shopping bags into ceiling lamps.

One of Bohlin's favourite stylistic devices is his juxtaposition of different materials, as in the *Zink* newspaper stand, a zigzag construction of wood and concrete: it is practical, in that it can be used on both sides, and is as striking as a totem pole. Bohlin adopted a similar approach with *Larv*, a leather 'worm' that turns out to be a halogen lamp. Among his interior design commissions are a number of high-profile Stockholm restaurants; he has also produced a delicate set of porcelain with a simple flower pattern for **Arabia**.

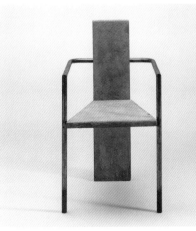

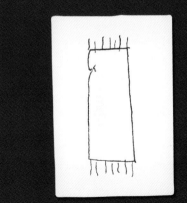

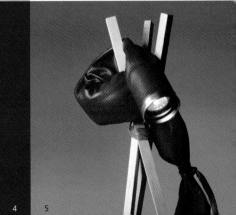

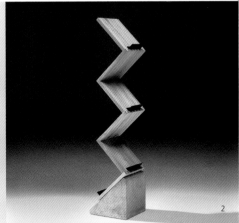

Ronan and Erwan **Bouroullec**

France | Furniture and product designers | **www.bouroullec.com**

Like a fresh breeze on the coast of their native Brittany, the objects designed by the brothers Ronan and Erwan Bouroullec have given fresh impulses to contemporary design. Within the space of just a few years the French designers have become a much sought-after double act. Their new-found fame is due in part to the Italian manufacturer **Cappellini**, which recognized their talent at a very early stage. At the beginning of the 1990s, in their studio near St Denis, the Bouroullecs devoted themselves, without any clearly defined programme, to the reinterpretation of diverse objects, all of which bore their unmistakable signature. They developed office systems and designed furniture, lamps, kitchens, kitchen equipment and other accessories for the home.

The Bouroullecs like surprises but not shock effects. Their work exhibits a high degree of formal harmony that goes hand in hand with a skilful choice of materials and multiple functionality. The fold-down shelf that is part of their *Glide* sofa, for example, is an additional function that adapts naturally to the shape of the sofa.

In their *Joyn* office system, designed for **Vitra**, which seats office employees at a long table, the Bouroullecs have sought to revolutionize the modern work environment. With its wide range of complementary features such as shelves, socket panels, lighting elements and partitions, this outstandingly elegant table is the epitome of modularity. Many other Bouroullec designs are equally well thought out, including the *Brick* shelf system and the *Combinatoires* vase system, which consists of eight freely combinable parts. Flexibility is high on the agenda of the Bouroullecs' approach to product design. The *Sans Titre* recumbent vase and the *Lit Clos* sleeping cabin both in their own way induce the observer to abandon his or her familiar attitude to objects – and this, together with flexibility, is the most important hallmark of the brothers' work. The Bouroullecs have become shooting stars of the new millennium.

78

1   *Brick* shelf system, 2001
2   *La Valise* briefcase, 2003
3   *Glide* sofa, 2001
4   *Sans Titre* vase, 1998
5   *Clouds* shelving, 2003
6   *Spring* chair, 2003
7   *Joyn* office system, 2002

1971	Ronan Bouroullec born
1976	Erwan Bouroullec born
1998	Ronan and Erwan Bouroullec receive International Critics Prize, Salon du Meuble, Paris
1999	Ronan Bouroullec receives ICFF Editors Award for Best New Designer, New York; brothers participate in *French Design and New Material* exhibition, Tokyo
2001	Exhibit at Miyake Design Studio Gallery, Tokyo
2002	Receive Designer of the Year Award, Salon du Meuble, Paris, and *Elle Decoration* Design Award
2003	Participate in *Ideal House* project at International Furniture Fair, Cologne; exhibit at Droog Design gallery, Amsterdam

Products

1992	Table for Christian Liaigre
1995	*Warsao* fruit bowl for Ardi
1997	*Combinatoires* vases
1998	*Sans Titre* vase for **Cappellini**; *Modular Kitchen*
1999	Fruit bowl for **Authentics**; *Square* vase for Cappellini; kitchen system for Units
2000	*Hole* chair, *Spring* armchair and *Lit Clos* sleeping cabin for Cappellini
2001	*Outdoor* folding armchair for **Ligne Roset**; *AIO* service for Habitat; *Brick* shelf system and *Glide* sofa for Cappellini; *Télé* vase for Galerie Kréo
2002	*Joyn* office system for **Vitra**; packaging design for Issey Miyake; *Samourai* armchair for Cappellini
2003	*Butterfly* cabinet with modular inserts, *Spring* chair and *Clouds* shelving for Cappellini; *La Valise* briefcase for **Magis**
2004	*Striped* furniture collection for ▶ Magis

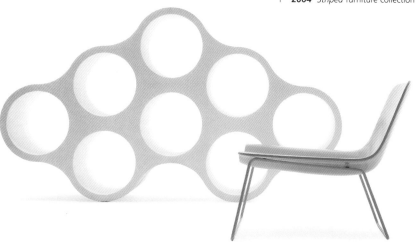

5   6

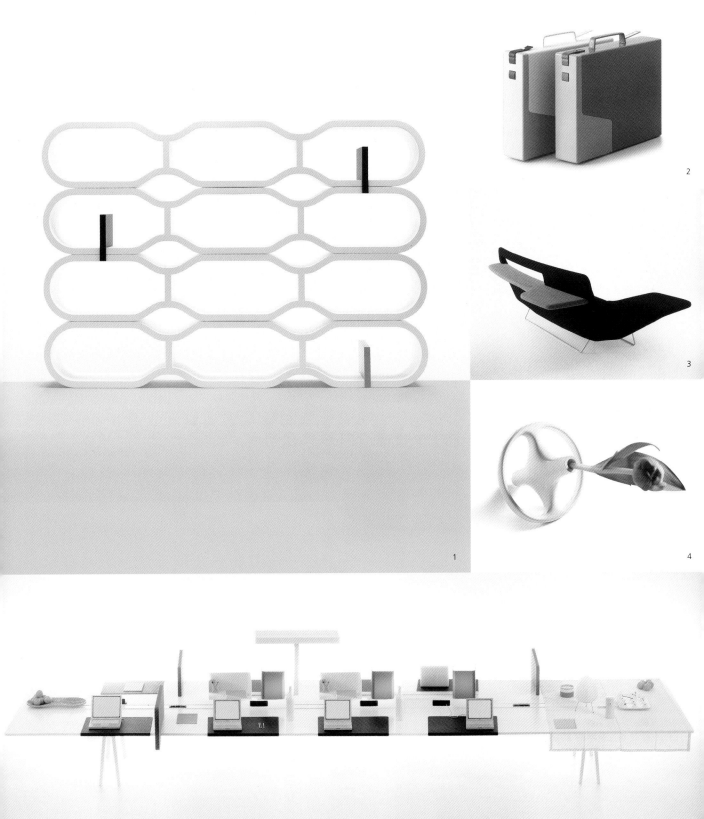

1

2

3

4

7

Marianne **Brandt**

Germany I Product and lamp designer I **www.mariannebrandt.de**

When the manufacturers **Alessi** and **Tecnolumen** began to revive Marianne Brandt's designs, few people knew her name. With great determination Brandt secured a place in the male-dominated metal workshop at the Bauhaus in the 1920s and proved to be an outstanding student. She created innovative designs and was highly productive. The famous *Tee-Extrakt-Kännchen* (tea infuser and strainer) is an excellent example of her metalwork, and clearly demonstrates her interest in the geometric forms of Constructivism. She experimented endlessly with such forms as the sphere and the hemisphere.

Brandt was highly influential in lamp design: of all the designs that she created (about seventy in total), half were of lamps. (Among the Bauhaus designers, however, **Wilhelm Wagenfeld**'s table lamp is now regarded as the ultimate classic.) Brandt's simple and functional ceiling lamp with a pull mechanism (designed with Hans Przyrembel) has remained a model of its kind. From the mid-1920s (around the same time as the Danish designer **Poul Henningsen**), Brandt devoted herself to the development of the table lamp, at that time still a relatively new product. Her *756* desk lamp (designed with Hin Bredendieck), with its reflector that can be tilted and swivelled from side to side, and the *702* bedside table lamp (with Bredendieck) were bestsellers.

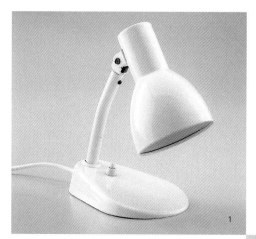

1

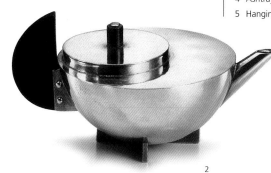

2

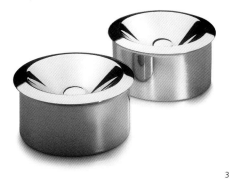

3

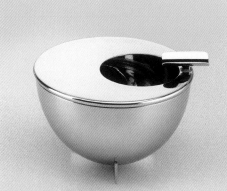

4   5

Andrea **Branzi**

Italy | Architect and furniture and product designer | www.andreabranzi.it

In the late 1980s Andrea Branzi was awarded the Compasso d'Oro, Italy's most coveted design prize. He was honoured not only for his work as a designer and an architect but also for his theoretical contributions to the field. Although he inclines towards the theoretical and intellectual, he has worked continuously as a product designer for more than three decades (among his clients are such leading Italian companies as **Artemide**, **Cassina**, **Poltronova**, **Zanotta** and **Alessi**) and has never lost sight of the basic conceptual issues surrounding his discipline. He was able to indulge his intellectual approach by working as editor-in-chief of the periodical *Modo*.

Branzi remains more interested in the language of objects than in questions of style. In the 1960s, as a co-founder of the Archizoom group, he was one of the most important representatives of the Radical Design movement. Archizoom engaged in practical criticism of functionalism with, for example, the ironic *Mies* chair (for ▶Poltronova), but it also developed such visionary architectural projects as *No Stop City*. In the mid-1970s Branzi was involved in the Global Tools project (planned as a series of experimental design laboratories) and, later, with the legendary design groups Studio Alchimia and Memphis. His recent projects, including the *Tano* clip-on table-top extension, continue to impress.

81

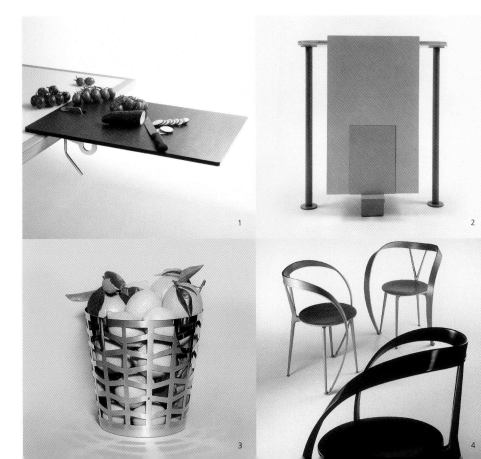

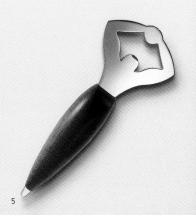

Braun

Germany | Braun GmbH, Kronberg im Taunus | Manufacturer of electrical appliances | **www.braun.com**

The *Phonosuper SK4* radio/record player, the *KM3* food processor, the *Studio 2* hi-fi system, the *Sixtant* electric shaver, the *ET22* pocket calculator, the *Nizo Integral* cine camera, the *Clean and Charge* self-cleaning shaving system – since the 1950s Braun has developed countless innovative domestic appliances, many of which have created a whole new product group. A large number of these design classics have become coveted collector's items.

The company's founder, Max Braun, died in 1951, and his sons Artur and Erwin took over the Frankfurt business. In the same year, the Hochschule für Gestaltung, an academy of design strongly influenced by the Bauhaus of the 1920s, was founded in Ulm. This historic coincidence gave twentieth-century design a new direction. Braun became synonymous with functionalism and formal asceticism. It was the first avant-garde audio brand, but it was soon followed by others, among them **Bang & Olufsen**, **Brionvega**, **Philips** and **Sony**. Artur Braun, who had initially also co-designed such products as the *SK1* radio, worked with the Hochschule für Gestaltung and appointed Ulm lecturers Otl Aicher and Hans Gugelot as consultants. Gugelot contributed impressive design ideas, including the *Phonosuper SK4* and the *Sixtant*. Freelance designers such as **Herbert Hirche** and **Wilhelm Wagenfeld** created a number of radios. As a result of Aicher's insight and vision, Braun, like **Olivetti**, became a shining example of a company with a rigorously defined corporate identity. At the same time, the company built up a design department – a novelty in Europe.

Young architects such as Gerd Müller, responsible for shavers and kitchen appliances, and, later, **Dieter Rams**, the long-standing head of design, and the Ulm graduate Reinhold Weiss, played decisive roles. Rams, who was the personification of functionalism, was responsible for several epoch-making developments, particularly in audio design, including the legendary *SK4* (with Gugelot) and *Studio 2*, the first hi-fi system. Further milestones followed: flashlights by Robert Oberheim, Florian Seiffert's archetypal *KF20* coffee machine and Roland Ullmann's *Micron Plus* shaver, which pioneered the combined use of hard and soft materials in appliance design. In recent years the company, as part of the Gillette group (now itself owned by Procter & Gamble), has focused on a range of body-care products. A rejuvenated design team led by Peter Schneider has constantly produced surprises while still remaining true to the Braun tradition.

82

1 *Micron Plus* electric shaver, 1982
2 *WK600 Impression* kettle, 2004
3 *KF20* coffee machine, 1972
4 *SK1* radio, 1955
5 *CSV13* amplifier, 1959
   (*Studio 2* hi-fi system)
6 *Nizo Integral 7* cine camera, 1979

1921	Established by Max Braun as manufacturer of radio components, with workshop for making equipment
1929	Develops complete radio sets
1932	Presents first radio/record player
1947	Presents first electric shaver
1950	Starts producing household appliances
1951	Artur and Erwin Braun take over management of company
1954	Collaborates with Hochschule für Gestaltung, Ulm, in particular, with **Hans Gugelot**, **Herbert Hirche** and **Wilhelm Wagenfeld**; **Dieter Rams** joins staff
1956	Fritz Eicher heads design department
1959	Develops modular hi-fi systems
1961	Rams becomes chief designer
1964	Exhibits product range at MoMA, New York
1967	Gillette acquires majority shareholding
1968	Introduces Braun Prize for Technical Design
1996	Takes over ThermoScan company

Products

1955	*Combi* radio/record player by ▶ Wilhelm Wagenfeld; *SK1* radio by Artur Braun and Fritz Eicher
1956	*Phonosuper SK4* radio/record player by Dieter Rams and ▶ Hans Gugelot
1957	*TS3* radio by ▶ Herbert Hirche
1958	*HF1* TV set by ▶ Herbert Hirche
1959	*Studio 2* hi-fi system by Dieter Rams
1962	*Sixtant* electric shaver by ▶ Hans Gugelot and Gerd Alfred Müller
1963	*T1000* world receiver by ▶ Dieter Rams
1968	*TFG2* table-top cigarette lighter by ▶ Dieter Rams
1972	*KF20* coffee machine by Florian Seiffert
1976	*ET22* pocket calculator by Dietrich Lubs and ▶ Dieter Rams
1979	*Nizo Integral 7* cine camera by Peter Schneider
1981	*ABW41* wall clock by Dietrich Lubs (▶ p. 51)
1982	*Micron Plus* shaver by Roland Ullmann; *Atelier* stereo system by Peter Hartwein
1984	*KF40* coffee machine by H. Kahlke; *oc3* dental care centre by Peter Hartwein
1991	*DB10* alarm clock by Dietrich Lubs
1996	*IRT1020* infra-red thermometer
1998	*Flex Integral* electric shaver; *Silk-épil* epilator
1999	*Syncro System* self-cleaning electric shaver by Roland Ullmann
2002	*FuturPro* hairdryer by Dietrich Lubs
2004	*Impression* domestic appliance series

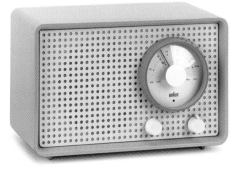

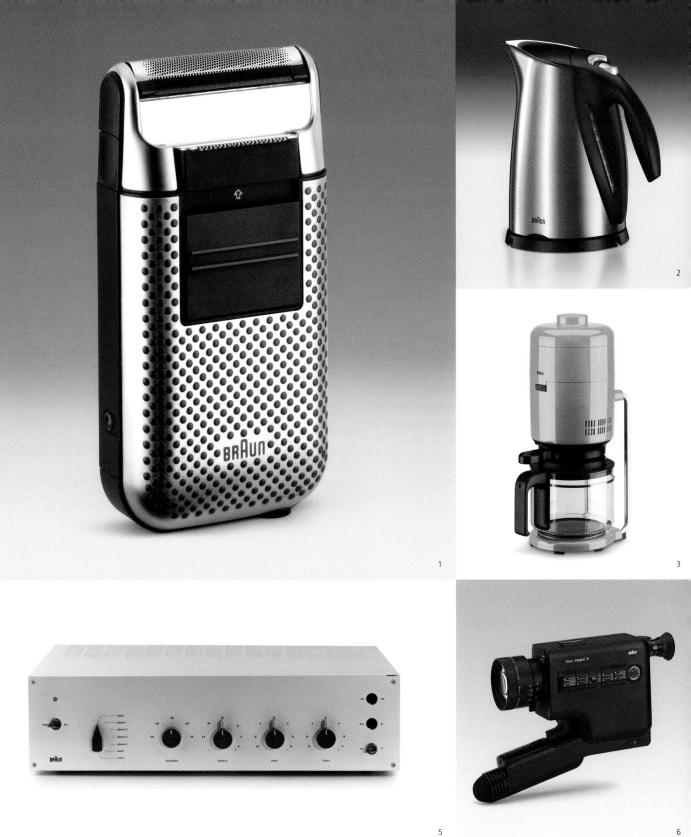

1

2

3

5

6

Wilhelm **Braun-Feldweg**

Germany | Architect, artist and product designer | **www.bf-berlin.de**

Wilhelm Braun-Feldweg was regarded as a perfectionist. He would often create more than twenty mock-ups for a single design before he finally found a form he liked. Starting out as a steel engraver and artist, he turned to design only after the Second World War and thereafter created a large variety of products, from cutlery to bottles, lamps and door handles. His *U 60* microphone set new standards and is still in production today. Glass and metal were his favoured materials, and he used them to create entire families of products that – whether liqueur glasses or a champagne flutes – were striking in their unusual, often cup-shaped design. Unlike **Wilhelm Wagenfeld**, with whom he was frequently compared, Braun-Feldweg regarded it as a constant challenge to endow different objects with specific forms and uses: his *Tokio* hanging lamp, for example, resembles an upside-down vase. Although his products were in keeping with the rationalism propagated by the Hochschule für Gestaltung in Ulm, the tenet of absolute predictability was too radical for him.

In the late 1950s Braun-Feldweg, who as a designer always shunned the limelight, finally accepted a chair at the Hochschule für Bildende Künste in Berlin, where he pioneered the newly created field of industrial design.

1908 Born in Ulm
1922 Begins apprenticeship as steel engraver
1928 Studies art at Staatliche Akademie der Bildenden Künste, Stuttgart
1935 Studies art history in Tübingen and Stuttgart
1937 Sets up teaching and project workshop at **WMF**
1949 Uses 'Braun-Feldweg' as pseudonym
1950 Publishes book *Metall: Werkformen und Arbeitsweisen* (Metal: industrial shapes and techniques)
1954 Publishes book *Normen und Formen industrieller Produktion* (Norms and forms of industrial production)
1958 Appointed professor of industrial design at Hochschule für Bildende Künste, Berlin
1966 Publishes book *Industrial Design Heute* (Industrial design today)
1998 Dies in Würzburg

Products
1952 *Erno 127* door handle
1955 *Marina* bowl for Hirschberg
1958 *Tokio* hanging lamp
1959 *Havanna* and *Mondello* hanging lamps and *15032* vase for Peill & Putzler
1960 *U 60* microphone; *Form 801 Alpha* cutlery for Heimendahl & Keller
1962 *Britz* wall lamp for Doria (later Mawa); *Avus* table lamp; *Tegel* wall lamp
1963 *Havel* ceiling lamp
1964 *Annette* cutlery for Carl Prinz
1966 *HFB 320* aeroplane armchair for Hansajet
2002 Re-edition of lamps (at Mawa) and door handles (at Ogro)

1 *Mondello* hanging lamp, 1959
2 *Marina* bowl, 1955, and vases, 1959
3 *Erno 127* door handle, 1952
4 *Britz* wall lamp, 1962
5 Vases and bowls, 1958–63

84

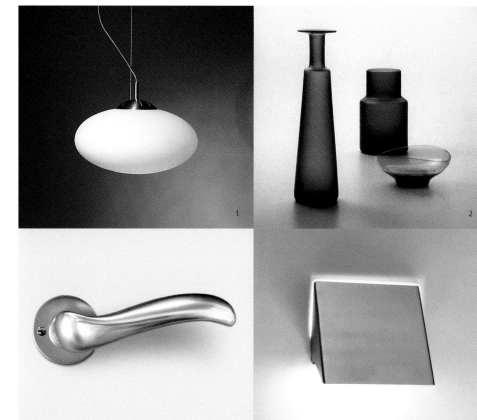

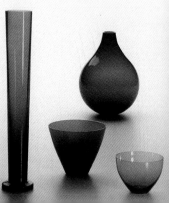

Bree

Germany | Bree Collection GmbH & Co. KG, Isernhagen | Bag manufacturer | **www.bree.de**

When Wolf Peter Bree began to create bags at the beginning of the 1970s, he aimed to produce 'classics' that were functional, simple and timeless in design. The self-taught designer specialized initially in the manufacture of traditional document cases in natural leather fitted with robust buckles. More recently, Bree has moved away from this no-nonsense image and extended its range to include new, more elegant and subtle nuances and accessories. The bestsellers of the early years, however, still sell successfully under the *Times* brand name. The family company employs in-house designers as well as more prominent external designers such as **Jasper Morrison**. The use of modern synthetic fibres and new production techniques has led to innovations in design. For example, for its *Punch* range of rucksacks, which is popular with cycle couriers, Bree used a waterproof and tear-proof fabric. The company has succeeded in bridging the gap between quality goods and mass-market products. Bree finally abandoned conservative designs with its futuristic *Cyber Sub* rucksack series, while the design of the *Conception* handbag was based on the folding technique used to create cardboard packaging, resulting in a pleasing lightweight bag in felt and leather.

85

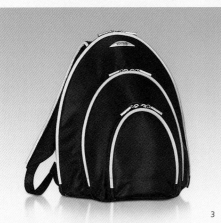
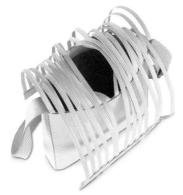
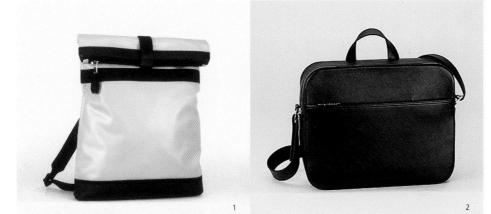
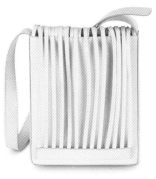

1

2

3 4

Marcel **Breuer**

Germany/USA I Architect and furniture designer I **www.marcelbreuer.org**

"I chose metal for this furniture", Marcel Breuer wrote at the end of the 1920s, "so that it would correspond with the characteristics of the modern room. The heavy upholstery of a comfortable armchair has been replaced by planes of tightly stretched fabric and a number of lightweight tubular bars." In this succinct appraisal of his approach to design, Breuer was actually referring to his most famous creation, the *B 3* chair (later renamed *Wassily*). He regarded his furniture as "the apparatus of modern living": it should be cheap, easily dismantled and hygienic. *Wassily* fulfilled virtually all these criteria but at that time was not a commercial success. Although Breuer had not created an object of everyday use, as he had hoped, it was nevertheless a sensational design that inspired a new genre of furniture. The importance of this lightweight chair went far beyond its use and the individual design, transforming tubular steel into a symbol of modernity for many years to come.

Breuer's first radical Modernist designs were the slatted chairs he created while at the Bauhaus in Weimar in the early 1920s. Similar to the designs of **Gerrit Rietveld**, these chairs, with their simple construction of juxtaposed slats of woods, had a machine-like appearance. Their backs and seats were fashioned from strips of fabric stretched across the frame, a concept that Breuer used again in the *Wassily* chair. He later also created an elegant tubular steel desk and a series of occasional tables that have become minimalist classics (and are now at ▸ **Tecta**).

A Hungarian Jew, Breuer had no future in Germany after Hitler came to power in 1933. He emigrated to the United Kingdom via Switzerland. In London he designed plywood furniture, reminiscent of designs by **Alvar Aalto**, for **Isokon**. This creative phase also brought a design for a radio. Finally, Breuer followed his mentor **Walter Gropius** to the United States, where within a short time he inspired an entire generation of design students at Harvard, among them Philip Johnson, Florence **Knoll** and Eliot Noyes. After the end of the Second World War he embarked on a second career as an architect and was very much in demand around the world.

86

1   *B 3* chair (later *Wassily*), 1925
2   *Isokon Long Chair* chaise longue, 1937
3   *Isokon Dining Chair*, 1936
4   *S 285* tubular steel desk, 1935
5   Slatted chair, 1924
6   *S 35* tubular steel armchair, 1929
7   *Radiogram* radio, 1936

1902	Born in Pécs, Hungary
1920	Studies art in Vienna; studies at Bauhaus carpentry workshop (until 1924)
1925	Heads Bauhaus carpentry workshop (until 1928); develops tubular steel chair
1928	Opens architecture practice in Berlin (until 1931)
1932	First building: Harnischmacher House, Wiesbaden
1935	Emigrates to United Kingdom
1937	Emigrates to USA; lectures at Harvard University
1938	Opens architecture practice in Cambridge, Massachusetts, with Walter Gropius (until 1941)
1946	Opens architecture practice in New York
1952	UNESCO headquarters, Paris; establishes Marcel Breuer and Associates in New York
1966	Whitney Museum of American Art, New York
1967	**IBM** Complex, Boca Raton, Florida
1981	Dies in New York

Products

1924	Slatted chair
1925	*B 3* chair (later *Wassily*)
1926	*D 4* folding chair
1927	*K 40* glass table; *B 9* tables
1928	*D 40* chair
1929	*S 35* tubular steel armchair and *S 32* and *S 64* tubular steel chair series (artistic copyright **Mart Stam**)
1930	*F 41* chaise longue
1932	*No. 301* aluminium chair
1935	*S 285* tubular steel desk
1936	Interior design for Highpoint apartments, London (incl. *Radiogram* radio); *Isokon Dining Chair* and *Dining Table* collection; *Coffee Table* and *Nesting Table;* collection of armchairs and sofas for ▸ **Isokon**
1937	*Isokon Short Chair* and *Isokon Long Chair* chaise longues for Isokon
	Some products available as re-editions at ▸ **Thonet**, ▸ **Tecta** and **Knoll**

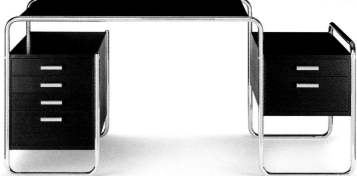

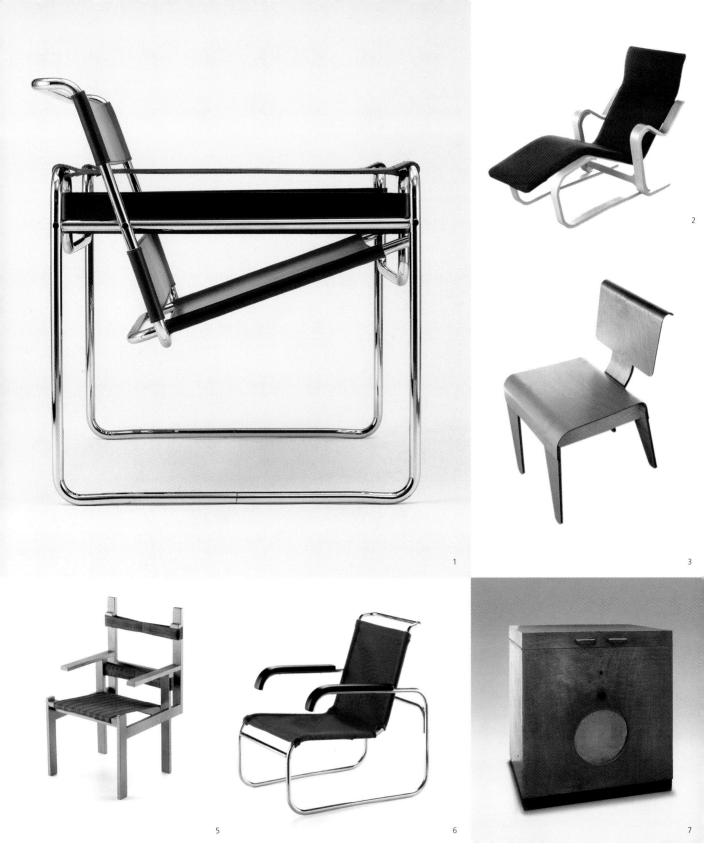

1

2

3

5

6

7

Brionvega

Itaiy I SIM2 Multimedia SpA, Pordenone I Manufacturer of electrical appliances I **www.brionvega.it**

Since the beginning of the 1960s Brionvega has proved that it is not absolutely essential to place radio and TV technology in boring boxes. These products can be transformed into display objects in their own right and at the same time awaken the playful instincts of their users. Such inspired designers as **Marco Zanuso** and **Richard Sapper** took advantage of this opportunity: the result was an intelligent, new and distinctly Italian variant of audio design that could hold its own with similarly ambitious manufacturers such as **Bang & Olufsen** and **Braun**. The *TS 502* folding radio conceals its functions in a colourful cube; the *Algol 11* TV set curves upwards towards the viewer; and the *Black ST 201* television, a dramatic cube, shrouds the charm of moving pictures in mystery. In **Mario Bellini** and the Castiglioni brothers Brionvega found sympathetic designers who shared its vision. **Achille Castiglioni** gave the *RR 126* radio set a control panel reminiscent of a cartoon character face. In the harsh reality of an audio market dominated by the Far East, however, a bold design strategy is, in itself, no longer sufficient to sustain demand. But what has remained constant is the cult surrounding a company that exalted technology and form to create a kind of poetry in its products. Brionvega still exists as a brand name within the Italian Formenti group, which has had great success with the reissue of a number of classics.

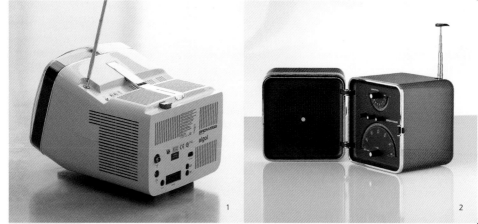

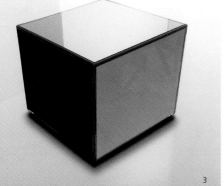

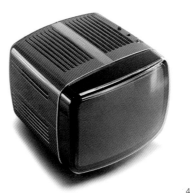

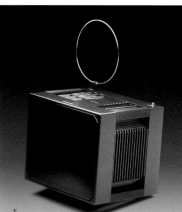

Bulo

Belgium | Bulo, Mechelen | Manufacturer of office furniture | **www.bulo.be**

At the end of the 1990s the furniture industry gradually became aware of an office furniture manufacturer in Belgium that combined a fresh marketing approach with unusual products. The *Pub & Club* office chair series in brown corduroy, which plays on associations with the lounge club scene, was a sensation. The Belgian avant-garde fashion designer Dirk Bikkembergs introduced a completely new type of furniture at the Milan International Furniture Fair in 2002: the *Mat* 'work mat' was a response to new, more flexible ways of working. This was also the concept behind Danny Venlet's *Easy Rider* armchair, which is mobile and does not force its user to sit on it in a particular way.

Company founder Walter Busschop's archive filing system was one of Bulo's early success stories in the 1960s. In the 1970s the firm specialized in office planning, but it did not establish its own design department until 1980. Since its breakthrough in the 1990s, Bulo has been determined to retain its unmistakable identity. The H_2O furniture collection by Claire Bataille and Paul Ibens was precisely what architects (Bulo's target group) wanted. For its *Carte Blanche* collection the company engaged such well-known architects and designers as Ann Demeulemeester, **Jean Nouvel**, **Hannes Wettstein** and **Maarten van Severen**. Their unusual perception of office work is reflected in a series of distinctive and novel products.

1963	Established by Walter Busschop
1970	Specializes in office planning and office furniture
1980	Establishes own design department
1987	Becomes market leader in Belgium
1999	Receives Good Design Award, Chicago, for *Schraag* desk
2003	Receives Red Dot Design Award and Good Design Award, Chicago, for *Easy Rider* armchair

Products

1980	*KRS* storage system
1989	*Buloflex* office system
1992	*Bulosafe* system for locking storage and drawer modules
1994	H_2O furniture collection by Claire Bataille and Paul Ibens
1996	*Carte Blanche* collection; *M2* workstation
1998	*Pub & Club* office chair collection
1999	*Schraag* desk by ▶ **Maarten van Severen**
2000	*Normal* collection by ▶ **Jean Nouvel**
2002	*Mat* work mat by Dirk Bikkembergs; *Double You* desk by **Hannes Wettstein**; *Easy Rider* armchair by Danny Venlet

1   *Easy Rider* armchair, 2002
2   *Pub & Club* office chair, 1998
3   Module from the H_2O collection, 1994
4   *Double You* desk, 2002

89

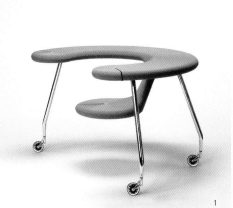

1

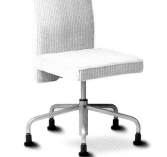

2

3   4

Bulthaup

Germany I Bulthaup GmbH & Co. KG, Bodenkirchen I Kitchen manufacturer I **www.bulthaup.com**

The factory-produced kitchen has become a standard feature of modern life. Bulthaup manufactured functional fitted kitchens such as *Typ 1* until the beginning of the 1980s, when it announced plans to produce more design-orientated models. Otl Aicher, who had already acted as consultant to **Braun**, Lufthansa and **Erco**, developed a design philosophy intended to revitalize the kitchen as a centre of social activity. The new kitchen concept was modelled on the flexible design of professional cookery studios and featured a central work table around which all activities were concentrated. Somewhat later, the central table evolved into a 'workbench' in stainless steel.

Bulthulp's radical reinterpretation of the kitchen called for the development of a different kind of furniture, such as shelving suspended from the ceiling. The almost sculptural ventilation systems were given greater prominence. The company also launched a range of high-quality kitchen utensils. Tables and chairs were added to the range in the mid-1990s, with the introduction of the *Korpus* and *Duktus* collections. The *25* and *20* systems designed by **Herbert H. Schultes**, with freely combinable elements equipped with ergonomically designed work surfaces and mobile kitchen containers, are regarded as the ultimate in kitchen design.

90

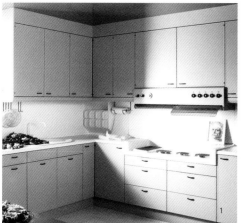

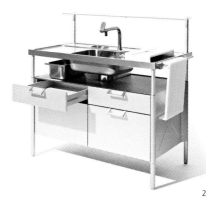

1

2

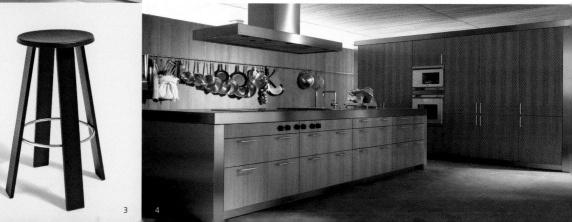

3   4

Rido **Busse**

Germany | Product designer | **www.busse-design-ulm.de**

Deeply influenced by his studies at the Hochschule für Gestaltung in Ulm, Rido Busse has developed more than two thousand products – from lawnmowers to pencil sharpeners and thermos flasks, all well-designed articles. Among his everyday classics are bicycle and car seats for children (for Römer Britax) and a set of mixing bowls for Krups (a design developed from a concept by **Sigvard Bernadotte**) that at one time was to be found in virtually every kitchen cupboard in Germany.

Busse, who has often received awards for his work, awards design prizes himself: his Longlife Design Award is given to products that have been on sale for at least eight years; the Plagiarius is awarded for the most audacious act of plagiarism. Both prizes underline Busse's basic philosophy that every article should be innovative, of practical use and have a long product life. The great names included on his list of clients – among them AEG, **Braun**, **IBM** and **Kodak** – demonstrate his success in meeting these aims. Companies appreciate the straightforwardness of Busse's designs and the range of services he provides, which includes graphics and communications design.

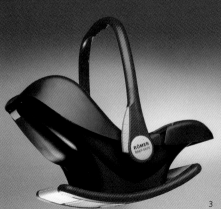

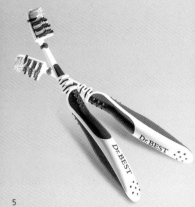

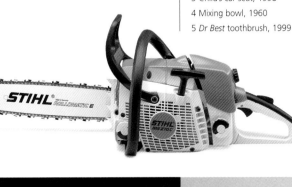

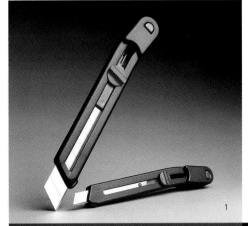

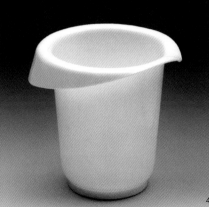

1

2

3

4

5

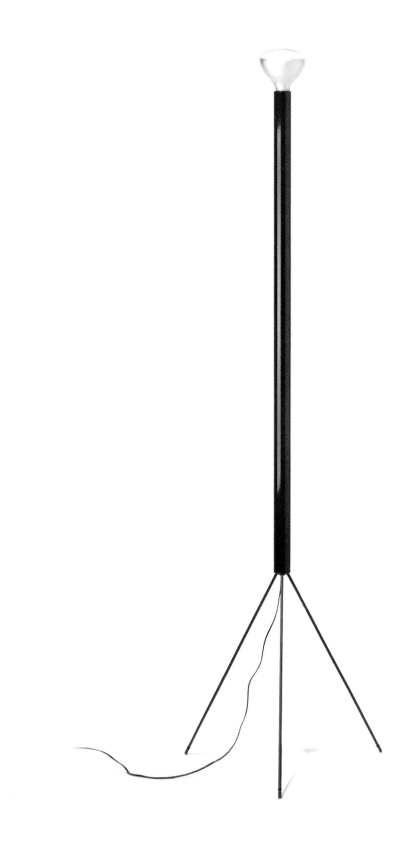

Fernando and Humberto **Campana**

Brazil | Furniture and product designers | **www.campanabrothers.com**

The sensational creations of the Campana brothers have been favourites of the design and home decoration periodicals for a number of years. The velvet upholstered *Boa* sofa and the *Sushi* rag chair are flagship products that underline the exceptional position of the Italian manufacturer **Edra** in the competitive world of design. The careers of the two brothers began quite conventionally: following his law degree, Humberto became a goldsmith and sculptor; Fernando became an architect. In the early 1980s they opened a studio together and started producing designs that transcended conventional limits, even as far as their choice of materials was concerned. While some of the materials were created in hi-tech laboratories, others seemed to come from the slums of São Paulo (the brothers' home town). Tubes, wooden slats, scraps of fabric, ropes and bamboo canes are often incorporated into the Campanas' work. A famous example is *Favela*, a chair made from small pieces of wood fixed together with glue and nails.

Many pieces of Campana furniture are assembled from a large number of identical parts. Sometimes these parts are assembled to form opulent, luxurious objects; at other times, they are fixed together to create much smaller products, as in the case of the *Blow Up* bowls and coasters for **Alessi** (▸ p. 7). This 'piecemeal' approach to design is combined with ingenious improvisation, a skill that is often crucial to survival in the slums of São Paulo. The elements of the individual pieces look as if they have not been fixed together in the usual industrial manner: arrangements sometimes appear arbitrary and spontaneous, as if determined by the hand of an artist. This random principle creates the impression of instability and liveliness – associations that arouse a feeling of uncertainty in the observer. The intertwined velvet tubes that make up the *Boa* sofa, for example, appear to form a mound of snakes. The effect is so convincing that one expects the object to move. The *Sushi* chair appears unfinished and looks as though someone has flung a pile of clothes on it. The successfully rebellious Campanas have also collaborated with the chemical company Bayer to develop a new kind of flooring made from a special artificial resin in which wooden slats have been integrated as though they have been strewn over the ground.

94

1953 Humberto Campana born in Rio Claro, São Paulo
1961 Fernando Campana born in Brotas, São Paulo
1972 Humberto studies law at Universidade de São Paulo (until 1977)
1979 Fernando studies architecture at Faculdade de Belas Artes de São Paulo (until 1984)
1983 Collaboration begins
1999 Receive George Nelson Design Award, USA
2003 Participate in *Ideal House* project at International Furniture Fair, Cologne, and *Air Craft* project at Vitra Design Museum

Products
1997 *Estela* lamp for **O Luce**
1998 *Azul* and *Vermelha* armchairs and *Verde* chair (all *Cotton String Collection*) for ▸ **Edra**
1999 *Cone* armchair for Edra
2000 *Bambù* and *Plastic* table lamps and *Tatoo* table for **Fontana Arte**; *Inflating Table* for MoMA, New York
2001 *Anemone* chair and *Zig Zag* bench for Edra; *Bambù Metal Chair* for Hidden; *Batuque* vase for **Cappellini**; pen collection for ACME
2002 *Boa* sofa and *Sushi* rag chair for Edra; *Bolas* child's chair for Bozart; *Peteca* cube toy for **Magis**; *California Rolls* chair
2003 *Favela* armchair for Edra
2004 *Blow Up* fruit basket for **Alessi** (▸p. 7); *Corallo* wire armchair for Edra; *Alligator* chair

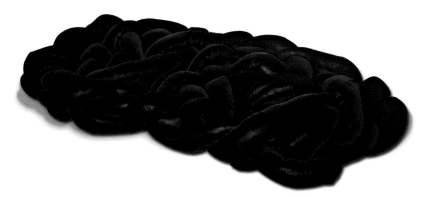

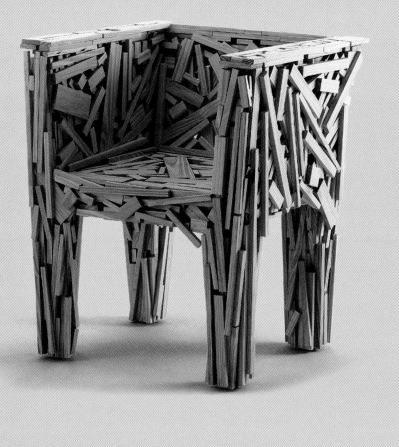

1

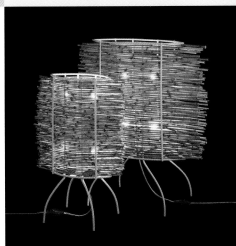

2

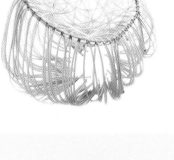

3

4

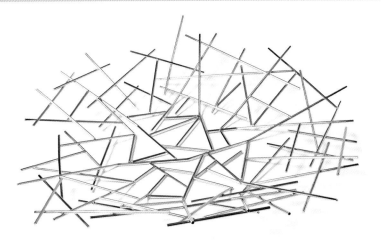

6

7

Cappellini

Italy I Cap Design SpA, Arosio I Furniture manufacturer I **www.cappellini.it**

Each April, when the International Furniture Fair lures the industry to Milan, an old warehouse in the southern part of the city used to attract design pilgrims. It was there that the Italian avant-garde furniture manufacturer Cappellini displayed its new products. In the 1970s the owner, Giulio Cappellini, sought to transform the company's fortunes. Giulio had a natural instinct for detecting young talent from all over the world, and his company has acted as the springboard for numerous successful careers, to the extent that the list of notable Cappellini designers reads like a *Who's Who* of modern design. ▶ **Shiro Kuramata** contributed his *Side 1* and *Side 2* curved chests of drawers to the collection; the Englishman **Tom Dixon** his delicate *S-Chair*, a style icon that is still available today in various versions. ▶ **Jasper Morrison** created characteristically minimalist designs, such as the elegant *Three* sofa system and the *Thinking Man's Chair*. Other stars engaged by Cappellini include **Marc Newson, James Irvine, Werner Aisslinger, Marcel Wanders, Ross Lovegrove, Rodolfo Dordoni, Christophe Pillet, Alberto Meda, Piero Lissoni** and the **Bouroullec** brothers. The Bouroullecs' shelf systems, which look like complex cellular units, have come to determine the company's more recent design programme in much the same way as Morrison's icons once did.

The Cappellini collection is characterized by powerful individual statements and is therefore extremely diverse. In this high-value market sector, the company relies on the cult status of exclusive objects. Anyone who buys Cappellini is purchasing a fetish object: Patrick Norguet's multicoloured *Rainbow Chair*, for example, is designed to be looked at rather than sat on. But practical objects are also available. The simple and functional storage and shelf systems by Giulio Cappellini himself have sold so well for the company that they have allowed it to take risks and experiment in other areas. This sophisticated furniture, which often places high demands on the manufacturing process, is produced by a network of factories that guarantees a high level of technical competence. Nevertheless, the bold range had its price: following the takeover of Cappellini by the Italian furniture company Poltrona Frau in 2004, it remains to be seen whether it will be possible to continue such experimentation.

96

1 *Side 1* chest of drawers, 1970

2 *Rainbow Chair*, 2000

3 *po 0035* lamp, 1998

4 *Three Sofa Deluxe*, 1991

5 *Felt Chair*, 1997

6 *S-Chair*, 1992

7 *Irkel* shelving, 2003

1946	Established in Arosio as manufacturer of handmade furniture
1960	Turns to modern design
1987	Launches Mondo subsidiary
2004	Poltrona Frau takes over company

Products

1970	*Side 1* and *Side 2* chests of drawers by ▶ **Shiro Kuramata**
1977	*Solaris* chest by ▶ Shiro Kuramata
1986	*Passepartout* shelf system by Giulio Cappellini and **Rodolfo Dordoni**
1988	*Thinking Man's Chair* by ▶ **Jasper Morrison**; *Pyramid* chest of drawers by ▶ Shiro Kuramata
1991	*Orgone* table by ▶ **Marc Newson**; *Satellite* table by **Konstantin Grcic**; *Three Sofa Deluxe* by Jasper Morrison
1992	*S-Chair*, *Pylon Chair* and *Bird* chaise longue by ▶ **Tom Dixon**
1993	*Proust* armchair by ▶ **Alessandro Mendini** (1978 design); *Figure of Eight* chair by **Ross Lovegrove**
1994	*ABC* shelf by **Alberto Meda**
1995	*Statuette* armchair by Lloyd Schwan; *Small Room* armchair by ▶ **Burkhard Vogtherr**
1996	*Juli* chair by ▶ **Werner Aisslinger**; *Knotted Chair* by ▶ **Marcel Wanders**
1997	*Felt Chair* by Marc Newson
1998	*Embryo Chair* by ▶ **Marc Newson**; *Big Shadow* standard lamp series by ▶ **Marcel Wanders**
2000	*Rainbow Chair* by Patrick Norguet
2001	*Glide* sofa by ▶ **Ronan and Erwan Bouroullec**
2002	*Pebbles* bench by ▶ **Claesson Koivisto Rune**; *Plan* cabinet collection by ▶ Jasper Morrison
2003	*None Rota* armchair by ▶ **Ron Arad**; *Clouds* shelving and *Spring* armchair by ▶ **Ronan and Erwan Bouroullec**; *Coupé* collection of upholstered furniture by ▶ **Piero Lissoni**; *Simplon* furniture system by Jasper Morrison; *Irkel* shelving by Lloyd Schwan

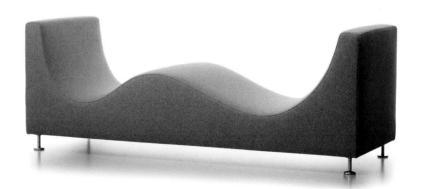

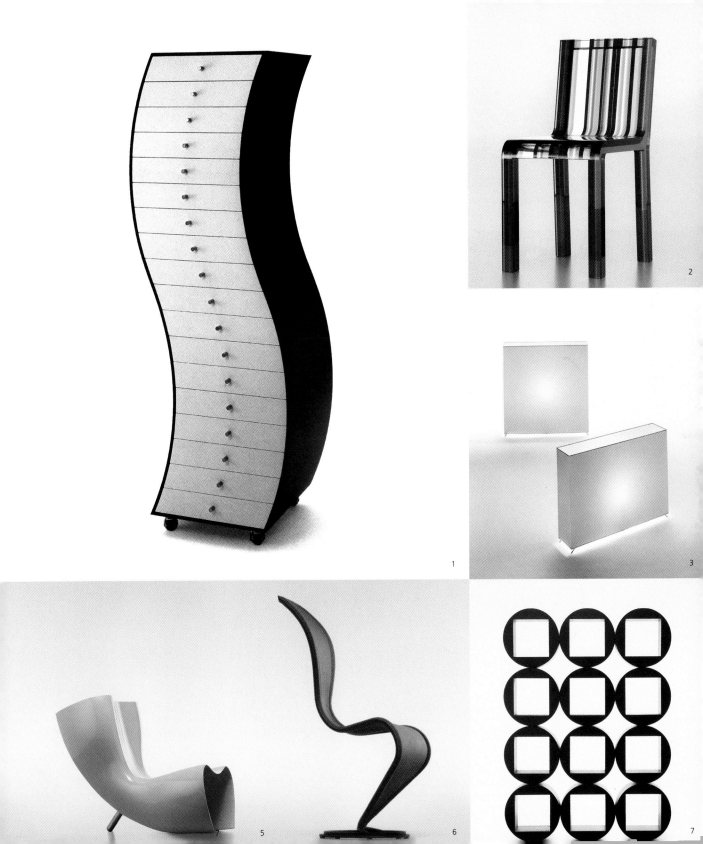

1

2

3

5

6

7

Cassina

Italy | Cassina SpA, Meda | Furniture manufacturer | **www.cassina.com**

Cassina was instrumental in the invention of the re-edition. Since the middle of the 1960s, furniture designed by such famous names as **Le Corbusier, Frank Lloyd Wright, Charles Rennie Mackintosh**, Gunnar Asplund, and **Gerrit Rietveld** has been revived as part of the company's impressive Masters Collection. As a result, these pieces have finally been acknowledged as design classics. The combination of tradition and avant garde is a theme that runs through the history of this company. The family firm was transformed after the Second World War from a traditional upholstery company into a leading manufacturer of modern furniture with a strong emphasis on quality craftsmanship. The elegant *Super-leggera* chair, a design by the architect ▸ **Gio Ponti**, was a milestone in the metamorphosis of the company. It was hailed as the lightest chair in the history of furniture and is still regarded as a shining example of modern Italian furniture design. Ponti took his cue from chairs made from such traditional materials as wicker and wood, but reduced the individual components so radically that the piece was ideally suited for industrial mass production.

For more than half a century Cassina has represented quality modern furnishings and has always sought to collaborate with the most influential contemporary designers, among them such figures as **Franco Albini, Mario Bellini, Vico Magistretti** and Afra and Tobia Scarpa. Leading designers working for the company today include **Hannes Wettstein, Jorge Pensi** and **Piero Lissoni**. Over the years Cassina has also aligned itself with design 'rebels', including **Gaetano Pesce** and Paolo Deganello, whose intentions were to bring about the downfall of the bourgeois interior with the introduction of their radical ideas. Deganello's *AEO* armchair, for example, had little in common with a traditional upholstered chair. It could be dismantled to create a separate base, cushions, two frames for the back and seat, and a tent-like throw. ▸ Gaetano Pesce's *Dalila* chair, made of polyurethane covered in polyester, was different in each production batch, and was thus an intentionally random product. **Philippe Starck** has recently designed successful products for Cassina, among them the *Lazy Working Sofa* (*LWS*), which, despite its traditional form, is highly contemporary in its ironic presentation of the sofa as a place of work.

98

1 *Nuvola Rossa* shelf, 1977
2 *Units* shelf and container system, 2000
3 *Meyer May* desk, 1986 (1908 design)
4 *La Rotonda* table, 1976
5 *LWS* armchair, 1998
6 *Ingram* chair, 1973 (1904 design)
7 *Cab* chair, 1977
8 *AEO* armchair, 1973
9 *Dodo* armchair, 2000

1927	Established by Cesare and Umberto Cassina in Meda
1947	Receives large commission from Italian navy
1965	Produces first classic re-editions
1989	**Steelcase** buys 50% share in company
2000	Fimalac Group takes over company

Products

1953	*Distex* armchair by **Gio Ponti**
1957	*Superleggera* chair by ▸ Gio Ponti
1965	Re-editions, incl. *LC 1* and *LC 2* armchairs, *LC 4* chaise longue, *LC 6* table and *LC 10-P* table by ▸ **Le Corbusier**
1973	Re-editions, incl. *Hill House, Argyle, Ingram* and *Willow* chairs by ▸ **Charles Rennie Mackintosh**; re-editions: *Zig-Zag* and *Red and Blue* chairs and *Schröder* table by ▸ **Gerrit Rietveld**; *AEO* armchair by Paolo Deganello; *Maralunga* sofa by ▸ **Vico Magistretti**
1976	*La Rotonda* and *La Basilica* tables and *Break* armchair by **Mario Bellini**
1977	*Nuvola Rossa* shelf by Vico Magistretti; *Cab* chair by Mario Bellini
1980	*Wink* easy chair by ▸ **Toshiyuki Kita**
1986	Re-editions, incl. *Johnson Wax* desk and chair and *Meyer May* desk by ▸ **Frank Lloyd Wright**
1987	*I Feltri* armchair by ▸ **Gaetano Pesce**
1993	*Revers* chair by ▸ **Andrea Branzi**
1996	*Met* sofa and *On-Off* table by **Piero Lissoni** and Sung Sook Kim
1998	*Duna* chair by ▸ **Jorge Pensi**; *LWS* furniture series by **Philippe Starck**
1999	*Nest* sofa by ▸ Piero Lissoni
2000	*Globe* sofa and *Units* shelf and container system by ▸ **Hannes Wettstein**; *Dodo* armchair by Toshiyuki Kita

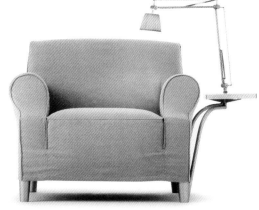

5

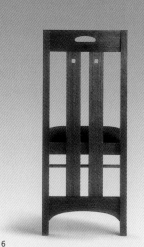

6

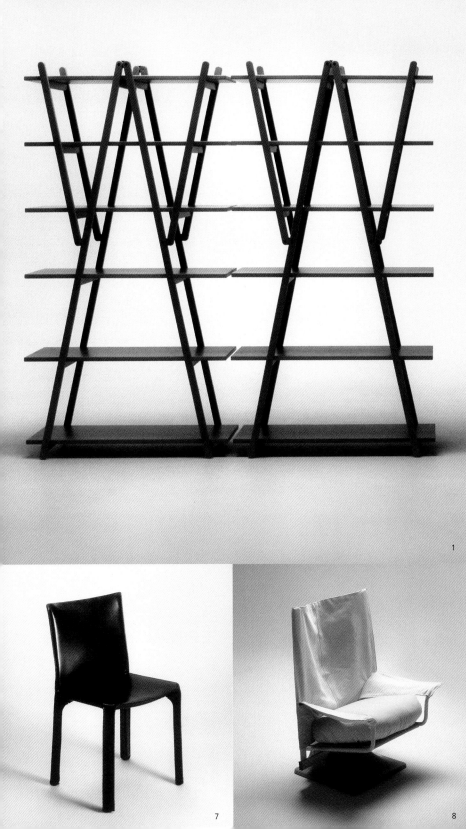

1

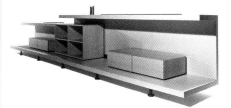

2

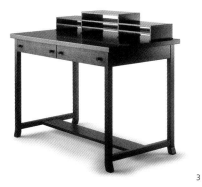

3

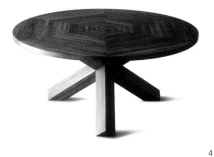

4

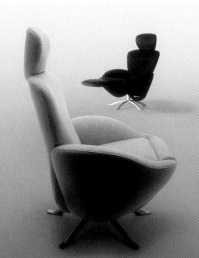

7

8

9

Anna **Castelli Ferrieri**

Italy | Architect and furniture and product designer

An advertising photograph depicts a group of Anna Castelli Ferrieri's *4870* polypropylene chairs, designed for **Kartell,** stacked up high, one on top of another. Such a supreme symbol of mass production will certainly have pleased the Italian designer and architect. Castelli Ferrieri is strongly influenced by rationalism, and throughout her career her aim has been to design products that are affordable and accessible to a large number of people. For this elegant, light and comfortable chair she received the Compasso d'Oro, Italy's most coveted design award. The use of plastics and technical experimentation are Castelli Ferrieri's hallmarks. She has always attempted to derive her designs from the inner logic dictated by the materials themselves. The *4970* container system in ABS plastic, dating from the late 1960s, was a completely new product, consisting of elements that can be stacked one upon the other without the use of a fastening mechanism. It was only recently that the chainstore Habitat included a model from this series in its range of classic designs. Castelli Ferrieri succeeded in producing another bestseller with the *4822/44* barstool in technopolymer, which marked a breakthrough in plastics technology at the end of the 1970s; it was only by means of a new polypropylene foam rubber reinforced with glass fibre that it became possible to insert metal parts into the stool that would guarantee the stability necessary for its long legs.

Castelli Ferrieri was influenced in the 1940s by the rigorous minimalism of the architect **Franco Albini**, in whose studio she took her first job. In the following decade she and her studio partner, Ignazio Gardella, devoted themselves to home and office interiors. Castelli Ferrieri also acted as a design consultant to Kartell during this period. She remained faithful to architecture long after she had become a celebrated designer of mass-produced articles. She designed the Kartell building in Binasco, the offices of **Alfa Romeo** in Arese, private houses, hospitals, churches and industrial buildings. In the 1990s she received commissions from such manufacturers as **Sambonet, Arflex** and Ycami. The voice of the grande dame of Italian design still carries weight, not least in ethical questions: Castelli Ferrieri is a human rights advocate and is committed to the conservation of natural resources.

100

1   *4966* and *4970* container units, 1967
2   *4310* table, 1983
3   *4810* plastic stool, 1987
4   Plastic salad set, 1976
5   *4822/44* barstool, 1979
6   *Hannah* cutlery, 1993
7   *4300* table, 1982

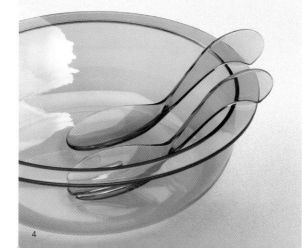

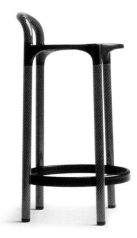

4

5

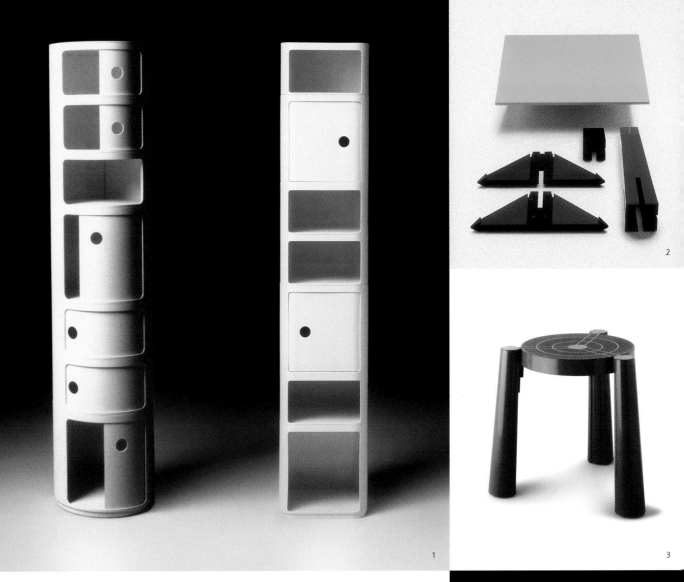

1

2

3

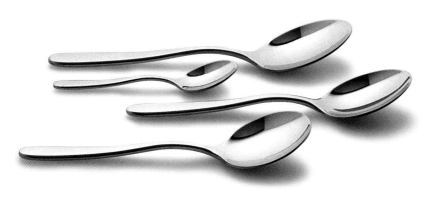

6

7

Achille **Castiglioni**

Italy | Architect and furniture, lamp and product designer

Achille Castiglioni was an inventor of genius and a designer of tremendous stature whose professional tenet was that form should always follow the inner logic of objects and that inspiration for their rejuvenation can be found through careful observation and analysis. An example is the modest *Cumano* table, designed for **Zanotta,** which was inspired by the French bistro table; Castiglioni 'improved' the object by punching a small hole in the top of the table so that it could be hung up and stored. Ordinary street lamps were the inspiration for his arch-shaped *Arco* lamp, which, like so many of his products, was designed in collaboration with his brother Pier Giacomo, who died at an early age in 1968. Another example of the brothers' innovative approach is the *RR 126* radio, designed in the 1960s for **Brionvega**. Castiglioni's product range also includes clocks, lamps and numerous furniture designs.

Castiglioni was commissioned to design for many notable Italian companies, ranging from **Alessi** and De Padova to Gavina and Zanotta. After the Second World War the Castiglioni brothers – initially in conjunction with the third brother, Livio – made a considerable impact on the world of design with their spectacular exhibitions for the Italian broadcasting network RAI. Until his death in 2002, exhibition design remained an important field of work for Achille. From the 1950s the brothers increasingly designed products that created a sensation, including a bicycle saddle mounted on a pivoting cast-iron base and a tractor seat transformed into a stool. Both objects were later put into production at ▶ Zanotta under the names *Sella* and *Mezzadro*. The Castiglionis transferred the ready-made concept to design, as in the case of the *Toio* standard lamp, which utilized a motor car headlamp as a light source. Almost all the Castiglioni lamps designed for ▶ **Flos** have become design classics, from *Luminator* (▶ p. 93) to the monumental *Taccia* table lamp, with its headlight-like reflector that turns upwards, and from *Parentesi*, an adjustable spotlight attached to a cable that hangs from a hook in the ceiling, and *Frisbi*, a hanging lamp with a flat plastic disc suspended by steel cords, to the elegant *Taraxacum* and *Fucsia* hanging lamps from the 1990s.

1 *Arco* standard lamp, 1962
2 *Frisbi* hanging lamp, 1978
3 *Taraxacum* hanging lamp, 1988
4 *Scrittarello* desk, 1996
5 *Cumano* folding table, 1979
6 *Sella* stool, 1957
7 Wall clock, 1965
8 *Servomuto* table, 1974

1918 Born in Milan
1944 Graduates in architecture from Politecnico, Milan
2002 Dies in Milan

Products with Pier Giacomo Castiglioni
1938 *Caccia* cutlery (with Luigi Caccia Dominioni; re-edition at ▶ **Alessi**)
1954 *Luminator* standard lamp (▶ p. 93)
1956 *Spalter* vacuum cleaner
1957 *Sella* and *Mezzadro* stools (re-editions at ▶ **Zanotta**, 1970, 1983)
1960 *San Luca* armchair for Gavina
1961 *Splügen Bräu* hanging lamp
1962 *Taccia* table lamp; *Arco* standard lamp; *Toio* standard lamp
          All for ▶ Flos
1966 *RR 126* stereo radio for **Brionvega**

Products by Achille Castiglioni
1965 Wall clock in glass for Alessi
1970 *Primate* seating for Zanotta; *Parentesi* lamp for Flos (with Pio Manzù)
1972 *Noce* floor/table lamp for Flos
1974 *Servomuto* table for Zanotta
1978 *Frisbi* hanging lamp for Flos
1979 *Cumano* folding table for Zanotta
1986 *Servento* screen for ▶ Zanotta
1988 *Taraxacum* hanging lamp for Flos
1991 *Sangirolamo* office furniture collection for **Olivetti** (with **Michele De Lucchi**)
1992 *Brera* lamp collection for Flos
1996 *Fucsia* hanging lamp for ▶ Flos; *Scrittarello* desk for De Padova
1997 *Basellone* occasional table for Zanotta

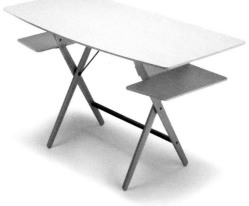

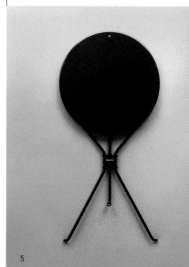

4

5

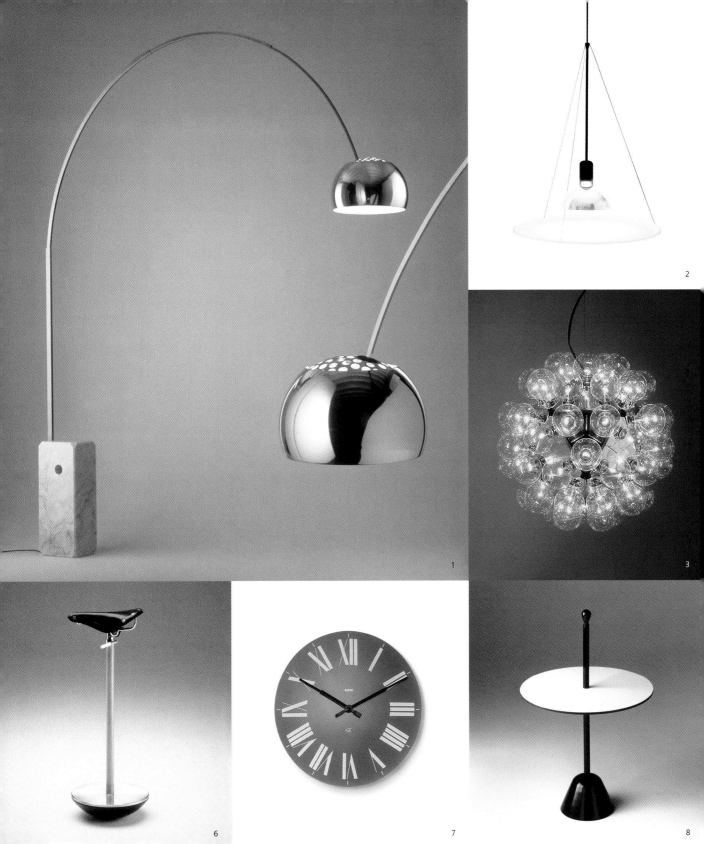

1

2

3

6

7

8

Cinelli

Italy | Gruppo SpA, Div. Cinelli, Caleppio di Settala | Bicycle manufacturer | **www.cinelli.it**

Italy is famously a country of *ciclismo*, a nation obsessed with cycling, and among its most impressive bicycle manufacturers is Cinelli – a highly innovative brand that has demonstrated endlessly its acute awareness of form and function. The Milan company was founded by the famous racing cyclist Cino Cinelli, who gave the sport, among other things, the first aluminium handlebars and the first saddle with a plastic frame. Well-known designers, including **Alessandro Mendini**, Alessandro Guerriero, Italo Lupi and Piero Fornasetti, have worked productively with this bold and creative manufacturer.

In the 1980s Cinelli's *Rampichino* model emerged as the Italian answer to the mountain bike and was instrumental in attracting the sport to Italy. The company succeeded in grabbing people's attention with its technical inventiveness, as demonstrated by the experimental *Laser* series. Cinelli was finally awarded the much-coveted Compasso d'Oro for its *Laser Evoluzione* racing bike. One of the company's most recent innovations is *Ram*, an integrated handlebar made from carbon fibre for increased comfort and grip. The *Spinaci* handlebar extension offers maximum ergonomic comfort during a race by improving the aerodynamic position of the cyclist.

1948 Established by Cino Cinelli
1978 Cinelli passes business on to Antonio Colombo
1991 Receives Compasso d'Oro for *Laser Evoluzione* racing bike
1997 Merges with handlebar manufacturer 3T (Tecno Tubo Torino) and frame specialist Columbus

Products
1962 *Unicantor* saddle with plastic frame
1963 First aluminium handlebar
1978 Fashion collection by **Alessandro Mendini**, Alessandro Guerriero and Studio Alchimia
1980 First *Laser* models (until 1995)
1985 *Rampichino* mountain bike
1991 *Laser Evoluzione* racing bike
1996 *Spinachi* handlebar extension
1998 *Soft Machine* bicycle
2000 *Bootleg* series
2002 *Ram* handlebar
2004 *XLR 8R* racing bike

1   *Bootleg* bicycle, 2000
2   *XLR 8R* racing bike, 2004
3   *Laser Evoluzione* racing bike, 1991
4   *Ram* handlebar, 2002

1

2

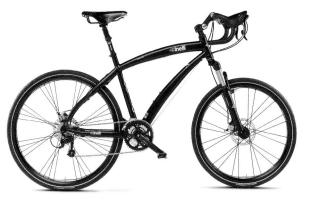

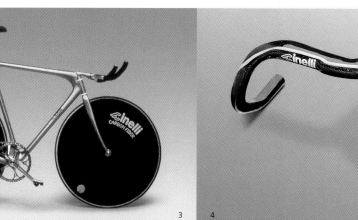

3   4

Citroën

France | Automobiles Citroën, Paris | Automobile manufacturer | **www.citroen.com**

Whether it is Citroën's 'goddess' that is under consideration, or its 'duck', the signature of one of the greatest automotive designers of the twentieth century is unmistakable. With the models *DS 19* and *2 CV* Flaminio Bertoni, an Italian by birth, created two of the best-known passenger cars. The eminent sociologist Roland Barthes described the *DS 19* as a goddess whose metal robe was the incarnation of 'organic' design and whose status as a cult object was shared by the utilitarian *2 CV*, nicknamed the 'duck'. Robert Opron, Bertoni's successor, introduced a new rectilinear quality. His designs for the *CX*, *SM* and *Visa* were also way ahead of their time. The *CX*, the successor of the *DS*, was in production for almost twenty years. The *SM*, which was created in collaboration with Maserati, is still impressive after three decades. After the merger with Peugeot, the *BX* saloon, created in the 1980s, was one of the most economically successful models in the history of the company. Designed in collaboration with **Bertone**, it was the first mass-produced vehicle with plastic body panels. In the middle of the 1990s Citroën opened up a new market segment with the *Berlingo* compact van. Under chief designer Jean-Pierre Ploué, the company returned to the formula of technical progress combined with bold design, as in the oviform *Xsara Picasso* van, the *Pluriel* convertible and the *C2* 'town sports car'.

1919	Established by André Citroën; produces *A Type*, first European assembly-line production
1924	Produces first all-steel body
1932	Flaminio Bertoni becomes chief designer
1935	Michelin takes over company
1976	Peugeot takes over company
2000	Jean-Pierre Ploué becomes chief designer

Products

1934	*Traction Avant* saloon
1948	*2 CV* small car by Flaminio Bertoni
1955	*DS 19* saloon by Flaminio Bertoni
1970	*SM* coupé
1975	*CX* saloon
1978	*Visa* compact car
	Last three by Robert Opron
1982	*BX* saloon by **Bertone**
1989	*XM* saloon by Bertone
1992	*XM* concept by ▶ **Jacob Jensen**
1996	*Berlingo* compact van
2000	*Xsara Picasso* compact van
2002	*C3* compact car
2003	*Pluriel* convertible; *C2* compact car
2005	*C1* small car

1 *DS 19* saloon, 1955
2 *C2* compact car, 2003
3 *XM* saloon, 1989
4 *BX* saloon, 1982

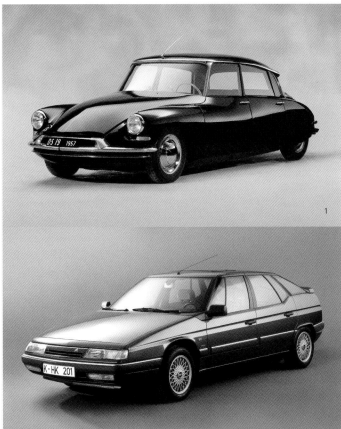

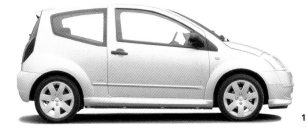

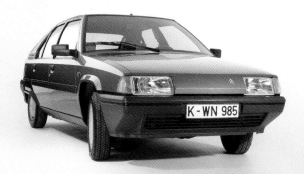

1

2

3

4

Antonio **Citterio**

Italy | Architect and furniture, lamp and product designer | www.antonio-citterio.it

Whether designing bathroom fittings for **Hansgrohe**, kitchens for Arclinea, cutlery for **Hackman**, lamps for **Flos** or office furniture for **Vitra**, the Italian designer–architect Antonio Citterio has never been concerned about showcasing his own individual style. He simply represents the image of the company for which he is working. It is doubtless this flexible attitude, along with his instinct for recognizing globally successful products, that has contributed to his elevated status as one of the leading designers of his generation.

Another decisive advantage is Citterio's impressive consistency: he has been working with the majority of his clients for many years, sometimes even decades, as in the case of ▸B&B Italia. Over the course of this particular collaboration he has developed significant sections of the company's collection, including such bestsellers as the *Sity* sofa from the 1980s, the *Charles* sofa from the 1990s, prestigious showrooms and most of the products of the traditional B&B label Maxalto. With the *Mart* armchair series he skilfully combined retro style with ironic purism. Citterio has thus decisively influenced the image of the internationally successful company for almost thirty years. One of his early successes, the apparently timeless *Diesis* sofa, seems as fresh today as when it was first created.

Architecture and interior design are among the other important focuses of Citterio's work. In the 1980s, in association with Terry Dwan, he undertook numerous building projects in Europe and Japan, among them the headquarters of Esprit in Amsterdam, Antwerp and Milan and an industrial building for Vitra in Germany. Citterio also has considerable experience in shop design. He has designed a Habitat store in London and several showrooms for B&B Italia and for such fashion companies as Cerruti in New York. Like any master designer, he takes a considerable interest in new technologies and materials: *Mobil*, a translucent plastic container trolley that he designed for **Kartell** (the manufacturer of plastic furniture), was a sensational novelty, despite its unspectacular form. Drawers on castors, stacked one upon the other, already existed, but the container's transparent matt plastic, in conjunction with its simple design, undoubtedly gave *Mobil* the distinctive aura of a modern classic.

106

1 *Lastra* hanging lamp, 1999
2 *Hal* wall lamp, 2003
3 *Mobil* container trolley, 1994
4 Cutlery (*Tools* collection), 1998
5 *T-Chair* office chair, 1994
6 *Mart* armchair collection, 2003
7 *Axor* tap, 2002

1950	Born in Meda
1973	Opens studio with Paolo Nava (until 1981)
1975	Graduates in architecture from Politecnico, Milan
1982	Showroom for **B&B Italia**, Milan
1985	Esprit headquarters in Milan (Amsterdam, 1987; Antwerp, 1988)
1987	Receives Compasso d'Oro (also 1995)
1999	Becomes art director at **Brionvega**; establishes studio Antonio Citterio and Partners
2000	Opens second studio in Hamburg

Products

1978	*Aria* sofa for **Flexform**
1980	*Factory* kitchen system for **Boffi**; *Diesis* sofa for ▸ B&B Italia (with Paolo Nava)
1986	*Sity* sofa for B&B Italia
1989	*AC* office chair system for **Vitra** (with Glen Oliver Löw)
1992	*Ephesos* office furniture system for **Olivetti**
1993	*Elettra* light system for Ansorg (with Glen Oliver Löw)
1994	*Mobil* container trolley for **Kartell**; *T-Chair* office chair for Vitra
1995	*Charles* furniture collection for B&B Italia
1997	*Dolly* folding chair for Kartell
1998	Cutlery (*Tools* collection) for **Hackman**; *ABC* armchair for ▸ Flexform
1999	*Lastra* lamp collection for **Flos** (with Glen Oliver Löw)
2002	*Axor* bathroom fittings for **Hansgrohe**; *George* sofa and tables for ▸ B&B Italia; *Spoon* barstool for Kartell; *Duo-Office* lamp for ▸ **Belux**; *Collective Tools* kitchen utensils for ▸ **Hackman** (with Glen Oliver Löw)
2003	*Mart* armchair collection for B&B Italia; *Hal* wall lamp for **Artemide**

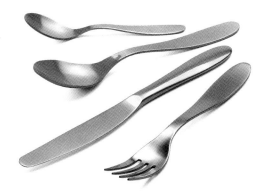

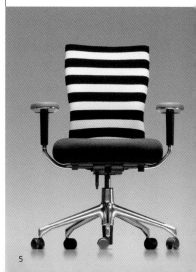

4

5

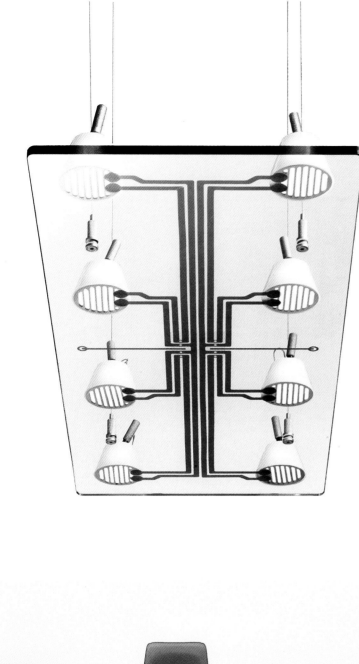

1

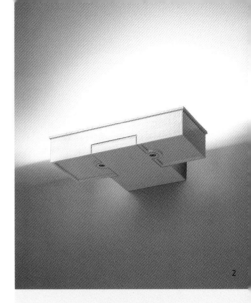

3

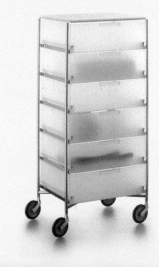

2

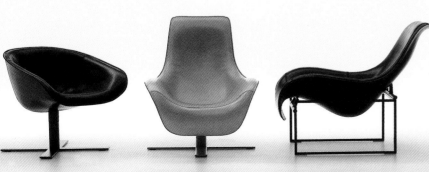

6

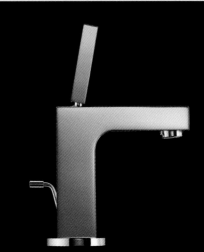

7

Claesson Koivisto Rune

Sweden | Interior and furniture design studio | **www.claesson-koivisto-rune.se**

Mårten Claesson, Eero Koivisto and Ola Rune are the representatives of a young and successful generation of Scandinavian architect–designers. The three like-minded individuals, who met during their studies at the Konstfack, Stockholm's art academy, form an exceptional team in terms of both their productiveness and their sense of purpose. Even prior to their graduation they had secured commissions to design office premises in Barcelona and two restaurants in Stockholm. They have also furnished the Berlin residence of the Swedish ambassador. Their aim is to unite interior design and architecture in a single art form. Most of their commissions have come from large Italian and Scandinavian furniture companies. The *Pebbles* bench, distributed by **Cappellini,** is a haven of peace. A bestseller at **David Design** is the *Byrne* chair, a very plain variation on **Arne Jacobsen**'s plywood classic.

Claesson Koivisto Rune is forthcoming about the fact that the *Bowie* bench was inspired by the Finnish designer **Alvar Aalto**. The trio in fact regard themselves as Aalto disciples. They anticipate a renaissance of Scandinavian Modernism, but in an even more progressive form. The predominance of linearity and right angles in their work, however, often leads to designs that have more in common with Bauhaus functionalism – as, for example, in the *Mood* bathtub, designed for **Boffi**. "There are plenty of brilliant ideas," says Koivisto, "but only a few of them are appropriate for industry". This insight surely inspired the design of the *Doppio* sofa, the seat and backrests of which appear to have been assembled in a similar way to a cardboard box. The studio remains faithful to the principle of extreme reduction, whether in its series of vases (for Skruf) or in the *Camp* wall clock, a minimalist variation on a classic by **Braun**. It combines formal aestheticism with playfulness, 'Nordic philosophy' with a polyglot perspective. The three young purists perceive their work as an alternative to global 'Disneyfication'.

108

1 *Doppio* sofa, 2000

2 *Scoop* armchair and ottoman, 2001

3 *Criss Cross* table, 2002

4 *Mood* bathtub, 2001

5 *Pebbles* bench, 2002

6 *Byrne* chair, 1999

7 Vases, 2001

8 *Camp* wall clock, 1998

9 *po 0018* fruit basket, 1992

1994 Mårten Claesson, Eero Koivisto and Ola Rune graduate from Konstfack, University College of Arts, Crafts and Design, Stockholm; present Villa Wabi experimental house in Stockholm

1995 Establish Claesson Koivisto Rune architecture practice; receive Forsnäs Prize, Stockholm; house for **Ingegerd Råman**

1998 Gucci store and McDonald's flagship restaurant in Stockholm

1999 Interior design of Swedish ambassadorial residence, Berlin

2000 Louis Vuitton fashion store, Stockholm

2003 Sfera Building, Kyoto, Japan

Products

1992 *po 0018* fruit basket for **Cappellini**

1995 *Maxply* chair; *Minimal* table for Nola

1996 *Polaris* lamps for Zero

1998 *Pine* furniture collection for Woodex; *Golden Section* carpet for **Asplund**; *Bowie* bench and *Camp* wall clock for ▸ **David Design**

1999 *Dropp & Dripp* armchair for Skandiform; *Byrne* chair collection and *Hockney* sofa for David Design; *Tinto* table and chair for **Offecct**; *Berliner* armchair and sofa and *Bend* furniture collection for ▸ **Swedese**

2000 *Doppio* armchair and sofa for Offecct; *Byrne* furniture collection for David Design

2001 *Mood* bathtub for **Boffi**; *Scoop* seating collection for Living Divani; vases for Skruf

2002 *Pebbles* bench and *Criss Cross* occasional table for Cappellini; *Swoop* chair for Offecct

2003 *DNA* modular tables and *Mono* chair collection for ▸ Offecct; *Unit* sideboard for ▸ Asplund

2004 *Pop* armchair for Offecct

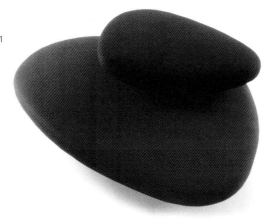

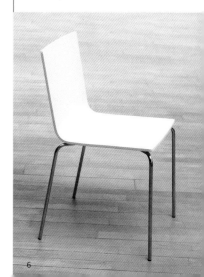

5

6

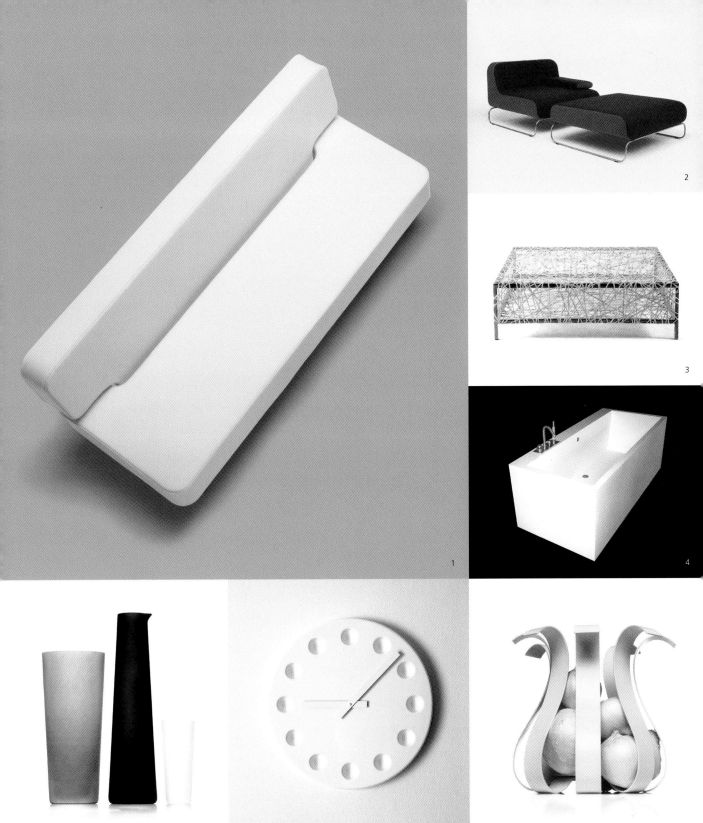

1

2

3

4

7

8

9

ClassiCon

Germany | ClassiCon GmbH, Munich | Furniture and lamp manufacturer | www.classicon.com

The product range of the German furniture and lamp manufacturer ClassiCon moves between the design tradition of the early twentieth century and present-day avant garde. The company originated in the Munich Vereinigte Werkstätten für Kunst im Handwerk (United Workshops for Art in Craft), and in the 1990s succeeded in developing a clearly defined profile that draws on the tension created from the dialogue between re-editions of Modernist classics and contemporary designs (hence the company's name). One designer whose work is central to the ClassiCon range of re-editions is ▶ Eileen Gray. Numerous well-known designs by this Irish, Paris-based designer (including her *E 1027* occasional table and less famous pieces such as the *Lota* sofa from the 1920s), often created to furnish her own houses and apartments, are now manufactured in Germany and sold worldwide. Gray's designs are complemented by a number of pieces from Otto Blümel, the former head of the drawing school at the Vereinigte Werkstätten, and, above all, by objects designed by Eckart Muthesius for the palace of the maharaja in Indore. Some of the most charming objects of the 1930s were created for this exotic project and were influenced by the aristocratic taste of the maharaja, who also favoured clear outlines. Contemporary designs by **Alfredo Häberli** take up the functional spirit of Modernism: his *Hypnos* armchair, for example, can be folded down and used as a chaise longue.

The designs of ▶ **Konstantin Grcic** give particular relevance to ClassiCon's programme in the present day. Grcic's *Chaos* series of sharply angular upholstered furniture – a particularly outstanding part of the *Contempora* collection of modern designers – demonstrates the courage of the designer and also that of the manufacturer. As well as being aesthetically pleasing, the products are characterized by functionality and sober forms, as demonstrated by the work of such designers as **Herbert H. Schultes**, the Swiss studio N2 and Gioia Meller Marcovicz. ClassiCon has emerged as one of the most ambitious and important design-orientated brands in Germany.

1 *Day Bed* chaise longue, 1925

2 *Juno* sofa, 2003

3 *Hypnos* armchair, 2004

4 *Nemea* sideboard, 2003

5 *Cherner* chair, 1958

6 *Mars* chair, 2003

7 *Ilos* table lamp, 1999

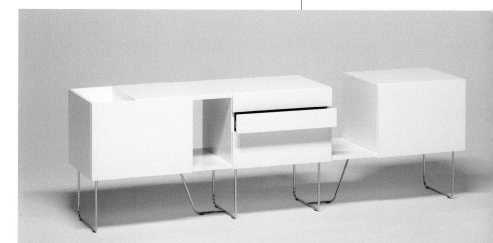

4

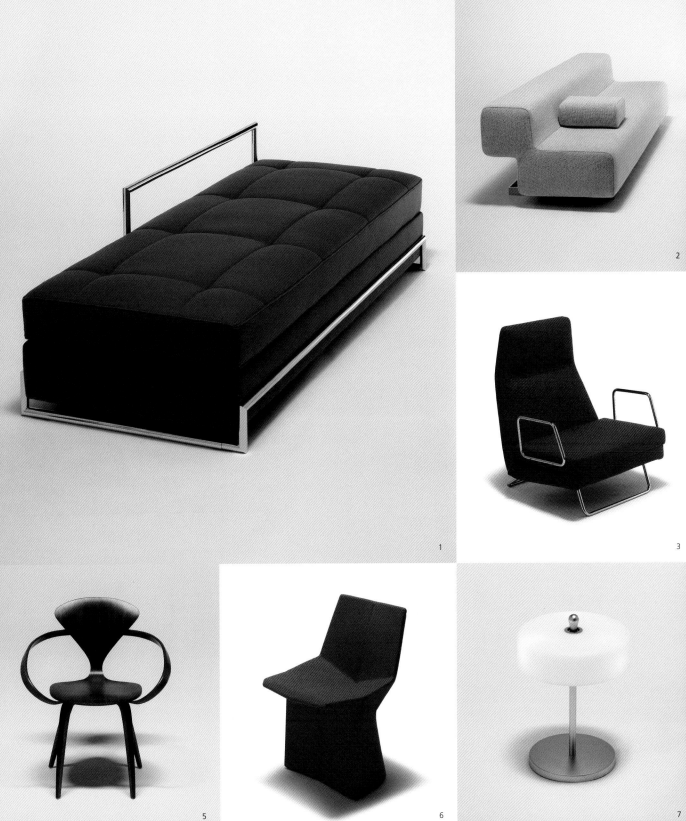

Joe **Colombo**

Italy | Artist and furniture and lamp designer | www.joecolombo.com

In the ten short years prior to his premature death in 1971, Joe Colombo not only created an impressive range of exciting products but also changed the course of Italian design history. Few designers strove more passionately, more optimistically and with greater results than Colombo to achieve integrated design concepts that went far beyond the creation of mere objects. Any hint of ostentation was anathema to him. His interests lay in such themes as flexibility and multifunctionality, which, from a modern perspective, makes him a pioneer. He was convinced that many of the problems that beset human civilization could be solved by reflection and technical progress.

Colombo studied art in Milan, and as a painter and sculptor in the 1950s he joined the avant-garde Nuclear Painting movement before finding his way to design via architecture. At the beginning of the 1960s he opened his own design studio and soon thereafter designed the *Uomo-Donna* modular container for **Arflex**, which accommodated an ashtray, lighter, pipe rack, lamp, record player and book shelf in a small space. The *Additional System* for Sormani consisted of individual modules that could be combined to form seating of different sizes and heights. With his *Carrellone Mini-Kitchen* (for **Boffi**), in which all the necessary kitchen utensils could be stored in a space-saving block on wheels, Colombo invented the mobile miniaturized kitchen. At the end of the 1960s he developed an integrated, futuristic living environment in plastic for the Bayer chemicals company that was inspired by science fiction and pop culture. Industrial products functioned as building blocks in Colombo's persistent theme of the 'integrated interior', as in his *Spider* table lamp (for **O Luce**), reminiscent of a small robot, in his *Elda* armchair upholstered in leather for Comfort and in his *4867* chair made entirely of plastic and produced by **Kartell**. This particular chair was one of the first in which Colombo focused attention on the technical aspects of the manufacturing process: the hole in the back of the chair was produced when the chair was extracted from the mould.

112

1 *Elda* armchair, 1963
2 *281* table lamp, 1966
3 *Spider* lamp, 1966
4 *Additional System* seat, 1967
5 *Birillo* barstool, 1971
6 *4867* chair, 1968
7 *Tubo* chair with combinable elements, 1969

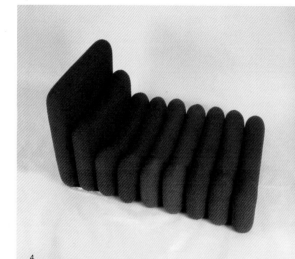

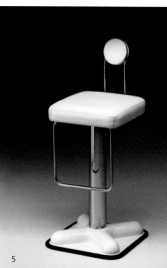

4

5

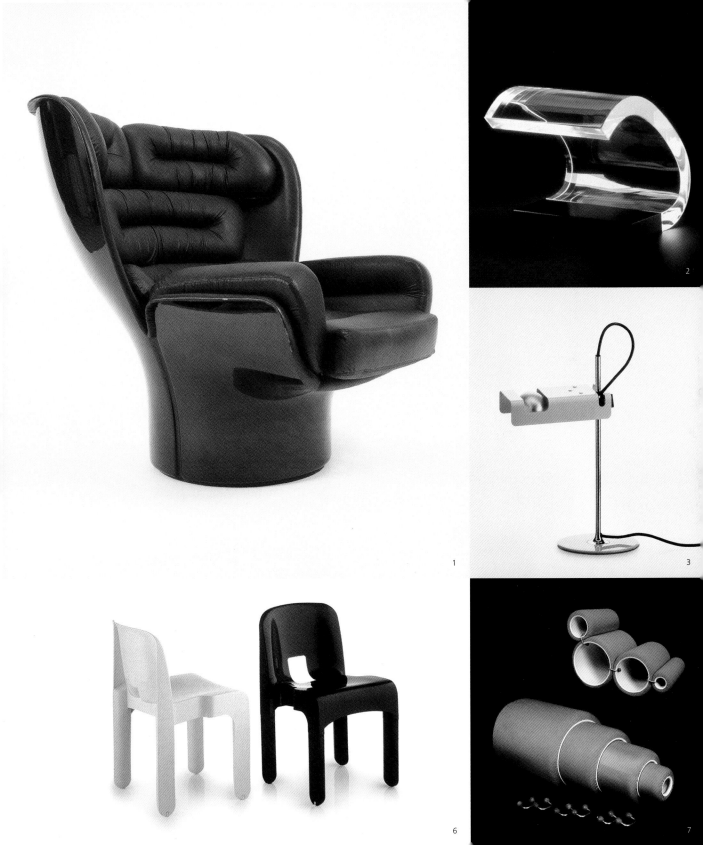

1

2

3

6

7

Conran & Partners

England | Architecture and product design studio | **www.conranandpartners.com**

Sir Terence Conran has dominated British design for more than fifty years. Without him, neither the Habitat chain nor the chic Conran Shop on the Fulham Road in London would exist. The Design Museum next to Tower Bridge would have been unthinkable without his involvement. This larger-than-life personality has played a key role in transforming the British way of life and in introducing a preference not only for high-quality modern design objects but also for good food. With the opening of the first Habitat store in London in the mid-1960s, Conran offered young customers radically new lifestyle options that were soon made available in other British cities and, eventually, throughout much of Europe. In 1990 the British design baron unexpectedly divested himself of shares in his various retail stores (although he subsequently bought back the Conran Shop) and opened a series of exclusive eateries in London; unsurprisingly, he was heavily involved in the design of these restaurants. He eventually returned to his roots with the opening of the design studio Conran & Partners. Included in its impressive product range are utensils that serve in the preparation and enjoyment of food – from the *Superwok* (for Ken Hom) and a set of kitchen scales with flowing lines (for Bliss) to the elegant cutlery for the Concorde aircraft.

114

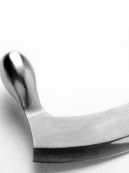

1

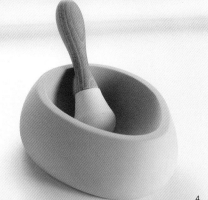

2

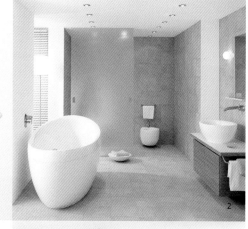

3

4

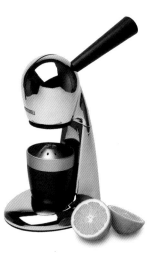

5

Continuum

USA I Communications and product design studio I **www.dcontinuum.com**

Gianfranco Zaccai, co-founder of Continuum, planned originally to study architecture but then became fascinated by the formula 'form follows function'. He eventually worked as an industrial designer for Instrumentation Laboratory, a company that manufactures appliances for medical diagnosis (and, indeed, medical instruments are included in Continuum's own product range). Continuum was founded by Zaccai and engineer Jerry Zindler in the early 1980s and today is one of the leading design service providers, with offices in Boston, Milan and Seoul. The company's holistic approach made it inevitable that it would join forces with such design-orientated companies as **Oxo** and with high-end brands, including Cambridge Soundworks. It has also collaborated with manufacturers that serve a wide market, among them **General Motors**, Procter & Gamble and Reebok. The versatile and compact *Pronta 1200 QD* camera – easy to hold, with soft, rounded lines and a non-technical appearance – was developed for the Korean electronics company Samsung. Continuum's briefs often extend far beyond pure product design, as demonstrated by the safe and effective fire extinguisher system (for Mija), the intelligent tool storage system (for Waterloo) and in the redesign of bowling alleys (for AMF).

1983 Established by Gianfranco Zaccai and Jerry Zindler
1986 Opens studio in Milan
2000 Opens studio in Seoul

Products
1998 Air-conditioning unit for Samsung
1999 *Cyclone XT* vacuum cleaner for Fantom; sunglasses for Zeiss
2000 *Titanium* U-lock for Masterlock
2001 *Scorpio* gas cooker and *Azzuro* grill for Campingaz; *QuickCam Pro* webcam for Logitech; *e-pc 40* computer for Hewlett-Packard; *Mio* digital camera for Polaroid
2002 *TTX1* record player for Numark; *Catapult* tennis racket for Völkl; *Pronta 1200 QD* camera for Samsung; *MadPlayer* MP3 player for MadWaves
2003 Digital thermometers for Samsung; *330* mobile telephone for **Philips**

1 *MadPlayer* MP3 player, 2002
2 *Pronta 1200 QD* camera, 2002
3 *Mio* digital camera, 2001
4 *TTX1* record player, 2002
5 Digital thermometers, 2003

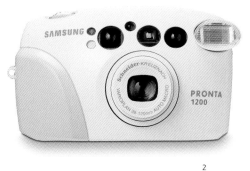

1

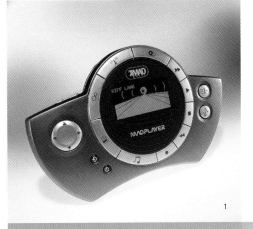

3

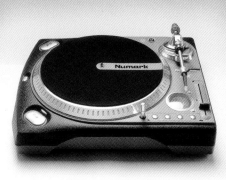

4

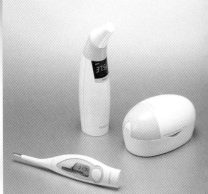

2

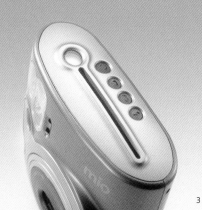

5

115

Cor

Germany | Cor Sitzmöbel, Helmut Lübke GmbH & Co. KG, Rheda-Wiedenbrück | Furniture manufacturer | **www.cor.de**

Rolf Heide, Peter Maly, Wulf Schneider, Luigi Colani: the list of eminent German furniture designers who have collaborated with Cor is impressive. The company is synonymous with modern upholstered furniture, and, together with Rolf Benz and one or two others, it is one of the few German manufacturers that is able to stand alongside the great Italian brands such as **Cassina** and **Moroso**. The company began working with designers as early as the 1960s: the charismatic Luigi Colani, for example, who for a while lived close to Cor's office, designed such futuristic models as *Polycor*, the one-legged shell-shaped chair, and the *Orbis* armchair on wheels.

The name ▸Peter Maly has been strongly linked with Cor since the beginning of the 1960s, and his designs are still an integral part of the company's programme. Among his many notable contributions are the *Zyklus* armchair, a classic of the 1980s; the solid *Nemo* armchair, a cube with a rounded headrest; and the *Circo* armchair, with its circular base and high, semi-circular armrest. The geometric components of Maly's *Cirrus* daybed can be combined to produce surprising formations. This is typical of Cor's programme, which features furniture consisting of different functional elements that can be freely, and ingeniously, combined. Wulf Schneider took up this idea in the design of *Clou*, a modular seating system comprising upholstered cubes that can be added to as desired, and backrests and armrests that can be clicked into place, depending on the layout of the interior. Among the less prominent names associated with Cor is Studio Vertijet. The studio's *Scroll* design can be transformed from a chaise longue into a sofa, and vice versa; its *Hob* chair gives the appearance of being upholstered, but in fact is not.

The *Conseta* sofa system by Friedrich-Wilhelm Möller (one of the very first modular furniture programmes) and the dynamic *Sinus* easy chair by Reinhold Adolf and Hans-Jürgen Schröpfer – a chain of plump cushions on a bent steel frame, the shape of which is echoed by a matching footstool – are examples of early designs that still have a place in the present-day collection. An excursion into a different sphere is the *Alto* table by Thomas Müller and Jörg Wulff: by means of an intelligent folding mechanism it can be transformed from a high table into a low coffee table, and vice versa.

116

1 *Conseta* modular seating system, 1964
2 *Hob* chair, 2003
3 *Circo* armchair, 1998
4 *Scroll* chaise longue/sofa, 2002
5 *Sinus* cantilevered easy chair, 1976
6 *Clou* seating system, 1994
7 *Cirrus* daybed, 1992

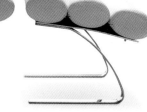

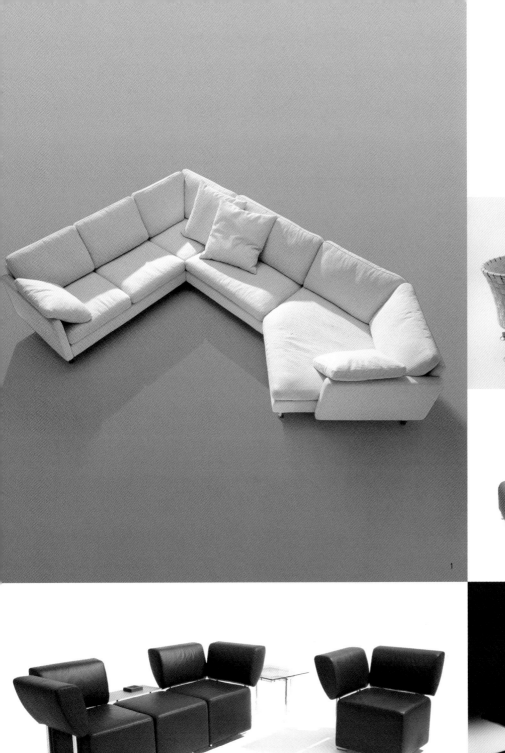

1

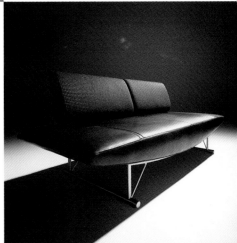

2

3

4

6

7

Matali **Crasset**

France | Product designer

Matali Crasset's rise to fame has been rapid, and she has undoubtedly secured a place for herself among the leading personalities of the design world. Nevertheless, the designs by this exceptional French designer from the Marne region are not as easy to market as those of some of her colleagues: her approach is strongly conceptual, and she has an interest in installations that fall somewhere between art and industrial design. Her work is not neatly categorizable; she clearly prefers to keep her design options open.

Crasset's farm upbringing has no doubt had some influence on her unique approach to design. In rural environments, all areas of life are interrelated, and problems tend to be viewed more pragmatically than in urban cultures. Crasset was accepted at one of France's élite universities, an experience that had a profound impact on her intellectual development. She wants to redesign the world, but at the same time to focus on traditional themes and values such as hospitality, empathy and generosity. Her designs are the epitome of imaginative sensuality. She often arrives at surprising solutions, such as an appliance for keeping food and drink hot (for Tefal) that is shaped a bit like a human torso, or the *Ici Pari* radio (for Thomson), which has a funnel as a loudspeaker.

During a period of practical training in Milan, Crasset met the innovative Italian designer **Denis Santachiara**, whose original design methods she studied for a year. Another influential personality has been **Philippe Starck**, under whom she worked on the design of radios and recorders for Tim Thom, the design department of the French electronics company Thomson. From the end of the 1990s she devised furniture for Domeau & Pérès, Domodinamica and Neotu; lamps for **Artemide** were created in her own studio. Crasset has also been involved in projects that explore the relationship between humans and their environment. The highly acclaimed interior of the Hi Hôtel in Nice is clear evidence of the fact that, despite her unconventional approach, she never loses her sense of reality.

1965 Born in Châlons-en-Champagne
1992 Works in Milan with **Denis Santachiara** and others
1993 Works in studio of **Philippe Starck**; develops projects for Thomson
1994 Becomes chief designer at Tim Thom, Thomson design department
1997 Receives Grand Prix du Design de la Ville de Paris
1998 Establishes own company in Paris
2002 Presents *Update/Three Spaces in One* bathroom project for **Dornbracht**

Products
1994 *O+O* walkman for Saba/Thomson
1995 *Ici Pari* radio (with Philippe Starck) and *Don-O* cassette radio for Thomson; *When Jim Comes to Paris,* portable sleeping installation for Domeau & Pérès
1996 *Cub* LCD projector for Thomson
1997 *Bicolor* beaker for **Authentics**
1998 *Petray* feeding trough for Authentics
2000 Glass and tray for Orangina; *Permis de Construire* sofa/toy; kitchen equipment collection for Tefal; *Daily Starting Block* shoe brush for DIM Berlin; *La Lampe Autogène* lamp
2001 *Ierace* lamp for **Artemide**; *Andy* CD burner for LaCie; *Air Corner 1* sofa
2002 *Omni* decanter and glass for Cristal Saint-Louis; *Sunic* perfume spray for Gandy Gallery; *Meeting Point* carpet
2003 *Hi.stone, Hi.bath* and *Ultrawhite* bathtubs for Aquamass
2004 *Evolute* lamp collection for **Danese**

118

1 Cable-free food and drink warmer, 2000
2 *Ierace* lamp, 2001
3 *Sunic* perfume spray, 2002
4 *Ici Pari* radio, 1995
5 *Daily Starting Block* shoe brush, 2000
6 *Omni* decanter and glass, 2002
7 Cable-free toaster, 2000
8 *Evolute* table lamp, 2004

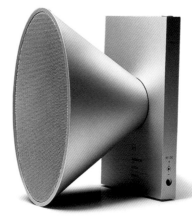

4

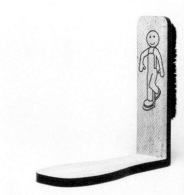

5

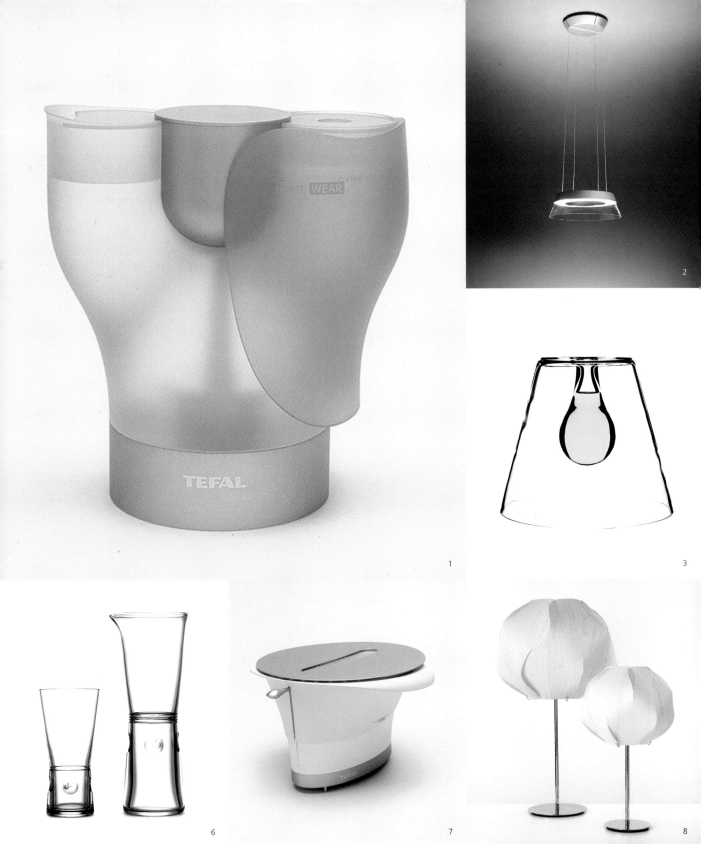

1

2

3

6

7

8

Dyson, *Dual Cyclone 02* (*DC02*) vacuum cleaner, 1995

For many years the designer–engineer James Dyson struggled to interest investors in his designs. When his greatest invention, the bagless vacuum cleaner, finally came on to the market it became an international bestseller. Dyson also changed people's ideas about what a vacuum cleaner should look like. The *Dual Cyclone 02* model is powerful and playful at the same time. Another novel feature is that the dust collected is visible in the transparent container.

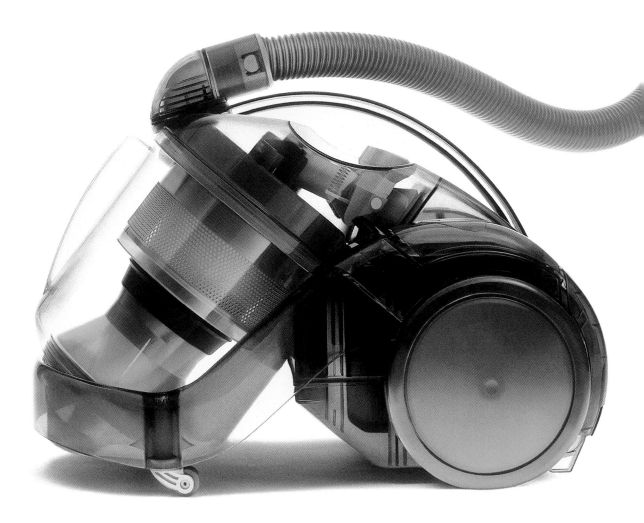

Björn **Dahlström**

Sweden | Furniture and product designer

Björn Dahlström trained originally as a graphic artist, but it was only when he ventured into furniture and product design that his career really took off. He is now Sweden's most successful industrial designer. His products have a charmingly naive, almost archaic quality about them (the designs for **Hackman**, for example, bear a close resemblance to children's drawings of cooking pots). Among his first works were toy scooters that look rather like colourful sketches on wheels. His furniture designs are similarly appealing: the *BD1* chair, another early piece, resembles a fragment of a letter drawn confidently with a broad-tipped pen. Other chairs, including the *BD5* – created by the versatile designer for CBI but subsequently sold by **David Design** – continue the classic line of Scandinavian design. It is evident that these reduced forms have been designed in the proven traditional manner. Dahlström is regarded as the golden boy of this sector who succeeds in everything he puts his hand to, including rigorous hard work: he spent no less than four years perfecting the design of a pneumatic drill. The end result was *Cobra mk1*, which is not only surprisingly quiet but also aesthetically pleasing – a Vespa among pneumatic drills.

122

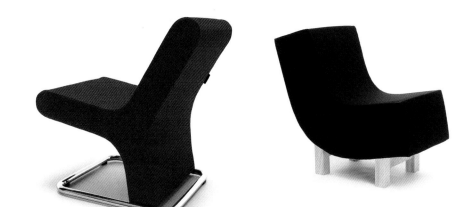

1

2

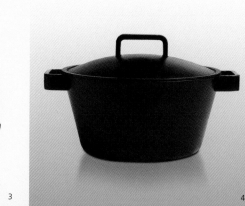

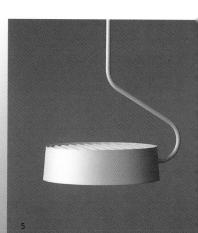

3

4

5

Danese

Italy I Danese Srl, Milan I Manufacturer of household items I **www.danesemilano.com**

Any discussion concerning Italian avant-garde design will, at some point, turn inevitably to the name Danese. During the 1960s the poetic and innovative products by **Enzo Mari** and **Bruno Munari** were instrumental in establishing the company's fame. These were simple yet ingenious designs, often involving experiment with new or unusual materials. The tubular shade of the *Falkland* hanging lamp by ▶ Munari is made from stocking material, while his *Cubo* ashtray is a simple black cube containing a thrice-folded strip of aluminium. For a long time Danese also produced Munari's art editions, among them his animated children's games. Mari's elegant *Ameland* letter opener (▶ p. 313) consists of nothing more than a twisted metal strip; his table and wall calendars are typographical masterpieces, highly valued today. **Achille Castiglioni**, **Angelo Mangiarotti** and Kuno Prey developed 'industrial art' for Danese, which was continued in the 1990s by Marco Ferreri, **Christophe Marchand** and **Alfredo Häberli**, among others. *Era Ora*, a wall clock by **James Irvine**, and *Stak*, stackable tableware by **Karim Rashid**, demonstrate the success of the Danese philosophy of giving mundane, everyday objects an unexpected twist.

1957 Established by Bruno Danese and Jacqueline Vodoz Danese in Milan
1994 **Alias** takes over company
1999 Carlotta de Bevilacqua heads company

Products
1957 *16 Animali* wooden toys by ▶ **Enzo Mari**; *Cubo* ashtray by ▶ **Bruno Munari**
1958 *Bali* lamp by ▶ Bruno Munari; *Putrella* tray
1961 *Camicia* vase
1962 *Ameland* letter opener (▶ p. 313); *Formosa* wall calendar
Last four by ▶ Enzo Mari
1964 *Barbados* ashtray by ▶ **Angelo Mangiarotti**; *Falkland* hanging lamp by ▶ Bruno Munari
1966 *Timor* table calendar by Enzo Mari
1971 *In Attesa* wastepaper basket by ▶ Enzo Mari
1983 *Paro* glass goblet by **Achille Castiglioni**
1986 *Milo Tino* concrete clock by Kuno Prey
1996 *Malvinas* bowl by **Alfredo Häberli** and ▶ **Christophe Marchand**
1997 *Pinocchio* bookends by Alfredo Häberli and Christophe Marchand
2001 *Humphrey* coat stand and shelves by Paolo Rizzato; *Super Hook* coat hook by ▶ **James Irvine**
2002 *Tano* clip-on table-top by ▶ **Andrea Branzi**; *Hold It* box set by ▶ James Irvine
2003 *Stak* stackable tableware by **Karim Rashid**; *Slice* desk set by Neil Poulton; *Oslo* desk set by **Harri Koskinen**
2004 *Evolute* lamp collection by ▶ **Matali Crasset**; *Era Ora* wall clock by James Irvine; *Spaziale* tableware by **Alberto Meda**

1 *Era Ora* wall clock, 2004
2 *Timor* table calendar, 1966
3 *Putrella* tray, 1958
4 *Stak* stackable tableware, 2003
5 *Pinocchio* bookends, 1997

123

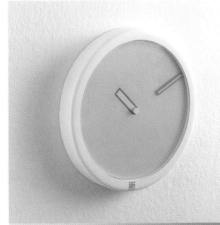

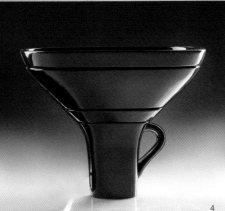

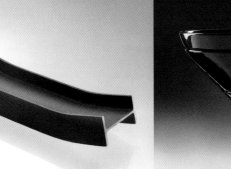

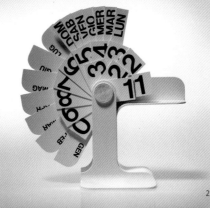

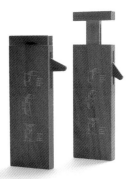

David Design

Sweden | David Design A/B, Malmö | Furniture and accessories manufacturer | **www.david.se**

With such names as *Funk*, *Vibe*, *Bowie* and *Beckham*, it is evident that David Design's products are heavily influenced by present-day pop culture. The company has contributed many ideas to Sweden's design revival, which started in the 1990s. Apart from contemporary furniture, it also offers a range of practical household goods. David Carlson, founder of the company, observes that "Sweden has produced so many simple, easy-to-use objects because it was an agricultural society for so long" – and this, in turn, has created a repertoire of different forms from which designers can draw inspiration.

The design studio **Claesson Koivisto Rune** has deliberately styled its *Bowie* bench in the tradition of the master **Alvar Aalto**. *Bowie* has a slit in the backrest, which makes it more flexible and comfortable. The bean-shaped *Bob* seat by Monica Förster and Nina Jobs's *Jungle* serving plate, decorated with a plant pattern, are inspired by the tradition of organic design. Carlson had a high regard for classic Danish design of the 1950s because it was, he claims, "humane and sensible". For David Design this does not, however, mean that it is humourless. Some of the company's designs are decidedly tongue in cheek: the *Glowblow* lamp, for example, inflates automatically when switched on, and an outsize clothes rack is named *Beckham*.

1 *Glowblow* standard lamp, 1997
2 *Bowie* bench, 1998
3 *Bob* seat, 2001
4 *Vibe* vases, 2000

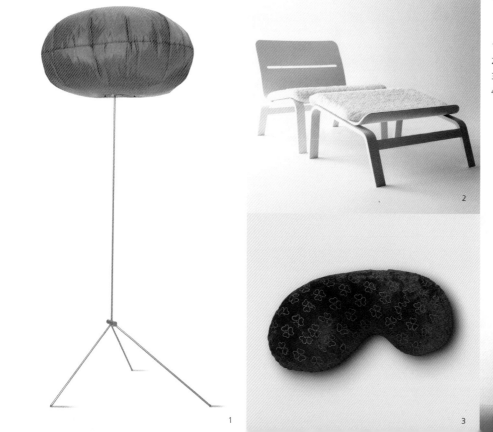

Robin and Lucienne **Day**

England | Furniture and textile designers

The revolt against the ubiquitous British country-house style in the 1950s was inextricably linked with Robin and Lucienne Day, who were regarded as the British answer to the American designer dream-team **Charles and Ray Eames**. From a stylistic point of view, the Days' work was strongly influenced by Scandinavian design, which in Britain was considered to be synonymous with 'contemporary'. The combining of unusual materials is characteristic of numerous designs by Robin Day, who often used steel tubes alongside plywood or plastic in order to reduce the manufacturing costs and the retail price. The *Polyprop* chair, named after the material, is an integral part of everyday life in Britain: easily stackable and of impressive simplicity, it can still be found in schools and offices across the country. The Eames *DAR* fibreglass chair may have served as an inspiration. Possibly even more popular than Robin's furniture are the textile and wallpaper patterns by Lucienne Day, whose designs were often influenced by abstract art. In the 1990s, however, the Days faded into obscurity. A revival of interest in designs of the 1950s and 1960s led to some of their works being re-edited by Loft, among them the *Polyarm* and *Q Stak* chairs and the *Club* upholstered furniture programme.

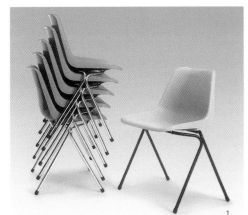

1

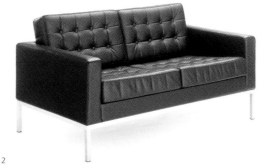

2

125

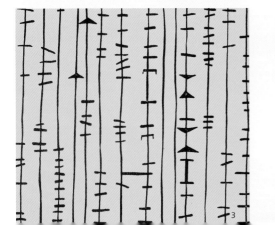

3

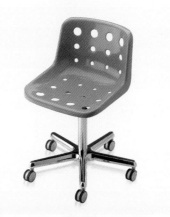

4

5

Michele **De Lucchi**

Italy | Architect and furniture and product designer | **www.amdl.it**

The Italian designer Michele De Lucchi is particularly popular with design enthusiasts on account of the experimental designs in his *Produzione Privata* collection, consisting of unusual vases, lamps and furniture in precious Murano glass, marble or metal. These objects are intended to appeal to connoisseurs who wish to enjoy valuable objects in a limited edition. In the early 1970s, however, De Lucchi was one of the young rebels fiercely opposed to the design establishment. Dressed as a Napoleonic general, the student of architecture stood watch outside the Milan Triennale in 1973 and protested against the over-abundance of superficial products. He joined the avant-garde experimental design group Studio Alchimia and in the 1980s the Memphis design group, for which he designed Post-modern furniture, furnishing accessories and laminates. During this period De Lucchi rejected the notion of functionality as the supreme principle of design – as evident, for example, in his *First* chair, the armrests and backrests of which consist simply of two balls and a brilliant blue disc fixed to a hoop. Comfort was the least consideration; the classical construction elements of the chair were regarded as all-important and were taken to extremes. At the end of the decade, however, De Lucchi turned increasingly to industrial products that could be mass produced. He succeeded in creating a bestseller with the elegant *Tolomeo* desk lamp for ▶ **Artemide**, with its matt aluminium construction, which today graces numerous offices and, after almost two decades, still embodies the illusion of timelessness.

At the end of the 1970s Italy's once legendary design company **Olivetti** engaged De Lucchi as a consultant. In the early 1990s he became head of its design department, responsible for product development. He also created product studies for Compaq, Siemens, **Philips** and **Vitra**. From the end of the 1980s De Lucchi undertook architectural projects in Japan and Europe. Also since this time, he and his teams in various offices have acted as consultants for large German service organizations such as Deutsche Bank and the railway company Deutsche Bahn, for which they have developed new ticket counters.

1951 Born in Ferrara
1973 Establishes Cavart group; develops experimental architectural projects
1975 Completes studies in architecture in Florence
1978 Joins Studio Alchimia
1979 Becomes consultant designer to **Olivetti**
1981 Becomes founding member of Memphis design group
1988 Establishes Studio De Lucchi
1992 Becomes chief designer at Olivetti
1993 Branches of Deutsche Bank
1997 Rail travel centre for Deutsche Bahn Frankfurt (with Nicholas Bewick)
1998 Establishes Studio aMDL with Angelo Micheli

Products
1979 Prototypes for the *Elettrodomestici* range of domestic appliances for Girmi
1981 *Oceanic* lamp and *Lido* sofa for Memphis
1983 *First* chair and *Antares* vase for Memphis
1987 *Tolomeo* desk lamp for ▶ **Artemide** (with Giancarlo Fassina)
1988 *Segmenti* office utensils for **Kartell**
1995 *OFX 1000* fax and *Echos 20* laptop computer for Olivetti
1997 *Tre Forchette* lamp
1999 *ArtJet 10* and *ArtJet 20* ink-jet printers for Olivetti
2000 *Attivo* office chair for Mauser
2001 *Gioconda* calculator range and *Copy Lab 200* copying system for ▶ Olivetti
2003 *Castore* and *Logico* lamp collections for Artemide (with Gerhard Reichert)
2004 *Layout* cupboard for **Arflex**

126

1 *First* chair, 1983
2 *Castore* ceiling lamp, 2003
3 *ArtJet 20* ink-jet printer, 1999
4 Prototype toaster from the *Elettrodomestici* domestic appliance range, 1979
5 *Antares* vase, 1983
6 *Tolomeo* desk lamp, 1987
7 *Attivo* office chair, 2000
8 *Segmenti* office utensils, 1988

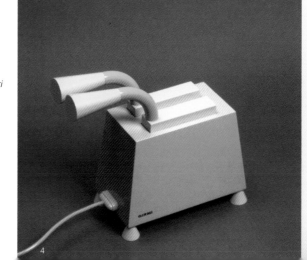

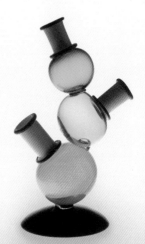

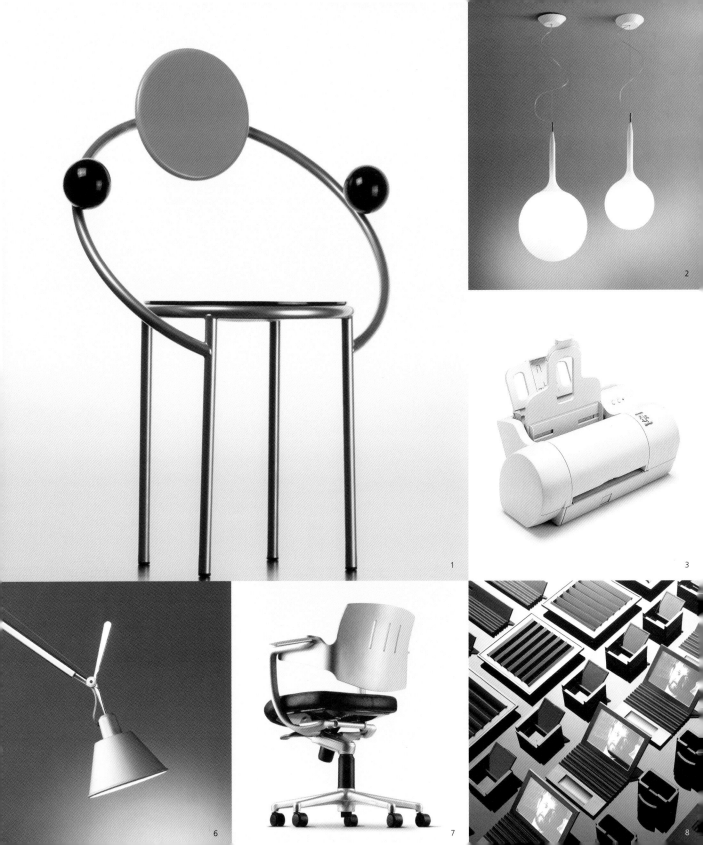

1

2

3

6

7

8

De Pas, D'Urbino, Lomazzi

Italy | Architects and furniture and product designers

The names Jonathan De Pas, Donato D'Urbino and Paolo Lomazzi are linked inseparably to two furniture design classics of the 1960s and 1970s: the inflatable PVC *Blow* armchair, manufactured by **Zanotta**, and the *Joe* baseball glove leather armchair designed for **Poltronova**, a tribute to the legendary Joe DiMaggio (the design was re-edited in a competitively priced polymer version by the American manufacturer **Heller**). These three young Italian architects were products of the Pop era, and their chairs and sofas effected an ironic break with the hitherto predominantly representational ideas of interior design. *Blow* was cheaper by far than most previous design objects from Italy: in the United States the transparent inflatable chair retailed at around ten dollars – a price that ensured its considerable popularity.

Another bestseller was the *Sciangai* coat stand for ▸**Zanotta**, composed of eight wooden rods fixed together in the middle, making it reminiscent of a bundle of chopsticks. Following the death of Jonathan De Pas in 1991, the studio has been managed by D'Urbino and Lomazzi. Their furniture is still able to surprise with its high degree of functionality, which often has a distinct tongue-in-cheek element. For the last couple of years the studio has been active for Zerodisegno and other manufacturers.

128

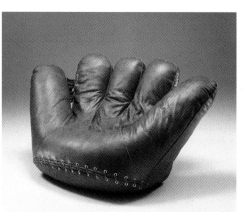

1

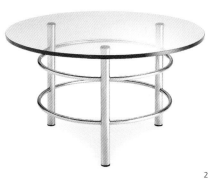

2

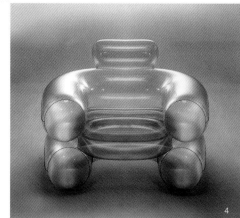

3

4

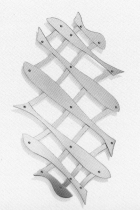

5

Designafairs

Germany | Communications and product design studio | **www.designafairs.com**

Design is "premonition rather than imitation", according to research by Designafairs into design trends. Alongside **Frogdesign**, this Munich-based company has become Germany's biggest and most famous think-tank for design solutions, and in addition offers its clients an all-round service. Formerly part of Siemens Design, it separated from the parent company in the late 1990s. A decade earlier, **Wilkhahn** had led the way in outsourcing design competence by establishing Wiege. As with the relationship between Wilkhahn and Wiege, Siemens remained the most important client for Designafairs after it became independent. The studio specializes in computer components and mobile telephones. The early mobile phone models, such as the *S 4*, are strongly reminiscent of the aesthetic principles of the cordless *Gigaset* series. The more recent *SL 55*, with its completely flat keypad, does not require a frame between the keys, and in this respect is similar to **Bang & Olufsen**'s hi-fi equipment. A partnership between Siemens and **Alessi** was established for the *Il Telefono* project. It comes as no surprise that, under the management of Christoph Böninger, the designer of the *Soest* stool, furniture has also become a strong point of the Designafairs range. A prime example is *Sax*, a patented series of height-adjustable tables on wheels (for **ClassiCon**).

1997 Established (formerly Siemens Design)
1998 Receives iF Design Award for *Gigaset* product family
2004 Receives iF Design Award for *S 55* mobile telephone

Products
1997 *S 4* mobile telephone for Siemens
1999 *Hexal* light system for Siteco; *Sax* table series for **ClassiCon**
2000 *Soest* stool for MABEG; *Idea* office chair for **Steelcase**
2001 *P.O.C.* conference furniture for MABEG
2002 *Delta Vita* light switch for Siemens; *Futurel* office lamp system for Siteco; *SX 45* pocket PC for Siemens; LCD monitor for Fujitsu; *Struc.Chair* for MABEG
2003 *SX 1, MC 60, M 55, S 55* and *SL 55* mobile telephones, *Gigaset A* and *C 250* wireless telephones for Siemens; *No. 1* mobile telephone for Xelibri; *Vistosa* table lamp and *DL 800* outside lighting for Siteco
2005 *Buga* rocking chair for Bundesgartenschau (German Garden Show) in Munich

1   *S 4* mobile telephone, 1997
2   *Soest* stool, 2000
3   LCD monitor, 2002
4   *Sax* mobile table, 1999
5   *SL 55* mobile telephone, 2003

129

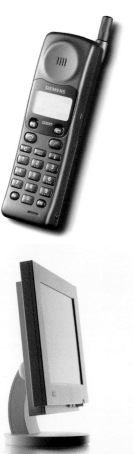

1

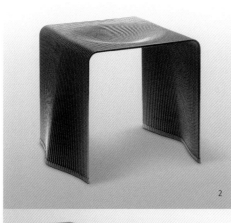

2

3

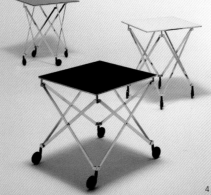

4

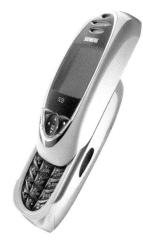

5

Nanna **Ditzel**

Denmark | Furniture, textile and jewellery designer | **www.nanna-ditzel-design.dk**

One obvious strand in Nanna Ditzel's work was a predilection for designing projects that encouraged activities on different levels, whether it be play areas for children or meeting points in public parks. Her guiding principle seemed to have consisted precisely in not becoming fixated on any particular concept: "When I start designing an object," she said, "anything is possible and permitted". The end result often comes as a surprise, as in the *Bench for Two*, which is a successful object in terms of both communication and graphics. Ditzel's career began in the post-war years. During this period, working with her husband Jørgen Ditzel, the young designer created practical furniture for small living spaces and was tremendously successful in Milan. After the death of her husband she embarked on a solo career, and was influenced initially by such personalities as **Verner Panton**, who had a profound impact on the innovative design of the 1960s. Ditzel moved in avant-garde circles, at the centre of which was the ambitious journal *Mobilia*. At that time she experimented with foam rubber, fibreglass and other materials, but also designed a hanging wicker chair (for Bonacina) and the subtle *Hallingdal* textile series, which has been produced in more than one hundred different colours. In the late 1960s she moved to London with her second husband, where she managed the company Interspace Furniture.

Two decades later, after the death of her second husband, Ditzel left London and returned to Copenhagen to start the fourth, and possibly the most interesting, phase of her career. For several years she worked with many distinguished Danish furniture manufacturers. Her designs were outstandingly popular: **Fredericia** is said to have increased its turnover by one-third, thanks to her successful *Trinidad* chair. Ditzel's method of working was sensual and direct. She proceeded quickly from first drafts on paper to full-scale models. "I cultivate the flowing form", she explained. Her favourite material, plywood, was often worked almost to splintering point. One of Ditzel's most exciting objects is the striped *Butterfly* chair on bent legs – an asymmetrical masterpiece and a refreshing antithesis to the minimalism characteristic of most Nordic furniture.

1 *Bench for Two*, 1989

2 *Stairscapes* room design, 2002

3 Corkscrew, 1957

4 *Butterfly* chair, 1990

5 *City* bench, 1997

6 *Temba* stackable chair, 1997

7 *Trinidad* chair, 1993

8 *Icon* easy chair, 2002

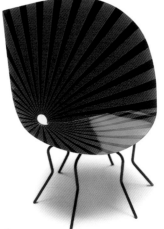

4

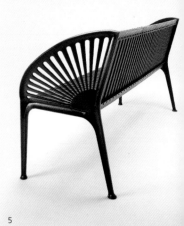

5

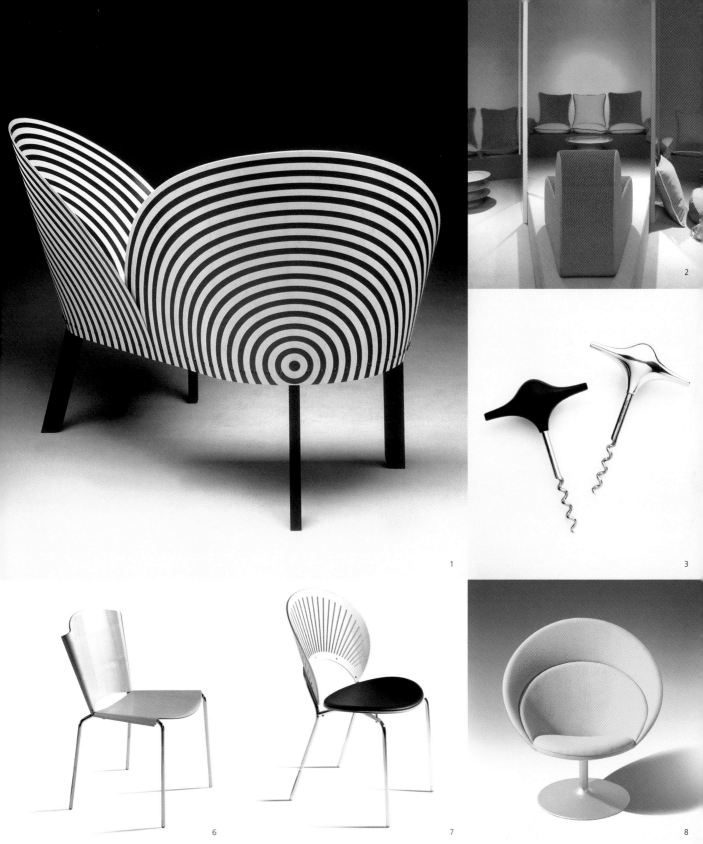

1

2

3

6

7

8

Tom **Dixon**

England | Furniture and lamp designer | www.tomdixon.net

Tom Dixon's training as a sculptor is reflected in his free choice of forms, as is true also of his colleague **Ron Arad**. Although both designers live in Britain, neither was born there. They nevertheless belong to the group of notable British designers who by the 1990s had risen into the premier league of the European design scene, thus endorsing Prime Minister Tony Blair's image of 'cool Britannia'. Dixon, born in Tunisia, is more than just the creator of such famous seating sculptures as the elegant *S-Chair* and the *Pylon Chair* (both for ▶ **Cappellini**). In his capacity as creative director of the Habitat furnishings chainstore, he has not only done much to further the careers of his young colleagues, including the **Bouroullec** brothers from Paris, but he has also contributed to the rediscovery of such forgotten masters as **Robin Day**.

From nightclub promoter to bass-guitar player, Dixon has had a varied career and finally came in a roundabout way to the production of furniture. His initial design methods were based on recycling, an approach again reminiscent of Arad's. The injection-moulded furniture *Fresh Fat Plastic,* with its restless colourfulness and frayed forms, still conveys the spontaneity of his early years and exists as a kind of halfway house between his 'wild' beginnings and the industrial perfection of his later designs. Dixon's Space studio in the East End of London became a design laboratory where several young designers, among them **Michael Young**, polished their skills. In *Jack* Dixon created a masterpiece, a magical and multifunctional design: the gleaming plastic object, the production of which entailed a number of technical finesses, is a source of light, a seat and a table all in one; a similar idea was taken up in the *Star Light* lamp. Later products, such as the *Serpentine* sofa system (for **Moroso**), which flows through the room like a bend in a river, also reflect the power and tremendous inventiveness of Dixon's unique designs.

132

1 *Pylon Chair*, 1992
2 *Paravent* room divider screen, 2002
3 Tables (*Stone* collection), 2004
4 Table (*Fresh Fat Plastic* collection), 2001
5 *Bird* chaise longue, 1992
6 *Star Light* lamp, 1996
7 *Serpentine* sofa system, 2003
8 *Jack* lamp, 1996

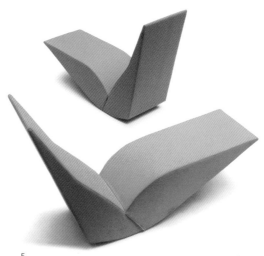

5

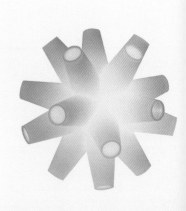

6

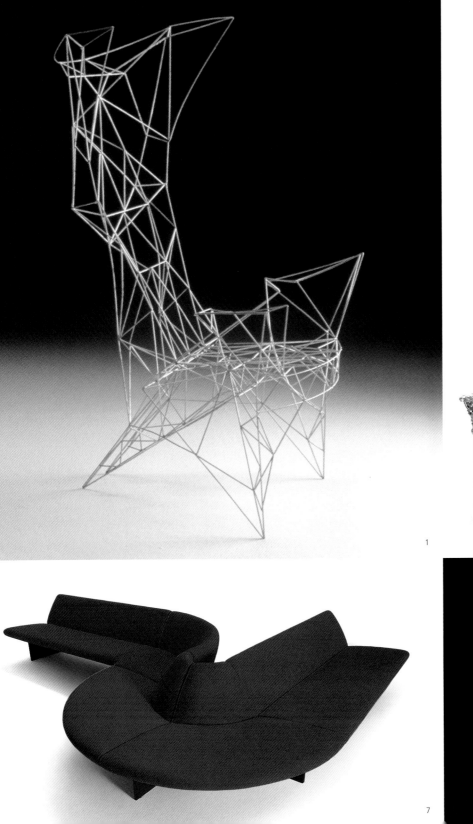

1

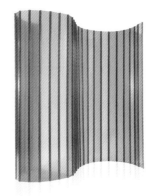

2

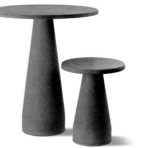

3

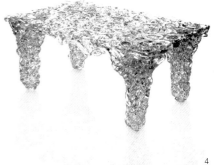

4

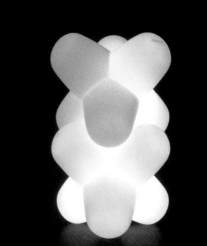

7

8

Rodolfo **Dordoni**

Italy | Architect and furniture and lamp designer

Balanced proportions, elegant functionality and formal rigour – these qualities characterize the furniture and lamps of the Milanese designer Rodolfo Dordoni, a representative of the established generation in contemporary Italian design. Convinced that objects have a powerful influence on mood, Dordoni designs products that are discreet yet pleasing and often include an unexpected feature. The special feature of the *Paco* table lamp (for Arteluce), with its sculptured polycarbonate colour shade, is a fluorescent switch that is easy to find in the dark. Dordoni's collection of beds developed for Flou is convincing in its consistent simplicity and high degree of comfort. He has also collaborated with other well-known Italian manufacturers, including **Artemide**, Crassevig, Minotti, **Moroso** and **Venini**, and worked as art director for **Cappellini** and **Foscarini**, among other companies. Dordoni's designs – whether the *Orione* table lamp, the *Regina Principe* vases, the *Diller* chair or the showrooms for fashion designers Dolce & Gabana – although rarely spectacular, are gently innovative and exhibit a confident command of the classic Modernist repertoire.

1954 Born in Milan

1979 Graduates in architecture from Politecnico, Milan; becomes art director at **Cappellini**, **Foscarini** and Imel, among other companies (until 1993)

Products

1981 *Colombia* chests for Cappellini (with Giulio Capellini)

1986 *Otero* table lamp for **Fontana Arte**

1990 *Waiting* sofa for **Moroso**

1992 *Orione* standard lamp and table lamp for **Artemide**

1993 *Buds 1, 2* and *4* hanging lamps for Foscarini

1994 *Halloween* and *Cina* hanging lamps for Arteluce/**Flos**

2000 *Flavignana*, *Marettimo* and *Levanzo* beds for Flou

2001 *Lipari* chest for Flou; *Lodgical* chest of drawers for **Molteni & C**

2002 *All Light* and *Pochette* lamps for Flos; *Float* towel rail for **Dornbracht**; *Diller* chair for Minotti; *Regina Principe* vases for **Venini**

2003 *Aliante* shelving for Cappellini; *Look* cupboard for Molteni & C; *Plaza* outside lighting for Flos; *Hockney* and *Nolan* sofas for Minotti; *Ambrosiana* light shelf for Fontana Arte

2004 *SL 120 XL* shelf for **Nils Holger Moormann**; *Bedroom* and *Bold* furniture series for Flou

1 *Aliante* shelving, 2003

2 *Orione* table lamp, 1992

3 *Cina* hanging lamp, 1994

4 *Diller* chair, 2002

5 *Regina Principe* vases, 2002

134

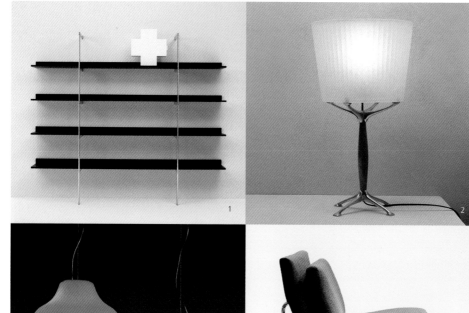

Dornbracht

Germany I Aloys F. Dornbracht GmbH & Co. KG, Iserlohn I Manufacturer of bathroom fittings I **www.dornbracht.com**

When Dornbracht, a manufacturer of bathroom fittings, began to work with such creative talents as **Matali Crasset**, **Massimo Iosa Ghini**, **Jean-Marie Massaud** and **Michael Graves**, the bathroom was transformed from a purely functional space into a place of contemplation, even pleasure. The company's collaboration with ▸ **Sieger Design**, which began in the 1980s, has been especially fertile, and led to the production of the *Domani* mixer tap, which has received numerous awards worldwide. *Domani* was followed by other equally sensational collections, among them *Meta*, *MEM* and, above all, *Tara*, with its characteristic cruciform handles, which became a huge success for Dornbracht. The modern bathroom of course also called for modern furniture. This was supplied by such models as the *Space Bar* wall cabinet by ▸ **Christophe Pillet**, and *Wave*, the transparent chaise longue in acrylic by ▸ **Massaud**. The *Meta Plasma* storage and shelf series by Sieger Design is striking in its use of bright colours, transparent plastic and light effects – all significant elements in the development of the contemporary bathroom.

135

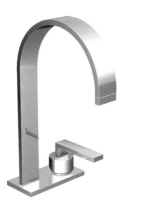

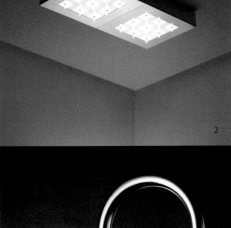

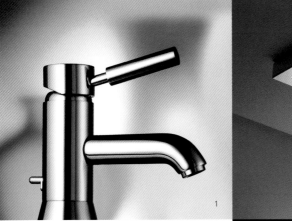

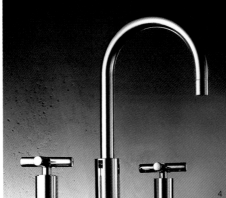

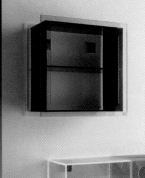

Christopher **Dresser**

England | Product designer and botanist

Christopher Dresser was a star student at the Government School of Design in London. After leaving college, he lectured in botanical studies. Had his application for chair of botany at the University of London been successful, British design history would have been deprived of one of its most fascinating representatives. Active in the second half of the nineteenth century, Dresser was ahead of his time, anticipating Modernist functionalism by several decades. He was also a great admirer of Japanese craftsmanship, however, and was equally interested in gentle, 'Oriental' shapes. Like William Morris, Dresser was an advocate of the "honesty of materials", as is particularly evident in his rigorously composed designs in silver, a material that held a special place in his work and one to which he turned increasingly in the 1870s. The geometric form of these everyday objects had a decisive influence on his public image: at a time when designers frequently indulged in excessive ornamentation, Dresser's clean and clearly structured creations must have seemed quite alien. He produced symmetrical designs in glass and porcelain and wallpapers for numerous British manufacturers. Commercially successful, he was very conscious of his role as an early industrial designer, and frequently voiced his opinions on design issues in books and periodicals.

136

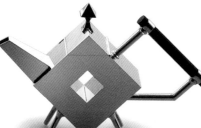

1

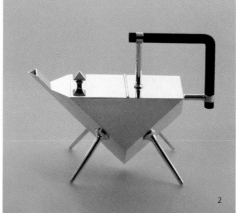

2

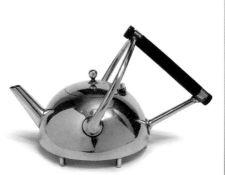

3

4

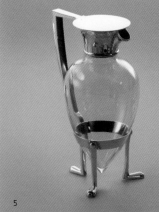

5

Henry **Dreyfuss**

USA | Industrial and product designer | **www.hda.net**

After serving an apprenticeship as a set designer with Norman Bel Geddes, Henry Dreyfuss changed to a completely new discipline. A career change from showman to product designer was not as unusual in the 1920s as it would be today. For ambitious young designers such as Dreyfuss, American industry offered boundless opportunities, and he took full advantage of them. His tributes to the 'streamlined' era, such as the *20th Century Limited* train, which many regard as the ultimate symbol of American design, proved to represent a transitional phase. What typified Dreyfuss was not so much a particular style as a particular approach. Among this first generation of designers (to which Geddes, **Raymond Loewy**, **Walter Dorwin Teague** and Russel Wright also belonged), he was the most precise. He made it his life's work to provide the nascent profession with a clear, methodological basis: he borrowed his way of working from statistics and the social sciences and catalogued his approach in a series of books. Some of Dreyfuss's most successful products were telephone handsets. Commissioned by the famous Bell Laboratory, they became the prototypes of the modern telephone. The tractors for John Deere were equally convincing. The last product Dreyfuss worked on before his death was the compact *SX 70* Polaroid camera.

1904 Born in New York City

1923 Works as stage designer with Norman Bel Geddes and others

1929 Opens own studio in New York (today Henry Dreyfuss Associates)

1930 Works for Bell Laboratories

1944 Becomes founding member of Society of Industrial Designers

1955 Publishes book *Designing for People*

1960 Publishes book *The Measure of Man*

1972 Dies in South Pasadena, California

Products

1936 *One Fifty* Bakelite vacuum cleaner for Hoover; *Mercury* locomotive for New York Central Railroad

1937 *300* and *302* telephone handsets for Bell

1938 *20th Century Limited* train for New York Central Railroad

1939 *Big Ben* alarm clock for Westclox

1940 *Constellation* aircraft for Lockheed

1950 *500* telephone handset for Bell; *62* vacuum cleaner for Hoover

1951 Furnishings for the *Independence* ocean liner

1952 Round thermostat for Honeywell

1956 *720* tractor for John Deere

1959 *Princess* telephone handset for Bell

1960 *New Generation of Power* tractors for John Deere

1963 *Automatic 100 Land Camera* for Polaroid

1965 *Trimline* telephone handset for Bell; *Swinger* camera for Polaroid

1972 *SX 70* instant camera for Polaroid

1 *SX 70* instant camera, 1972
2 *Mercury* locomotive, 1936
3 *720* tractor, 1956
4 *500* telephone handset, 1950
5 Round thermostat, 1952

137

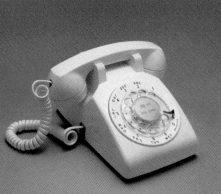

1

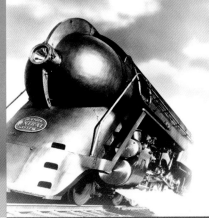

2

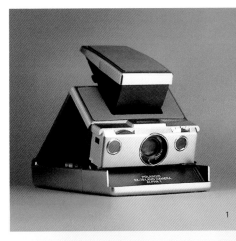

3

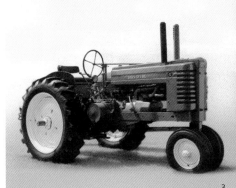

4

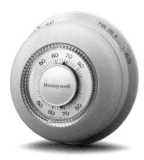

5

Driade

Italy I Driade SpA, Fossadello di Caorso I Furniture manufacturer I **www.driade.com**

Driade is a major protagonist among the leading north Italian manufacturers that have made numerous notable contributions to furniture design. The company's product range, devised by owners Adelaide Acerbi and Enrico and **Antonia Astori**, has always had a decisively Modernist focus. An equally major factor in ensuring Driade's commercial success, however, has been its emphasis on effective communication and on slick advertising and publicity strategies, including the early company logo designed by Acerbi, the creative promotional campaigns that accompany each new product line, and the publication of *Driade Edizioni*, the company's own magazine.

The distinctive *Oikos*, *Kaos*, *Pantos* and *Epiplos* shelf and storage systems by ▸ Astori are important products for Driade. From the same decade – the 1970s – as *Oikos*, and, like *Oikos*, a crucial component of the company's range, is Astori's *Chef* kitchen system, which has been updated several times since its launch. In the 1970s Driade also produced furniture with clearly defined contours, including Rudolfo Bonetto's sturdy *Melaina* monobloc armchair and **Enzo Mari**'s delicate *Delfina* chair.

In the 1980s the company launched the *Aleph* furniture collection. A continuation of the revolution begun by the Memphis group of avant-garde designers, *Aleph* became a legend in the history of design. Today's leading designers are still drawing inspiration from the immensely successful series, among them **Ron Arad**, **Matthew Hilton** and **Mario Bellini**. In 1984 **Philippe Starck** contributed *Costes*, a three-legged coffee-house chair that also assumed cult status.

Driade's *Atlantide* collection is marketed under the Driadestore label and was introduced as a response to the trend towards simplicity that emerged in the mid-1990s. The range targets a young, price-conscious consumer and includes practical yet beautifully designed products with distinctive, innovative detailing; there is also an emphasis on the use of plastic. Many international designers, including Starck – with, among other models, his famous *Lord Yo* chair – **Jorge Pensi**, **Konstantin Grcic**, Marco Zanuso Jr and **Tokujin Yoshioka** have all created products for *Atlantide*. The *Follies* accessories series also retails under the Driadestore label.

138

1 *Oikos I* storage system, 1972
2 *Bed*, 2002
3 *Gemini* sofa, 1995
4 *Tokyo Pop* sofa, 2003
5 *Melaina* armchair, 1970
6 *Delfina* chair, 1974
7 *Zigo* chair, 1992
8 *Costes* chair, 1984
9 *Bluebelle* chair, 1997

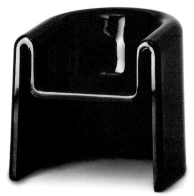

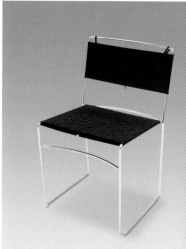

5

6

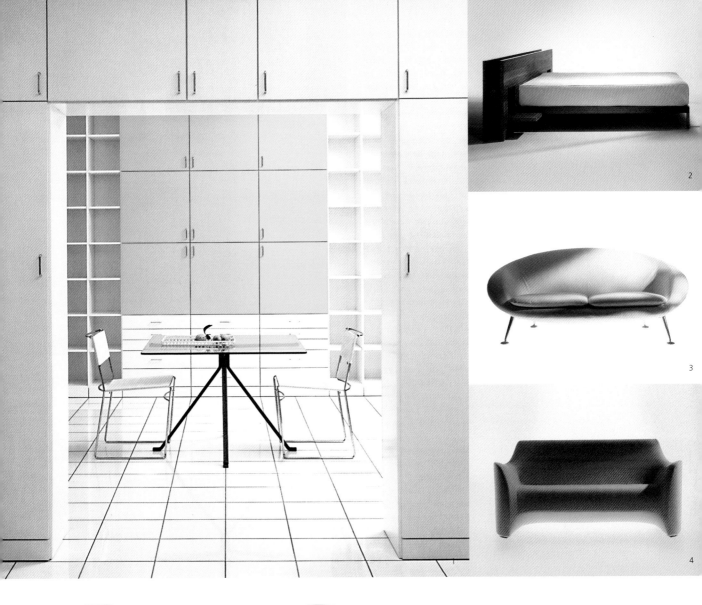

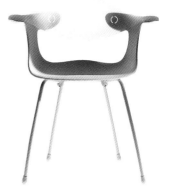

2

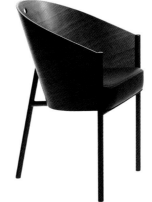

3

4

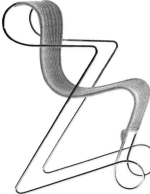

7

8

9

Droog Design

The Netherlands | Design agency | www.droogdesign.nl

Probably no design label of the last decade has had a greater influence on a generation of up-and-coming designers than Droog. The agency is responsible for having discovered and nurtured creative talents who went on to produce some of the most important works of the 1990s. Droog's founders, designer Gijs Bakker and design historian Renny Ramakers, met at the beginning of that decade. Both were looking to find ways of redefining traditional designer–producer relations. Their support of gifted designers and their self-conscious reflection on the creative process immediately bore impressive results: designs presented at the Milan International Furniture Fair in 1993 were greeted with great enthusiasm. Some of the products exhibited, including *85 Lamps*, a chandelier of lightbulbs by Rody Graumans, set design trends for the entire decade.

At a single stroke, Droog appeared to sweep away the superficial Post-modernism of the 1980s, replacing it with an approach that not only moved with masterful ease between form, functionality and materials, but also reflected critically on the conditions of its own production. Droog's dry, pleasingly restrained design aesthetic made the tone of the preceding decade appear loud and garish in comparison (it also served to emphasize the significance of the agency's name, which in English translates as 'dry'); its attendant humour was refreshingly understated. **Marcel Wanders**, **Hella Jongerius**, **Arnout Visser** and **Richard Hutten** – the leading lights of the new Dutch design generation – were all supported by Droog. Bakker and Ramakers have always kept a watchful eye on potential talent in design colleges and educational establishments.

From the mid-1990s, DMD, a Dutch manufacturer, was commissioned to produce designs under the Droog label. Projects with such large companies as **Rosenthal**, commissions from **Mandarina Duck** and Levi Strauss, and acquisitions by museums do not appear to have adversely affected Droog's overall philosophy or its original approach to designer–producer relations. The *Simply Droog* exhibition was organized in Munich in 2003 to mark the company's tenth anniversary and was a spectacular media event.

1993 Established by design historian Renny Ramakers and designer Gijs Bakker

Products

1989 *Set Up Shades* standard lamp by ▶ **Marcel Wanders**

1990 *Salad Sunrise* oil and vinegar bottles by ▶ **Arnout Visser**; coat stand by Jan Konings

1991 *Table Chair* and *Table-On-Table* barstool by ▶ **Richard Hutten**; *Milkbottle Lamp* and *Rag Chair* by Tejo Remy

1993 *85 Lamps* chandelier by Rody Graumans; *Urn* vase and bath mat by **Hella Jongerius**

1994 *Easy Chair* by Martijn Fransen; *S(h)it-On-It* and *The Cross* benches by Richard Hutten; *Sugar and Milk* glasses by ▶ **Arnout Visser**

1995 *Salt Glass* salt shaker by Arnout Visser; *Stop* tap by Dick van Hoff

1996 *Knotted Chair* by ▶ **Marcel Wanders** (edition by **Cappellini**)

1997 Multifunctional wall tiles by ▶ Arnout Visser, Peter van der Jagt and Erik Jan Kwakkel; *Porcelain Stool* and *Pushed* and *Soft* washbasins by ▶ Hella Jongerius; *Bronto* child's chair by Richard Hutten

1998 *Optic Glass* by ▶ Arnout Visser; plastic tablecloth by Jan Oosterhof

1999 *Treetrunk* bench and *Lightshade Shade* lamp by Jurgen Bey; *Birdhouse* bird table by Marcel Wanders; *CM* chair by Richard Hutten; *B Set* service by Hella Jongerius

2000 *Wallpaper Lamp* by Jaap van Arkel; *Latex Cupboard* by Chris Slutter; *Do* project and fixtures collection, including the *Do Swing* lamp by Thomas Bernstrand and *Do Hit* armchair by Marijn van der Poll

140

1 *85 Lamps* chandelier, 1993

2 Bath mat, 1993

3 Plastic tablecloth, 1998

4 *Latex Cupboard*, 2000

5 *CM* chair, 1999

6 Coat stand, 1990

7 *Salt Glass* salt shaker, 1995

8 Multifunctional wall tiles, 1997

9 *Urn* vase, 1993

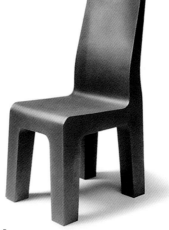

5

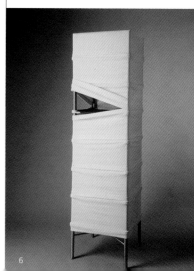

6

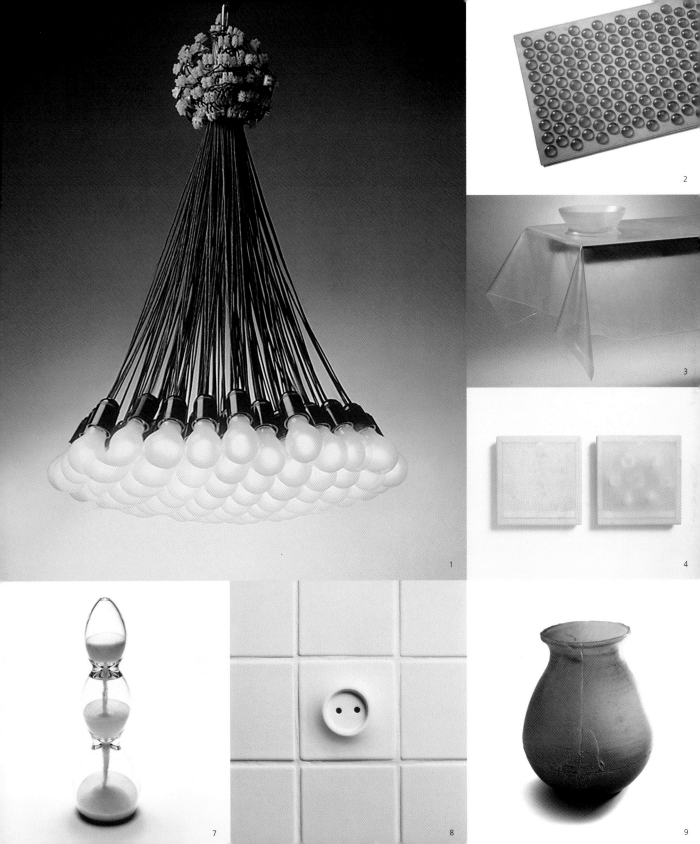

1

2

3

4

7

8

9

Ducati

Italy I Ducati Motor SpA, Bologna I Motorcycle manufacturer I **www.ducati.com**

Ducati's first major breakthrough in the motorcycle industry came directly after the Second World War with *Cucciolo* (Pup). Initially sold as a small auxiliary motor for bicycles, *Cucciolo* soon acquired a frame of its own. This modest vehicle secured the company's initial racing successes, which have been its trademark ever since. More technically ambitious motorbikes began to be developed in Bologna in the 1950s. The 'desmodromic' valve-control system, a technological innovation that rendered valve springs superfluous and increased efficiency, was an almost certain guarantee of success. Its designer, Fabio Taglioni, continued to determine model policy until well into the 1980s.

The victory of the *750 Imola Desmo* in the Imola 200 race in 1972 heralded the start of the Desmo L-twin era, which continues to the present day. The cross-mounted V-twin engine essentially determines the appearance of the machines. The change to a more design-orientated brand began with such carefully styled models as the *750 SS*. Among the details that created a distinctive look were the slim C-shaped front section, the deep-cut seat and the exhaust tapered towards the front. The *850 GT* model by **Giorgetto Giugiaro**, created a short time later, was not popular among the 'Ducatisti' because of serious quality defects. The final step towards improvement came in the early 1990s with the *Monster*. Created by Miguel Galluzzi, it introduced a new paradigm into motorcycle design with the 'naked machine'. This feature, evident in such models as the *998* and the *800 SS,* has distinguished Ducati from all other manufacturers, particularly the Japanese, right up to the present day. The fundamental design principle of these models is the visibility of the construction, a style associated with such architects as Norman Foster (of **Foster and Partners**). The unconcealed bar frame in the *Monster* series is a symbol of this transparency. The art of Ducati's designers consists, above all, in the skilful shaping of the bikes' irregular components to produce a harmonious appearance. An important factor in the overall impression is the use of different colours for individual parts. The deep, throaty sound of the Ducati engine is also an unmistakable brand characteristic.

142

1 *998*, 2002
2 *750 SS*, 1974
3 *800 SS*, 2004
4 *Monster S4 Fogarty*, 2001

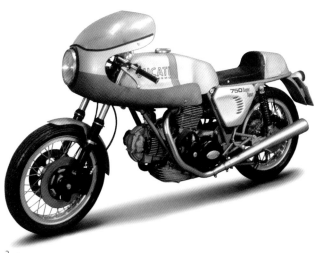

2

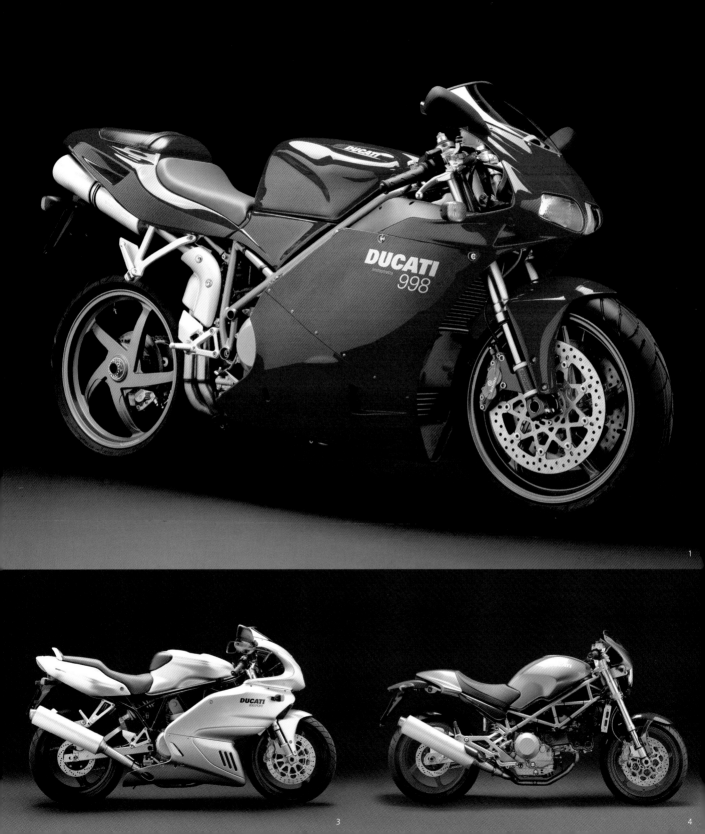

Duravit

Germany I Duravit AG, Hornberg I Manufacturer of bathroom fittings I **www.duravit.com**

Founded in the early nineteenth century as a stoneware and porcelain factory, Duravit has transformed into an internationally renowned brand. Since the 1980s the company's style has been decisively influenced by the **Sieger Design** studio. Sieger is responsible for devising the distinctive outline of the letter D, representing Duravit's name, which appears on each individual item in the *Happy D* bathroom series.

Duravit is notable for having brought elementary design back into the bathroom, and was assisted greatly in this task by ▶**Philippe Starck**. His *Starck 1* series, which came on to the market in the mid-1990s, represented a return to simplicity and signalled an entirely new approach to bathroom design. The famous French designer has since presented a further two series of his minimalist designs for the company. Like Starck's creations, the products of the *Giorno* series, designed by ▶**Massimo Iosa Ghini**, whose characteristic motif is the circle, project timeless elegance. A number of other well-known designers, including Norman Foster (of **Foster and Partners**), **Michael Graves**, **James Irvine** and the **Phoenix Design** studio, have also made notable contributions to the product range of this long-established company.

144

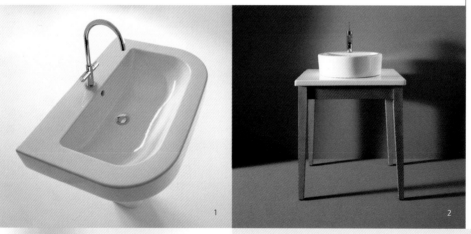

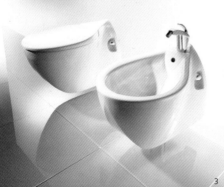

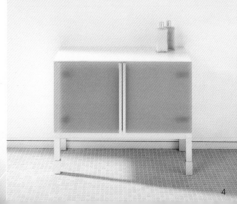

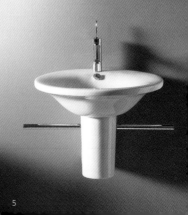

James **Dyson**

England | Entrepreneur and product designer | **www.dyson.com**

The inventor and entrepreneur James Dyson is among the most fascinating personalities of the British design scene. He has successfully demonstrated that, after a long period of design abstinence, British industrial products are more than able to compete with both German and Japanese designs. In the late 1970s, with characteristic perseverance, Dyson devised a bagless vacuum cleaner, a radically new idea that would eventually revolutionize the industry. None of the major manufacturers showed any interest in his concept, however, and it was only much later that he was able to produce the machine in his own factory. Even before **Apple**, Dyson paved the way for translucent aesthetics combined with high-performance technology. His most ingenious and provocative move was to make the vacuum cleaner's dust compartment transparent. The cleaner was marketed as a high-tech product, which also made it attractive to male customers. Inventions that can make people's lives easier have always fascinated Dyson. In the mid-1970s he developed a wheelbarrow that used a sphere instead of a conventional wheel, allowing it to ride over muddy ground without getting stuck. Among his more recent inventions is a washing machine with two contra-rotating drums – a simple principle that almost halves the washing time.

1 *DC08 Root¹² Cyclone* vacuum cleaner, 2003

2 *DC05* vacuum cleaner, 1998

3 *CR01* washing machine, 2000

4 *DC11 Telescope* vacuum cleaner, 2004

5 *DC06* robot vacuum cleaner (prototype), 1999

145

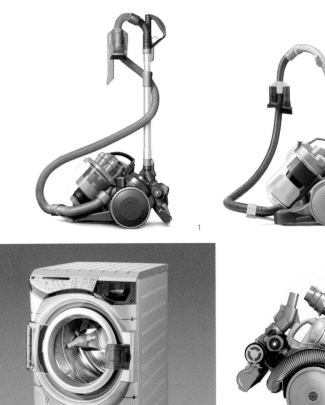

1

2

3

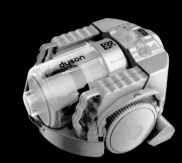

4

5

Ray Eames, *La Chaise*, 1948

Ray Eames studied in New York in the 1930s under the artist Hans Hoffman, a pioneer of Abstract Expressionism who raised his students' awareness of three-dimensional forms and their flexibility. This influence can be seen in Eames's plywood sculptures and in such works as her *La Chaise* chaise longue: the extraordinary white plastic cloud, which might have been plucked from a Surrealist painting, played a key role in the development of the 'organic' style.

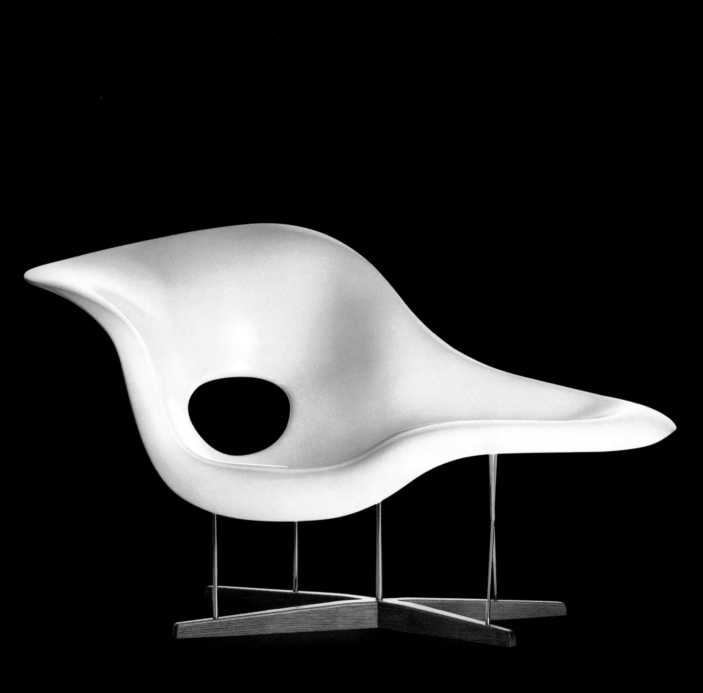

Charles and Ray **Eames**

USA | Furniture designers, architects and film-makers | **www.eamesoffice.com**

Charles and Ray Eames were the dream couple of American design and, after **Raymond Loewy**, perhaps its greatest exponents. They were not only successful photographers, film makers and architects but also talented furniture designers. Over a period of forty years the innovative couple produced compact shelf systems, folding sofas, stackable chairs and multi-purpose furniture, all notable for their versatility and technological finesse. Charles's first moulded-plywood chair, designed in collaboration with **Eero Saarinen** for the Museum of Modern Art's *Organic Design in Home Furnishings* competition in 1940, was an instant success. The *LCW* (Lounge Chair Wood), with its rounded forms, is an example of the shift away from the angular Bauhaus style towards a functionalism that was tempered by more organic elements. The most commercially successful model, a plywood chair with tubular steel legs, was given a name of military precision: *DCM* (Dining Chair Metal). Like the tubular steel furniture of the 1920s, it inspired an entire generation of designers to experiment with new techniques.

The ambitious manufacturer **Herman Miller** included furniture by the Eameses, such as the *RAR* (Rocking Armchair), in its programme. Almost overnight the couple found themselves at the centre of an intellectual circle that was to redefine American design. Such was the significance of their work that the Museum of Modern Art (MoMA) devoted a special exhibition to Charles Eames in 1946. Ray's contribution was for a long time ignored, as was her artistic career, which had its roots in the bohemian world of New York's immigrants.

Among the highlights of the couple's furniture collection are the leather-upholstered lounge chair and ottoman, an almost perfect 'seating machine' that looks good in both offices and private homes. The *Tandem Sling* bench set aesthetic standards for lounges at international airports, while the *Aluminum Group* chair collection (for ▸ Herman Miller) has remained popular to the present day. The Eameses' furniture can be seen as an interpretation of the belief in progress and of American cultural dominance. Even their own home reflected their avant-garde approach. The legendary Case Study House No. 8, a steel and glass cube on stilts, which is strikingly reminiscent of the *ESU* (Eames Storage Unit), became a showcase for the modern lifestyle.

148

1 *ESU* (Eames Storage Unit), 1950
2 *Hang It All* coat rack, 1953
3 *DSR* dining chair with wooden legs, 1950
4 Lounge chair and ottoman, 1956
5 *LCW* (Lounge Chair Wood), 1945
6 *LTR* side table with wire base, 1950
7 *RAR* (Rocking Armchair), 1950

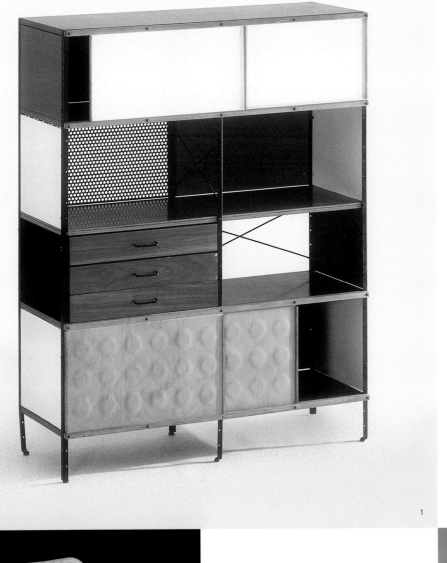

1

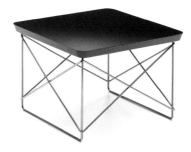

2

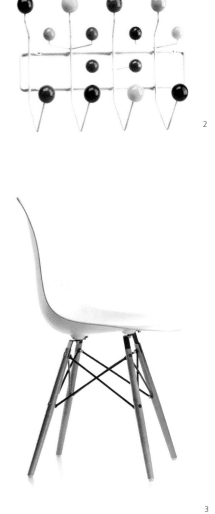

3

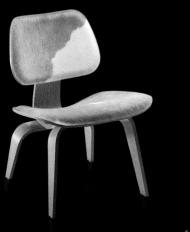

5

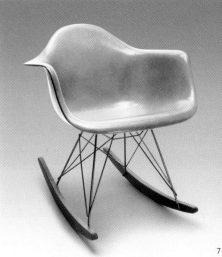

6

7

Ecart

France | Ecart International, Paris | Furniture manufacturer | **www.ecart-international.com**

When the interior designer Andrée Putman founded Ecart, her intention was to take classic designs out of museums and archives and bring them back in living-rooms. Like **Cassina** and **ClassiCon**, Ecart has enjoyed commercial success with re-editions and, it could be argued, is making a positive contribution to cultural history. The re-editions focus specifically on the 1920s and 1930s, a productive phase in French design, when Art Deco was still in its heyday. The product range also includes contemporary designs by Putman herself and other designers. In addition to furniture, the Paris-based company offers lamps and textiles for the home.

The foundation of the Union des Artistes Modernes in France at the end of the 1920s marked a departure from the decadent luxury of Art Deco towards more functional design ideas. Designs by two members of this avant-garde movement, Robert Mallet-Stevens and Pierre Chareau, are represented in the Ecart range. The *Transat* armchair, the *Satellite* mirror and numerous carpet designs by **Eileen Gray** are among other re-editions. Also available are creations by designers whose work had largely been forgotten: Michel Dufet, Mariano Fortuny, Jacques-Henri Lartigue and the design team Jean-Michel Frank and Adolphe Chanaux. One of the most distinctive designs is Fortuny's standard lamp. The lamp stands on a tripod, and the light is reflected by a parasol, creating the impression of a photographic studio. The piece still appears modern, even after almost a century.

The high-quality furniture in Ecart's 'Editions' collection of contemporary designs is clearly influenced by classic models and is characterized by its clean lines. The range uses interesting combinations of materials: the tops of the *Art d'Ecart* cabinet and occasional table are, for example, covered in enamelled ceramic tiles. Ecart also offers prestigious pieces, such as the *Lotus* collection of upholstered furniture by Putman. Some designs deliberately venture into the eclectic, as in the desk that accompanies the well-known *T* stool by Chareau, which echoes both the shape and materials of the original stool.

1978 Established by Andrée Putman in Paris
1997 Putman leaves the company

Products
1903 Table lamp by Mariano Fortuny
1907 Standard lamp by Mariano Fortuny
1925 Table lamp by Félix Aublet
1927 Armchair by Robert Mallet-Stevens; *Transat* armchair and *Satellite* mirror by **Eileen Gray**; *T* stool by Pierre Chareau
1930 *Club* furniture collection and *President* desk by Jean-Michel Frank and Adolphe Chanaux; stackable chair by Robert Mallet-Stevens; metal chair by Michel Dufet; *Fan* table by Pierre Chareau
1932 *Footstool*
1934 *X* occasional table
1935 *Rattan Chair*
     Last three by Jean-Michel Frank and Adolphe Chanaux; all as re-editions since 1980
1990 *Kraft* lamp collection
1992 *Glaçon* standard lamp
1993 *Damier* occasional tables
1996 *Damier* coffee table
1998 *Lecture* and *Duplex* standard lamps
2002 *Traversante* coffee table

150

1 *T* stool, 1927
2 Standard lamp, 1907
3 *Kraft* standard lamp, 1990
4 *Transat* armchair, 1927
5 Stackable chair, 1930
6 Metal chair, 1930
7 Table lamp, 1925
8 *Satellite* mirror, 1927

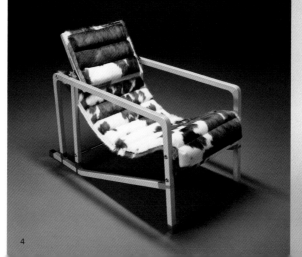

4

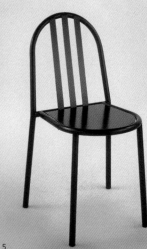

5

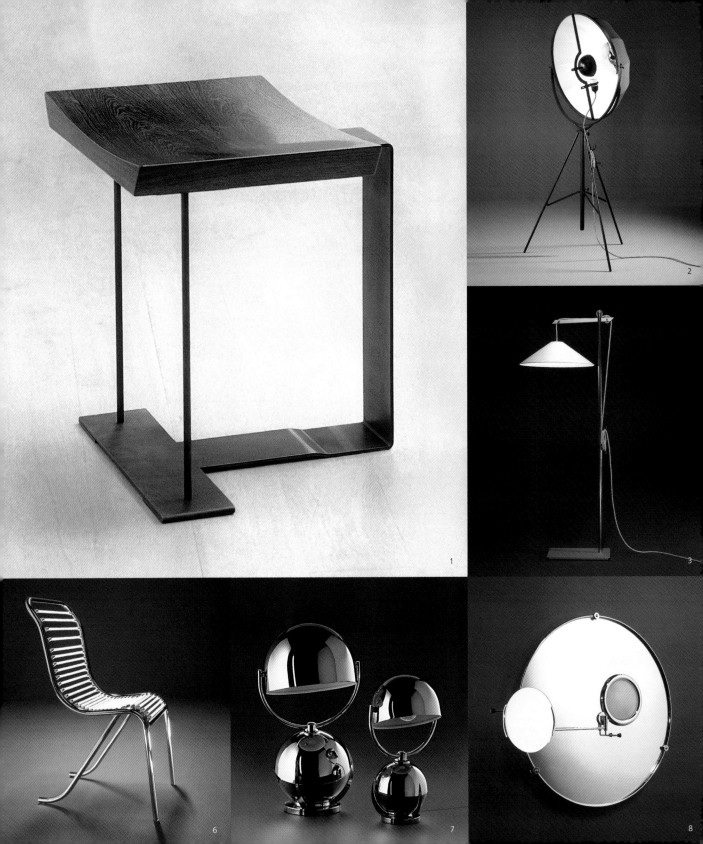

Edra

Italy I Edra SpA, Perignano I Furniture manufacturer I **www.edra.com**

Edra is famous not only for unusual furniture but also for brilliant stage management. The presentation of its new products is always a grand theatrical event. The Tuscany-based company, which was founded at the height of the boisterous 1980s, places an emphasis on beautifully flashy and eccentrically exclusive style. Its debut range, *I Nuovissimi*, was an experiment. Edra commissioned several young designers and was the first company to manufacture their designs. Since then, art director **Massimo Morozzi** and his team have scouted for creative talent at the international trade fairs. The collection is rich in contrasts and eye-catching creations: the spiral-shaped *Tatlin* sofa by Mario Cananzi and Roberto Semprini and the sculptural 'flower furniture' by ▶**Masanori Umeda**, including his famous *Rose Chair,* have left their mark on Edra's image, as have the *Flap* sofa by Francesco Binfaré and the *Elysée* sofa system by **Christophe Pillet**, which uses textiles by **Hella Jongerius**. The designs by the Brazilian brothers ▶**Fernando and Humberto Campana** caused a sensation. Among their contributions are the *Vermelha* cord armchair, the *Sushi* 'rag' chair and the *Favela* armchair, made from glued chips of wood (the chair's construction is a reference to the urban slums of Brazil). ▶Massimo Morozzi himself has contributed to the company's successful product range: his almost infinitely expandable *Paesaggi Italiani* shelf and cupboard system (based on a simple rectangular module) is highly flexible and functional, but at the same time indulges in an uninhibited play with form and colour (▶p. 13).

Despite the theatricality and flamboyance often associated with Edra, the company undertakes intensive research into its materials prior to serial production, and sometimes even develops entirely new materials. It is precisely this sustained effort that has not only helped secure its reputation but has also made its unusual designs highly popular with television and film directors, who regularly use the furniture as props. The company's bold advertising strategies undoubtedly contribute to its success. Its catalogues epitomize the phrase 'sex sells': Edra believes in creating a sensual home environment. Rooms are transformed into grand stages upon which its furniture plays the leading role.

152

1 *Elyseé* sofa system, 2001
2 *Passepartout* seating, 1998
3 *Paesaggi Italiani* storage system, 1995
4 *Flap* sofa, 2000
5 *Tatlin* sofa, 1989
6 *Rose Chair*, 1990
7 *Vermelha* armchair, 1998

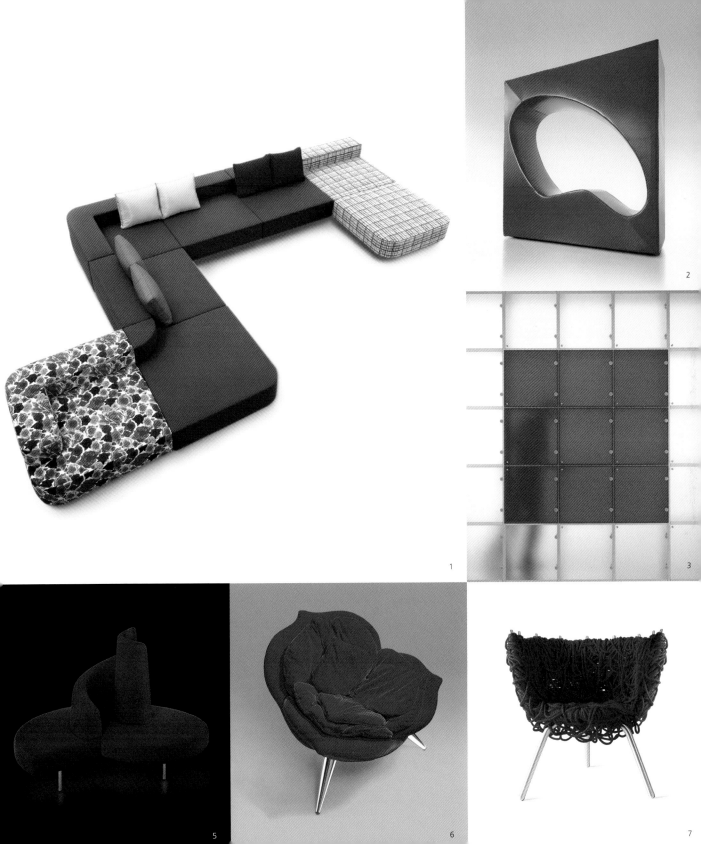

1

2

3

5

6

7

Egon **Eiermann**

Germany | Architect and furniture designer | **www.wilde-spieth.de**

Egon Eiermann earned international renown for his interior design of the German Pavilion at *Expo '58* in Brussels, for which he created the ceiling spotlights (now produced by ▸ **Tecnolumen**), ashtrays, glasses, lanterns and occasional tables. His contributions to German post-war Modernist architecture included the new building of the Gedächtniskirche in Berlin, the high-rise office block for members of the West German parliament in Bonn and the German headquarters of **Olivetti** in Frankfurt am Main. Eiermann focused on the smallest details in his projects as well as the larger context. Most of his furniture was influenced by his architectural designs, and in this, as in other respects, he resembled his Danish colleague and contemporary **Arne Jacobsen**. However, Eiermann discovered plywood – a material that had been used before the Second World War by **Alvar Aalto** and was eventually to trigger a revolution in chair design – a little earlier than Jacobsen. In the late 1940s and early 1950s, a time of new departures, he designed the greatest number of his plywood chairs. During the later economic boom in West Germany these chairs – among them the models *SE 41*, *SE 42*, *SE 68* and *SE 18* – became an integral part of many public buildings.

Transparency, appropriate use of materials and high-quality design, down to even the most minute detail, were the perfectionist standards that Eiermann demanded of both his buildings and his furniture. One of his most famous designs is the hugely successful *SE 18* folding chair made from beech and plywood. Its harmonious proportions, restrained curves and legs that widen towards the middle are reminiscent of Danish designs by Finn Juhl or **Hans J. Wegner**. With this design in particular, and also his early wicker armchairs, Eiermann provided a link between modern German design and up-and-coming Scandinavian design. The avant-garde designer was also well aware of design trends in the United States. His *SE 42* bentwood chair and the *SE 68* stackable chair, which combines light tubular steel with an ergonomically moulded plywood seat, were modelled on designs by **Charles and Ray Eames**. Eiermann's chairs and his practical table frames are today produced by Wilde & Spieth and, after having almost faded into obscurity, are now regarded as classics in design-conscious circles.

154

1   *SE 42* bentwood chair, 1949
2   *Eiermann* shelving, 1932
3   *E 10* wicker chair, 1948
4   Table frame, 1953
5   *SE 41* swivel chair, 1949
6   *SE 68* stackable chair, 1950
7   *SE 68* stackable chair (detail), 1950
8   *SE 18* wooden folding chair, 1952

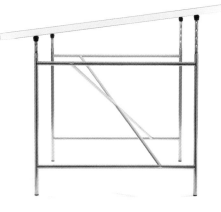

4

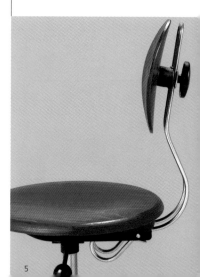

5

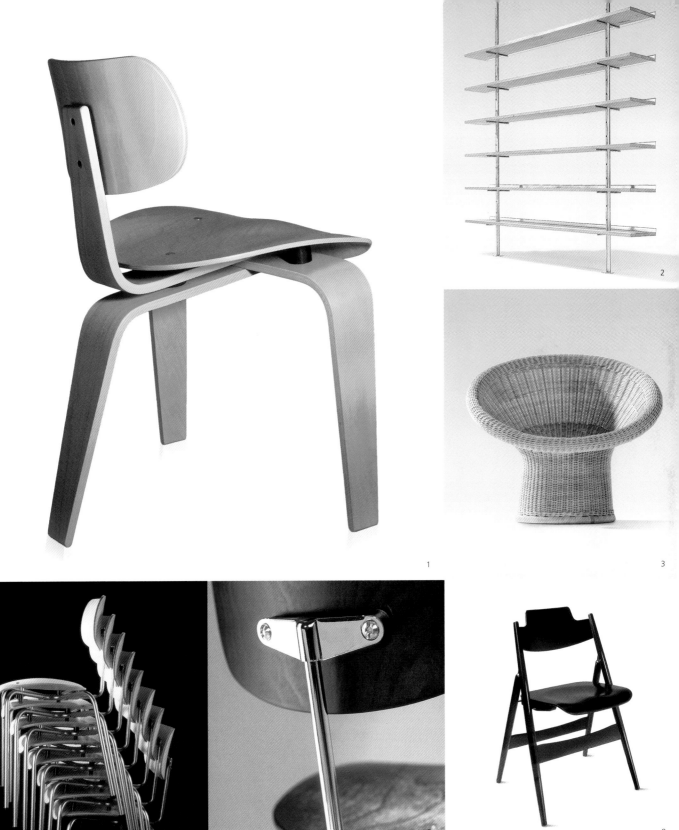

1

2

3

6

7

8

Erco

Germany | Erco Leuchten GmbH, Lüdenscheid | Lamp manufacturer | **www.erco.com**

"We sell light, not lamps" is the motto of the Erco company. Erco calls itself the 'Light Factory' and regards the 'software' of light as more important than the 'hardware' of the high-tech lamps and luminaires it manufactures. Until the beginning of the 1960s the company focused on kitchen and bathroom lighting; it then began to conquer the newly emerging market for architectural lighting, in which it now competes with such firms as **Louis Poulsen** and **iGuzzini**. Erco became a specialist in complex lighting solutions and was responsible for new lighting schemes in the Reichstag in Berlin, the Musée du Louvre in Paris and the Vatican in Rome. Collaboration with such international designers as Roy Fleetwood from Britain and **Knud Holscher** from Denmark was a logical progression. The Italian designer ▸ **Mario Bellini** created the extremely versatile *Eclipse* modular spotlight, which resembles an SLR camera both in appearance and technical construction. Fleetwood's *Emanon* spotlight has an austere technological beauty. The graphic designer Otl Aicher acted as a consultant to the company for many years and developed its entire corporate identity, from the logo to the pictograms on illuminated information signs. Erco's no-nonsense 'light machines' have thus become the equivalent of the black, white and grey iconography that dominates the company's image.

1934 Established as supplier of lighting components
1959 Lighting programme encompasses kitchen, bedside and bathroom lamps
1963 Klaus Jürgen Maack joins company
1968 Formulates company doctrine: light is the product, not the lamps ('Light Factory')
1974 Erco lamps selected for permanent collection of MoMA, New York
1975 Collaborates with Otl Aicher; introduces new corporate design
1988 Opens Centre for Light and Electronics
1997 **Verner Panton** designs London showroom

Products
1962 *6000* hanging light series by Alois Dworschak
1973 First *Downlight* collection
1982 *Optec* wall floodlight by Hans Hollein; *Osiris* spotlight by Giancarlo Piretti
1986 *Eclipse* spotlight by ▸ **Mario Bellini**
1988 *Axis* and *Gantry* lighting support systems by Roy Fleetwood and Ove Arup
1991 *Emanon* spotlight by Roy Fleetwood
1992 *Quinta* spotlight collection by ▸ **Knud Holscher**
1995 *Lucy* desk lamp by Franco Clivio
1998 Emergency light by Henk Kosche
2001 *Beamer* spotlight (in-house design)
2002 *Stella* spotlight by Franco Clivio

1 Emergency light, 1998
2 *Emanon* spotlight, 1991
3 *Beamer* spotlight, 2001
4 *Stella* spotlight, 2002
5 *Lucy* desk lamp, 1995

156

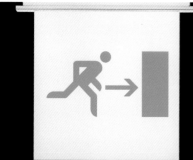

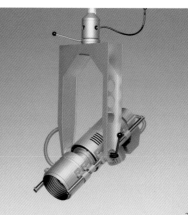

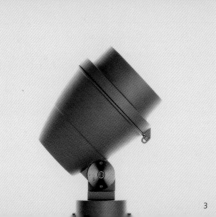

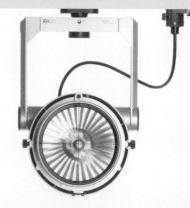

Ergonomidesign

Sweden | Product design studio | www.ergonomidesign.com

In the late 1980s the Museum of Modern Art (MoMA) in New York presented the *Design for Independent Living* exhibition, which provided the first international platform for designs for the sick and people with disabilities. One of the most striking objects was a kitchen knife with a handle that enables users to cut a slice of bread with the minimum physical effort. The product was designed by the Stockholm-based industrial design consultancy Ergonomi Design Gruppen (now Ergonomidesign), which had its roots in the hippy subculture. The best-known members of this team, Maria Benktzon and Sven-Eric Juhlin, were unchallenged masters in their field. Like **Oxo**, Ergonomidesign does not impose strict limits on its areas of activity. It argues that, when it comes to the relationship between humans and machines, very often the same problems arise in hospitals, factories or the home. At the beginning of every project, intensive research is undertaken to ensure maximum user-friendliness. More than three hundred ergonomically designed tools, for example, have been developed in collaboration with the manufacturer Bahco. Whether the *Speedglas 9000* welding helmet, with its automatically darkening shield, or the comb with an extended handle, each design treats the independence of the user as the most important consideration. Ergonomi thus sees itself in the tradition of the 'democratic design' of the 1960s.

1969 Ergonomi Design established in Stockholm
1973 Maria Benktzon and Sven-Eric Juhlin present project on ergonomic handles for people with disabilities
1979 Designgruppen and Ergonomi Design merge to form Ergonomi Design Gruppen (EDG)
1988 Participates in *Design for Independent Living* exhibition at MoMA, New York
1999 Company name changes to Ergonomidesign
2002 Opens studio in Japan

Products
1974 *Ideal* kitchen knife with handle for **Hackman**
1979 Ballpoint pen for people with rheumatism
1980 Cutlery for people with disabilities
1986 *Ergo* tools for Bahco
1987 *Beauty* brush and comb series
1988 Coffee service for SAS
1989 Ergonomic crutches; cutlery for children with multiple disabilities
1996 *Speedglas 9000* welding helmet for Hörnell
2003 *Frame 319* saw for Bahco
2004 Bicycle handles for RTI Sports

1 *Beauty* brush and comb, 1987
2 *Frame 319* saw, 2003
3 Bicycle handle, 2004
4 *Ideal* kitchen knife, 1974
5 *Speedglas 9000* welding helmet, 1996

157

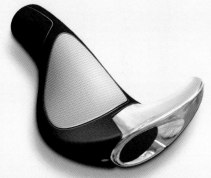
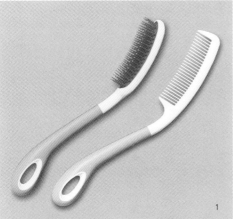
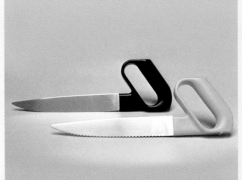
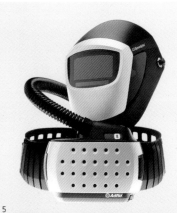
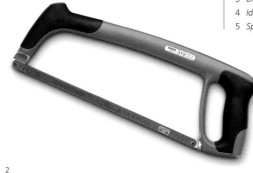

Ericsson

Sweden I LM Ericsson AB, Stockholm I Manufacturer of telecommunications equipment I **www.ericsson.com**

Against a background of falling sales figures and the fast-moving nature of the mobile telephone market, Sweden's largest telecommunications company decided to join forces with the entertainment giant **Sony**. This alliance resulted in designs – for example, the *T 300* and *T 610* models, with their clear, sleek surfaces – that were in stark contrast to the more expressively designed models of some competitors. Ericsson's very first telephones enjoyed long-term success: a desk model, introduced in 1892, was replaced only seventeen years later. The follow-up model was a product that set standards across Europe. Jean Heiberg gave the Bakelite phone a simple, rational design with pronounced angles and edges. In the mid-1950s Ericsson introduced the *Ericofon*. With its distinctive rounded contours and innovative design, it anticipated much of the comfort and convenience offered by later generations of telephones. It was also the first one-piece telephone set in that the dial and the receiver were not separate. Ericsson's mobile phones were initially quite different from the more biomorphic style of its competitors' models, but they gradually changed to keep abreast of new trends, despite their potentially short product life. *GF 768*, the classic model with a flap, was available in various colourful versions, and the clock in the top shell of the *Z 200* model was also a highly contemporary feature.

1876 Lars Magnus Ericsson establishes workshop for telegraphic equipment in Stockholm
1885 Produces first Ericsson telephone handset
1923 Introduces telephone dial
1932 Makes losses in the Great Depression; ITT acquires 34% share of business (bought back in 1960)
1950 Introduces world's first automatic international exchange, between Stockholm and Copenhagen
1981 Establishes Ericsson Information Systems
1989 Establishes mobile communications division
2001 Establishes Sony Ericsson Mobile Communications with **Sony**

Products
1892 First desk telephone
1931 Bakelite telephone by Jean Heiberg
1956 *Ericofon* telephone
1966 Telephone handset with keypad
1991 First digital mobile telephone system
1997 *DT120* wireless telephone handset and *GF 768* mobile telephone by Richard Lindahl
1998 *SH 888* mobile telephone
2003 *T 610* mobile telephone; *Z 200* mobile telephone
2004 *Z 500* mobile telephone
2005 *K 300i* mobile telephone

1 *Z 500* mobile telephone, 2004
2 *Ericofon* telephone, 1956
3 *T 610* mobile telephone, 2003
4 *Z 200* mobile telephone, 2003
5 *GF 768* mobile telephone, 1997

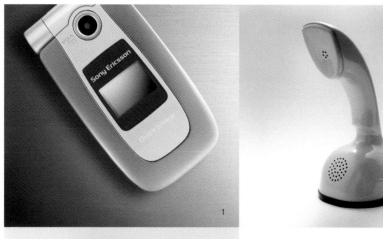

1

2

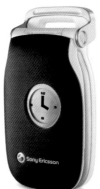

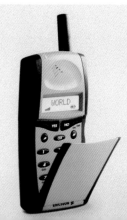

3

4

5

Thomas **Eriksson**

Sweden l Architect and furniture designer l www.stockholmdesignlab.se

Audi, **Cappellini**, H&M, **Ikea**, SAS (the Swedish national airline), Virgin – even a partial list of Thomas Eriksson's clients reveals that he is very much in demand, despite the fact that he prefers to keep a low profile. In Cappellini's *Progetto Ogetto* collection, products created by this designer–architect include strikingly unpretentious bathroom fittings and a clothes rack in the shape of a ladder, as well as more symbolic objects, such as *Crosscabinet*, a bright red medicine chest with a Red Cross design, and E-shaped shelving units, a clear allusion to the designer himself. The same idea is behind the angular *E-Seat* sofa, the first signature sofa (for **Offecct**). Eriksson's contributions to Ikea's *PS* furniture series are similarly restrained and have a distinctive graphic quality, rather like furniture by **Björn Dahlström**. Eriksson is eager to give Swedish style a contemporary interpretation.

For a number of years Eriksson was responsible for the design of SAS airport lounges, which now offer their passengers open fires and other neo-Nordic touches, not just at Stockholm and Copenhagen airports, but also at Heathrow and Newark. Other Swedish institutions are also keen to commission Eriksson. The cosmopolitan Scandinavian designer gave the crisis-ridden Moderna Museet (Museum of Modern Art) in Stockholm a new corporate identity and thus helped it to completely revitalize its image.

1959 Born in Örnsköldsvik

1985 Completes architecture studies at Konstfack, University College of Arts, Crafts and Design, Stockholm

1988 Works as freelance architect

1992 Presents furniture exhibitions in Milan, New York and Cologne for **Cappellini**

1995 Receives award for Excellent Swedish Design

1998 SAS Euroclass Lounge, Milan and London

Products

1992 *Skeleton* towel rack for **Asplund**; *Crosscabinet* medicine chest for Cappellini

1994 *E* trolley and *TE 1* coffee table for Cappellini

1995 Candlestick, TV table and table clock (*PS* collection) for **Ikea**

2001 *F-Seat* sofa for **Offecct**

2002 *E-Seat* sofa and *I-Seat* chaise longue for Offecct

1 *Skeleton* towel rack, 1992

2 *E-Seat* sofa, 2002

3 *Crosscabinet* medicine chest, 1992

4 *E* trolley, 1994

5 Table clock (*PS* collection), 1995

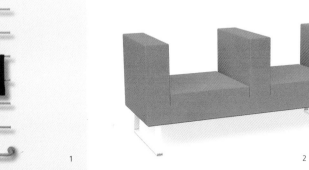
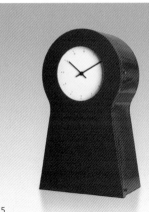

1

2

159

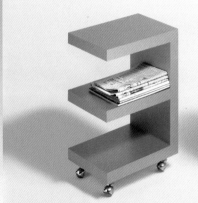

3

4

5

Ford, *Mustang Fastback*, 1967

At the beginning of the 1960s Lee Iacocca, at that time vice-president of Ford, called for a sports coupé that would also appeal to families. The *Mustang* was presented in 1964 and proved to be an outstandingly successful automobile concept. The styling – stumpy back, long bonnet and low lines – soon attracted an enthusiastic following. The favourable price and numerous model variants, such as the *Fastback*, also contributed to its success.

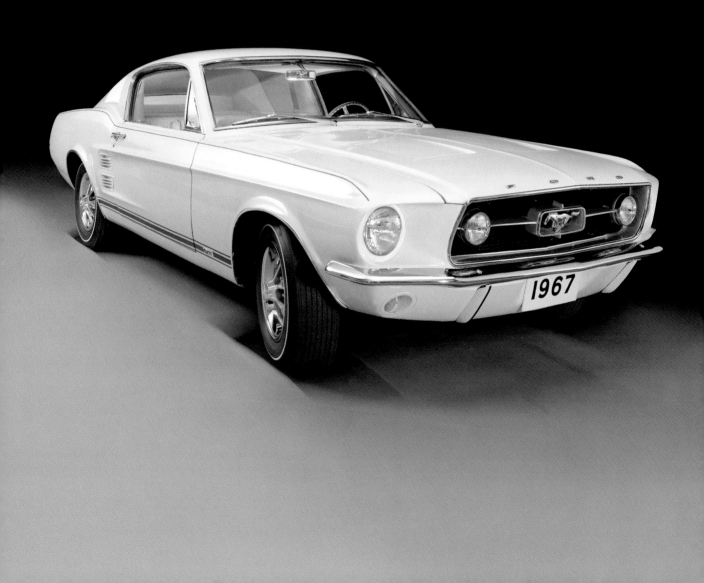

Ferrari

Italy | Ferrari (Fiat Auto SpA), Turin | Automobile manufacturer | www.ferrariworld.com

The story of this legendary company begins at the end of the 1920s, when Enzo Ferrari, a former employee of **Alfa Romeo**, established a racing workshop. The production of road vehicles began after the Second World War with the *Spider Touring*, which was soon given the nickname *Barchetta* (Little Boat). The golden decades of the post-war era were characterized by the gentle waves of Italian 'bel design'. The *250 GT*, designed by **Pininfarina**, the in-house designer, contributed significantly to the worldwide success of the marque in the mid-1950s. Subsequent versions, such as the *250 GT Tour de France* and the *250 GT SWB* from the early 1960s, were among the most beautiful cars of this period. They were, however, still racing cars driven on ordinary roads by enthusiasts. At the end of the 1960s the *365 GTB/4* – also called *Daytona*, after the famous Daytona races – with its powerful appearance and impressively long bonnet, similar to that of the **Jaguar** *E-Type*, was received by the growing number of Ferrari fans with tremendous enthusiasm.

The 1970s were dominated by the *308 GTB* and *GTS*. The *GTS* became famous thanks to its appearances in the TV series *Magnum, PI*. The extrovert *Testarossa* is regarded as the ultimate symbol of Italian automobile design of the 1980s. Once again, an American TV series – in this case, *Miami Vice* – brought worldwide fame. The dream car – together with the rival model *Countach* from Lamborghini, designed by **Bertone** – ushered in an age of extreme vehicles that were previously only familiar from comics. At the turn of the century, however, the *360* (available as a *Modena* coupé and a *Spider* convertible) signified a return to the restrained lines of the *308*. Its V8 engine, which can be admired through the rear window, is glorified in a way that is disarmingly honest. The *Enzo Ferrari* is a tribute to the founder of the firm and is a line that is repeated each decade (it began with the *F 40* in the 1980s and was continued with the *F 50* in the 1990s). Technologies and materials from Formula One cars have been introduced into the more recent production models. The inside of the *Challenge Stradale*, for example, more obviously resembles the cockpit of Michael Schumacher's racing car than the interior of a classic sports car.

162

1 *Enzo Ferrari* (detail), 2003
2 *550 Maranello*, 1996
3 *360 Spider*, 1999
4 *Testarossa*, 1985
5 *250 GT SWB*, 1960
6 *308 GTB*, 1975
7 *Challenge Stradale*, 2003

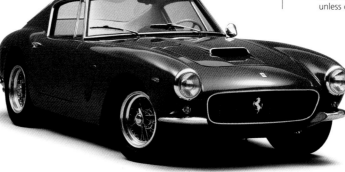

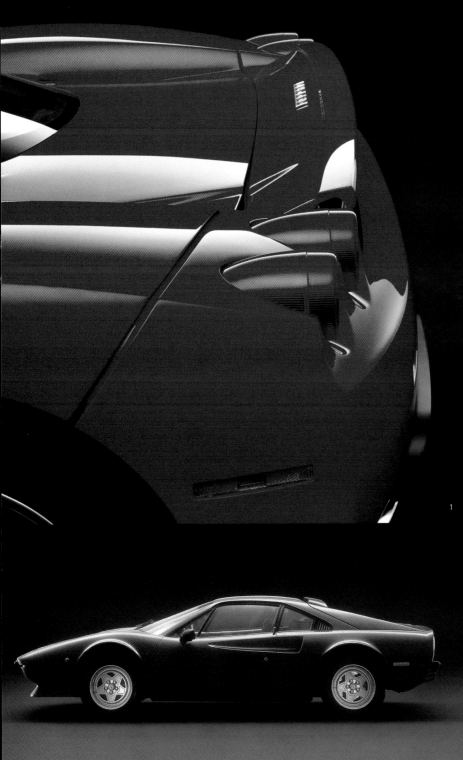

1

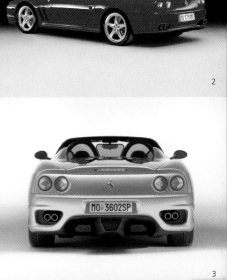

2

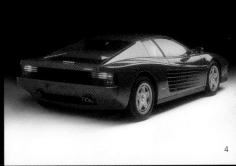

3

4

6

7

Fiat

Italy I Fiat Auto SpA, Turin I Automobile manufacturer I **www.fiat.com**

The Fiat Group – to which the once independent marques **Lancia**, **Alfa Romeo** and, in a somewhat different league, **Ferrari** and Maserati now belong – not only manufactures lorries, buses and other commercial vehicles, but also dams, satellites and turbines, and is active in such fields as medical equipment and robot technology. Cars, however, remain its core focus. Founded shortly before the end of the nineteenth century, the company, like all motor manufacturers, concentrated initially on the production of expensive, hand-built luxury and racing cars. Just before the First World War, however, Italy's first mass-produced car, the Fiat *Zero*, the answer to Henry **Ford**'s *Model T*, went into production. By the end of the 1920s Fiat was the leading car manufacturer in the country. In the midst of the Great Depression the elegant *Balilla* family saloon was a huge sales success. A few years later, the first *500* model, the *Topolino*, ushered in the era of attractive small cars, which was continued in the 1950s with the super compact *Nuova 500* and *600* models, echoing the soft lines of the *Vespa*.

By the mid-1950s the Fiat company had come to epitomize the Italian economic miracle. In 1956 it presented the *Multipla* microbus, based on the *600* model. The *Multipla* anticipated present-day SUVs and was particularly appealing because of its flexibility and spaciousness. In the early 1970s Fiat launched the *X 1/9*, designed by **Bertone**. It was the first affordable sports car with a centrally mounted engine and was a bestseller in Japan and the United States. The 1980s brought Fiat two more major successes. The Fiat *Panda*, designed by **Giorgetto Giugiaro**'s Italdesign, was a practical box on wheels that caused something of a sensation. Giugiaro's economical *Uno*, the Italian equivalent of **Volkswagen**'s *Golf*, likewise caused something of a sensation. In the 1990s the exciting designs of the *Coupé Fiat* and the *Barchetta* roadster, both by Chris Bangle, gave new life to the marque. However, a protracted sales crisis, combined with the threat of a takeover by **General Motors** after the death of Giovanni Agnelli (grandson of the founder of the firm and father of Italian industry), assumed dramatic proportions. At the same time, interesting models, such as the new version of the *Multipla*, proved that Fiat could still play on its old strengths. With the *Punto*, *Panda 2* and *Seicento* – all of them reinterpretations of the small-car theme – the elegantly curved look of the early years was revived on home territory.

164

1 *Punto 2* compact car, 2001

2 *Barchetta* roadster, 1997

3 *Coupé Fiat*, 1994

4 *Croma* saloon, 1985

5 *500* small car (*Topolino*), 1936

6 *X 1/9* sports car, 1972

7 *Panda 2* small car, 2004

1899	Società Anonima Fabbrica Italiana Automobili Torino (FIAT) established by Giovanni Agnelli in Turin
1939	Opens Mirafiori factory
1945	Giovanni Agnelli dies
1958	Establishes Centro Stile (design centre)
1963	Giovanni Agnelli, grandson of founder, becomes managing director
1969	Acquires **Lancia** and **Ferrari**
1982	Lingotto factory closes down
1987	Acquires **Alfa Romeo**
1992	Chris Bangle becomes chief designer (moves to **BMW** in same year)

Products

1912	*Zero* small car
1932	*Balilla* saloon
1935	*1500* sports car
1936	*500* small car (*Topolino*)
1952	*8 V* racing car
1955	*600* small car
1956	*600 Multipla* microbus
1957	*Nuova 500* small car
1959	*1800/1900* saloon
1964	*850* small car
1966	*124 Spider* convertible by **Pininfarina**
1971	*127* compact car
1972	*X 1/9* sports car by **Bertone**
1980	*Panda* small car
1983	*Uno* small car
1985	*Croma* saloon
	Last three by ▶ **Giorgetto Giugiaro**
1989	*Tipo* compact saloon
1993	*Cinquecento* small car; *Punto* small car
1994	*Coupé Fiat* by Chris Bangle
1997	*Barchetta* roadster by Chris Bangle
1998	*Seicento* small car; *Multipla* MPV
2001	*Stilo* compact saloon; *Punto 2* compact car
2004	*Panda 2* small car

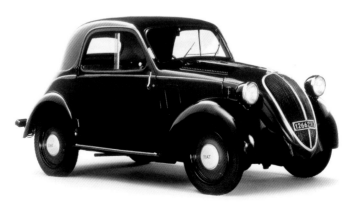

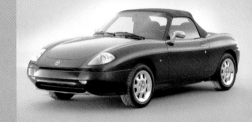

2

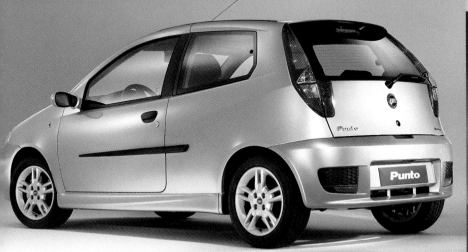

1

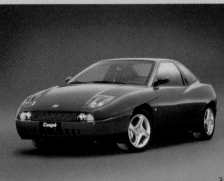

3

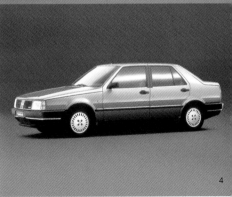

4

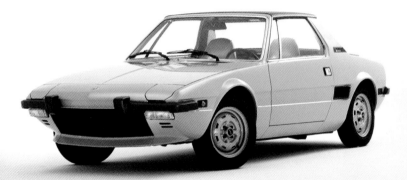

6

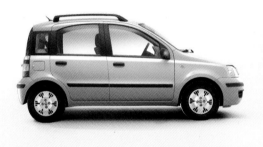

7

Uwe **Fischer**

Germany | Furniture and lamp designer

After completing his studies, Uwe Fischer had to decide which path his future career in the design industry should take: he could pursue the profit-orientated mass market or focus on the exclusivity of individual pieces. In fact, he chose a middle path, and together with Achim Heine founded Ginbande Design, which eventually made one of the most subtle and individual contributions to the Neues Deutsches Design movement in the 1980s. Ginbande's pieces are striking for the manner in which they function. The best-known design is probably *Tabula Rasa*, an extremely flexible table/bench construction that can be extended from half a metre in length to five metres (1' 6"–16' 4") and is able to accommodate up to twenty people. It is particularly fascinating for its unusual combination of high-tech and 'beer tent' aesthetics. Flexibility is also paramount in Fischer's later products. The design of the *Take Five* hanging lamp, for example, was inspired by an accordian. The lamp can be altered in length, and its five neon tubes can be adjusted to suit the light conditions. After Ginbande split up in the late 1990s, Fischer designed furniture and lamps for, among others, **B&B Italia** and **Serien**. His experimental functionalism, intended to encourage reflection on everyday objects, has remained an important feature of his work. The perception of objects has also been the focus of his research as a professor in Nuremberg and Stuttgart.

1958 Born in Offenbach
1978 Studies design at Hochschule für Gestaltung, Offenbach
1985 Establishes Ginbande Design with Achim Heine
1992 Establishes own design office in Frankfurt am Main
1993 Appointed professor at Akademie der Bildenden Künste, Nuremberg
2001 Appointed professor at Staatliche Akademie der Bildenden Künste, Stuttgart

Products

1985 *Tabula Rasa* pull-out table/bench combination for **Vitra** (with Achim Heine)
1990 *Nexus* table system for Vitra (with Achim Heine)
1993 Children's furniture for Anthologie Quartett; *Take Five* hanging lamp for **Serien Lighting** (with Achim Heine)
1995 *Wogg* folding table (with Achim Heine)
1998 *Tama* stackable chair and *Zoom* table collection for **B&B Italia**; *Shut Up* canister for **Authentics**
1999 *Sina* swivel armchair for B&B Italia; *Jones* standard lamp for Serien Lighting
2001 *Lotus* armchair and sofa for B&B Italia; *Funnel* glass bowls for Vitrocristal
2002 *Starter* coffee mug for Satira; *Molecullar* jewellery collection for Biegel Jewellery

1 *Take Five* hanging lamp, 1993
2 *Sina* swivel armchair, 1999
3 *Tabula Rasa* pull-out table/bench combination, 1985
4 *Nexus* table system, 1990
5 *Jones* standard lamp, 1999

166

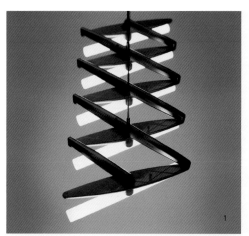

1

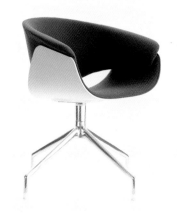

2

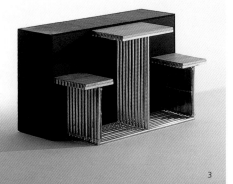

3

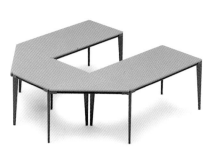

4

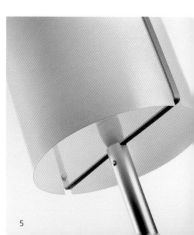

5

Fiskars

Finland I Fiskars Brands Finland Oy A/B, Helsinki I Tool manufacturer I **www.fiskars.com**

It is sometimes claimed that when Finns travelling abroad see a pair of scissors with an orange handle, they feel a sense of national pride and then check discreetly to see whether it is the original – the *Classic* model by Fiskars. The combination of the plastic handle and the metal blade, which makes the scissors lightweight and easy to use, was a novelty in the late 1960s. Today the *Classic* remains a cult object of Finnish design.

In the design of scissors, knives, axes and other tools, ergonomic considerations are paramount, and it is this basic philosophy that has ensured Fiskars's success. The company has, among other things, reinvented the axe. Traditionally, the handle of a metal axe has been attached by means of a hole in the blade. In Fiskars's axes this principle has been reversed: the plastic handle grips the blade, resulting in a far more stable construction. Similarly innovative is the lever mechanism of the *Anvil* garden pruners, which increases cutting power considerably. In order to differentiate its products from the inevitable host of copy-cat manufacturers, Fiskars eventually refrained from focusing on purely simple, dynamic forms. The new, more complex line is emphasized by the company's black, orange and silver colour scheme.

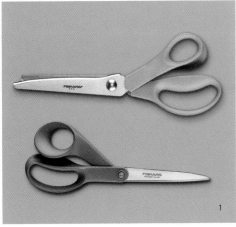

1

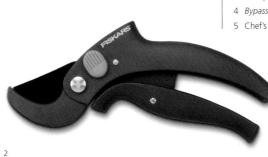

2

167

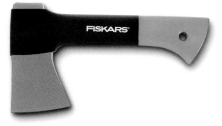

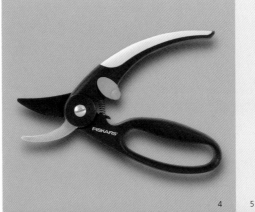

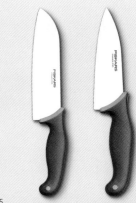

3

4

5

Fitch

USA | Product, interior and communications design studio | www.fitch.com

The designers from the Fitch studio are masters of creating products with beautiful, organic forms and complex, modern textures. They have even removed sharp edges from computers and television sets and given them flowing lines. The company's *Zip* drive, designed for Iomega, was awarded a prize in the United States for one of the best-designed products of the 1990s. The development of the sleek, flat appliance was inspired by the technology used in laptop computers, transforming what was originally a utilitarian box into an aesthetically pleasing design object that looked good on any desk.

Fitch has also developed a range of grooming products in the *Equine Care* series for Oster that combine a distinctive, contemporary look with advanced materials for maximum comfort and grip. The studio sees itself as a service that provides total design solutions, including graphics and interior design. The division for corporate identity plays a key role here. Its rebranding of the hitherto somewhat unexciting Hush Puppies range of shoes is a good example of its work: after Fitch refocused attention on the famous basset hound logo – which was put at the centre of all the graphic components – and redesigned the product range, the footwear company's share price soared by 150 per cent.

1 *Zip* drive, 1995
2 *Titanium CD Boombox* radio/CD player, 2000
3 Brush (*Equine Care* series), 2003
4 *Hermes* Internet telephone, 1998
5 Food processor (*Attrezzi* collection), 2004

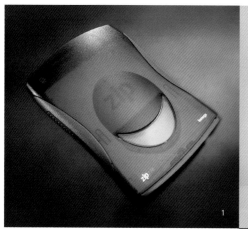

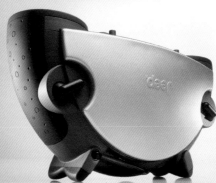

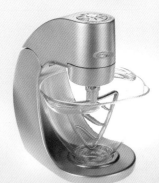

Flexform

Italy | Flexform SpA, Meda | Furniture manufacturer | **www.flexform.it**

For almost half a century some of the world's best designers – from **Cini Boeri, Joe Colombo,** Sergio Asti and Rodolfo Bonetto to **Antonio Citterio** and Paolo Nava – have found their way to Meda, near Milan, in northern Italy to collaborate with Flexform. The company was founded in the 1950s by Romeo, Agostino and Pietro Galimberti and has since grown to become one of the great Italian brands, known in particular for its elegant and comfortable seating systems. Flexform's furniture successfully combines innovative design with high-quality technical production.

Although traditional stylistic elements are often incorporated in Flexform's designs, the range also features strictly Modernist models by the Italian Rationalists Mario Asnago and Claudio Vender, including the famous *Letto Piano* bed. The company excels in the play of opposites, as in the distinctive *Tubo* chair by ▸ Joe Colombo, a Pop icon from the late 1960s, and in its successful range of simple sofas, such as *Max, Glenn* and *ABC* by Citterio. The classic *Mood* furniture series, by the American designer John Hutton, encapsulates Flexform's general philosophy: elegant but not conventional, harmonious but not bland.

1959 Established by Romeo, Agostino and Pietro Galimberti

Products

1969 *Tubo* chair by ▸ **Joe Colombo**

1980 *Filiberto, Doralice* and *Ugomaria* sofa collections by **Antonio Citterio** and Paolo Nava

1983 *Eva* chair by Paolo Nava; *Max* sofa by Antonio Citterio

1984 *Victor* sofa collection; *Nonnamaria* sofa collection by Antonio Citterio

1985 *Mokka* glass cabinet collection; *Patrik* sofa collection; *Mixer* chair

1987 *Le Canapé* furniture collection

1991 *Amadeus* armchair, *Press* chair and *Poggiolungo* sofa by Antonio Citterio

1995 *Spider* armchair by Giulio Manzoni

1996 *Rosetta* armchair, *Pierre* sofa, *Status* sofa collection and *Zanzibar* occasional table by Antonio Citterio; *Letto Piano* bed by Mario Asnago and Claudio Vender; *Linda* chair

1997 *Bob* and *Greta* armchairs, *Pat* chair, *Glenn* sofa, *Carlotta* furniture collection and *Sem* armchair and occasional tables by Antonio Citterio

1998 *ABC* armchair and sofas and *Theo* sofa and occasional table collection by Antonio Citterio

1999 *Winny* sofa bed by Guido Rosati

2000 *Mood* furniture collection by John Hutton

2001 *Alexander* sofa, *Sally* chair, *Atlantic* armchair, *Thomas* chair by Antonio Citterio

2002 *Morgan* armchair; *Jenny* chair; *Lightpiece* furniture collection

2003 *Magnum* sofa by Antonio Citterio

1 *ABC* armchair, 1998
2 *Carlotta* armchair, 1997
3 *Lightpiece* sofa, 2002
4 *Cool* armchair (*Mood* collection), 2000

169

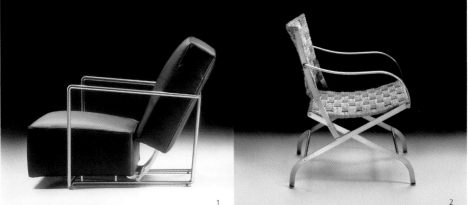

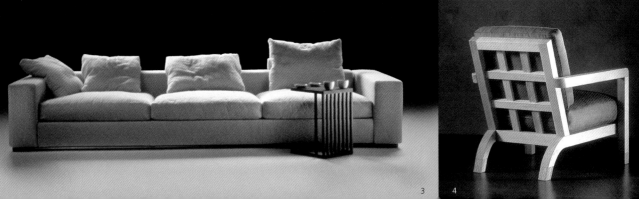

Flos

Italy | Flos SpA, Bovezzo | Lamp manufacturer | **www.flos.com**

From the 1960s until his death in 2002, the great Italian designer ▸ **Achille Castiglioni** shaped the identity of the lamp manufacturer Flos, initially with his brother Pier Giacomo. From the modest *Splügen Bräu* to the revolutionary *Parentesi* and the *Frisbi*, *Brera*, *Fucsia* and *Diabolo* hanging lamps, the Castiglioni products in the Flos programme made history in modern lamp design. In 1962, the year in which the company was founded, three products were created that today are regarded as classics. Perhaps the most famous is the arched *Arco* lamp, inspired by street lamps. With its solid marble base, it combines the advantages of a standard lamp with those of a hanging lamp. The other two classics are *Taccia,* the monumental table lamp, and the *Toio* ceiling spotlight, fashioned from a car headlight mounted on a pole.

Subtle touches of humour frequently distinguish great design. This is evident not only in the work of the Castiglionis but also in the products of numerous other designers who collaborate with Flos. For example, the *Ará* table lamp, created in the 1980s by ▸ **Philippe Starck**, the star of modern French design, has a characteristic pointed form. In the 1990s Starck contributed the small *Miss Sissi* table lamp, the base, stand and shade of which are all made of the same inexpensive coloured plastic.

In the 1960s and 1970s Tobia Scarpa produced several simple but highly distinctive designs, including the *Ariette 1-2-3* ceiling lamp, the reflector of which consists of a semi-transparent material that makes the cable and fittings visible when the lamp is switched on. In the early 1970s Flos took over the legendary lighting manufacturer Arteluce, founded by **Gino Sarfatti**. Some of Sarfatti's designs are still in production today. The Flos range also includes works by a younger generation of designers, among them Marc Sadler and **Rodolfo Dordoni**. The balloon-shaped *Glo-Ball* collection by the British designer **Jasper Morrison** has opened up new avenues in lamp design.

1 *Taccia* table lamp, 1962
2 *Fucsia* hanging lamp, 1996
3 *Splügen Bräu* hanging lamp, 1961
4 *Archimoon* table lamp, 1998
5 *Gibigiana* table lamp, 1980
6 *Glo-Ball* table lamp, 1998
7 *Ará* table lamp, 1988
8 *May Day* portable lamp, 1998

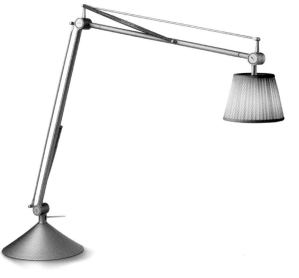

4

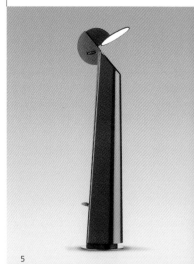

5

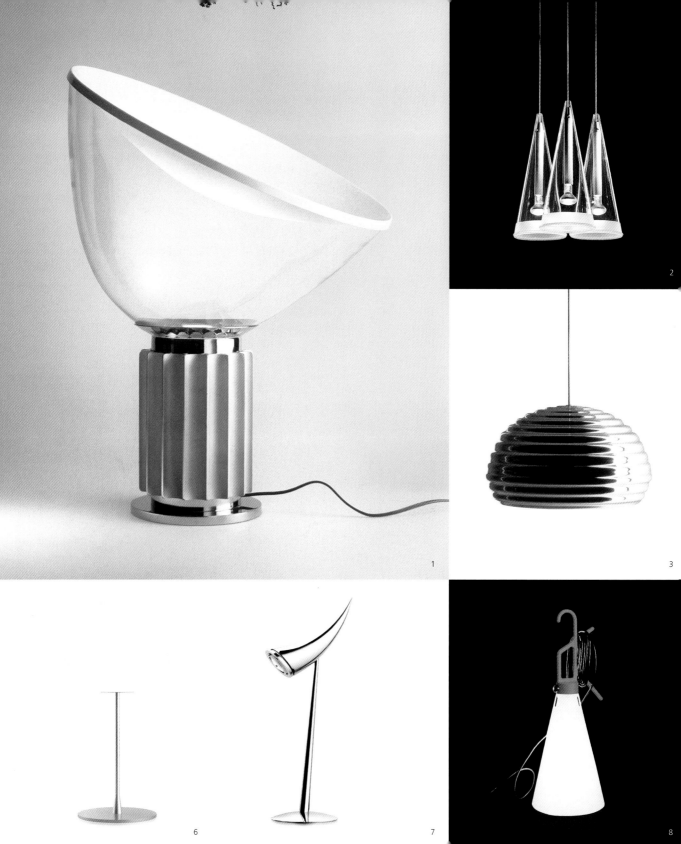

1

2

3

6

7

8

Fontana Arte

Italy | Fontana Arte SpA, Corsico | Lamp and furniture manufacturer | **www.fontanaarte.it**

In the early 1930s the famous architect **Gio Ponti** established Fontana Arte as the artistic division of the Luigi Fontana glassworks. Ponti was fascinated by the delicate and malleable properties of glass and by its design possibilities. In those days, the company's core business was the manufacture of stained-glass windows, which it had produced for the cathedral in Milan, among many other churches. Ponti gradually began to develop high-quality furniture and lamps for Fontana Arte. He invited the architect Pietro Chiesa to contribute a number of simple lamps to the collection, including the well-proportioned *Luminator*, which seems as modern today as when it was first produced in 1933.

Although Fontana Arte soon made a name for itself in its early years, this advantage was lost after the Second World War. An international company bought Luigi Fontana, including Fontana Arte, and turned towards mass production using inferior materials. In its attempt to create a purely commercial product range, however, it diluted the company's hitherto unmistakable design image. It was not until Carlo Guglielmi bought Fontana Arte with a private group of investors at the end of the 1970s that the company returned to its origins. Fontana Arte resumed the use of high-quality glass and again sought to work with designers and architects. Gae Aulenti became art director, while Daniela Puppa and Franco Raggi were responsible for exhibitions and special events, and Pierluigi Cerri handled advertising. Various renowned designers and architects, including **Ettore Sottsass**, **Vico Magistretti**, Umberto Riva and Renzo Piano, were commissioned to develop such high-quality and original products as the *Franceschina* table lamp and the *Morocco* hanging lamp. In the 1980s and 1990s Fontana Arte earned its place among the leading Italian design companies with a well-defined range of furniture and lamps. It launched the *Candle* lighting series, aimed at a younger market, in the early 1980s and the *Schopenhauer* collection of furniture and glass objects (now called *Arredo* and *Oggetti*) in the early 1990s. Today **Rodolfo Dordoni** is the most important consultant for these collections. Since the mid-1990s office lighting has been marketed under the *Naskaloris* brand.

1932 Established by **Gio Ponti**
1979 Bought by a private group, headed by Carlo Guglielmi

Products
1931 *0024* hanging lamp by Gio Ponti
1933 *Luminator* standard lamp by Pietro Chiesa
1954 *Fontana* table lamp by Max Ingrand
1967 *Pirellone* floor lamp by ▸ Gio Ponti
1980 *Parola* lamp collection by Gae Aulenti and Piero Castiglioni
1988 *Velo* hanging lamp by Franco Raggi
1989 *Franceschina* lamp collection by Umberto Riva
1992 *Piccola San* table lamp by Daniela Puppa; *Koi* and *Nobi* lamp collections by Metis
1993 *Tour* and *Tavolo con Ruote* occasional tables by Gae Aulenti
1994 *Falena* lamp collection by Alvaro Siza
1998 *Morocco* hanging lamp by **Vico Magistretti**
1999 *Flute/Magnum* standard lamp by Franco Raggi
2000 *Bambù* table lamp by ▸ **Fernando and Humberto Campana**
2001 *Colour* table lamp by Riccardo Giovanetti; *Zoe* table lamp by Paolo Zani
2002 *S. Vigilio* hanging lamp by ▸ **Matteo Thun**
2003 *Charms* table lamp and *Maya* vase by Daniela Puppa; *Loop* table lamp by Voon Wong; *Bruco* wall lamp by Vico Magistretti; *Ambrosiana* light shelf by **Rodolfo Dordoni**

1 *Franceschina* table lamp, 1989
2 *Velo* hanging lamp, 1988
3 *Charms* table lamp, 2003
4 *Luminator* standard lamp, 1933
5 *0024* hanging lamp, 1931
6 *Morocco* hanging lamp, 1998
7 *Parola* wall lamp, 1980
8 *Tavolo con Ruote* occasional table, 1993

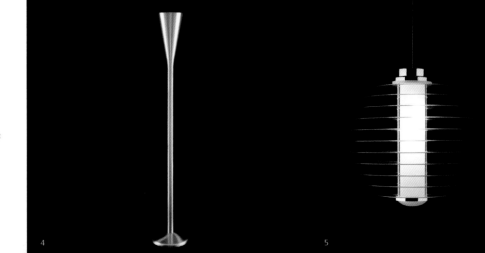

4   5

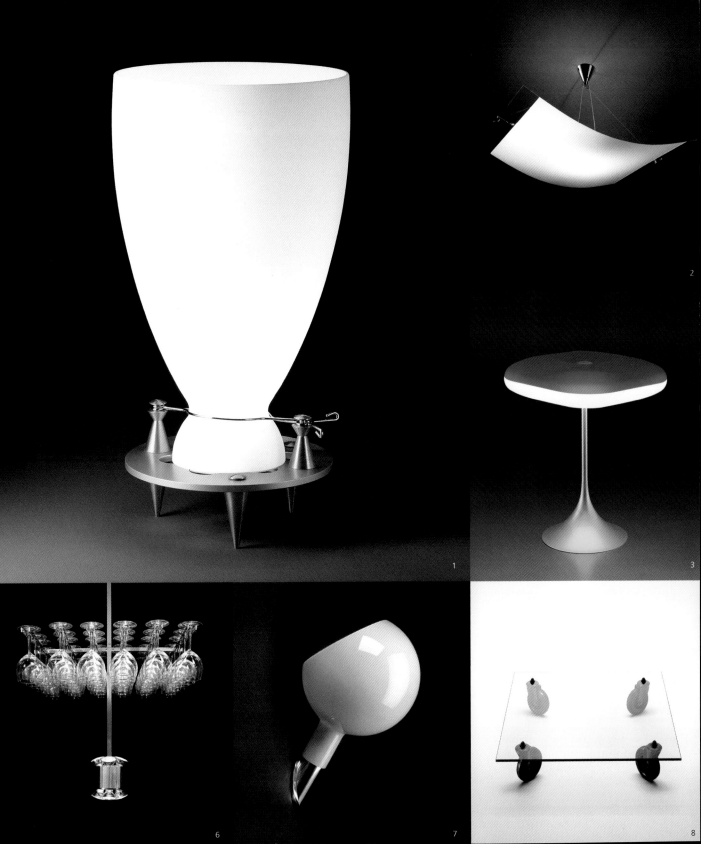

1

2

3

6

7

8

Ford

USA/Europe | Ford Motor Company, Dearborn, Michigan | Automobile manufacturer | **www.ford.com**

The first motor car produced by Ford was also the first automobile in the world to sell by the millions. With this car, the *Model T*, Henry Ford created a universal symbol of mobility. The downside of the success story was, however, that, unlike **General Motors**, Ford initially failed to recognize the importance of industrial design. This failure was remedied in the early 1940s, when chief designer Eugene Gregorie finally had great success with the Lincoln *Continental*, a luxury saloon that is regarded as one of the most aesthetically pleasing cars of its time. In the middle of the following decade Ford presented the *Thunderbird* sports car, which also became a classic. It was particularly distinctive for being almost European in design. The late 1950s saw Ford's biggest flop thus far – the *Edsel*. The *Mustang* came to the company's rescue in the mid-1960s. Its design became the prototype for the 'pony car' class of affordable, performance-orientated vehicles. When J. Mays was engaged as the company's chief designer in 1997 he launched re-editions of both the *Thunderbird* and the *Mustang*. Mays is a great advocate of retro design, and was involved in the development of the *New Beetle* (for ▶ **Volkswagen**).

Until well into the 1980s, the German and British subsidiaries of the American parent company were relatively independent, although the first post-war model for the German market, the *Taunus 12M*, was still produced in Detroit. In the early 1960s the Cologne-based German subsidiary ventured a stylistic solo turn with the functional *Taunus 17M*, popularly referred to as the 'Bathtub'. By contrast, the *Capri*, a fastback coupé that was in production for sixteen years, clearly shows the influence of the American *Mustang*. The designs that followed were not particularly exciting. It was all the more surprising, therefore, that in the mid-1990s a small car was presented that heralded a visual revolution – the Ford *Ka*. It had been developed under chief designer Claude Lobo and stood out for its unusual proportions and uninterrupted lines. This style was appropriately referred to as 'New Edge'. Under Lobo's successor, Chris Bird, the design offensive continues with such models as the *StreetKa* roadster (by ▶ **Pininfarina**), the second generation of the mid-range *Focus* and the *Focus C-Max* MPV.

1 *Ka* small car (detail), 1996
2 *SportKa* small car, 2003
3 *Focus* compact saloon, 1998
4 *Capri* coupé, 1969
5 *Thunderbird* convertible, 1954
6 *Mustang* coupé, 1964
    and *Mustang* coupé redesign, 2004
7 *Mustang* coupé (detail), 2004

1903	Established by Henry Ford in Michigan
1913	Introduces moving assembly lines
1919	Son Edsel succeeds Henry Ford
1925	Acquires Lincoln Motor Company
1938	Launches Mercury marque
1945	Henry Ford II becomes president
1970	Lee Iacocca becomes president
1987	Claude Lobo becomes chief designer (Europe)
1997	J. Mays becomes chief designer (USA)
1999	Acquires **Volvo** car division; establishes Premier Automotive Group (Aston Martin, Jaguar, Lincoln and Volvo); Chris Bird becomes chief designer (Europe)
2000	Acquires Land Rover

Products

1908	*Model T* (first model)
1927	*Model A*
1940	*Continental* saloon
1954	*Thunderbird* convertible
1960	*Taunus 17M* saloon ('Bathtub')
1964	*Mustang* coupé and convertible
1969	*Capri* coupé
1974	*Fiesta* small car
1975	*Granada* saloon
1981	*Escort* compact saloon
1982	*Sierra* saloon
1986	*Scorpio* saloon
1994	*Mondeo* saloon
1996	*Ka* small car
1998	*Focus* compact saloon
2003	*SportKa* small car; *StreetKa* roadster by ▶ **Pininfarina**; *Focus C-Max* MPV
2004	*Mustang* coupé and convertible; *GT* sports car (both redesigns)

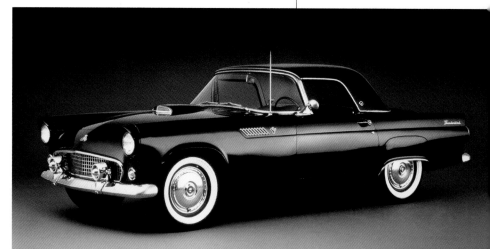

5

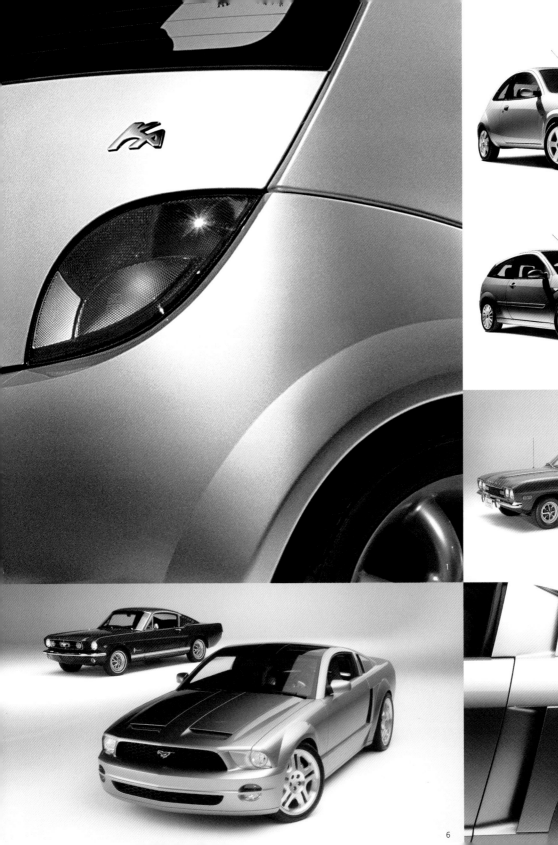

1

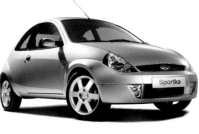

Sportka

2

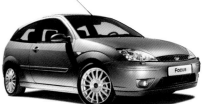

Focus

3

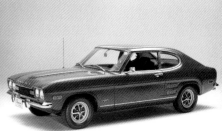

4

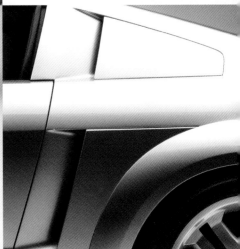

6

7

Foscarini

Italy | Foscarini Srl, Marcon | Lamp manufacturer | **www.foscarini.com**

The elegant Murano glass that is produced on a group of islands in the Venice lagoon is legendary in Italy. When Foscarini was founded in the city at the beginning of the 1980s, it concentrated exclusively on developing the potential of this precious and traditional material. The company soon began to look further afield, however: its management not only made contact with such leading international designers as Jozeph Forakis, **Tom Dixon**, **Rodolfo Dordoni**, Defne Koz, Ferrucio Laviani, **Denis Santachiara** and Roberto and Ludovica Palomba, but also extended its range of materials quite considerably. For many years now Foscarini's designers have been working in a range of different media, including satin glass, wood, plastics, aluminium and various patented special textures. Foscarini's catalogue reflects this variety and contains a diverse range of original designs, including the *Bague* table lamp by ▶ **Patricia Urquiola** and Eliana Gerotto, which exhibits the design duo's characteristic high-tech appeal; the *Esa* table lamp by ▶ **Lievore Altherr Molina**, a reinterpretation of a classic format; the award-winning *Mite* and *Tite* lamps by Marc Sadler; and the *Havana* 'cigar' standard lamp by Forakis. The *Lumiere* table lamp by Rodolfo Dordoni has already become a classic.

1 *Blob* lamp, 2002
2 *Orbital* standard lamp, 1992
3 *Lumiere* table lamp, 1990
4 *Havana* standard lamp, 1993
5 *Mite* standard lamp, 2000

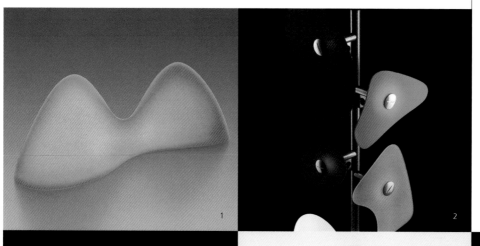

Foster and Partners

England | Architecture and furniture and product design studio | www.fosterandpartners.com

Modernism in aluminium, glass and steel: the designs of the renowned British architect Sir Norman Foster radiate optimism and celebrate faith in technology. The *Nomos* glass table series for the Italian manufacturer Tecno has legs that are reminiscent of a plane's under-carriage, an aesthetic allusion to Foster's most famous building of the 1980s, the headquarters of the Hongkong and Shanghai Bank. After studying in Manchester, where he was born, Foster rose through the ranks to enjoy a dazzling career: he is now an architect of considerable international standing whose services are in great demand. In 1997 he was awarded a knighthood for his achievements.

Foster's products often emerge out of architectural commissions, as in the lighting system developed in collaboration with **Erco** for the Hongkong and Shanghai Bank and the *A 900* chair programme produced with **Thonet** for the Reichstag in Berlin. The hallmark of these products, and of others designed independently of building projects, is the cool elegance of matt metal, as used in the office accessories series for ▶ **Helit**, the *Airline* seating system for **Vitra** and the *Focus* outdoor lamp series for **Artemide**.

1 *A 900* chair, 1999
2 *Focus* outdoor lighting, 2003
3 *Nomos* table, 1987
4 Pen stand (*Foster Series* collection), 2000

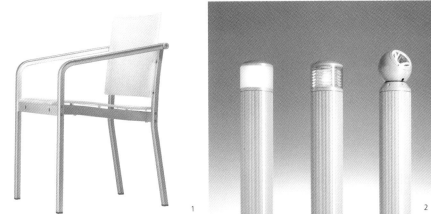

1

2

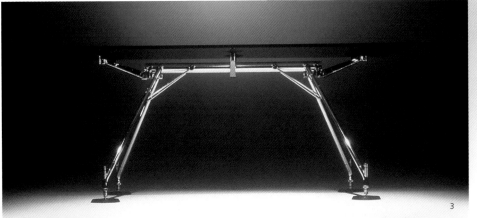

3

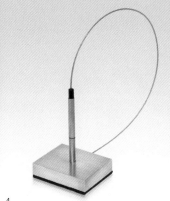

4

Kaj **Franck**

Finland I Ceramics and glass designer I www.iittala.com I www.arabia.fi

Although Kaj Franck's classic designs in ceramic and glass were taken out of production in the 1970s, today they are bestsellers at both **Arabia** and **Iittala**. The *Kartio* glass series from the 1950s (▶ p. 235), for example, was revived by Iittala at the beginning of the 1990s. Franck's work is characterized by distinct colours, simplicity of form, combinable elements and multifunctionality – design principles derived from classical Modernism. Franck not only inspired a revolution in tableware but also became an influential teacher, largely on account of his role as design director of the Institute of Industrial Arts in Helsinki in the 1960s. His career as a designer began in earnest after the Second World War at Arabia, where he later became artistic director. Franck was initially regarded as a controversial figure: he criticized traditional Scandinavian design, preferring the "geometrical principles of the 1930s" inspired by the Bauhaus. His motto was "radical and social", and his aim was to achieve a new material culture for all. His plates, dishes and glasses were as practical as stackable chairs. He drew inspiration for his designs from early industrial goods and from the Samen people's simple, robust tableware.

Franck had overwhelming success with *Kilta* (today known as *Teema*, for ▶ Arabia), an 'anti-service' designed to counter the prevailing trend in European tableware. Ironically, its pieces were fired in the same kilns as Arabia's washbasins and toilets. The attraction and the novelty of these pieces lay in the fact that they had not been designed as a complete service: they consisted of more than thirty individual items that could be combined at will. 'Mix and match' became a popular activity, first in Europe and then in Finland itself. It was the mass production of the avant garde. Of the twenty-five million items sold, a few are to be found in illustrious surroundings, such as the cafeteria at the Picasso Museum in Paris.

The glassware that Franck designed (for Iittala and Nuutajärvi) is also significant. He made a clear distinction between art and items for everyday use. Among his staff were such well-known Finnish glass designers as Oiva Toikka, Heikki Orvola and Kerttu Nurminen. Franck was adamantly opposed to his name being used for advertising purposes, arguing that it distracted unnecessarily from the objects themselves.

1   *Kilta* service, 1952 (reissued as *Teema*, 1981)

2   Cup and bowls from the *Kilta* (*Teema*) service, 1952

3   Large drinking glass from the *Kartio* series, 1958

4   Pitchers and small glasses from the *Kartio* series, 1958

5   *Prisma* vase, 1954

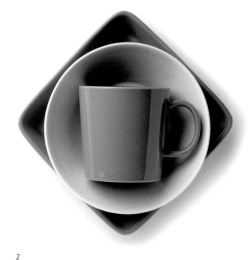

2

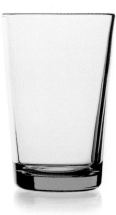

3

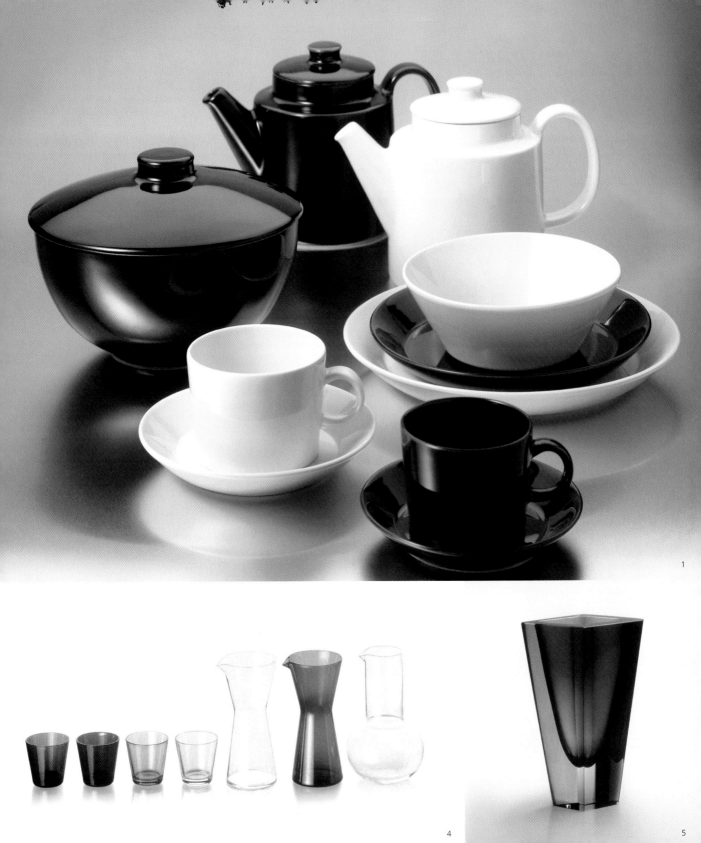

1

4

5

Josef **Frank**

Sweden | Architect and furniture and product designer | **www.svenskttenn.se**

The prominent Austrian architect and designer Josef Frank, who emigrated to Sweden in 1933, belonged to the inner circle of European Modernists. Unlike his contemporaries **Walter Gropius** and **Le Corbusier**, however, Frank did not set out to rationalize interiors in a radical fashion – a home was not a machine, in his view. The very fact that he did not explain the principles that lay behind his work was, in itself, an important aspect of his approach to design. A humanist and connoisseur of historic furniture, Frank arranged rooms as though "chance had played the most important part [in them]". He viewed purism as "anaemic" and the products of the Swedish Arts and Crafts Association, which was based on Bauhaus principles, as "boring". His designs caused a sensation when they were presented in 1939 at the *Golden Gate International Exposition* in San Francisco and the *New York World's Fair*, and may have given credence to his claim of having "invented the Scandinavian style".

Frank owed much to the support of his patron and colleague Estrid Ericson, who appointed him as chief designer of her furnishings company, Svenskt Tenn. He developed a design aesthetic that was colourful, witty, surprising and, above all, wholly new – as evident in his *Blue Chest* and *Knuten* intertwined candelabra. Frank often used walnut and mahogany in his designs instead of the ubiquitous birch and elm. The extravagantly flowing lines of his *Liljevalch* oversized sofa, which he presented in the mid-1930s, were an affront to those who favoured a functional approach to design. Inspired by Oriental furniture (particularly Chinese pieces), Frank preferred such lightweight, natural materials as cane and rattan. One of his favourite models was the traditional English Windsor chair. His furniture generally had a light and airy quality and was designed to make rooms appear as open and spacious as possible.

A remarkably prolific designer, Frank produced around two thousand pieces of furniture throughout his career, as well as numerous textile designs. Under his management, Svenskt Tenn developed an unprecedented variety of furniture and materials and remained committed to his slogan: "Whatever style we use, Baroque or tubular steel, is unimportant. What Modernism has given us is freedom."

1885	Born in Baden, near Vienna, Austria
1903	Works as architect in Vienna
1911	Marries Anna Sebenius, a Swede
1925	Establishes Haus & Garten company
1927	House for Weissenhofsiedlung, Stuttgart
1932	House for Werkbundsiedlung, Vienna
1933	Emigrates to Sweden
1937	Designs Swedish Pavilion at *Exposition Internationale*, Paris, and again in 1939 at *New York World's Fair*, making 'Swedish Modern' popular
1967	Dies in Stockholm
1996	Retrospective held at Bard Graduate Center, New York

Products

1920	*G 2548* standard lamp
1925	*300* chair in walnut and leather; *Primavera* printed textile; *2025* chair
1930	*592* garden chair in red lacquered metal; cupboard with *Mirakel* pattern; iron plant stand
1934	*Liljevalch* armchair and sofa for Svenskt Tenn (as are all products below)
1936	*542* armchair
1938	*Knuten* candelabra; *965* mahogany table; three-legged standard lamp
1939	*San Francisco* standard lamp
1940	*311* rattan chair
1944	*Gröna Fåglar*, *Manhattan* and *Terrazzo* textile patterns
1948	*2215* chest in birch and tropical hardwood; *300* and *1165* chairs
1949	*2073* table
1950	Jewellery box in glass; coloured candlestick in wood
1954	*Blue Chest 2192*

1 *Blue Chest 2192*, 1954

2 *2215* chest, 1948

3 *592* garden chair, 1930

4 *Knuten* candelabra, 1938

5 Three-legged standard lamp, 1938

6 *Liljevalch* sofa, 1934

7 *San Francisco* standard lamp, 1939

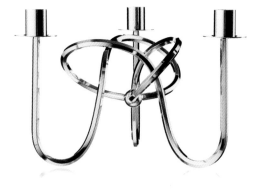

4

5

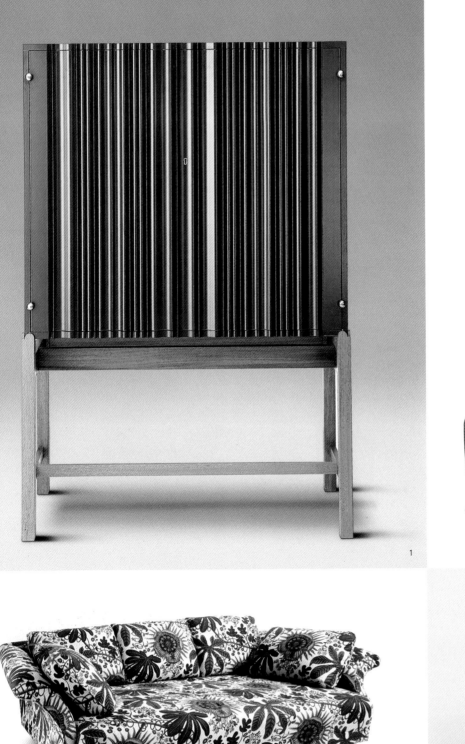

1

2

3

6

7

Fredericia

Denmark | Fredericia Furniture A/S, Fredericia | Furniture manufacturer | **www.fredericia.com**

Fredericia today belongs to the premier league of the furniture industry. In the unsettled period following the Second World War, however, the Danish chair factory found itself on the brink of bankruptcy. Andreas Graversen, owner of a furniture workshop in the same town, bought his ailing competitor for a nominal sum and soon transformed the company into one of the most distinguished furniture manufacturers in the business. Several factors contributed to this success, including the emergence and subsequent popularity of Danish design around the same period and the fact that Graversen was acquainted with Børge Mogensen, a highly sought-after cabinetmaker, whom he persuaded to work for Fredericia. The craftsman–carpenter designed a new collection almost overnight. His furniture was practical and unpretentious, and represented the finest of the well-crafted Danish furniture that was being exported around the world. Mogensen's 'Spanish armchair' and his rustic 'hunting chair' are still among the company's best-known products.

Mogensen, the creative designer, and Graversen, the businessman, had joined forces at precisely the right moment, a stroke of luck that was to be repeated some four decades later. The end of the 1980s saw the start of Fredericia's collaboration with ▶ **Nanna Ditzel**, who had just returned to Denmark from Britain. Ditzel's prize-winning *Trinidad* chair – reminiscent of the wooden architecture of the colonial period and of her lengthy stay on the Caribbean island of the same name – increased turnover rapidly. Fredericia had hitherto been known for the pronounced Danish solidity of its furniture, but Ditzel's involvement introduced a more avant-garde element into the programme. Her novel designs, such as the *Bench for Two* and, later, the shell-shaped *Icon* easy chair, stirred the industry out of its complacency. Fredericia now has a team of established designers who are continuing Ditzel's innovative approach. The V-form frame of the *V2* table by Kasper Salto, for example, guarantees considerable stability and allows the best use of space. The *Mobili* line, created by a group of younger designers, has been added to the product range. Fredericia's traditional furniture also continues to make an impact: the elegant desk by Rud Thygesen and Johnny Sørensen is to be found in the study of the queen of Denmark.

1911	Established in Fredericia
1955	Andreas Graversen takes over company (headed since 1995 by son Thomas)
1971	Receives Danish Furniture Prize
1995	Receives ID Prize for *Trinidad* chair

Products

1958	*2226* 'Spanish armchair'; *2254* armchair
1962	*2212* and *2213* chairs
1965	*Shaker* table
1971	*2333* sofa
	All by Børge Mogensen
1989	*Bench for Two* by ▶ **Nanna Ditzel**
1990	*Butterfly* chair by ▶ **Nanna Ditzel**; desk by Rud Thygesen and Johnny Sørensen
1993	*Trinidad* chair by ▶ **Nanna Ditzel**
1995	*Max* sofa by **Pelikan Design**
1996	*Tuba* chair; *Tobago* conference table
1997	*Temba* stackable chair
1998	*Tempo* chair
2000	*Sonar* stackable chair
	Last five by ▶ Nanna Ditzel
2001	*2229* 'hunting chair' by Børge Mogensen (1950 design)
2002	*Zip* cabinet by Andreas Lund and Carlo Wolf; *Mirror* coffee table and *Icon* easy chair by ▶ **Nanna Ditzel**; *Pingo* chair by Hans Sandgren Jakobsen; *B2* chair and *V2* table by Kasper Salto
2003	*Easy Bean* chair by Nicholai Wiig Hansen
2004	*Distance* armchair and sofa by Niels Jørgen Haugesen; *StingRay* rocking chair and *Spacemaker* partition by Thomas Pedersen

182

1 *2229* 'hunting chair', 2001 (1950 design)

2 *Pingo* chair, 2002

3 *Distance* sofa, 2004

4 *Icon* easy chair, 2002

5 *2226* 'Spanish armchair', 1958

6 Desk, 1990

7 *V2* table, 2002

8 *Zip* cabinet, 2002

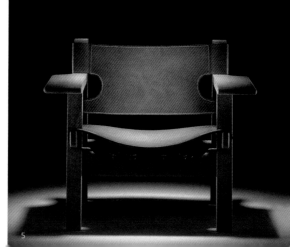

5

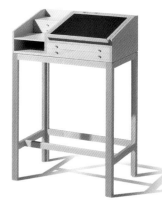

6

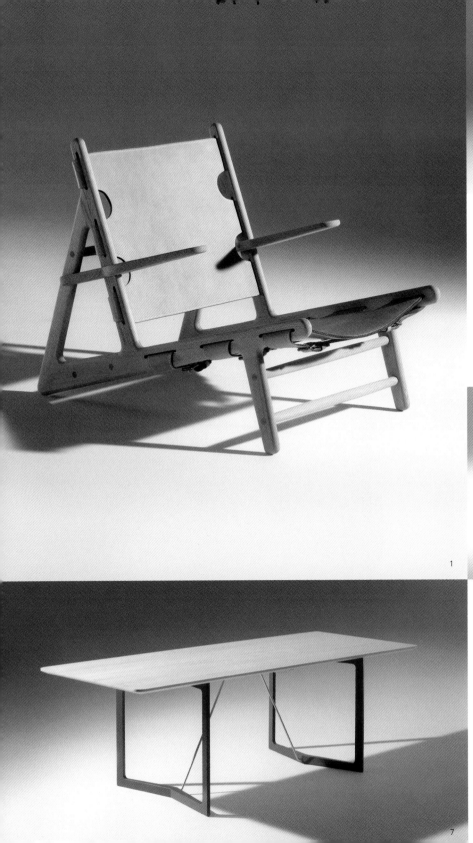

1

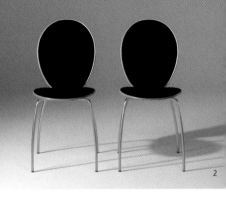

2

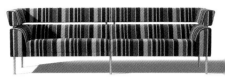

3

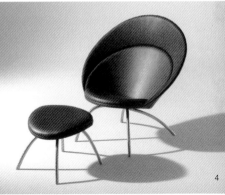

4

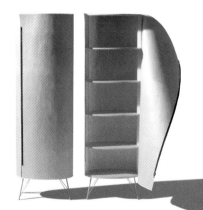

7

8

Fritz Hansen

Denmark | Fritz Hansen A/S, Allerød | Furniture manufacturer | **www.fritzhansen.com**

"Objects are not created on the drawing board. They are the result of close cooperation between the designer and the manufacturer", declared **Vico Magistretti**. The eminent Italian designer thus made many trips to provincial Denmark in the 1990s, when he started working with Fritz Hansen. Magistretti's chairs consciously took up and extended the range of products that had been initiated by **Arne Jacobsen**. Bent tubular steel, as in the *Vicoduo* line, today forms an essential part of the company's programme. In the 1950s the collaboration with Jacobsen had marked a turning point for the traditional Danish furniture manufacturer. The company's previous commercial success had derived mainly from the production of seating for large cinema auditoria. Over the years, the business association with ▶ Jacobsen produced more than fifty different models; of these, seven are still in production. The three-legged *Ant* chair and its successor, the *Series 7* chair, are not only the company's most successful products but are among the bestselling pieces of furniture in the world. The daring curves of Jacobsen's *Swan* and *Egg* chairs symbolized his break with traditional furniture design.

Although Fritz Hansen was taken over in the late 1970s, following a period of declining sales, the company now has a healthy profit margin and in fact has a bigger turnover than any other furniture manufacturer in Denmark. In keeping with its image as a successful international company, it has begun collaborating with renowned designers from outside Scandinavia, including Magistretti and **Burkhard Vogtherr** from Germany. A large part of its programme is made up of designs by ▶ **Poul Kjærholm**, one of the great, though still lesser-known, Danish Modernists. The *Superellipsis* table by the Swedish designer **Bruno Mathsson** is another classic design. Kasper Salto and Hans Sandgren Jakobsen are among the younger Danish designers who work for Fritz Hansen. Room dividers, such as *Viper* by Jakobsen and *Wing* by **Pelikan Design**, are a relatively new product line. The company's basic formula, however, has remained the same: furniture should be economical and practical.

184

1 *Swan* armchair, 1958
2 *Decision* sofa, 1986
3 *Vicoduo* chair, 1997
4 *Superellipsis* table, 1968
5 *Series 7* chair, 1955
6 *3300* sofa, 1956
7 *LA 150* partition, 1992

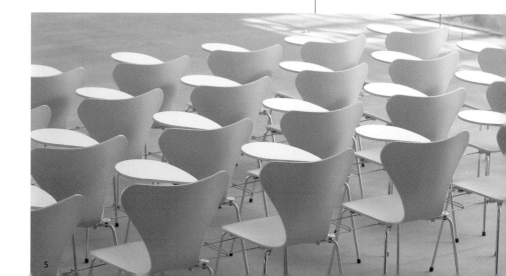

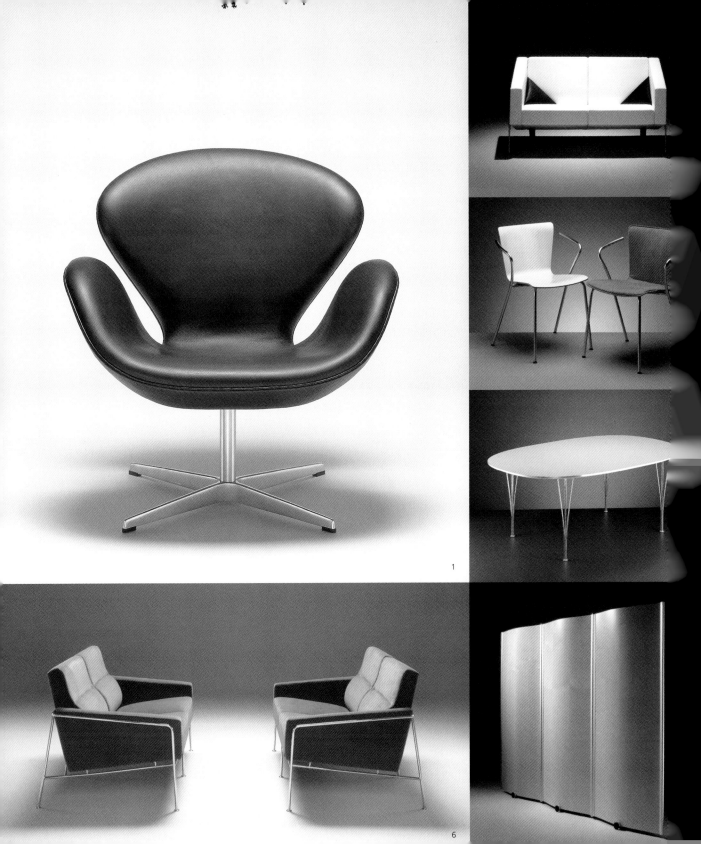

1

6

Frogdesign

Germany/USA | Communications and product design studio | **www.frogdesign.com**

Hartmut Esslinger, the founder of Frogdesign, has followed a career path that has taken him from the Black Forest to Sunnyvale in California via the offices of ▶ **Apple**. In the early 1980s the computer giant wanted to give an appropriate stylistic form to its innovative products. Esslinger's response was the *Macintosh*, the first truly user-friendly computer. The product was so successful that Apple retained his design until well into the 1990s.

Esslinger believes that communication and close collaboration with his clients are important aspects of his work; he also enjoys contributing his views on general design issues. The Frogdesign slogan "form follows emotion" represents only one aspect of the company's approach to projects. The acronym (Frog) that forms part of the company's name stands for the Federal Republic of Germany, and clients are aware of the significance of the reference: alongside **Designafairs** and Wiege, Frogdesign is one of the few large German studios that has developed contemporary designs for such diverse products as bathroom fixtures (for ▶ **Hansgrohe**), answering machines (for AT&T), computers (for Micron), TV sets (for Wega and **Sony**), hi-fi equipment (for the relaunch of the traditional Dual brand) and tableware (for Fissler). Like other similar studios, the company has developed an integrated approach to design that today encompasses digital design and corporate identity.

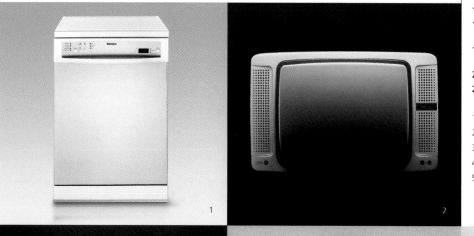
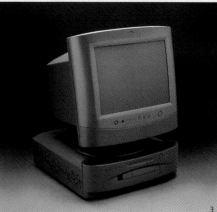
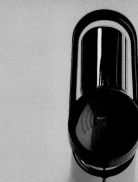
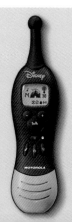

FSB

Germany | Franz Schneider Brakel GmbH & Co. KG, Brakel | Manufacturer of door handles | **www.fsb.de**

FSB has turned the manufacture of door handles into an art form. In the 1980s the graphic designer Otl Aicher created an entirely new image for the company (just as he had done for **Erco** a decade earlier), from the logo down to the development of its own publications series. With a clear design strategy, FSB succeeded in making a name for itself in architectural and marketing circles. The company has enjoyed success with *ErgoSystem*, an ergonomically designed series of handles that is also suitable for use by people with physical disabilities. FSB's restrained style has contributed to its upmarket image and has served also to emphasize its expertise in the field. Since door handles are intended to be extremely long-lasting products, it is important to achieve a neutral, 'timeless' design. Although there may not appear to be a tremendous amount of scope for the design of such products, FSB has challenged this view by offering a range comprising more than one hundred different models. It focuses on developing a high-quality product line using first-class designers from various countries, embracing the whole spectrum of European design culture. **Dieter Rams**, **Philippe Starck**, **Erik Magnussen** and **Jasper Morrison** have all worked for FSB. The company's real star, however, is Johannes Potente, the FSB in-house designer of the 1950s and 1960s, whose door handles are probably the most frequently copied in the world.

187

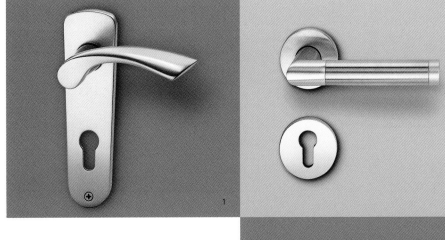

1

2

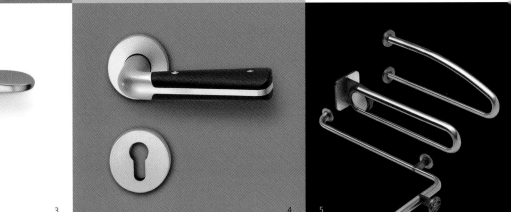

3

4

5

Eileen Gray, *Tube Light* standard lamp, 1927

In her early, more decorative lamps, Eileen Gray used such natural materials as leather straps and parchment. The first piece of furniture in which she used metal, her *Day Bed* chaise longue, was created in 1925. The free-standing *Tube Light* lamp, in which a neon tube was held in place by a chrome tube of the same height, seemed all the more radical – a strip of light as a symbol of Modernism.

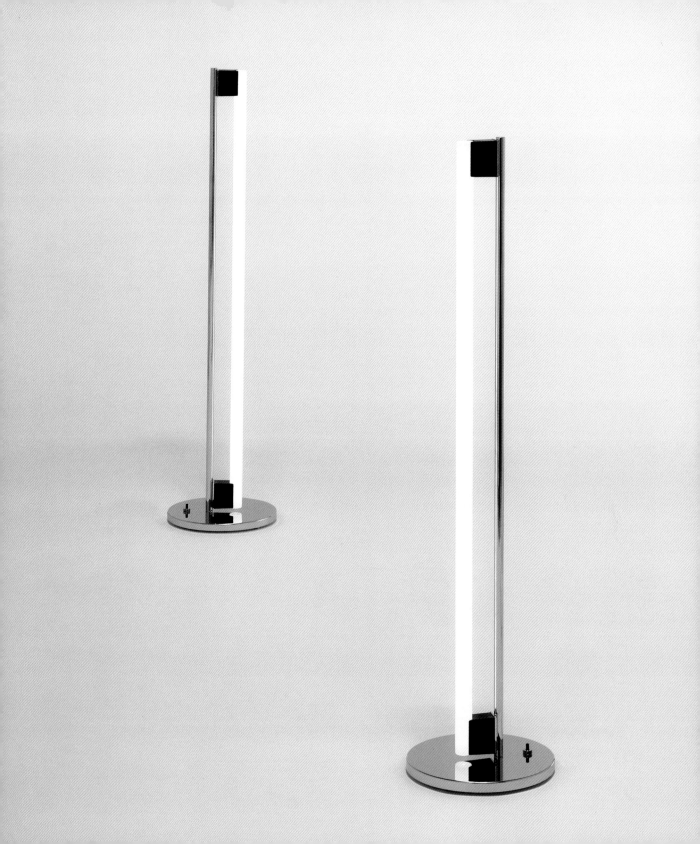

Gaggenau

Germany I Gaggenau Hausgeräte GmbH, Munich I Manufacturer of kitchen appliances I **www.gaggenau.com**

Whether ultra-quiet extractor fans, spacious ovens or ingenious hobs – technical innovation and elegant design in the kitchen is automatically associated with Gaggenau. The Munich-based company has a reputation as a top-quality manufacturer that has succeeded in transferring the standards required of professional kitchen appliances into the home. In particular, it has turned the manufacture of modular hobs into an art form, in recognition of the fact that timing is vital in cooking. The company was founded in the late seventeenth century as an ironworks. Its products included enamelled stove casings and, somewhat later, bicycles. Eventually, however, it began to specialize in stoves and cookers. The 'economy cookers' of the late 1920s reflected the functional style of the period. It was only in the 1960s, when the flawless functionality and timeless design aesthetic favoured by **Braun** began to influence industrial design as a whole, that Gaggenau began to pay serious attention to the look of its products. However, the company has always chosen to keep its designs anonymous. The fact that the prominent designer **Jacob Jensen**, who worked for **Bang & Olufsen** for many years, has produced beautifully crafted appliances for Gaggenau, is not central to its corporate identity. The Danish designer's preference for sleek surfaces and invisible seams is nevertheless unmistakable.

1681 Ironworks established by Count Ludwig Wilhelm von Baden in Gaggenau
1873 Produces agricultural machinery, metal goods and machine tools
1894 Produces bicycles and gas cookers
1931 Produces first electric cookers
1961 Georg von Blanquet heads company and establishes a new line
1991 Collaborates with **Jacob Jensen Design**
1994 Bosch and Siemens take over company
1999 Collaborates with the designer H. Reinhard Segers
2003 Headquarters transfers to Munich

Products
1956 EB 218 and EB 208, first built-in kitchen appliances in Europe
1974 First Vario series; first glass ceramic hob
1975 EB 600 built-in oven
1978 CK 025 electric glass ceramic hob
1982 AH 250 extractor hood
1986 Vario 300 modular cooktop series
1988 EB 388 built-in oven
1990 IK 900 integrated fridge-freezer
1992 EB 900 built-in oven by ▶ Jacob Jensen Design
1999 Vario 200 modular cooktop series by Jacob Jensen Design and H. Reinhard Segers
2001 AW 530 wall extractor hood
2003 IK 360 wine cooler
2004 Vario 400 modular cooktop series

1   AW 530 wall extractor hood, 2001
2   EB 388 built-in oven, 1988
3   Vario 200 modular cooktops, 1999
4   EB 900 built-in oven, 1992
5   IK 360 wine cooler, 2003

190

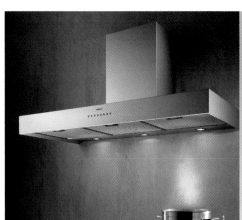

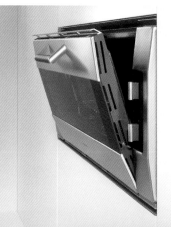

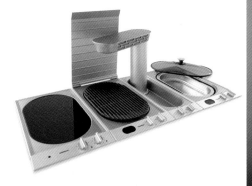

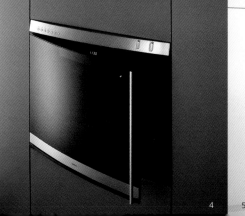

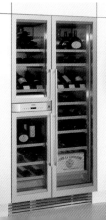

Niels **Gammelgaard**

Denmark I Furniture and product designer I **www.pelikan.dk**

Although an imposing portrait of Niels Gammelgaard was once on display in **Ikea**'s stores, the influential Danish designer is not generally one to seek the limelight. He nevertheless works behind the scenes to considerable effect. In the mid-1970s, when still a young architect with just a few years' experience, he designed a lamp for **Louis Poulsen**. He was already collaborating with Ikea at this time and was one of the few designers that the Swedish furniture company decided it could afford. The decision was no accident: whether the *Ted* folding chair, the *Moment* table or the *Nevil* plastic swivel chair, Gammelgaard's designs are extremely simple yet utterly convincing constructions, and they often became bestsellers. Plastic is one of his preferred materials. Although his main focus is furniture design, his product range is quite diverse and also includes, for example, children's bicycles. Since the end of the 1970s Gammelgaard has been a partner at **Pelikan Design**, a studio that has worked with some of Denmark's leading furniture manufacturers, including Bent Krogh, **Fritz Hansen** and **Fredericia**. His design principles are in keeping with those of many of his compatriots: from **Arne Jacobsen** to **Knud Holscher**, the central concerns in Danish design are to achieve simplicity without compromising form or function, a faithfulness to the materials used and a respectful attitude towards humans and the environment.

191

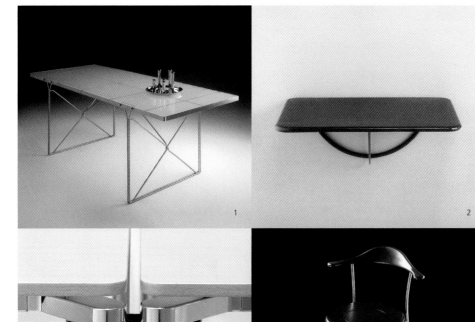

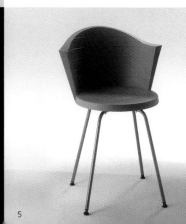

Frank O. **Gehry**

USA I Architect and furniture designer

Frank Owen Gehry is undoubtedly one of the world's foremost architects. His eccentric, artistically influenced style, which contributed to the development of Deconstructivism, has produced such sensational buildings as the Vitra Museum in Weil am Rhein in Germany and the Guggenheim Museum in Bilbao, Spain. Gehry also has a reputation as one of the most original minds in furniture design.

It is immediately evident from Gehry's designs that he perceives both furniture and buildings as sculptures. The everyday materials he incorporates into his architectural commissions – corrugated iron, roughcast, rectangular mesh, steel and iron girders – appear far from conventional by virtue of the unusual and unexpected contexts in which they are placed. His furniture exhibits a similarly bold approach. The chairs in the *Easy Edges* series consist of glued layers of laminated corrugated cardboard – an allusion to packaging. This process, patented by Gehry, solves the long-standing problem of instability that beset earlier versions of cardboard chairs. The exposed edges of the furniture mimic the texture and appearance of corduroy. Gehry, an eminently practical designer, also perfected an efficient manufacturing technique that enabled his chairs to be sold at affordable prices. Seventeen different models were manufactured in total – not only his free-form styles, but also more graphic designs, such as the undulating *Wiggle Side Chair*.

Gehry later presented an ironic interpretation of the *Easy Edges* series with the *Little Beaver* chair (for **Vitra**), a design reminiscent of a conventional upholstered armchair. In the 1990s he produced the highly successful *Cross Check* series, the chairs and tables of which were made of interwoven strips of maple. The complex, ribbon-like design involved the technicians at **Knoll** in the production of more than one hundred prototypes over a period of two and a half years. Gehry's basket-weave furniture is today regarded by some as the most radical design innovation to have come from the United States since the days of **Charles and Ray Eames**.

192

1 *Cross Check* furniture collection, 1991
2 *Little Beaver* armchair, 1987
3 *Wiggle Side Chair*, 1972
4 *Side Chair*, 1990
5 *FOG* stackable chair, 1999

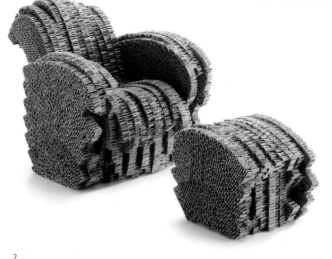

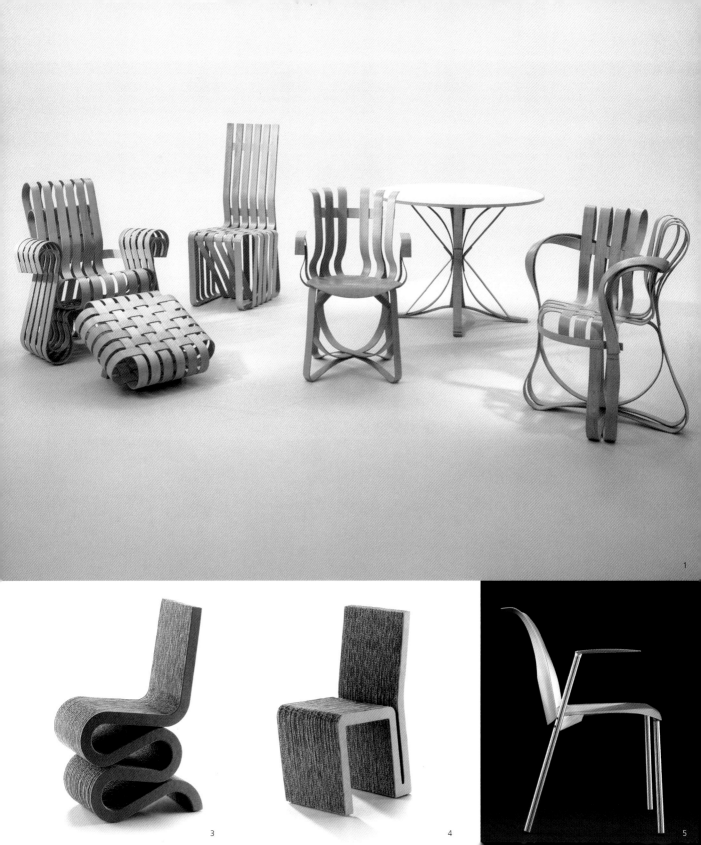

1

3

4

5

General Motors

USA I General Motors Corporation, Detroit, Michigan I Automobile manufacturer I **www.gm.com**

The 1959 Cadillac *Eldorado*, with tail fins that point upwards like rockets, was the climax of a stylistic development that could be described as jet-fighter Baroque. Chief designer Harley Earl was a pioneer of automotive design and a luxuriant stylist. He started working with General Motors in the mid-1920s. The company was the first automobile manufacturer to establish a design department, and it proved to be a hotbed of uniquely American industrial design. GM – which includes the marques Buick, Cadillac, Chevrolet, Oldsmobile and Pontiac, with **Opel**, Vauxhall and Saab in Europe – remains the largest automobile manufacturer in the world. Despite various crises over the years, it is essentially an American success story, with Earl as one of its most symbolic figures. The company produced the first prototypes in clay and the first concept cars. The 1953 *Corvette*, which seemed almost European in style, became a classic of automobile design. Earl was succeeded by his pupil, Bill Mitchell, who preferred a more aggressive stylistic approach, as in the lethal-sounding *Corvette Stingray* or the more simple 'muscle cars' (mid-size, high-performance models), such as the Pontiac *GTO*. GM spent much of the 1970s and 1980s attempting to fight off foreign competitors, but in the early 1990s had respectable success in the luxury car class with the Cadillac *Seville*. To this day GM continues to produce surprises with its concept cars.

1904	William C. Durant buys Buick Motor Company
1908	Durant establishes General Motors
1909	Acquires Cadillac
1911	Durant and Louis Chevrolet establish Chevrolet Motor Car Company
1926	Introduces Pontiac marque; Harley Earl becomes chief designer
1929	Acquires Adam **Opel**
1959	Harley Earl leaves GM; Bill Mitchell succeeds him

Products

1908	Buick *Model 10* Roadster
1927	Cadillac *La Salle*
1935	Chevrolet *Suburban* saloon
1951	Buick *LeSabre* (concept)
1953	Chevrolet *Corvette* sports car
1955	Chevrolet *Bel Air* model series
1958	Chevrolet *Impala* model series
1959	Cadillac *Eldorado* executive saloon; Chevrolet *Corvair* compact car
1963	Chevrolet *Corvette Stingray*
1964	*Futurama* concept car exhibition; Pontiac *GTO* coupé
1967	Chevrolet *Camaro* and Pontiac *Firebird* sports cars
1976	Chevrolet *Chevette* small car
1986	Cadillac *Allanté* (with **Pininfarina**)
1992	Cadillac *Seville* executive saloon
1999	Cadillac *EVOQ* coupé (concept)
2000	Chevrolet *Impala* and Buick *LeSabre* (both relaunches)
2001	Chevrolet *Corvette Z 06*
2003	Cadillac *XLR* roadster; Buick *Park Avenue Ultra* saloon

1 Chevrolet *Corvette* sports car, 1953
2 Cadillac *EVOQ* coupé (concept), 1999
3 Pontiac *GTO* coupé, 1964

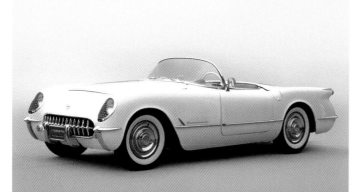

1

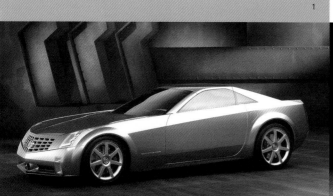

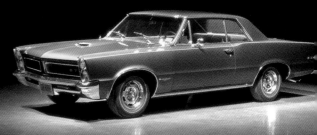

2   3

Georg Jensen

Denmark I Georg Jensen A/S, Frederiksberg I Cutlery and tableware manufacturer I **www.georgjensen.com**

Georg Jensen had always wanted to pursue a career as an artist; he actually became a successful potter and then a famous silversmith. In 1904 he founded a silversmith workshop in the centre of Copenhagen. While many similar companies still worked in the ornamental style of *Skønvirke* (Danish Arts and Crafts), Jensen was influenced by Art Nouveau: the precision and restrained ornamentation of the style lent discreet elegance to his designs.

Jensen's collaboration with his friend the artist Johan Rohde, who became his first in-house designer, was extremely productive. Following the Second World War, a new generation of designers took over the task of developing contemporary designs. Henning Koppel is particularly associated with this phase in the company's history. His famous serving dish for fish is very distinctive: its gentle lines and soft shape, typical of the 1950s, have reappeared in a twenty-first century reinterpretation – in the form of a thermos jug – by Maria Berntsen. Koppel also initiated a series of numberless or 'timeless' clocks. In more recent years, such leading Danish designers as **Nanna Ditzel**, **Knud Holscher**, Jørgen Møller and Alan Scharff have considered it an honour to work for the brand. Cutlery by ▸**Arne Jacobsen** and ▸**Jean Nouvel** adds further interest to the range. It is no accident that arguably the most important Danish design award is named after the company's founder.

195

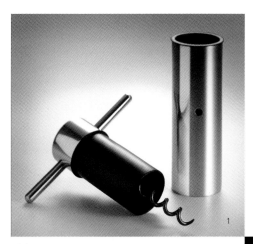

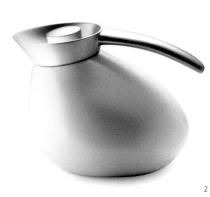

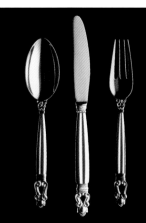

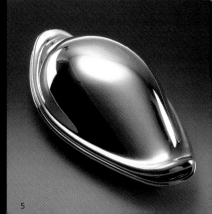

Stefano **Giovannoni**

Italy | Architect and furniture and product designer | www.stefanogiovannoni.it

The Italian architect and product designer Stefano Giovannoni has always enjoyed experimenting with bright colours and bold, rounded shapes. There are no severe lines or sharp angles in his designs. On the contrary, his work is often populated by cartoon-like forms and characters. Since the late 1980s these cheerful figures and unexpected, playful forms have enlivened our everyday world: from *Nutty the Cracker* nutcracker in the shape of a squirrel and salt and pepper shakers designed as little ovoid men, to the flamboyant *Merdolino* 'potted-plant' toilet brush and the jolly *Mary Biscuit* biscuit-box collection. These and many other delightful plastic objects were all designed for ▶**Alessi**. Giovannoni's long-standing collaboration with the north Italian manufacturer has had a significant influence on his career, and the relationship has remained friendly and productive.

Giovannoni's design philosophy is based on the principle that products should be in keeping with their time and should appeal to people's emotions. Although his motto is "form follows fun", it would be a mistake to reduce his work to the level of mere 'fun design'. The determination with which he combines the unconventional and the practical is remarkable, as can be seen in his successful *Bombo* barstool design for **Magis**: the hula-hoop footrest and unusual plastic seat add a completely new dimension to this type of furniture. The ingenious tableware products in the *Girotondo* series for Alessi (developed with Guido Venturini), which incorporate lines of cut-out figures holding hands, have sold in their millions. This one idea generated an entire family of products, with the figure motif appearing on items as diverse as jewellery and ice-cube trays. Giovannoni has succeeded in producing a new bestseller at Alessi with *Mami*, the pleasantly bulbous series of cookware, cutlery, crockery and accessories. The *Il Bagno Alessi* bathroom collection, characterized by a surprisingly high degree of elegant symmetry, reveals that the *enfant terrible* of Italian design has come of age.

196

1 Washbasin (*Il Bagno Alessi* collection), 2002
2 *SG 66* kitchen scales, 2004
3 *Mami* service, 2003
4 *Fruitscape* bowl, 2002
5 Plate (*Girotondo* collection), 1987
6 *Merdolino* toilet brush, 1993
7 *Bombo* barstool, 1997
8 Wireless telephone handset, 2003
9 *Magò* broom, 1998

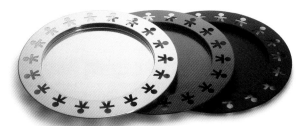

5

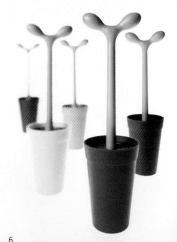

6

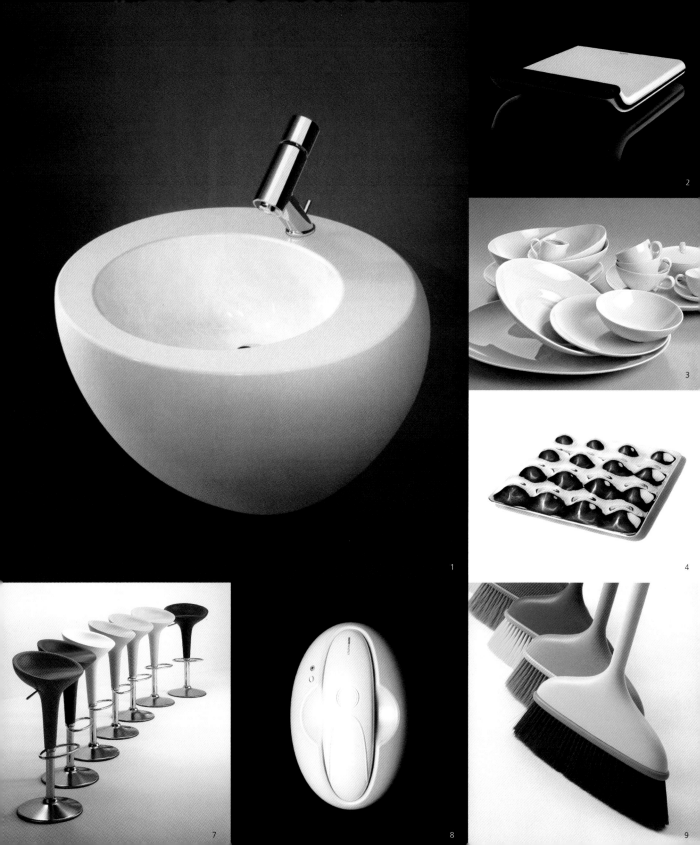

1

2

3

4

7

8

9

Giorgetto **Giugiaro**

Italy | Automobile and product designer | www.italdesign.it | www.giugiarodesign.it

The *Golf*, one of the most popular cars in the world, has a multicultural pedigree. The design of this revolutionary German model is by Giorgetto Giugiaro, who, alongside **Bertone** and **Pininfarina**, is a legendary name in Italian automotive design. The sharp-edged *Golf* and *Scirocco* (for ▸ **Volkswagen**) – models that contributed to the description of Giugiaro's work as the 'folded-paper' style – were brought on to the market at exactly the right time. Giugiaro had accurately interpreted the mood of the early 1970s: the oil crisis and a general recession had created a demand for compact, practical and inexpensive small and medium-sized cars.

Descended from a family of artists, Giugiaro was originally to have become a fresco painter. In the mid-1950s, however, he joined the design centre at **Fiat**; from there he moved to Bertone and then to Ghia, where his main focus was luxury cars. Giugiaro was not only interested in creating beautiful forms, however; he was also eager to develop new concepts, and in the late 1960s he founded the design company Italdesign. With its modern, comprehensive range of cars, it ushered in a new era in the automobile industry. Not only were the major manufacturers able to order a design from Giugiaro, but they could also commission mock-ups, prototypes, bodies, mechanical parts, cost analyses and reports on estimated times and methods of production. Other bestsellers produced by Italdesign include the legendary *Alfasud*, the Fiat *Panda* and the Fiat *Uno* (the Italian equivalent of the *Golf*), which also achieved cult status. To date, Italdesign has developed more cars than any comparable studio and has worked for all the well-known marques: not only Fiat, Alfa Romeo and Volkswagen (the *Passat* and the *W 12* sports car concept, as well as the *Golf* and the *Scirocco*), but also **Audi**, **BMW**, Hyundai and **Renault**.

In the early 1980s Giugiaro founded Giugiaro Design, a studio specializing in industrial and product design. At the end of the decade it created the *F4* professional camera for Nikon and also had considerable success with watches, dishwashers, furniture, racing yachts, trains, telephones, sewing machines and, perhaps somewhat more surprisingly, new varieties of pasta.

1938 Born in Garessio
1955 Joins **Fiat** design centre after graduating from Accademia Albertina delle Belle Arti, Turin
1959 Becomes chief designer at **Bertone**
1965 Becomes director at Ghia
1968 Establishes Italdesign
1981 Establishes Giugiaro Design

Products
1961 *3200 CS* coupé for **BMW**
1963 **Alfa Romeo** *Giulia GT* (at Bertone)
1965 **Fiat** *850 Spider* (at Bertone)
1967 *Ghibli* sports car for Maserati
1970 *Boomerang* (concept) for Maserati
1971 *Cheetah* (concept) for Karmann
1972 *Alfasud* for Alfa Romeo; Fiat *X 1/9* sports car (at Bertone)
1973 *Passat* estate for **Volkswagen**
1974 *Scirocco* and *Golf* for ▸ Volkswagen
1975 *Esprit* sports car for Lotus; *F3* camera for Nikon (until 1999)
1978 *M1* sports car for BMW
1979 *Quattroporte* saloon for Maserati
1980 *Panda* small car for Fiat
1982 *Speedmaster Sport* watch for Seiko; *Logica* sewing machine for Necchi
1983 *Uno* small car for Fiat; *Marilla* pasta for Barilla
1986 *21* saloon and estate for **Renault**
1988 *F4* camera for Nikon
1991 *Toledo* saloon for Seat
1997 *W 12* sports car (concept) for Volkswagen
1998 *3200 GT* coupé for Maserati
2002 *Spyder* for Maserati
2003 *Alfa Brera* coupé (concept) for Alfa Romeo

1 Volkswagen *W 12* (concept; detail), 1997
2 Volkswagen *W 12* (concept), 1997
3 Maserati *3200 GT* coupé, 1998
4 Alfa Romeo *Alfa Brera* (concept), 2003
5 Alfa Romeo *Alfasud*, 1972
6 Volkswagen *Scirocco*, 1974
7 Fiat *Uno*, 1983

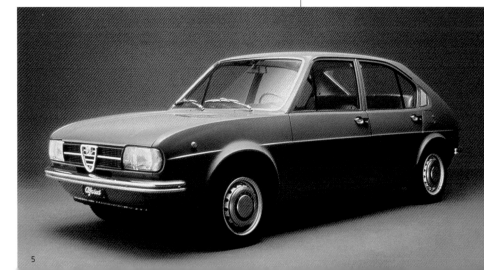

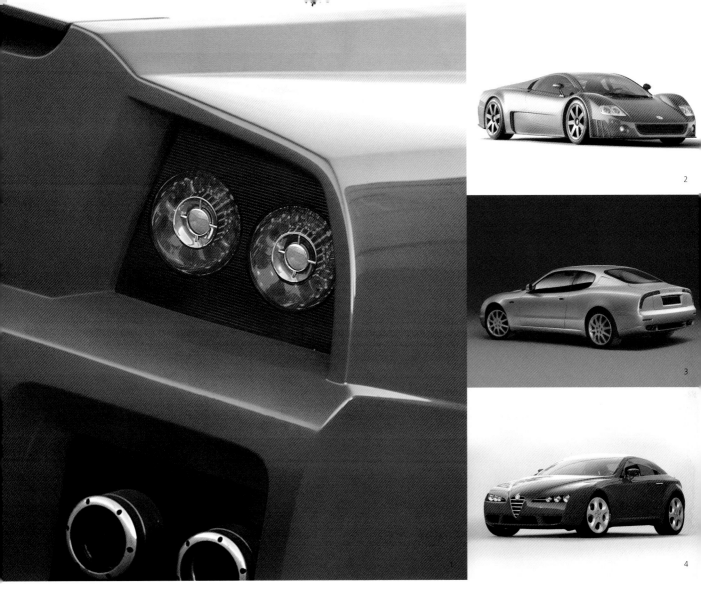

1

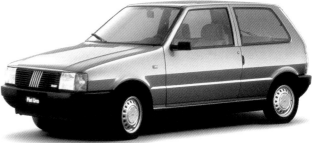

2

3

4

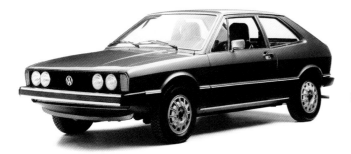

GK Design Group

Japan | Product design studio | **www.gk-design.co.jp**

From a soy sauce bottle to a high-speed train, from motorbikes to furniture, and from orientation systems to packaging and mobile phones: GK Design Group's range of products is vast and includes commercial goods as well as household items. There are few articles that the company has not designed in the last five decades. After breaking off his training as a Buddhist priest, the founder of the firm, Kenji Ekuan, studied design in Tokyo and Pasadena before becoming spokesman for the GK Studio, a group of designers who had been influenced by the teachings of university professor Iwataro Koike (the company's initials, GK, stand for 'Group of Koike'). The studio, which primarily looked to the West for inspiration, became the most important creative centre for product design in Japan. Its reliance on Western ideas was short-lived. The highly successful company now has branches in Europe and the United States.

Although GK does not have a prescribed approach to design, it has developed an extensive design process in order to create products that target a specific market or group of users. In the case of the soy sauce bottle, this process led to a design that is reminiscent of the traditional *sake* bottle, an item that appears on every Japanese dining table. The *Morpho* motorbike concept for **Yamaha** produced a vehicle with perfect ergonomic features. Whether mobile telephones for **Motorola**, washing machines for the Haier group or folding bicycles for Maruishi, the company endeavours to develop products that reconcile the interests of industry with those of consumers.

Ekuan, the leading figure at GK Design, is well known not only as a former president of the international design association ICSID and as a juror for many design competitions, but also as a publicist who frequently contributes to debates on design. Perhaps as a result of his having witnessed the dropping of the atomic bomb on Hiroshima in 1945, both Ekuan's professional life and private life reflect a profound sense of social and ecological responsibility.

1929 Kenji Ekuan born in Tokyo
1955 Graduates from Tokyo National University of Fine Arts and Music
1956 Studies at Art Center College of Design, Pasadena, California
1957 Returns to Japan; establishes GK Industrial Design Associates
1966 Establishes GK Sekkei, GK Dynamics, GK Graphics, GK Tech, GK Kyoto, Design Soken Hiroshima and GK Design International
1989 Studio renamed GK Design Group
2003 Ekuan receives Lucky Strike Designer Award

Products
1961 Soy sauce bottle for Kikkoman
1985 *V-Max* motorbike for ▶ **Yamaha**
1990 *Shuttle Chef* cooking pot collection for Thermos Nissan
1991 *Morpho* motorbike (concept) for Yamaha; *Narita Express* train for East Japan Railway
1992 *YST-DC 11* stereo system for Yamaha
1994 *Rumina 3000* sewing machine for Singer
1997 *SRX 700S* snowmobile, *Grizzly* all-terrain vehicle and *YZF R-1* (▶ p. 527) and *YZ 400 F* motorbikes for Yamaha; *Akita Shinkansen* train for East Japan Railway
1998 *Formio* children's furniture for Sanyei; *EZ Ripple* CD rack for Nikkei Products
1999 Bus shelter for Wall
2001 *Gel Mountain Express* sports shoes; *T-300 Echolac* suitcase set; *Marvelous* cooking pot collection
2002 *AFina Style* computer for Sotec; refrigerator and washing machine for Haier; *iDen* mobile telephone for **Motorola**

200

1 Washing machine (prototype), 2002
2 *EZ Ripple* CD rack, 1998
3 *AFina Style* computer, 2002
4 *Morpho* motorbike (concept), 1991
5 Soy sauce bottle, 1961
6 *iDen* mobile telephone, 2002
7 *YZF R-1* motorbike, 1997
8 *Shuttle Chef* cooking pot collection, 1990

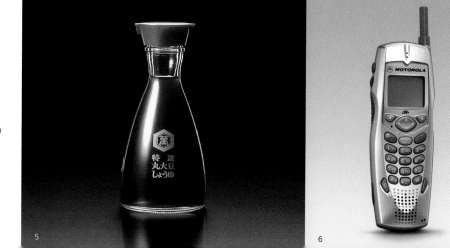

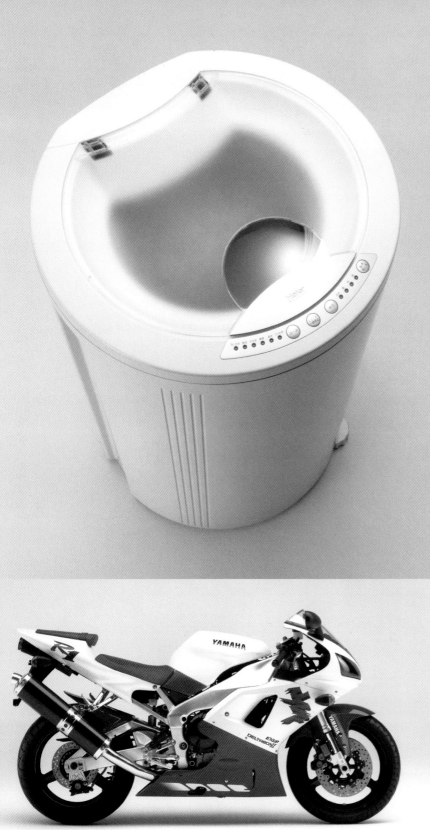

1

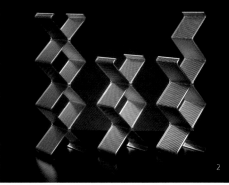

2

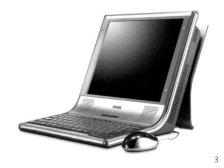

3

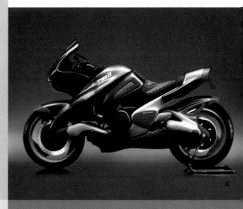

4

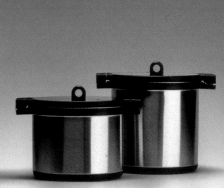

8

7

Kenneth **Grange**

England | Product designer

No other industrial designer has had a more decisive influence on everyday life in Britain than Kenneth Grange. The products designed by this Londoner over the last five decades range from a high-speed train to an iron. There is one commission, however, that must have been particularly special for him. In the late 1990s Grange redesigned a world-famous British icon – the London taxi. Without altering its distinctive silhouette, he created an entirely new body for the vehicle, revitalizing its hitherto somewhat dated design.

In the early 1970s Grange co-founded the internationally renowned Pentagram agency, Britain's first interdisciplinary design consultancy. Whether creating wet razors for Wilkinson Sword or packaging for Shiseido, Japan's largest cosmetics company, Grange often cultivates a style in which basic geometric forms convey a sense of permanency. He became well known for his kitchen blenders for Kenwood, the manufacturer of household goods, and for the *Instamatic* camera series for **Kodak**. With his *Brownie 44A* he designed a camera that was not only practical but that could, on account of its plastic parts, be manufactured competitively and therefore profitably. Grange worked with Kodak for more than two decades and with Kenwood for thirty-five years.

1929 Born in London
1947 Begins training as illustrator
1958 Opens own design studio
1969 Elected Royal Designer for Industry
1972 Co-founds Pentagram consultancy, London
1984 Appointed Commander of the British Empire (CBE)
1999 Leaves Pentagram

Products
1959 *Brownie 44A* camera for **Kodak**
1960 Domestic appliance collection for Kenwood (including *Chef* food processor)
1964 *Brownie 44B* camera for Kodak
1966 *Instamatic* camera for Kodak; *Chefette* handmixer for Kenwood
1972 *804* sewing machine
1977 *Intercity 125* high-speed train for British Rail
1979 *25* fountain pen for Parker
1992 *Protector* razor for Wilkinson
1995 *Discovery* iron for Kenwood
1997 London taxi (redesign)

1 *Chef* food processor, 1960
2 London taxi (redesign), 1997
3 *Discovery* iron, 1995
4 *Brownie 44B* camera, 1964
5 *Protector* razor, 1992

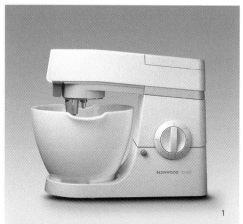

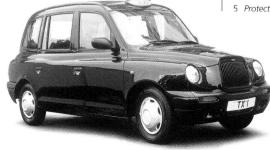

202

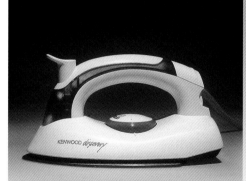

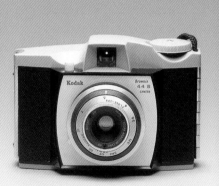

1

2

3

4

5

Tobias **Grau**

Germany I Lamp designer and manufacturer I **www.tobias-grau.com**

Tobias Grau argues that our desire for individuality is increasing and that designers should therefore focus on unconventional and seemingly uncommercial projects. Hence a wooden tripod lends his *George* standard lamp stability, and his *Ufo* hanging lamp really does look like a flying saucer. Grau's very first endeavours as a lamp designer were so successful that the decision to concentrate exclusively on lighting design was a not difficult one. The positive response to the *Luja* low-volt lighting system in particular was sufficient reason for the economist and interior designer to build up a design-orientated brand of his own – one that turned out to be a match for Italian competitors such as **Artemide** and **Flos**.

With a staff of around forty in his own company, and a team of some two hundred specialists among his suppliers to whom he can turn for support, Grau has freedom and flexibility as far as his choice of materials is concerned. His designs, which each take between one and two years to develop, are distinguished by their technical ingenuity and eccentric forms. These features are reflected in such models as *Soon,* a caterpillar-like, transparent desk lamp, *Twist*, a table lamp with a convex base attached to a wooden ring, and *Flux*, a wall and ceiling lamp that radiates soft light.

203

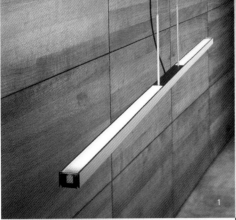

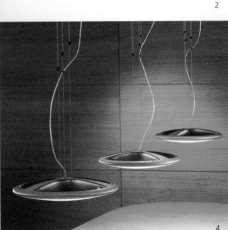

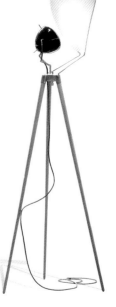

1

2

3

4

5

Michael **Graves**

USA | Architect and product designer | **www.michaelgraves.com**

During the 1960s Michael Graves was a member of the New York Five group of Modernist architects who took their inspiration from the buildings of the 1920s and 1930s. By the end of the 1970s, however, he had become a leading proponent of Post-modernism. The purism of his early work gave way to a more figurative approach, resulting in such ironic designs as a Mickey Mouse teapot. Among Graves's more recent architectural projects are hotels for Walt Disney and an annex for the Whitney Museum of American Art in New York.

Prior to designing his first Post-modern building (a company headquarters in Portland, Oregon), Graves was well known both for his position as a Princeton University professor and for his impressive drawings. Unlike other representatives of the new eclecticism that was emerging in design, he successfully translated his skills into producing items suitable for everyday use. A notable example is the stainless steel *Bird* kettle, an icon of Post-modern design, with its colourful whistling bird on the spout. It was with this product that the Italian manufacturer **Alessi** made its breakthrough into the design industry in the 1980s. The ingeniously stylish object was bought by more than half a million people, marking the entry of Post-modern design into the home of the average consumer. The bird is reminiscent of earlier designs in porcelain and of decoration characteristic of nineteenth-century American tea services. The kettle's conical shape is timeless and is accentuated by a subtle pattern of raised dots towards the base and by a black ball that serves as a knob on the lid. The successful collaboration between Graves and Alessi continued with such products as espresso cups, an egg timer, a corkscrew, a thermos jug and a range of kettles and jugs.

The name Michael Graves stands for sophisticated product design. The all-round designer has created porcelain, lamps, carpets, jewellery and numerous clocks. Among his earliest furniture designs was the Art Deco-inspired *Plaza* dressing table. More recent designs include the *Dreamscape* bathroom series (for **Duravit**), the playful fittings of which counterbalance the formal severity of the washbasin. For other similarly unique, sophisticated and occasionally witty creations, Graves's studio has received more than one hundred design awards.

204

1 *Bird* kettle, 1984

2 *Dreamscape* washbasin, 1999

3 Egg timer, 1992

4 Milk jug, 1988

5 *Mantel* clock, 1986

6 *Dreamscape* fitting, 1999

7 Wall clock, 1999

8 *Euclid* thermos jug, 1994

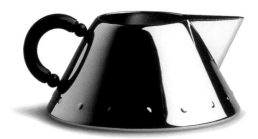

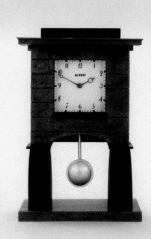

4

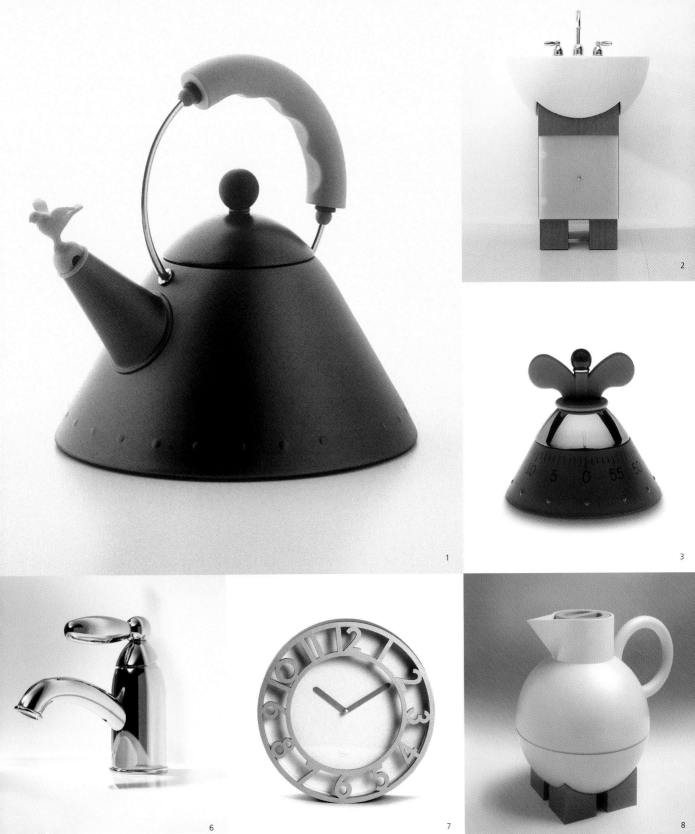

1

2

3

6

7

8

Eileen **Gray**

Ireland/France | Interior, furniture and lamp designer | **www.classicon.com**

The Irish designer Eileen Gray is today recognized as one of the outstanding creative talents of the 1920s. Her Modernist creations in chrome, steel and glass are notable for their elegance and simplicity. Among her classic designs are the *E 1027* occasional table, the *Tube Light* standard lamp (▶p. 189) and the *Monte Carlo* sofa. The simple geometry and clean lines of these pieces create an aesthetic timelessness that only few designers have been able to achieve. Sadly, however, Gray's tremendous contribution to product design was only truly appreciated after her death in 1976.

Having completed her studies at the Slade School of Fine Art in London (a significant achievement for a woman in those days), Gray moved to Paris in 1902. During this period she was greatly influenced by Japanese design. One of her main interests lay in lacquerwork, which she incorporated in Art Deco-inspired furniture and accessories. It was, however, Gray's tubular steel furniture (in advance of designs in this medium by such eminent names as **Marcel Breuer** and **Ludwig Mies van der Rohe**) that was to bring about a truly dramatic shift in early twentieth-century design. Prior to this radical breakthrough, tubular steel was a familiar sight in factories and hospitals, but had certainly not been deemed suitable for use in living-rooms. Gray's *Day Bed* (now at ▶ **ClassiCon**) from the mid-1920s shows the extent of her success in disproving this assumption. The appeal of this unusual bed lies in its simplicity and in the tension created between the soft upholstery and the tubular steel framework.

In the 1920s Gray worked with two other design revolutionaries, **Le Corbusier** and J.J.P. Oud, and began to devote more of her time to architecture. Her first house, *E 1027*, was her most important building, a Modernist masterpiece, located in a picturesque site on the cliff-lined coast at Roquebrune, Monte Carlo, in France. She designed numerous furnishings for it; today these are available at ClassiCon.

206

1 *E 1027* occasional table, 1927
2 *Castellar* mirror, 1927
3 *Rivoli* bar, 1928
4 *Roquebrune* chair, 1932
5 *De Stijl* table, 1922
6 *Monte Carlo* sofa, 1929
7 *Non Conformist* armchair, 1926

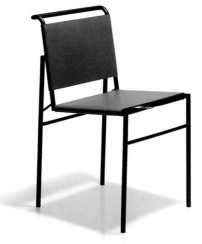

4

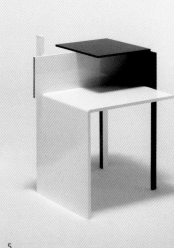

5

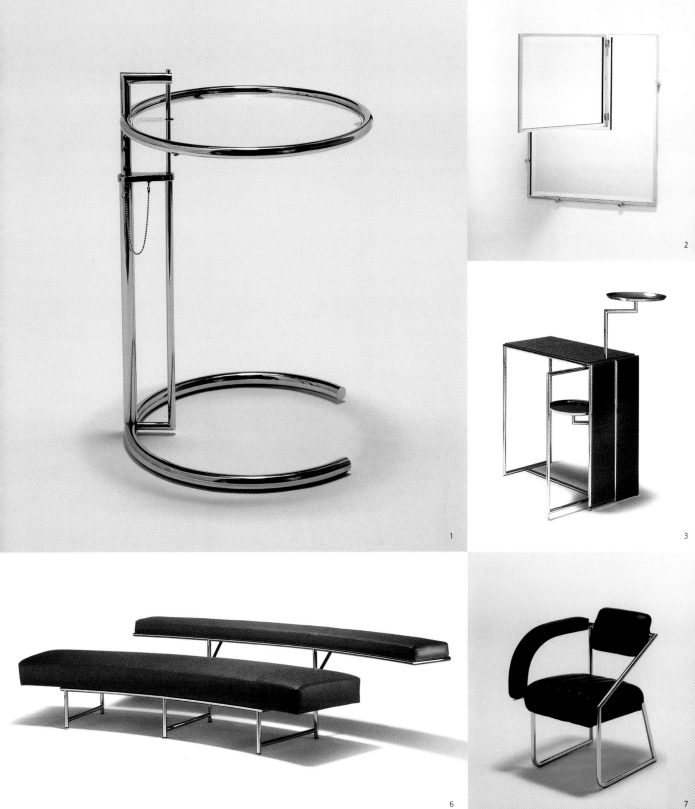

Konstantin **Grcic**

Germany | Furniture and product designer | www.konstantin-grcic.com

Konstantin Grcic's introduction to the world of furniture and product design began in the mid-1980s at Parnham College in Dorset, England, where he studied cabinetmaking. From there he moved to the Royal College of Art to study furniture design. It was there that he met **Jasper Morrison**, in whose London office he later worked. He returned to his native Germany in the early 1990s, opened his own design studio in Munich and has been highly productive ever since. At the beginning of his career Grcic was identified, inaccurately, as a minimalist. Although almost all his designs exhibit a pleasing restraint, they are nevertheless conceptually complex and reflect logic and intellectual rigour. Grcic's varied range of products includes a drinking glass with a groove that aids stacking and gripping; rubbish bins enlivened with interesting details; the portable, multi-purpose *May Day* lamp (for ►**Flos**); the *Coup* tableware series (for **Rosenthal**/Thomas), which combined porcelain and metal for the first time; and the crooked *Es* shelving unit, with vertical supports that resemble broom handles – an ironic comment on the cult of form and functionality.

Among connoisseurs, Grcic is regarded as the only world-class young German designer. **Philippe Starck** has claimed that he is one of the few interesting designers of the present day. Grcic's impressive client list includes such names as **Agape, Driade, Flos, Magis** and Montina from Italy, **Iittala** from Finland, **Authentics** and **ClassiCon** from Germany, **Muji** from Japan and **SCP** from England. Grcic is prepared to experiment boldly with materials and to display individuality; he is far more interested in complex projects than straightforward tasks. His products always take their cue from the challenges posed by industrial processes. This innovative approach is particularly evident in his *Chair_One* (for Magis), which has a die-cast aluminium seat. With this design, Grcic has created a radically new skeletal–sculptural form. It succeeds in simultaneously surprising and provoking feelings of confusion in the observer.

1 *Grcic* glass, 1999

2 *Magnum* spotlight, 2000

3 *Osorom* seat, 2004

4 Microwave hob (concept), 2000

5 *Chaos* chair, 2002

6 *Hut ab* coat stand, 1998

7 *Diana E* occasional table, 2002

8 *Es* shelf, 1999

9 *Chair_One*, 2003

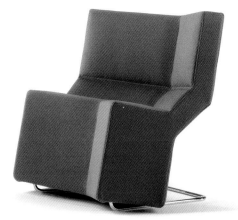

5

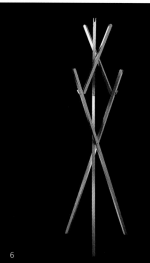

6

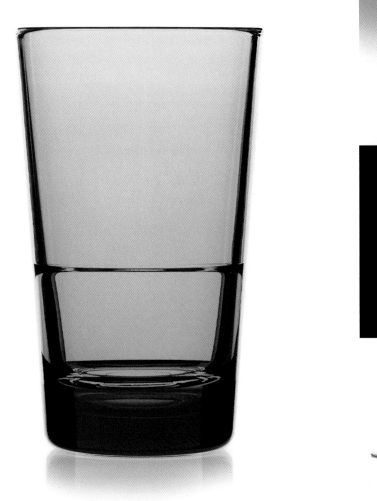

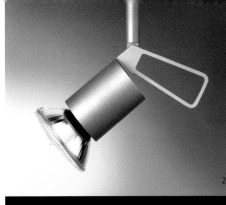

2

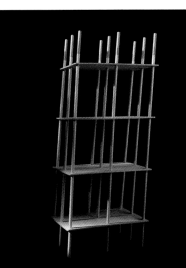

3

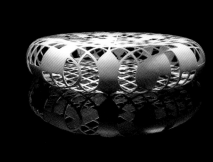

1

4

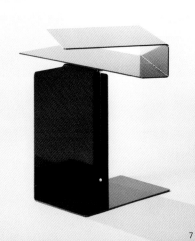

7

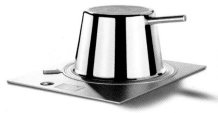

8

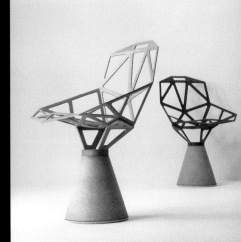

9

Walter **Gropius**

Germany | Architect and furniture and product designer

Despite the fact that his designs are relatively few in number, the work of the legendary Walter Gropius altered the course of design history. Alongside **Ludwig Mies van der Rohe**, Gropius was one of the most influential figures in the development of Modernist architecture. Among the most important projects in his career were the Fagus factory near Hanover, the Bauhaus complex in Dessau and the house he designed for himself in Lincoln, Massachusetts, during his exile in the United States.

Gropius became famous as the founder and first director of the Bauhaus, the most famous art and design school of the twentieth century. It was a radically new learning environment, and provided a major forum in which artists, craftspeople and clients could all work together. In his writings on Bauhaus principles in the mid-1920s Gropius called for design "to restrict itself to typical basic forms". This approach greatly inspired such fellow designers as **Marianne Brandt**, **Marcel Breuer** and **Wilhelm Wagenfeld**. Of Gropius's own functional product designs, his cylindrical door handles (today at **FSB**) and the *TAC 1* tea service, a late design for **Rosenthal**, perhaps came closest to fulfilling the high-minded requirement that the useful object should also be 'timeless'.

1883 Born in Berlin
1903 Studies architecture in Munich and Berlin (until 1907)
1908 Works in office of Peter Behrens
1910 Establishes architecture practice with Adolf Meyer in Berlin; joins Deutscher Werkbund
1911 Fagus factory, Alfeld, near Hanover
1919 Appointed director of the Bauhaus, Weimar (until 1928)
1926 New Bauhaus building and director's house, Dessau; writes *Grundsätze der Bauhausproduktion* (Principles of Bauhaus production)
1928 Works as architect in Berlin
1934 Emigrates to England; establishes architecture practice with E. Maxwell Fry
1937 Emigrates to USA; becomes professor of architecture at Harvard University, Massachusetts
1938 Collaborates with **Marcel Breuer**
1946 Co-founds The Architects' Collaborative
1963 PanAm Building, New York
1969 Dies in Boston

Products
1910 *D 51* armchair and *D 51-2* bench for Fagus factory, Alfeld (today at **Tecta**)
1920 *F 51* armchair and *F 51-3* sofa (today at Tecta)
1922 Cylindrical door handle (with Adolf Meyer; today at **FSB**)
1930 Cars for Adler
1936 Plywood chair and table for **Isokon**
1969 *TAC 1* tea service for **Rosenthal**

1 *TAC 1* tea service, 1969
2 Cylindrical door handle, 1922
3 *D 51* armchair ('Fagus armchair'), 1910
4 *F 51-3* sofa and *F 51* armchair, 1920

210

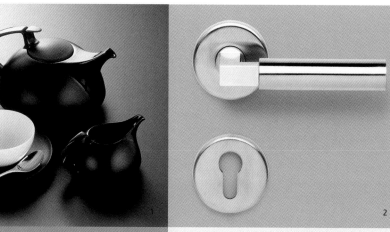

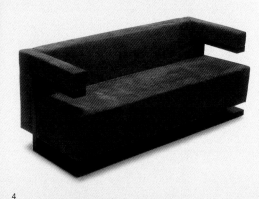

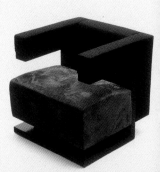

1

2

3   4

Gufram

Italy I Gufram Srl, Balangero I Furniture manufacturer I **www.gufram.com**

At the beginning of the 1970s the *I Multipli* collection of limited-edition furniture by the Turin company Gufram started to appear in shop windows. The effect was sensational. Dramatic, outsize, figurative sculptures, such as the bright red, lip-shaped *Bocca* sofa, thrust themselves into view, displacing ordinary chairs and cupboards, which appeared mundane in comparison. This was Pop design staging a spectacular event. A waist-high piece of rubber lawn called *Pratone* invited people to lie down and rest. A cactus in expanded polyurethane purported to be a coat stand. The broken capital of a Greek pillar masqueraded as a chair that, if you ventured to sit on it, was unexpectedly soft and was made of plastic, not stone. These crazy pieces of furniture, which, depending on one's point of view, were either a postscript to the Italian Radical Design movement of the 1960s or an attempt by Pop art to move into the world of industrial products, found a niche precisely at the boundary between art and product design. A number of young Turin artists, among them Studio 65, Gruppo Strum, the duo Guido Drocco and Franco Mello, and Piero Gilardi were responsible for the designs. The *I Multipli* range is still available and has already become something of a legend. Since the late 1970s Gufram has also furnished cinemas, theatres, hotels and universities.

1952 Established as chair manufacturer
1966 Starts producing high-design furniture
1972 Starts producing *I Multipli* furniture collection in limited editions
2004 Becomes part of Charme Group (with **Cappellini**, **Cassina** and Poltrona Frau, among others)

Products
1967 *Pavé Piuma* carpet by Piero Gilardi
1968 *Sassi* stool by Piero Gilardi; *Torneraj* armchair by Giorgio Ceretti, Pietro Derossi and Riccardo Rosso
1969 *Mozza* armchair by Giuseppe Raimondi; *Babele* table by Gianni Pettena
1971 *Puffo* stool and *Pratone* seat by Giorgio Ceretti, Pietro Derossi and Riccardo Rosso; *Bocca* sofa and *Capitello* seat by Studio 65
1972 *Cactus* coat stand by Guido Drocco and Franco Mello
1974 *Masolo* seat by Piero Gilardi; *Wimbledon* armchair by Giorgio Ceretti, Pietro Derossi and Riccardo Rosso
2004 *Siedi Tee* stool by Laura Fubini, Francesco Mansueto and Marco Verrando; *Bill* sofa by Franco Mello (both re-editions)

1 *Cactus* coat stand, 1972
2 *Bocca* sofa, 1971
3 *Capitello* seat, 1971
4 *Pratone* seat, 1971
5 *Masolo* seat, 1974

211

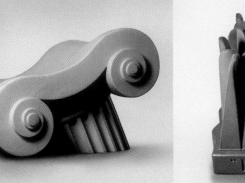

1

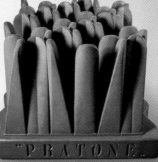

2

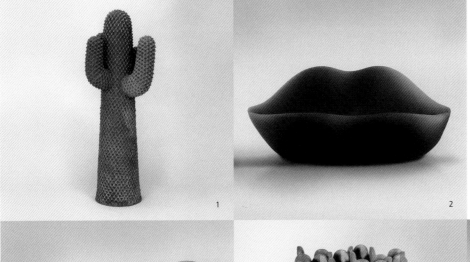

3

4

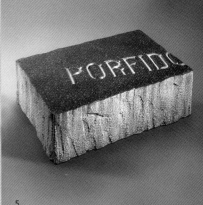

5

Hans **Gugelot**

Switzerland/The Netherlands | Architect and furniture and product designer

Hans Gugelot had a short but active life. When the Ulm Museum devoted an exhibition to him in 1960 he was forty years old and, as a result of the war, had only ten years' professional experience behind him. In those few years, however, he had made a considerable impact on the design world. The pioneering designer worked for such companies as Bofinger, Pfaff and the Hamburg underground. He also acted as a consultant for **Braun**, the manufacturer of electrical appliances and audio systems, and in the late 1950s developed a series of exemplary radio and television sets in a combined system. The relationship with Braun was of outstanding importance in the history of design. Gugelot's simple yet highly innovative concept of combinable elements, based on a building-block principle, indicated an entirely new direction in industrial design. His compact *Studio 1* was Braun's first grey radio and record player unit. He later introduced the silver-and-black scheme, first used for the *Sixtant* electric shaver; the scheme remains a significant feature of the company's corporate identity to the present day.

The son of a Swiss mother and a Dutch father, Gugelot was born on Celebes (now Sulawesi, Indonesia), and spent his childhood on the island. The family later moved to The Netherlands, then Switzerland, where Gugelot studied architecture and played jazz guitar in a band. After the Second World War he went on a number of long trips to Italy. He took a job in **Max Bill**'s office in Zurich and later followed Bill to the new Hochschule für Gestaltung in Ulm, where he led the product design programme. Among Gugelot's first designs was the *M 125* storage system, based on his building blocks principle. In the late 1950s, together with Otl Aicher, Herbert Lindinger and Helmut Müller-Kühn, he started work on his biggest project – the design of trains for the Hamburg underground. Some four hundred of these trains are still in service today. Gugelot's design was later adopted by the underground systems in Amsterdam and Dublin. His most commercially successful project, the *Carousel-S* slide projector, was developed in the early 1960s for **Kodak** and set the industry standard. The projector's innovative rotary action proved to be extremely reliable. Somewhat later, Gugelot designed an object that at some point in their lives almost everyone will have held in their hands – a plastic crate for bottles.

212

1 *Phonosuper SK 4* radio/record player, 1956
2 *Studio 1* control unit, 1956
3 *Carousel-S* slide projector, 1963
4 *Sixtant* electric shaver, 1962
5 *FS-G* TV set, 1955

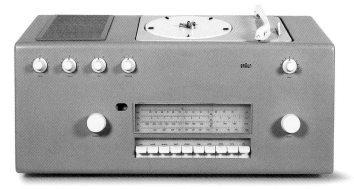

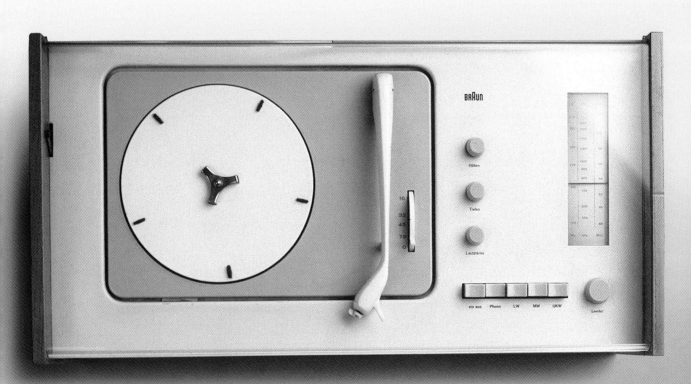

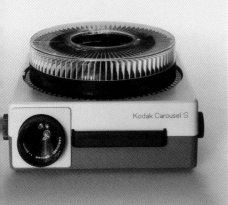

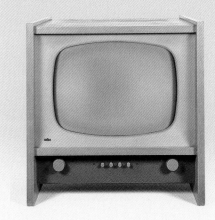

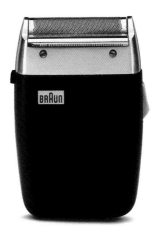

1

3

4

5

Helit, pen holder, 1966

Prior to teaching at the famous Hochschule für Gestaltung in Ulm, Walter Zeischegg had trained as a sculptor. He was particularly interested in geometric structures. In the late 1960s he designed a series of office items in Bakelite for Helit, including filing systems, index-card systems, a stackable ashtray and a pen holder that is cylindrical on the inside and octagonal on the outside, making it easier to handle.

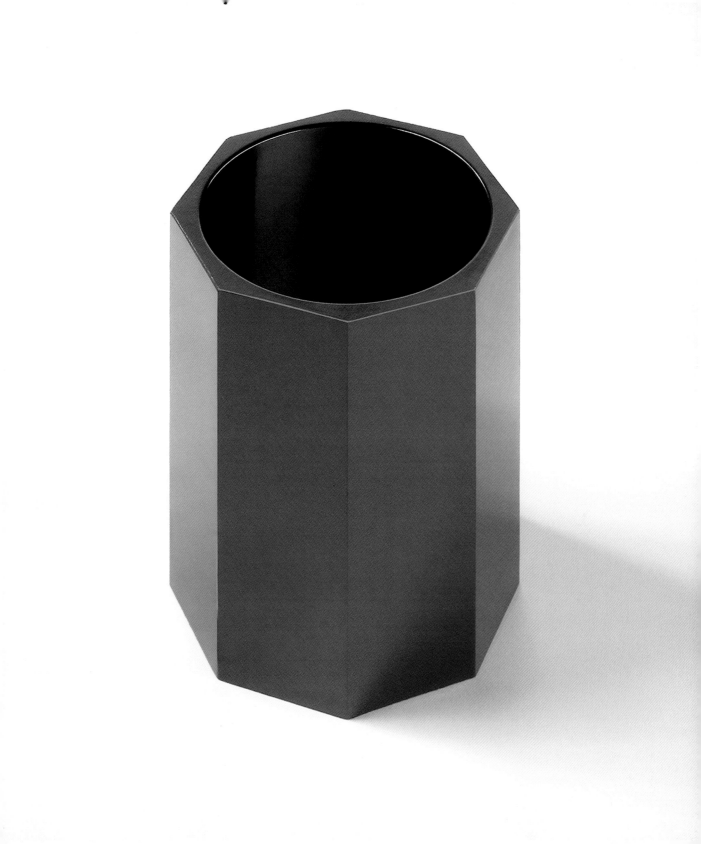

Alfredo **Häberli**

Switzerland | Furniture and product designer | **www.alfredo-haeberli.com**

From a sofa that can be used as either a lounger or place to work and a barstool with a handy built-in shelf to a piece of furniture on wheels that functions as a chair, container and trolley all in one – Alfredo Häberli's imaginative designs are not only multifunctional but are also brimming with wit and irony. Despite their apparent frivolity, however, all these designs have been created with careful thought and observation. Many leading manufacturers appreciate such qualities.

Häberli has designed beds for **Alias**, chairs for **Cappellini**, lamps for **Luceplan**, accessories for **Driade** and tubular steel chairs for **Thonet**. Until the late 1990s he created many products in collaboration with his partner, **Christophe Marchand**. Häberli's designs are easily recognizable by their highly individual style, which, according to his fellow designer **Björn Dahlström**, is characterized by elongated proportions and the use of archetypal forms. More recent products include the *Essence* wineglass series for **littala** and the *Nais* chair for **ClassiCon**, which can be interpreted as a radically simplified version of **Harry Bertoia**'s *Diamond* chair. Häberli has also designed numerous exhibitions.

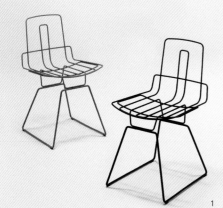

1

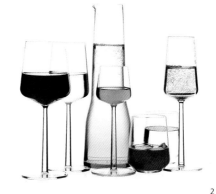

2

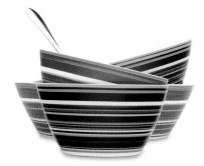

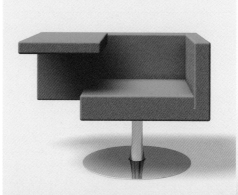

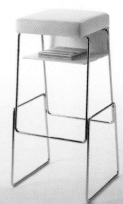

3
4
5

Hackman

Finland | Hackman, Iittala Oy A/B, Helsinki | Manufacturer of cutlery and kitchenware | **www.hackman.fi**

"What do optimal kitchen appliances look like?" This was the rhetorical question posed by Hackman, Scandinavia's leading manufacturer of household goods, to the readers of its catalogue. The answer was the "functional, innovative and simple" *Tools* series from the late 1990s. Together with the Swedish industrial designer **Björn Dahlström** and a team of materials specialists, technicians and professional cooks, the company developed an elegant range of kitchen utensils that was designed to optimize each stage in the preparation of food. Hackman has a long and complex history and is now part of a large conglomerate. The company was founded more than two centuries ago by Johan F. Hackman, a German immigrant. In 1990 it took over **Arabia** and **Iittala** and rose to become the leading Danish design company. Its household products are today exported worldwide under the Iittala brand. Hackman has sought to introduce new products into its range by such internationally renowned designers as **Alberto Meda** and **Harri Koskinen**, as well as Glen Oliver Löw and **Antonio Citterio**, who has contributed several notable creations, including a plump, ergonomic salt and pepper set.

217

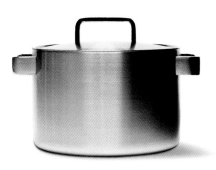

1

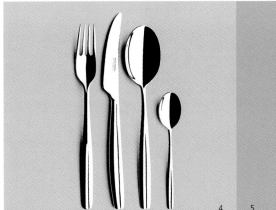

2

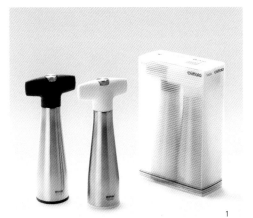

3

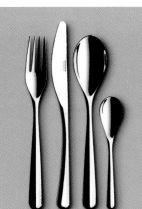

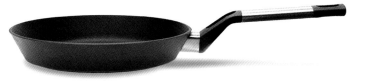

4

5

Hansgrohe

Germany | Hansgrohe AG, Schiltach | Manufacturer of bathroom fittings | **www.hansgrohe.com**

Hansgrohe was the first company in the bathroom fittings industry to enlist the help of product designers. As early as the end of the 1960s it was collaborating with the young designer Hartmut Esslinger, who later founded **Frogdesign**. Esslinger's very first design, *Tribel*, a compact three-way shower attachment, was successful and won an award. Since then Hangrohe has received numerous other awards for its products. As in the case of its competitor **Dornbracht**, design has become an integral part of the company's marketing and corporate culture.

Hansgrohe's products are divided into three brands: the Pharo range adds luxury to the bathroom with its pre-assembled 'shower temples'; Axor is the company's high-end design brand, and offers a series of stylish products; and a comprehensive range of solid, functional fittings for both the bathroom and the kitchen is sold under the Hansgrohe name. Esslinger determined the company's approach to design until well into the 1980s, a role that was subsequently taken over by **Phoenix Design**. Such leading talents as **Philippe Starck** and **Antonio Citterio** have designed complete series of fittings for the Axor brand. The *Raindance* plate-sized shower attachment, which can be adjusted from a concentrated jet of water to a rain-soft spray, adds a further individual touch to the bathroom.

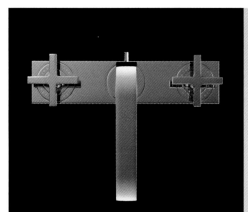

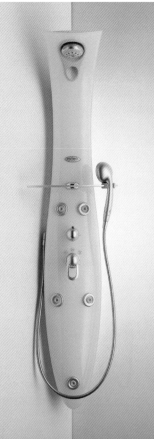

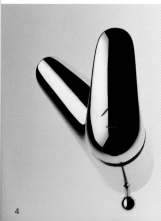

1

2

3

4

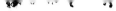

Rolf **Heide**

Germany | Interior, furniture and exhibition designer

"If one could not afford an **Eames** in the 1960s, one simply indulged in a Heide", wrote an expert about one of the most colourful characters on the German design scene. Rolf Heide's name is rarely mentioned in specialist literature because his work defies neat categorization. Like **Peter Maly** (his colleague and fellow German), the versatile designer trained as a cabinetmaker and interior designer. He also acquired considerable experience working for magazines. His designs for exhibition stands and corporate identity concepts have often attracted critical acclaim.

Although it is sometimes claimed that Heide's products do not have the same status as his presentations and exhibition designs, his contribution as a designer of furniture and lamps is undoubtedly remarkable. Over the last five decades he has worked for such manufacturers as Anta, **Cor**, De Padova, Wohnbedarf, WK, Vorwerk and, in recent years, increasingly for **Interlübke**. Some of his designs are regarded as classics, including a stackable bed from the 1960s, a self-assembly sofa bench and the *Travo* furniture series (for ▶Interlübke). According to Heide, "Too many superfluous things are designed". His preference is for clear shapes, and he has a particular interest in unconventional and mobile living.

1934 Born in Kiel
1950 Begins apprenticeship as cabinetmaker
1953 Studies interior design at Muthesius-Werkschule, Kiel
1959 Works on freelance basis at *Brigitte* magazine (from 1970 also for *Schöner Wohnen*; from 1980 for *Architektur & Wohnen*)
1978 Works for **Gaggenau**, kitchen manufacturer
1986 Creates stands for trade fairs, advertisements and presentations for Vorwerk and **Bulthaup**; publishes book *Die Küche als Lebensraum* (The kitchen as living area)
1993 Retrospective held in Berlin
1999 Receives Karl Schneider Prize for Design

Products
1968 Stackable bed for Wohnbedarf
1971 *Container* storage system for Wohnbedarf
1989 *Dialog* carpet collection for Vorwerk
1992 *Milch* milk-glass collection for Ritzenhoff
1995 *Aruga* lamp collection for Anta
1998 *Futo* standard lamp for Anta; *Schnaps* glass and *Bier* beer-glass collection for Ritzenhoff; *Campa* bed system, *Travo* cabinet system and *SL* storage system
2000 *Travo* table
2002 *Travo* chair
Last five for ▶ **Interlübke**
2004 *Tender* hanging lamp for Anta; *Malo* bed for Interlübke

1 *Futo* standard lamp, 1998
2 *Container* chest of drawers, 1971
3 Stackable bed, 1968

219

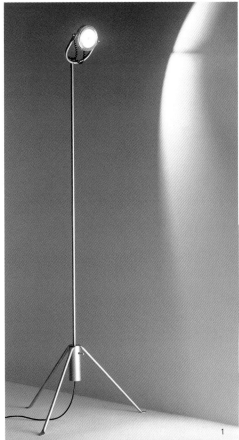

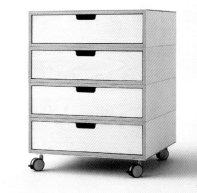

2

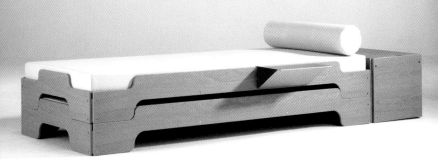

1   3

Helit

Germany I Helit innovative Büroprodukte GmbH, Kierspe I Manufacturer of office equipment I **www.helit.de**

Helit was originally a metal workshop, but after some fifty years it switched to manufacturing office products made from Bakelite. In the mid-1960s the company – like **Braun** a decade earlier – started collaborating with the Hochschule für Gestaltung in Ulm and, in particular, with Walter Zeischegg, who was a lecturer at the school and a specialist in product design and geometry. Until well into the 1980s Helit worked with Zeischegg to develop around seventy products, including a pen holder and a stackable ashtray, both of which are today well known around the world. For a long time these classics determined the company's image.

At the end of the 1990s Helit decided to diversify by introducing a range of products by leading designers. **Porsche Design**, for example, has contributed an ingenious metal trolley on castors for moving items between desks. **Foster and Partners** has developed numerous desktop utensils, including index-card boxes, hole punches, clocks and tape dispensers, all of which take the form of boxes and are designed to resemble building blocks. A surprising contrast in Helit's programme is represented by **Stefano Giovannoni**'s range of small objects, such as a magnetic cactus for holding paperclips.

220

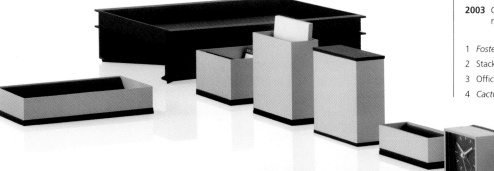

1

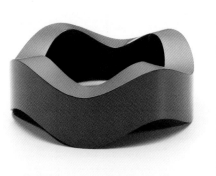

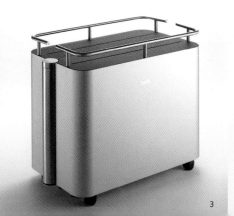

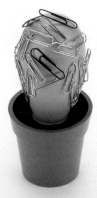

2

3

4

Heller

USA I Heller, Inc., New York I Furniture manufacturer I www.helleronline.com

The career of Alan J. Heller, founder of the Heller company, took a decisive turn when he was introduced to Lella and Massimo Vignelli (of **Vignelli Associates**) in New York. Soon thereafter the Italian design duo devised his company's corporate image, using **Knoll** as a model. The Vignellis' series of stackable plastic tableware from the 1960s was one of the first re-editions to be introduced into Heller's programme. Alan Heller became increasingly interested not only in Italy, which he began visiting regularly, but also in the world of design. His former experience in synthetic materials finally convinced him, in the early 1990s, to start producing furniture himself.

"**Charles Eames** would today work for Heller", Heller speculated confidently. In the absence of Eames, however, who better than ▶**Mario Bellini** to produce the first chair in which the Heller concept was realized. The *Bellini* chair, a mixture of polypropylene and fibreglass, is moulded using a special process that allows the legs to be hollow, making the chair lighter and more stable. The fact that the multi-purpose chair is to be found in the cafeteria of the Museum of Modern Art (MoMA) in New York is a notable mark of its success. The *MB 1* plastic armchair, produced five years later, is also manufactured using an unusual moulding procedure, this time to produce a seat that is surprisingly pliable and springy.

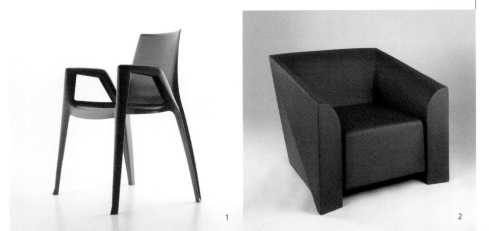

1

2

221

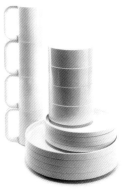

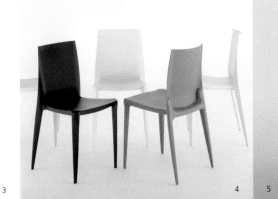

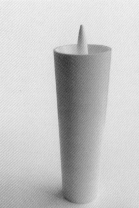

3

4

5

Poul **Henningsen**

Denmark | Architect, writer and lamp designer

Poul Henningsen's lamps are essentially 'reflection machines' with ingeniously complex shades that not only prevent glare but also direct the light so that it falls in exactly the right place. Henningsen varied this design principle over and over again and also experimented with different materials, such as glass and copper, so that the principle could be refined and tailored to meet specific situations. The impressive *Artichoke*, from the 1950s, is a complex variation on this theme, with overlapping leaves that cast the light over a large area; the use of copper in the shade creates a warm and inviting glow. Henningsen's constructions were almost always striking, aesthetically imposing and sometimes confusing objects, as in the series of *PH* lamps that are still manufactured by **Louis Poulsen**.

Henningsen, who also had considerable success as an architect, critic, writer and songwriter, had been an attentive observer of the urban scene since the 1920s. He was particularly interested in electric light, which was still a new development at that time. His lamps were among the first modern products to be exported Europe-wide, and they merit comparison with the more or less contemporary creations by **Marianne Brandt** and **Wilhelm Wagenfeld**, both Bauhaus designers. Henningsen's models were based on the scientific analysis of the ways in which lampshades distribute light, and were carefully designed using detailed sketches that took reflection into account. They were suitable for mass production and could be used in virtually any imaginable application – from nightclubs to indoor tennis courts, and from churches to the Tivoli Gardens. Moreover, they remain genuinely popular lamps, at least in Denmark.

In the early 1930s Henningsen also designed tubular steel furniture, including the *Snake Chair*, which was made from a single bent tube; the chair anticipated similar designs by several decades. At an advanced age, and as the editor of one of the first consumer magazines, Henningsen attempted to encourage young artists to protest publicly against improper treatment. One of his favourite slogans was "We are strong in disunity!"

1894 Born in Ordrup
1917 Breaks off architecture studies in Copenhagen; writes for art magazines
1924 Experiments with multishade lamps
1925 Receives gold medal at *Exposition Internationale des Arts Décoratifs et Industriels Modernes*, Paris
1926 **Louis Poulsen** produces *PH* series of lamps; edits *Kritisk Revy* journal (until 1928)
1930 Designs new range of *PH* lamps; builds villa in Gentofte
1935 Makes documentary film about Denmark
1941 Edits Louis Poulsen's *Nyt* magazine (until 1967)
1951 Publishes book of poetry, *Springende Vers*
1955 Publishes collection of aphorisms
1964 Publishes first Danish consumer magazine
1967 Dies in Copenhagen

Products
1919 Crystal chandelier for Carlsberg
1921 *Slotsholm* street light
1924 *Snowball* hanging lamp
1926 *PH 3/2*, *PH 2/1* and *PH 41* lamp collections
1931 *Circular* lamp; *Sepina* hanging lamp; *PH 6* lamp
1932 *Snake Chair*; surgery lights
1933 *2/1* desk lamp
1943 *Spiral* hanging lamp
1949 Lamp for Tivoli Gardens; ball lamps
1957 *PH Louvre* hanging lamp
1958 *PH 5* hanging lamp; *PH Artichoke* hanging lamp
1961 *PH 5* table lamp
1966 *PH 4-3* lamp collection

1 *Sepina* hanging lamp, 1931
2 *PH 5* hanging lamp, 1958
3 *Snake Chair*, 1932
4 *PH 3/2* table lamp, 1926
5 *PH Artichoke* hanging lamp, 1958
6 *2/1* desk lamp, 1933

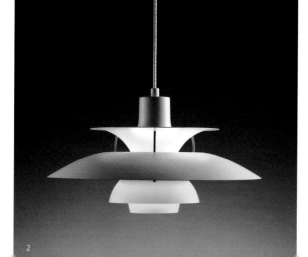

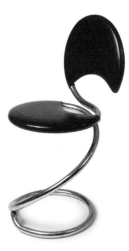

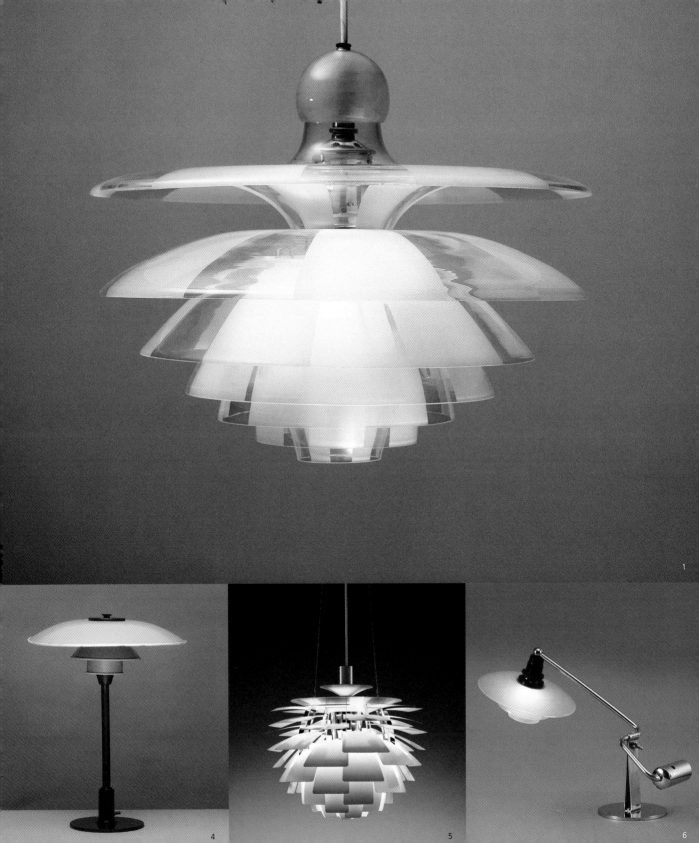

1

4   5   6

Herman Miller

USA | Herman Miller, Inc., Zeeland, Michigan | Furniture manufacturer | **www.hermanmiller.com**

With operations and sales offices on four continents and a comprehensive range of first-class office furniture, Herman Miller is one of the few furniture manufacturers (together with **B&B Italia** and **Knoll**) that is active worldwide. The company features products by leading designers in its collection, including the legendary **Alvar Aalto**, **George Nelson** and **Charles and Ray Eames**. Among the company's best-known designs are the Eameses' lounge chair and ottoman, shelving unit, *Aluminum Group* chairs and the *DKR* wire chair (▶p. 9).

Such contemporary American designers as Bruce Burdick, Don Chadwick, Bill Stumpf and Jeff Weber have contributed a number of highly functional pieces. Stumpf presented the *Ergon* office chair in the mid-1970s and later followed up with the *Equa* and *Aeron* models. Largely as a result of its shape and the innovative material used in the backrest, the *Aeron* office chair resembles an insect. The *Caper* chair by Weber is a lightweight, stackable multi-purpose chair, available in a range of different colours.

The first creative designer to work for Herman Miller was Gilbert Rohde, whose furniture was celebrated in the 1930s as the "furniture of the future". After the Second World War the company was still small, but was beginning to be noticed outside Michigan by those in the industry. The turning point came with the appointment of George Nelson as design director after Rohde's death. The combination of a highly gifted chief designer with the right timing and a rare degree of team spirit (to which Charles and Ray Eames soon contributed) made the Herman Miller brand, alongside Knoll, one of the best known in the industry in the United States. Playful designs, including Nelson's *Marshmallow* sofa and **Isamu Noguchi**'s *Articulated Table*, contrasted with rational systems furniture, such as the *ESU* (Eames Storage Unit) and the *Storagewall* shelf system by Nelson. Such concepts as the *Action Office* furniture system from the early 1960s became the models for the 'office landscapes' that were gradually developed. Today, at the Herman Miller National Design Centers in various large cities across the United States, customers are able to view the latest furniture and learn about the creative design process.

224

1 Management chair (*Aluminum Group*), 1958
2 *Goetz* sofa, 1999
3 *Tandem Sling* seating, 1962
4 *Platform* bench, 1946
5 *Aeron* office chair, 1992
6 *Mirra* office chair, 2003
7 *Burdick* table, 1980

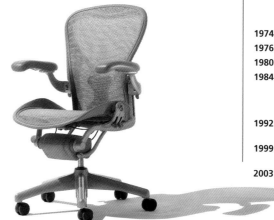

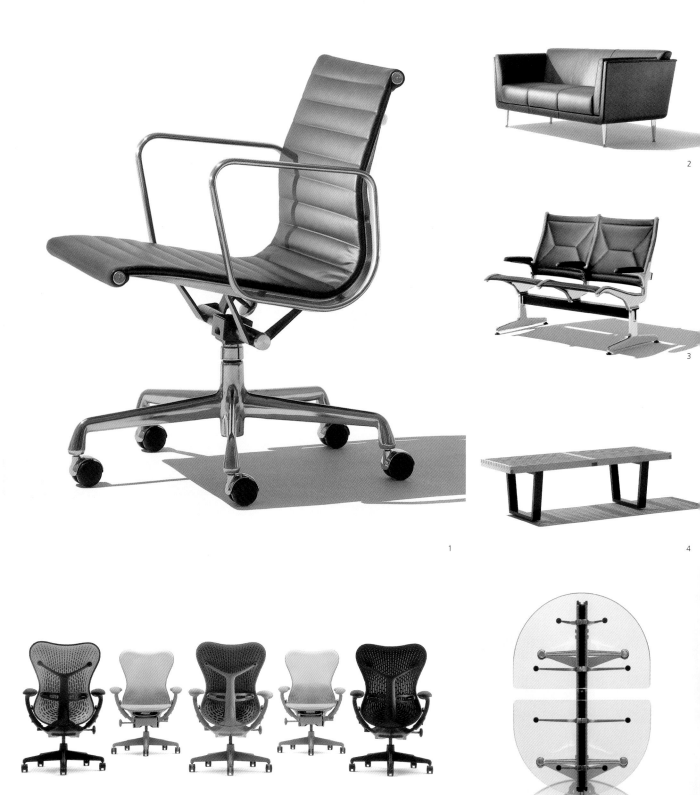

1

2

3

4

6

7

Matthew **Hilton**

England | Furniture designer

Alongside **Jasper Morrison**, Matthew Hilton is one of the leading furniture designers of the what has been called the British 'neo-objectivity' movement. Sheridan Coakley, the founder and head of the English furniture manufacturer **SCP**, was among the first people to support the two designers in the 1980s. The relationship between Coakley and Hilton produced a considerable number of innovative products, including the curvilinear *Buffalo* armchair and the asymmetrical *Kerouac* sofa. The *Orford* sofa measures 2.5 metres (8' 2") in length, but can be extended to form an even larger upholstered seating system.

Hilton does not believe in the concept of design trends, but considers that every product should be developed from its own logic. His products are therefore quite diverse and include such pieces as the light, multi-purpose *Wait* chair (for **Authentics**), made of translucent plastic, and the *Puff* seat (for **BD Ediciones**), the footstool of which can be placed in the hollow of the seat itself to form a single unit, or ottoman, with rounded edges. While Hilton still acts as in-house designer at SCP, for a long time he has also worked with other European manufacturers, including **Driade**, Disform, Montis, XO, **Sawaya & Moroni**, Perobell, Lusty's Lloyd Loom and Habitat.

1957 Born in Hastings, East Sussex
1975 Studies at Portsmouth College of Art (from 1976 at Kingston Polytechnic, Surrey)
1984 Opens own studio

Products
1985 *Oval Bowl*
1986 *Bow* shelf
1987 *Antelope* table
1989 *Flipper* table; *Swan* candlestick
1991 *Auberon* table; *Club* and *Balzac* armchairs
1993 *Kerouac* sofa
All for ▶ **SCP**
1995 *Voyager* chair, *Antares* and *Orion* armchairs and *Gemini* and *Mercury* sofas for ▶ **Driade**; *Reading Chair* and *Orwell* sofa for SCP
1999 *Wait* plastic chair for **Authentics**
2002 *Buffalo* armchair for SCP
2003 *Orford* sofa collection for SCP; *Puff* ottoman for **BD Ediciones**
2004 *Britten* table and *Baude* and *Underneath* armchairs for SCP

1 *Puff* ottoman, 2003
2 *Orford* sofa, 2003
3 *Buffalo* armchair, 2002
4 *Reading Chair*, 1995
5 *Wait* plastic chair, 1999

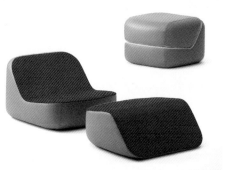

1

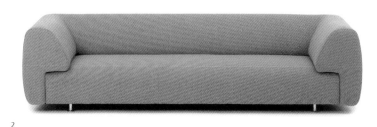

2

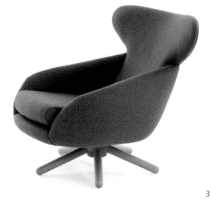

3

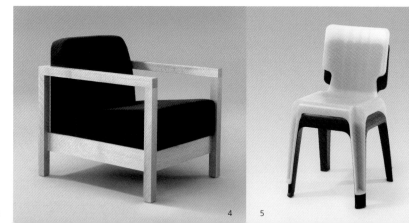

4   5

Herbert **Hirche**

Germany | Furniture and product designer

With a seat and upholstered backrest made from two flat cubes resting on a tubular steel frame, Herbert Hirche's *Lounge Chair* (today available at Richard Lampert) appears as severe as chairs by **Marcel Breuer** and **Ludwig Mies van der Rohe**. Hirche studied at the famous Bauhaus school for three years, until its closure in 1933. Thereafter he worked in the offices of Mies van der Rohe, **Egon Eiermann**, and Hans Scharoun. After the Second World War he became involved in the reconstruction of Berlin with Scharoun and presented examples of new German design in the epoch-making exhibition *Wie Wohnen* (How to live), which was held in Stuttgart (where he was a professor at the Staatliche Akademie der Bildenden Künste). Hirche was one of the Modernist designers of the German post-war period who had a significant influence on style and taste. For such manufacturers as Holzäpfel, Walter Knoll and **Wilkhahn** he produced numerous pieces of furniture that were based strictly on the principle of 'good design', among them modular storage systems that also functioned as room dividers. Together with **Hans Gugelot** and **Wilhelm Wagenfeld**, Hirche also developed a new, rational product range for **Braun**. His grey, sharp-edged *HF1* television set represented a decisive break with the traditional television cabinet.

1   *HF1* TV set, 1958
2   *Lounge Chair*, 1953
3   *TS3* radio, 1957

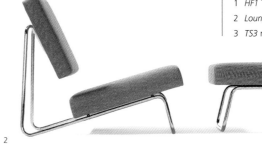

2

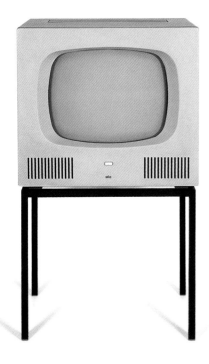

227

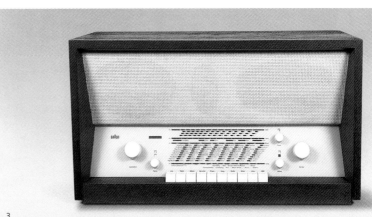

1   3

Josef **Hoffmann**

Austria | Architect and furniture and product designer | **www.wittmann.at**

The lofty ambition of Austrian architect Josef Hoffmann was to achieve a union of art, architecture, craftsmanship and design, to create an integrated approach that would encompass everything, from a building to interior design and furniture design to a teaspoon. Inspired by the Arts and Crafts Movement in England, Hoffmann (a former student of Otto Wagner), together with like-minded artist Koloman Moser, founded the Wiener Werkstätte (Vienna Workshops; a co-operative group of painters, sculptors, architects and decorative artists) shortly after the turn of the twentieth century. During the same period Hoffmann and Moser designed the Purkersdorf Sanatorium, near Vienna, the first masterpiece of rational Modernism and a design that, in many respects, anticipated the basic principles of the Bauhaus.

Hoffmann was born in Pirnitz, Moravia (now Brtnice in the Czech Republic). He studied architecture in Munich and then in Vienna, where he joined the avant-garde Secession movement, to which Gustav Klimt, Joseph Maria Olbrich and other important representatives of Viennese Modernism also belonged. Hoffmann was enthused by the Secessionist idea of art as a regenerative force. One of his most important commissions, in collaboration with Moser, was the Palais Stoclet in Brussels, a truly integrated concept for which he designed the building, interiors and furnishings. After visiting **Charles Rennie Mackintosh**, a kindred spirit, Hoffmann renounced the flowing ornamentation typical of the time and developed instead a style characterized by basic geometric forms. This style is particularly evident in his *Kubus* upholstered furniture collection. Hoffmann's well-known *Sitzmaschine* (Sitting machine) expressed his affinity with the world of industry, which for him represented rationality. With the Kohn company he produced a chair that formed part of the furnishings for the Purkersdorf Sanatorium. Its construction is reminiscent of the bentwood chairs by **Thonet**. Although Hoffmann rejected superfluous ornamentation in his designs, he was not an aesthetic revolutionary, unlike his fellow countryman Adolf Loos; he was more concerned with making everyday objects more beautiful. The high quality of his designs contributed to his role as a central figure in the internationally respected German Werkstätte movement.

228

1870	Born in Pirnitz, Moravia (now Brtnice, Czech Republic)
1897	Becomes founding member of Vienna Secession
1899	Appointed professor at Kunstgewerbeschule, Vienna
1903	Establishes Wiener Werkstätte with Koloman Moser; Purkersdorf Sanatorium, also with Moser
1905	Palais Stoclet, Brussels, with Koloman Moser
1932	Wiener Werkstätte close
1935	Retires from academia
1956	Dies in Vienna

Products

1900	*Satztische* nest of tables
1903	*JH* lamp (re-edition at **BD Ediciones**); *Purkersdorf* chair
1905	*Sitzmaschine* armchair; *Kunstschau 1908* armchair
1906	*Fledermaus* chair; *Rundes Modell* cutlery (re-edition at **Alessi**)
1908	*Armlöffel* armchair
1910	*Club* and *Kubus* upholstered furniture collections
1912	*Alleegasse* collection of upholstered furniture; *Broncia* armchair; *Villa Ast* armchair
1913	*Villa Gallia* armchair
1915	*Cabinett* furniture collection
1923	*Oval* tray (re-edition at Alessi)
1955	*86* cutlery for **Pott**
	All furniture in re-edition at ▶**Wittmann**

1 *Sitzmaschine* armchair, 1905

2 *Cabinett* sofa, 1915

3 *86* cutlery, 1955

4 *Oval* tray, 1923

5 *Satztische* nest of tables, 1900

6 *JH* lamp, 1903

7 *Kubus* sofa, 1910

8 *Purkersdorf* chair, 1903

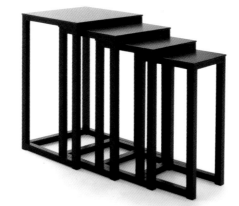

5

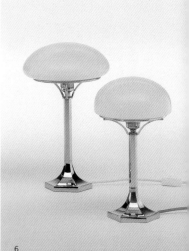

6

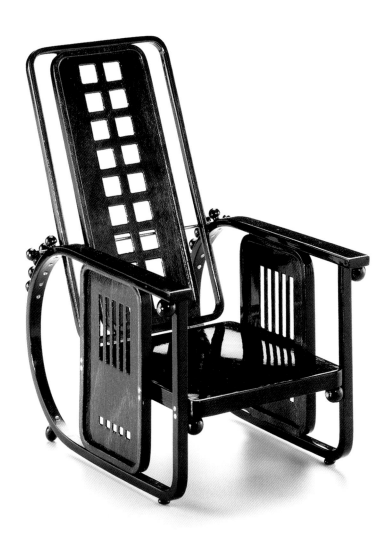

1

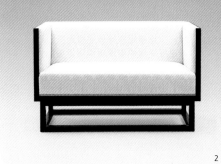

2

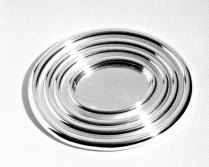

3

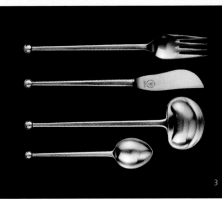

4

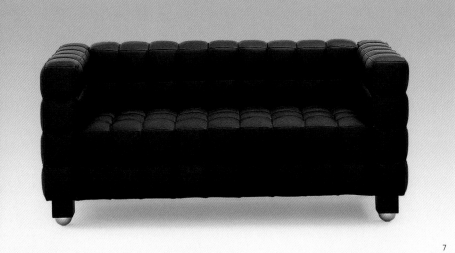

7

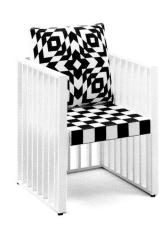

8

Geoff **Hollington**

England | Furniture and product designer

Geoff Hollington has enjoyed a highly successfully collaboration with the American furniture manufacturer **Herman Miller** since the late 1980s. Hollington's work is characterized by functional, well-conceived designs; quality is more important to him than the visual excesses favoured by some other British designers. Hollington, who was born on the outskirts of London, made a name for himself shortly completing his studies at the Royal College of Art. He worked with the Milton Keynes Design Team in the mid-1970s and then founded a consultancy with Michael Glickman in 1978. Two years later he opened his own design studio, which, among other products, has developed pens for Parker, furniture for **SCP** and cameras for **Kodak**.

Hollington's pragmatic approach to design could perhaps be described as that of the 'English gentleman': his products must fulfil their function but otherwise should be understated and elegantly restrained. It almost goes without saying that Hollington pays considerable attention to technical details.

230

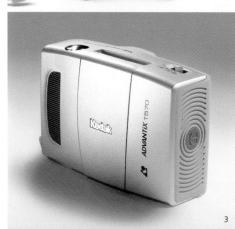

1

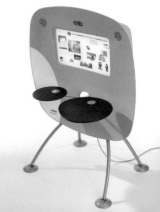

2

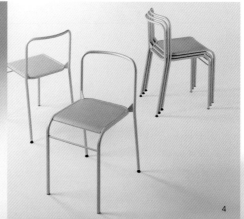

3   4   5

Knud **Holscher**

Denmark | Architect and product designer | www.knudholscher.dk

Knud Holscher's portfolio includes a disparate range of projects: lamps, bathroom fittings, office furniture, sign systems for the visually impaired and the corporate image for a design museum. Although Holscher began his career as an architect, he is now one of Scandinavia's most sought-after product designers. When he contributed a thermos jug to the **Georg Jensen** collection, the company and the designer alike profited from each other's good name. Holscher is a pupil of the legendary designer **Arne Jacobsen**, from whom he not only adopted the puritan work ethic and the principle that quality always prevails, but also learned "which red wine to drink". The quality of his designs can be seen in such products as *D-line*, his simple fittings in stainless steel. The series, which includes bottle openers, soap dispensers and coat hooks as well as door handles, was successfully launched in Japan some thirty years after it was originally introduced.

Although Holscher's work is characterized by the use of straight lines, now and again his designs go beyond the purely functional: the high-precision spotlights and lamps that Holscher developed (in the spirit of his fellow countryman **Poul Henningsen**) for **Erco**, for example, incorporate decorative lines.

231

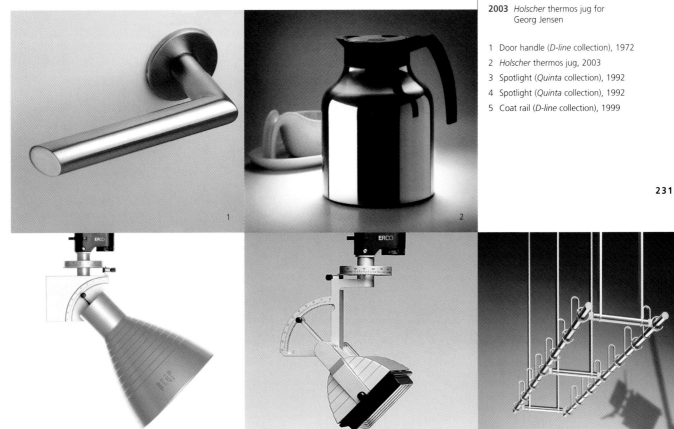

Richard **Hutten**

The Netherlands | Furniture designer | **www.richardhutten.com**

The Dutch designer Richard Hutten is an avowed minimalist: even in such hybrid objects as the *3 Minus 1* desk, which includes an integrated chest of drawers, he has managed to create a design that is completely bereft of ornamentation. That such severity can go hand in hand with humour has been demonstrated time and again by the new generation of Dutch designers who quickly went from being up-and-coming names at the beginning of the 1990s to established figures in the international design scene. Hutten shares his compatriots' approach to design: the noses on his Murano vases have a definite clown-like elegance to them.

Hutten graduated from the Academy of Industrial Design in Eindhoven in 1991. Two years later, a selection of his work was presented in **Droog Design**'s first exhibition. As well as designing furniture and household articles, Hutten has also been involved with interior and exhibition design. In all his projects, his intention is to achieve distinctive effects by simple means. His *Coattrunk* coat stand, for example, produced by Pure Design, uses mass-produced coat hooks of different lengths that are fixed together to resemble the branches of a tree. Here, as in the furniture created for the manufacturers Hidden and E&Y, Hutten executes clever ideas through very simple designs.

1967 Born in Zwollerkerspel
1991 Graduates from Academy of Industrial Design, Eindhoven
1993 Works at **Droog Design**

Products
1991 *Table Chair* and *Table-On-Table* barstool for Droog Design
1994 *S(h)it-On-It* and *The Cross* benches for Droog Design; *Skyline Rotterdam* storage system (in-house production)
1995 *Thing I* chair (in-house production); fruit bowl for DMD
1996 *Split Level* bench for Droog Design
1997 *Bronto* child's chair for Droog Design; *Straight Down and Up* sideboard for Harvink; *3 Minus 1* desk
1998 *Table Lamp* standard lamp with table for E&Y
1999 *CM* chair and *Longdrink* glass series for ▸ Droog Design; *One of a Kind* chair and *Wheels* cupboard for Hidden; *Table Sofa* sofa for **Sawaya & Moroni**
2000 *Zzzidt* glass object (in-house design); *Think 7* bench for Droog Design
2001 *Sexyrelaxy* chair for Hidden

1 *Table Chair*, 1991
2 *Think 7* bench, 2000
3 *Sexyrelaxy* chair, 2001
4 *Zzzidt* glass object, 2000
5 *One of a Kind* chair, 1999

232

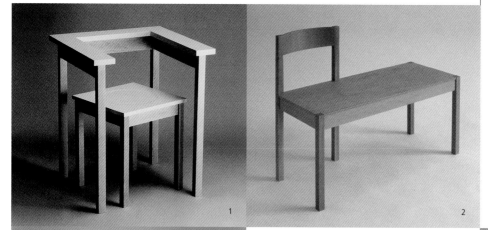

1

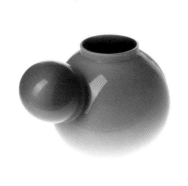

2

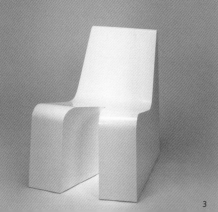

3

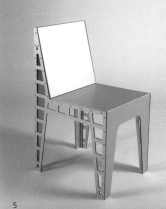

4

5

Niels **Hvass**

Denmark | Furniture designer | **www.strand-hvass.com**

Niels Hvass has a good reputation among organizers of trade fairs. His eye-catching designs, such as his *Wicker Chair* made from the branches of trees, are always popular for press photos. Hvass has nothing against the hustle and bustle of such events, even though he considers other issues to be more important. According to him, the essential thing about design is "the idea behind it". The numerous chairs that "are only designed to make money" are anathema to him. In the late 1980s, as part of the Octo design group, Hvass created works that bridged the gap between art and design. His chairs, which he began designing in the early 1990s, are multilayered, sometimes ironic objects, such as *Yesterday's Paper*, a chair made of sheets of newspaper piled waist-high; from this mass Hvass simply carved out a cube to make a seat. The geometric block is a virtual parody of **Le Corbusier**'s *LC 2* armchair, but at the same time intrudes into present-day reality: the user literally sits down on a headline.

Hvass eventually found his way back into the world of everyday objects. In 1998 he founded the Strand & Hvass studio with Christina Strand. The studio has developed such carefully thought-out, contemporary furniture as the *Tingstedet* shelf system; *Mix-It* (for BCI), a computer and office furniture programme; and the *Straight* table for Tranekær.

233

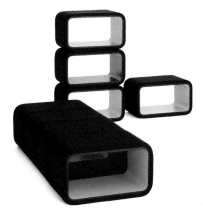

1

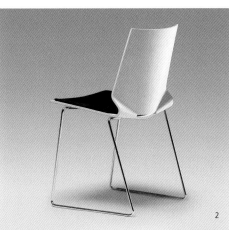

2

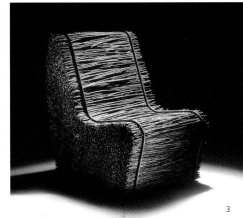

3

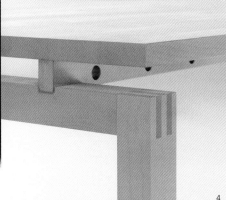

4

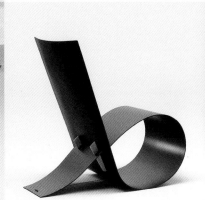

5

Iittala, glass from *Kartio* series, 1958

Finland's most coveted design prize is not named after the world-famous Alvar Aalto, but after his fellow countryman, Kaj Franck – a clear indication of the significance that has been attributed to the work of this industrial designer. In the *Kartio* series of glasses Franck designed for Iittala in the late 1950s, he succeeded in creating a design classic out of an everyday object.

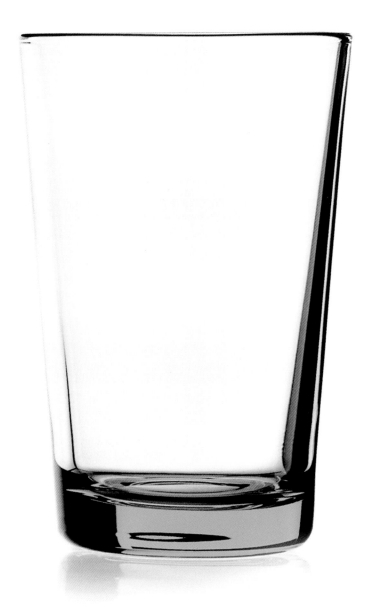

IBM

USA | IBM Corporation, White Plains, New York | Computer manufacturer | **www.ibm.com**

When the black *Aptiva SE 7* personal computer was introduced in the 1990s, it was greeted with surprise. The bold design of the prize-winning desktop computer was part of a repositioning of IBM, not the first in the company's unusual history. IBM's story began at the end of the nineteenth century, with the invention of punch-card technology. The biggest upheaval took place in the 1940s, during the advent of computer technology. Eliot Noyes, who was to reform the company on the model of **Olivetti**, was the first designer to be appointed to the management board. He invited Paul Rand to join the company. The avant-garde graphic designer soon created a radically new visual image for the firm, including its famous logo. IBM also collaborated with the legendary **Charles and Ray Eames**, who produced a number of films to explain the workings of computers. Noyes himself designed a series of forward-looking electric golf-ball typewriters, among them the *Selectric* model.

IBM's tremendous burst of creative activity was met with widespread admiration. However, the company arguably missed the boat completely as far as the shift towards desktop computers was concerned. It was not until the beginning of the 1990s that it managed to recover from the mistake. A charismatic designer was appointed for the next new start: **Richard Sapper** was commissioned to develop the *ThinkPad 700C* laptop computer and the *Flat Panel* screen. Both were in black, the new signature colour – the same colour, in fact, that **Braun** had introduced a few years previously to lend a more upmarket image to its products. IBM's new design-orientated strategy was accompanied by a willingness to experiment (as evident, for example, in its presentation of prototypes that reflected new ideas and technologies). An important aim for the company was to gain the confidence of Internet users, who regarded it with a certain degree of scepticism: unlike **Apple** and Hewlett-Packard, it did not belong to the self-made culture of Silicon Valley, and for a long time had a monopoly of the computer market. IBM remains the biggest information technology company in the world and produces laptops, PCs, monitors and pocket computers. It has coined the slogan "ThinkVantage Design" in order to communicate its fundamental aims: to make working in front of the screen easier and to cut costs for the consumer.

236

1 Personal computer, 2003
2 Personal computer, 1981
3 Telephone handset, 1980
4 *ThinkPad 700C* laptop computer, 1992
5 *Selectric* typewriter, 1961
6 *ThinkPad X-Series* laptop computer, 2000
7 *L 200* flat-screen monitor, 2001
8 *e-Server* mainframe computer, 2000

1896	Tabulating Machine Company established by Herman Hollerith
1911	Series of mergers leads to establishment of Computing-Tabulating-Recording Company
1914	Thomas J. Watson Sr joins company as general manager
1924	Company name changes to International Business Machines (IBM) Corporation
1956	Eliot Noyes develops corporate identity (until 1977); Paul Rand designs logo
1981	Rand creates 'Eye, Bee, M' campaign
1993	Louis V. Gerstner Jr becomes CEO and turns around failing company
1997	Launches e-business campaign
2001	Invests in *Linux* technology

Products

1944	*Mark I* Automatic Sequence Controlled Calculator (with Harvard University)
1947	*Model A* typewriter by Norman Bel Geddes
1952	*701* computer
1957	*305* computer with disk storage system
1959	*7090* transistorized data-processing system
1961	*Selectric* typewriter by Eliot Noyes
1962	*1440* data-processing system (with Eliot Noyes and Walter Furlani)
1964	*System/360* model series
1981	First IBM personal computer (processor chip by Intel, DOS by Microsoft)
1992	*ThinkPad 700C* laptop computer and *Leapfrog* computer by ▶ **Richard Sapper**
1997	*Aptiva S* series
1998	*ThinkPad 600* laptop computer and flat-screen monitor by Richard Sapper
2000	*ThinkPad X-Series* laptop computer; *eServer* mainframe computer
2001	*City Companion IntelliStation R Pro* mobile telephone; *L 200*, *T 210* and *T 220* flat-screen monitors
2002	*MetaPad* minicomputer

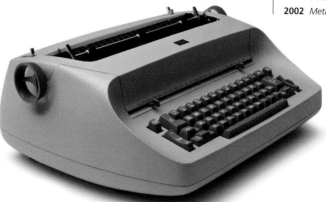

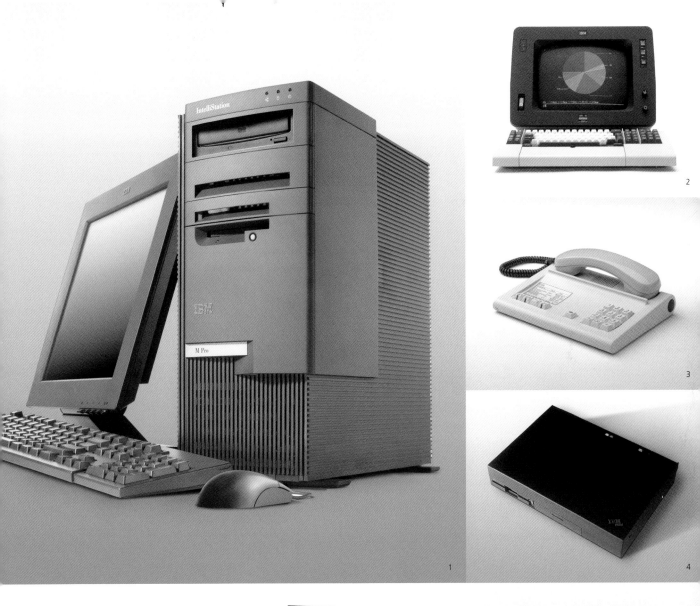

1

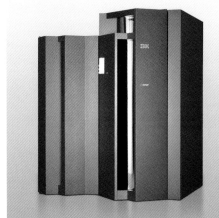

2

3

4

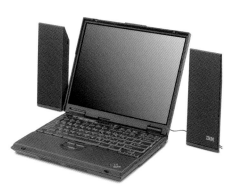

6

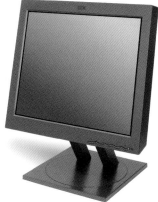

7

8

Ideo

England/USA I Product design studio I **www.ideo.com**

When the British industrial designer Bill Moggridge created the computer mouse for Microsoft in the mid-1980s, he unearthed nothing less than a seam of gold. In its heyday, up to seven million copies of Moggridge's mouse were produced every year. Moggridge had moved from London to California, the centre of the digital revolution, in the 1970s. Some fifteen years later he founded Ideo with partners David Kelley and Mike Nuttall. By the end of the 1990s Ideo had become one of the most successful design agencies in the United States. Today it also has branches in Germany, Great Britain and Japan. Computers have always been Moggridge's main focus. His studio designed *Compass*, the first laptop-style computer (for GridSystems), which formed part of the equipment in the NASA Space Shuttle. He also devised the first computer mouse for **Apple**, following this with the first mouse for Microsoft. In the late 1990s Ideo introduced the *SoftBook*, the first electronic book (for Gemstar eBook). The *Palm V* organizer, designed for Palm Computing, was also innovative and successful.

Consumers come into daily contact with the creative ideas of Ideo not only when they click on their mouse but also in other routine tasks, such as cleaning their teeth. The toothpaste tube developed for Procter & Gamble promises a "neat squeeze"; one of the *Xelibri* mobile telephones created for Siemens can be worn as a clip. Moggridge combines British originality with American business sense, a formula that perhaps represents the original concept behind the founding of the company. Time and again this successful combination has generated products that not only sell unusually well but are radically new, as in the case of the minimalist wall-mounted CD player developed for **Muji**. This item emerged as a best-seller for the Japanese trading company, breathing fresh air into one of the more unexciting product categories. Also included in Ideo's portfolio are such projects as *Heimspiel* (Home play), a study of everyday objects from which new products can be generated. The project has given rise to such innovations as a door handle that sinks into the door when it is locked and a radiator with a thermostatic light that indicates temperature.

238

1 Wall-mounted CD player, 2002

2 *Xelibri 7* mobile telephone, 2003

3 Wireless control terminal, 2003

4 *Mouse* for Microsoft, 1987

5 *SoftBook* electronic book-reader, 1999

6 *Palm V* organizer, 1998

7 *Xelibri 8* mobile telephone, 2003

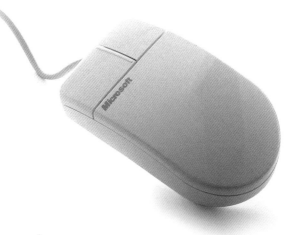

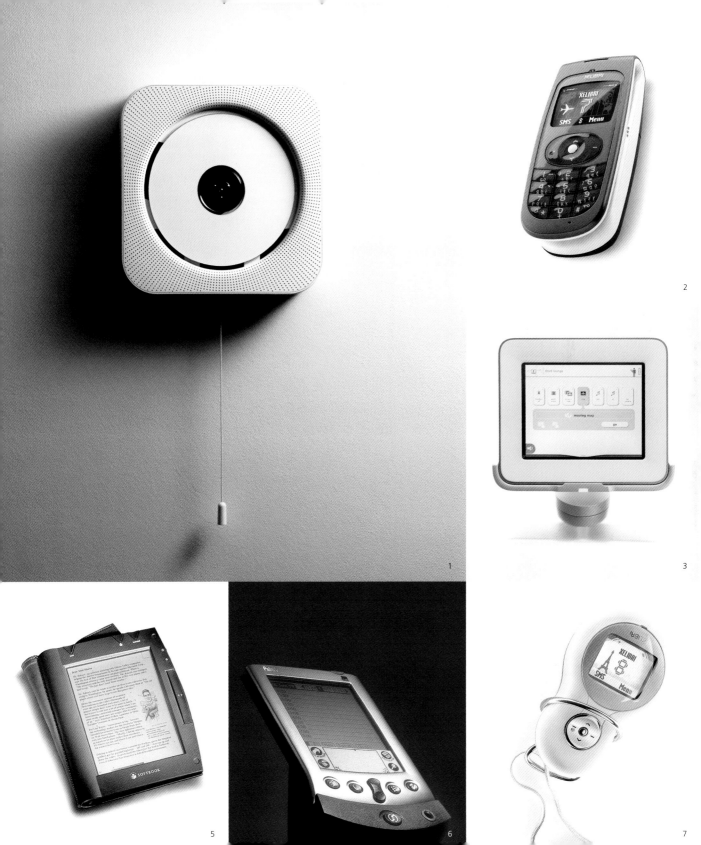

1

2

3

5

6

7

iForm

Sweden I iForm A/B, Malmö I Furniture manufacturer I **www.iform.net**

Voxia, a seating programme designed for iForm by the Danish architect Peter Karpf, represents a new and unexpected chapter in the exciting history of plywood furniture. These laminated chairs, moulded in one piece, possess sculptural qualities that are reminiscent of designs by **Ron Arad**, but can equally be described as high-tech versions of classic chairs by **Arne Jacobsen**. The *Voxia* collection is the result of intensive experimentation. Karpf, who knew Jacobsen personally and formerly worked at **Fritz Hansen**, developed the series over three decades. The chairs have a patented combination of veneered layers that are cut on the bias to provide stability, strength and flexibility. Although highly effective, the process is neither particularly complex nor excessively expensive. When iForm (previously a specialist in office furniture) launched the series in the early 1990s, it caused something of a sensation. The company then continued cautiously on its new design-orientated course. The *Voxia* collection was followed by *Pocket* shelving by the Swedish designers Helena Allard and Cecilia Falk. These shelves are dedicated to paperback enthusiasts: their height and depth correspond exactly to the international standard measurements of the paperback format.

240

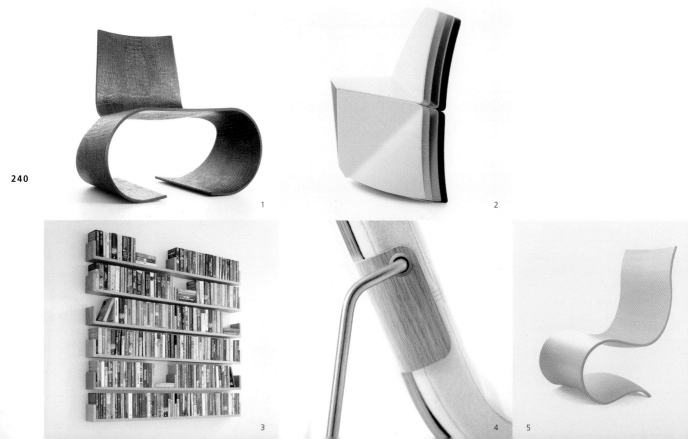

iGuzzini

Italy I iGuzzini Illuminazione SpA, Recanati I Lamp manufacturer I **www.iguzzini.com**

A specialist in technical and architectural lighting, the Italian lamp manufacturer iGuzzini has impressed international juries for many years with its innovative and technically sophisticated designs – to the extent that it has had to insert a separate page on its website in order to accommodate a list of its numerous design prizes. Founded in the late 1950s, the now globally active company had its roots in the manufacture of craft products in copper. More and more products, including lamps, were added gradually to its range, and the company also began to work with new plastics. Since the early 1970s it has concentrated exclusively on the manufacture of lamps. Many leading architects have worked for iGuzzini, including Norman Foster (of **Foster and Partners**), Renzo Piano, Gae Aulenti and Luigi Massoni. The company is more concerned with providing effective lighting solutions than with simply producing lamps; in this respect it is reminiscent of the German manufacturer **Erco**. A good example is the *Cestello* lighting system, which was the first product of its kind to unite several lamps in one element, thus providing tremendous flexibility. In outdoor lighting, the *ColourWoody* projector combines functionality with individual design; its variable colours make it possible to achieve special lighting effects.

1958 Harvey Creazoni established by Raimondo, Giovanni, Virgilio, Giuseppe and Giannunzio Guzzini for the production of artistic objects in enamelled copper

1973 Company restructured and renamed iGuzzini

1989 Receives Compasso d'Oro for *Shuttle* spotlight

1995 Opens Research and Study Centre

Products

1986 *Cestello* lighting system by Gae Aulenti and Piero Castiglioni

1988 *Shuttle* spotlight collection by Bruno Gecchelin

1993 *Lingotto* lamp collection by Renzo Piano

1994 *Gabbiano* spotlight collection by Bruno Gecchelin

1995 *Emilia* street-lamp collection by Valerio Sacchetti

1998 *Berlino* hanging lamp by Piano Design; *Sivra* lighting system by D. Skene, P. Scuri and D. Bedini

1999 *Greenwich* hanging lamp by Norman Foster (of **Foster and Partners**)

2000 *Le Perroquet* lamp collection by Piano Design

2002 *ColourWoody* projector by Mario Cucinella; *Flaminia* street-lamp collection by Jan Wickelgren

2003 *Gem* hanging lamp by Paul Andreu; *Metro* spotlight collection by Bruno Gecchelin; *Sirrah* lamp collection by **Vignelli Associates**

2004 *Lavinia* and *Pavinia* street lamps by Massimiliano and Doriana Fuksas

1 *Cestello* lighting system, 1986
2 Hanging lamp (*Sirrah* collection), 2003
3 *Lingotto* lamp, 1993
4 *ColourWoody* projector, 2002
5 *Shuttle* spotlight, 1988

241

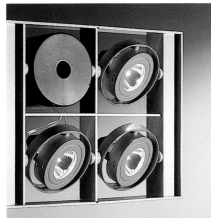

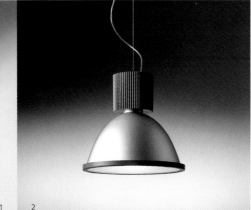

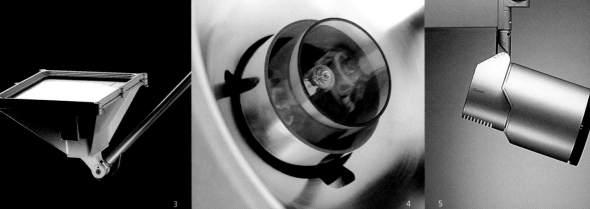

Iittala

Finland I Iittala Oy A/B, Helsinki I Glassware manufacturer I **www.iittala.fi**

In 1956 ►**Timo Sarpaneva** designed a new glass collection for Iittala and at the same time provided the company with its distinctive corporate logo: a white 'i' in a red circle. Sarpaneva had already been successful with his unusual artworks in glass, but these were pieces that could be admired only in galleries and at exhibitions. The *I-line* series for Iittala was a completely new departure for him: it was different from anything else he had designed previously and also meant that his work could be enjoyed by a wider public. It had a wider significance, too: it represented not only the beginning of modern product design in the Finnish glass industry, but also a turning point in the history of Iittala.

The company was founded by Swedish glass-blowers in the 1880s and for decades had focused exclusively on the manufacture of everyday glassware. During the First World War it became part of the Ahlström group, and some modernization of the plant took place. From the 1930s onwards the company organized a number of artistic competitions; Aino and **Alvar Aalto** were among the regular participants. Their designs – above all, the *Savoy* vase, renamed *Aalto* – experienced a renaissance in the 1980s and have today acquired almost mythical status.

Iittala's golden era began after the Second World War. At that time it was recruiting such young artists such as **Tapio Wirkkala**, **Kaj Franck** and Göran Hongell, whose work was notable for its originality. Hongell's *Aarne* series is an early example of the functional design of the post-war years. Wirkkala and Franck both started working for the company in 1946 after winning a glass competition, and the young Sarpaneva joined in 1950. Sarpaneva set a new trend with the *Finlandia* art-glass collection, which was blown in special wooden moulds. In 1990, following a decade of decline, Finland's independent glass manufacturers were absorbed by the **Hackman** group. Today Iittala functions as Hackman's design brand. Alongside such names as Oiva Toikka and the celebrated Kerttu Nurminen, such young designers as Annaleena Hakatie and **Harri Koskinen** are updating the collection. In recent years the company has also started working with various international guest designers, including **Konstantin Grcic**, **Alfredo Häberli** and **Marc Newson**.

242

1 *Aarne* glass series, 1948
2 *Aino Aalto* pressed glass series (formerly *Bölgeblick*), 1986 (1932 design)
3 *Gaissa* glasses, 1972
4 *Atlas* candlestick, 1996
5 *Aalto* vases (formerly *Savoy*), 1986 (1936 design)
6 *Halo* tealight holder, 2001
7 *Senta* glass series, 2000
8 Vase (*Claritas* collection), 1984

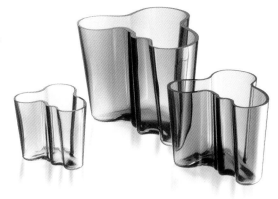

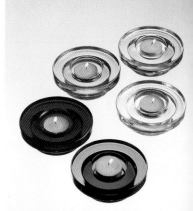

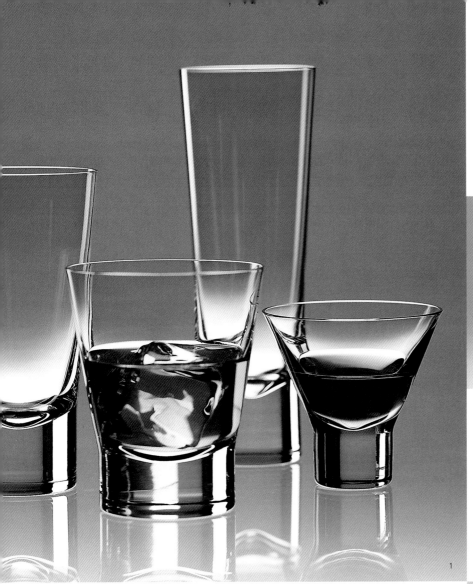

1

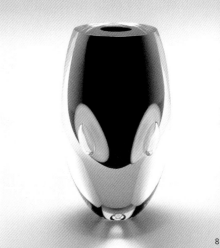

2

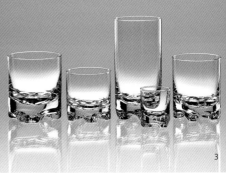

3

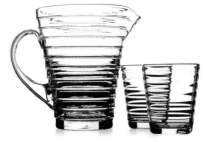

4

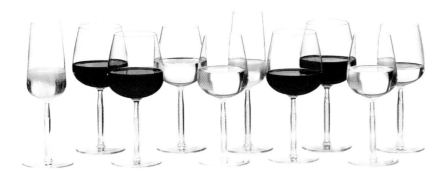

7

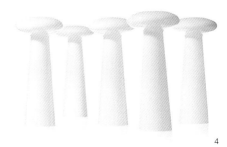

8

Ikea

Sweden I Ikea International A/S, Humlebæk I Furniture and accessories manufacturer I **www.ikea.com**

For Ikea the era of mattresses and wooden shelving did not end until the beginning of the 1980s. In the 1970s the company, today the largest furniture chain in the world, sold millions of pieces of basic furniture such as the *Ted* folding chair. It gradually transformed itself into a lifestyle brand that had a tremendous influence on popular taste, with products that were affordable for the majority of people. With a constant flow of new products and ranges and a comprehensive collection of fabrics and lamps, the blue-and-yellow giant progressed from hallways and children's rooms into living-rooms and bedrooms. At the same time, the quality of its products improved, and external designers were hired. One of the first was the Dane **Niels Gammelgaard** from **Pelikan Design**, who introduced a considerable number of designs. Products such as Gammelgaard's *Moment* sofa, as well as in-house designs such as Tomas Jelinek's *Stockholm* glass cabinet, typify the move away from provincial respectability to international modernity. For many years Ikea has been a genuine alternative for people who, to quote its advertising, "have more taste than money". In the 1990s the process of globalization moved at a furious pace, but there was also a return to Swedish traditions, the clearest expression of which was the *PS* furniture series launched by Stefan Ytterborn, **Thomas Eriksson** and **Thomas Sandell**.

1 *Moment* sofa, 1985
2 *Ilen* tea trolley, 2003
3 *PS* armchair, 1999
4 *Brum* child's seat, 2003
5 *Jules* swivel chair, 1998

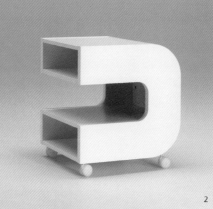

1

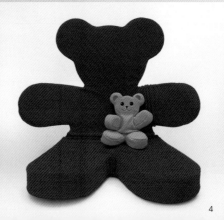

2

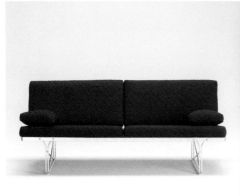

3

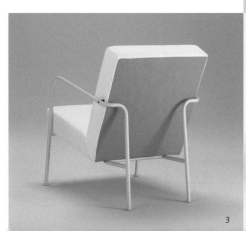

4

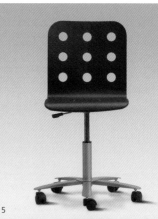

5

Inflate

England | Furniture and product design studio | **www.inflate.co.uk**

Take an idea from the 1950s and exaggerate it to such an extent that it becomes a trend – such is the basic premise of Inflate, the furniture and product design company that has made a success out of inflatable vinyl objects. Inflate's designers offer a surprisingly wide range of products – from vases, picture frames and fruit bowls to postcards. The collection also includes furniture and lamps, and even an eggcup (by ▶**Michael Sodeau**) that has almost achieved the status of a design classic. With these unusual objects the company seeks to create nothing less than "a popular, global brand that stands for originality, fun, functionality and affordable design and that makes everyday life more agreeable".

In the mid-1990s three young design graduates – Nick Crosbie and the brothers Mark and Michael Sodeau (Michael is no longer part of the team) – joined forces. They had attracted considerable attention with the designs they produced for their final college exams – furniture in the the style of lifebelts. When the well-known Italian company **Alessi** made the British newcomers an offer, they rejected it, as they wanted to remain independent. In the late 1990s, in order to create new, original products, they approached other designers to collaborate with them, including Steve Bretland, Mark Garside, **Michael Marriott** and **Michael Young**.

245

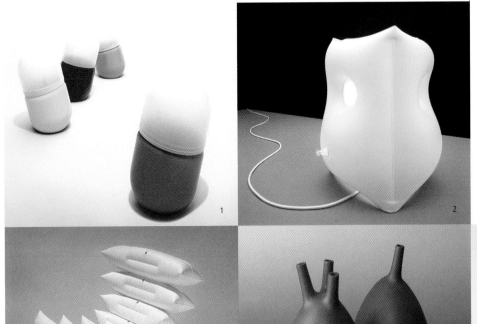

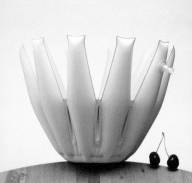

Interlübke

Germany I Gebr. Lübke GmbH & Co. KG, Rheda-Wiedenbrück I Furniture manufacturer I **www.interluebke.de**

Chance undoubtedly played a part in the emergence of Interlübke as one of Germany's limited number of furniture brands. The company was founded by the brothers Hans and Leo Lübke in the town of Wiedenbrück and specialized originally in polished bedroom furniture. Its first financial crisis came at the beginning of the 1960s, but it was rescued by the introduction of a single product – the 'endless cupboard' storage unit (known today as *SL*). The Swiss furniture designer Walter Müller and his office, Team Form, had developed a simple storage system that could be assembled from just a few parts. The base and the top were identical, and if the cupboard was turned 180 degrees, the top became the base. One cupboard could be added to another to form a series of wall units in which, for the first time, all the doors opened in the same direction. Since it extended from wall to wall and could be adapted according to individual circumstances, the system provided for an optimum use of space. Shelves, baskets and drawers offered additional storage within the cupboard. This product proved to be very successful for the company, and has since inspired many imitations.

The *Cube* and *Travo* cabinet systems, by **Werner Aisslinger** and **Rolf Heide** respectively, are typical Interlübke products. Both systems can either be stacked up or wall-mounted, as required. *Travo*'s internal units in aluminium or leather are easy to move or take out; its distinctive U-shaped handle is striking, and can be operated easily with one finger. Heide is also responsible for the modern, revised version of the *SL* storage system. Maintaining collaboration with designers helps the company ensure continuity in its product range. Thus Karl Odermatt and Franz Hero from the new Team Form designed both the *Aparo* walk-in storage system and the *Studimo* shelf system.

In the late 1990s Interlübke's poorly defined corporate profile and a disappointing balance sheet led to another crisis within the company. The internally illuminated *EO* storage system, developed by Wulf Schneider, was a response to this situation: the *EO* is an ingeniously designed light cube, with different colours that can be programmed and changed according to mood and environment.

246

1 *EO* storage system, 2001
2 Shelving (*Center* system), 1992
3 *Aparo* storage system (detail), 2000
4 *Cube* cabinet system, 2002
5 *SL* storage system, 1998
6 Cabinet (*Travo* system), 1998

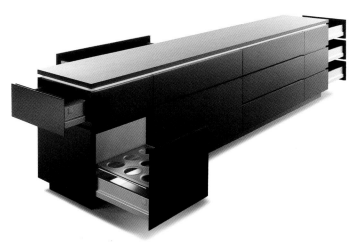

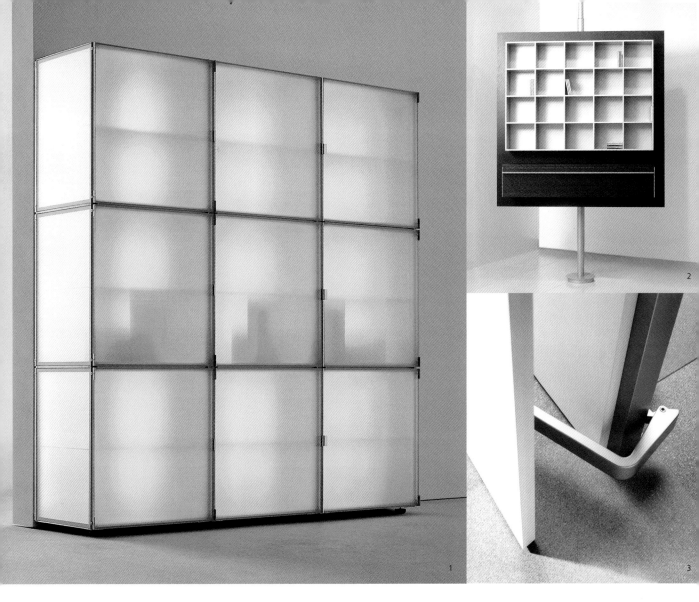

1

2

3

5

6

Massimo **Iosa Ghini**

Italy | Architect and furniture and product designer | **www.iosaghini.it**

Dynamic, curvilinear shapes are characteristic of almost all the products designed by Massimo Iosa Ghini, including his bathroom fittings for **Dornbracht**, sanitary ware for ▶**Duravit** and espresso machines for Tuttoespresso. Today the architect and designer, whose head office is in Bologna, advises many different companies on their product strategies and corporate identity. Although his primary focus is therefore not on objects, he nevertheless still has a preference for designing classic consumer goods. Iosa Ghini started out as a cartoon artist and then became involved in the design of studio sets for Italian television. His collaboration with the Memphis design group in 1986 proved to be a tremendous inspiration. Also at this time, he co-founded the Bolidismo movement with a group of like-minded architects and designers whose points of reference were Futurism, American streamlined forms and 1950s aesthetics. Curves, ellipses and flowing lines also characterized his *Dinamic* range in the mid-1980s, his first collection of upholstered furniture for ▶**Moroso**. Iosa Ghini still collaborates with Moroso and designs kitchens for Snaidero and furniture for Bonaldo. He has designed numerous showrooms for Fiorucci, **Renault**, **Ferrari**, Maserati and Omnitel.

248

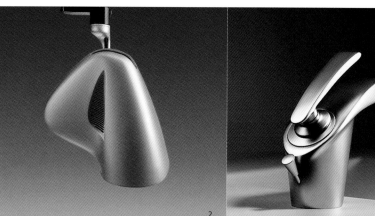

1

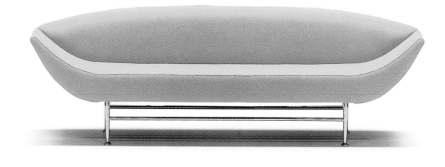

2

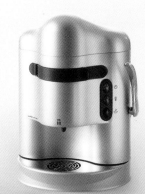

3   4

Isokon Plus

England | Isokon Plus, London | Furniture manufacturer | **www.isokonplus.com**

In the period between the two world wars, British furniture manufacturers still had a conservative approach to design. Isokon was the great exception. The company – directed by Jack Pritchard, and founded with his wife, Molly, and the architect Wells Coates – was poised to introduce modern furniture to the British market. Pritchard was conscious of the fact that the taste of British consumers was also very conservative, and he therefore decided on the use of bent plywood in the furniture rather than tubular steel. The designs were created by the German émigrés **Marcel Breuer** and **Walter Gropius**, Bauhaus teachers who were already internationally renowned. Breuer, in particular, was to design a considerable number of the products that are strongly associated with the Isokon brand, including a plywood version of his tubular steel chaise longue, a model reminiscent of designs by **Alvar Aalto**. The company resumed furniture production in the early 1960s, continuing its tradition of restrained functionalism with such products as the *Penguin Donkey* bookcase by Ernest Race, a redesign of Egon Riss's original from the 1930s. Windmill took over furniture production in the early 1980s. In more recent years, following a transformation in British taste, new designs by such contemporary talents as **Michael Sodeau** and **Barber Osgerby** have been added to the range to complement the collection of design classics.

1 Armchair by Marcel Breuer, 1936
2 *T 46* coffee table, 2001 (1946 design)
3 *Stretch Dining Table* pull-out table, 2002
4 *Penguin Donkey Mark 2* bookcase, 1963
5 *Shipshape* container, 2003

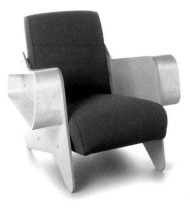

1

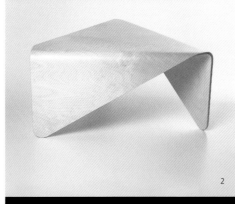

2

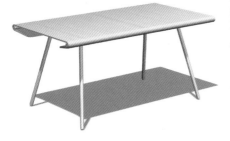

3

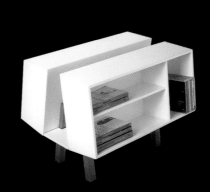

4

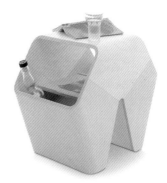

5

James **Irvine**

England/Italy | Furniture and product designer | **www.james-irvine.com**

James Irvine's varied portfolio includes glass objects for Egizia and a bus for **Mercedes-Benz**. Irvine is one of the multitalented industrial designers who have given Britain its reputation as 'the world's creative workshop'. He is, indeed, mainly active outside his own country, in Sweden and Germany, for example, and his list of clients includes such companies as **Thonet**, **Vitra**, **WMF** and **Artemide**.

After graduating from the Royal College of Art in London, Irvine moved to Italy. His first job was with **Olivetti** in Milan. He then lived in Tokyo for a while and worked for the electronics company Toshiba. Irvine returned to Italy in the late 1980s and later worked for several years as a partner in **Ettore Sottsass**'s studio – a period that was particularly formative as far as his career as a designer was concerned. When Irvine set up on his own in Milan in the late 1990s, he was able to look back on an impressive list of projects. Close co-operation with such leading Italian manufacturers as **Alessi**, **B&B Italia** and **Cappellini** (the *Progetto Oggetto* collection of which Irvine developed in collaboration with **Jasper Morrison**, a friend from his student days) encouraged him to give up his nomadic life and settle permanently in Italy.

Irvine is held in high esteem for his disciplined approach to design and is regarded as one of the most important, yet undogmatic, protagonists of the 'new simplicity'. This may also account for the fact that he has become one of the most sought-after designers in the world. While Irvine once stood in Morrison's shadow, in his more recent designs, such as a bus shelter for Ströer, he demonstrates stylistic independence. Above all, Irvine's work is characterized by its creative individuality, which he has achieved through a conscious use of colour and form. Irvine attracted much critical attention with his *A 660* chair for ▶ Thonet, which combines, for the first time, modern plastic mesh upholstery with a bentwood frame.

1958 Born in London

1978 Studies design at Kingston Polytechnic, Surrey

1981 Studies furniture design at Royal College of Art, London

1984 Works with **Michele De Lucchi** and **Ettore Sottsass** for **Olivetti** in Milan

1988 Opens own design studio

1993 Becomes partner at Sottsass Associati in Milan (until 1997)

1999 Exhibits at **Asplund**, Stockholm

2004 Elected Royal Designer for Industry

Products

1991 *Piceno* chair and table for **Cappellini**

1995 *Span* and *Archiver* shelving for **SCP**

1996 *Spider* armchair for Cappellini; *JI* sofa bed for CBI; *Tubo* chair for BRF

1998 *Lunar* sofa bed for **B&B Italia**; *Flik* chair for **Magis**; *Luigi* bottle opener/corkscrew for ▶ **Alfi**

1999 *Üstra* city bus for **Mercedes-Benz**; *Dozo* stacking trays for Marutomi

2000 *Float* hanging lamp for **Artemide**

2001 *Radar* armchair for B&B Italia; *One-Two* standard lamp for Artemide; *Earth* plant pots for **Arabia**; *Uno* collection of drinking glasses for WMF; *EB15* fax machine for Canon; *Centomila* table and chair for Magis; *Super Hook* coat hooks for **Danese**; *Sonia* chair for ▶ **Swedese**

2002 *X3* and *X4* tables for ▶ **Swedese**; *Lounge* bar accessories and *Il Meglio* kitchen utensils for ▶ **WMF**; *Hold It* box set for Danese

2003 *A 660* chair and *A 1660* table for ▶ **Thonet**; *Change* mirror for **Duravit**; *Hjälltön* armchair for **Ikea**

2004 *Era Ora* wall clock for ▶ Danese

250

1 *One-Two* standard lamp, 2001

2 *Super Hook* coat hooks, 2001

3 Grater (*Il Meglio* collection), 2002

4 *Earth* plant pots, 2001

5 *Lunar* sofa bed, 1998

6 *Hold It* box set, 2002

7 *Radar* armchair, 2001

8 *Centomila* chair, 2001

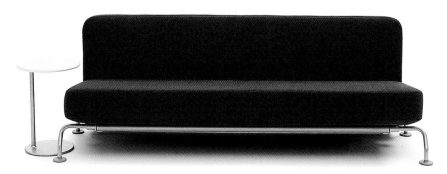

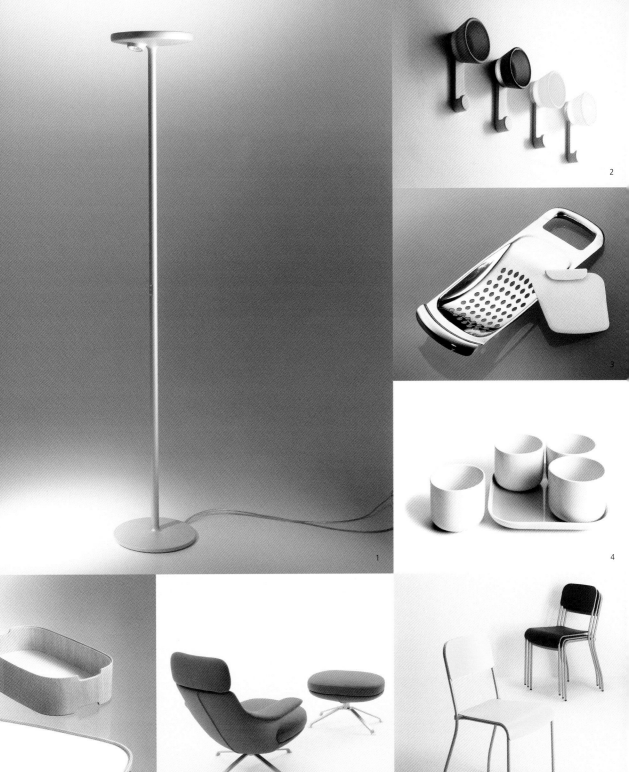

1

2

3

4

6

7

8

J

Hella Jongerius, *Groove* and *Longneck* vases, 2000

Hella Jongerius has consistently expanded the boundaries of ceramics. Among the new generation of Dutch designers, she is regarded as an alchemist, keen to experiment with new ideas. Her *Groove* and *Longneck* vases confirmed her reputation as an artist who manages to extract new properties from the materials she uses. The vases consist of a novel mixture of glass and porcelain.

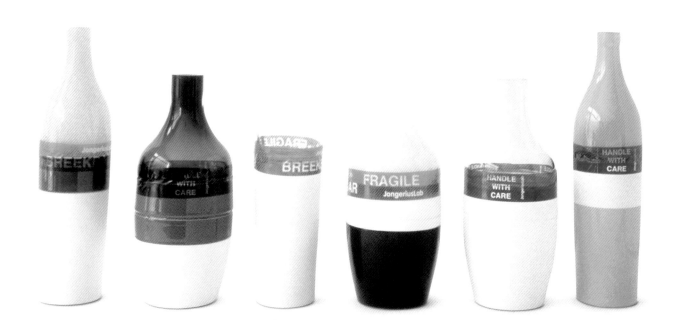

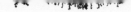

Jacob Jensen Design

Denmark I Product design studio I **www.jacob-jensen-design.dk**

Jacob Jensen's *Beogram 4000* – the first record player with tangential tracking – revolutionized turntable technology. There is nothing awkward or obtrusive in the appearance of this elegant cuboid: the silver-coloured plate is flush with the turntable casing; rubber supports radiate from the centre; the flush-mounted rectangular control pad is operated with a light touch of the fingertips. The turntables, radios and stereo systems designed by Jensen for **Bang & Olufsen** from the 1960s onwards did not resemble traditional appliances. Their sleek, immaculate surfaces conveyed the impression of absolute perfection. Jensen created a new species of audio equipment and in doing so, radically changed the idea of what such equipment should look like: his designs could be hung on walls or placed on a pedestal as icons of the Pop era.

As a young man, Jensen worked in his father's upholstery workshop. He attended the School of Applied Arts in Copenhagen, where his instructors included **Hans J. Wegner** and Jørn Utzon. After completing his studies, Jensen worked at the design office of Bernadotte & Bjørn. He was oblivious to the fact that **Sigvard Bernadotte** was the brother of Queen Ingrid of Denmark until she visited him at work one day. Jensen's foundation course in industrial design, his experience in dealing with professional clients, and the long time he spent in the United States during the 1950s, all helped to transform the boy from the suburbs of Copenhagen into a designer of worldwide renown. When the Museum of Modern Art (MoMA) exhibited twenty-eight of Jensen's designs for hi-fi equipment in the late 1970s, the *New York Times* wrote that he deserved to be considered one of the great industrial designers of the twentieth century. Today Jensen's design office is a family enterprise, managed by his son Timothy. The casual synthesis of utility and elegance is still a successful formula, as the vacuum cleaner for Nilfisk, kitchen appliances for **Gaggenau** and a towering wind turbine on the Danish coast demonstrate. The Jensens emphatically reject the notion that their designs have a particular style: "It is all about the ability to think", says Timothy Jensen. "It is the idea that is of interest."

1926 Jacob Jensen born in Vesterbro, Copenhagen

1951 Graduates from School of Applied Arts, Copenhagen; works at Bernadotte & Bjørn (from 1954, head of studio)

1958 Opens own studio

1963 Works for **Bang & Olufsen**, product and design strategy (until 1991)

1978 *Bang & Olufsen: Design for Sound by Jacob Jensen* exhibition held at MoMA, New York; son Timothy Jensen joins company (director since 1991)

Products

1950 *Margrethe* plastic bowls for Rosti (with ► **Sigvard Bernadotte**)

1967 *Beovox 2500* loudspeaker

1970 *Beomaster 1200* receiver; *Beomic 2000* microphone

1971 *Beolit 400* portable radio

1972 *Beogram 4000* record player

1974 *Beomaster 2000*

All for ► **Bang & Olufsen**

1979 *Comet* telephone handset for Alcatel

1988 Wristwatch

1989 *Beocenter 9000* hi-fi system for Bang & Olufsen

1990 *Beosystem 6500* hi-fi system for Bang & Olufsen

1992 *Quintessence* glasses for Rodenstock; *GM 200* vacuum cleaner for Nilfisk; *XM* concept car for **Citroën**; *EB 900* built-in oven for **Gaggenau**

1993 Desk for Boform

1994 *EB 100* oven for Gaggenau; *T-3* telephone for DRS Electronics

1995 Wind turbine for Nordtank/NEG

1999 *Weather Station* series

2000 *Vario 200* modular cooktop series for ► Gaggenau (with H. Reinhard Segers)

2002 *Linear* and *Symbolic* jewellery series

1 *Beogram 4000* record player, 1972
2 Citroën *XM* concept car, 1992
3 Alarm clock (*Weather Station* series), 1999
4 Desk, 1993
5 *Beocenter 9000* hi-fi system, 1989
6 *EB 900* built-in oven, 1992
7 *T-3* telephone, 1994
8 *Beolit 400* portable radio, 1971

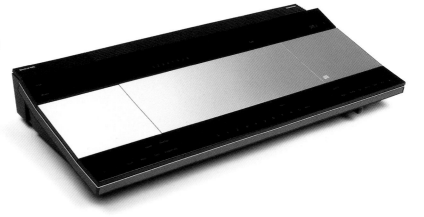

5

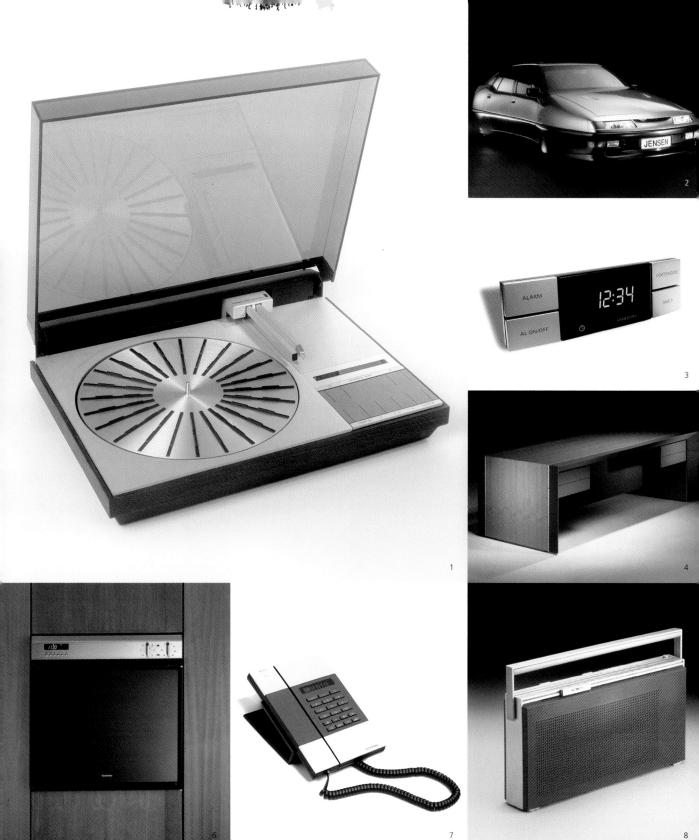

Arne **Jacobsen**

Denmark I Architect and furniture and product designer I **www.arne-jacobsen.com**

Arne Jacobsen first achieved international recognition in the early 1950s with his design for the Søholm development of terraced houses in Klampenborg. The project represented a laid-back, Modernist style that was regarded as typically Scandinavian. Around this time Jacobsen was also working on a chair made from plywood, a material he had used before the Second World War in seats for cinemas. In order to ensure that his design was not too similar to the moulded-plywood chairs designed by **Charles and Ray Eames**, he had a model sent to him for comparison from the United States. Jacobsen's *Ant* chair was a stroke of genius. Its design was a clear rejection of the conventions of Danish furniture, which were rooted in traditional craftsmanship, as well as of the austere functionalism of the pre-war period. It was also the one of the first chairs that was suitable for mass production. *Ant* consisted of just two main components – the seat and the legs – and an additional connecting element. This simplicity, together with the minimal use of materials, made it extremely economical. Yet the chair's design was considered so avant garde that the manufacturer **Fritz Hansen** was initially sceptical as to whether it would lend itself to mass production. In fact, well over five million *Ant* chairs have been sold since production began in the early 1950s. (However, Jacobsen, a purist, would doubtless not have approved of the fact that the chair was later produced in a variety of colours.) In the mid-1950s Jacobsen repeated the successful concept with the slightly more robust *Series 7* model. This light, stackable chair is to be found in seminar rooms, dining-rooms and cafés around the world.

In the late 1950s Jacobsen realized his largest project – the SAS Royal Hotel in Copenhagen, for which he designed everything, from the building itself to sofas and bathroom taps. The most spectacular designs of that period were his curved armchairs: *Egg*, *Swan*, *Drop* and *Pot*. According to **Knud Holscher**, a former member of his staff, Jacobsen "designed chairs in the same way that Matisse painted his pictures – in a free, playful manner". The introduction of an abstract design vocabulary into Jacobsen's work is reminiscent of **Alvar Aalto**. Like Aalto, Jacobsen created most of his objects for particular building projects, and they were largely designed during a short productive period. His products sold well, proving his critics wrong. Jacobsen received a significant number of commissions in the 1960s. The *Cylinda Line* series from that period was based on a concept by ▶ **Stelton**.

256

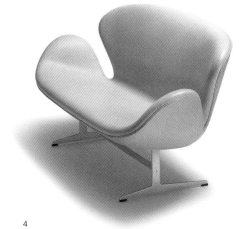

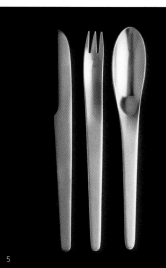

4

5

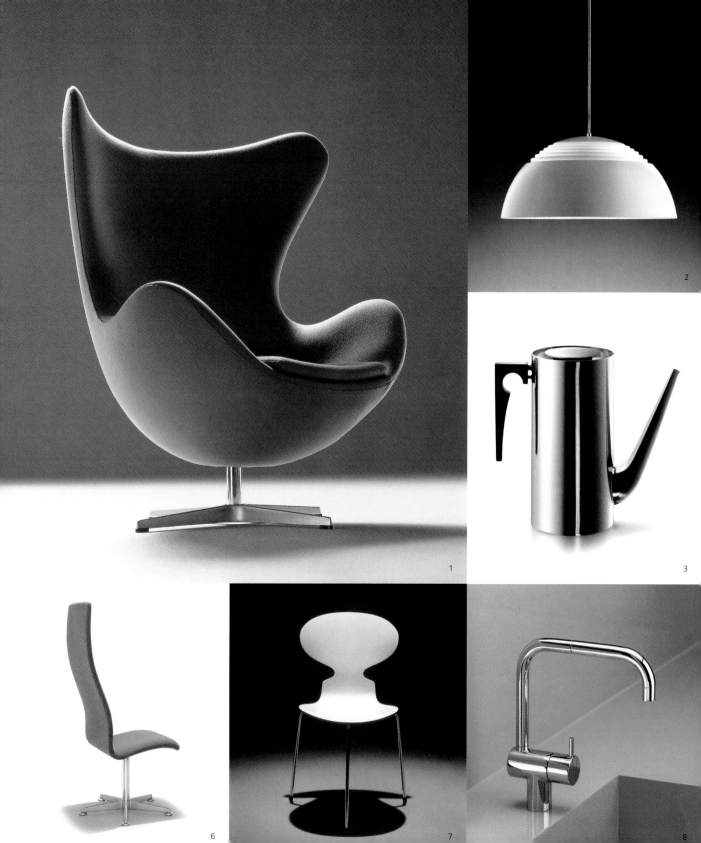

1

2

3

6

7

8

Jaguar

England | Jaguar Cars Ltd, Coventry | Automobile manufacturer | **www.jaguar.com**

The *XK 120* sports car reached a mind-boggling speed of 193 kph (120 mph) and was the star of the London Motor Show in 1948. The car's success was due largely to its unitary chassis, unbroken line and protruding headlights. This was not the first time that Jaguar had made the headlines. Established as the Swallow Sidecar Company, it had earned a place alongside Aston Martin, MG and Morgan as one of Britain's most prestigious sports car manufacturers before the Second World War. It sold its cars initially under the SS logo, but this subsequently became unusable because of its Nazi connotations. Its international debut came in the mid-1930s with the *SS 100* model, characterized by a flat and extremely elongated bonnet and elegantly curved wings. The two-seater, with its legendary robust six-cylinder engine, was designed for rallies, and for this reason the headlights were protected with wire mesh.

The marque achieved cult status with the *E-Type*, a slender sports car from the early 1960s that included the novel feature of headlights that were integrated into the chassis. The headlights of the *C-Type* racing car, from a decade earlier, were protected by a Plexiglas cover. The *C-Type*'s aerodynamic body, in the 'organic' style of the period, was designed by Malcolm Sayer, who had previously worked in the aircraft industry. In subsequent years Jaguar gradually ceased to be associated with speed records and exciting styling, and turned to traditional British design, with the result that a series of somewhat nondescript models was produced. Since the company was taken over by Ford, however, Jaguar has rediscovered its old qualities and attempted to revive the former glory of its motor sports era. It has returned to the Formula One circuit, where the cream of racing car manufacturers compete with each other. Hopes of renewed success were pinned on the sleek *XK8* sports car and, above all, on the *S-Type*, a completely new sports saloon: the car's elongated shape emanates dynamism, an impression emphasized by such details as the tapering bulges on the bonnet, which take the rounded form of the headlights. The design harks back to the styling of the 1950s and 1960s and appeals to a young, well-heeled clientele; it is also the official car for members of the British government.

1922 Swallow Sidecar Company established
1945 Jaguar Cars Ltd established by William Lyons
1951 Achieves first of seven victories at Le Mans 24-hour race
1966 Merges with British Motor Corporation
1984 Company privatized; Geoff Lawson becomes chief designer
1988 **Ford** takes over company
1999 Ian Callum becomes chief designer (also at **Aston Martin**); establishes Advanced Design Team
2000 Returns to Formula One racing

Products
1935 *SS 100* roadster
1948 *XK 120* roadster
1951 *C-Type* racing car
1954 *XK 140* roadster
1955 *D-Type* racing car
1956 *MKI* saloon
1958 *XK 150* roadster
1961 *E-Type* coupé and roadster; *MK10* saloon
1968 *XJ6* saloon
1972 *XJ12* saloon
1974 *E-Type Series III V12* roadster
1979 *XJ* saloon by **Pininfarina**
1996 *XK8* coupé and convertible
1999 *S-Type* saloon
2000 *F-Type* roadster (concept) by Geoff Lawson
2001 *R-Coupé* (concept) by Julian Thomson and Matthew Beaven
2003 *XJ6* and *XJ12* saloon
2004 *X-Type* estate; *XJ LWB* saloon

1 *S-Type* saloon (detail), 1999
2 *R-Coupé* (concept), 2001
3 *F-Type* roadster (concept), 2000
4 *XK8* coupé, 1996
5 *E-Type* coupé, 1961
6 *C-Type* racing car, 1951
7 *XJ LWB* saloon, 2004

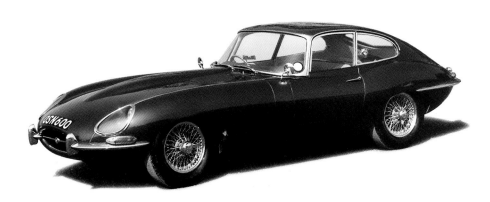

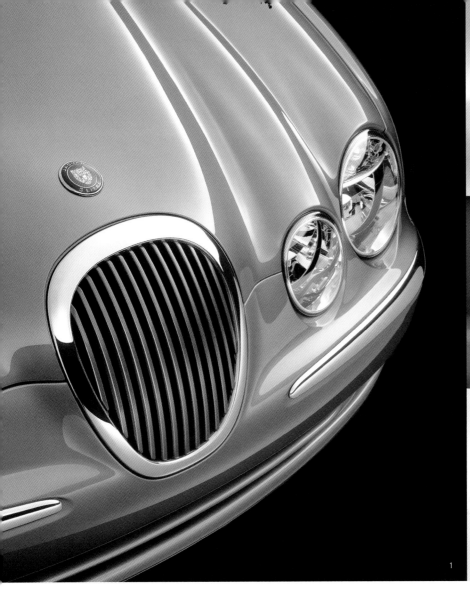

1

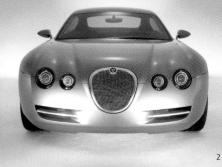

2

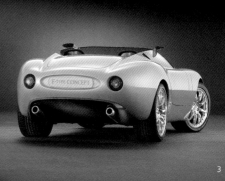

3

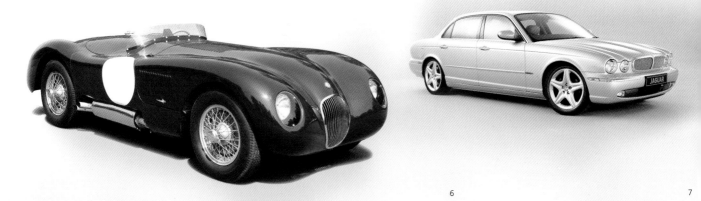

4

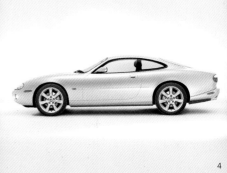

6

7

Hella **Jongerius**

The Netherlands | Product and furniture designer | **www.jongeriuslab.com**

The workshop of the Dutch designer Hella Jongerius conjures up images of an alchemist's secret laboratory: shelves are laden with boxes, jars, materials and tools, all of which give an impression of creative order. Experimentation with different materials, objects and techniques forms the basis of Jongerius's work, so it therefore makes complete sense that the word 'lab' (short for 'laboratory') has been added to the end of her company name. The results of Jongerius's experiments are a pleasure to look at and to touch. The idea of breaking away from visual and tactile expectations has been a major feature of her work since such early products as the *Urn* vase and a washbasin made of silicon, both of which are sold through ▶ **Droog Design**. Jongerius undertakes meticulous research, provokes debates on the environment and, quite effortlessly (or so it seems), develops unconventional solutions. Among her original designs are a traditional African three-legged chair, which she combines with the distinctly high-tech materials neoprene and carbon fibre, and the *My Soft Office* installation at the Museum of Modern Art (MoMA) in New York – an extreme interpretation of the home office. Thanks to her productive curiosity, Jongerius has a reputation as one of the most innovative designers in Europe.

260

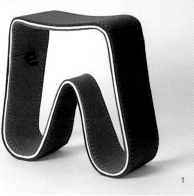

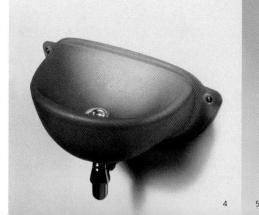

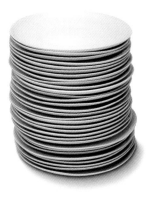

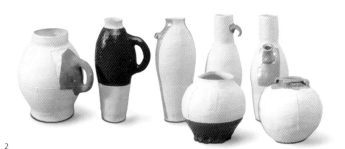

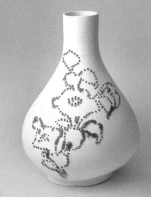

1   2

3   4   5

Patrick **Jouin**

France | Furniture and product designer | www.patrickjouin.com

The flexible spatula that Patrick Jouin designed specifically for jars of Nutella hazelnut spread is an ideal tool for anyone with a sweet tooth. Jouin's product designs are always characterized by *esprit* and elegance. The same is true of his furniture, which demonstrates the young designer's talent for developing distinctive forms that have a particularly sensual quality, as in his *Mabelle* chair, which softly enfolds the human body and is supported by a delicate tubular frame. The leading Italian manufacturer **Cassina** is among Jouin's most notable clients.

After graduating from the Ecole Nationale Supérieure de Création Industrielle (ENSCI) in Paris, Jouin followed a similar career path to **Matali Crasset**: in the early 1990s he started working for Tim Thom, the design department of the French electronics company Thomson, where he gained considerable practical experience under the professional guidance of **Philippe Starck**. He then worked for Starck's studio for some time before setting up on his own. As well as creating toys, household goods, furniture and interior designs, all of which have attracted considerable public attention, Joiun is active as a car designer for **Renault**. He has also designed several motor shows in collaboration with Imaad Rahmouni.

1967	Born in Nantes
1992	Graduates from ENSCI, Paris; works for Compagnie des Wagons-Lits
1993	Joins Tim Thom, design department of Thomson
1995	Works at studio of **Philippe Starck**
1998	Opens own studio

Products

1999	*Wave* service for Alain Ducasse
2000	*CuteCut* sofa for Moderno
2002	*Fol.D* folding chair for XO
2003	*Kami* sofa, *Rond* container, *Lebeau* table and *Mabelle* chair for **Cassina**; *Nutella* spatula/spoon; *Tagine* bowl for Vallauris
2004	*D.I.Vox* radio and *D.I.Math* calculator for Lexon

1 *Mabelle* chair, 2003
2 *Nutella* spatula/spoon, 2003
3 *Wave* service, 1999
4 *Lebeau* table, 2003

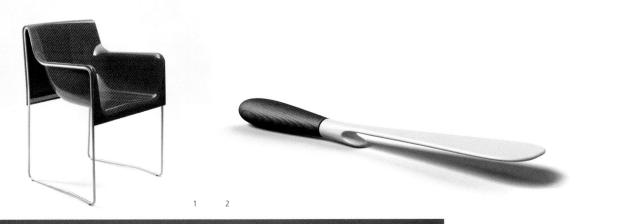

1 2

261

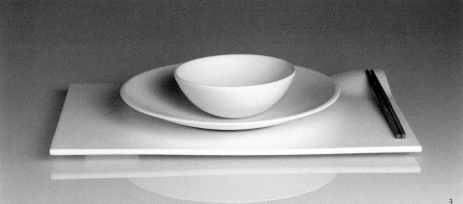

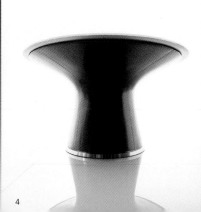

3 4

K

Knoll, Wire table, 1966

In the mid-1960s the American designer Warren Platner felt that there was "room for the kind of decorative, gentle, graceful design that appeared in the period style of Louis XV". In a range of models with frames that consisted of a large number of parallel steel wires, he attempted a twentieth-century reinterpretation of the design style of the *ancien régime*. Although the principle itself was simple, the furniture proved time-consuming and expensive to manufacture. The highlight of the collection was the dining table, one of a series of dining tables and low tables Platner designed for Knoll in the 1960s.

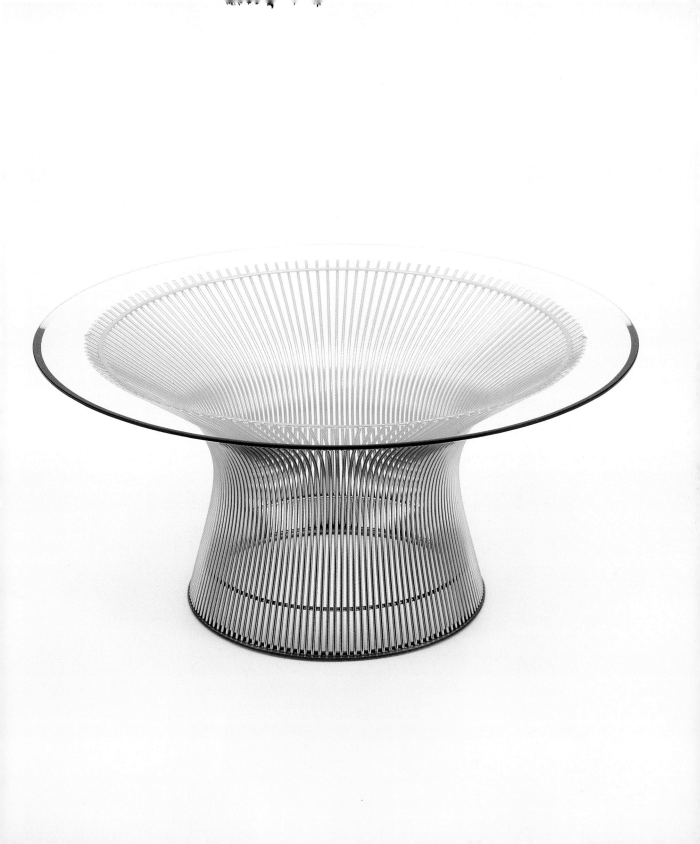

Källemo

Sweden I Källemo A/B, Värnamo I Furniture manufacturer I **www.kallemo.se**

Småland is one of the most austere areas in Sweden, and its inhabitants are often depicted as shrewd and careful with money. The region is also notable as being the cradle of the Swedish furniture industry: it is not only where the furniture giant **Ikea** started business, but also where the counteroffensive was launched by Källemo, one of the most unconventional furniture manufacturers north of the Alps. Sven Lundh, founder of the company, regarded furniture not just as a commodity, but also as a work of art. His ideas were met with scepticism in the industry and were considered almost sacrilegious in a land in which functionalism was so highly prized. Nevertheless, Lundh – art connoisseur, owner of an art gallery and active in the field of business administration – succeeded in creating a haven for unorthodox design in the harsh climate of the furniture industry. His models, which are produced in small editions, represent the antithesis of "anything that is mass-produced, faceless and anonymous". The company's product range includes re-editions of furniture by Gunnar Asplund and **Bruno Mathsson**, Sweden's leading furniture designers.

Källemo initiated a new era in Swedish furniture design. The *Concrete* chair by ▸**Jonas Bohlin**, dating from 1980, marked a revolutionary change, although today it is difficult to understand how this delicate piece of furniture could have caused such a tremendous stir. The company's furniture range is evocative of an art collection. Co-operation with a large number of highly original designers, among them **Mats Theselius**, means that its catalogue comprises such unusual showpieces as a chair design based on a motorbike built in India. Many of the designs have a poetic quality and subvert our traditional way of looking at objects: Sigurdur Gustafsson's *Take Away* lamp, which takes the form of a carrier bag, is nothing less than a metaphor that produces light; the books on John Kandell's *Pilaster* shelf are sloping; the *Gute* chair by Mattias Ljunggren is in vibrant orange. Needless to say, these objects set out deliberately to cause confusion. Lundh is convinced that "the things that are really important have always been met with a lack of appreciation in their time". However, Källemo's programme is not just about originality for originality's sake. The *Non* chair, for example, is not only a fascinatingly simple design, but is also robust and extremely versatile.

264

1 *Non* rubber chair, 2000
2 *Take Away* hanging lamp, 2000
3 *Nonting* chaise longue, 1987
4 *Window* shelf, 1995
5 *Chaise Longue*, 1992
6 *Pall Asplund* chair, 1930
7 *Gute* chair, 1998
8 *Puma* chair, 1996
9 *Rex* armchair, 1995

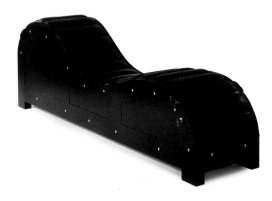

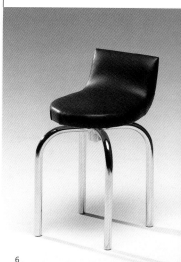

5

6

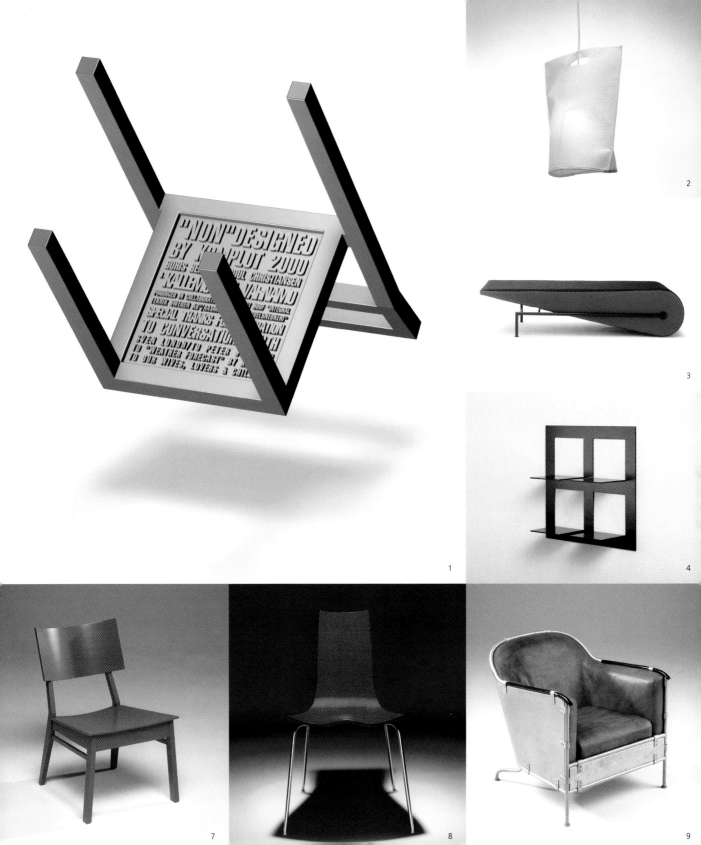

"NON" DESIGNED
BY KOMPLOT 2000
BORIS BER... ...OUL CHRISTIANSEN
L'KALLEVIG ...VARNAVO
PRODUCED IN COLLABORATION... ...FRNIK ...
PERNIK ...OTSEN AFTERNOON... ...RUNS "INTEGRAL
SPECIAL THANKS FO... ...RATION
TO CONVERSATION... ...ITH
SVEN LORENTO PETER S... ...
TO "WEATHER FORECAST" BY ...
TO OUR WIVES, LOVERS & CHIL...

1

2

3

4

7

8

9

Kartell

Italy | Kartell SpA, Noviglio | Manufacturer of plastic furniture and accessories | **www.kartell.it**

The Italian manufacturer Kartell owes its tremendous commercial success to plastic, which for many years was regarded as an inferior material. The company made a major contribution to the re-evaluation of the material, to the extent that it now enjoys equal status with other materials – a fact that has been of great financial benefit to such companies as **Authentics** and **Heller**. Kartell has been leading the plastics revolution since the 1950s. Household goods that were previously considered boring and bland were transformed by bold splashes of colour from the company's chief designer, Gino Colombini, who was awarded numerous prizes for stylish lemon squeezers, rubbish bins and other kitchen utensils. By the beginning of the 1960s, the plastic materials that had been developed were so strong that it became possible to use them in the production of furniture. The stackable, weatherproof *K 4999* child's chair made of polyethylene, by **Marco Zanuso** and **Richard Sapper**, is a pioneering example that heralded the decade of plastic furniture. Kartell undertook research in its own laboratories, enabling designers to develop their creations using a variety of new, patented materials. Among these designers were the stars of the Italian design scene, including **Joe Colombo**, Gae Aulenti, **Vico Magistretti**, **Anna Castelli Ferrieri**, Ignazio Gardella, **Achille Castiglioni**, Giotto Stoppino and Sergio Asti. They produced many classic designs. The *4867* stackable chair by ▶Colombo is, for example, one of the company's long-runners. Numerous designs by ▶Castelli Ferrieri (Kartell's artistic director for many years), such as her *4970/84* container units, which can be assembled without bolts and catches, are still in production today. ▶**Philippe Starck**'s radical *La Marie* and *Dr No* chairs, ▶Magistretti's *Maui* chair, **Ron Arad**'s *Bookworm* shelf, ▶**Antonio Citterio**'s *Mobil* container trolley and Ferruccio Laviani's *Take* table lamp are among the many other successful designs that have contributed to Kartell's image as a designer label for affordable products. Since the late 1980s Claudio Luti, originally from the fashion industry, has managed the company and turned it into an international brand. Kartell's success lies, in part, in its combining of two apparently disparate worlds: technological invention and industrial design on the one hand, and, on the other, the world of fashion, where the concept of collections plays an important role.

266

1949	Established by chemical engineer Giulio Castelli in Milan
1953	Produces small household objects
1958	Establishes Labware division
1964	Experiments with furniture
1972	Relocates to Noviglio, near Milan
1988	Giulio Castelli leaves company; Claudio Luti becomes chairman

Products

1953	Thermos by Gino Colombini
1959	Colander by Gino Colombini
1964	*K 4999* child's chair by **Marco Zanuso** and **Richard Sapper**
1967	*4970/84* container units by **Anna Castelli Ferrieri**
1968	*4867* chair by ▶ **Joe Colombo**
1971	Magazine rack by Giotto Stoppino
1976	Plastic salad set
1979	*4822/44* barstool
1983	*4310* table
1986	*4873* plastic chair
	Last four by ▶ Anna Castelli Ferrieri
1989	*Dr Glob* chair by **Philippe Starck**
1994	*Mobil* container trolley by **Antonio Citterio** and Glen Oliver Löw; *Bookworm* shelf by ▶ **Ron Arad**
1996	*Dr No* chair by ▶ Philippe Starck
1997	*Maui* chair collection by ▶ **Vico Magistretti**
1998	*Ero(S)* chair by Philippe Starck; *FPE* chair by Ron Arad
1999	*La Marie* chair by Philippe Starck; *One* shelf system by ▶ **Patricia Urquiola** and **Piero Lissoni**
2001	*Bubble* furniture collection by Philippe Starck; *LCP* plastic chair by ▶ **Maarten van Severen**
2002	*Louis Ghost* chair by Philippe Starck; *Spoon* stool by Antonio Citterio
2003	*Take* table lamp by Ferruccio Laviani

1 *Take* table lamp, 2003

2 *FPE* chair, 1998

3 *Bubble* armchair, 2001

4 Colander, 1959

5 *K 4999* child's chair, 1964

6 *4970/84* container units, 1967

7 *Ero(S)* chair, 1998

8 *Bookworm* shelf, 1994

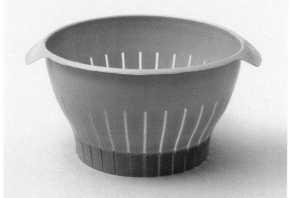

4

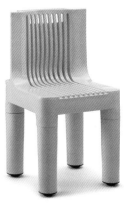

5

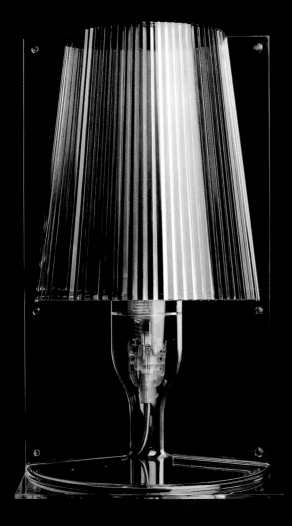

1

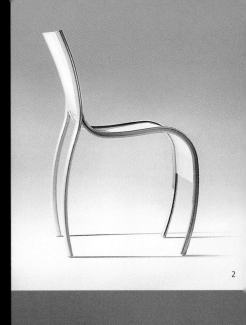

2

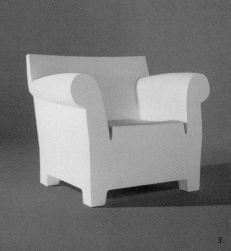

3

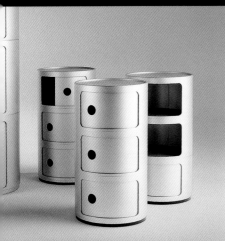

6

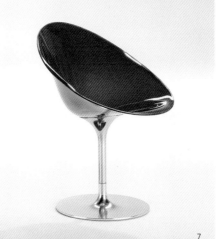

7

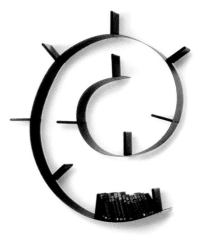

8

Kazuo **Kawasaki**

Japan | Product designer

It is rare that an industrial designer is awarded a doctorate in medicine for the development of a particular product. However, the eminent Japanese designer Kazuo Kawasaki was honoured with this prestigious academic degree for his pioneering work on the design of artificial hearts. He has also been an exceptional figure in the fields of teaching, research and practical work, and has received numerous international design awards. Kawasaki's career began in the early 1970s in the design department of the electronics giant Toshiba, where he learned the importance of precision. He subsequently established a studio in the vicinity of a craftsmen's village. Japanese cultural traditions are an important focus of his work. The knives of the *Artus* series, made from one single piece of steel, and without the traditional wooden handle, were one of his early successes and have made the Japanese kitchen knife almost as famous as the Samurai sword. His circular egg timers, with their small display windows and grooved edges, are a lesson in concentration on the essential. Kawasaki, who is himself physically disabled as the result of a car accident, caused a sensation in the late 1980s when he presented his collapsible *Carna* wheelchair, which has a tubular titanium frame and weighs as little as 20 kilograms (44 lb).

1949 Born in Fukui City
1972 Graduates from Kanazawa College of Art; joins design department of Toshiba
1981 Establishes Kazuo Kawasaki Design Studio in Fukui
1985 Establishes ex-Design
1996 Lectures at Nagoya University
1999 Receives doctorate in medicine for work on design of artificial hearts

Products
1983 *Artus* knife collection for Takefu Knife Village
1984 *Clipeus* loud speakers for Maruichi Trading Company
1985 *X & I* scissors for Takefu Knife Village
1989 *Carna* wheelchair for SIG Workshop
1993 Clock; *Cano* egg timer
1996 *CRT FlexScan* monitor for Eizo
1997 *LCD FlexScan* monitor for Eizo

1 *Carna* wheelchair, 1989
2 *Artus* knife collection, 1983
3 *LCD FlexScan* monitor, 1997
4 *Cano* egg timer, 1993
5 Clock, 1993

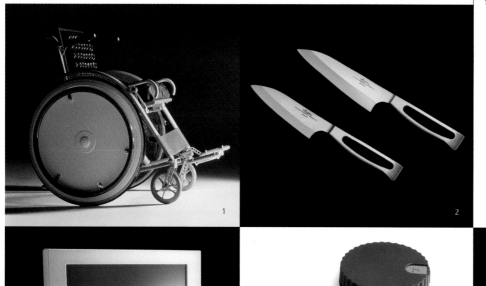

268

King-Miranda Associati

Italy | Furniture and product design studio | **www.kingmiranda.com**

In the mid-1970s Perry A. King and Santiago Miranda set up a studio together in Milan, the design capital of Europe. Since that time, the design duo (King is English, Miranda Spanish) have developed their projects in close collaboration. They design not only products, furniture and lamps, but also services, communications and exhibitions. Their client list features such manufacturers as **Olivetti**, **Ericsson**, **Flos** and **Baleri Italia**. For Baleri Italia they designed *Lisa*, an unpretentious, mass-produced stackable chair that is convincing down to the very smallest detail. King-Miranda places emphasis on its client's success; in other words, the designers' main focus is not on themselves or on the development of their own image through stylistically identifiable designs. It came as a surprise to the industry when the renowned Danish lamp manufacturer **Louis Poulsen** entrusted the two non-Scandinavian designers with the development of an outdoor lamp. King-Miranda has a successful track record designing lamps, and its unpretentious, elegant *Jill* standard lamp (for Flos), dating from 1979, is still a bestseller. The interface the company designed for Olivetti received considerable praise in the 1980s. The studio undoubtedly profited from King's experience working for Olivetti in the 1960s and 1970s, when he designed the bright red *Valentine* portable typewriter and helped develop the company's corporate identity.

1974 Perry A. King and Santiago Miranda write *Typeface Design,* a manifesto for **Olivetti**

1976 King and Miranda establish studio in Milan

1978 Work shown at *Design Process Olivetti 1908–1978* exhibition, Los Angeles

1980 Corporate identity for Arteluce

1983 Interfaces for Olivetti office machines

1984 Interior of Sogno A disco in Tokyo

1990 Establishes EDEN (European Designers Network)

Products

1978 *Donald* table lamp for Arteluce

1979 *Jill* standard lamp for **Flos**

1986 *Beato* armchair for Disform

1990 *Sedia N* chair for Atelier International

1995 Mobile telephones for **Ericsson**

1996 *Tam Tam* lamp for Sirrah; *Borealis* outdoor light for **Louis Poulsen**

1999 *Diogenes* standard lamp for ▶ **Belux**

2001 *Lisa* stackable chair for **Baleri Italia**

2003 *Luxit* lamp collection for Luxo Italiana; *KM 501* office furniture collection for IB Office

1 *Borealis* outdoor light, 1996
2 *KM 501* office furniture collection, 2003
3 *Lisa* stackable chair, 2001
4 Wall lamp (*Luxit* collection), 2003

269

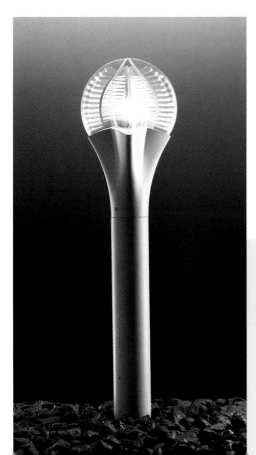

2

3

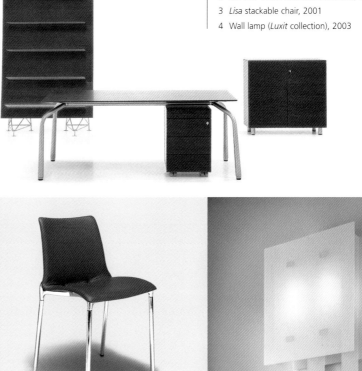

4

Rodney **Kinsman**

England | Furniture designer

The work of the British furniture designer Rodney Kinsman ranges from Pop art to designs for public seating. The *F Range* armchair was produced in the swinging sixties, at the beginning of his career. The chair has a shimmering vinyl cover that gives the appearance of being wet, and, despite its graphically simple structure, it could well serve as an eye-catching prop for a film set. Kinsman's bestselling *Omkstak* stackable chair was created six years later and is also characterized by clear lines and a high degree of functionality. Some of its details are typical of Pop art, such as the punched-out holes in the seat and backrest.

After graduating from the Central School of Arts and Crafts in London, Kinsman, together with Jerzy Olejnik and Bryan Morrison, founded the OMK design studio. Before long, OMK became a specialist in furnishing public spaces. The studio was commissioned to design interior fittings for British Rail trains and seats for Gatwick Airport. Kinsman presented *Seville*, a robust yet elegant aluminium bench, for the British Pavilion at *Expo '92* in the Spanish city of the same name. The seating system has a restrained, slightly surgical style reminiscent of furniture designs by the leading British designer Norman Foster (of **Foster and Partners**). The *Vienna* tubular steel chair and *Graffiti*, a slanting coat rack and shelf system, both clearly exhibit Kinsman's rationalism.

270

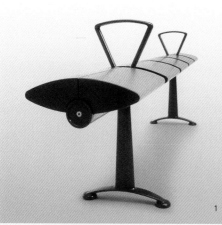

1

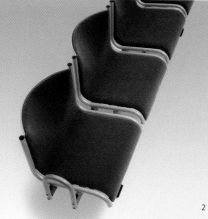

2

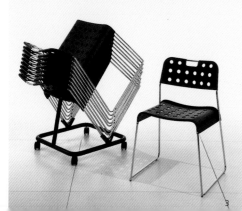

3

4

5

Toshiyuki **Kita**

Japan /Italy | Furniture and product designer | **www.toshiyukikita.com**

Toshiyuki Kita's famous *Wink* chair resembles a cartoon character. However, it is not the chair's Pop colour scheme or its zoomorphic form that make it extraordinary. Kita designed *Wink* as a highly versatile piece of furniture that is always comfortable, whether it is used for sitting, lying or kneeling on. The ten years of hard work that went into the design were not in vain: the different elements of the chair – for example, the headrests – can be folded in various ways and can thus be adapted to different moods and situations.

Like other Japanese designers of his generation, Kita went to Italy, the world's design Mecca, to study architecture. There he collaborated with Giotto Stoppino, **Mario Bellini** and others before he opened his own design studio. In the late 1980s he designed the *On Taro* and *On Giro* tables with the artist Keith Haring from the United States. Such renowned manufacturers as **Moroso**, **Magis**, **Wittmann** and **Cassina** bought more of his designs, which combine poignant wit with a return to Japanese traditions. The *Dodo* chair (for ▸ Cassina) and the *Hop* furniture collection (for ▸ Wittmann) are among Kita's most famous pieces. In his *Kyo* series of lamps (for **iGuzzini**) the cosmopolitan designer offers a reinterpretation of traditional handcrafted lanterns made from hand-dipped paper. Kita has offices in Osaka and Milan, and in the last few years has focused increasingly on architectural projects.

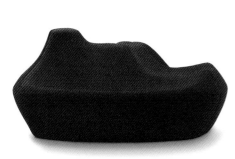

1

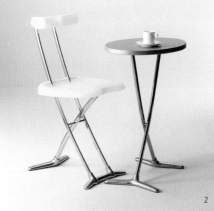

2

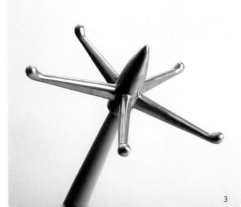

3

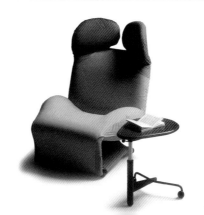

4

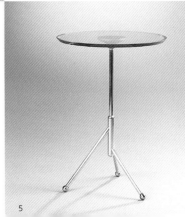

5

Poul **Kjærholm**

Denmark | Furniture designer | **www.kjaerholmproduction.dk**

The 1950s were a golden era for Danish furniture, and design experts agree that it was Poul Kjærholm who was largely responsible for maintaining the furniture industry's good reputation throughout the following decade. Kjærholm was without doubt a designer of exceptional talent. Always remaining true to his principles, he worked exclusively for E. Kold Christensen, whose company was later taken over by **Fritz Hansen**. Unlike the furniture of many other designers, Kjærholm's pieces were almost exclusively created for mass production, despite the fact that he had started his career as an apprentice in a cabinet-maker's workshop. He shared his belief in the benefits of mass production with his contemporary **Arne Jacobsen**, with whom he had otherwise very little in common. While Jacobsen was keen to improvise, Kjærholm always followed a clear and decisive plan: his designs were based on experiments, were coherent down to the smallest detail and distinguished themselves by their clarity of concept and honest construction, which concealed nothing.

Kjærholm started experimenting with aluminium, wire and other unusual materials at a very early stage in his career. A combination he often used was a steel frame with a covering of natural material such as leather, wicker or a textile for the seat. An example is the *PK 24* chaise longue, which has a frame of chrome-plated steel and a woven cane seat – a delicate structure with sweeping lines and a silhouette that is reduced to a single stroke. A close examination of the design details does not destroy the positive overall impression: The seat is not welded to the frame, but held in position by elegant clamps. The *PK 61* coffee table is equally striking and unusual. The staggered position of the legs, visible through the rectilinear glass top, lends the table a highly original appearance. This design can be regarded as a development of the glass table by **Ludwig Mies van der Rohe**, who inspired many of Kjærholm's designs. An early piece of furniture is the *PK 0* chair, which, much like a Saab design from the same period, radiates the dynamism of the optimistic post-war years. The chair consists of just two plywood shells that are screwed together – another example of Kjærholm's masterful reductionism.

1 *PK 9* shell chair, 1960
2 *PK 31* armchair, 1961
3 *PK 20* easy chair, 1967
4 *PK 61* coffee table, 1955
5 *PK 22* chair, 1956
6 *PK 24* chaise longue, 1965
7 *PK 0* chair, 1952

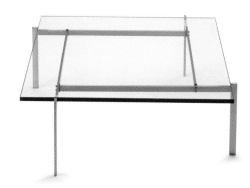

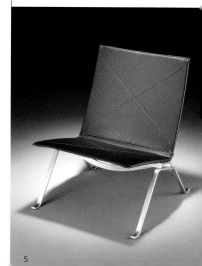

4

5

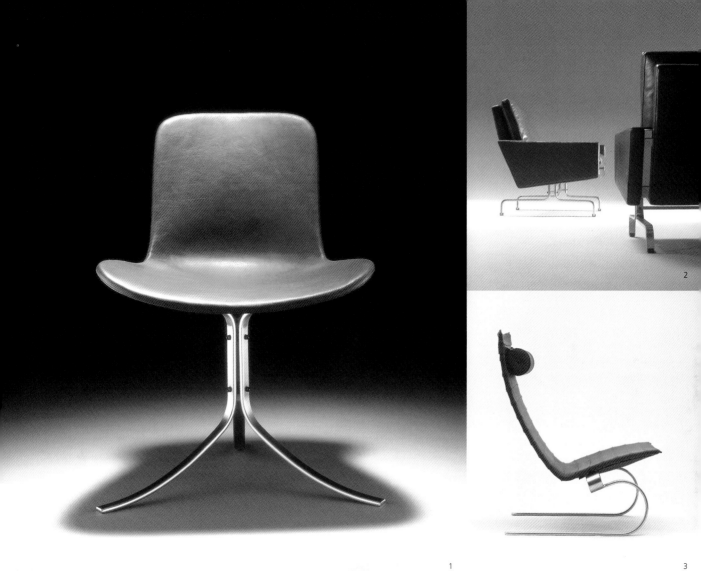

1

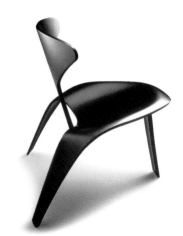

2

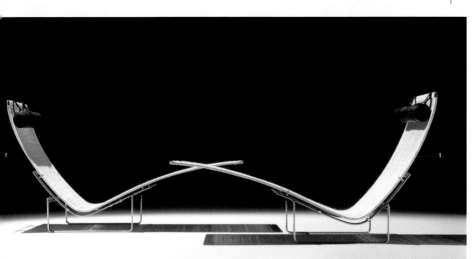

3

6

7

Knoll

USA I Knoll, Inc., East Greenville, Pennsylvania I Furniture manufacturer I **www.knoll.com**

The design philosophy of the furniture manufacturer Knoll is influenced by two different schools – the Bauhaus and the prestigious Cranbrook Academy of Art in Michigan. Florence 'Shu' Knoll (née Schust), the American first lady of design, was the embodiment of this dual influence. While studying at the Kingswood School on the Cranbrook campus, she became a protégée of **Eero Saarinen**. She studied architecture at Cranbrook and later in London and Chicago. Her first practical work experience was with **Walter Gropius** and **Marcel Breuer** in Cambridge, Massachusetts. She joined the Hans G. Knoll Furniture Company in the early 1940s and assumed responsibility for the Planning Unit, where she revolutionized interior design planning. A few years later she married Hans Knoll. The Knolls were a like-minded couple, comparable to **Charles and Ray Eames**. After the death of her husband in the mid-1950s, Florence took over the management of Knoll for several years. The company was sold in 1959, and she became chief designer, adopting a restrained design aesthetic.

In the 1940s and early 1950s Knoll took the lead in design development with such furniture as the *Womb* chair by ▸Eero Saarinen, textile-covered chairs by the Danish designer Jens Risom and ▸**Harry Bertoia**'s wire furniture collection. In the 1960s a number of Bauhaus designs were introduced, including the *Brno* chair by ▸**Ludwig Mies van der Rohe** and ▸Breuer's *Wassily*, the prototype of all tubular steel chairs.

Together with **Herman Miller**, Knoll remains a top player in modern American furniture design. The great Bauhaus designs still form the core of the company's programme, which also includes comprehensive office furniture systems. A gallery of great designers from all over the world add an international dimension: **Cini Boeri**, **Richard Sapper** and **Ettore Sottsass** from Italy; Marc Alessandri and **Pascal Mourgue** from France; and Charles Pfister, **Warren Platner** and **Frank O. Gehry** from the United States. With their seats of interwoven strips of maple, ▸Gehry's *Cross Check* chairs were tremendously innovative in the early 1990s, and introduced an entirely new construction principle into furniture design. Knoll is famous for its modern classics, but also for its carefully designed corporate identity, for which **Vignelli Associates** is responsible.

274

1 *Tulip* armchair, 1956

2 *Diamond* armchair, 1952

3 Chaise longue (*MR* collection), 1965
(1931 design)

4 Oval table (*Florence Knoll Executive
Collection*), 1961

5 Lounge chair (*Risom* collection), 1941

6 *A3* office system, 2001

7 Sofa (*Florence Knoll Lounge Seating*), 1954

8 *Pollock* executive chair, 1965

1938	Hans G. Knoll Furniture Company established by Hans Knoll in New York
1943	Establishes Knoll Planning Unit; Florence Schust becomes director
1946	Florence Schust marries Hans Knoll; company name changes to Knoll Associates
1955	Hans Knoll dies; Florence Knoll assumes directorship
1959	Art Metal buys company

Products

1941	*Risom* furniture collection by Jens Risom
1945	Cylindrical table lamp by ▸ **Isamu Noguchi**
1948	*Barcelona* armchair by ▸ **Ludwig Mies van der Rohe** (1929 design); *Womb* chair by ▸ **Eero Saarinen**
1952	*Diamond* armchair by ▸ **Harry Bertoia**
1954	*Florence Knoll Lounge Seating*
1956	*Tulip* tables and chairs by ▸ Eero Saarinen
1960	*Brno* chair by ▸ Ludwig Mies van der Rohe (1930 design)
1961	*Florence Knoll Executive Collection*
1965	*MR* tubular steel furniture collection by ▸ Ludwig Mies van der Rohe (1931 design); *Pollock* executive chair by Charles Pollock
1966	Wire furniture collection by ▸ **Warren Platner** (▸ p. 263)
1969	*Wassily* armchair by ▸ **Marcel Breuer** (1925 design)
1970	*Lunario* table by Cini Boeri
1984	Chair collection by Robert Venturi
1986	*Mandarin* chair by ▸ **Ettore Sottsass**
1988	*Toledo* stackable chair by ▸ **Jorge Pensi**
1991	*Cross Check* furniture collection by ▸ **Frank O. Gehry**
1994	*Paperclip* table by ▸ **Vignelli Associates**
1999	*FOG* stackable chair by ▸ Frank O. Gehry
2001	*A3* office system by Asymptote

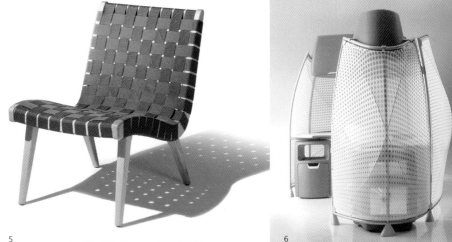

5

6

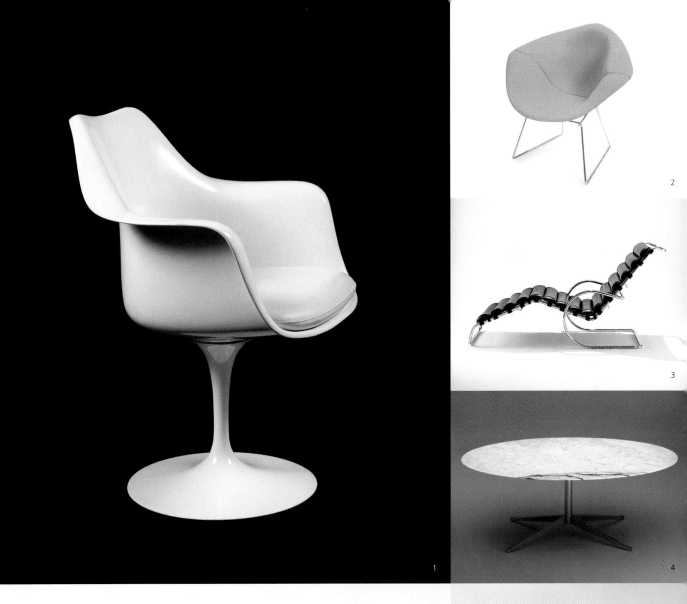

1

2

3

4

7

8

Kodak

USA I Eastman Kodak Company, Rochester, New York I Camera and film manufacturer I www.kodak.com

Kodak's famous *Brownie* camera, launched at the beginning of the twentieth century, was extremely easy to operate. It was one of the first pieces of technology that could be used without having to be understood. The camera cost just one dollar; Kodak's real profits came from the film that was sold with it. The company was thus responsible for the advent of amateur photography. Three decades later, Kodak returned to the successful concept: the *Baby Brownie*, designed by **Walter Dorwin Teague**, was technologically simple and was intended to boost the sales of film. The compact, black plastic casing housed a mechanism that was fixed to the top of the casing and could be pulled out like a drawer when the film was loaded. The vertical ribs at the front of the camera were a characteristic feature. Around the same time, Kodak took over the German camera manufacturer Nagel. Its *Retina* 35mm camera, which combined a high degree of precision with a competitive price, quickly found a ready market. The *Instamatic 100*, designed by **Kenneth Grange** in the early 1960s, was an even greater success. Its integrated design is still regarded as an icon of industrial styling. Kodak reaped the benefits, selling more than 70 million cameras. The company's original motto – "You press the button, we do the rest" – has found renewed relevance in the age of digital photography.

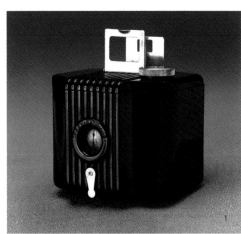

1

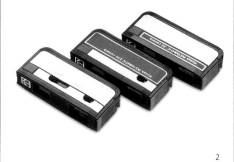

2

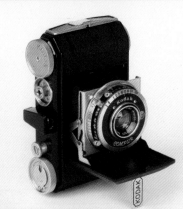

3

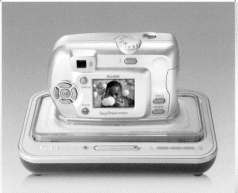

4

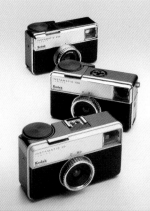

5

Harri **Koskinen**

Finland | Product designer | www.harrikoskinen.com

1970 Born in Karstula
1989 Studies at Lahti Institute of Design
1998 Completes studies at University of Art and Design, Helsinki
2000 Named Young Designer of the Year, Design Forum Finland

In the mid-1990s Harri Koskinen presented his *Block* lamp at the great furniture fairs in Cologne and Milan. *Block* consisted of a single bulb encased in a slab of glass that had been designed to resemble a block of ice. The Finnish designer became famous virtually overnight, and the Museum of Modern Art (MoMA) in New York ordered the lamp for its permanent collection. Koskinen is one of those young, innovative Scandinavian designers who in Finland are associated with the **Snowcrash** group and in Sweden with such companies as **David Design**. After his success with *Block*, he began working for Finland's leading design brands. In their simplicity and versatility, his stackable kitchen containers (for **Arabia**) follow in the design tradition of works by **Kaj Franck**, and represent the Scandinavian equivalent of **Tupperware**. His *Relations* storm lantern (for **Iittala**), which has symmetrical upper and lower sections and a 'waist', hovers on the boundary between a work of art and an everyday object – a balancing act that such Finnish glass designers as **Tapio Wirkkala** frequently managed to carry off. In recent years Koskinen's portfolio has become more international. For the Japanese watch manufacturer Seiko, for example, he designed *Vakio* (in Finnish, 'reliable'), the second watch series for the Issey Miyake fashion label.

Products

1996 *Block* lamp for Design House Stockholm; *Atlas* candlestick for ▸ **Iittala**

1998 *Pick Up* shelf for **Källemo**

1999 *Relations* storm lantern for Iittala

2000 *Koskinen 2000* barbecue cookware for **Hackman**; *Folded* carpet for **Asplund**

2001 *Air* kitchenware collection for **Arabia**; *6040/7060 A* loudspeaker system for Genelec; *Lumières d'Issey* case for Issey Miyake; *Halo* tealight holder and *Muotka* vase for Iittala

2002 *All Steel* collection of cooking utensils for Iittala

2003 *Gotico* and *Orbital* vases for ▸ **Venini**; *k* chair for Woodnotes; *Lamppu* standard lamp for ▸ **O Luce**; *Muu* table and chair for Montina

1 *Koskinen 2000* barbecue cookware, 2000
2 Containers (*Air* kitchenware collection), 2001
3 *Block* lamp, 1996
4 *Pick Up* shelf, 1998
5 *Relations* storm lantern, 1999

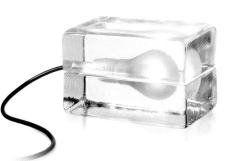

1

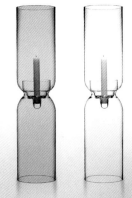

2

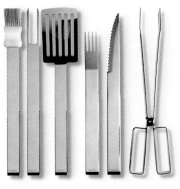

3

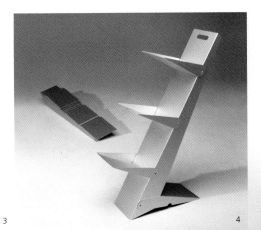

4

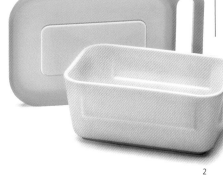

5

Kosta Boda

Sweden | Orrefors Kosta Boda A/B, Kosta | Glassware manufacturer | **www.kostaboda.se**

Behind the famous brand name Kosta Boda are three glassworks: Åfors, Boda and Kosta. Throughout their histories, they have often changed owners and names. Although they were acquired by their former competitor **Orrefors**, which subsequently merged with **Royal Copenhagen**, the glassworks have nevertheless managed to retain their independence. At Kosta, the artists Gunnar Wennerberg and Alf Wallander began to produce original designs around the beginning of the twentieth century. This period of creativity was, however, not repeated again until the 1950s, when Vicke Lindstrand produced versatile and experimental designs. In the 1960s, the age of liberalization, design was finally recognized as being an important factor in the manufacture of glassware. Numerous artists therefore moved to the Swedish glass-making district, among them such leading designers as Monica Backström, Bertil Vallien and Göran Wärff. Following the concentration of creative talent in the region in the 1970s and the art-glass boom of the 1980s, two young designers working in the United States, Gunnel Sahlin and Ann Wåhlström, were engaged. Since that time, the traditional technique of glass painting has experienced an artistic and commercial renaissance. Works by Ulrica Hydman-Vallien are particularly popular.

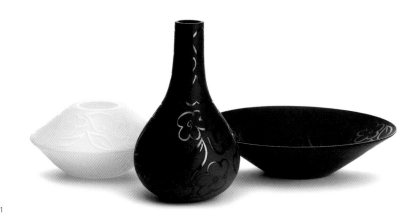

278

1

1742	Kosta Glassworks established by Anders Koskull and Georg B. Staël von Holstein
1864	Boda Glassworks established by Kosta glass-blowers
1876	Åfors Glassworks established by Kosta glass-blowers
1929	Elis Bergh becomes first artistic director at Kosta (until 1950)
1946	Kosta and Boda merge
1950	Vicke Lindstrand becomes artistic director at Kosta (until 1973)
1990	**Orrefors** takes over company
1997	Merges with **Royal Copenhagen**

Products

1836	Bottle with engraving
1896	*Odelberg* glass series
1899	Vase with black orchids by Gunnar Wennerberg
1929	*Koh-i-noor* glasses by Elis Bergh
1934	*Moiré* glasses by Elis Bergh
1953	*Trees in Fog* vase by Vicke Lindstrand
1955	*Mambo* glasses by Vicke Lindstrand
1973	*Gras* vase by Lisa Bauer and Sigurd Persson
1980	*Utopia* vase by Göran Wärff
1986	*Cat Lady* stained glass by Ulrica Hydman-Vallien
1992	*Amazon* jugs by Gunnel Sahlin
1996	*Kaboka* glass series by Ulrica Hydman-Vallien
1998	*Tonga* bowls by Monica Backström
2002	*Amber* vase collection by Göran Wärff
2003	*Duo* glass collection by Anne Nilsson
2004	*Atoll* bowl collection and *Barcelona* vase collection by Anna Ehrner

1 *Duo* glass collection, 2003
2 *Amber* vase collection, 2002
3 *Trees in Fog* vase, 1953
4 Bowl (*Kaboka* glass series), 1996

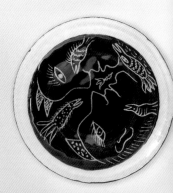

2   3   4

Koziol

Germany | Koziol Ideas for Friends GmbH, Erbach im Odenwald | Manufacturer of household items | **www.koziol.de**

Balduin, the humidifier, takes the form of a likeable ghost; *Lucy*, the hole-punch, is a colourful butterfly; the punk hairstyles of the washing-up brushes *Tim* and *Tweety* are designed to deal with dirty crockery. The everyday products of Koziol, eyed somewhat suspiciously by many in the design industry, lie somewhere between kitsch and cult. These "ideas for friends", as the enterprising and marketing-conscious owner of the firm, Stephan Koziol, calls his colourful range of internationally successful gift articles and household goods, are certainly not purist. The company, based near Frankfurt am Main, has adopted the motto "design is life". Stephan and Bernhard Koziol took over the firm from their father, also called Bernhard, in 1980. The origins of the company were in souvenirs, figurines and wall-paintings. In the late 1920s Bernhard Koziol senior founded a workshop in which he initially carved brooches and figurines from ivory. In the mid-1930s the company switched to an innovative injection-moulding system. At the beginning of the 1950s Koziol invented a bestseller that has already taken its place in popular cultural history: the highly collectable transparent 'snow globes' that send down showers of glitter on to miniature plastic versions of famous landmarks when they are shaken.

1927 Ivory-carving workshop established by Bernhard Koziol in Erbach im Odenwald

1935 Uses first hand-operated injection-moulding system

1980 Bernhard Koziol retires and hands over management to sons Stephan and Bernhard

Products

1950 First snow globe

1986 *Rio* collection by Thomas Etzel

1992 *Manhattan Tower* CD rack

1994 *Sharky* clothes peg by Rainer Lehn

1996 *Tim* and *Tweety* washing-up brushes by Jan Hansen and Frank Person

1997 *Frog King* bottle opener by Rainer Lehn; *Gina* pasta server by Orange

1998 *Balduin* humidifier by Jan Hansen and Frank Person; *Shopper* bag by **Alessandro Mendini** and Maria Christina Hamel; *Speedy* tape dispenser by Peter Naumann; *Aroma* espresso cup by ▶ **Matteo Thun**; *Powerflower* watering system by Designpartners; *Elise* watering can

2001 *Gonzales* stapler by Peter Naumann; *Toq* toilet brush by Platt & Young

2003 *Elvis* tape dispenser by Serge Atallah; *Algue* partition for *Ideal House* project of **Ronan and Erwan Bouroullec** at International Furniture Fair, Cologne

1 *Elise* watering can, 1998
2 *Elvis* tape dispenser, 2003
3 *Gonzales* stapler, 2001
4 *Balduin* humidifier, 1998
5 *Tweety* brush, 1996

279

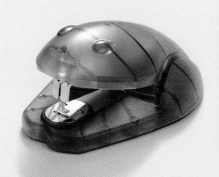

1

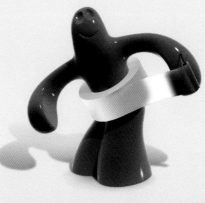

2

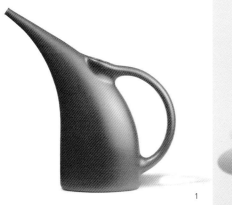

3

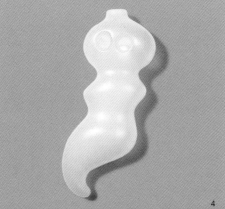

4

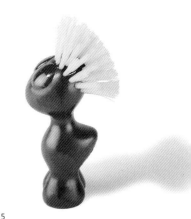

5

Axel **Kufus**

Germany | Furniture designer | **www.kufus.de**

In the mid-1980s Axel Kufus designed a 'cellar-window cupboard' as part of his *Ad Hoc* furniture collection in collaboration with the sculptor Ulrike Holthöfer. It consisted of a concrete box (the 'cellar') balanced on the long, rough branches of a tree, which acted as legs. Metal bars represented the cellar window. Young designers often attempted to challenge the dominant functionalism of the era with such unwieldy object-collages as this cupboard. At that time, Kufus, who is now a professor of product design, was embarking on his design course at the Hochschule der Künste in Berlin, which was then a centre of the New German Design movement. The path he eventually took, however, was determined decisively by his previous training as a cabinetmaker. The work of this master carpenter reveals ecological sensitivity, a focus on simple forms and a profound knowledge of materials and their properties. His designs represent functionalism on a higher plane – or, as in the name of the company he co-founded with **Jasper Morrison** and Andreas Brandolini, Utilism International. Kufus's own products often have equally concise names, such as the immensely successful *FNP* shelf system (for **Nils Holger Moormann**) and the *Kufus* table collection.

1958 Born in Essen
1977 Begins apprenticeship in cabinetmaking
1985 Studies design at Hochschule der Künste, Berlin
1986 Produces and markets his own furniture
1990 Establishes studio in Berlin with Sibylle Jans
1993 Becomes professor of product design at Bauhaus-Universität, Weimar
2001 Receives Good Design Award, Chicago, for *Office Kitchen* and iF Design Award for *FNP* shelf system
2003 Receives iF Design Award for *Egal* shelf system

Products
1984 *Ad Hoc* furniture collection (with Ulrike Holthöfer)
1987 *Kufus* table collection (in-house production; later at Magazin); *Lattenschrank* cupboard and *Lattentisch* table (in-house production)
1989 *FNP* shelf system for **Nils Holger Moormann**
1993 *Stöck* chair for Atoll
1996 *Lader* drawers for Nils Holger Moormann
2000 *Office Kitchen* for Casawell Service Gruppe; *Stand By* multifunctional shelves for **Magis**
2001 *Egal* shelf system for Nils Holger Moormann
2002 *Container* (concept) for Manufactum; *Just 3* cigarette case for Magis; *proArc* revolving circular shelves for kitchen cupboards for Ninkaplast

1 *FNP* shelf system, 1989
2 *Stöck* chair, 1993
3 *Lader* drawers, 1996
4 *Kufus* tables, 1987
5 *Stand By* shelves, 2000

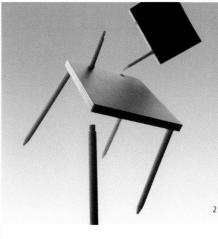

1

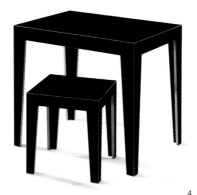

2

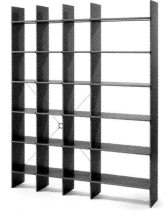

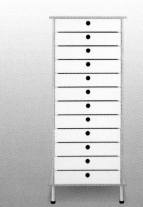

3

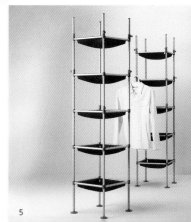

4   5

Yrjö **Kukkapuro**

Finland | Interior and furniture designer | **www.avarte.fi**

Yrjö Kukkapuro grew up in a three-roomed flat with his parents, grandmother and three siblings. This living arrangement doubtless accounts for his love of nature and free space (today he lives in a large 1960s Modernist house on the outskirts of Helsinki) and his respect for a team spirit. His success, he says, has nothing to do with working on his own, but is due to the fact that "the designer, the entrepreneur and the marketing people pursue the same aims". Along with Antti Nurmesniemi, Kukkapuro has made a significant contribution to raising the profile of Finnish furniture design around the world. For more than two decades the uncompromising Modernist has been head of design at Avarte, a furniture company that has never accepted the traditional division between "saleable run-of-the-mill design and avant-garde showpieces". By the mid-1960s Kukkapuro, who shares a predilection for steel and leather with **Poul Kjærholm**, had already created a masterpiece: his *Ateljee* armchair was swiftly included in the collection of the Museum of Modern Art (MoMA) in New York and has been in production ever since. Kukkapuro became well known as a result of his bold design for the *Karuselli* swivel chair and for his skeletal chairs made from metal rods screwed together. He later used plastic, plywood and even solid Finnish wood in his designs.

281

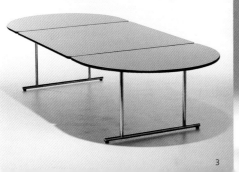

1

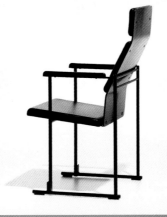

2

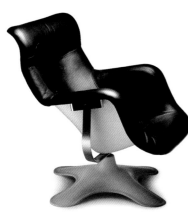

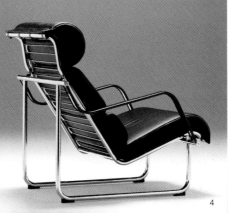

3

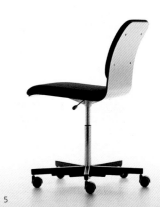

4

5

Shiro **Kuramata**

Japan | Furniture designer

Shiro Kuramata's furniture, executed in a range of industrial materials, is highly original. His designs often seem exotic, even poetic: cupboards stand on long, thin legs; a chest of drawers dances the tango; a chair entitled *How High the Moon* appears as an elegant, strangely ghost-like structure of interwoven steel mesh (at **Vitra**). The Japanese 'furniture Surrealist' studied woodworking at the Municipal Polytechnic High School in Tokyo and then furniture design at the Kuwasawa Design Institute. He presented his first works towards the end of the 1960s. The bold forms of even these early pieces challenge our habitual modes of perception and ideas about seating. In such designs as the *Pyramid* chest, a skyscraper on wheels, his passion for drawers is apparent. The use of acrylic for the outer casing underlines the impression of storeys.

The novelty value of Kuramata's work often lies in the use of unusual combinations of materials. A glass table rests on spherical rubber legs. The back and seat of the *Miss Blanche* chair consist of transparent acrylic in which paper roses have been cast. *How High the Moon*, the voluminous but transparent chair that appears weightless and almost as if it is floating, is made of expanded steel mesh covered with a paint containing nickel. The smooth, reflective surface of the metal emphasizes the chair's ethereal quality, as if the moon is shining down on it. The chair takes its name from a Duke Ellington jazz classic.

In the 1980s Kuramata created designs for numerous well-known international companies, including Memphis, **Cappellini**, Vitra and XO. He also designed boutique interiors for the Japanese fashion designer Issey Miyake in Tokyo, Paris and New York. His premature death at the age of fifty-seven ended a unique career in which he moved constantly between East and West, both geographically and conceptually.

1934 Born in Tokyo
1953 Graduates from Municipal Polytechnic High School, Tokyo
1956 Graduates in furniture design from Kuwasawa Design Institute, Tokyo
1965 Establishes own studio in Tokyo
1981 Receives Japan Culture Design Award; works at Memphis design group
1984 Interior design of Issey Miyake boutiques in Paris, Tokyo and New York
1991 Dies in Tokyo

Products
1968 *Pyramid* chest of drawers (re-edition at **Cappellini**)
1970 *Furniture in Irregular* cabinet for Fujiko; *Revolving Cabinet* (re-edition at Cappellini); *Side 1* and *Side 2* chests of drawers (re-edition at Cappellini)
1972 *K* lamp collection for Yamagiwa
1976 *Glass Chair* for Mihoya Glass
1977 *Solaris* chest for Cappellini
1979 *01* chair for Ishimaru
1982 *Sofa with Arms* for Cappellini
1983 *Kyoto* table for Memphis
1984 *Sedia Seduta* armchair
1985 *Sing Sing Sing* chair for XO
1986 *Homage to Josef Hoffmann Vol. 2* armchair; *Ko-Ko* occasional table for Cappellini
1987 *Sally* table for Memphis; *F.1.86* umbrella stand for UMS Pastoe; *How High the Moon* armchair for **Vitra**
1988 *Miss Blanche* chair for Ishimaru
1989 *Ephemera* vases for Ishimaru
1991 *Laputa* bed; *Placebo* table for Cappellini; washbasin for Rapsel

282

1 *Pyramid* chest of drawers, 1968, and *Revolving Cabinet*, 1970
2 *Side 2* chest of drawers, 1970
3 *How High the Moon* armchair, 1987
4 *Ko-Ko* occasional table, 1986
5 *Sofa with Arms*, 1982
6 *Solaris* chest, 1977

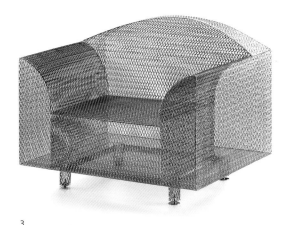

3

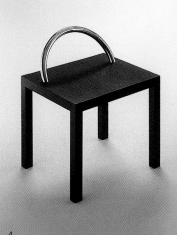

4

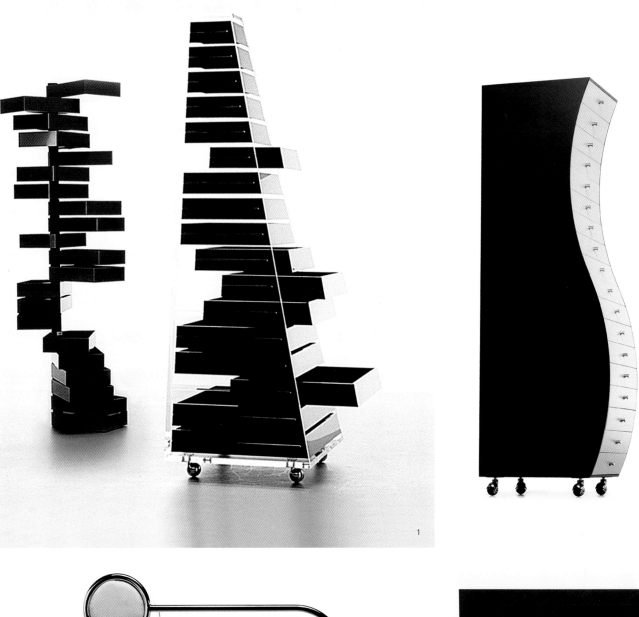

1

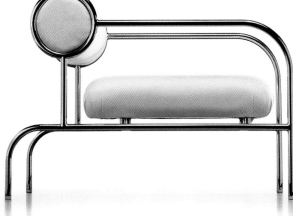

2

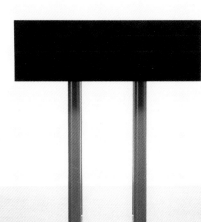

5

6

Loewe, *Mimo* TV set, 2003

When the television manufacturer Loewe decided that it wanted to produce a set for young people, the Phoenix Design studio responded with the *Mimo* series. The fascia of the set is available in various colours and can be changed to suit its surroundings. The set can be positioned as required: on a base, fixed to the wall or on a tripod stand – a step towards the creation of a customized television set.

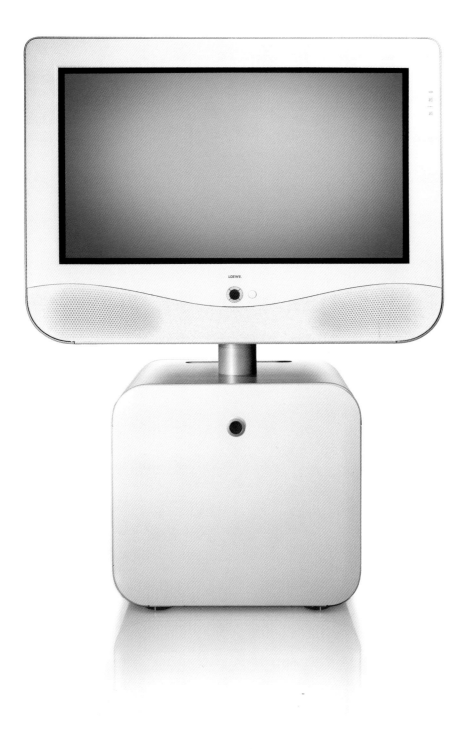

Lammhults

Sweden I Lammhults Möbel A/B, Lammhult I Furniture manufacturer I **www.lammhults.se**

Over the years Lammhults has developed from a small provincial furniture manufacturer into a design-orientated and internationally respected company. Although unmistakably Swedish, it differs from **Ikea** and **Källemo**, two other firms that were both founded in the same part of the country. Lammhults enjoyed its first design successes in the 1960s. Collaboration with Börge Lindau and Bo Lindekrantz, in those days the revolutionaries of Swedish furniture design, gave the company a clearer profile. With such products as the *X 75* director's chair, the company's exhibition displays became local events. Today Lammhults cultivates its reputation for contemporary, tasteful, quality design, and continues to receive many awards: the Danish architects Johannes Foersom and Peter Hiort-Lorenzen, specialists in office and upholstered furniture who have been associated with Lammhults since the 1980s, were awarded the Bruno Mathsson Prize in Copenhagen; Gunilla Allard received the prestigious Georg Jensen Prize. Familiar with different styles and materials in her capacity as a film-set designer, Allard stepped into the limelight with her elegant retro furniture, such as the *Cinema* and *Casino* chair series. She also presents minimalist works, including the *Saturn* table, an ellipse that appears to float. Also in the Lammhults team are representatives of new Swedish furniture design, including **Jonas Bohlin** and Love Arbén.

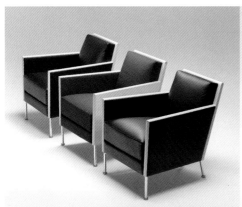

1

2

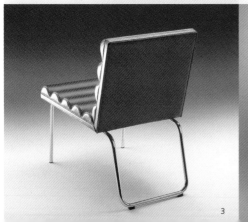

3

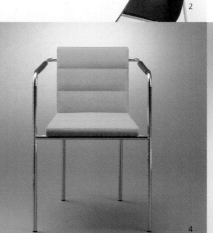

4

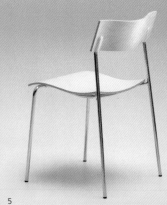

5

Lamy

Germany I C. Josef Lamy GmbH, Heidelberg I Manufacturer of writing utensils I **www.lamy.com**

Lamy is the leading manufacturer of writing utensils in Germany, both in terms of sales and in the number of design awards the company has received. For many years the family business remained relatively unknown. In the mid-1960s, however, Gerd A. Müller translated the purism he had learned during his employment at **Braun** into the design of fountain pens, pencils and ballpoint pens. He created a fountain pen in stainless steel and plastic with a slightly bulbous form and a distinctive colour combination of black and silver, which remain the company's corporate colours. The pen was given the forward-looking name *Lamy 2000*. It triggered a successful attempt to find a common visual denominator that indicated not only strict functionality but also an innovative corporate culture.

Lamy's approach to design pervades everything from its advertising campaigns to the futuristic architecture of its new development centre. Every Lamy product is designed to be innovative. In the 1990s Wolfgang Fabian's super-slim *Spirit* ballpoint pen, made from a single piece of metal and with a perforated surface, created something of a stir. **Mario Bellini**, with his grooved *Persona* fountain pen, and **Richard Sapper**, another Italian master, with his triangular-shaped *Dialog 1* ballpoint pen, have made Lamy synonymous with top-quality design.

1930 Established by C. Josef Lamy
1933 Patents fountain pen/pencil combination
1986 Manfred Lamy takes over company
1996 Receives Bundespreis Produktdesign for *Spirit* series

Products
1966 *2000* series by Gerd A. Müller
1984 *Unic* ballpoint pen by Gerd A. Müller
1987 *ABC* fountain pen by Bernt Spiegel
1990 *Persona* fountain pen by **Mario Bellini**
1994 *Spirit* ballpoint pen and mechanical pencil and *Lady* fountain pen and ballpoint pen by Wolfgang Fabian
1997 *AL-Star* pen series by Wolfgang Fabian
1998 *Accent* pen series by ▶ **Phoenix Design**
2000 *2000 Blackwood* rollerball pen (new collection of *Lamy 2000*); *Scribble* mechanical pencil and ballpoint pen by ▶ **Hannes Wettstein**
2001 *Pico* pocket pen by Franco Clivio
2003 *Dialog 1* ballpoint pen by **Richard Sapper**

1 *2000* series, 1966
2 *Pico* pocket pen, 2001
3 *Spirit* ballpoint pen and mechanical pencil, 1994
4 *Dialog 1* ballpoint pen, 2003

287

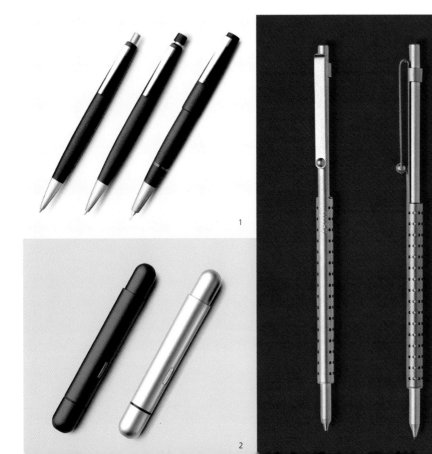

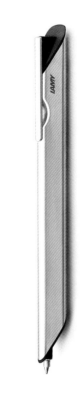

Lancia

Italy | Lancia (Fiat Auto SpA), Turin | Automobile manufacturer | **www.lancia.com**

The history of the Italian marque Lancia, founded by the racing driver Vincenzo Lancia, is not only one of racing successes but also, perhaps less famously, one of tremendous achievement in the development of automobile design. Lancia's models ranged from the *Lambda* in the early 1920s, which was one of the first cars to feature a monocoque-type body, and the elegant *Aprilia*, with its distinctive 1930s body (which, in the coupé version by **Pininfarina**, represented the Italian equivalent of American streamlining), to the successful and elegant post-war models such as the *Aurelia* coupé, the *Aurelia B 24 Spider* and the *Flaminia* luxury saloon, with an attractive panoramic window.

For many years Lancia was a symbol of a jet-set lifestyle. Among its clients were such luminaries as Prince Rainier of Monaco and the film stars Brigitte Bardot and Marcello Mastroianni. From the end of the 1960s, when the company became part of the **Fiat** group, the name stood for elegant, mid-range models. Lancia was able to regain its profile in the luxury class with the forward-looking *Thesis*. Styled closely on its historically successful forerunners, the *Thesis* manages to be a modern car that is aesthetically unusual yet also has definite emotional appeal.

1906	Established by Vincenzo Lancia
1969	**Fiat** acquires Lancia

Products

1921	*Lambda* saloon
1937	*Aprilia* coupé
1951	*Aurelia B 20* coupé
1954	*Aurelia B 24 Spider*
1959	*Flaminia* coupé
1969	*Flavia 2000* coupé
	Last five by ▶ **Pininfarina**
1971	*Stratos* sports car by ▶ **Bertone**
1974	*Beta Montecarlo* coupé by Pininfarina
1975	*Beta* with Targadach by Pininfarina
1980	*Delta* compact car; *Gamma* coupé by Pininfarina
1997	*Kappa* saloon and estate
1999	*Thesis* saloon
2004	*Ypsilon* small car

1 *Aurelia B 20* coupé, 1951
2 *Beta Montecarlo* coupé, 1974
3 *Thesis* saloon, 1999
4 *Gamma* coupé, 1980

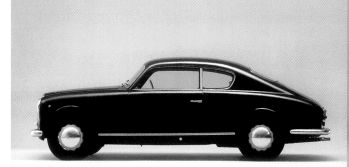

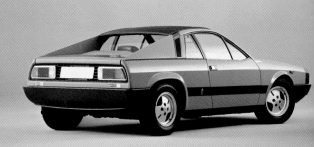

1

2

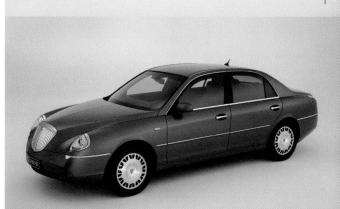

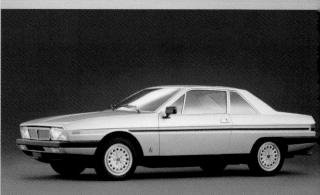

3

4

Lapalma

Italy I La Palma Srl, Cadoneghe I Furniture manufacturer I **www.lapalma.it**

Modern furniture design is the reservoir from which Lapalma, founded at the end of the 1970s near Padua, draws inspiration. Functional proportions and high-quality materials and finishes characterize the furniture and accessories that are created by the company for private homes and public buildings. Natural and clear materials predominate in its collection: wood from sustainable plantations, glass, leather, metal and wickerwork. The typical Lapalma style, developed by such notable designers as Enzo Berti, Karri Monni, Fabio Bortolani and **Shin and Tomoko Azumi**, can best be described as calm, understated, almost modest. Berti had a particularly strong influence on the product range, with, among other designs, numerous distinctive chairs and *Hole* – a simple but extremely elegant barstool.

Lapalma is notable above all for the tremendous range and diversity of its seating. Most pieces are purist, many are angular, but all are created using a minimum of material. It is perhaps no accident that neither the company nor its designers are based in Milan. Lapalma's profile is independent, light, Mediterranean and, at the same time, subtly charming. Many of its products have been awarded prizes, and deservedly so.

289

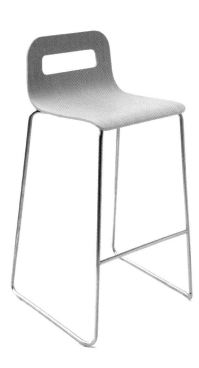

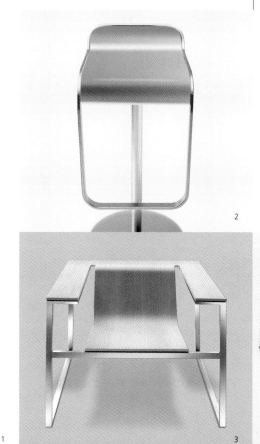

Le Corbusier

France | Architect and furniture designer | **www.fondationlecorbusier.asso.fr**

Modernism in architecture and design is strongly associated with the name Le Corbusier, a pseudonym used by the Swiss architect Charles-Edouard Jeanneret from about 1920 onwards. The son of a watchmaker from the Jura mountains, he was eventually to emerge as one of the most influential architects of the twentieth century. As well as his tremendous architectural achievements, however, he created a series of furniture classics. Although Le Corbusier did not invent Purism, he was a vehement advocate of this clean Modernist aesthetic. The puritan severity of his designs was highly influential, and his numerous theoretical works became obligatory reading.

Following the completion of his architectural studies, Le Corbusier began travelling extensively throughout Europe, visiting Italy, Vienna, Paris, Berlin, Istanbul and Athens. His travels were to have a significant influence on his professional development. In Vienna he was introduced to **Josef Hoffmann**, and in Paris to Auguste Perret, a specialist in the use of reinforced concrete. In Berlin Le Corbusier worked in the office of the architect and designer Peter Behrens, where he became familiar with industrial production.

A building of key importance for Le Corbusier was the Pavillon de l'Esprit Nouveau, created for the 1925 *Exposition Internationale des Arts Décoratifs et Industriels Modernes* in Paris. The structure's bare walls and moveable furniture demonstrated his idea of futuristic living. Some of his projects were controversial, such as the Plan Voisin for the systematic demolition and rebuilding of large sections of Paris. The project was never developed. For Le Corbusier, the modern house or apartment was "a machine for living in" that should function with the least possible difficulties. Although this was little more than a metaphor, one of his most famous designs, the *Chaise Longue à Réglage Continu* (today available as *LC 4* at **Cassina**), is in fact reminiscent of a machine. Le Corbusier developed his furniture from the mid-1920s onwards in collaboration with his cousin Pierre Jeanneret and the architect Charlotte Perriand. At the end of the decade he created, with his partners, the *LC* series in tubular steel with leather upholstery (initially for **Thonet**, France). One of the best-known classics is the *Grand Confort* (*LC 2*) armchair, produced today by Cassina – a product that has become particularly popular with designers for use in foyers.

290

1 *LC 2* armchair, 1928

2 *LC 1* armchair, 1928

3 *LC 7* swivel chair, 1928

4 *LC 4* chaise longue, 1928

5 Sideboard (*LC-Casiers Standard* system), 1925

6 *LC 6* table, 1928

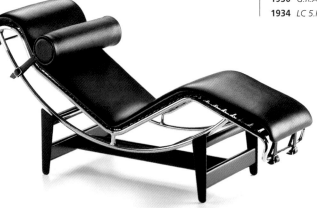

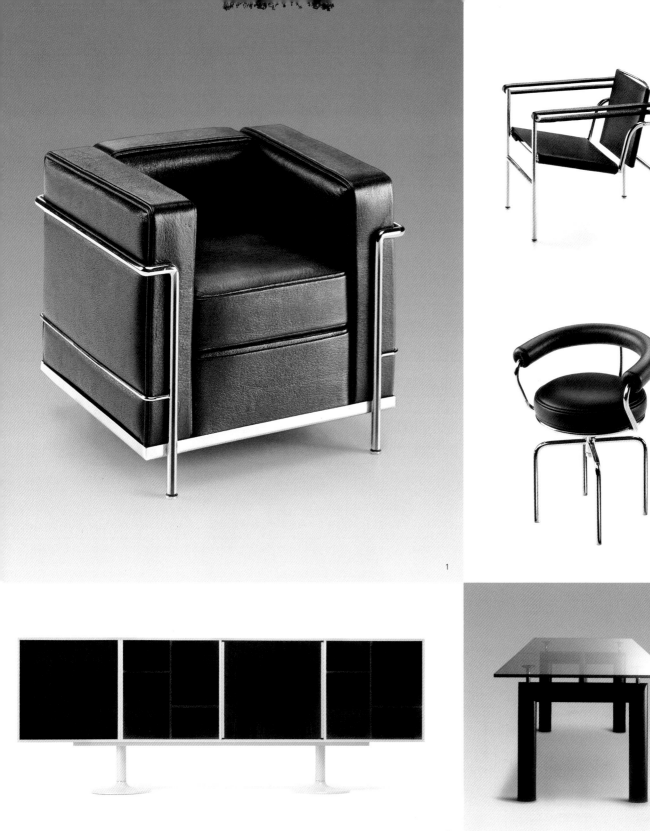

1

2

3

5

6

Leica

Germany I Leica Camera AG, Solms I Camera manufacturer I **www.leica.com**

The development of the world's first 35mm camera in the 1920s revolutionized documentary photography and photo journalism: it gave birth to the snapshot and also enabled photographers to become mobile. The new camera, *Leica 1*, manfactured by Leitz, was robust and was equipped with the very finest quality lenses. Its flat, cuboid shape, central lens, controls that were arranged on the top of the casing, and its distinctive black-and-silver colour combination created an entirely new type of camera. As with the tubular steel chair by **Marcel Breuer** and the **Ford** *Model T* car, the purest industrial form had emerged from everyday life. The Leica camera and its successors were for a long time standard equipment for professional photographers, but gradually became niche products as a result of significant competition from Asia. Since it introduced the *C1* model in the late 1990s, the company has attempted to regain its profile with strikingly simple lines. In the highly competitive field of digital cameras, Leica has commissioned designs from the Heine Lenz Zizka studio. Achim Heine's small but extremely elegant *D-Lux* has the potential to become a classic. The *Digilux 2* is impressively user-friendly and unites the benefits of digital technology with those of analogue photography: settings can be adjusted like those on a traditional SLR camera by means of setting rings on the lens and a shutter speed dial.

1849 Optisches Institut established by Carl Kellner in Wetzlar to develop lenses and microscopes

1865 Ernst Leitz becomes a partner in company

1914 Oskar Barnack develops Leica 'miniature camera' (series produced from 1925)

1986 Establishes Leica GmbH from company's photographic division

1996 Acquires camera division of Minox; becomes a public company, Leica Camera AG

1999 Launches special *M6* model to mark company's 150th anniversary

Products

1925 *Leica I* (1930 with screw-in lens)

1932 *Leica II*

1954 *M3* 35mm camera

1965 *Leicaflex* single-lens reflex camera

1971 *M5* camera with rangefinder

1996 *S1* and *R8* digital cameras

1997 *Z 2X* compact camera

1999 *C1* compact camera by Achim Heine; *Digilux Zoom* digital camera

2000 *LRF 800* rangefinder

2003 Leica *MP* 35mm camera; *Ultravid 50 BR* binoculars; *D-Lux* digital camera by Achim Heine

2004 *Digilux 2* digital camera by Achim Heine

1 *C1* compact camera, 1999
2 *M3* 35mm camera, 1954
3 *Z 2X* compact camera, 1997
4 *Digilux 2* digital camera, 2004
5 *Ultravid 50 BR* binoculars, 2003

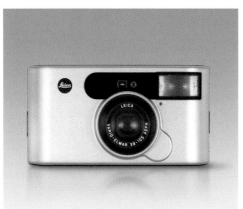

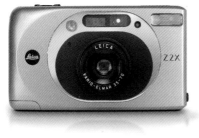

1

2

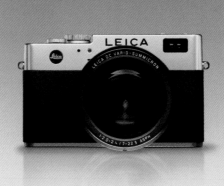

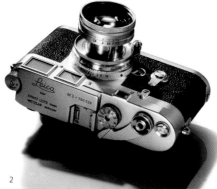

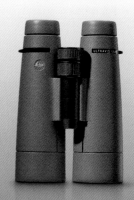

3

4

5

Lensvelt

The Netherlands I Lensvelt BV, Breda I Furniture manufacturer I **www.lensvelt.nl**

Lensvelt, a medium-sized company from the south of The Netherlands, regards itself as a specialist in providing unique manufacturing solutions in furniture production: anything that can be folded, punched, stamped or lasered in steel seems to be within its capabilities. The company is notable not only for its versatility and flexibility in responding to its clients' various unusual requirements but also for its careful observance of costs and prices. Aside from the furniture manufacturing firm, a wood-processing factory and two steel-processing plants also fall under Lensvelt's umbrella. Its comprehensive range of products includes Piet Hein Eek's *PHE* aluminium furniture collection, based on a classic Dutch design from the 1990s. The aluminium chair from the series is among the furnishings featured in the Dutch Design Café at the Museum of Modern Art (MoMA) in New York.

Shelves, chairs, tables and a trolley in the Lensvelt collection are assembled by means of screws, nuts and rivets. The *Rizzatto* office furniture system by the Italian designer Paolo Rizzatto is equally easy to assemble. Dirk van Berkel's *The Wall* container system is an ingenious minimalist design, only the sliding doors of which are visible: when opened out, they reveal space for hanging files and storage. Lensvelt's furniture can always be relied on to bring an intelligent twist to familiar, everyday objects.

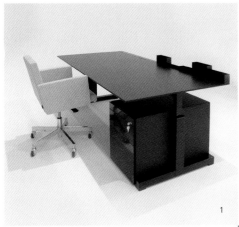

1   2

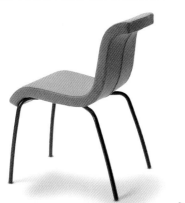

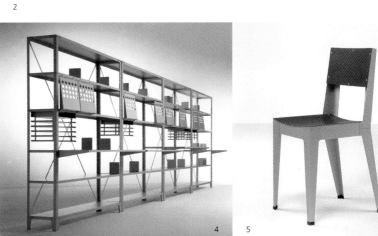

3   4   5

Arik **Levy**

Israel/France | Furniture and product designer | **www.ldesign.fr**

Arik Levy began his career as a graphic designer and sculptor. Born in Israel, he studied industrial design in Switzerland and then worked for Seiko in Japan. At the beginning of the 1990s he taught at the Ecole Nationale Supérieure de Création Industrielle (ENSCI; the leading French design institute) and later held design workshops in various European universities. During this period he designed sets for various dance ensembles, among them the Nederlands Dans Theatre. In 1996 Levy co-founded the Ldesign studio in Paris with Pippo Lionni, from the United States. "Just as when giving birth, it can be painful to generate real ideas", Levy has observed. Apart from devising corporate identity programmes for such eminent clients as the Kieler Woche (the annual sailing regatta in Kiel, northern Germany), the Bibliothèque of the University of Paris and the Louisiana Museum in Denmark, he has designed numerous pieces of furniture and lamps for **Authentics**, **Vitra** and **Ligne Roset**, one of his major customers. Levy is notable for creating ingenious products, among them his striking *Light Pocket* hanging lamp, which has a shade in the shape of a carrier bag that opens in a slit at the bottom; behind the shade the bulbs produce atmospheric, shadowy forms. The legless *XL 1* chaise longue, a double-bend silhouette, unites the elegance of Modernism and French chic.

294

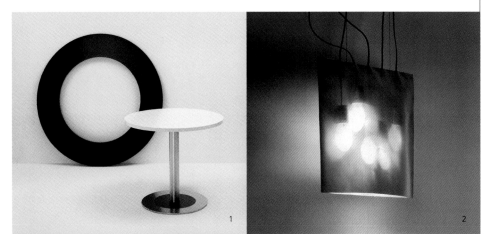

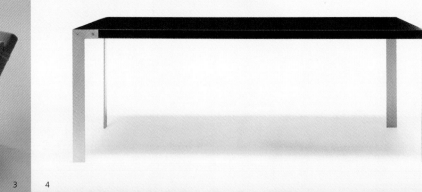

Lievore Altherr Molina

Spain I Furniture design studio I www.lievorealtherrmolina.com

The work of the Lievore Altherr Molina studio in Barcelona is unmistakably Mediterranean in its beauty and harmony, but it also places an emphasis on technological innovation. The furniture and lamps created by Alberto Lievore, Manel Molina and the German designer Jeannette Altherr do not appear spectacular at first sight. They are nevertheless innovative pieces and highly convincing in their sensitive use of colours and materials. The *Catifa* chair, for example, has a moulded seat that consists of a single seamless sheet of polypropylene processed using a special technique that makes it possible to produce the seat and back in two different colours. *Catifa* is typical of the work of this impressive design trio: the chair matches precisely both the requirements and the image of the company for which it was designed – in this case, the Italian firm Arper.

The success of Lievore Altherr Molina, a relatively young company, owes much to its 'holistic' approach: apart from furniture, the studio has designed exhibition displays and visual communications for Arper. Other clients include Halifax, Santa & Cole, Sellex and Verzelloni. For **Thonet**, the studio devised the simple *S 890* chair programme, with its open, inviting but at the same time protective form.

295

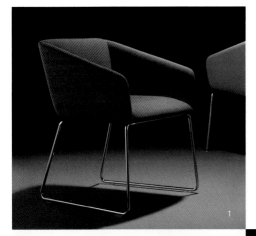

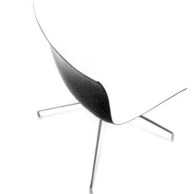

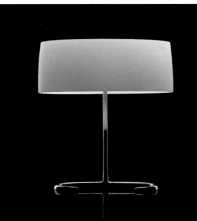

Ligne Roset

France I Ligne Roset SA, Briord I Furniture manufacturer I **www.ligne-roset.com**

With a contemporary interpretation of elegance that is typically French, the furniture manufacturer Ligne Roset has succeeded in appealing to a wide clientele. For more than thirty years the company's programme has been notable for a sophisticated style that avoids the design extremes and fetish objects that have become part of corporate policy in many Italian firms. The original company, Roset, was established in the 1860s and produced walking sticks and umbrella handles, a range that was gradually expanded to include upholstered furniture. The Ligne Roset brand name was established in the early 1970s, and from the outset followed a clearly defined aesthetic. The collection offers a comprehensive range of not only furniture but also accessories, textiles and lamps. At the end of the 1980s the firm had success with the bestselling flexible *Multy* sofa by Claude Brisson, which is still in production. Since the end of the 1990s the hitherto cautious company has been working with a new generation of designers, and today offers furniture and accessories by **Jeffrey Bernett**, **Christophe Pillet** and **Arik Levy**. The German designer Christian Werner adopts a restrained Modernist approach. His *Pop* chair is reminiscent of the 1960s, when the reduced forms of upholstered furniture were combined with gentle curves and delicate legs. Werner's *Kloc* rug, which has a hillock-shaped backrest, is not only a striking object but is also probably one of the first multifunctional floor coverings.

Furniture by such established designers as Didier Gomez, **Pascal Mourgue** and **Peter Maly**, all of whom have had a decisive influence on Ligne Roset's range, is still part of the collection. Many of their designs have become recognized classics. With his *Brera* shelf system, Maly has contributed a simple but imposing piece of furniture architecture. Another design that is both conceptually and visually unusual is the *Lover* sofa by Mourgue, which has a distinctive flexible backrest that can be turned up or down.

296

1 *Pop* chair, 2001
2 *Crescendo* table, 1999
3 *Kloc* rug with backrest, 2000
4 *Togo* sofa, 1973
5 *Lover* sofa, 2003
6 *Bianca* table/lamp, 2000
7 *Saint James* armchair, 1996
8 Flower pot, 2001
9 *Brera* shelf system, 1999

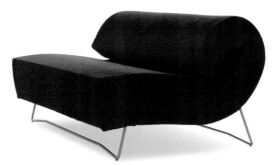

5

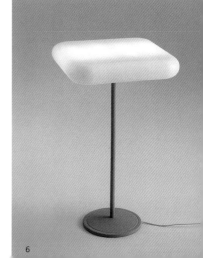

6

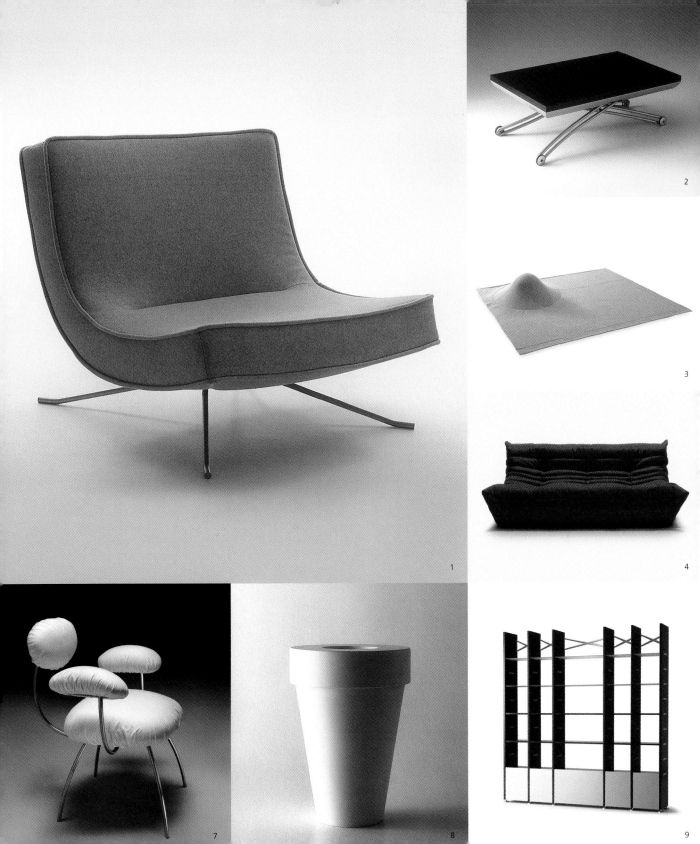

1

2

3

4

7

8

9

Piero **Lissoni**

Italy | Architect and furniture designer

The creations of the Italian architect and furniture designer Piero Lissoni are distinctive for their stark minimalism and strict simplicity of line and form. Lissoni has no interest in the cult of celebrity; his products rather than his personality take centre stage. Since the early 1990s he has been one of the most sought-after furniture designers in Italy, the country that is firmly at the forefront of the industry. Apart from interior design and architecture, his commissions often include corporate identity design and public relations – an all-round approach that contributes to his tremendous success. From **Artemide**, **Boffi**, **Cappellini**, **Cassina**, **Kartell** and Living Divani to **Moroso** and **Porro**, Lissoni and his team of about thirty designers work for the very finest Italian manufacturers.

Lissoni's versatility in his use of materials and styles within his strictly Modernist aesthetic is reflected in his kitchens for Boffi. Whereas in the *Works* kitchen from 1995 he relied exclusively on warm wood, creating a relaxed workshop atmosphere, in the *WK6* system, designed two years later, he alludes more to the style of the 1960s. Citing **Charles Eames**, **Ludwig Mies van der Rohe** and **Eileen Gray** as his points of reference, Lissoni describes his own designs as "quiet". This understated approach is evident in such minimalist pieces as the simple *Aero* bed, the elegant *Modern* storage system for Porro, which is based on square modular elements, and in the *One* plastic shelf system for Kartell (designed in collaboration with ▶**Patricia Urquiola**). The *Aviolux* shelf system for Cappellini, a development of the *Avio* shelf system designed in 2001, is a restrained but nevertheless practical and versatile wall sculpture. Lissoni also adopts a minimalist approach with his *Uno* seating system, the rectangular, upholstered 'building blocks' of which can be grouped casually or used separately. An equally reduced form can be found in the clocks he designed for **Alessi**, which once again are impressive for their lack of ornamentation.

298

1 *Aviolux* shelf system and *Coupé* armchair, 2003
2 *Nest* sofa and *Flat* sideboard, 1999
3 *Aero* bed, 2003
4 *Uno* seat, 2003

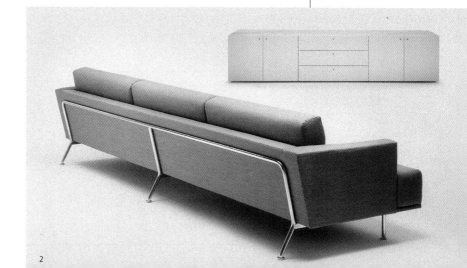

2

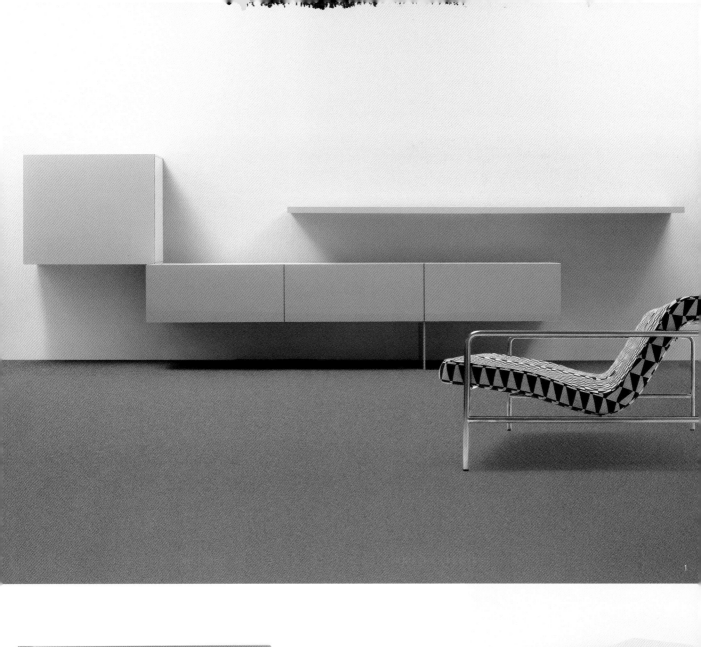

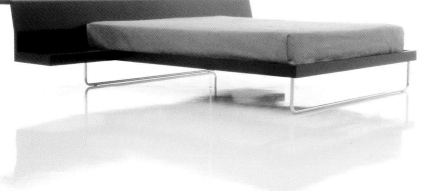

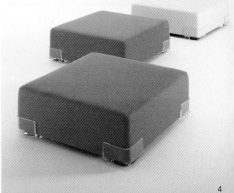

1

3

4

Loewe

Germany | Loewe AG, Kronach | TV and hi-fi manufacturer | **www.loewe.de**

Founded in the early 1920s, Loewe was among the group of companies that entered the market in the early days of radio. Its history is one of German technological invention, competition from the Far East and innovative design. In the 1930s Loewe attempted to develop a television set that could be mass-produced, but it was not until after the Second World War that there was a dramatic boom in business in Kronach, Bavaria, where the company is based. Consistently one of the most forward-looking electronics companies, Loewe launched a portable tape recorder at the beginning of the 1950s and a decade later the first video recorder. The machine was monstrous in size, but it took just ten years to shrink to a small box with a plain rectilinear design, in keeping with the rational style of the time. The 1980s proved to a difficult period for the industry, with strong competition coming from Japanese manufacturers that were able to offer goods at cheaper prices. Once again, however, Loewe put its faith in technological innovation, and produced the first stereo television set and the *MultiTel TV 10*, an integrated all-rounder that united the telephone and the TV set and was quite possibly too ahead of its time. The *Art 1* television set met with greater success. Created by Alexander Neumeister, it heralded a new era in TV set design and was as epoch-making as the sets produced by **Braun** in the 1950s and **Brionvega** in the 1960s. Above all, it was a milestone for Loewe: the decision to employ an external designer had turned out to be the right one. While almost all other German manufacturers were gradually squeezed out of the market, Loewe, like **Bang & Olufsen**, managed to secure a niche for itself with its winning formula of good design coupled with technological innovation.

Since the 1990s **Phoenix Design** has provided Loewe with state-of-the-art designs for multimedia living rooms, including the *Mimo* series (▶p. 285) and the flat-screen *Spheros*, one of the first plasma TV sets. Loewe has increasingly combined audio-visual technology in its products, providing complete home entertainment systems. It has also developed the *RC 1* bi-directional remote control, an intelligent, universal remote that can be programmed to operate a variety of appliances around the home.

1923 Established by Siegmund and David Ludwig Loewe in Berlin
1964 Establishes Loewe Opta
1981 Launches first stereo TV set in Europe
1988 *Art 1* TV set selected for permanent collection of MoMA, New York
1999 Becomes public limited company
2000 Receives Bundespreis Produktdesign for *Spheros 37* plasma TV
2004 Receives iF Design Award for *Articos 55 HD* and *Mimo 15* and *28* TV sets

Products
1926 *OE 333* local receiver with 'triple tube', first integrated circuitry
1931 First electronic TV set ('Braun tube')
1951 *Optaphon*, first tape recorder
1955 *Palette* 'music table'
1961 *Optacord 500* video recorder
1985 *Art 1* TV set by Alexander Neumeister
1991 *Art Vision* TV set by Alexander Neumeister
1995 *CS1*, first recyclable TV set; *Ergo* TV set by **Phoenix Design**
1998 *Spheros* plasma TV set series by Phoenix Design
1999 *Aconda* TV set
2002 *Certos* system, integrating video and audio expertise
2003 *Mimo* TV set series (▶ p. 285) and *Xelos SL 20* LCD TV set by ▶ Phoenix Design
2004 *Spheros R 37 Masterpiece* LCD TV set; *Articos 55 HD* TV set

300

1 *Spheros 42 HD C* plasma TV set, 1998
2 *Mimo 20* TV set, 2003
3 *Aconda* TV set, 1999
4 *Art 1* TV set, 1985
5 *Spheros 42 HD S* system with *Certos* system control unit and *Concertos 1* loudspeakers, 2002
6 *Mimo 20* TV set (detail), 2003

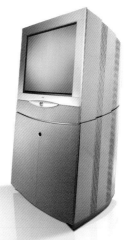

3

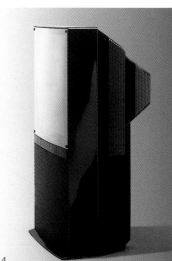

4

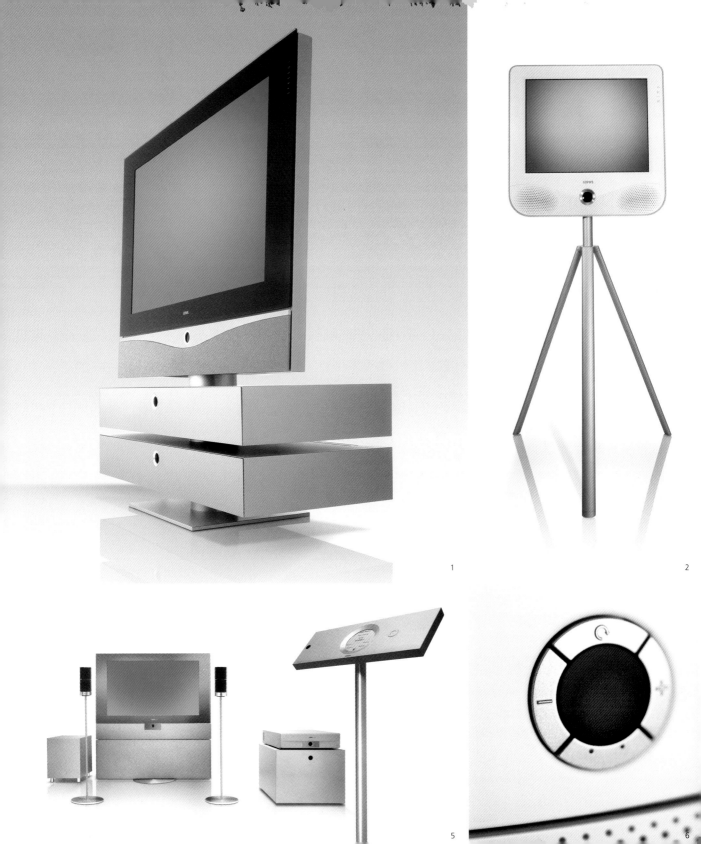

1

2

5

6

Raymond **Loewy**

USA | Product designer | www.raymondloewy.com | www.raymondloewyfoundation.com

Raymond Loewy's inexhaustible creativity, coupled with his business acumen, made him the model for an entire generation of designers. Like his contemporaries **Henry Dreyfuss** and Russel Wright, he represented the professionalization of the design industry. An immigrant, he initially earned his living as a window-display designer and fashion illustrator. His meteoric rise began at the end of the 1920s, when he established one of the first industrial design consultancies, in New York City. In the mid-1930s his company opened satellite offices, first in London and later in Paris. At the end of his career, the late 1960s, Loewy acted as a consultant to NASA, working on the interior design of the Skylab space station. This somewhat unconventional commission served to underline his almost legendary status. Designs by Loewy's studio included office and kitchen utensils, radios and furniture, logos, packaging, filling stations and vehicles of all kinds, from cars, buses and locomotives to planes and passenger ships.

At the beginning of Loewy's career streamlining was in vogue, and he produced several archetypes of the sleek style, including rocket-shaped pencil sharpeners and the *Coldspot Super Six* refrigerator, which gave new impetus to an ailing sector. From the 1930s he worked for Studebaker, the car manufacturer, for which he later designed the legendary *Avanti*. The racy model, with its sharply angular, flowing lines and striking, button-like 'eyes', was a design that Loewy himself regarded as one of his best. The *Scenicruiser* bus for Greyhound was another classic on wheels.

Loewy's eye-catching design for the Lucky Strike cigarette packet from the beginning of the 1940s ushered in a new phase during which he shaped the image of many companies. Among new clients were the food and beverage companies Nabisco, Heinz and Coca-Cola and the oil multinationals BP, Shell and Exxon. Loewy designed their filling stations and improved their brand identity. For Exxon he created the striking, overlapping double X logo. For Shell he removed the company's name from inside the seashell emblem to make the logo more distinctive – an early example of a strikingly powerful pictograph. (Saul Bass had already used a similar idea successfully at the Bell company.) Loewy's most significant innovation, however, was the creation of his consultancy.

302

1 Pencil sharpener (prototype), 1933
2 *GG-1* electric locomotive, 1936
3 *Purma Special* roll-film camera, 1937
4 *Starliner* coupé, 1953
5 *Avanti* coupé, 1962
6 *Scenicruiser* bus, 1954
7 Packaging for Lucky Strike, 1941

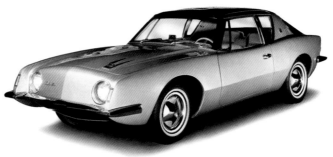

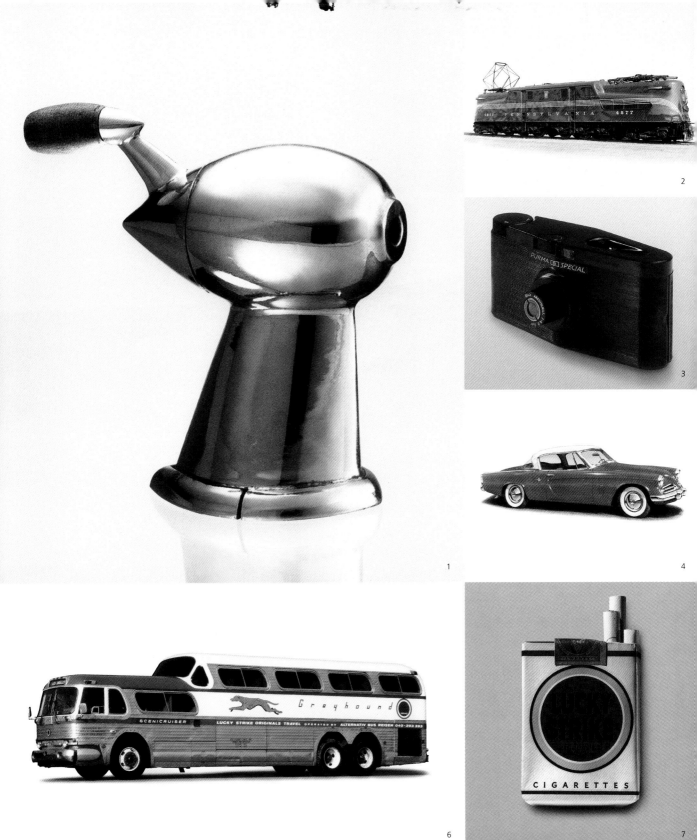

1

2

3

4

6

7

Louis Poulsen

Denmark I Louis Poulsen Lighting A/S, Copenhagen I Lamp manufacturer I **www.louis-poulsen.com**

The company known today as Louis Poulsen started out as a wine importer. It moved into the wholesale electrical equipment business when Copenhagen's first power station was built in 1892, and traded from an old town house on the quay at Nyhavn. The company began making lamps as a result of its collaboration with the designer **Poul Henningsen** in the mid-1920s. Lamp production now accounts for roughly one-third of its annual turnover. Henningsen's *PH* lamps, ubiquitous throughout Denmark but not widely known beyond Danish borders, have made the company something of a national institution.

Louis Poulsen's products have been sold around the world since the 1960s. Like **BEGA** and **iGuzzini**, the company focuses on functional lighting concepts for both indoors and outdoors that are designed by well-known architects and designers. ▶ Henningsen's originals, from the imposing *Artichoke* hanging lamp to the graceful *PH 3/2* table lamp, remain the showpieces of the collection. In the 1950s, 1960s and 1970s several new classics came into production, including ▶ **Arne Jacobsen**'s brilliantly simple *AJ* series, **Verner Panton**'s Pop-inspired *Panthella* collection and the *Albertslund* lamp by the architect Jens Møller-Jensen, which must have seemed like the work of a kindred spirit to Henningsen, who had one installed in his own garden. Møller-Jensen also designed a similar steel version for use indoors – the *Orbiter Micro* ceiling lamp. In more recent collections, white still predominates over colour, and rigorous attention is paid to geometric form. These principles also apply to the lamps that Poulsen designed himself. There is one product from the 1990s, however, that seems somewhat out of place: the *Borealis* outdoor bollard light by ▶ **King-Miranda Associati** is in white but has an expressive budlike head that is unusual among Poulsen designs. The *Charisma* hanging lamp (by PLH Design), made of polycarbonate and aluminium, points the way towards new lighting effects. A similarly modern combination of materials was used in the *Kipp* outdoor post light by Alfred Homann, a futuristic-looking construction combining an aluminium frame with such synthetic materials as polycarbonate and acrylic.

304

1   *AJ* floor and table lamps, 1959
2   *PH 41* hanging lamp, 1926
3   *VP Globe* hanging lamp, 1970
4   *Munkegaard* ceiling lamp, 1954
5   *Charisma* hanging lamp, 2001
6   *Kipp* post light, 1998
7   *Panthella* floor and table lamps, 1971
8   *Orbiter* ceiling lamp, 1963

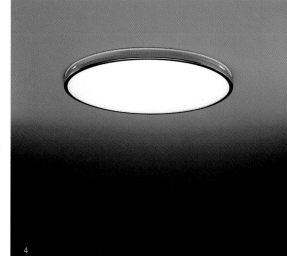

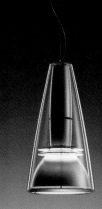

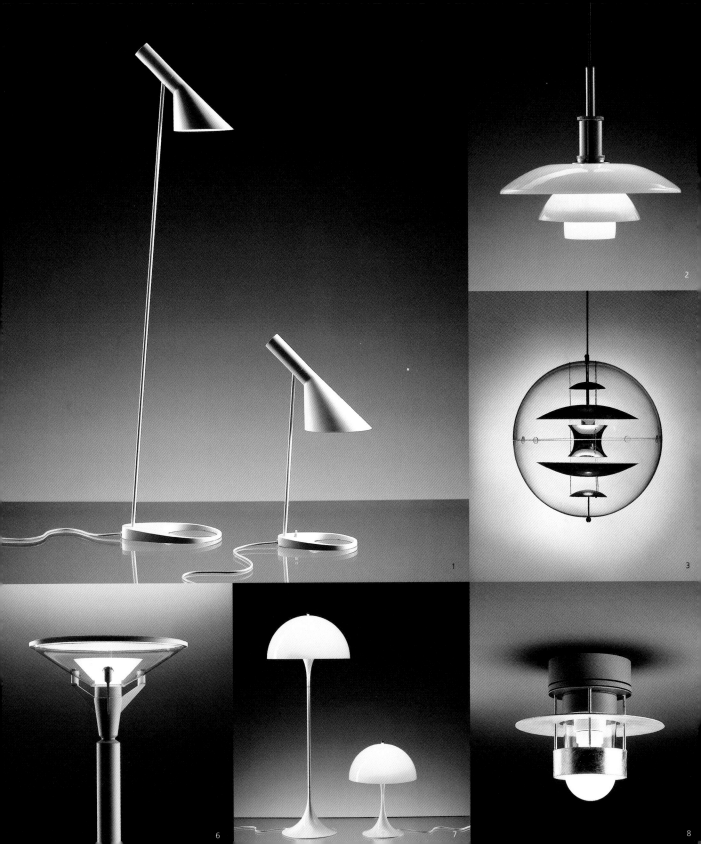

1

2

3

6

7

8

Ross **Lovegrove**

England | Furniture and product designer

Since graduating from the Royal College of Art in London in the early 1980s, Ross Lovegrove has become one of the world's most successful product designers and, together with **Ron Arad**, **Tom Dixon** and **Jasper Morrison**, forms part of Britain's design élite. Although he has always been fascinated by British craftsmanship (which forms the basis of many of the objects he has created), today he is regarded more as a furniture and industrial designer. His works include the *Coachline* luggage collection for Connolly, purveyor of leather goods to the royal family. Throughout his career he has created something of a stir with such designs as the *Eye* camera for Olympus, the *Go* plastic chair for Bernhardt Design, the *Basic* thermos jug for **Alfi** (with Julian Brown; ▶p. 15), lamps for **Luceplan** and furniture for Frighetto.

Lovegrove is a versatile talent who frequently draws inspiration from the repertoire of forms provided by nature, as is evident in his gently curvilinear chaises longues for Lloyd Loom in which sensuality and ergonomics are united. His objects are created specifically to cater to the needs of their users – a focus that is not typical of contemporary British design. According to one critic, "everyday activities such as eating, combing one's hair, typing data, pouring out coffee, nurture [Lovegrove's] thinking and acting". His interest in linking tradition and modernity is reflected in the design of his studio, a cool steel and concrete construction in which African art is exhibited.

Lovegrove left Britain immediately after having completed his degree, and gained considerable experience abroad. His first position was at **Frogdesign** in Germany. From there he moved to Paris, where he was an adviser to **Knoll**. While in France, along with **Jean Nouvel** and **Philippe Starck**, he was invited to join the Atelier de Nîmes, where he worked with a number of leading French manufacturers, including Cacharel, Louis Vuitton and Hermès. By the end of the 1980s Lovegrove's name had become famous. He returned to London in 1988 and set up studio in a converted warehouse in Notting Hill. Since then he has attracted clients from all over the globe: **Cappellini**, **Driade** and **Luceplan** from Italy; **Sony** and Olympus from Japan; **Herman Miller** from the United States; and **BD Ediciones** from Spain. Lovegrove continues to be convinced that "design can improve our lives".

306

1 *Go* plastic chair (detail), 2001
2 Chaise longue (collection for Lloyd Loom), 1998
3 Bicycle (concept), 2000
4 *Brasilia* easy chair, 2003
5 *Air One* styrofoam easy chair, 2000
6 Lamp (*bd.love* street furniture collection), 2002
7 *Go* thermos flask, 2000
8 *Basic* thermos jug, 1989
9 *Solar Bud* lamp, 1998

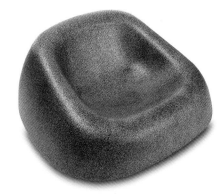

5

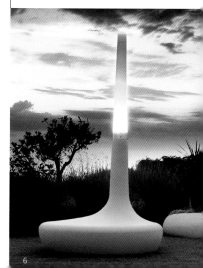

6

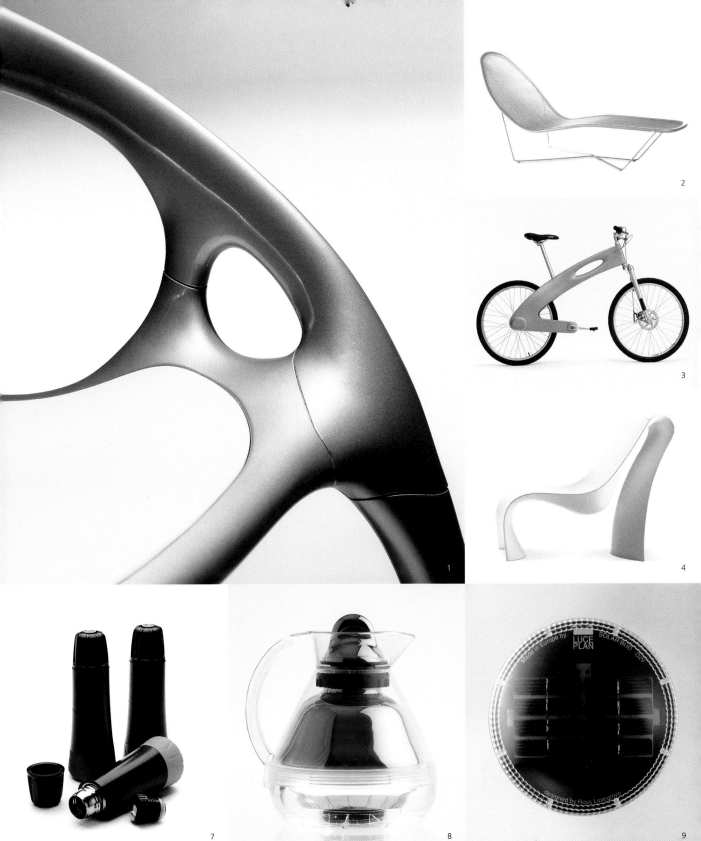

1

2

3

4

7

8

9

Luceplan

Italy I Luceplan SpA, Milan I Lamp manufacturer I **www.luceplan.com**

The distinctive, high-tech designs of the architect Paolo Rizzatto and the engineer **Alberto Meda** have given the products of the Italian lamp manufacturer Luceplan an unmistakable profile. Despite the diversity of the designs, all exhibit technical innovation, transparent construction and a distinctive approach to form, as is evident in *Titania*, the UFO-like hanging lamp that allows you to select your own colour effect using easy-to-change filters. The *Costanza* lamp series, which has undergone continuous development since the 1980s, conceals subtle and highly effective technology that has only recently become widely available. The standard, table and wall lamps in the series can all be turned on by a mere touch of the metal dimmer rod that is fixed close to the shade. In 1998 Meda and Rizzatto designed *Fortebraccio*, the first halogen table lamp that does not require a transformer. Rizzatto is also responsible for the creation of the ingenious *GlassGlass* hanging lamp, which is designed so that various shades (coloured or clear, round or pointed) can be fitted into an aluminium ring suspended from a steel cable that carries the electric lead. The lamp is practical in that the shades are interchangeable and can be cleaned separately. It is typical of Luceplan to offer its customers such choice.

Luceplan was founded in the late 1970s by three architects: Riccardo Sarfatti, the son of the lighting pioneer **Gino Sarfatti**, Sandra Severi and Paolo Rizzatto. Meda joined the partnership in the mid-1980s. Architecture is still the main point of reference for the continued development of the company's designs. The belief that a reasonably priced product is an essential feature of good design is also very much part of Luceplan's ideology. Every project is preceded by years of research. Teamwork is a crucial part of this process. Apart from Meda and Rizzatto, since the second half of the 1990s numerous renowned designers have increasingly worked for the company, including **Ross Lovegrove** and **Alfredo Häberli**, who contributed the *Carrara* standard lamp to the collection.

308

1 *Titania* hanging lamp, 1989
2 *Carrara* standard lamp, 2001
3 *Fortebraccio* table lamp, 1998
4 *GlassGlass* hanging lamp, 1998
5 *Costanza* table lamp, 1986
6 *Berenice* desk lamp, 1985
7 *Pod Lens* lamp, 1998

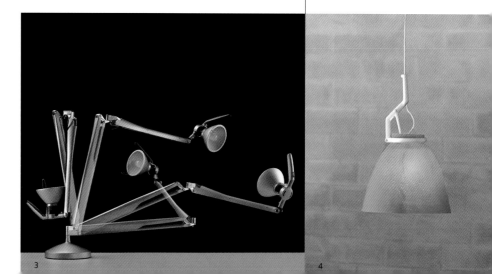

3

4

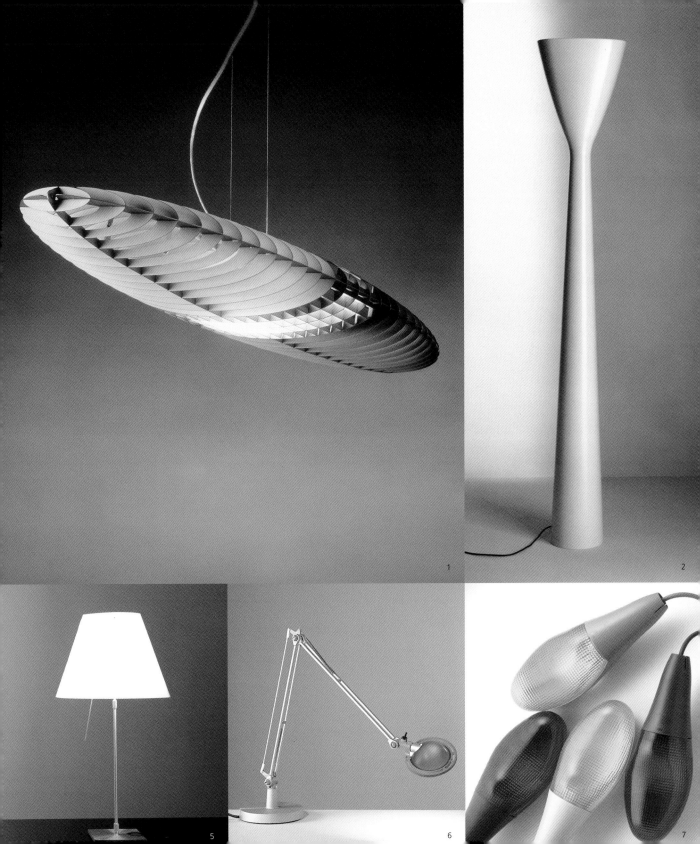

1

2

5

6

7

Lunar Design

USA | Product design studio | **www.lunar.com**

It is no accident that Lunar Design, founded in the mid-1980s, is based in California, where new technologies are constantly giving rise to new firms and products. The company has secured itself a place alongside **Continuum**, **Ideo** and **Ziba** as one of the most successful design studios in the United States. Lunar's CEO is Jeffrey Smith, to whom *Inc.* magazine devoted an article entitled 'How to Get Rich in America'. The studio is actively involved in shaping the new products of the digital age.

Among Lunar's product designs are computers of all shapes and sizes, an electronic 'softbook' and monitors both with and without cathodes. The studio's list of clients reads like an encyclopedia of American design, and includes such companies as **Apple**, **Motorola**, Hewlett-Packard, Palm, Polaroid, Samsung and **Sony**, all of which have increasingly put their faith in design and understand the need to keep a firm grasp of the rapidly changing market. Lunar does not deal exclusively with electronics, however. Its novel *Kerve* bicycle saddle features a split seat with an air-filled pocket on each side to improve comfort. The *Lush Lily* trays, which have no sharp corners or edges, are other everyday items that have received Lunar's ergonomic design treatment.

1984 Established by Jeffrey Smith and Gerard Furbershaw

2002 Receives American Graphic Design Award

2003 Receives Industrial Design Excellence Award (IDEA) for *Xootr eX3* electro-scooter for Nova Cruz

Products

1991 *PowerBook 100* laptop computer for **Apple**

1993 *Laserwriter 600* and *630* printers for Apple

1995 *Lush Lily* tray collection for Absolut Vodka; *Pavilion* multimedia PC for Hewlett-Packard

1996 *Velo 1* hand-held computer

1999 *HMD 100* monitor for **Sony**; *Cross Action* toothbrush for Oral-B; *Xootr* scooter for Nova Cruz; *TalkAbout* mobile telephone for **Motorola**; *Pavilion FX70* flat panel display for Hewlett-Packard

2000 *Palm m100* organizer for Palm Computing

2002 *Kerve* bicycle saddle; *zx 6000* computer for Hewlett-Packard

1 *HMD 100* monitor, 1999
2 *Kerve* bicycle saddle, 2002
3 *Lush Lily* tray collection, 1995
4 *zx 6000* computer, 2002
5 *Xootr* scooter, 1999

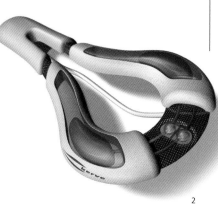

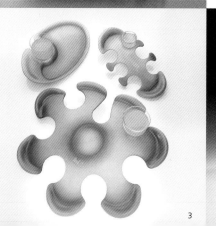

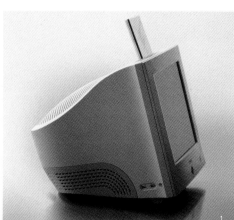

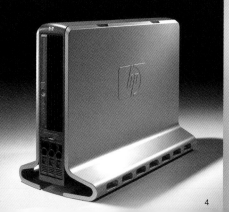

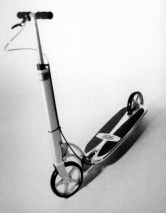

Claus **Luthe**

Germany | Automobile designer

1932 Born in Germany
1960 Works as designer at NSU
1976 Becomes chief designer at **BMW** (until 1990)

Products
1961 NSU *Prinz 4* small car
1967 NSU *Ro 80* saloon
1970 **Volkswagen** *K 70* saloon
1978 *6 Series*
1981 *5 Series* (new series in 1988)
1982 *3 Series* (new series in 1990)
1986 *7 Series*
1989 *850i* coupé
    Last five for ► BMW

1 NSU *Ro 80* saloon, 1967
2 BMW *750i* saloon, 1986
3 BMW *750i* saloon, 1986

Claus Luthe's career began in the mid-1950s at **Fiat**, but soon thereafter he moved to NSU, a manufacturer of compact small cars recognizable by their striking 'bathtub' shape. Luthe, a metalworker, coachbuilder and automotive engineer, used this shape for the first time in the *Prinz 4* car. At the end of the 1960s he created a sensation: the *Ro 80* was the first saloon with a Wankel engine and was also epoch-making in aesthetic terms. Giving the car a low bonnet, rising line and short back, Luthe introduced an entirely new design phenomenon – the wedge form.

Following NSU's acquisition by **Volkswagen**, Luthe worked for a time with **Audi**–NSU before moving to **BMW**. As chief designer there, he succeeded in strengthening the visual identity of the marque. In the early 1980s BMW's most successful model series up to that point, the *3 Series*, was launched. It was followed a few years later by the *7 Series*, with which the company established itself, alongside **Mercedes-Benz**, in the luxury class. BMW cars have always been compact and dynamic, and for this reason the company has tended to avoid aesthetic experimentation. This policy has made BMW an internationally renowned, elegant marque that, like an Armani suit or a music system by **Bang & Olufsen**, projects a certain lifestyle image.

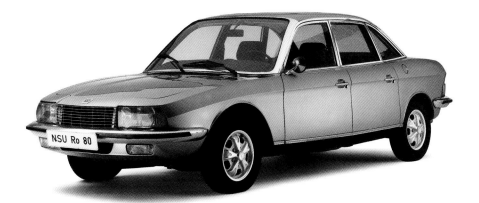

1

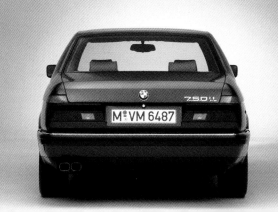

2   3

311

Enzo Mari, *Ameland* letter opener, 1962

Enzo Mari's first design for Danese was a wooden jigsaw puzzle for children. It marked the beginning of many years of collaboration between Mari and the Italian manufacturer. The partnership gave rise to a wealth of uncompromising product designs, among them the *Ameland* letter opener. With its double blade, twisted form and lack of handle, it is reminiscent of the type of optical illusion devised by the twentieth-century graphic artist M.C. Escher.

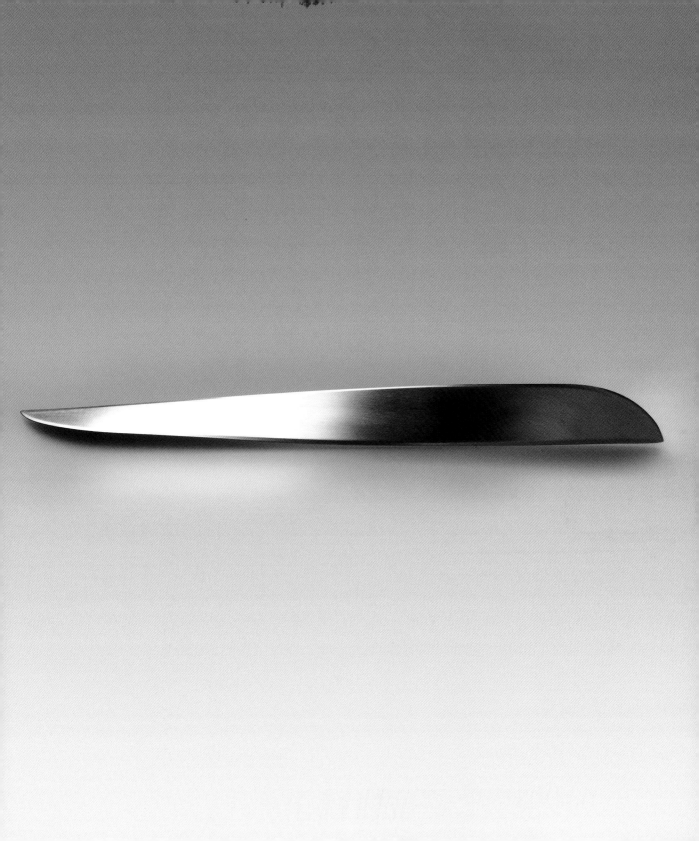

Charles Rennie **Mackintosh**

Scotland | Architect and furniture designer | **www.crmsociety.com**

The work of the Glaswegian architect and designer Charles Rennie Mackintosh made a significant contribution to British design in the twentieth century. With Herbert MacNair and the sisters Frances and Margaret Macdonald, all fellow students at the Glasgow School of Art, he formed the 'Glasgow Four'. From around 1900 this group was successful in creating a modern design style that is instantly recognizable and is today widely acknowledged as being way ahead of its time in Britain.

Mackintosh is a representative of a period that produced many outstanding designers, among them Antoni Gaudí, **Frank Lloyd Wright** and **Josef Hoffmann**, with whom he was in close contact. The unconventional architect created a body of work that, although derived from Continental Art Nouveau in style, displayed graphic differences. His bold furniture, with its reduced lines, is still impressive today. The high-backed chair, with its extreme proportions, which Mackintosh varied over and over again, is particularly famous. The *Argyle* chair exhibits the same stylistic features. In the *Argyle* he was still using floral motifs typical of Art Nouveau; his later works, however, are characterized by geometric severity and a preponderance of right angles. This can be seen most clearly in the *Willow* chair, which rests on a box instead of legs; its broad, curved back has a pattern of rectangles and parallel lines. This grid pattern is taken up again in the *DS 322* table.

Mackintosh's most important architectural commission was for a new building for the Glasgow School of Art, for which he also designed the furniture and fittings. Like many Scots, he left his home country for a period to seek design inspiration on the Continent. On his return, he began to export his views on design, especially to Vienna. His interior designs were nothing less than integrated works of art. Hill House in Helensburgh, Miss Catherine Cranston's tea rooms and his own apartment at 120 Main Street, Glasgow, are examples of his ingenuity. Later in his career he had difficultly finding new clients and so moved to France. Mackintosh's genius has, however, been preserved: the Italian company **Cassina** has been reproducing a number of his furniture designs since the early 1970s.

314

1 *Ingram* chair, 1904, and *Hill House* chair, 1902
2 *Argyle* chair, 1897
3 *Berlino* table, 1905
4 *DS 322* table, 1918
5 *Willow* chair, 1904

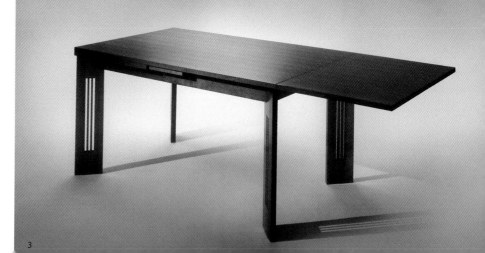

3

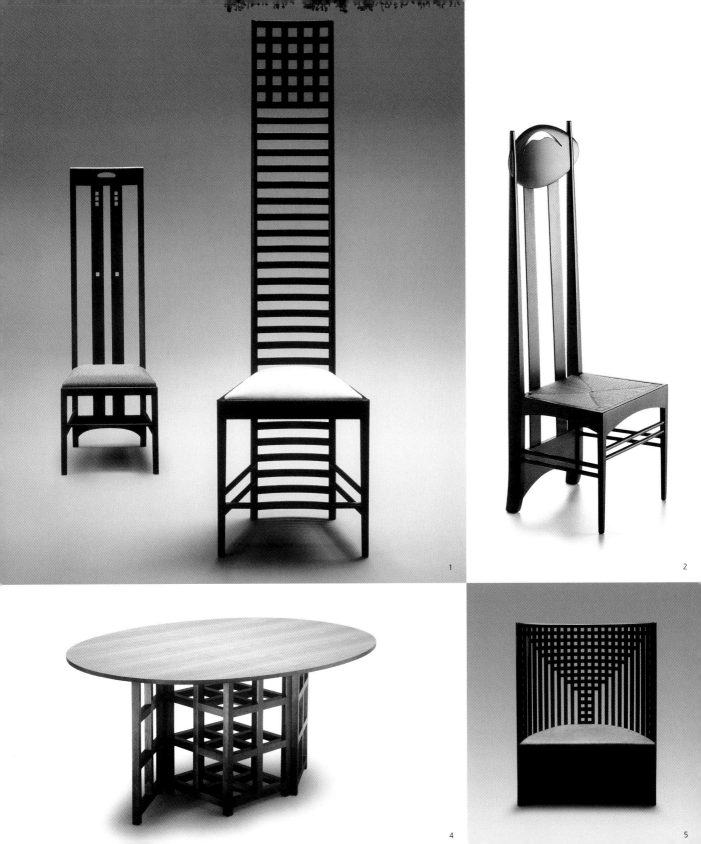

1

2

4

5

Magis

Italy I Magis SpA, Motta di Livenza I Furniture and accessories manufacturer I **www.magisdesign.com**

According to its founder, Eugenio Perazza, Magis is a firm of designers. Based near Venice, the company views itself as a kind of product publisher, one that gathers together the different languages and styles of international designers. Perazza gives his designers considerable free rein and is himself passionately involved in the creative process of each individual product. Magis has a team of hand-picked specialists and suppliers who are ready to react flexibly and quickly to the ideas of external designers; the firm is thus basically a design factory, minus the manufacturing side. Over three decades it has built up a range of fresh, vivid furniture and everyday objects created by such illustrious designers as **Konstantin Grcic, Jasper Morrison, Karim Rashid, Stefano Giovannoni, Marc Newson, Werner Aisslinger, James Irvine** and **Michael Young**.

Magis was founded in 1976 and is therefore not one of those legendary Italian companies that heralded the beginning of modern Italian design in the 1950s and 1960s. It is, however, one of those that profited from this development and was able to embark on its own distinctive course. The firm decided to focus on two materials – plastic and metal – and to use them to create a permanent flow of new and innovative products. The casual *Bombo* barstool by ▸Stefano Giovannoni, with its 'hula hoop' footrest and slanting, rounded seat, has become a bestseller. The *Bottle* wine rack from 1994, designed by Jasper Morrison, and his elegant *Air* chair, from 2000, are among the company's other success stories. One of the more recent products that has aroused a lot of interest is ▸Konstantin Grcic's *Chair_One*, with its skeletal aluminium frame. For this chair series, Grcic used high-tech die-cast aluminium, a material that is completely new to the Magis range. The German designer created a furniture collection that is exotic and expressive, but does not look particularly inviting. The response was therefore somewhat mixed, although it must be conceded that the design is highly individual and courageous – in other words, a typical Magis product. Another recent design for Magis is *Striped*, by **Ronan and Erwan Bouroullec**, an appealing series of chairs with stretchy plastic straps that support the weight of the body.

1976 Established by Eugenio Perazza

Products

1979 *X-Line* chair

1984 *Cricket* chair and *Step* ladder by Andries and Hiroko van Onck

1992 *Amleto* ironing board by Design Group Italia; *Rondine* folding table and chair by ▸ **Toshiyuki Kita**

1994 *Bottle* wine rack by **Jasper Morrison**

1997 *Bombo* barstool by ▸ **Stefano Giovannoni** (series extended between 1999 and 2003 to include various tables and easy chairs)

1998 *Dish Doctor* drainer and *Rock* doorstop by ▸ **Marc Newson**; *Magò* broom by ▸ Stefano Giovannoni

2000 *Hercules* coat hanger by Marc Newson; *Air* chair by Jasper Morrison; *Stand By* shelf by ▸ **Axel Kufus**

2001 *Pebbles* stool/container by **Marcel Wanders**; *Centomila* table and chair by ▸ **James Irvine**; *Plus Unit* drawer system by ▸ **Werner Aisslinger**

2002 *MY 080* tray/table by **Michael Young**; *Aida* folding table and chair by ▸ **Richard Sapper**; *Tam Tam Family* stool and table by ▸ **Matteo Thun**; *Technotable* by ▸ **Christophe Pillet**

2003 *Chair_One* by ▸ **Konstantin Grcic**; *Butterfly* chair and *Kase* briefcase by ▸ **Karim Rashid**; *La Valise* case by ▸ **Ronan and Erwan Bouroullec**; *Nic* chair by Werner Aisslinger; *Flare* table by ▸ Marcel Wanders; *Pilastro* table by ▸ **Enzo Mari**; *Magis Wagon* mobile table by Michael Young

2004 *Striped* furniture collection by Ronan and Erwan Bouroullec

2005 *Puppet XL* child's seat by **Eero Aarnio**

1 *Bombo* barstool, 1997 (available in aluminium since 2002)
2 *Striped* furniture collection, 2004
3 *Aida* folding table, 2002
4 *Bottle* wine rack, 1994
5 *Hercules* coat hanger, 2000
6 *Magis Wagon* mobile table, 2003
7 *Dish Doctor* drainer, 1998
8 *Air* chair, 2000

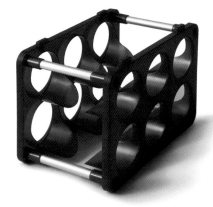

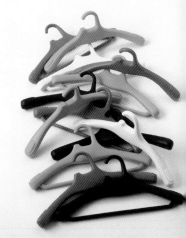

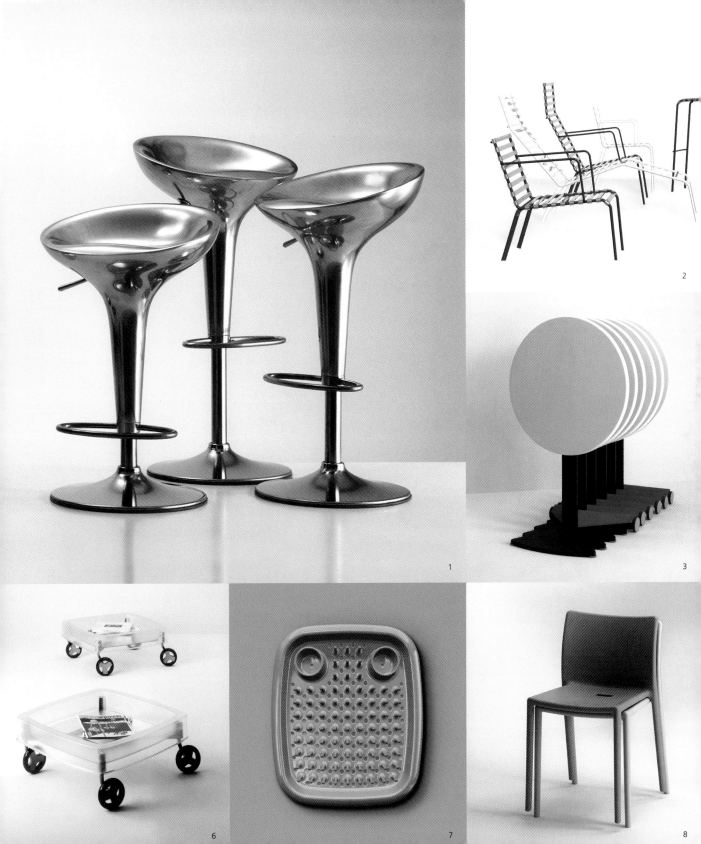

1

2

3

6

7

8

Vico **Magistretti**

Italy | Architect and furniture and lamp designer

The softly curved *Maui* plastic chair is one of the leading products of the Italian manufacturer **Kartell**. Designed by Vico Magistretti, the grand master of restrained Italian design, the chair combines innovative technology with practicality, and is a courageous statement; it is also beautifully designed, competitively priced and unpretentious. There is one further distinctive feature about the chair that makes it a typical Magistretti product: it has been a bestseller for many years.

There is an incredibly long list of Magistretti designs that tells a similar success story. As early as 1960 he created *Carimate* for **Cassina**. This farmhouse-style wooden chair had a woven raffia seat and made Magistretti famous virtually overnight as the master of simple, almost austere forms. In the late 1960s he had another success, this time with *Selene* (for ▶ **Artemide**), a plastic chair made from a single cast that almost undoubtedly helped the material to shed its cheap, downbeat image. Magistretti has designed a vast number of other objects that today are regarded as classics. These include, from the 1960s, the small, poetic *Eclisse* lamps, with their simple but effective means of adjusting the light by turning the reflector to half moon, full moon or new moon position, and the *Chimera* standard lamp, a beautiful, curved light sculpture (both for Artemide); from the 1970s, *Atollo*, an exquisitely sculpted table lamp for **O Luce**; and from the 1980s, the multi-purpose *Silver* chair for De Padova, an aluminium–plastic redesign of **Marcel Breuer**'s *811* wooden chair for **Thonet** dating from 1925. Magistretti has left his mark on De Padova's range of high-quality, elegant furniture and has also exerted a strong influence on the Cassina programme. He once said that he had tried to avoid creating peculiar things. His name does not stand for formal excess and short-lived ideas, but rather for subtle design quality that constantly reveals new dimensions in everyday use.

318

1 *Atollo* table lamp, 1977

2 *Louisiana* armchair, 1993

3 *Variantes* sofa, 1996

4 *Lester* table lamp, 1988

5 *Maui* swivel armchair, 1997

6 *Mezzachimera* standard lamp, 1965

7 *Maralunga* sofa, 1973

8 *Silver* chair, 1989

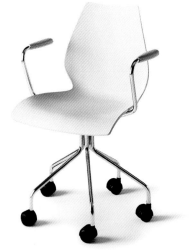

5

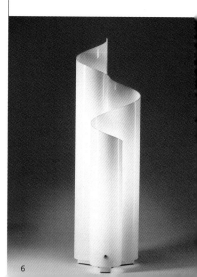

6

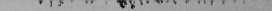

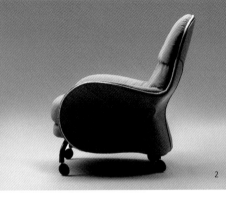

1

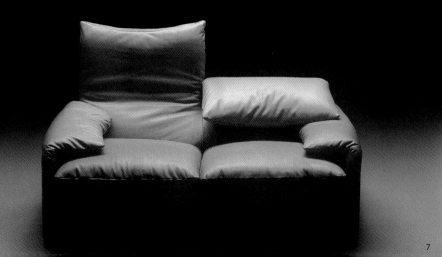

2

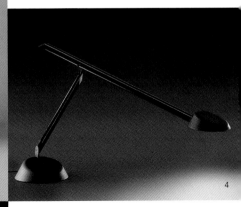

3

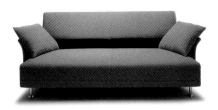

4

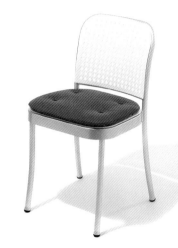

7

8

Erik **Magnussen**

Denmark | Product and furniture designer | www.magnussen-design.dk

In his early career Erik Magnussen was a successful ceramicist, but his stated interest was in "real things" – and in his view, these were produced in factories. In the mid-1960s he designed his first service for Bing & Grøndahl, which broke with convention and drew inspiration from the stackable crockery produced by **Kaj Franck** and Hans Roericht for **Rosenthal**. In the 1970s he was appointed as **Arne Jacobsen**'s successor at **Stelton**. Magnussen's appointment was an appropriate one since he, along with **Knud Holscher**, is widely regarded as representing the best in Danish industrial design. The partnership with Stelton continues to this day. His very first product for the company, a cylindrical thermos jug that was intended to complement Jacobsen's famous *Cylinda Line*, was a bestseller. Magnussen developed a unique lid that automatically opens when the jug is positioned for pouring. With this jug, today found in any self-respecting upmarket furnishing store, he created a product that was the absolute embodiment of his design principles. Magnussen believes that a product should be original, durable, economical to manufacture and, at the same time, as simple and easy to handle as possible. Such simplicity requires time, however: "I have never spent less than a year on a product", he claims.

In his furniture designs, Magnussen, a rationalist, favours tubular steel for its ability to be bent as required. His stackable chair (for Paustian), which consists of a single bent tube reminiscent of **Poul Henningsen**'s *Snake Chair*, is striking in its simplicity. Steel legs form the backbone of the plastic chair he designed for **Thonet**. Magnussen's work, which often hovers on the verge of anti-design, rarely has anything fashionable about it. His scientific approach has proved beneficial in a somewhat unexpected field of activity: among the technical appliances he has designed is a navigation instrument for ships that combines satellite-based technology with digital data processing. Magnussen's approach shows that the classic principle 'less is more' is still applicable in the twenty-first century.

320

1 Thermos jug, 1977
2 Compact hi-fi system, 1995
3 Knife set, 2001
4 Kettle, 1986
5 *1127* door handle, 1991
6 Chair, 1989
7 Cake servers, 1981
8 *K 818* chair, 2000

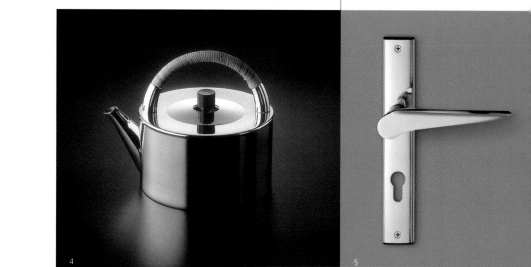

4

5

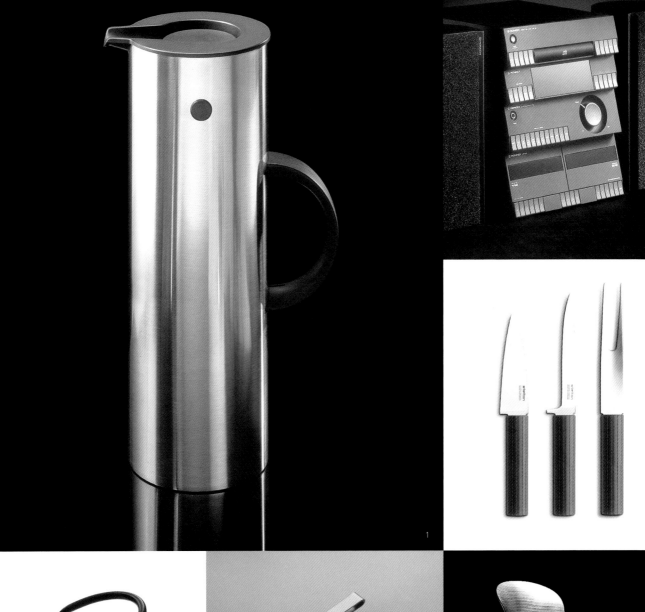

1

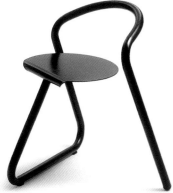

2

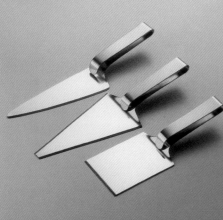

3

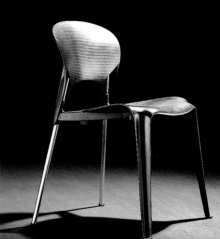

6

7

8

Peter **Maly**

Germany | Interior and furniture designer | **www.peter-maly.de**

Peter Maly was regarded by his colleague **Verner Panton** as a perfectionist. It is unlikely that Maly himself would disagree with this observation, particularly given that his role model is Johann Sebastian Bach. Following his apprenticeship as a cabinetmaker and interior designer, Maly worked for the Hamburg periodical *Schöner Wohnen*, Germany's biggest interior design magazine. While as working as an editor, he began producing his first designs for **Tecta** and **Cor**. Later in his career, he also designed exhibition stands and showrooms for Cor.

Maly set up his own company in the 1970s. His early work was influenced by contemporary Danish furniture design and by Pop art. He later discovered the Bauhaus, which had an even greater impact on his designs. Since then, carefully measured geometric forms have become an integral part of Maly's work, as in his *Zyklus* armchair, a cult object from the mid-1980s; his carpets for JAB Anstoetz; and *Le Ballon* series of lamps (for **Ligne Roset**). Even though he is inspired by basic forms, Maly's primary interest lies in functionality: "A chair is made for the bottom and not for the head", he once stated baldly. Durability is also an important element in his work. As a committed environmentalist, he believes that furniture should be worth passing on to one's heirs.

1936 Born in Trutnov, Bohemia (now Czech Republic)
1960 Graduates in interior design from Fachhochschule, Detmold; works for *Schöner Wohnen* magazine
1970 Opens own studio in Hamburg
1995 Receives Red Dot Design Award for *737* chair collection

Products

1967 *Series 1* furniture collection for **Tecta**
1969 *Trinom* armchair for **Cor**
1976 *Logo* armchair for Cor
1983 *Maly* bed for **Ligne Roset**
1984 *Delta* table and *Zyklus* armchair for Cor; *Duo* system furniture for **Interlübke**
1990 *Tarbo* sofa and armchair for Cor
1992 *Cirrus* daybed for ► Cor
1993 *Biblia* bookcases for Ligne Roset; *737* chair collection for **Thonet**
1996 *Menos* chest for Behr
1997 Fireplace accessories for Conmoto; *Vivace* grand piano for Sauter
1998 *Circo* armchair for ► Cor; *Screen* lamps for Anta
1999 *Alas* furnishings programme for Behr; *Le Ballon* lamps and *Brera* shelf system and table for ► Ligne Roset
2000 *Medio* multimedia cabinet for Interlübke
2001 *Traversale* seating system for Ligne Roset; *Nemo* armchair and sofa and *Circo* table for Cor
2002 *Lumeo* bed for Ligne Roset
2003 *Circo-solo* armchair for Cor; *Flexus* sofa for Ligne Roset

1 *Zyklus* armchair, 1984
2 *737* chair, 1993
3 *Vivace* grand piano, 1997
4 *Flexus* sofa, 2003
5 *Le Ballon* standard lamp, 1999

322

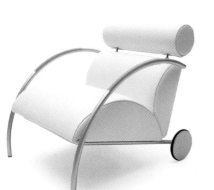

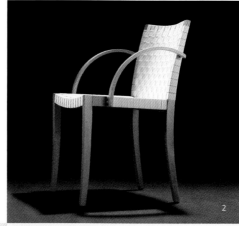

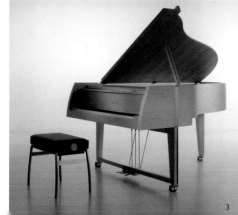

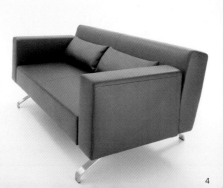

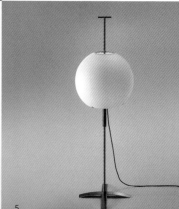

Mandarina Duck

Italy I Plastimoda SpA, Cadriano I Bag manufacturer I **www.mandarinaduck.com**

Research into new and unusual materials, together with collaboration with outstanding designers, is Mandarina Duck's formula for success. To date, the bag and accessories manufacturer from Bologna has registered around one hundred technical patents. The brand was introduced in the mid-1970s and was bold in its designs at a time when natural materials in subdued colours dominated the market. *Utility*, its first colourful series in synthetic materials, proved extremely popular, thus validating the company's unorthodox research, design, and marketing policies.

In the early 1980s the Italian designer **Alberto Meda** adopted technology used in the automobile industry for his *Tank* bags, which incorporate a ribbed material made from strong, lightweight rubber. Around twenty years later, the Dutch designer **Marcel Wanders** presented the spectacular *Murano* bag series, notable for its exceptional strength and stability. The bags were developed from a unique thermo-sensitive material. Each bag is individually 'oven-baked' in a kiln, where the material becomes elastic. Mandarina Duck also has a fashion collection and a range of spectacles and watches (developed in collaboration with Seiko). It has commissioned various leading designers and studios to design its stores, including **Michele De Lucchi** and **Droog Design**.

1968	Established by Paolo Trento and Pietro Mannato in Bologna
1977	Launches Mandarina Duck label
2001	Opens store in Paris, designed by **Droog Design**
2002	Opens store in Rome, designed by Angelo Micheli
2003	Receives iF Design Award for *Elastic* keyholder
2004	Opens store in Berlin, designed by **Michael Young**

Products

1977	*Utility* collection
1981	*Tank* collection by **Alberto Meda**
1984	*Sistema* collection
1988	*Hera* collection
1994	*Wink* collection
1998	*Linea Twice* bag
2000	*Frog* collection
2002	*Murano* collection by **Marcel Wanders**; *Clique* collection; wristwatch collection (with Seiko)
2003	*Spin*, *Keep* and *Mandarina* collections
2004	*Lamandarina* ballpoint pen by Giulio Lacchetti; *Impronta* ballpoint pen by **Ross Lovegrove**

1 Shopper (*Murano* collection), 2002
2 Shoulder bag (*Murano* collection), 2002
3 Holdall (*Sistema* collection), 1984
4 *Lamandarina* and *Impronta* ballpoint pens, 2004
5 Travel bag (*Tank* collection), 1981

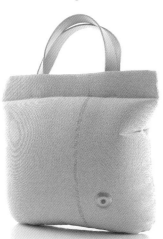

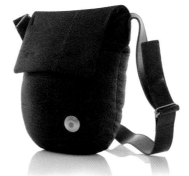

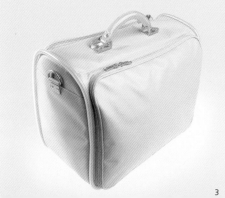

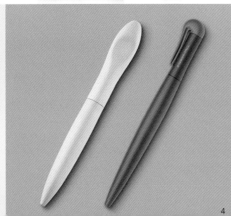

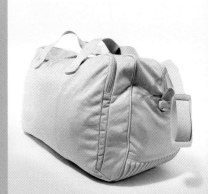

323

Angelo **Mangiarotti**

Italy | Architect and furniture and product designer

The materials most loved and most often used by the Italian architect, designer and artist Angelo Mangiarotti are plastic, wood and glass. He rarely combines them in individual designs but allows them to stand alone so that their beauty and distinct qualities can be fully appreciated. For Mangiarotti, the material "is to design what the brain is to thinking". This basic principle is evident in the entire range of his work, from elegant, mouth-blown glass lamps, such as *Lesbo* for **Artemide**, and solid marble tables, such as *Eros* and *Fiorera* for Skipper, to precious crystal objects for Colle Cristalleria and the *T-Table* in aluminium for **Baleri Italia**. The remarkable shapes he managed to tease out of fibreglass in the creation of the *Chicago* chair are particularly audacious.

The simple form of such a basic everyday object as the *Barbados* ashtray (for **Danese**) enhances the effect of the shiny red plastic. Architecture and sculpture have remained important focal points in Mangiarotti's work. Since the 1950s he has been one of a number of eminent designers providing new impulses in post-war Italian design, as demonstrated not only by his objects but also by his research into the development of new materials, particularly plastics. The Milan Triennale in 2002 devoted an entire exhibition to Mangiarotti's work.

1921	Born in Milan
1948	Graduates in architecture from Politecnico, Milan
1955	Collaborates with Bruno Morassutti
1956	Co-founds Associazione per il Disegno Industriale (ADI)
1989	Certosa and Rogoredo stations, Milan; opens office in Tokyo
1996	Begins collaboration with **Baleri Italia**

Products

1960	*Section* table clock with Bruno Morassutti
1963	Armchair for **Cassina**
1964	*Barbados* ashtray for **Danese**
1965	*Multiuse* cupboard for **Poltronova**
1966	*Lesbo* table lamp for **Artemide**
1971	*Eros* and *Fiorera* marble tables for Skipper
1973	*Cruscotto* kitchen for Snaidero
1977	*Incas* stone table for Skipper
1980	*Chicago* fibreglass chair for Skipper
1982	*Status* kitchen for Snaidero
1986	*Kyatos* and *Askos* decanters for Colle Cristalleria
1990	*Clizia* seat for Skipper; *Ergonomica* cutlery for Mepra
1996	*Ypsilon* shelf system for Baleri Italia
1998	*T-Table* and *Ad Lovis* table lamp for ▶ Baleri Italia
2003	*AML-White/Black* wristwatch for Pierre Junod
2004	Wall clock and table clock for Klein & Co.

1   *T-Table*, 1998
2   *Barbados* ashtray, 1964
3   *Lesbo* table lamp, 1966
4   *Chicago* fibreglass chair, 1980

324

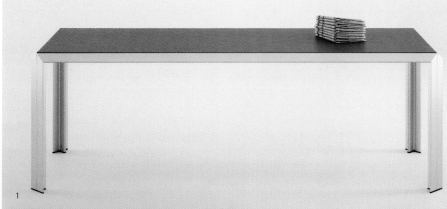

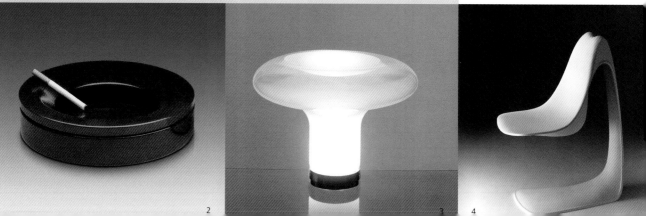

Christophe **Marchand**

Switzerland | Furniture and product designer | **www.christophemarchand.ch**

Precision and lightness are among the distinctive qualities evident in the work of the Swiss designer Christophe Marchand. The restraint typical of the Swiss design scene is reflected in his *Wave* chair (for Ycami), with its armrests that stretch out to greet the user; in the slim modules of the *Wogg 25* hanging shelf (for Wogg); and in the precise tubular steel aesthetic of the folding tables and coat stands (for **Thonet**) that he developed in collaboration with his long-standing partner, **Alfredo Häberli**.

Born in Fribourg, Marchand is one of the most sought-after designers in the industry. He completed an apprenticeship as a cabinetmaker before attending the Hochschule für Gestaltung und Kunst in Zurich. He then devoted himself to product design and opened a studio in Zurich. His *MaRe* chaise longue (for ▸ **Wellis**) combines a strong graphic effect with the lightness characteristic of his work. Marchand contributed *Happening*, a comprehensive and flexible system of modular elements, to the collection of ▸ **Steelcase**, a manufacturer of office furniture from the United States. He also attracted considerable attention with *PAC* (for ICF), his futuristic office swivel chair constructed from materials that had hitherto been used to make sports equipment.

325

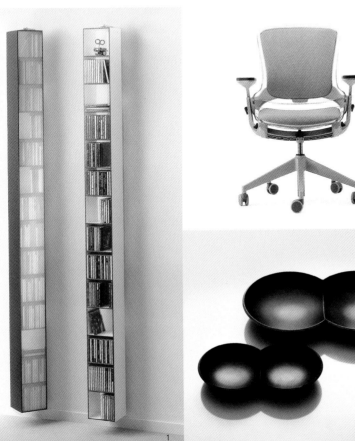

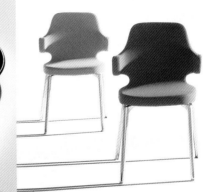

Enzo **Mari**

Italy | Artist, theoretician and furniture and product designer

"Good design for everybody at affordable prices" is the motto of the Italian designer, artist and theoretician Enzo Mari. Mari came to design via the world of art and approached it as a critic of the consumer society. Having contributed to debates on design for more than fifty years now, he is regarded by many as the chief ideologue of the industry. Mari believes that, rather than simply giving expression to the ideas and ideologies of others and confining themselves to questions of aesthetics, designers should participate in debate and develop their own ideologies. He regards functionality as important and abhors senseless or kitsch products. Mari is always concerned that his designs may be perpetuating the *status quo* and is therefore suspicious when people praise them. He cannot escape acclaim entirely, however, as his products are among the most poetic and beautiful ever produced by an Italian designer. His table and wall calendars, created for ▶ **Danese** in the 1960s, are typographical masterpieces that succeed in lending a sensitive and sensual dimension to time. His early children's games were produced in wood and can be dismantled. They are particularly attractive for their tactile and educational qualities.

In the early 1960s Mari published his first theoretical works on the psychology of visual perception, aesthetics and design. Since then he has designed roughly 1400 pieces of furniture and other objects, including book covers, household articles and wall tiles. Among his furniture, which has been produced by such well-known manufacturers as **Driade** and **Zanotta**, the light, stackable *Delfina* chair and the practical *Day-Night* sofa bed deserve special mention. A large number of his designs, including the older ones, are still in production. In the early 1990s Mari became chief designer at the renowned Königliche Porzellan-Manufaktur (KPM) in Berlin. There, in close collaboration with craftsmen, he developed a small number of designs that could be produced in intelligent variations. For his *Berlin* service he reinterpreted the traditional values of porcelain – individuality of design, lasting value and the fine quality of the material – in the context of modern design. Mari recently presented a series of chairs for the Japanese label **Muji**. Its distinctive mix of forms and materials created something of a stir.

1 *Formosa* wall calendar, 1962
2 *Pilastro* table, 2003
3 *Tela* lamp collection, 2002
4 *Ulm* shelf system, 1996
5 *16 Animali* wooden toys, 1957
6 *In Attesa* waste bin, 1971
7 Teapot (*Berlin* tea service), 1996
8 *Sof Sof* chair, 1972

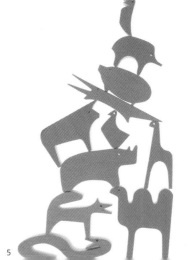

5

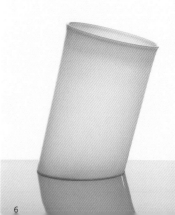

6

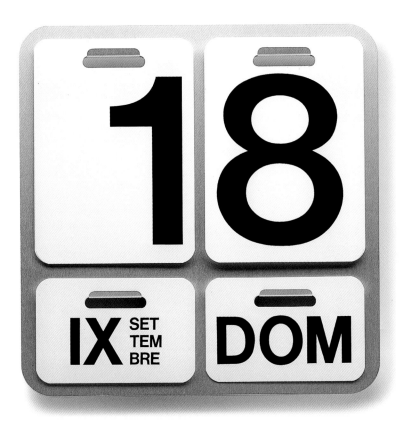

1

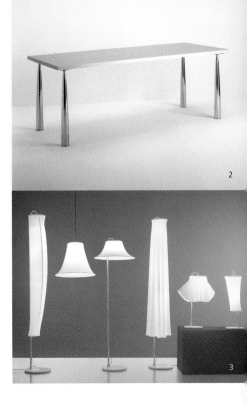

2

3

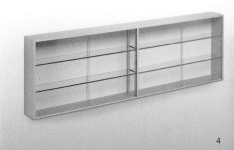

4

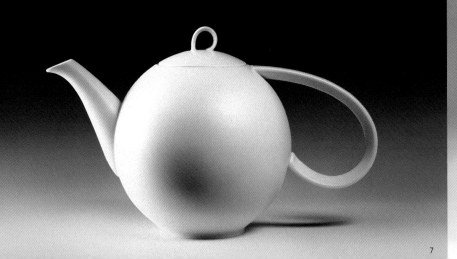

7

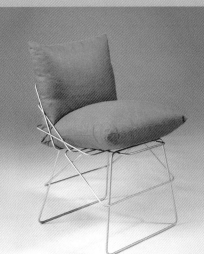

8

Javier **Mariscal**

Spain | Furniture and product designer | www.mariscal.com

Twipsy, the mascot of the Hanover *World Exposition 2000*, has a big mouth, a gigantic nose, arms that differ in length and three fingers on each hand. The figure was created in the Barcelona studio of Javier Mariscal, an artist, graphic designer and furniture and product designer. One of the high-profile leaders of the international design scene, Mariscal has succeeded in establishing an extremely eccentric style. He claims that "Calder and Vázquez, Miró and Mickey Mouse, Matisse and Crumb" have influenced his work in equal measure. While a student of design, he made a name for himself as an artist for underground comics. His first furniture design, the *Duplex* barstool from the early 1980s, seemed like a three-dimensional version of his comics. The *Hilton* serving trolley, a bold metal and glass combination that he co-designed with Pepe Cortés in 1981 for the legendary Memphis design group exhibition in Milan, aroused tremendous interest. Mariscal has remained faithful to his unique style. His *Duplex* stool, for example, appears to be dancing, and the *Alessandra* armchair is one of the cheeky outsiders in the **Moroso** product range. His lamps also demonstrate his rejection of simple geometry, as in the freely designed polyethylene shades in the *Domine* series, a recent project produced by Santa & Cole.

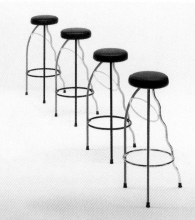

1

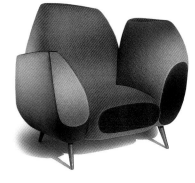

2

328

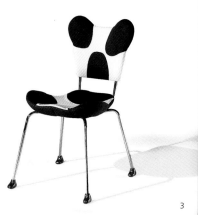

3

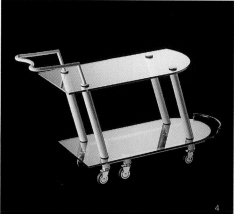

4

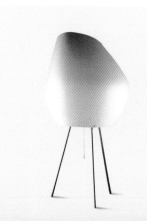

5

Michael **Marriott**

England | Furniture and product designer

Like his fellow Britons **Ron Arad** and **Tom Dixon**, Michael Marriott started his career with designs made from recycled materials. In the 1990s he created such furniture as the *Seven Series* miniature drawers made from sardine tins and the *Citrus Light* container on wheels, with drawers made from cardboard boxes. The recycling idea arose originally from financial necessity. During his studies at the London College of Furniture and the Royal College of Art Marriott worked part-time for an antiques dealer, and he tried his hand as a graphic designer, exhibition designer and head of a furniture workshop before he became a proponent of modern British design. Towards the end of the 1990s he started using more orthodox materials without, however, completely losing his typically British sense of humour. His *Skittle* table, for example, which for a time was sold by **SCP**, has baseball bats as legs. For the same manufacturer he designed the *Croquet – floor* and *Croquet – wall* shelving units and the *Missed* chaise longue. All are simple designs that can be classified as minimalist. It comes as no surprise to learn that Marriott was enthusiastic about the Bauhaus as a student. He has also remained faithful to a principle that was important to him in his use of second-hand materials: the rejection of the wastefulness of industry.

329

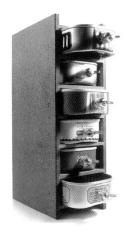

1

2

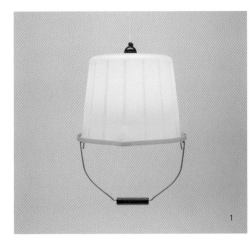

3

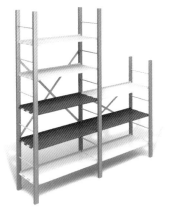

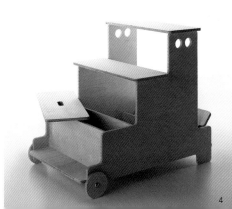

4

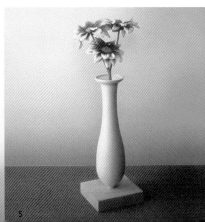

5

Jean-Marie **Massaud**

France | Furniture designer | www.massaud.com

How Sigmund Freud, the father of psychoanalysis, would have reacted if he had learned that his name would be given to a shimmering gold couch in the early twenty-first century can only remain a matter of speculation. The naming of a chaise longue (for **Moroso**) after Freud is typical of the tongue-in-cheek approach of the French designer Jean-Marie Massaud, who clearly regards playfulness as a positive value in design. Massaud is one of a number of new French designers – among them **Matali Crasset**, **Christophe Pillet** and the brothers **Ronan and Erwan Bouroullec** – who are finally moving out of the shadow of the grand master **Philippe Starck**. In 2000, following his training at the prestigious Ecole Nationale Supérieure de Création Industrielle (ENSCI, which has produced many renowned designers) and a period in Hong Kong, Massaud set up his own studio in Paris. His partner is the Romanian-born architect Daniel Pouzet. Today such prestigious companies as **Authentics**, **Cassina**, Habitat, Lancôme, **Ligne Roset**, **Renault** and **Yamaha** feature on the studio's lengthy client list. Massaud's work focuses on domestic furniture, lamps and furnishings. His *Outline* and *In-Out* sofas, designed for **Cappellini**, show that he is not afraid of expressive gestures. There is another side to the designer, however: in such works as *Wave*, a Perspex chaise longue (for **Dornbracht**), Massaud demonstrates considerable discipline.

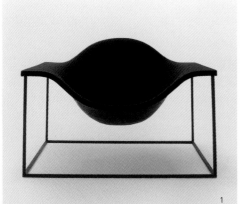

1

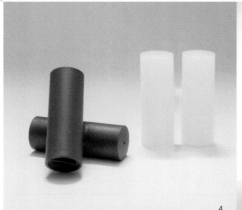

2

330

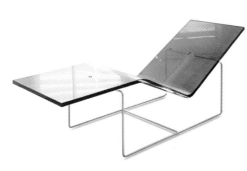

3

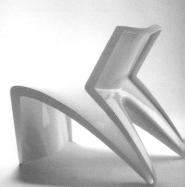

4

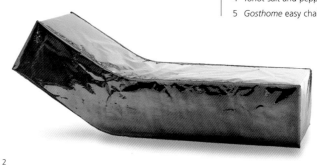

5

Bruno **Mathsson**

Sweden | Furniture designer | www.bruno-mathsson-int.com

Bruno Mathsson came from a family of cabinetmakers. He used the skills he learned at an early age not only to perfect his craftsmanship but also to develop forward-looking ergonomic seating based on anatomical studies. These innovative methods made him Sweden's most famous designer. His *Eva* chair from the mid-1930s was conceptually different from any other chair created before. Its bentwood frame was made of beech, and its seat consisted of woven webbing. It was particularly notable for its soft, flowing lines, which gave it an unusual dynamism, and for the fact that it represented a completely new concept in seating. The body is pressed into the seat as a result of the chair's comfortable design, which affects the user's centre of gravity, pushing it down much lower than usual. Mathsson produced a number of variations on this successful design over the course of several years. The same principle lay behind his *Pernilla* chaise longue from the 1940s.

Mathsson constantly ventured into new terrain, whether with shelving on wheels; with his *Superellipsis* from the 1960s, an ingenious oval table based on complex calculations undertaken by the inventor Piet Hein; or with the work tables he designed in the 1980s. Mathsson's approach to marketing was also entirely new; he was one of the first designers to ship his furniture direct to customers.

331

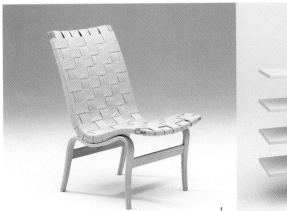

1

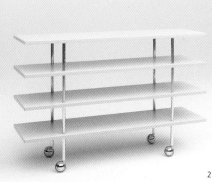

2

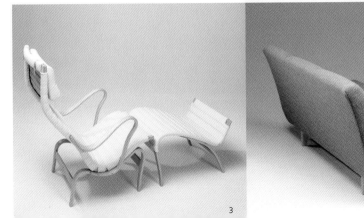

3

4

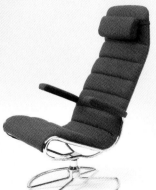

5

Ingo **Maurer**

Germany | Lamp designer | **www.ingo-maurer.com**

Cryptic, subtle, not exactly minimalist, on the border between kitsch and poetry: the lamps by the German designer Ingo Maurer are communicative sculptures that provoke comment, a smile or even an expression of surprise. *Wo bist du, Edison …?*, for example, consists of a hologram of a light bulb 'caught' inside a lampshade, creating a lamp within a lamp. The reflector of the *Mozzkito* table lamp is made from an outsize tea strainer, to which spidery metal rods have been attached. When switched on, it immediately conjures up the image of a mosquito, as suggested by its name. For *Lucellino*, Maurer adorned a naked light bulb with goose feathers; *Zettel'z* is a collection of different pieces of paper with writing on them, suspended in mid-air; *Porca Miseria!* resembles a set of crockery frozen at the moment of bursting apart; the charm of the *MaMo Nouchies* lamps lies in their gracefulness. Many of Maurer's products make subtle use of paper, wire mesh or other inexpensive materials, and every design hints at his unbridled pleasure in playing with the various properties of light. Maurer, Bernhard Dessecker and the other lighting experts of the Munich team are obviously concerned with designing light rather than lamps.

Maurer's career as a prize-winning lamp designer began in the 1960s. At that time he was already successful as a graphic designer. He moved to the United States in 1960 but returned in 1963, and in 1966 founded his design studio, Design M, in Munich. In the same year he created *Bulb*, his first lamp. Inspired by Pop art, it consisted of a light bulb within another outsize bulb; it was a lamp and sculpture at the same time. The *YaYaHo* low-voltage halogen lighting system, which Mauer developed in 1984, also broke new ground, both in its design and in its technology: not only shades, but also birds, moons and other 'flying' objects can be suspended from its wires. Maurer designs lamps for both private houses and public places and has, for example, created gigantic light bells for the Westfriedhof underground station in Munich. Numerous museums, including the Centre Georges Pompidou in Paris and the Museum of Modern Art (MoMA) in New York, have taken a lively interest in his work.

1932 Born Reichenau, Lake Constance
1954 Studies graphic design in Munich (until 1958)
1960 Moves to USA (remains until 1963)
1966 Establishes Design M studio in Munich
1969 Products selected for permanent collection of MoMA, New York
1985 YaYaHo light system features in *Lumière, je pense à vous* exhibition at Centre Georges Pompidou, Paris
1999 Opens showroom in New York
2000 Receives Lucky Strike Designer Award
2002 *Ingo Maurer: Light – Reaching for the Moon* exhibition held at Vitra Design Museum

Products
1966 *Bulb* table lamp
1970 *Light Structure*
1983 *Willydilly* hanging lamp
1984 *YaYaHo* low-voltage lighting system
1989 *One From the Heart* standard lamp
1990 *Zero-One* wall lamp
1992 *Lucellino* wall lamp
1994 *Hot Achille* and *Porca Miseria!* hanging lamps
1996 *Mozzkito* table lamp
1997 *Wo bist du, Edison …?* hanging lamp with hologram; *Zettel'z* hanging lamp
1998 *MaMo Nouchies* lamp collection incl. *Wo-Tum-Bu, Kekeli, Con-Qui*
1999 *XXL Dome* hanging lamp
2000 *Max. Mover* wall and hanging lamp; *Bob* table lamp; *Holonzki* wall lamp
2001 *Ball Park* lamp (with **Ron Arad**); *El.E.Dee* table lamp
2002 *Pixel Birds* lamp (with Ron Arad); *Campari Light* hanging lamp
2003 *Prototype* lamp

1 *Zettel'z* hanging lamp, 1997
2 *Campari Light* hanging lamp, 2002
3 *Porca Miseria!* hanging lamp, 1994
4 *Lucellino* wall lamp, 1992
5 *Bulb* table lamp, 1966
6 *El.E.Dee* table lamp, 2001
7 *Mozzkito* table lamp, 1996
8 *Wo-Tum-Bu* standard lamp, 1998

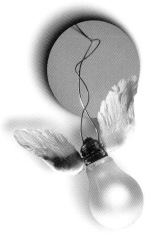

4

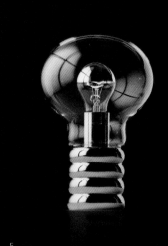

5

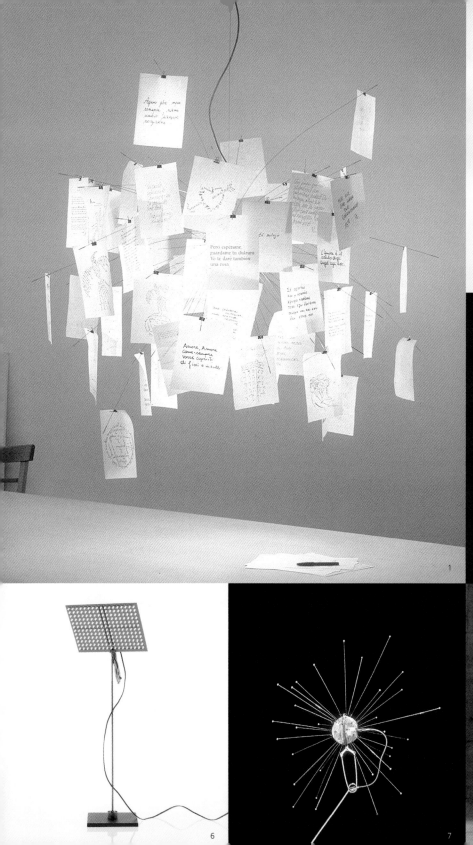

1

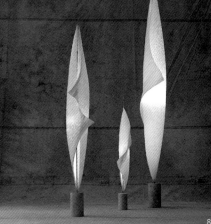

2

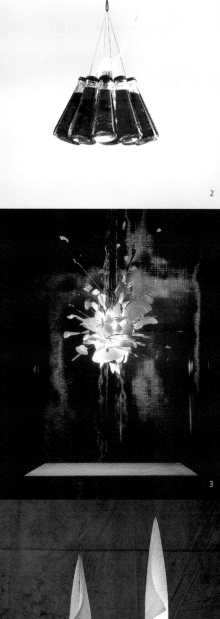

3

6

7

8

Sergio **Mazza**

Italy | Architect and furniture and product designer

Toga, the throne-like armchair designed by Sergio Mazza for **Artemide**, came on to the market in 1968, at the height of the craze for plastics. It was a showpiece of the Pop furniture movement and today can be found in numerous design collections. Mazza is among the many designers who were strongly influenced by Modernism and rationalism. He was particularly interested by new plastics technologies. Together with Giuliana Gramigna, his long-standing partner, he has designed furniture for Cinova, Full and Frau, as well as numerous lamps for Artemide and Quattrifolio that are based on simple geometric forms.

Mazza and Gramigna also developed a number of minimalist door handles for Olivari. As architects as well as designers, they always take the concept of space into consideration when developing their products. The impact of Mazza's designs – whether furniture, lamps or bathroom fittings – unfolds in the tension between the initial idea and the industrial process. The partners have a joint studio, SMC Architettura, in Milan. They have undertaken many projects together, although they sometimes work independently. In the mid-1960s Mazza and Gramigna also founded the periodical *Ottagono*, which they edited until the late 1980s.

1 *Toga* plastic armchair, 1968
2 *Alfa* table lamp, 1959
3 *Rubin* table lamp, 1989
4 *Bacco* container trolley, 1967
5 *Cilindro* lamps, 1976

334

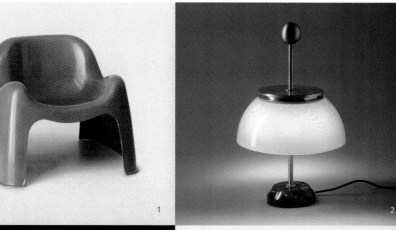

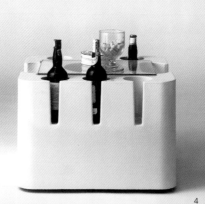

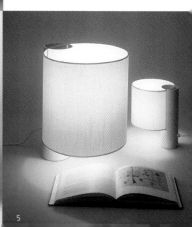

MDF Italia

Italy | MDF Italia Srl, Milan | Furniture manufacturer | **www.mdfitalia.it**

Bruno Fattorini, owner of the successful Milan-based furniture manufacturing company MDF Italia, cultivates a form of simplicity that at times verges on spectacular minimalism. Fattorini, who took over the company in the early 1990s, gave it a dynamic strategy in which innovation and an international approach to design are of paramount importance. Many of the designs are by Fattorini himself, who is also the company's art director. The purist collection of shelves, beds, tables and sofas is easily identifiable by the combination of neutral aluminium, plain wood and the occasional careful use of colour.

Apart from Fattorini himself, Ennio Arosio, Donato D'Urbino and Paolo **Lomazzi,** For Use, Emilio Nanni and **Patricia Urquiola**, among others, also design for MDF Italia. The company's more recent products continue to reflect a typically Italian version of the philosophy 'less is more'. The delicate *FU 09* chair by For Use, for example, renounces all superfluous detail, as does the simple *Nicole* armchair by Fattorini, and the minimalist *Aluminium Bed* by Francesco Bettoni represents the underlying approach of the entire product range.

1939 Bruno Fattorini born in Domodossola
1992 Takes over MDF Italia
1998 Receives Compasso d'Oro
     for *Minima* shelf system

Products

1992 *Bookcase* storage system;
     Déjeuné chair
1997 *Minima* shelf system
1999 *Aluminium Cabinets* storage system;
     Pad sofa

     All by Bruno Fattorini

2000 *Aluminium Bed* by Francesco Bettoni;
     Minima 60 chest by Bruno Fattorini
2001 *Allen* sofa collection and *Newcase*
     storage system by Bruno Fattorini;
     Le Banc bench by Xavier Lust
2002 *Lowboard* chest by Ennio Arosio;
     La Grande Table and *La Chaise*
     chair by Xavier Lust; *Clover* table
     by **Patricia Urquiola**
2003 *M1* chair by Piergiorgio Cazzaniga;
     Minima 03 shelf system by Bruno
     Fattorini; *FU 09* chair by For Use
2004 *Colors* tables and *Laccato* sideboard
     by Bruno Fattorini; *Lofty* armchair by
     Piergiorgio Cazzaniga; *Nicole* armchair
     and sofa by Bruno Fattorini

1 *Clover* table, 2002
2 *Laccato* sideboard, 2004
3 *FU 09* chair, 2003
4 *Aluminium Bed*, 2000

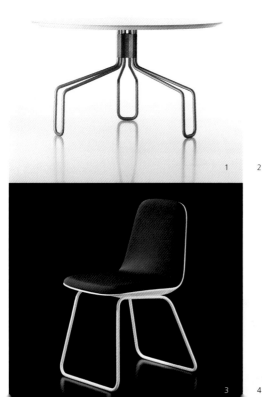

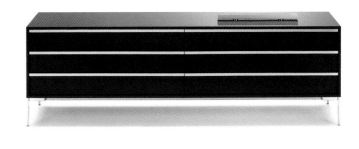

335

Alberto **Meda**

Italy | Furniture and product designer | **www.albertomeda.com**

The Italian furniture and product designer Alberto Meda alludes explicitly to **Charles Eames** in his motto "Less form, more constructive ideas". Meda graduated in mechanical engineering in the late 1960s and is notable as the engineer among Italy's designers. Since the end of the 1980s he has emerged as one of the most interesting personalities in the industry. After gaining technical experience at **Kartell** in the 1970s and at **Alfa Romeo** in the 1980s, he began increasingly to design his own products. New technologies became the inspiration for such highly innovative designs as the *Light Light* chair prototype for **Alias**, which weighed barely 2 kilograms (4.4 lb), but which, unlike Meda's high-tech *Frame* furniture collection for the same manufacturer, never went into production. The main construction principle – the combination of woven material and aluminium – triggered a series of successful designs. Meda's lamps (including *Lola*, *Berenice*, *Metropoli* and *Titania*, the 'UFO' light, all developed for ▶**Luceplan**), many of which were designed in collaboration with Paolo Rizzatto, are sometimes described as technological poetry. Other well-known Meda products include the sturdy *Tank* luggage collection for ▶**Mandarina Duck**, the *Meda* office and conference chair for **Vitra**, and tableware and kitchen utensils for **Arabia**, **Alessi** and **Iittala**.

336

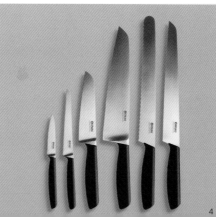

1

2

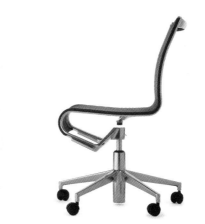

3

4

5

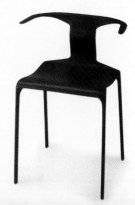

David **Mellor**

England | Product designer | www.davidmellordesign.com

David Mellor was born in Sheffield, the very heart of the English cutlery industry. Considering that he trained as a silversmith, it would have seemed logical for him to have spent his career crafting exquisite silverware for Britain's stately dining tables. However, Mellor chose instead to become an industrial designer. Active in both the Arts Council and the Crafts Council, he has played a central role in the development of 'good design'.

When the British government expressed an interest in commissioning new cutlery for its canteens, Mellor produced *Thrift*, a cutlery set made of steel that is notable both for its simple form and its low manufacturing cost. Indeed, simplicity and elegance based on Scandinavian and German models are among Mellor's principal design concepts. Some of his cutlery services in stainless steel have become design classics. His best-known series include *Provençal* from the 1970s, *Café* and *Savoy* from the 1980s and *City* from the 1990s. *Minimal*, a recent, extremely flat cutlery set, does honour to his name. Always faithful to his principles, Mellor manufactures his cutlery in his purpose-designed factory in Derbyshire. For a number of years he has been working with his son, the furniture and product designer Corin Mellor, who has contributed, among other products, a range of plywood furniture called *Birch* to the collection.

337

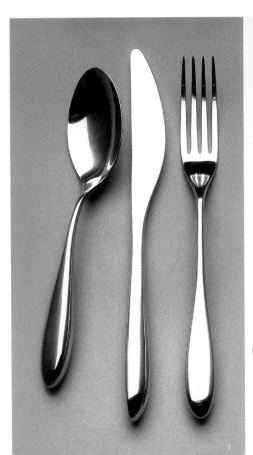

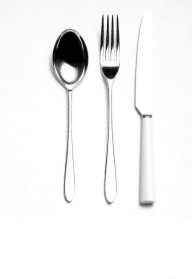

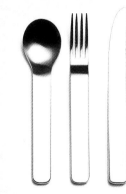

Alessandro **Mendini**

Italy | Architect and furniture and product designer | **www.ateliermendini.it**

Without exception, all the products created by the Italian designer and architect Alessandro Mendini are based on careful thought, intellectual rigour and considerable historical knowledge. It is therefore not surprising that his work should be so multidimensional and rich in associations. Yet, at the same time, it is precisely this wealth of historical allusion that sometimes leads critics to question why his designs are held up as symbols of the modern age. Mendini's work includes vases for **Venini**, furniture for **Zanotta**, watches for Swatch and the famous *Anna G.* and *Alessandro M.* corkscrew figures for ▶**Alessi**, whose heads have literally been turned millions of times. Mendini has acted as consultant to Zanotta and Alessi for many years. The creations of this author–designer undoubtedly polarize opinion and are difficult to classify in terms of taste, and for this reason, they stimulate passionate discussion. A prime example is his controversial design for Groningen Museum in The Netherlands. Highly colourful and decorative, it consciously avoids neutral exhibition rooms. In the 1960s, however, it would have been thought inconceivable that Mendini, who was employed by the **Olivetti** designer Marcello Nizzoli, would one day be considered one of the most eccentric figures of a revolutionary design culture.

It was only at the beginning of the 1970s that Mendini began criticizing the design scene, which he believed had become too complacent and settled in its ways. He published articles in the periodicals *Casabella*, *Modo* and *Domus* and was a supporter of the avant-garde design school Global Tools and of Studio Alchimia, the pioneering experimental design group. Since the end of the 1970s Mendini's name has been associated with the concepts of Redesign (combining existing designs) and Banal Design (how everyday objects can inspire new design). He has created ironic interpretations of **Thonet** and Bauhaus chairs, kitted out with flags and elaborate ornamentation. Decoration – anathema to functionalists – continues to play an important role for Mendini. His comfortable *Proust* armchair, the craftsman-like products of his *Collezione Privata* and the laminates he has developed for Abet are all covered in patterns and grids. Mendini's designs have never fitted into the category of one-dimensional, functional design. They encourage communication and raise fundamental questions concerning the meaning and purpose of design.

338

1931 Born in Milan
1959 Graduates in architecture from Politecnico, Milan
1960 Becomes partner in Nizzoli Associati industrial design studio, Milan
1970 Becomes editor of *Casabella* magazine (until 1976)
1973 Co-founds Global Tools design group
1974 Creates *Lassù* performance
1977 Establishes *Modo* magazine
1979 Becomes managing editor of *Domus* magazine (until 1985); joins Studio Alchimia
1980 Participates in *L'oggetto banale* exhibition at Venice Biennale
1989 With brother Francesco, opens Atelier Mendini in Milan; Paradise Tower in Hiroshima with Yumiko Kabayashi
1993 Groningen Museum, The Netherlands

Products
1978 *Proust* and *Vassilij* armchairs for Studio Alchimia (re-edition at **Cappellini**, 1993)
1979 *Kandissi* sofa and *Ondoso* table for Studio Alchimia
1983 Tea and coffee service for **Alessi**
1984 *Zabro* table/chair and *Cantaride* cabinet
1985 *Papilio* table
1988 *Bisanzio* sofa
Last three for **Zanotta**
1990 *Cosmesis* and *Metroscape* wristwatches for Swatch
1991 *Guerrier de Verre* vase for **Venini**
1994 *Philips by Alessi* coffee machine; *Anna G.* corkscrew for ▶ Alessi
1996 *Scala* armchair for Mastrangelo
2003 *Grande Alzata* vase for Venini; *Alessandro M.* corkscrew for Alessi

1 *Lassù* chair (from Mendini's performance of the same name), 1974
2 *Philips by Alessi* coffee machine, 1994
3 *Alessandro M.* corkscrew, 2003
4 *Kandissi* sofa, 1979
5 *Zabro* table/chair, 1984
6 *Papilio* table, 1985
7 *Guerrier de Verre* vase, 1991
8 *Proust* armchair, 1978

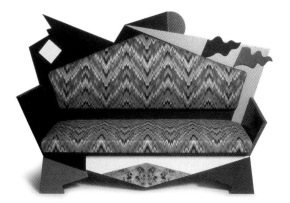

4

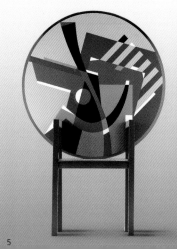

5

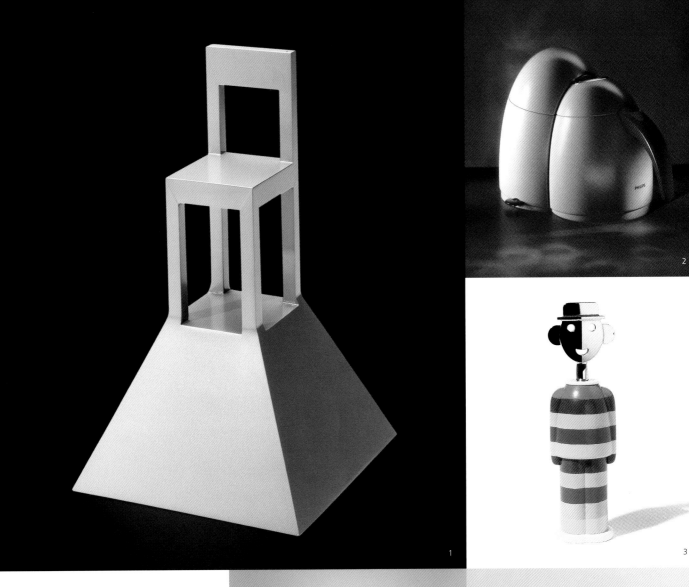

1

2

3

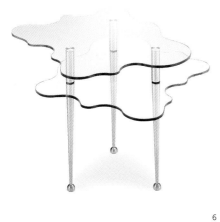

6

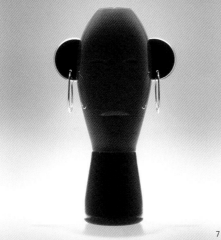

7

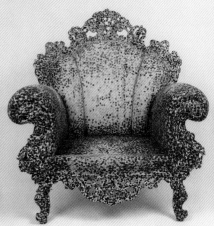

8

Mercedes-Benz

Germany | DaimlerChrysler AG, Stuttgart | Automobile manufacturer | **www.mercedes-benz.com**

Named after Karl Benz, who is credited with the invention of the automobile, Mercedes-Benz was one of the first companies to produce such aerodynamic models as the *Simplex* before the First World War. By the 1920s cars that had the famous Mercedes star badge were already regarded as status symbols. The first newly developed car of the period following the Second World War was the *Type 180*, which had a step-style body. Externally, it had little in common with its predecessors, with one exception: the shape of the grille was retained, even though it often served no practical purpose. Today the grille is sometimes only subtly hinted at, but it is nevertheless the undoubted emblem of the marque and the symbol of tradition. The most famous model from the 1950s was the *300 SL* coupé, which was based on an idea by Rudolf Uhlenhaut, the racing car constructor. Uhlenhaut, Karl Wilfert (chief stylist), Béla Baróny (development engineer) and, later, the young Italian Bruno Sacco formed an impressive team at Mercedes that was notable for its concentration of design expertise. The successor model, the *230 SL*, known as the 'Pagoda' on account of the characteristc shape of the roof, represented a stylistic break with the past. With its body designed by Paul Bracq – who also designed the *600*, *Strich 8* and *220 SE* coupé (*W 111*) – it was the archetype of the restrained convertible. The 1970s began with the third generation of the *SL* roadster (*R 109*) and the *C 111* experimental car by Bruno Sacco, which was a significant departure from the company's traditional designs. In the 1980s Mercedes expanded its range and started to produce a new series of compact models.

Towards the end of the 1980s a group of creative designers worked on alternative designs in the newly created Advanced Design Department. They began their work cautiously by defining individual series, such as the *E-Class* and *C-Class*, which, with their four elliptical headlights, were something of a sensation. In the late 1990s more radical designs appeared – a move that once few critics would have thought the Stuttgart company capable of making. By this time, however, Mercedes was a global player and Germany's biggest industrial organization. The *Smart* city runaround sold under its own brand name; the *A-Class* models – which targeted a young market and were distinctive for their unusual proportions and Post-modern appearance – were launched with a great deal of imaginative marketing. Since the merger with Chrysler in 1998, the range of models has become even more diverse under the guidance of chief designer Peter Pfeiffer.

340

1 *300 SL* coupé, 1954
2 *SLR* super sports car (detail), 2003
3 *SL* roadster, 2002
4 *CLK* coupé, 1998
5 *A-Class* compact car, 2004 series
6 *280 SE* coupé, 1969
7 *SL* roadster (*R 109*), 1972

1886	Karl Benz patents his first motor car, powered by an internal combustion engine
1896	Develops 'contra' engine, forerunner of the boxer engines
1902	Mercedes first used as marque
1926	Daimler merges with Benz
1934	Enters racing with *W 25* 'Silver Arrow'
1936	Introduces first diesel passenger car
1974	Bruno Sacco (with company since 1958) becomes chief designer
1987	Advanced Design Department develops compact car
1998	Merges with Chrysler
2000	Peter Pfeiffer becomes chief designer

Products

1901	Mercedes *S* sports car by Ferdinand **Porsche**
1902	*Simplex* touring car
1927	Mercedes-Benz *S* sports car (1928 *SS* and *SSK*)
1935	*150 H* sports car
1936	*500 K* roadster; *260 D* saloon with diesel engine
1951	*300* 'Chancellor Limousine' ('Adenauer')
1953	*180* saloon
1954	*300 SL* coupé ('Gullwing')
1955	*190 SL* roadster
1961	*220 SE* coupé
1963	*230 SL* coupé; *600* saloon
1969	*280 SE* coupé
1972	New *SL* (formative for future models); *S-Class* series by Bruno Sacco
1975	*123* series
1981	*SEC* coupé
1982	*190* saloon
1989	*SL* roadster
1993	*C-Class*
1995	*E-Class* models with four elliptical headlights
1997	*SLK* roadster
1998	*A-Class* compact car; *CLK* coupé; *Smart* small car
2003	*SLR* super sports car
2004	*CLS* four-door coupé; *SLK* roadster
2005	New *S-Class*

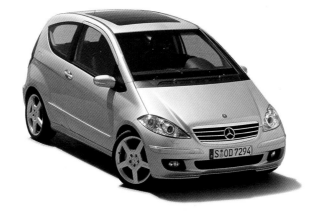

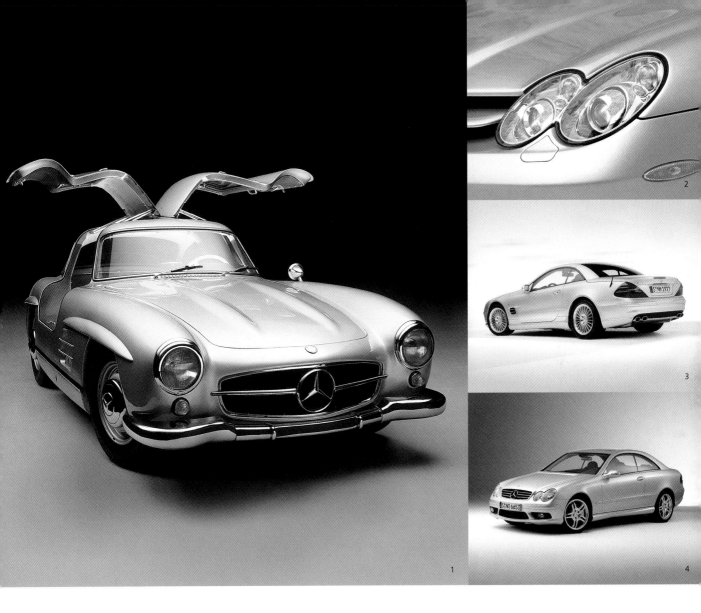

1

2

3

4

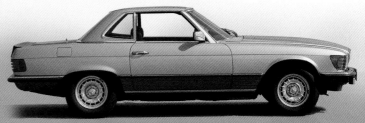

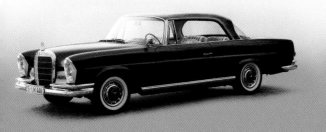

6

7

Ludwig **Mies van der Rohe**

Germany/USA | Architect and furniture designer

Ludwig Mies van der Rohe was born into a family of stonemasons. In the late nineteenth century he attended the Domschule in Aachen and then the local trade school. In 1905 he began an apprenticeship in the studio of the furniture designer Bruno Paul in Berlin, and a few years later joined the office of the architect Peter Behrens. During this period he produced his first designs for skyscrapers made of steel and glass. The high-rise structures he later designed, such as the Seagram Building in New York, are among the high points of modern architecture. His approach to his furniture was very similar to his approach to architecture; he insisted on "no trivial ornamentation". All his furniture designs were created as by-products of his architectural commissions.

Mies van der Rohe's work for the Weissenhofsiedlung housing project in Stuttgart, which he headed, and his designs for the German Pavilion at the *Exposición Internacional de Barcelona* in 1929 and the Tugendhat House in Brno, in the present-day Czech Republic, made important contributions to the history of design. His career in furniture design began in the mid-1920s with the cantilever chair, a concept he borrowed from **Mart Stam**. The idea of using tubular steel for the chair came from **Marcel Breuer**. Mies van der Rohe combined both approaches and produced a successful synthesis. He referred to the prestigious *Barcelona* chair, designed for the international exposition, as a "monumental object". The use of steel for the frame, which, although heavy, made the elegant scissor form possible, was remarkable. Despite the relatively small number of his designs that went into production, Mies van der Rohe nevertheless created a new style. This is evident not only in the huge number of imitations and their successful marketing by such firms as **Thonet** and **Knoll**, but also in the development of his ideas by such leading designers as **Franco Albini**, **Poul Kjærholm** and the Anti-Designers Archizoom, creators of the *Mies* chair for ▶**Poltronova**.

Although Mies van der Rohe is usually associated with the Bauhaus, he had already developed his own style before becoming the school's director in 1930. In 1938 he emigrated to the United States, where he headed the architecture department of the Illinois Institute of Technology. He remained a much sought-after architect right until his death in 1969. With Breuer and **Walter Gropius**, he was regarded as one of grand masters of the International Style.

1886	Born as Ludwig Mies in Aachen
1897	Attends Domschule, Aachen; works as stonemason in family business
1903	Designs stucco ornamentation
1905	Begins furniture apprenticeship at Bruno Paul's studio in Berlin
1908	Joins Peter Behrens's architecture practice in Berlin
1912	Establishes own architecture office in Berlin (until 1937); adopts mother's maiden name, van der Rohe
1921	Joins Deutscher Werkbund
1927	Heads Werkbund's model housing project in Weissenhof, Stuttgart
1928	Tugendhat House, Brno (now in Czech Republic)
1929	Designs German Pavilion at *Exposición Internacional de Barcelona*
1930	Appointed director of Bauhaus, Dessau, later Berlin (until 1933)
1938	Emigrates to USA; appointed director of Department of Architecture at Armour Institute of Technology, Chicago (until 1958; became Illinois Institute of Technology, 1940)
1951	Lake Shore Drive Apartments, Chicago
1958	Seagram Building, New York
1968	Neue Nationalgalerie, Berlin
1969	Dies in Chicago

Products

1925	Veneered wooden furniture
1927	*MR 10*, *MR 20* and *MR 534* cantilever armchairs; tubular steel stool; tubular steel table with glass top; collection of upholstered furniture for Ester in Krefeld
1929	*Barcelona* easy chair, stool and glass table; *248* chaise longue
1930	*Brno* cantilevered armchair; *Tugendhat* armchair and table
1931	Tubular steel furniture with upholstery for Bamberg Metallwerkstätten
	Re-editions at ▶ **Knoll** and **Thonet**

1 *MR 10* armchair, 1927
   (Knoll re-edition, as *MR* chair, shown)
2 *Brno* cantilevered armchair, 1930
3 *Tugendhat* table, 1930
4 *248* chaise longue, 1929
5 *Barcelona* easy chair, 1929
6 *Barcelona* glass table, 1929

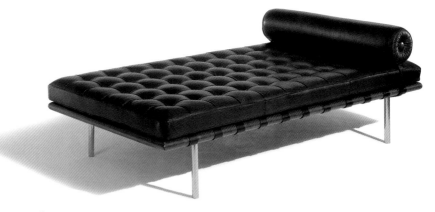

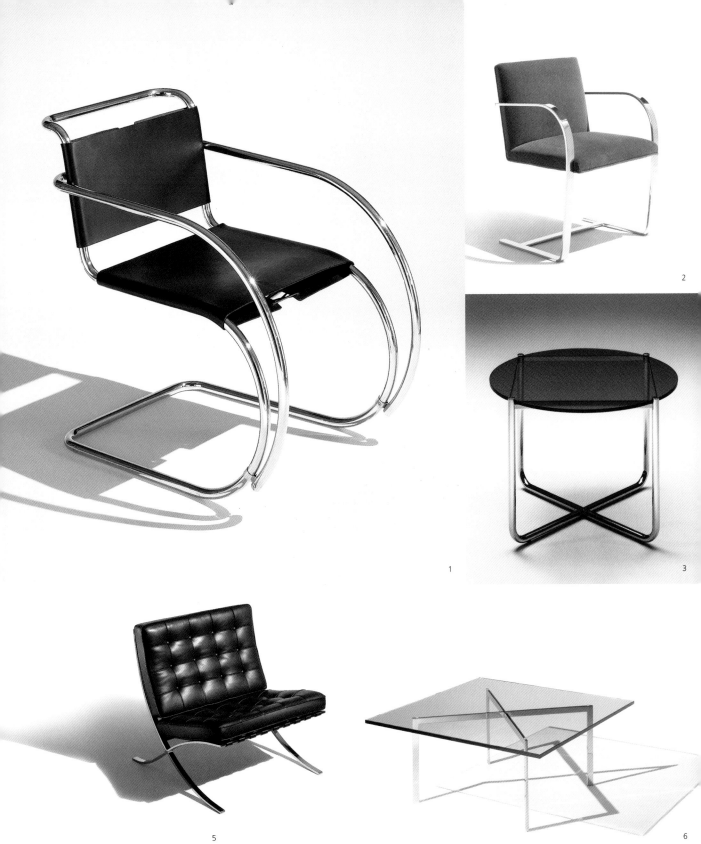

1

2

3

5

6

Milani Design

Switzerland | Product design studio | **www.milani.ch**

Attractive and efficient, the *Symphony* breast pump is proof that medical appliances need not be unexciting or even frightening. The same is true of the *Caleo* incubator, which helps to ensure the survival of premature babies, but does not have a cold, disconcerting machine aesthetic. Both these products were designed by the highly successful Swiss studio Milani Design. Today based in Erlenbach, near Zurich, the company was founded in Ticino in the early 1960s by Francesco Milani. The designer Britta Pukall has managed the company since 2002. Pukall was successful originally in her native Germany, first at **Frogdesign**, then in her own studio in Wiesbaden and finally at the Schott Glassworks in Mainz, where she was head of marketing for consumer goods. She also studied business management in St Gallen, which probably accounts for her holistic approach. Before Pukall and her team actually start designing, they spend time analysing the client's specific requirements and developing a strategic approach.

Apart from medical appliances, Milani Design also develops everyday consumer goods. Its products include a tennis racket for Völkl, cooking pots for Fissler and the Musis underwear collection.

1963 Studio for Industrial Design & Visual Communication established by Francesco Milani in Giubiasco

1997 Studio relocates to Zurich; Britta Pukall becomes partner (formerly design manager at **Frogdesign**, Germany); receives Red Dot Design Award for *Babytherm 8000* warming bed and *Julian* anaesthetic machine

2002 Pukall becomes managing director (also president of **Raymond Loewy** Foundation, Switzerland)

2003 Receives Medical Design Excellence Award for *Symphony* breast pump

Products

1997 *Babytherm 8000* warming bed and *Julian* anaesthetic machine for Dräger Medical

1999 Mobile fluid-management pump for Medela; osteosynthesis nail-holding pliers for Sulzer Medica

2000 *Caleo* incubator for Dräger Medical; *PerioStar 3000* dental instrument sharpener for Hawe-Neos Dental

2001 Parking-ticket machine for Zeag

2002 *Symphony* breast pump for Medela

2003 Carrying box for *Symphony* breast pump for Medela; *Catapult 10* tennis racket for Völkl

2004 *Zeus* anaesthetic machine for Dräger Medical

1 *Symphony* breast pump, 2002

2 Osteosynthesis nail-holding pliers, 1999

3 Carrying box for *Symphony* breast pump, 2003

4 Mobile fluid-management pump, 1999

5 *Catapult 10* tennis racket, 2003

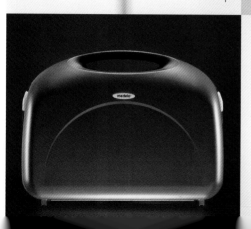

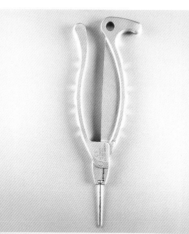

1

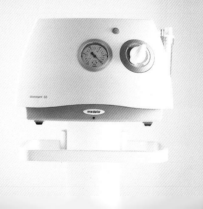

2

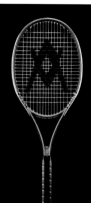

Molteni & C

Italy I Molteni & C SpA, Giussano I Furniture manufacturer I **www.molteni.it**

Molteni & C is a world of warm beige and brown tones. Experimental and spectacular designs do not form part of the company's ethos. What is evident, however, is a traditional philosophy that aims to achieve elegant, comfortable and high-quality furnishings. The company's product range offers clean lines, clear forms and impressive standards. Such well-known designers as Pierluigi Cerri, **Michele De Lucchi**, **Rodolfo Dordoni**, Ferruccio Laviani, Afra and Tobia Scarpa and **Hannes Wettstein** have all worked for this prestigious brand. In recent years Molteni has attempted to introduce more avant-garde design into its collection, with, for example, the *Clip* bed by **Patricia Urquiola** and the *Marais* family of upholstered furniture by **Paola Navone**.

Founded in the 1930s as an upholstery workshop, the company changed to industrial production in the 1950s. Today Unifor, the office furniture manufacturer, and Dada, the kitchen furniture manufacturer, both belong to the Molteni group. For many years Molteni has been known for its modular systems. In particular, Luca Meda, a specialist in creating distinctive furniture, has contributed exemplary designs. Since the 1970s he has produced top-quality individual pieces that are always developed with a view to their position in the collection as a whole.

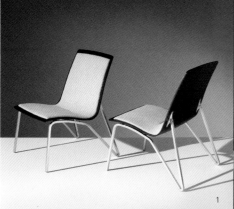

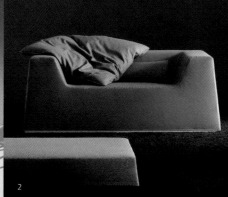

345

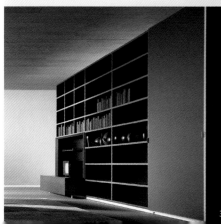

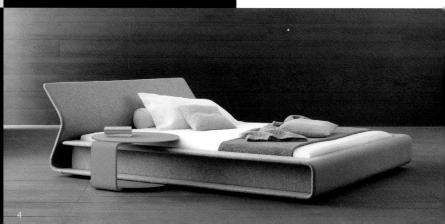

Carlo **Mollino**

Italy | Architect, engineer, photographer and furniture designer

Carlo Mollino was undoubtedly one of the most eccentric and enigmatic design personalities of the twentieth century. Throughout the course of his extraordinary life, whatever Mollino turned his hand to, he always emerged victorious. He learned to ski and within a short time became one of the best skiers in Italy; he was involved in the Italian winter sports association and in 1951 published a book on modern skiing techniques. As an internationally recognized racing driver he won numerous races in the 1950s, including the prestigious Le Mans. He also built his own racing cars, such as the stylish *Bisiluro*. He had considerable success as an enthusiastic aerobatic pilot and aeroplane constructor and as a gifted art photographer of the nude body. He sketched women's shoes and fashions. An accomplished inventor, Molino applied for some fifteen patents during his lifetime. He also worked as an essayist and as a stage- and film-set designer. Additionally, he was one of the most unorthodox architects and furniture designers of his time.

Interiors magazine in the United States once described Mollino's style as "Turin baroque". Although some critics regard his furniture as tasteless, his forms are never static; on the contrary, they swell and luxuriate. For his furniture designs – the majority of which were created in the 1940s and 1950s – he developed a patented process that enabled plywood to be bent at low temperatures. Mollino never hesitated to take on ambitious projects. The unusual results of these ventures included three-legged, curved chairs and uninhibited imitations of the female body translated into pieces of furniture. The backs of some of his chairs are reminiscent of women's dresses or of tongues curved in lust; seats are divided down the middle to resemble human bottoms. Despite their opulent splendour, Mollino's pieces of furniture are always precise constructions, often inspired by aeroplanes or automobiles. However, his furniture was not suitable for mass production (although the Italian firm **Zanotta**, for example, still has some models in its range). Like many other great designer–architects, Mollino designed his furniture largely in the context of specific building projects.

346

1 *Ardea* armchair, 1944
2 *Milo* mirror, 1937
3 Chair for Faculty of Architecture in Turin, 1962
4 *Arabesco* table, 1949
5 *Reale* table, 1946
6 *Gilda* armchair, 1954

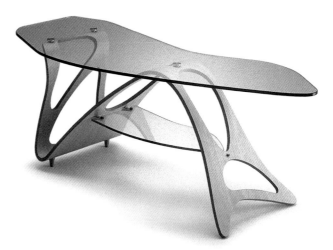

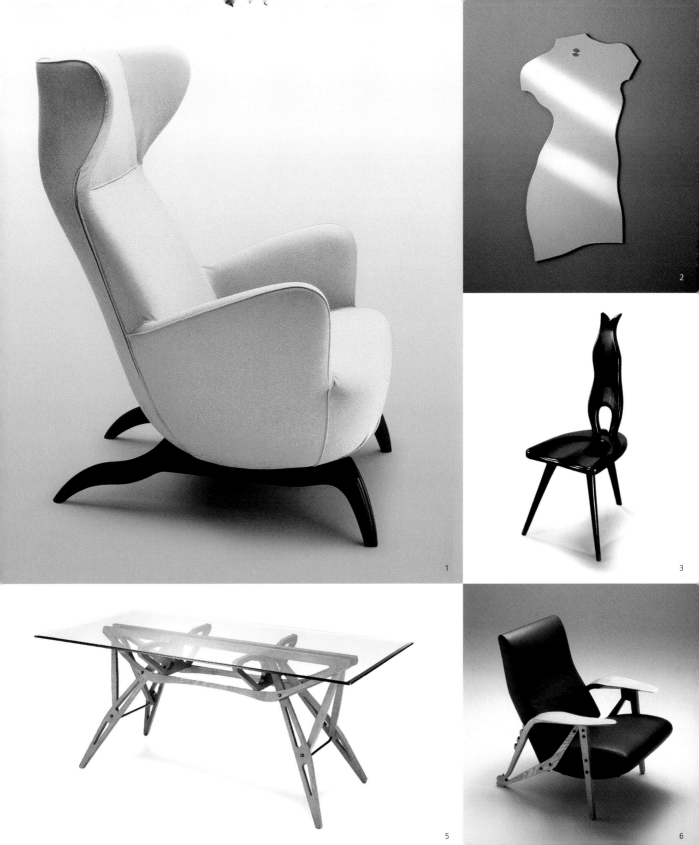

1

2

3

5

6

Mono

Germany | Seibel Designpartner GmbH, Mettmann | Cutlery manufacturer | **www.mono.de**

Cutlery and table accessories have been manufactured in Mettmann, near Düsseldorf, for generations. Founded at the end of the nineteenth century, the family firm Mono was not known beyond the immediate region until 1936, when it supplied the cutlery for the Olympic village in Berlin. In the late 1950s, inspired by the success of such companies as **Braun** and **Rosenthal**, Herbert Seibel, the head of the firm, decided to start manufacturing design-orientated products. This new approach meant that all superfluous ornamentation had to be abandoned. The company soon produced a bestseller in *Mono-a*, a set of cutlery designed by Peter Raacke. Practically overnight, the Mono brand, like **Pott**, became synonymous with elegant German cutlery design. Almost fifteen years later, the *Classic* teapot by Tassilo von Grolman, a modern version of **Wilhelm Wagenfeld**'s glass teapot, also proved to be a design classic.

Following the lead of the Italian metalware manufacturer **Alessi**, Mono expanded its range of products in the 1980s. Apart from cutlery, it began producing teapots, espresso cups, candlesticks, nut crackers and other accessories for everyday use. Products from the 1990s, such as the *Filio* cutlery by Ralph Krämer or the cheese and tomato knives from the *Mono-tools* series by Michael Schneider, are organic in form and as elegantly simple as ever.

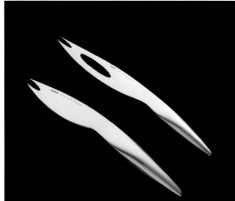

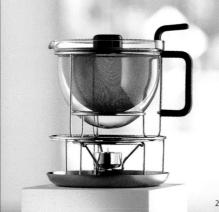

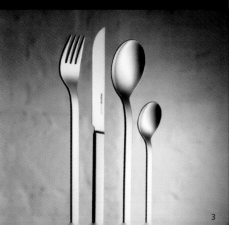

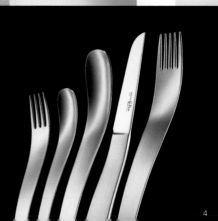

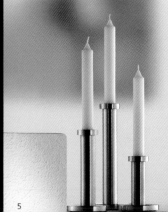

Moooi

The Netherlands | Moooi BV, Breda | Furniture and lamp manufacturer | **www.moooi.nl**

Moooi (meaning 'beautiful', but with ironic undertones) brings together the very best in contemporary Dutch design from Amsterdam to Rotterdam. Whether created by such famous names as Joep van Lieshout, or by relatively unknown young designers such as the Monkey Boys, all items in the Moooi product range are highly individual. The collection focuses on furniture and lamps. Casper Vissers and Hans **Lensvelt** bought the company, known originally as Wanders Wonders, in 2001 from **Marcel Wanders**. Wanders became Moooi's art director and has contributed a large number of designs, from the *Ming* ceramic vase, with its slightly unnerving sloping shape, and the *Flower Chair*, which consists of delicate individual flowers crafted out of wire and then welded together, to *City*, an elegant storage system available in white, brown or red painted steel. The individual containers in the system can be assembled on an aluminium platform, like a collection of architectural building blocks. A glance at the long list of creative talents associated with the company shows the extent to which Moooi reaps the fruits that flourish in the hothouse of Dutch architecture, art and design.

2001 Casper Vissers and Hans **Lensvelt** buy Wanders Wonders from **Marcel Wanders** and rename company Moooi; Wanders becomes art director

2002 Receives Elle Decoration Design Award

Products

1989 *Set Up Shades* standard lamp

1996 *Card Case* shelf

1997 *Sponge*, *Egg* and *Ming* vases; *Foam Bowl* (▶ p. 507)
All by ▶ Marcel Wanders

1999 *Fake Lamp* by Sophie Krier; *Lightshade Shade* lamp by Jurgen Bey; *AVL* chair, barstool and table by Atelier van Lieshout

2000 *V.I.P. Chair* by ▶ Marcel Wanders

2001 *Flower Chair* and *Flower Table* by ▶ Marcel Wanders

2002 *Square Boon* hanging lamp by Piet Hein (▶ p. 2); *Container* table and *City* storage system by Marcel Wanders; *Cork* stool by **Jasper Morrison**; *Lovenet* armchair by **Ross Lovegrove**; *Random Light* hanging lamp by Monkey Boys

1 *Random Light* hanging lamp, 2002
2 *Lovenet* armchair, 2002
3 *AVL* chair, 1999
4 *Ming* vase, 1997
5 *Container* table, 2002

349

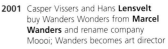

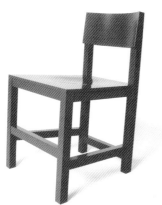

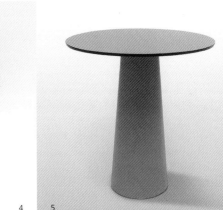

Moroso

Italy | Moroso SpA, Udine | Furniture manufacturer | **www.moroso.it**

Moroso, like many other Italian design companies, relies on a tried-and-tested formula: a string of internationally renowned designers coupled with a considerable degree of entrepreneurial spirit. The furniture manufacturing company is based not in Milan, like numerous others, but in Friuli, near Udine. Founded in the 1950s, it has always played an important role in the export of Italian products. It sells both furniture for the home and a range of accessories. The use of high-quality materials is complemented by a clear design strategy, producing a collection of elegant chairs and sofas that includes the avant garde as well as the traditional. **Massimo Iosa Ghini** from Bologna has been designing for Moroso for the last twenty years. His contributions range from the spectacular *Dinamic* collection to the restrained *Hi Pop* sofa. **Ron Arad**, the London-based sculptor–designer, developed the *Victoria & Albert* series, with its distinctive bathtub shape; the compact *Little Albert* plastic chair, which is part of the range, has become a bestseller.

Enrico Franzolini's *Jules* and *Jim* collections offer a purist interpretation of traditional living, whereas **Marc Newson** from Australia has evoked his generation's lounge culture with *Gluon*, a high-tech chair programme. The *Saruyama* seat by ▸**Toshiyuki Kita** impresses with its sculptural strength, while the *Los Muebles Amorosos* collection by the Spanish designer ▸**Javier Mariscal** is reminiscent of comic characters and clearly relies on eccentricity. In the last few years the successful designs *Springfield*, *Lowland*, *Lowseat*, *Malmö* and *Fjord* by the young Spanish designer ▸**Patricia Urquoila** have created something of a sensation. In *Springfield* the approach is fresh and generous; in *Lowseat* it is cool and sensual. The Swiss designer **Alfredo Häberli** has contributed an unusual chair called *Take a Line for a Walk*. Although the chair is as protective as a child's seat, its retro look makes it as cool as a piece of lounge furniture. The *I Classici* range, which draws on historic styles, offers upholstered furniture that is pitched at a distinguished rather than an avant-garde style of living. **Antonio Citterio** and the Moroso studio itself have designed for this particular collection.

350

1 *Take a Line for a Walk* armchair, 2003
2 *Alessandra* armchair (*Los Mueblos Amorosos* collection), 1995
3 Barstool (*Dinamic* collection), 1986
4 Sofa (*Victoria & Albert* collection), 2000
5 *Lowseat* chaise longue, 2000
6 Armchair (*Victoria & Albert* collection), 2000

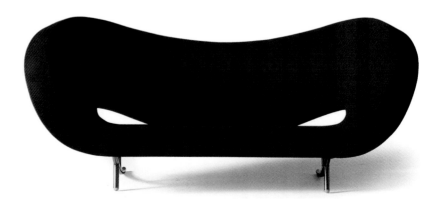

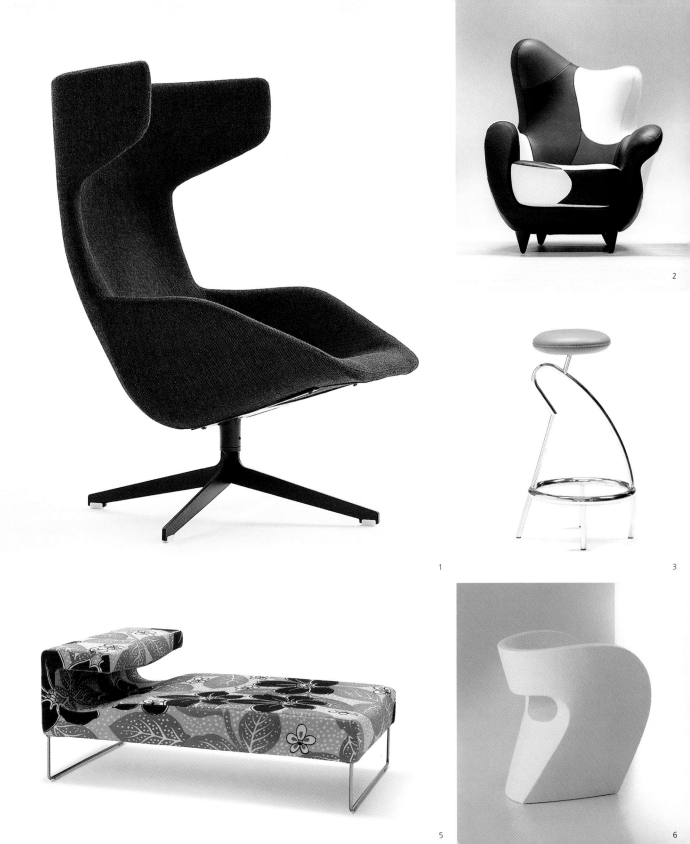

1

2

3

5

6

Massimo **Morozzi**

Italy | Furniture and product designer

Massimo Morozzi's roots lie in the Radical Design movement. In the mid-1960s the young architect founded Archizoom with his friends **Andrea Branzi**, Gilberto Corretti and Paolo Deganello. The avant-garde group's unusual projects were designed specifically to provoke the establishment, which at that time revered functionalism. In the 1970s Morozzi became involved in developing new textiles before founding his own studio in Milan in the early 1980s. He devoted himself mainly to product and furniture design. Morozzi has always taken care to view design within its rightful context and not to reduce it to questions of aesthetics. His designs range from an innovative concept car for Nissan, the Japanese automobile manufacturer, and functional kitchen products for **Alessi** to successful furniture for the Italian companies **Driade**, Fiam and **Edra**, where he is art director.

In the world of interior design, Morozzi's name represents versatility, and he is regarded internationally as one of the most agile and original personalities in the field. His speciality lies in the combination of striking forms and practical innovation. An example is the *Nuovo Domino* sofa for Edra, the backrest elements of which can be folded down to create a chaise longue. Morozzi also has a distinct sense of humour; his *Topolone* sofa, for example, took its inspiration from Mickey Mouse.

One of Morozzi's most successful products is undoubtedly the *Paesaggi Italiani* (Italian landscapes) storage system (▶p. 13), which functions not only as a versatile cupboard, but also as a wall, a partition or as shelving. The original design consisted of a basic square module that could be combined with other modules in any number of ways, giving the individual user complete freedom to create his or her own personal furniture system. Today the system is available in a remarkable range of seventy-five colours, as well as in five different types of wood and in acrylic and metal. Thanks to the recent addition of rounded elements, it is now possible to extend the 'landscapes' around corners, creating organic, curvilinear compositions.

352

1 *Paesaggi Italiani* storage system (collection 2003)
2 *Paesaggi Italiani* storage system (collection 2001)
3 *Pasta Set* cooking pot, 1985
4 *Nuovo Domino* sofa, 1985
5 *Cubista* sofa, 1998

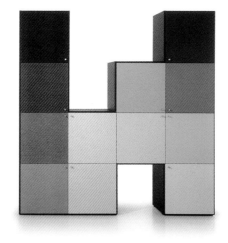

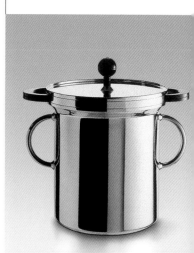

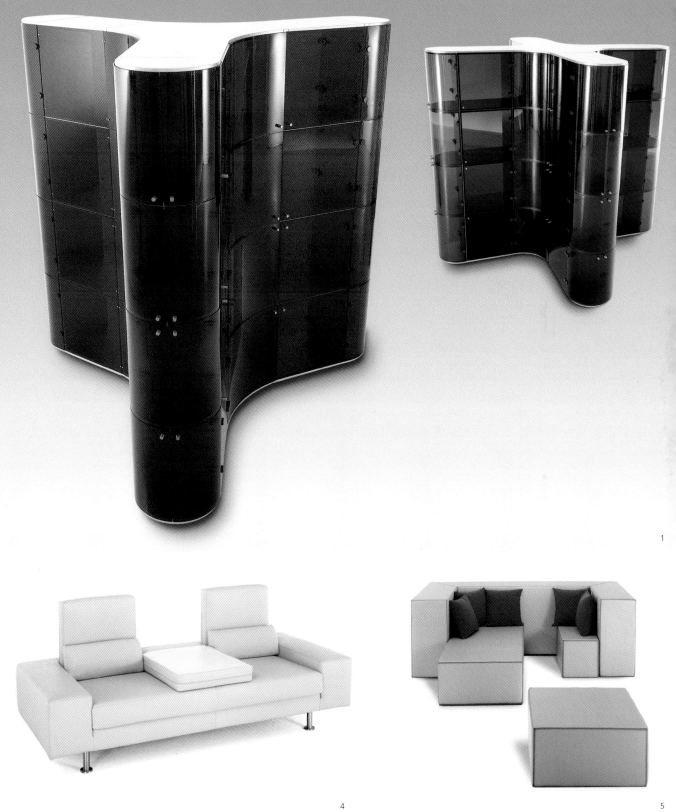

1

4

5

Jasper **Morrison**

England | Furniture and product designer | www.jaspermorrison.com

As a critical voice who advocated a more moderate approach to the consumer and design excesses of the 1980s, Jasper Morrison became something of a moral arbiter. This is not the only characteristic he shares with his fellow countryman William Morris, a leading figure of the British Arts and Crafts movement of the nineteenth century. Morrison's search for permanence pervades his entire work. With this basic approach he helped establish a new sensual minimalism in the 1990s, of which he himself was the chief proponent. Morrison first attracted attention as a furniture designer. His *Plychair* (for ▶ **Vitra**) and *Thinking Man's Chair* (for **Cappellini**) from the 1980s became well known. He later worked increasingly in other fields: he designed the *Moon* dinner service for **Rosenthal** and the *1144* door handle for ▶ **FSB**. Throughout his successful career, Morrison has remained true to his convictions, from his examination project at the Royal College of Art to the tram system he designed for the German city of Hanover.

Morrison almost undoubtedly owes his early fame to **SCP**, the furniture company that snapped up his designs even before he had graduated from college. Design and manufacture form a conceptual unity in Morrison's work. In fact, it is this reciprocal relationship, above all else, that explains the strength of his designs. His colours, like his shapes, are always neutral and restrained, creating a calm backdrop to his surprisingly simple innovations. Such simplicity characterizes his work, whether in the gentle curve of an armrest, as in *Plychair*, or in the strikingly painted architecture of the *Plan* series of cabinets. Morrison has increasingly designed tubular steel furniture, including the graceful *SIM* stackable chair (for Vitra) and the *Vega* chair series (for **Artifort**). He is not only a star at the great furniture fairs, but has also become a truly all-round designer, constantly venturing into new fields, whether with a design for a contemporary whisky bottle or in the development of electrical appliances (for ▶ **Rowenta**). With the *Morrison* domestic appliances, in particular – which bear his initial, despite the fact that he prefers to keep a low profile – he succeeded in setting purist standards.

354

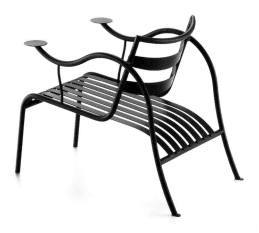

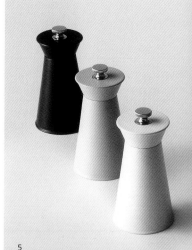

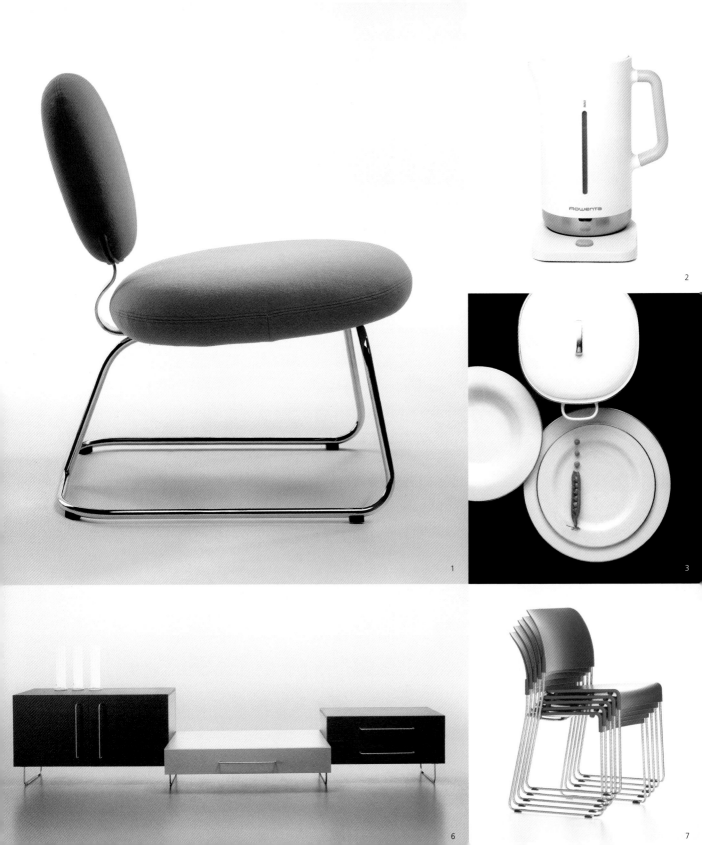

1

2

3

6

7

Motorola

USA | Motorola, Inc., Schaumburg, Illinois | Manufacturer of telecommunications equipment | **www.motorola.com**

Motorola's *StarTAC* flip-top mobile phone is so tiny that you can conceal it in your bikini, or so the advertising blurb claims. What is more certain, however, is that it was one of the first cult phones ever to be produced. Motorola's chief designer, Al Nagele, was responsible for this sensation in the mid-1990s. The functional separation of the keyboard and microphone on the one side, and the receiver and battery on the other was made possible by miniaturization. The previous *MicroTAC* model had established the flip-top mechanism at the end of the 1980s, and it was taken up by other manufacturers, including **Ericsson**, Siemens and **Sony**; Motorola retained the feature in later models.

The Motorola company is not only a pioneer in the field of mobile telephones. In the 1930s it built the first radios for automobile manufacturers in the United States, including Chrysler, **Ford** and **General Motors**. (The company name was given originally to its car radios.) The legendary walkie-talkie designed by Dan Noble in the early 1940s has recently found a worthy successor in the prize-winning *TalkAbout Two Way* radio communication equipment. The company is also associated with another historic moment: the words spoken by astronaut Neil Armstrong, the first human to set foot on the moon – "One small step for man, one giant leap for mankind" – were transmitted by a Motorola transponder.

1928	Galvin Manufacturing Corporation established by Paul and Joseph Galvin
1943	Company goes public
1947	Company name changes to Motorola, Inc.
1948	Begins collaboration with **Ford**, Chrysler and **General Motors** (until 1987)
1986	Establishes Motorola Training and Education Center (MTEC)
2001	UDC (Urbana-Champaign Design Center) moves into new premises at University of Illinois
2004	Provides digital security systems for Olympic Games in Athens

Products

1936	*Police Cruiser* mobile radio
1940	*Handie-Talkie* two-radio for US Army
1943	*Walkie-Talkie* portable FM radio
1983	*DynaTAC,* first commercial mobile telephone; *Sensar* pager
1989	*MicroTAC* mobile telephone
1992	*International 3200* mobile telephone
1996	*StarTAC* mobile telephone
1997	*TalkAbout Two Way* radio equipment
1999	*v.3688* mobile telephone; *TalkAbout T 2288* mobile telephone by **Lunar Design**
2002	*Starline SG900 Optical Mode* and *V 70* mobile telephones
2003	*C 330, V 300, V 525* and *V 600* mobile telephones
2004	*A 630, E 680, MPx 200* and *V 400* mobile telephones

1 *MPx 200* mobile telephone, 2004
2 *StarTAC* mobile telephone, 1996
3 *A 630* mobile telephone, 2004
4 *V 300* mobile telephone, 2003
5 *TalkAbout T 2288* mobile telephone, 1999

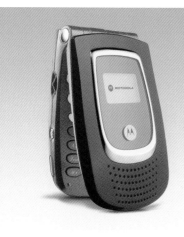

1

2

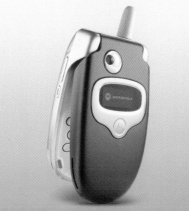

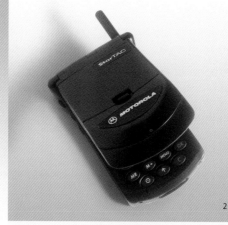

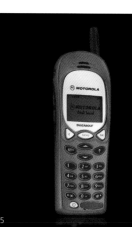

3

4

5

Pascal **Mourgue**

France I Furniture designer I www.pascalmourgue.com

"When it rolls up, you can relax in its embrace." This is how Pascal Mourgue describes the special feature of his *Lover* sofa, an ode to rounded shapes and soft lines. In this series of upholstered furniture, which also includes a chaise longue, an easy chair and a stool, the French designer has used the flexibility of foam rubber to create backrests that can be easily rolled up or down. And when rolled up, *Lover* literally embraces you. This graphically striking piece of furniture, produced by ▸**Ligne Roset**, looks as though it could itself be dozing when its backrest is lowered. Mourgue has designed a number of flagship stores and numerous pieces of upholstered furniture for Ligne Roset with such names as *Calin*, *Petit Calin* and *Cuddle* (the French word *calin* translates as 'caress' or 'embrace'). Mourgue, a Parisian, is a trained sculptor and much sought-after interior designer. He combines a predilection for simplicity with a pronounced appreciation of comfort. As a designer from the country that invented the comfortable upholstered armchair, he is continuing a time-honoured tradition with his contemporary interpretations. It is therefore no wonder that sofas and beds are his strong points. However, his studio also produces designs for lamps and glass and ceramic objects.

1943 Born in Neuilly

1966 Studies design and sculpture in Paris

2001 Receives iF Design Award for *Smala* sofa collection

2004 Receives iF Design Award for *Lover* seating collection

Products

1991 *Rio* chair for Artelano

1994 *Pascal Mourgue* collection, *Offrande* glass collection, *Lamp* lamp collection and *Calin* easy chair for **Ligne Roset**

1996 *Dolce Vita* sofa for Ligne Roset

1997 *Moove* sofa collection for **Cassina**; *Ten Line* stackable chair for Artelano

1998 *Shanghai* sofa for Artelano; *In Fine* upholstered furniture; *Roller* mobile furniture

1999 *Le Paresseux* easy chair; *Les Trois Terres* vases

2000 *Smala* furniture collection

2003 *Lover* seating collection

2004 *Cuddle* seating collection

Last seven for ▸Ligne Roset

1 *Les Trois Terres* vases, 1999

2 *Smala* sofa, 2000

3 *Le Paresseux* easy chair, 1999

4 *Calin* easy chair, 1994

5 *Rio* chair, 1991

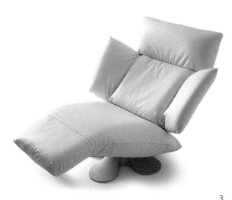

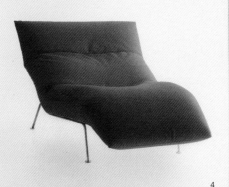

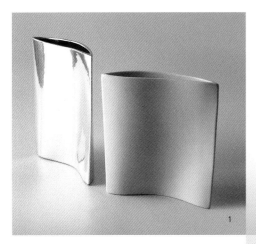

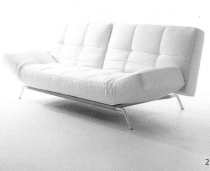

357

Muji

Japan | Ryohin Keikaku Co., Ltd, Tokyo | Product and furniture manufacturer | www.muji.net

The products of the Japanese company Muji are regarded by many people as cult objects, even though they are neither spectacular nor expensive nor even particularly unique. The secret of this department store with a difference, which sells its products in the Far East, France, Ireland, Britain and via the Internet, is concealed in the name of the firm: *Mujirushi Ryohin* translates as 'good no-brand goods' and reflects the business principle by which the company has increased its turnover many times since the beginning of the 1980s. Muji looks set to be never-ending success story. Its products are useful, affordable and beautifully designed everyday objects. They also have an ecological bias, which in itself conceals a Japanese version of the familiar 'less is more' principle. Muji's range runs to some 9000 products. It includes boxes, stationery, household utensils, bottles of all sizes, clothes, small pieces of furniture and bicycles, and is characterized by subdued colours and a restrained approach to design. After praise from such established designers as **Jasper Morrison** had enhanced the company's reputation, Muji began to employ named designers. The Italian maestro **Enzo Mari** began with a table and chairs. ▶**Ideo** contributed a brilliantly simple wall CD player. It has an open turntable framed by a rectangular loudspeaker and, like a lamp, is turned on by means of a pull cord.

1980 Established as a brand at Seiyu, discount store for household goods
1981 Clothing included in product range
1983 First Muji store opens in Aoyama; Muji boutiques open as outlets in department stores
1990 Ryohin Keikaku assumes control of company
1991 First overseas store opens, in London
1997 Sells non-traditional products, such as inflatable furniture
2002 Strengthens collaboration with external design studios
2004 Product range totals more than 9000 items

Products
1982 22-inch bicycle
1983 Modular shelf system
1984 Tricycle
1988 Bag in sponge rubber
1989 Business-card case in aluminium
1990 Indoor footwear
1991 Mattress with legs
1992 Bicycle with cardan shaft; desk calendar
1996 Camping stove
1997 Hanging lamp in aluminium; portable CD radio
1998 Wireless telephone/fax machine
1999 Children's furniture in cardboard; plastic modular storage system
2002 Wall CD player by ▶**Ideo**
2003 Table and chairs by **Enzo Mari**
2004 Make-up brushes in aluminium

1 Tricycle, 1984
2 Mattress with legs, 1991
3 Plastic modular storage system, 1999
4 Make-up brushes, 2004
5 Business-card case, 1989

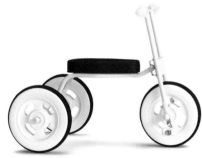

1

2

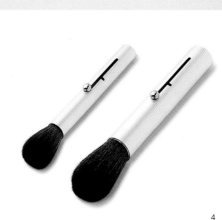

3

4

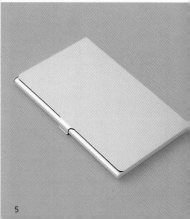

5

Bruno **Munari**

Italy | Artist and furniture and product designer

'Useless machines', 'illegible books', studies on visual perception, toys, ice boxes and lamps: the unassuming but poetic objects created by the Italian designer Bruno Munari have enhanced our awareness of the world around us. Over a period of about seven decades, Munari – a painter, draughtsman, abstract artist, poet, designer, graphic artist, teacher and theoretician – gave new impetus to Italian culture. His began his career in the 1920s as a Futurist painter, and in the 1930s he worked as a graphic artist for **Olivetti**, Campari and other companies. It was not until the 1940s that he became known to a wider public with his first children's books. In the early 1950s he created *Zizi*, an ingenious flexible toy monkey for children and adults alike. It also proved to be an ideal way of demonstrating the qualities of Pirelli's newly developed foam rubber. At about the same time Munari began a highly productive collaboration with **Danese**. Some of the imaginative designs from that period remain popular to the present day, including the *Cubo* ashtray, a black cube containing a strip of folded aluminium, and the *Falkland* hanging lamp, which is constructed from large metal rings and an elastic material usually associated with hosiery.

1 *Bali* self-assembly lamp, 1958
2 *Cubo* ashtray, 1957
3 *Falkland* hanging lamp, 1964
4 *Zizi* toy monkey, 1953

359

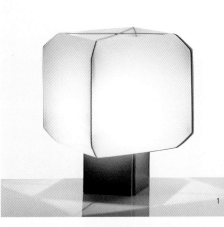

1

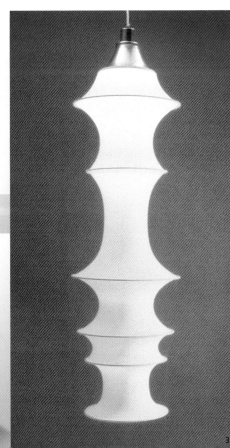

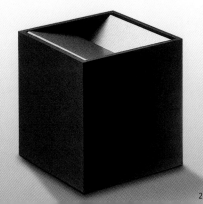

2

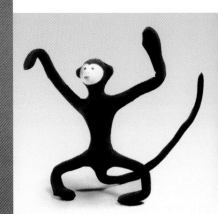

3   4

N

George Nelson, *Atomic* wall clock, 1949

When George Nelson was commissioned by the Howard Miller Clock Company to design a series of wall clocks, he used the collage principle, combining contrasting colours and materials, on which his later design for the *Marshmallow* sofa is based. The *Atomic* wall clock is the best-known design from the series, and, as its name suggests, is inspired by the molecular structure of an atom. The hour hand is shaped like an arrow, the minute hand like a metronome – playful details that heralded the style of the 1950s.

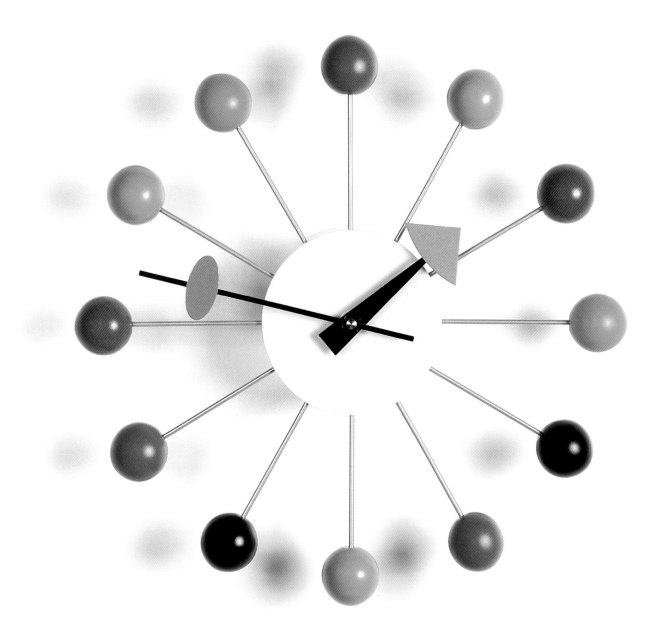

Nambé

USA | Nambé Mills, Inc., Santa Fe, New Mexico | Metalware, glassware and ceramics manufacturer | **www.nambe.com**

In the early 1950s a group of young artists founded a studio near Santa Fe, New Mexico. They were committed to creating elegant, simple everyday objects such as cookware. They started using a metal alloy that had originally been developed at the nearby Los Alamos National Laboratory. Pauline Cable, a member of the group, worked as a secretary for the inventor of this special alloy and acquired the production rights. Eva Zeisel, another member of the group, was one of the best-known ceramicists of the time. Born in Budapest, Zeisel worked in Germany and then in the Soviet Union until she was forced to go into exile, and emigrated to the United States. Her archetypal designs have since become an important part of the company's product range.

Over the years, Nambé has grown to be one of the most ambitious, design-orientated companies in the field of decorative objects. Its present programme comprises more than four hundred pieces, all of them tastefully elegant. Such contemporary designers as **Karim Rashid** have contributed to the product range, which is continuously expanding. The late 1990s saw the launch of a crystal glass collection, followed by a range of lighting in 2001 and a porcelain collection in 2003.

1951 Established in Nambé, near Santa Fe, New Mexico

2003 Receives Metropolitan Home Modernism Award

Products

1967 *Butterfly* bowl (in-house design); *Tri-Corner* collection (inc. bowls and candlesticks)

1994 *Kissing* salt and pepper shakers and *Wave* picture frames by **Karim Rashid**

1998 First crystal glassware collection (including *Planar* bowl by Karim Rashid)

2000 *Freedom* vase by Eva Zeisel (re-edition)

2001 *Flame* collection by Fred Bould; first lamp collection

2002 *Twist* collection by Fred Bould

2003 *Butterfly* collection (bowls, cutlery, tableware, lamps) by Mikaela Dörfel; *Grande* collection (bowls, trays, platters; in-house design); *Peek-a-Boo* vase by Eva Zeisel (re-edition); *Bias* decanter by Neil Cohen

1 *Freedom* vase, 2000
2 *Twist* salt and pepper shakers, 2002
3 *Butterfly* bowl, 1967
4 *Peek-a-Boo* vase, 2003
5 *Kissing* salt and pepper shakers, 1994

362

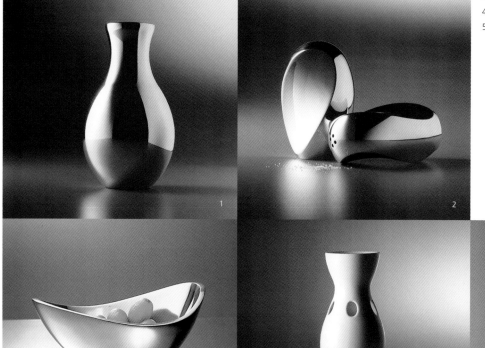

Paola **Navone**

Italy | Furniture designer

The Milan-based designer Paola Navone is a true cosmopolitan who is equally at home in Hong Kong, Morocco or Malaysia. Her furniture reveals a preference for an international mix of styles, and she is always on the lookout for inspiration. In the early 1980s she was influenced by **Alessandro Mendini**, **Ettore Sottsass** and the Studio Alchimia design group. During the same period she worked as a consultant for the carpet manufacturer Abet Laminati. Despite her background in experimental design, Navone has shown little interest in the formalism that dominates avant-garde interior design. In the late 1980s, together with Giulio Cappellini, she established the Mondo furniture division of **Cappellini**. The company produces multicultural, ethnic designs, and Navone has been heavily criticized for her obvious liking for exotic handicrafts. Such criticism, however, does not disconcert her. She has developed exclusive accessories for **Driade**, and, as creative director of such top-range companies as Gervasoni, **Molteni & C** and Orizzonti, the bed manufacturer, she has proved that she is not tied to restrictive design philosophies and fixed styles. "We need new medicines and technologies, but certainly not any new chairs", she says with conviction. "We should just remember those that have already been created."

1950 Born in Turin

1979 Begins collaboration with Abet Laminati

1987 Establishes Mondo division within **Cappellini** (with Giulio Cappellini)

1997 Appointed creative director at Gervasoni

Products

1988 *M 3002* easy chair for Mondo

1992 *Dejà Vu M101/0* wicker chair for Mondo

1995 *Posh Pots* aluminium vases for **Driade**

1998 *Helva 03* sofa for Gervasoni; *Zita I–III* bedspreads for Driade; *Adaman Tatami* bed for Orizzonti

1999 *Black* and *Inout* seating collections for Gervasoni; *Milos* bed for Orizzonti; furniture collection for Casamilano; *Grass* vases for Arcade; *Paloma P.* salad servers for Driade

2001 *Morgana* chandelier series for Swarovski

2003 *Cite* bed and *Passy*, *Odeon* and *Rivoli* upholstered furniture collections for **Molteni & C**; *Punto Rosso* upholstered furniture collection for Baxter Contemporary

2004 *Marais* sofa and bed for Molteni & C

1 *Rivoli* sofa, 2003

2 *Istanbul* floor cushions, 2003 (*Punto Rosso* collection)

3 *Passy* armchair, 2003

4 *Vienna* chair, 2003 (*Punto Rosso* collection)

363

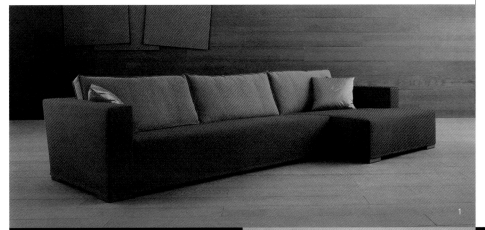

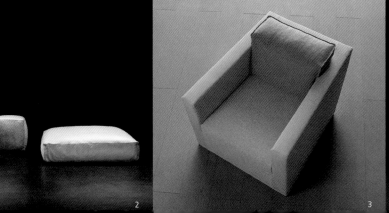

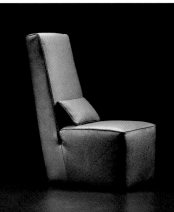

George **Nelson**

USA | Architect and furniture and product designer

George Nelson took a degree course in architecture at Yale University and then studied fine arts. He had barely started graduate work at the Catholic University in Washington, DC, when he was awarded the Rome Prize in architecture. Nelson had an exceptional creative talent. He was a highly regarded critic, influential author and respected commentator on design issues. He designed several pavilions for the *New York World's Fair* in 1964, when there was still a strong and optimistic belief in progress. Nelson gave an ambitious definition of 'good design' when he said that it is the ability of the human spirit to go beyond its limits – which is something that he himself certainly did. His *Storagewall* shelf system of 1945, which could also be used as a partitioning wall, revolutionized the office environment and was so exciting and original that the furniture manufacturer **Herman Miller** became eager to collaborate with the ingenious designer. Nelson worked together with the young designers **Charles Eames** and Alexander Girard to give Herman Miller its new, highly innovative image. From 1946 to 1965 he was the company's design director.

Although Nelson specialized in storage systems and packaging, he created some remarkable designs in other areas. One of his classics is the *Marshmallow* sofa from the 1950s, which anticipated Pop design. Its seat consists of eighteen round cushions, just like those typically used on barstools. The *Atomic* wall clock (▶p. 361) was a sophisticated combination of symbolism and modern simplicity. The spheres marking the hours represent atoms – the most potent metaphor of an era with a strong faith in technological progress. Nelson's works are often metaphorical statements: the *Coconut Chair*, with its striking shell shape, for example, was designed not only for comfort; it can also be interpreted as a reference to the more relaxed, less formal lifestyle that was becoming popular in the late 1950s. Nelson continued his multidisciplinary approach in the 1960s and, together with Robert Propst, developed the *Action Office* furniture system, which was so successful that it was soon found in every progressive office in the United States.

1908	Born in Hartford, Connecticut
1931	Graduates in architecture from Yale University, Connecticut
1932	Studies at American Academy in Rome
1935	Becomes associate editor of *Architectural Forum* journal
1942	Teaches at Columbia University, New York
1945	Collaborates with **Herman Miller** Furniture Company (design director from 1946 to 1965)
1947	Establishes own architecture and design office in New York
1957	Publishes book *Problems of Design*
1964	Designs number of pavilions for *New York World's Fair*
1983	Plans *Design since 1945* exhibition at Philadelphia Museum of Art
1986	Dies in New York

Products

1945	*Storagewall* shelf system
1946	*Platform* bench
1947	*Kite* and *Sunburst* wall clocks
1949	*Eye* and *Atomic* wall clocks (▶ p. 361)
1952	*Bubble* hanging lamp
1954	*Steelframe Group* office furniture collection
1956	*Marshmallow* sofa; *DAF* chair; *Coconut Chair*
1958	*Comprehensive Storage System*
1962	*Action Office* furniture system (with Robert Propst)
1964	*Sling Sofa*
	All for ▶ Herman Miller
1968	*Editor* typewriter for **Olivetti**
1975	*Table Tray* occasional table

1   Desk, 1962 (*Action Office* furniture system)
2   *Kite* wall clock, 1947
3   *Sunburst* wall clock, 1947
4   *Eye* wall clock, 1949
5   *Coconut Chair*, 1956
6   *Swivel* chair, 1962 (*Action Office* furniture system)
7   *Marshmallow* sofa, 1956
8   *Table Tray* occasional table, 1975

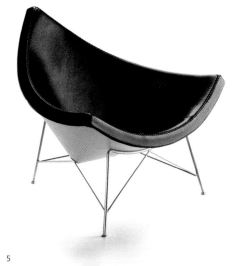

5

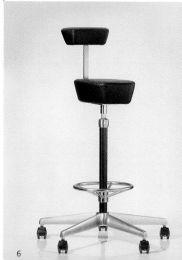

6

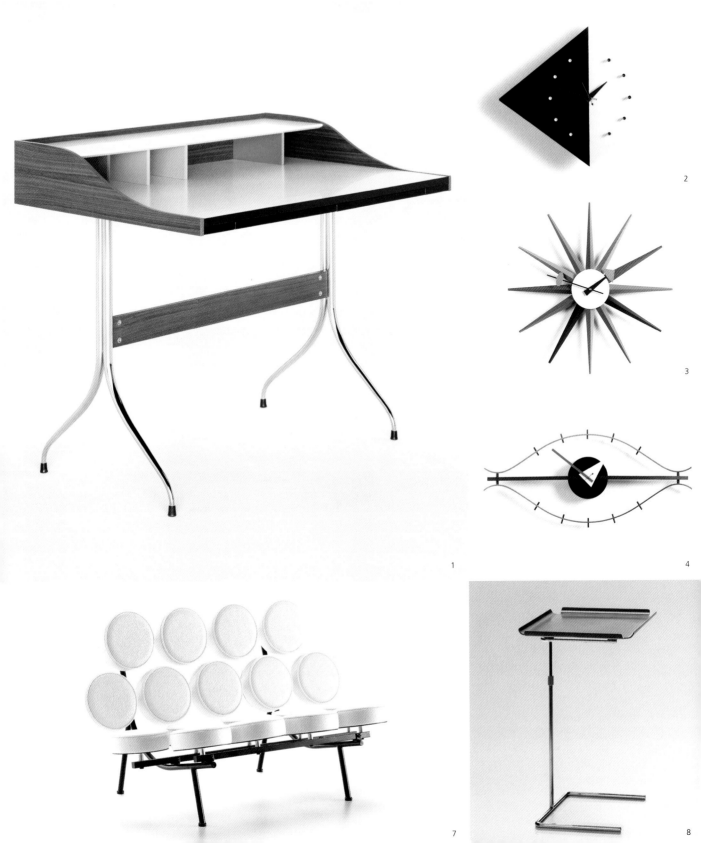

1

2

3

4

7

8

Marc **Newson**

England | Furniture and product designer | **www.marcnewson.com**

After working in Tokyo and Paris, the Australian-born designer Marc Newson settled in London, where he creates designs for his international clients, among them **Alessi**, **Cappellini**, **Flos**, **Magis** and **Moroso**. It has been suggested that Newson's fondness for smooth, flowing forms is related to his passion for surfing. The cosmopolitan designer took a degree in jewellery design and sculpture in Sydney in the mid-1980s, a qualification also held by **Tom Dixon**. Newson was influenced by **Ron Arad**, with whom he collaborated for some time. His eclectic approach is a typically British trait, and he is quite content to borrow from different stylistic periods of design history. The result is an amalgam of styles that includes streamlining in the manner of **Raymond Loewy**, with its glorification of the machine age, and the organic forms of the 1940s and 1950s, which were introduced into international design by **Alvar Aalto** and **Josef Frank**. Newson gives these elements a futuristic touch and fuses them miraculously into a stylistic whole. The *Lockheed* chaise longue, with its visible rivets, is a parody of aeroplane aesthetics and a good example of this stylistic fusion. Newson always produces exciting designs, whether he is creating a bicycle for ▸ **Biomega** or the interior of a jet plane. His stylistic repertoire includes understatement and discipline, as demonstrated by the glass series *Relations*, which he designed for **Iittala**, and by the *Strelka* cutlery series for Alessi.

An extremely versatile designer, Newson has also created a collection of wristwatches sold under the brand name Ikepod, a collaboration between Pod, his furnishings company, and Ike, the Swiss watch manufacturer. In addition, he has designed numerous restaurants and shops throughout the world, including the Pod Bar in Tokyo, the Crocodile Boutique in Hong Kong and the restaurant in the Lever Building in New York. Like Arad, Dixon and **Ross Lovegrove** – all of whom are also London-based – Newson is a designer who plays on the imagination and emotions of consumers by translating bold visions of the past into present-day objects. This approach has become something of a trademark of British design. It therefore comes as no surprise to learn that Madonna has featured Newson's furniture in her videos and that such companies as **Ford** have asked him to produce visionary designs.

366

1 *Strelka* cutlery, 2003
2 *Nimrod* chair, 2003
3 *Relations* glass series, 1999
4 *Embryo Chair*, 1998
5 *Wood Chair*, 1992
6 *Rock* doorstop, 1998
7 *Lockheed* chaise longue, 1986
8 *Orgone* table, 1991
9 Ford *021 C* small car (concept), 1999

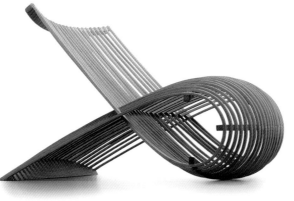

5

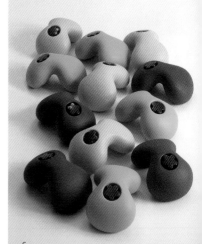

6

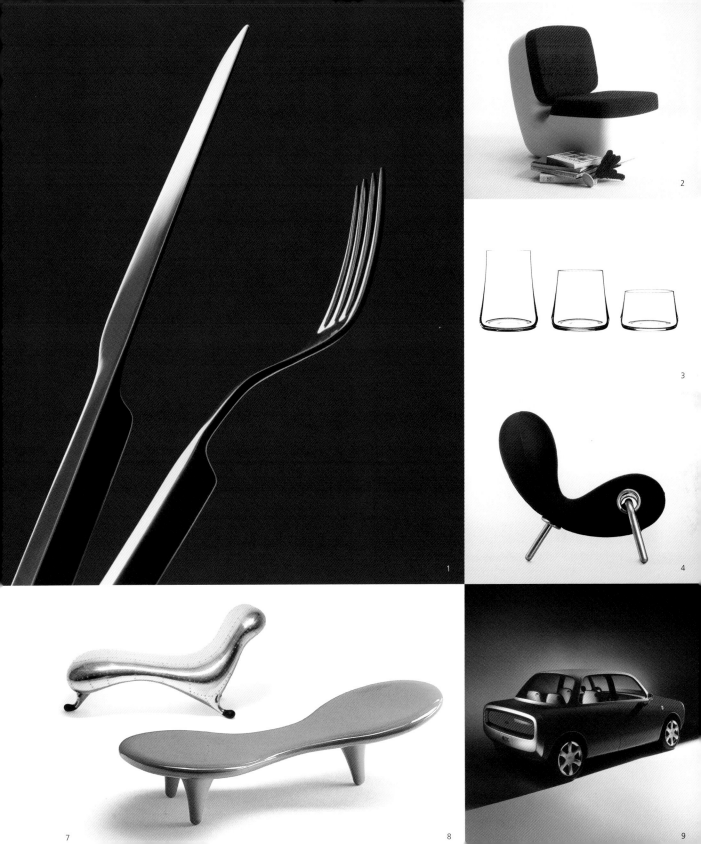

1

2

3

4

7

8

9

Nils Holger Moormann

Germany | Nils Holger Moormann GmbH, Aschau im Chiemgau | Furniture manufacturer | **www.moormann.de**

The business magazine *Econy* has spoken of Nils Holger Moormann's "creative–chaotic marketing", and the German edition of the *Financial Times* has referred to him as a "design entrepreneur". Moormann is an unconventional figure who has made a name for himself on the European design scene with his purist furniture. He attracted media attention with his lawsuit for plagiarism against the furniture giant **Ikea**. He went through the courts and eventually won his case. This defiant entrepreneur has a CV that is not exactly typical of a designer. In the early 1980s he dropped out of law school and switched to design. After several years without much success he finally made a breakthrough with two products. Wolfgang Laubersheimer's *Gespanntes Regal* shelf system made from sheet steel created a wave of enthusiasm throughout the industry and is regarded as a German design classic. Hanspeter Weidmann's *Schuhkippe*, an innovative shoe cupboard, also became a huge bestseller. *Schuhkippe* is extremely flat, with a height of just 16 centimetres (6.3 in.), and has a tilting mechanism that opens and closes all its compartments at once. Its simplicity epitomizes Moormann's production concept. The same is true of the *Zoll D* shelving, a modular system made from sheet aluminium. The awards jury for the Bundespreis Produktdesign in 1996 praised the basic principle behind the product: "the maximum reduction of material and effort needed to produce and assemble the shelf".

Moormann has a reputation for taking young, unknown designers seriously, which is why he receives many unsolicited design samples. When a new product is being developed, he not only invests capital but also a great amount of time and energy into getting the right design. This investment has produced a number of bestsellers, such as the *FNP* shelf system by ►**Axel Kufus**, a minimalist and flexible construction made from hardboard that reveals the intellectual effort put into the design process. The same holds true for almost all Moormann products, including the lightweight *Spanoto* table by Jakob Gebert and the *Step* ladder, designed by **Konstantin Grcic** to make life easier for librarians and bookworms. The *Kant* desk, designed by Patrick Frey and Markus Boge, has a V-shaped trough in the top, where files and books can be securely stored for easy access. This product has been very popular with office workers. All of Moormann's furniture – whether in metal, plywood or chipboard – has the austere elegance frequently associated with top-quality products.

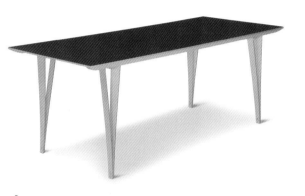

3

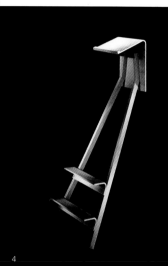

4

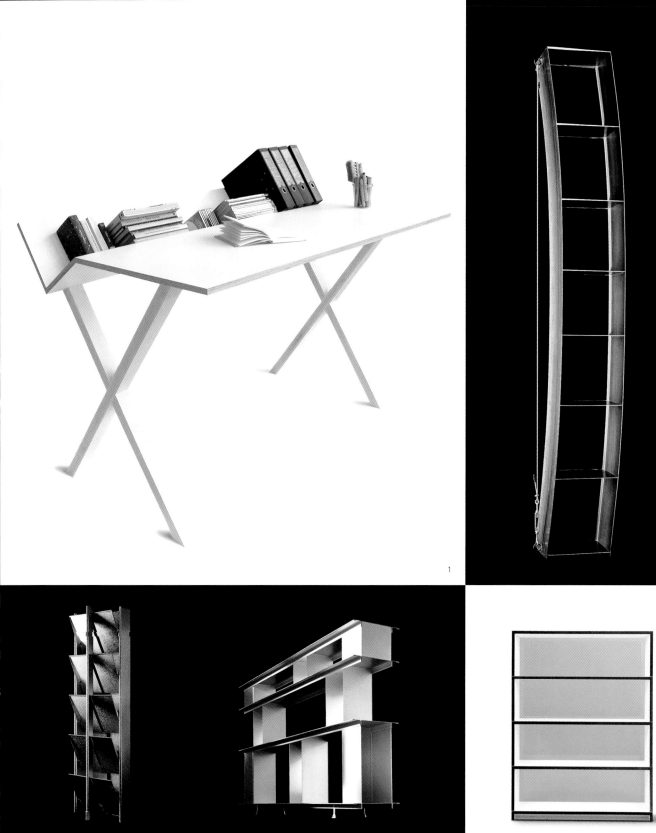

1

2

5

6

7

Isamu **Noguchi**

USA/Japan | Artist and furniture and lamp designer | www.noguchi.org

Isamu Noguchi was born in Los Angeles, the son of an American writer and a Japanese poet. He spent his childhood in Japan and his high school years in the United States. After switching from a degree course in medicine to one in sculpture and then gaining some work experience in France and Japan, the nomadic artist finally settled in New York in the late 1920s. Like **Ray Eames**, Noguchi belonged to a bohemian circle that in those days still had a low profile. He created playgrounds and stage sets and was also reasonably successful as a garden designer. Like his Japanese–American colleague George Nakashima, Noguchi always regarded himself as an artist–designer, but this did not prevent him from creating mass-produced objects.

Noguchi's collaboration with **Herman Miller** was particularly fruitful, and towards the end of the 1940s the company launched his *Articulated Table*, a combination of an amoeba-like glass top and two identical, linked legs. The ensemble, regarded by many as a modern sculpture, radiates the tension characteristic of Surrealist paintings from the same period. The ingenious mixture of free design and rational construction – the weight of the glass top stabilizes the two legs – turned Noguchi's table–sculpture into a design icon that anticipated the style of the 1950s. Among his other best-known works are the *Nurse* Bakelite radio and his lamp designs for **Knoll**. Noguchi failed to patent his designs and was repeatedly a victim of plagiarism. Although the resulting financial loss did bother him, he was more concerned about the poor artistic quality of the imitations. In the 1950s he triggered an avalanche of copycat designs with his *Akari* (Japanese for 'light') lamp collection. He had discovered paper lanterns in the Japanese town of Gifu, a traditional centre of paper lamp production, and made some crucial technical improvements: he replaced the wooden sticks with wire and used paper made from the bark of mulberry trees because it facilitated optimum light distribution. The result was an elegant series of lamps, some very plain, some playful, but all of them light, delicate, glowing objects that appeared to float in space.

370

1 Table lamp (*Akari* collection), 1950
2 Tea cup with large saucer, 1952
3 *70* sofa and *71* footstool, 1946
4 *Cyclone* table, 1954
5 *Articulated Table*, 1947
6 Cylindrical table lamp, 1945
7 *Fin* coffee table, 1944
8 *Nurse* radio, 1938

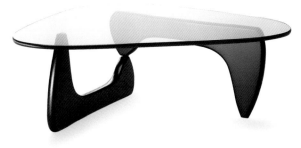

5

6

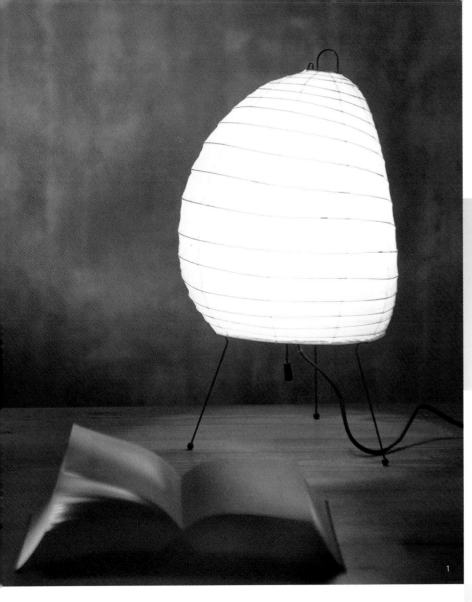

1

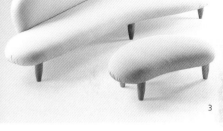

2

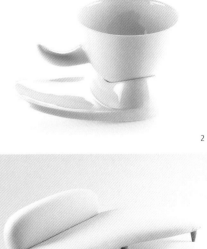

3

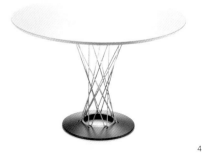

4

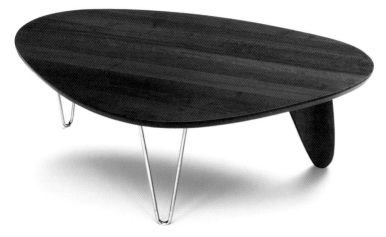

7

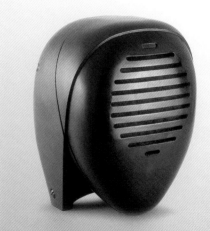

8

Nokia

Finland | Nokia Group, Espoo | Manufacturer of telecommunications equipment | **www.nokia.com**

The top-of-the-range Nokia *Communicator* phone can be flipped open to reveal a keypad and screen that enable users to access all their office work from a street café. The *9500* model comes in a stylish black-and-silver shell, a colour scheme that is also used by **Braun** and **Lamy** to signal serious elegance. A mobile phone with a silver casing caused a stir as early as the late 1990s. The *8810* model was intended to convey the same image as an elegant watch or a stylish fountain pen, said chief designer Frank Nuovo when the phone was launched. The days when owning a mobile was the preserve of the privileged classes were definitely over, most certainly for the Finns, who have a particular passion for mobile phones. Nokia caught on to the idea a bit earlier than its competitors **Ericsson**, **Motorola** and **Sony** that there was a market for high-fashion mobiles. A telecommunications giant with subsidiaries in more than one hundred countries, Nokia is Finland's most successful company by far. Its marketing keeps relatively quiet about the fact that it started out as a paper manufacturer. Mobile phones are the most important part of the company's product range. Dozens of new models are introduced every year. Nokia's design strategists took their cue from the world of fashion, and from a very early stage recognized the trend towards using form, colour and styling to target specific consumer groups.

1865 Nokia Company established as paper manufacturer in south-western Finland
1898 Finnish Rubber Works established
1912 Finnish Cable Works established
1967 Three companies merge to form Nokia Corporation
1979 Establishes mobile phone division
1988 Launches first ISDN network
1995 Sells off cable and television divisions; Frank Nuovo becomes chief designer
1996 Establishes Smart Traffic Products division
1997 New headquarters open in Espoo
1999 Develops study on design of multimedia mobile phones
2002 Establishes Vertu, brand for luxury mobile phones

Products
1996 *Communicator 9000*
1997 *5510* coloured mobile telephones
1998 *6100* mobile telephone collection; *8810* mobile telephone with silver-surfaced casing by Frank Nuovo
2000 *8210* mobile telephone
2002 *Communicator 9210*; *3650* mobile telephone
2003 *7600* mobile telephone
2004 *6630, 6260* and *2650* mobile telephones; *Communicator 9500*

1 *Communicator 9210*, 2002
2 *7600* mobile telephone, 2003
3 *8810* mobile telephone, 1998
4 *3650* mobile telephone (detail), 2002
5 *6110* mobile telephone, 1998

372

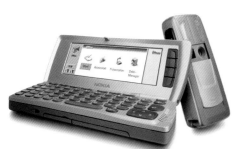

1

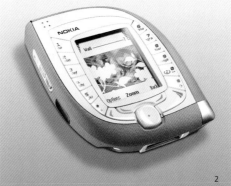

2

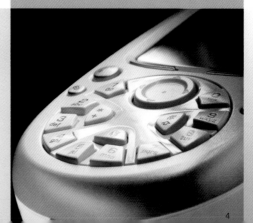

3

4

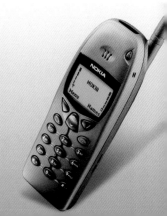

5

Jean **Nouvel**

France | Architect and furniture and product designer | www.jeannouvel.com

The upmarket Danish company **Georg Jensen** has traditionally worked with Scandinavian designers, so the commissioning of a French designer for a new cutlery series was unprecedented. Yet Jean Henri Nouvel's approach to design is modern, disarmingly unpretentious and perfectly in line with the company's philosophy. The star architect, who refuses to be stylistically pigeon-holed, has created several unusual architectural landmarks, including the Institut du Monde Arabe, the Fondation Cartier pour l'Art Contemporain (both in Paris) and the Kultur- und Kongresszentrum on Lake Lucerne in Switzerland. While still studying at the prestigious Ecole Nationale Supérieure des Beaux-Arts, Nouvel took a job at the Paris offices of the architect Claude Parent. In the late 1970s he co-founded the Syndicat de l'Architecture, a national professional organization. None of his buildings, in which he makes ample use of glass and concrete, resembles any other. Each is unique in its sophisticated and subtle design, and what they all have in common is elegant functionality. The same is true of Nouvel's furniture, which betrays the designer's architectural background: for example, the *Elémentaire* armchair (for **Ligne Roset**), the *TBL Inox* table (for ▶ **Sawaya & Moroni**) and the *Normal* office furniture series (for **Bulo**). The *Normal* desk has moveable cabinet elements that are reminiscent of office blocks connected by a bridge.

1945 Born in Fumel
1971 Graduates in architecture from Ecole Nationale Supérieure des Beaux-Arts, Paris
1979 Co-founds Syndicat de l'Architecture
1981 Institut du Monde Arabe, Paris
1993 Opéra, Lyon
1994 Fondation Cartier pour l'Art Contemporain, Paris
1995 Galeries Lafayette, Berlin
1998 Musée de la Publicité, Paris
1999 Schutzenberger brewery, Strasbourg
2000 Kultur- and Kongresszentrum, Lucerne, Switzerland

Products
1990 *Elémentaire* armchair for **Ligne Roset**
1994 *Less System* office furniture collection for Unifor; *Less* table for **Molteni & C**
1995 *TBL Inox* table and *Milana* armchair for ▶ **Sawaya & Moroni**; *Mass* armchair for **Moroso**
1996 *Saint James* armchair for ▶ Ligne Roset
1999 *1=2* table and *Compact* shelf for Zeritalia
2000 *Normal* office furniture collection for **Bulo**
2001 Wine cooler for Sawaya & Moroni
2002 *4 SPR* table and *MM* chair for Matteograssi
2003 *Waterborn* fabric for Kvadrat; *Touch* armchair for Poltrona Frau; door and window handles for Valli & Valli; *Tea & Coffee Towers* service for **Alessi**
2004 *Nouvel* cutlery for **Georg Jensen**

1 *Tea & Coffee Towers* service 2003
2 *Elémentaire* armchair, 1990
3 Desk (*Normal* collection), 2000
4 *Nouvel* cutlery, 2004

373

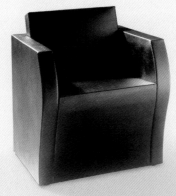

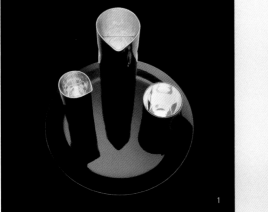

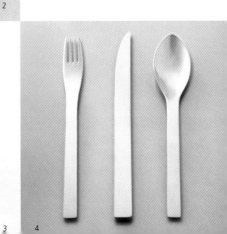

NPK

The Netherlands | Product and graphic design studio | **www.npk.nl**

No other contemporary design firm in The Netherlands plays such a large part in public life as the creative NPK studio, which is based in Leiden, in the metropolitan area between Amsterdam and The Hague. Among the projects that have left their mark is the Dutch traffic orientation system, including all the motorway signs, which were redesigned by NPK in the late 1990s. One of the company's first classic designs was a letterbox from the mid-1980s for the Dutch national mail. It consists of a red container suspended between two poles. Its design was a departure from the traditional, simple box and aimed to reflect the new emphasis on service, which caught on somewhat earlier in The Netherlands than in other European countries.

The studio was founded in the late 1970s, and today, along with **Ideo**, **Fitch** and **Ziba**, is among the leaders in the international design industry, with branches in Boston and Hamburg. The abbreviation NPK comes from the names of the partners: Ninaber van Eyben, Peters and Krouwel. The studio has come to be associated with a comprehensive, integral approach that focuses on detail and process, including market and product analyses and collaboration between designers and engineers. This approach has also led to the studio working in a wide range of areas. It has designed such technical appliances as X-ray equipment and a meat-slicing machine; numerous everyday products, including toboggans, toys, children's seats for cars and bicycles; furniture and, being a Dutch company, a handy water-bottle clip for bicycles. Other NPK designs that have become ubiquitous are radios, pens and vacuum cleaners. The *Yachtboy 500* world receiver (for Grundig) combines a variety of different functions with high sound quality in a minute casing. Its control panel has a clear and logical design. Sales figures for the new highlighter pen for Edding have surpassed all expectations. Its slim, ellipsoidal form is easily recognizable, and gives the pen an unmistakable identity. The *Art* vacuum cleaner for Miele has such an attractive design that it need not be tucked away in the cupboard after hoovering the carpet.

1978 Peters en Krouwel established by by Wolfram Peters and Peter Krouwel
1985 Bruno Ninaber van Eyben becomes partner
1991 NPK exhibition held at Stedelijk Museum, Amsterdam
1997 Ninaber van Eyben leaves studio; Jan Witte and Jos Oberdorf become new partners
1999 Establishes studio in Hamburg, Germany
2004 Establishes studio in Boston, USA

Products

1985 Child's seat for Dremefa
1986 Diabetes management system for Diva Medical Systems
1987 Viewphone for KPN Telecom
1989 Halogen spotlight for Siemens
1990 Office furniture system for Aspa
1991 *Bobob* child's seat for Dremefa; *PX* home telephone exchange for Alcatel
1993 Desk accessories for Randstad
1994 Chair for Kembo; *Yachtboy 500* world receiver for Grundig
1995 *Plato* office furniture for Kembo
1996 Meat slicer for Avery Berkel
1998 *Kiss* child's bicycle seat for Hamax; *Oiva* coat hanger for MK-Tresmer; *Point* office table system for Haworth
1999 Coffee dispenser for Douwe Egberts; *Sno-Shark* child's sledge for Hamax; *Sonic* lamp system for Wila
2001 *Let's B* office chair for **Steelcase**
2002 Highlighter pen for Edding; *Sno-Cross* sledge for Hamax; bottle carrier for Tacx
2003 *Art* vacuum cleaner for Miele; *Ofro* robot for Robowatch
2004 *Beertender* home draught system for Heineken; *Please 2* office chair for Steelcase

374

1 *Sno-Cross* sledge, 2002
2 *Art* vacuum cleaner, 2003
3 Highlighter pen, 2002
4 *PX* home telephone exchange, 1991
5 Coffee dispenser, 1999
6 Meat slicer, 1996
7 *Yachtboy 500* world receiver, 1994

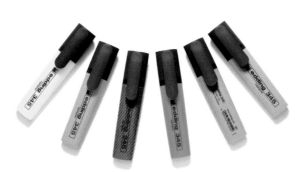

3

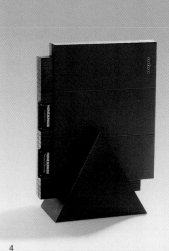

4

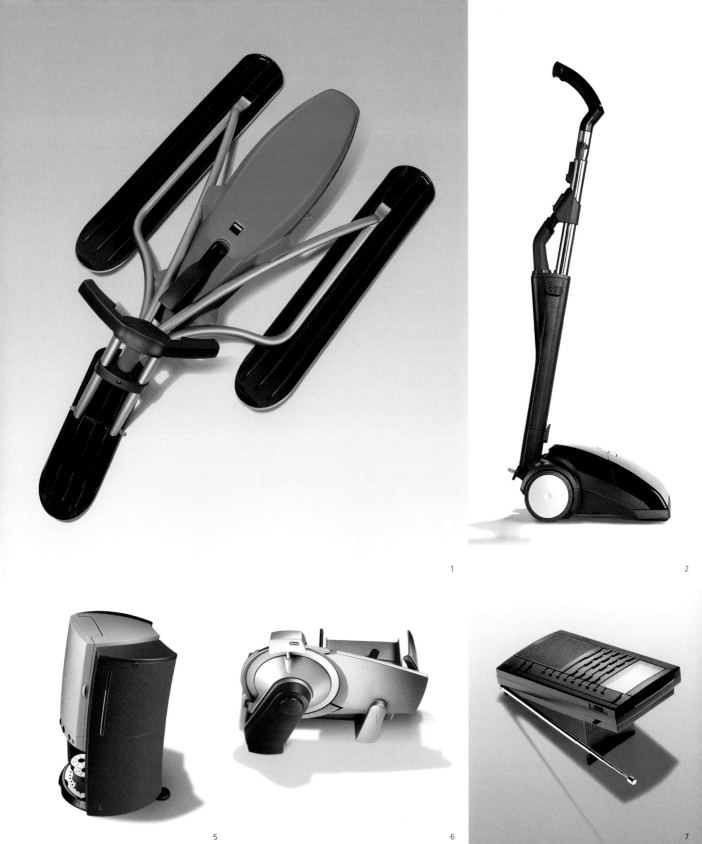

1

2

5

6

7

Oxo, *Gel-e* gardening tools series, 2004

Oxo takes a scientific approach to developing household items.
The design studios **Continuum** and **Ideo** have transformed Oxo
products such as the *Gel-e* gardening tools series into design icons.
The handles of these tools are manufactured using multicomponent
technology. The material is slightly elastic so that users are able to get
a firm grip and the tools do not slip, even when their hands are wet.

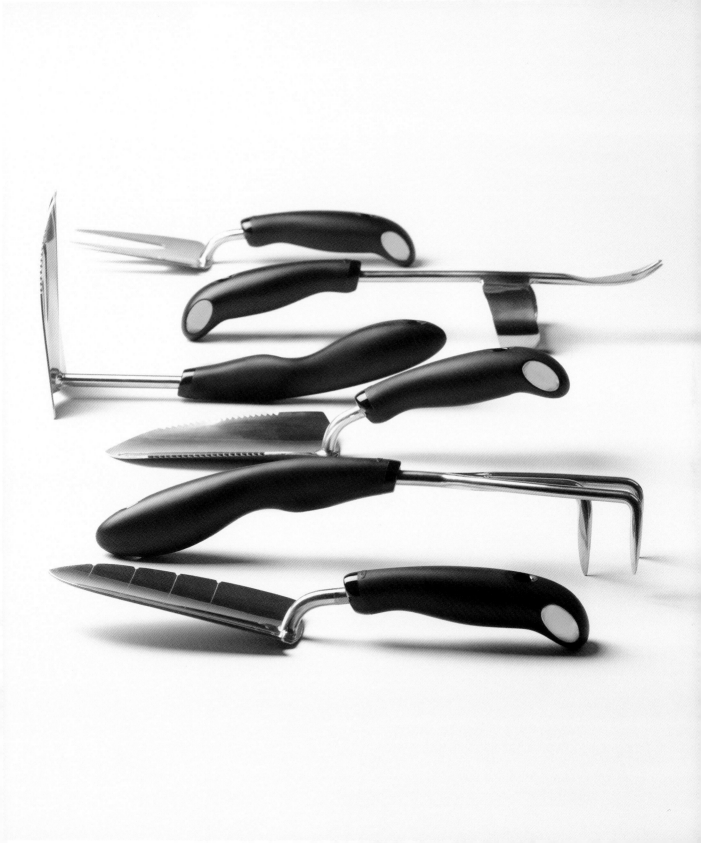

O Luce

Italy I O Luce Srl, Milan I Lamp manufacturer I **www.oluce.com**

The *Atollo* table lamp is a masterly composition with a hemispherical shade that hovers weightlessly above a cylindrical base. It was designed for O Luce by ▸ **Vico Magistretti**, the grand master of Italian design. In the 1960s and 1970s in particular, Magistretti had a substantial influence on the company's product range and made an important contribution to establishing the reputation of Italian lamp design in general. Another designer who contributed to the company's success was ▸ **Joe Colombo**. His *281* table lamp, consisting of a curved Perspex diffuser, his small *Spider* table lamp, with its robotic features, and his *626* standard lamp, the first halogen lamp to be produced in Italy, were the highlights of a series of innovative and imaginative designs. Bruno Gecchelin also created products for the company, including the elegant *Dogale 512* desk lamp and the *Gemma* standard lamp.

In the 1980s and 1990s O Luce collaborated with a new generation of designers, among them Marco Romanelli, Marta Laudani, **Sebastian Bergne, Fernando and Humberto Campana**, and the Finnish designer **Harri Koskinen**, whose *Lamppu* standard lamp, with its cool, futuristic design, is untypical of the company's programme.

378

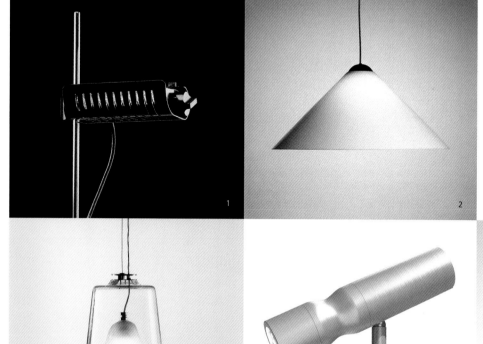

Offecct

Sweden | Offecct A/B, Tibro | Furniture manufacturer | **www.offecct.se**

The Swedish design boom of the 1990s had a profound impact on office furniture. Some of the most important representatives of a new generation of Swedish designers have contributed to the Offecct product range, among them Monica Förster, Eero Koivisto, Ola Rune and **Thomas Sandell**. Unlike the companies **Ikea**, **Lammhults** and **Källemo**, which have their roots in the province of Småland, Offecct is based in Skaraborg, in central Sweden. Its impressive range of seventeen sofas, which it describes as "meeting points for creative people", demonstrates that an office can be turned into a snug and relaxing place. Offecct's designs include a wide variety of different styles, such as the C-shaped *Orgy* sofa by **Karim Rashid** and **Jean-Marie Massaud**'s rectangular *Easy Block* module sofa, which omits one armrest, allowing different modules to be fitted together. Following the lead of many Italian companies, Offecct has recently started collaborating with a group of renowned international designers. It succeeded in recruiting the Swiss designer **Alfredo Häberli**, who created the *Yakin* sofa and *Pick Up*, a magazine rack on castors in the shape of a van. Offecct is always keen to remain at the forefront of progress. It has launched a joint research project with the Royal Institute of Technology in Stockholm with the aim of investigating health matters at the workplace.

1990 Established in Tibro

Products
1999 *Tinto* table and chair by **Claesson Koivisto Rune**
2000 *Doppio* armchair and sofa by ▶ Claesson Koivisto Rune
2001 *F-Seat* sofa by **Thomas Eriksson**; *Easy Block* sofa by **Jean-Marie Massaud**; *Solitaire* armchair by ▶ **Alfredo Häberli**
2002 *E-Seat* sofa and *I-Seat* chaise longue by ▶ Thomas Eriksson
2003 *Orgy* sofa by **Karim Rashid**; *DNA* modular tables, *Dual* table and *Mono* chair collection by Claesson Koivisto Rune; *Pick Up* magazine rack/chair/trolley by Alfredo Häberli; *K-Line* rubbish bin, coat stand and tea trolley by Khodi Feiz
2004 *Pop* armchair and *Flower* stool by Claesson Koivisto Rune; *Yakin* sofa by Alfredo Häberli; *Tray* table by Monika Förster; *Metro* chair by ▶ **Thomas Sandell**; *Orbit* seating system by Claesson Koivisto Rune

1 *Easy Block* sofa, 2001
2 *Pick Up* magazine rack/chair/trolley, 2003
3 *Orgy* sofa, 2003
4 *DNA* modular tables, 2003
5 *Mono* chairs, 2003

379

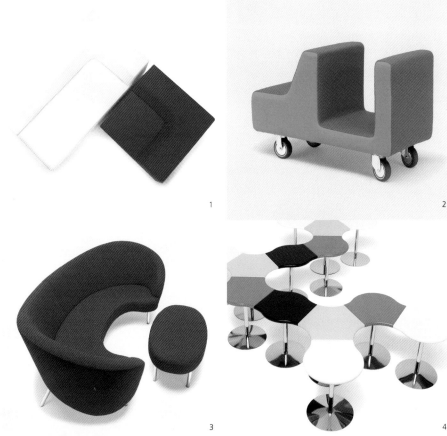

1

2

3

4

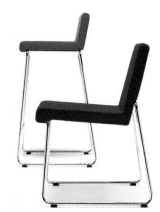

5

Olivetti

Italy | Olivetti SpA, Ivrea | Manufacturer of office equipment and computers | **www.olivetti.com**

Adriano Olivetti was one of the first and most successful design managers. He made Olivetti famous the world over and created an exemplary corporate culture. Along with **Fiat**, Olivetti is probably Italy's best-known manufacturer. It was founded by Camillo, Adriano's father, who designed the *M1*, the first Italian typewriter, in 1911. Adriano joined the company in the 1920s and went on to establish an advertising department that employed the best artists of the period. Olivetti also developed an enlightened social welfare infrastructure for its staff that included company flats, libraries and nurseries. The basis of the company's success was of course its exemplary product designs. Different decades are associated with different great designers. In the 1940s and 1950s Marcello Nizzoli gave typewriters and adding machines a pleasantly flowing design. His *Lettera 22* from 1950 is an extremely lightweight, flat machine. In the same decade it was awarded the prize for 'best industrial product of the last one hundred years' by a jury of one hundred of the world's best-known designers. During the same period, under Giovanni Pintori, the advertising department became renowned for its modern Italian graphic design. Even Olivetti's showrooms and factories were designed by acclaimed artists and architects. In the late 1950s ▸**Ettore Sottsass** produced the *Elea 9003*, the company's first mainframe computer, which became a technological and aesthetic icon. In the 1960s he created such typewriters as the unconventional, bright red *Valentine*.

At the end of the 1960s Hans von Klier took over responsibility for the company's corporate identity and summarized his instructions in the legendary 'red books'. It was also during this period that ▸**Mario Bellini** joined the Olivetti team. He designed the *Divisumma 18* desktop calculator, with its rounded casing, the successful *Logos* calculator series and the *Praxis 35* typewriter. The 1970s marked a period of financial difficulty for Olivetti. The company branched out into new areas such as office automation and telecommunications. In 2003 it became part of the Telecom Italia group. Recent designs include laptop computers and multimedia equipment by **Michele De Lucchi** and his team.

380

1 *Summa 19* calculator, 1970
2 *ArtJet 10* ink-jet printer, 1999
3 *Gioconda* desk calculator, 2001
4 *Copy Lab 200* copying system, 2001
5 *Lettera 22* typewriter, 1950
6 *MC 45 Summa* calculator, 1940
7 *Divisumma 18* calculator, 1973
8 *Logos 60* calculator, 1973

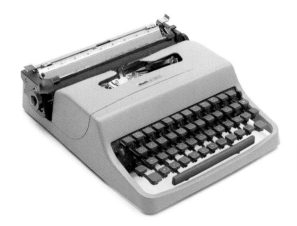

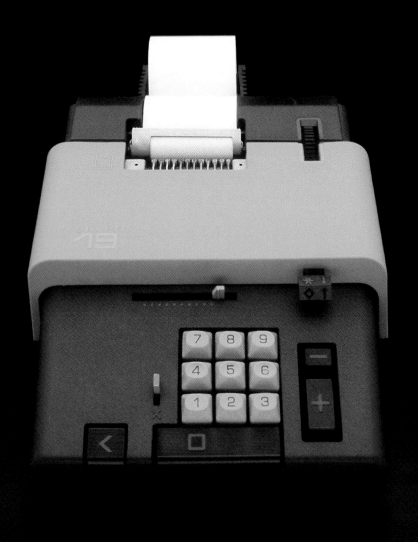

1

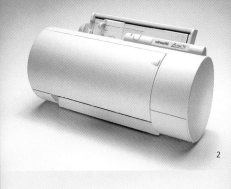

2

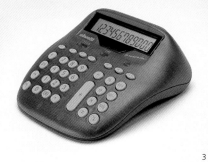

3

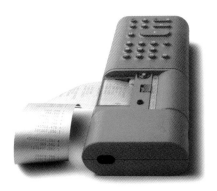

4

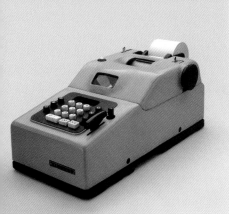

6

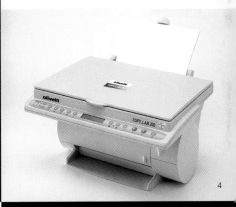

7

8

Opel

Germany | Adam Opel AG, Rüsselsheim | Automobile manufacturer | **www.opel.com**

The *Kapitän*, manufactured by Opel, was one of the dream cars of the German post-war economic boom. In the 1950s its image was, for a while, even more distinguished than that of **Mercedes-Benz**. The *Kapitän* acquainted Germans with styling from the United States, including tail fins, chrome trim and wrap-around screens. Opel started out as a manufacturer of sewing machines and bicycles and soon developed into one of the most progressive German carmakers; in the 1920s it even built the first rocket-powered automobiles. Assembly-line production was introduced as early as the mid-1920s. In 1929 the company was taken over by **General Motors**. The models of the 1930s were influenced by the streamlined cars from the United States, while the names were derived from naval ranks. The *Kadett*, *Commodore* and *Admiral* ranges stayed in production until well into the 1980s. The first model with a more European design was the *Rekord* from the early 1960s, which had a clean and uncluttered look. A year later, the *Kadett*, a scaled-down version of the *Rekord*, was launched as an answer to **Volkswagen**'s *Beetle*. With its straight lines and no-frills design, it was another step towards a more European style. This sober 1960s design was used in the restyling of the *Kapitän* and *Admiral* models. The flowing lines of the *Commodore B* and *Rekord C* coupés targeted a different group of consumers, and the extremely low-slung *GT* – Opel's first sports car – boasted retractable 'frog-eye' headlights and was advertised with the slogan "Only flying is more exciting".

Three decades later, in the early twenty-first century, Opel again took up the production of a sports car, this time with the robust *Speedster*. In the last few decades the company has been good at marketing its products, even though the cars themselves have not been particularly inspiring. There are, however, two notable exceptions: the *Astra* coupé, designed by **Bertone**, and the *Calibra*, with its high waistline and arc-shaped roof. Both cars anticipated the emotional style of the 1990s. The later 1990s saw some successful designs, including the *Zafira* and *Tigra*, although their sales figures were less than satisfactory. The more angular look of the *Meriva* and *Signum* models combines detail and stylistic unity and heralds a new trend defined by chief designer Bryan Nesbitt.

382

1 *Meriva* minivan (detail), 2003
2 *Insignia* executive saloon (concept), 2003
3 *Signum* saloon, 2003
4 *Calibra* coupé (detail), 1989
5 *Rekord C* coupé, 1967
6 *GT* sports car, 1968
7 *Speedster* sports car, 2001

1862	Established in Rüsselsheim by Adam Opel as manufacturer of sewing machines
1887	Begins producing bicycles
1895	Adam Opel dies
1899	Begins producing automobiles
1911	Begins producing aircraft engines
1929	**General Motors** acquires company
1967	Chuck Jordan becomes chief designer
1983	Wayne Cherry becomes chief designer (later chief designer at General Motors)
2002	Martin Smith becomes chief designer
2004	Bryan Nesbitt becomes chief designer

Products

1899	*Lutzmann* patent motor car
1909	4/8 hp 'Doktorwagen' (Doctor's car)
1924	4/12 hp 'Laubfrosch' (Tree frog)
1930	*Blitz* lorry
1935	*Olympia* saloon
1953	*Olympia Rekord* saloon
1955	*Kapitän* saloon
1961	*Rekord* saloon and coupé
1962	*Kadett* saloon and coupé
1964	*Kapitän*, *Admiral* and *Diplomat V8* saloons
1967	*Rekord C* coupé
1968	*GT* sports car
1970	*Ascona A* saloon; *Manta A* coupé
1975	*Ascona B* saloon; *Manta B* coupé
1977	*Senator* saloon; *Monza* coupé
1979	*Kadett D* compact car
1982	*Corsa* small car
1984	*Kadett E* compact car
1986	*Omega* saloon
1988	*Vectra* saloon
1989	*Calibra* coupé
1991	*Astra* compact car; *Frontera* SUV
1994	*Tigra* coupé
1999	*Zafira* van
2001	*Speedster* sports car
2003	*Meriva* minivan; *Signum* saloon; *Insignia* executive saloon (concept)
2004	*Tigra* roadster
	Models are sold under the Vauxhall marque in the United Kingdom

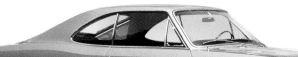

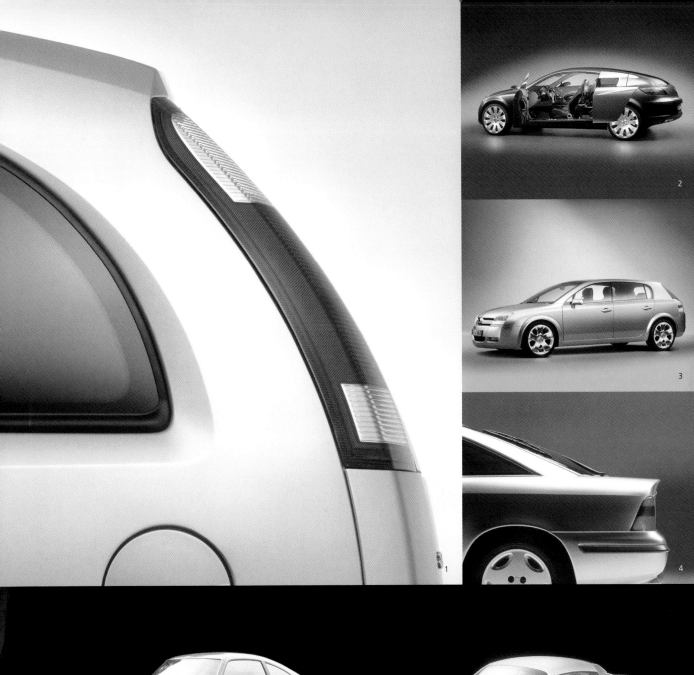

1

2

3

4

6

7

Orrefors

Sweden I Orrefors Kosta Boda A/B, Orrefors I Glassware manufacturer I **www.orrefors.se**

Orrefors was founded originally as an ironworks in the eighteenth century and began producing glass bottles in 1898. Johan Ekman, the company's new owner, hired the artists Simon Gate and Edward Hald in 1916 and 1917 respectively as the firm's first designers. Orrefors's glassware became a Swedish export success after its delicate engravings caused a stir at the 1925 *Exposition Internationale des Arts Décoratifs et Industriels Modernes* in Paris. These engravings were figurative motifs in an elegant Neo-classical style, for which the term 'Swedish Grace' was coined. Within just a few years the small glassworks from Småland developed into a company of international renown. It gained its reputation as a result not only of the high quality of its products, but also of a circumspect management that established its own school of glass-making.

In the 1930s Edwin Öhrström and Vicke Lindstrand developed the sophisticated Ariel technique of glass design, a variant of the innovative *graal* technique. By this time, Orrefors had become world famous and, in the eyes of the Swedes, a national institution. Alongside **Ikea** and **Volvo**, it remains one of Sweden's best-known companies. The golden years of the 1950s saw the creation of such design icons as the *Apple* vase by Ingeborg Lundin and the subsequent consolidation of Orrefors's success. It came as a shock when the company – which had acquired **Kosta Boda** in 1990 – merged with the Danish manufacturer **Royal Copenhagen** seven years later. There had been indications of a looming crisis long before the takeover. The turbulent 1960s, when Gunnar Cyrén created his *Pop* glasses, were a turning point. The second generation of designers left the company, among them Lundin and the photographer and glass designer John Selbing. Orrefors has never been associated with experimental gimmicks, but has always striven to create "beauty for everyone". Since the late 1990s a young team of designers has decisively influenced the company's style. Among the new talents are Martti Rytkönen and Lena Bergström, who finds "beauty in imperfection". The beginning of the twenty-first century witnessed a new, larger design studio and fresh design trends, including the expressive collage technique of Per B. Sundberg and the sophisticated minimalism of **Ingegerd Råman**.

384

1 *Apple* vase, 1955
2 *Cirkus* vase, 1930
3 Vase, 1972
4 *Babuschka* bowl, 2001
5 *A Drop of Water* carafe, 2001
6 Art glassware (*Planet* collection), 2002
7 *Squeeze* vase, 1997
8 *Difference* glass series, 2002

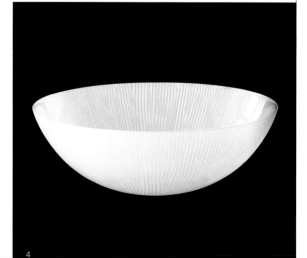

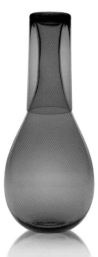

4

5

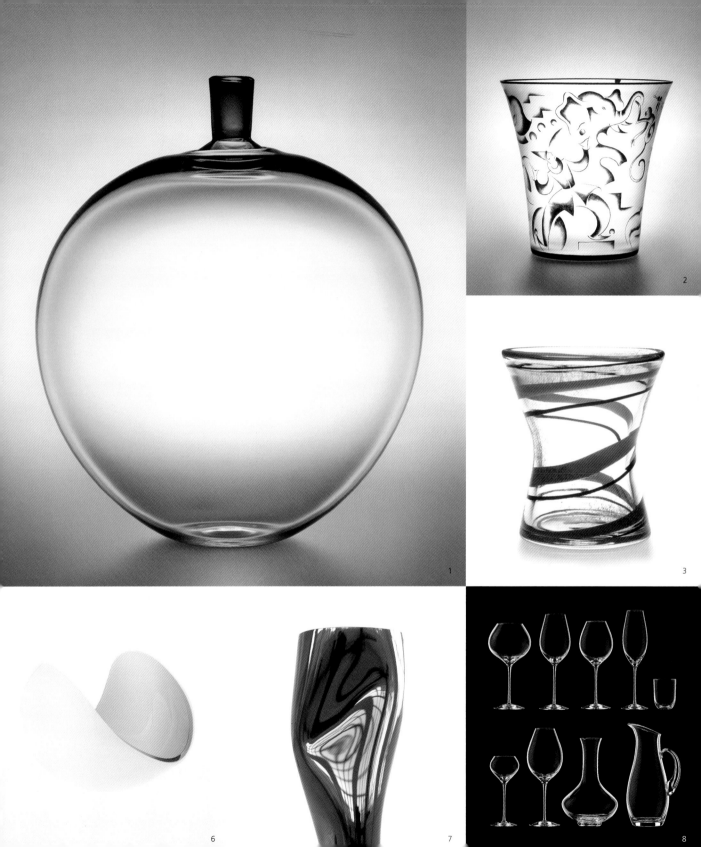

Oxo

USA I Oxo International Ltd, New York I Manufacturer of kitchenware and household items I **www.oxo.com**

"Why hasn't someone come up with this before?" This is a common reaction when people use tools such as Oxo's vegetable peeler for the very first time. With its swivel blade and ridged handle, it makes the task of peeling vegetables so much simpler. Cooking experts in the United States were wildly enthusiastic about the handy gizmo, and the simple peeler triggered Oxo's success. The company was established in 1990 after the entrepreneur Sam Farber witnessed his arthritic wife's frustrating struggles with standard household utensils. Farber developed the concept of 'universal design', which goes a step beyond the idea of design for people with disabilities that was developed by the Swedish studio **Ergonomidesign**. Oxo products are designed for *all* users: the physically disabled, the elderly and infirm, left-handed people and for the majority of right-handed users. The concept turned out to be a highly profitable commercial idea and caught on quickly in the United States. It combines innovation, ergonomic design, good marketing and a philanthropic approach. Farber, who has since retired from the company, took up the long-standing tradition of inventiveness in the United States, one that has been particularly evident in the design of tools and household utensils.

Since its foundation Oxo has developed around five hundred innovative products in collaboration with such renowned studios as Smart Design, **Ideo** and **Continuum**. In almost all cases the product was not exactly reinvented, but it was certainly redefined. Examples include a highly efficient tin opener with a tomahawk head and a measuring jug with a wrap-around scale that enables users to read it without having to lift the jug. Very often it is the small details that make all the difference, as in the case of a lemon squeezer that can be adjusted to fit the size of the fruit. Oxo commissioned the Smart Design team from New York for its *Good Grips* range of products, which established the company's reputation. These designers created, among other items, the *Soap Squirting Palm Brush*, a washing-up brush with a built-in soap dispenser that can be operated single-handedly. The ingenious gadget appeals, in particular, to those keen on saving time – and, of course, it also helps save water, soap and energy.

386

1 *Smooth Edge* tin opener, 2002

2 *i-Series* jar opener, 2003

3 Carwash brush, 1998

4 *i-Series* garlic press, 2003

5 *Soap Squirting Palm Brush*, 2000

6 Corkscrew, 1993

7 Lemon squeezer, 2001

8 1.0 litre measuring jug, 2002

9 Coloured spatulas, 2003

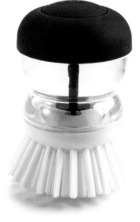

5

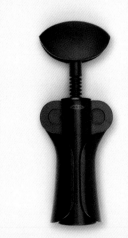

6

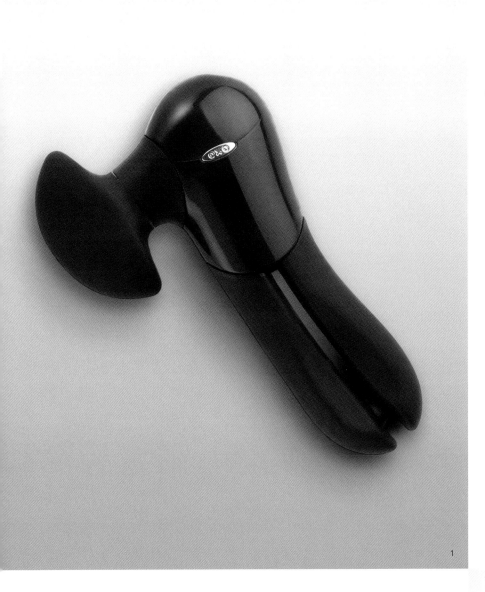

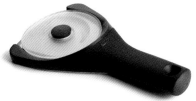

2

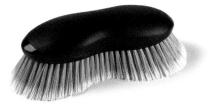

3

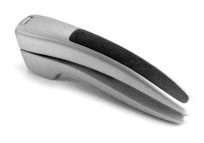

4

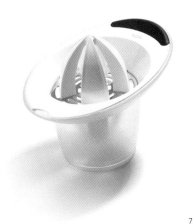

1

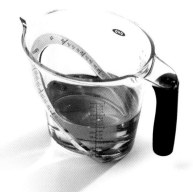

7

8

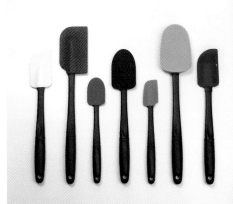

9

Porsche, *911* coupé, 1963

The design of Porsche's *911* coupé was a stroke of genius. It combined the stylistic features of the older *356* model with the more sober look of the 1960s. The body was designed by Ferdinand Alexander Porsche, while Erwin Komenda was responsible for the technical aspects of the design. The car's clean, straight lines and characteristic eye-shaped headlights have ensured its continued popularity.

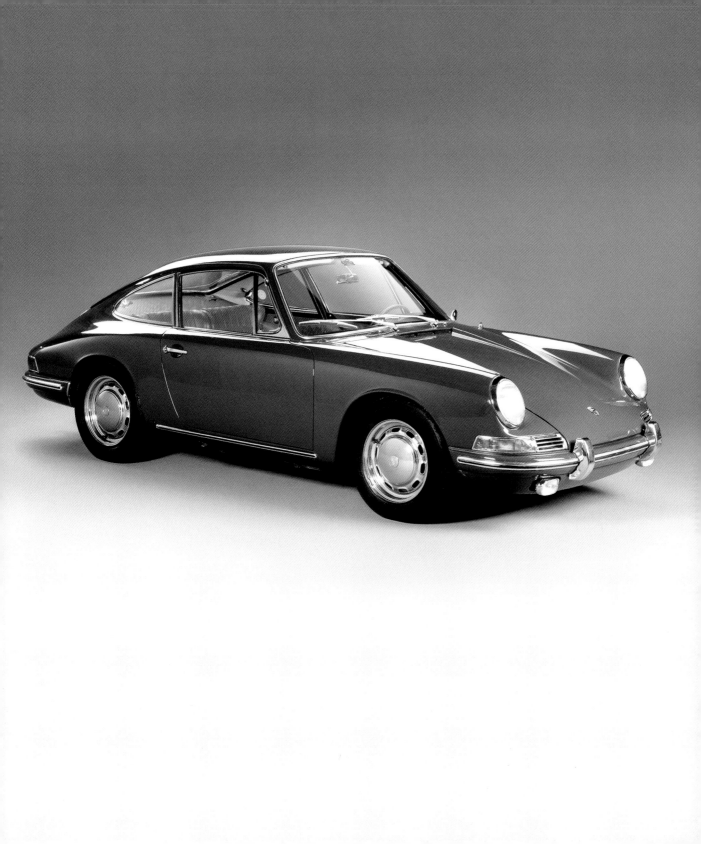

Verner **Panton**

Denmark | Architect and furniture designer | www.panton.ch | www.vernerpanton.com

After working as an assistant to **Arne Jacobsen**, Verner Panton travelled extensively throughout Europe in his ▶**Volkswagen** *Transporter*. His eccentricity earned him a lasting reputation as Denmark's most controversial designer. At a furniture fair in the late 1950s, his *K1 Cone Chair* was shown fixed upside down on the ceiling. Panton also created inflatable furniture, a transportable, inexpensive plastic house and a spherical house – a glass sphere reminiscent of R. Buckminster Fuller's geodesic dome. The lighting designer **Poul Henningsen** remarked on his colleague's "instinct for lighting" and "feeling for darkness". Above all, Henningsen considered Panton to be a talented creator of atmosphere.

In the early 1960s Panton escaped the confines of Denmark and worked in Paris and Cannes. He eventually settled in Basel in Switzerland. His explosive use of colour and bold experimental designs, hitherto regarded as somewhat preposterous, set a new trend. The International Furniture Fair in Cologne became Panton's stage, and soon Bayer, the German chemicals giant, hired him to showcase its innovative technologies. The company wanted to demonstrate the versatility of plastic, polyurethane foam and new synthetic fibres. Panton responded by designing an impressive fantasy landscape entitled *Visiona 2* for the 1970 Cologne fair. The real sensation, however, was the *Panton Chair*, a cantilever chair created from a single piece of plastic. A number of other designers had experimented with a similar technically and aesthetically sophisticated concept, but Panton was the first to realize it. In the previous year he had designed the *S Chair* for **Thonet**, a plywood design that anticipated the basic form of the *Panton Chair*; it was later further refined for his *Art Chair* series. Like the Finnish designer **Eero Aarnio**, Panton was highly successful in shaping flowing forms into stunning plastic creations, but he also went a step further. The *Visiona 2* installation was the first complete synthetic landscape, a futuristic environment that, one year after the Apollo moon landing, clearly showed the influence of the space age. The Danish culture magazine *Mobilia* once wrote that Panton set out to stimulate all the senses, re-creating a range of different experiences, "from claustrophobia to erotic desire".

1 *Panton Chair*, 1967
2 *Moon Lamp*, 1960
3 *Ring Lamp*, 1969
4 *Visiona 2* installation, 1970
5 *Barboy* container trolley, 1963
6 *K2 Wire Cone Chair*, 1959
7 *K3 Heart Wire Chair*, 1959
8 *Geometri* carpet, 1961

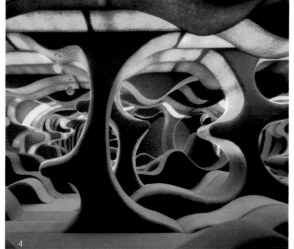

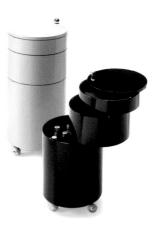

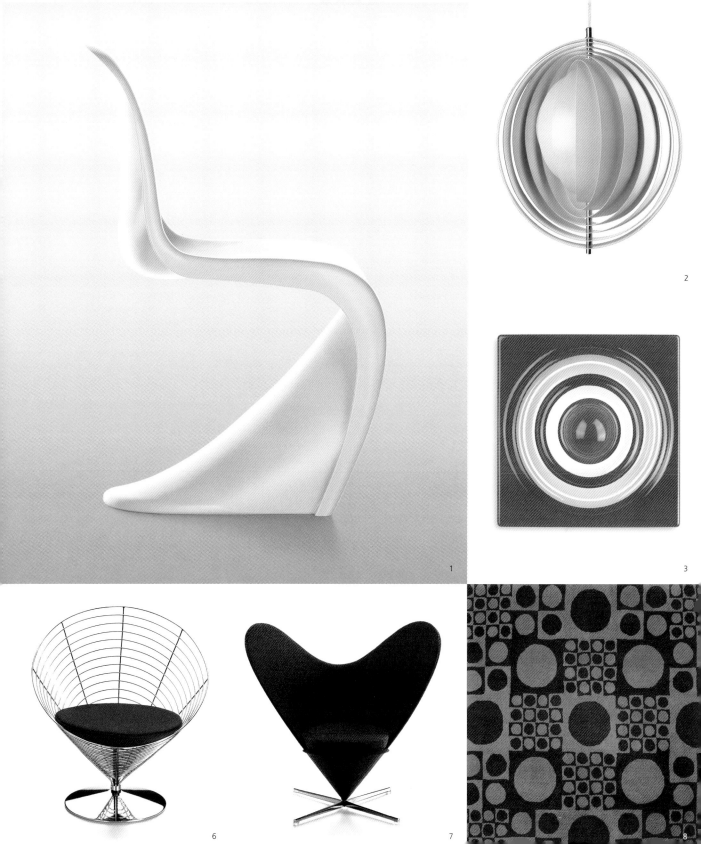

1

2

3

6

7

8

Pierre **Paulin**

France | Furniture designer | www.artifort.com

Oranges, tulips, tongues and butterflies: it is not only the names of Pierre Paulin's designs that are taken from the plant and animal kingdoms, but also their shapes, which reflect the tremendous variety of natural forms. Paulin had great success with this 'organic' style, characterized by its soft outlines and sculptural expressiveness. His designs from the 1960s, which saw a revival a quarter of a century later and today serve as a source of inspiration for modern designers, epitomized the heady atmosphere of the Pop era. His favourite materials were leather and foam.

Paulin designed his first chairs for **Thonet**. The German manufacturer had become aware of the self-taught, talented designer from Paris in the early 1950s. It was only towards the end of that decade, however, that Paulin found a congenial client in the Dutch furniture company **Artifort**, and it was there that he was able to realize his most innovative designs. His armchairs are a fusion of French and Scandinavian design elements. Even though his *Orange Slice*, *Tulip* and *Tongue* chairs show influences from **Arne Jacobsen**'s sculptural furniture, Paulin found his own unique style. His sophisticated *Ribbon* chair from 1966 caused something of a stir internationally, and anticipated the expressionist designs of **Ron Arad**, who created furniture from sheets of bent metal in the 1980s and 1990s.

The climax of Paulin's career came when he was engaged to furnish the private apartments of Georges Pompidou, the conservative French president. His *Elysée* chair from the early 1970s was a product of this commission. François Mitterrand, Pompidou's socialist successor, later also hired Paulin to design furniture for his office. Paulin gained even greater prominence when he redesigned the Denon Wing of the Musée du Louvre in Paris. In the mid-1970s he focused his activities on industrial design, which led to a long-term collaboraton with the French designer Roger Tallon.

1927 Born in Paris
1970 Designs seating for *Japan World Exposition*, Osaka
1971 Furnishes private apartments of President Georges Pompidou, Elysée Palace, Paris
1975 Establishes ADSA & Partners with Roger Tallon

Products
1954 Furniture for **Thonet**
1960 *Oyster*, *Orange Slice* and *Globe* armchairs
1963 *Mushroom* armchair
1964 *Butterfly* armchair
1965 *Tulip* and *Little Tulip* armchairs
1966 *Ribbon* chair
1967 *Tongue* chair; *F 302* plastic lounger
1968 *ABCD* armchair and sofa
All at **Artifort**
1971 *Elysée* chair for Alpha International
1973 *F 598* armchair for Artifort
1978 *Dangari* garden chair for Allibert

392

1 *Orange Slice* armchair, 1960
2 *Ribbon* chair, 1966
3 *Tongue* chair, 1967
4 *F 302* plastic lounger, 1967
5 *Little Tulip* armchair, 1965
6 *Butterfly* armchair, 1964
7 *Mushroom* armchair, 1963

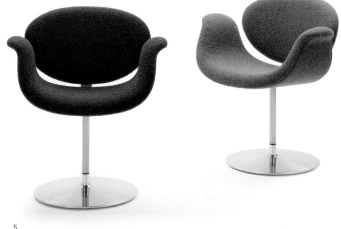

5

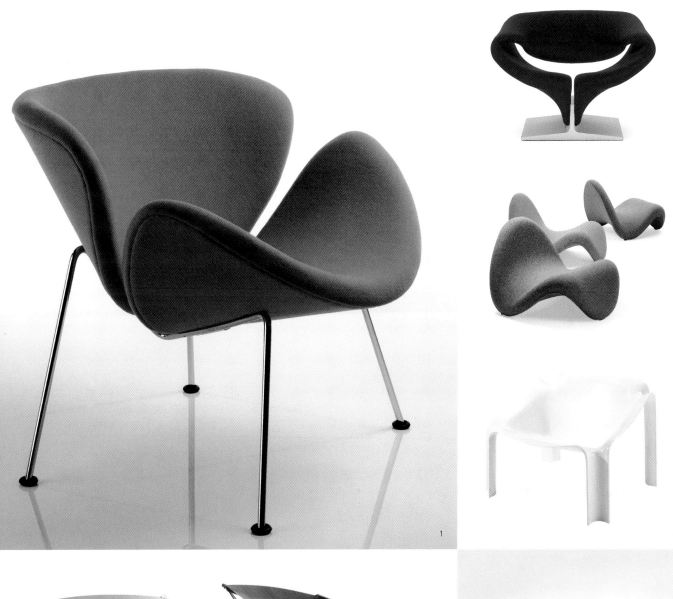

1

2

3

4

6

7

Pelikan Design

Denmark | Furniture and product design studio | **www.pelikan.dk**

One of the mottoes of the Pelikan Design studio can be translated as: "Details are what counts, because design is measured in pounds and pence." The company has always distanced itself from traditional Danish cabinetmaking and has focused instead on tubular steel chairs and sofas. Pelikan Design consists of the architects **Niels Gammelgaard** and Lars Mathiesen and a handful of staff. The Copenhagen-based studio regards furniture as an industrial product, and it is therefore no surprise to learn that it has been working for **Ikea** for many years. Among the designs developed for the Swedish furniture giant are *Ted*, the inexpensive plastic folding chair from the 1970s (one of Ikea's bestsellers), the popular *Moment* table and various mirrors, shelf systems, upholstered suites, coat hangers and a series of storage boxes for records, computer disks and CDs.

The Pelikan studio has designed an exceptionally wide range of products, including ashtrays, trailers for bicycles, hospital beds, children's bikes, lamps, blinds and a seating system for railway carriages. At the centre of the studio's activities have always been furniture designs commissioned by **Fritz Hansen,** Erik Jørgensen, Bent Krogh, **Fredericia** and **Stokke**. For Fritz Hansen, Pelikan created various partition screens and the versatile *Plano* table series.

1978 Established by **Niels Gammelgaard** and Lars Mathiesen in Copenhagen
1980 Receives ID Prize (also 1991, 1996)
1993 Receives Danish Furniture Prize
1994 Establishes Pelikan Copenhagen, developing products for **Ikea**

Products
1977 *Ted* folding chair for Ikea
1980 *Tribike* child's tricycle for Rabo
1983 *Café Chair* for **Fritz Hansen**
1985 *Moment* sofa for ▸ Ikea
1986 *Decision* sofa for ▸ Fritz Hansen; *PK 7* armchair for **Cappellini**
1987 *Kräsen* candlestick for Ikea
1990 Transit carrier for Copenhagen Airport (with Komplot Design); *Oasis* upholstered furniture for Erik Jørgensen
1992 *LA 150* partition for ▸ Fritz Hansen
1993 *Wing* partition for Fritz Hansen
1994 *Nevil* chair for Ikea
2000 *Plano* table collection for Fritz Hansen; *Sirkus* dining and kitchen table for **Stokke**
2001 *Kämpe* shelf for Ikea
2002 *Ice* and *Runner* chairs; *Moment* table and table for *PS* product collection for Ikea; *Mimmi* hanging lamp for Zero
2003 *Gubbo* swivel armchair for Ikea

1 *Plano* table, 2000
2 *Gubbo* swivel armchair, 2003
3 Table (*PS* collection), 2002
4 *Tribike* child's tricycle, 1980
5 *Mimmi* hanging lamp, 2002

394

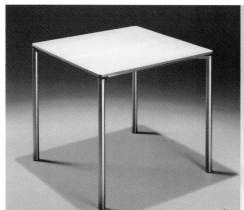

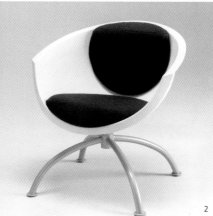

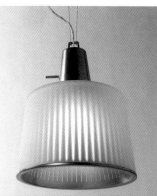

Jorge **Pensi**

Spain | Furniture designer

The lightweight yet robust *Toledo* is an elegant aluminium stackable café chair created by the Spanish designer Jorge Pensi for **Knoll**. With its distinctive rib structure, it has brought Mediterranean flair on to European high streets since the late 1980s. In the mid-1970s, after studying architecture in Buenos Aires, Pensi emigrated to Spain. Settling in Barcelona, which had already emerged as the country's design capital, he founded the design consultancy Grupo Berenguer with Alberto **Lievore**, Norberto Chaves and Oriol Pibernat. The group designed furniture – including the *Latina* range for Perobell – and also concepts for exhibitions.

Pensi founded his own design studio in 1984 and since then has been working on his own. He has remained faithful to his material of choice, aluminium, and has focused on furniture and lamp designs. His clients include such Spanish companies as Amat, B. Lux and Disform, and such Italian and German manufacturers as **Cassina** and **WMF**. He developed a comprehensive range of chairs for the office furniture manufacturer Kusch + Co, including the *Ona* and *¡Hola!* series.

395

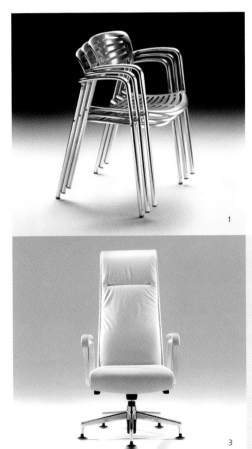

1

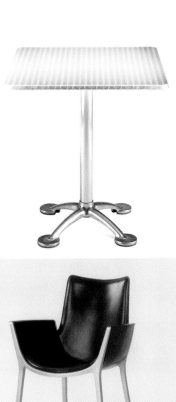

2

3

4

5

Gaetano **Pesce**

Italy | Architect, artist and furniture and product designer | **www.gaetanopesce.com**

Interaction and communication are keywords for the unorthodox Italian designer Gaetano Pesce. The pioneer of Pop design made a name for himself in the late 1960s with his *Up* series, which he designed for C&B Italia (now **B&B Italia**). It consists of seven seats made from polyurethane foam (at that time, a new and innovative material) that pop out of their packaging to take on rounded, anthropomorphic forms. *Up* made Pesce famous almost overnight and turned him into one of leading proponents of the Radical Design movement, which opposed purely functional design. Pesce has always been more interested in an object's meaning than in its function. He continues to comment ironically on the principles of mass production by developing objects that are mass-produced yet not identical. He applied this principle as early as 1980, in the polyurethane/resin armchairs from the *Dalila* series. Each of the slightly amorphous chairs is unique, differing slightly from the others in its detailing. This principle is also incorporated in his *Sansone* resin table from the same year (both products for **Cassina**). The manufacturer's craftsmen were given free rein to decide on the design of the upper section of the table. Some of Pesce's more recent designs have taken up this idea once again. His *Nobody's Perfect* furniture collection (for Zerodisegno) is made from his favourite material, synthetic resin, and is a further ironic comment on mass production and individuality. Each piece in the collection is unique in terms of colour, shape and decoration; imperfection is the guiding design principle.

Pesce began his career as an artist and took up design only in the late 1960s. He still succeeds in creating products that are innovative and contain an element of surprise, as in the *543 Broadway* chair (for Bernini), which incorporates springs in its frame, or the *Umbrella Chair* (for Zerodisegno), which indeed resembles a closed umbrella and can be opened when required. His unconventional *I Feltri* furniture series in felt has become a symbol of rebellious Post-modernism. In 1980 Pesce moved to New York. Architecture has recently become the major focus of his work.

396

1   *I Feltri* armchair, 1987

2   Urethane bowl, 1995

3   *Tre Piede* vase, 2002

4   Bowl (*Suza Cruz* collection), 1997

5   *Up* armchair, 1969

6   *Dalila* armchair, 1980

7   *Greene Street* chair, 1984

8   *Alda* standard lamp, 2003

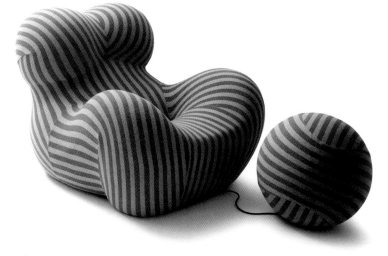

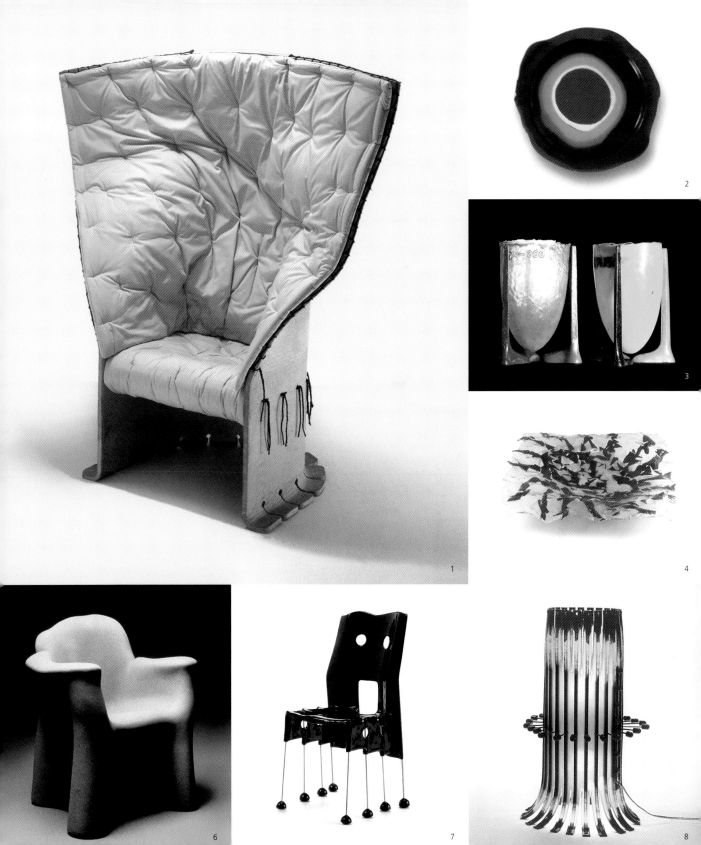

Philips

The Netherlands I Koninklijke Philips Electronics NV, Amsterdam I Manufacturer of electrical appliances I **www.philips.com**

Philips's *KEY007* digital camera, which is a similar size and shape to a mobile phone, can also be used as a memory stick to store data. The same is true of the *KEY004* digital audio player, which delivers music free of any sound skipping. The player comes with a neck strap that has an integrated remote control. The most conspicuous feature of these portable devices is a silvery control disc with a coloured rim that makes a complicated array of control buttons superfluous. These two items are also examples of Philips's recent endeavour to enlarge and update its product range, as it has done successfully in the past. In the 1960s, for example, Philips developed the first compact audio tape cassette. The 1980s saw a similarly revolutionary development, with the introduction of the compact disc, which marked the demise of the vinyl record and changed the way we listen to music. The company that started out with a modest series of radio sets and electric shavers today offers a product range of sufficient diversity to rival even that of the Japanese giant **Sony**. Philips products extend from monitors, hi-fi equipment and television sets to kitchen appliances, vacuum cleaners, electric shavers and medical equipment. For a global company of this calibre, product design has always played an important role. The list of design awards for recent products is impressive and includes the *190B4* LCD flat-screen monitor and the *Elance 3000* steam iron, which offers simple yet sophisticated styling and exemplary ergonomics.

One of Philips's greatest successes has been the development of multiple-head shaving technology, which is as effective as **Braun**'s six-edged blade. The award-winning *Philishave Cool Skin*, with its striking curved design, is a top-of-the-range wet/dry shaver that is kind to the skin. Both this model and the *Philishave Quadra Action* electric shaver have three heads. Chief designer Stefano Marzano regularly devises futuristic projects that blur the lines between different product types. *Nebula*, for example, an interactive projection system, not only projects the time on to the bedroom ceiling, but also flashes up images of sheep. A more recent headline-making project is *Letto ZZZ*, developed in collaboration with **Cappellini**, which integrates the latest Philips home theatre technology into a range of furniture.

398

1 *KEY007* digital camera, 2003
2 *GC3126 Elance 3100* steam iron, 2004
3 *Philishave Cool Skin* electric shaver, 2004
4 Video projector, 2003
5 *20PF 9925* plasma TV set, 2002
6 *Senseo* coffee machine, 2001
7 *HD 4672* kettle, 2001
8 *SA220* MP3 player, 2002

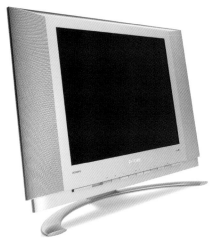

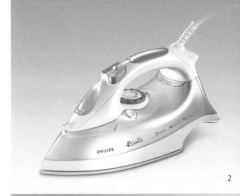

2

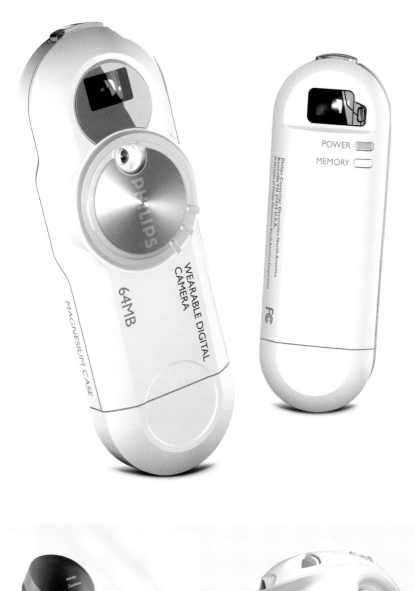

WEARABLE DIGITAL CAMERA

64MB

MAGNESIUM CASE

PHILIPS

POWER

MEMORY

Philips Consumer Electronics North America
Knoxville, TN 37914 U.S.A.
A Division of Philips Electronics North America Corporation

FC

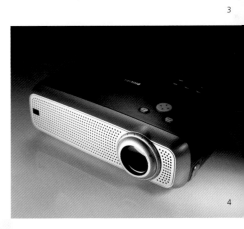

3

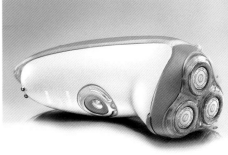

1

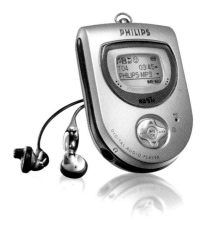

4

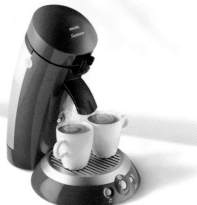

6

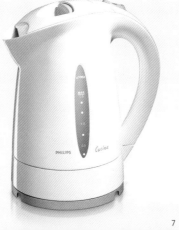

7

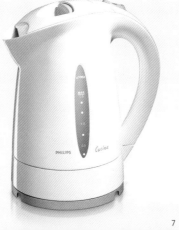

8

Phoenix Design

Germany | Product design studio | **www.phoenixdesign.de**

The taps found in some old cellars and sculleries are often pipe-shaped. Phoenix Design has taken this archetypal shape and transformed it into a contemporary form. The *Arco* tap (for **Hansgrohe**) is a bent pipe topped by an arched lever. The minimalist fitting is very much in keeping with the manufacturer's design concept and is also typical of products by Phoenix. The two founders of the studio, Andreas Haug and Tom Schönherr, who had previously both worked for **Frogdesign**, do not try to impose an expressive style on their clients. Instead, they offer tailor-made solutions for each project.

Whether mobile phones, stereo systems or bathtubs, Phoenix presents designs to its clients as prototypes, a service that makes it considerably easier for clients to formulate their specific requirements. The lively dialogues generated by this process often lead to the development of highly innovative products. In this way Phoenix designed *Xelos* for the television and hi-fi manufacturer **Loewe**, an LCD television that is forward-looking yet also fits neatly into Loewe's existing range of products. Phoenix also developed the exclusive *Accent* pen series for **Lamy**, elegant writing utensils with a high-gloss, brilliant black coating and with holders available in a range of finishes (Bruyère wood, elegant palladium or gleaming platinum) that can be swapped according to taste and mood.

400

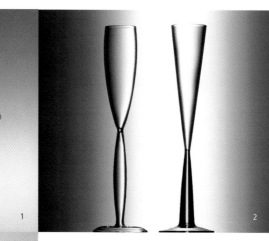

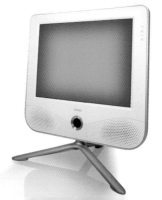

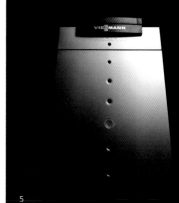

Christophe **Pillet**

France | Furniture designer | **www.christophepillet.com**

Starck's Kids is the title of a book by Pascale Cassagnau and Christophe Pillet in which they describe a new generation of designers in France who have been greatly influenced by the grand master and PR genius **Philippe Starck**. Pillet, who worked for Starck for five years, is part of this new wave of French design. His work is characterized by a functionalism that is not excessively serious and by soft shapes, harmonious colour combinations and sculptural expressiveness. He has designed furniture and lamps for such well-known manufacturers as Domeau & Pérès, **Dornbracht** and **Cappellini**, electrical appliances for Whirlpool and house-hold products for Tanita, as well as various stage sets. His work has been influenced not only by Starck. Pillet studied for a masters degree at the Domus Academy in Milan in the mid-1980s, and there is a definite Italian grace that characterizes many of his pieces of furniture, such as the *Y's* chair for Cappellini, making his designs ideal for the elegant collections of Italian manufacturers. The designs Pillet has been creating in his Paris studio since the early 1990s are, however, more than just seductive objects. A skilful combination of wit and well thought-out design – of which the *Elysée* seating system for **Edra** is a prime example – makes Pillet one of the leading designers of his generation.

401

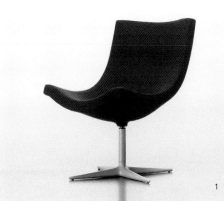

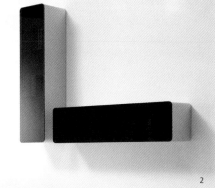

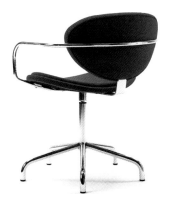

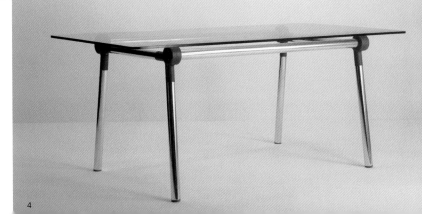

Pininfarina

Italy | Automobile design studio | **www.pininfarina.it**

Battista 'Pinin' Farina was regarded as an 'automobile artist'. In 1930 he founded a workshop for luxury coachbuilding. The company has remained a family business, and today is managed by the third generation. Together with **Bertone** and **Giorgetto Giugiaro**, Pininfarina is an aristocrat of Italian automotive haute couture and is still one of the most prestigious studios for automobile design in the world. With such cult coupés as the *Cisitalia* and the ▶ **Lancia** *Aurelia* and the ▶ **Alfa Romeo** *Giulietta Spider*, Pininfarina did more than create enthralling cars; it also accomplished a brilliant translation of the aesthetics of the post-war period – which were celebrated in Italy as 'bel design' – into glass, chrome and painted metal. Pininfarina also applied these aesthetics to the Peugeot *403*, a mid-range saloon, and gave the car a waistline that would become a standard feature of other models in the decades to come.

Pininfarina's clearly defined cars of the 1960s and 1970s, such as the Rolls-Royce *Camargue* or the Peugeot *504* coupé, also set high standards. Models that took a longer time to build, such as the Alfa Romeo *Spider Duetto*, became classics of Italian design and still attract attention today. Among the company's eye-catching innovations were two unusual concept cars: the 1976 *Peugette*, with its symmetrical body (the front and rear bodywork sections were identical), and, from the early 1990s, the *Ethos*, described by Pininfarina as an "ecological, high-tech niche sports car".

Pininfarina is **Ferrari**'s in-house designer (Bertone, in comparison, has designed only two Ferrari models). The histories of the two companies are therefore inextricably intertwined, and it is a collaboration that has had a profound influence on both parties. The sports car specialist also designs more pedestrian models, however, such as the *StreetKa* for **Ford** of Europe. The *StreetKa* is a contemporary version of the 'New Edge' design once hailed as revolutionary. The grille and front spoiler are bigger and squarer than those of its predecessor, and the large, round clear-glass headlights have been replaced by narrow slits. The bulbous wings are a characteristic feature. The dynamic rear also contributes to the sporty look.

402

1 Ferrari *Enzo Ferrari*, 2003
2 Ford *StreetKa*, 2003
3 Alfa Romeo *Spider*, 1995
4 Ferrari *360 Modena*, 1999
5 *Cisitalia* coupé, 1947
6 Peugeot *504* coupé, 1969
7 Lancia *Aurelia B 24 Spider*, 1954

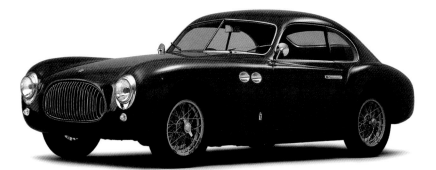

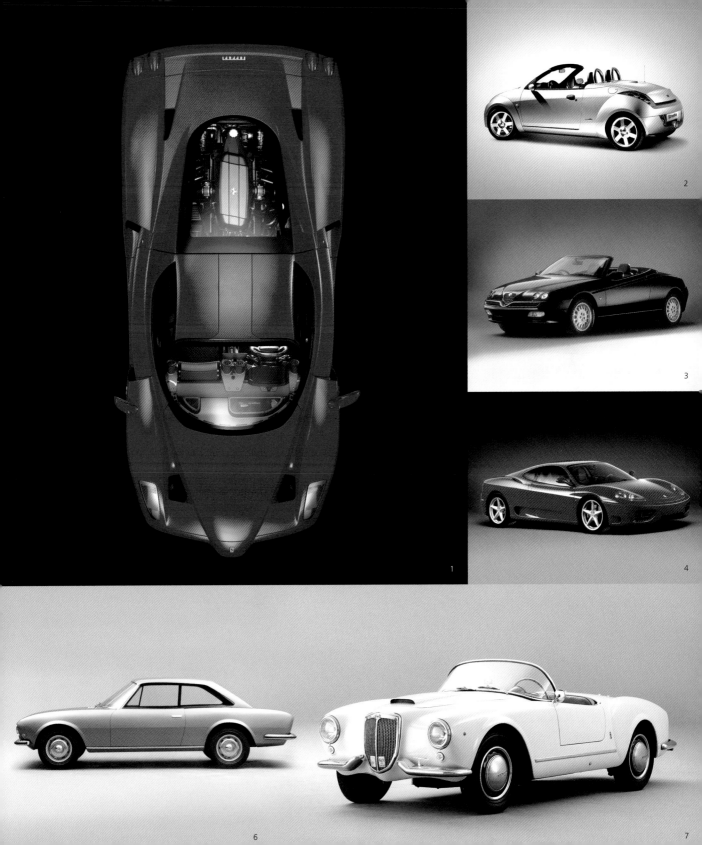

1

2

3

4

6

7

Warren **Platner**

USA | Furniture designer | www.knoll.com

"You always hope to design a classic", admitted the furniture designer Warren Platner, expressing what others only dare to think. For several years Platner studied the works of leading American designers for ideas on what made their products so successful. He drew inspiration, in particular, from such creative talents as **Raymond Loewy** and **Eero Saarinen**, in whose studios he worked. During the 1950s Platner became interested in wire furniture, producing a collection for **Knoll** that, after a lengthy series of experiments (similar to those carried out on ▶ **Frank O. Gehry**'s *Cross Check* woven furniture), went into production in the following decade.

Platner's wire creations appear light and transparent and bear some resemblance to ▶ **Alessi**'s elegant wire baskets from the 1950s. Their complex construction, consisting of hundreds of bent steel rods, produces a *moiré* effect similar to that sometimes seen in printed photographs. A single chair contains no fewer than 1400 welded points. Towards the end of the 1960s Platner established his own studio, with a view to concentrating on interior design for corporate clients. His most spectacular commission, on which he collaborated with Milton Glaser, was the glamorous Windows on the World restaurant at the top of the World Trade Center in New York.

1919 Born in Baltimore, Maryland
1938 Studies architecture at Cornell University, Ithaca, New York
1945 Works in office of **Raymond Loewy** (until 1950)
1950 Works in office of **Eero Saarinen**, Birmingham, Michigan (until 1965)
1967 Establishes interior design studio in North Haven, Connecticut
1968 Interior design of Georg Jensen Design Center, New York
1974 Showroom for **Steelcase**
1975 Interior design of Windows on the World restaurant in World Trade Center, New York (with Milton Glaser)
2006 Dies in Connecticut

Products
1966 Wire furniture collection for **Knoll** (▶ p. 263)
1967 Furnishings for **Ford** Foundation Building, New York
1973 *Executive Office* furniture collection for Knoll

1 Armchair, 1966
2 Armchair, 1966
3 Table, 1966
  All from Knoll wire furniture collection
4 Office furniture (*Executive Office* collection), 1973

404

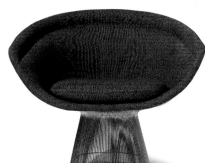

1

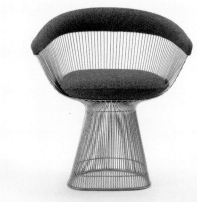

2

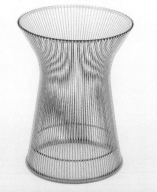

3   4

Poltronova

Italy | Poltronova Srl, Montale | Furniture manufacturer | **www.poltronova.com**

Some of Poltronova's most famous pieces of furniture date from the 1960s: *Sgarsul*, Gae Aulenti's decisive reinterpretation of the traditional rocking chair; *Mies*, the provocative tubular steel chair that was the avant-garde Archizoom group's ironic comment on functionalism; the *Superonda* plastic sofa; and the *Safari* sofa covered in a leopard-skin pattern. In the early 1970s the company presented a number of Pop icons, including the *Joe* 'baseball-glove chair' by ▶ **De Pas, D'Urbino, Lomazzi**; the Post-modern *Mitzi* and *Marilyn* sofas by Hans Hollein appeared in the early 1980s. At the beginning of the 1990s a series of striking and unconventional seating was added to the collection, including *Galleggio* by Nigel Coates, *Split* by **Ron Arad** and *She* by Prospero Rasulo.

Rich in notable modern classics, Poltronova's early range of furniture resembles a museum of Italian design. The company lives off its history, and in recent years surprisingly little has been added to the range. In the 1960s **Ettore Sottsass** was a very important influence on Poltronova. As art director, he developed the *Mobili Grigi* (Grey furniture) range, experimented with laminates and ceramics and paved the way for unconventional design, to which the company subsequently remained faithful.

1957 Established by Sergio Cammilli

Products
1962 *Sgarsul* rocking chair by Gae Aulenti
1964 *Saratoga* furniture collection by Massimo and Lella Vignelli (▶ **Vignelli Associates**)
1965 *Loto* table by **Ettore Sottsass**; *Multiuse* cupboard by **Angelo Mangiarotti**
1966 Laminated furniture by Ettore Sottsass; *Superonda* plastic sofa by Archizoom
1969 *Mies* chair and *Safari* sofa by Archizoom
1970 *Mobili Grigi* (incl. *Elledue* fibreglass bed and *Ultrafragola* fibreglass mirror) by Ettore Sottsass; *Joe* armchair by ▶ **De Pas, D'Urbino, Lomazzi**
1976 *Insieme* seating group by De Pas, D'Urbino, Lomazzi
1981 *Marilyn* and *Mitzi* sofas by Hans Hollein
1990 *Galleggio* sofa by Nigel Coates; *Split* armchair by **Ron Arad**
1991 *Split* table by Ron Arad
1992 *She* upholstered furniture collection by Prospero Rasulo
1997 *Able* table by Tim Power; *Nella* chair by Biagio Cisotti

1 *Ultrafragola* mirror, 1970
2 *Sgarsul* rocking chair, 1962
3 *Mies* chair, 1969
4 *Marilyn* sofa, 1981

405

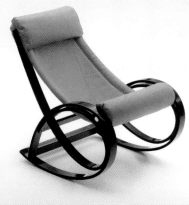

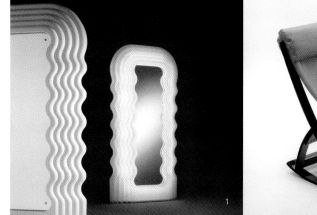

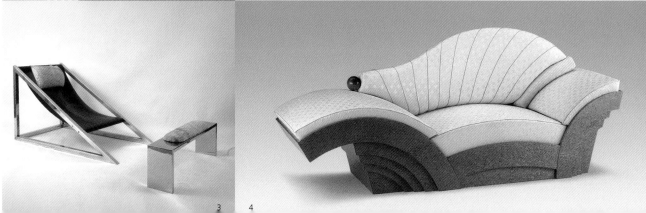

Gio **Ponti**

Italy I Architect and furniture and product designer I **www.gioponti.com**

In the late 1950s **Cassina** presented the *Superleggera*, which was acclaimed as "the world's lightest chair". It outshone even the most ingenious Scandinavian chairs. It was created by Gio Ponti, one of the most famous of all Italian architects. Ponti claimed that "the past does not exist. Everything is simultaneous. In our culture only the present exists in our idea of the past and our vision of the future." He set out to unite the old and the new in his own product designs. When he was designing the *Superleggera*, he carefully analysed the simple wooden chairs he found in one Italian fishing village and chose traditional materials – wood and wicker – for his own chair. The end result was a modern industrial product that was suitable for mass production.

Ponti was also responsible for such architectural milestones as the Milan headquarters of the Montecatini company (1936) and the Pirelli Tower (1956), also in Milan. In the mid-1920s he was one of the founding members of the Novecento movement, which favoured a return to traditional aesthetics and the great Italian representational art of the past. Ponti loved traditional materials and craftsmanship. Nevertheless, he was a modernizer, and, as a result of his interest in new techniques and mass-production processes, he was an important supporter of Italian industrial design.

Ponti is often referred to as the first universal Italian designer: he created a variety of products, from railway carriages to textiles for Vittorio Ferrari, and lamps and furniture for **Fontana Arte**, which he established in 1932. Before that time, in the early 1920s, he was artistic director at the ceramics manufacturer Richard Ginori. In 1928 he founded *Domus*, the influential architectural magazine, which he edited with few interruptions until his death. After the Second World War, Ponti put his stamp, above all, on the profile of the furniture manufacturer Cassina. He later developed, among numerous other products, bathroom suites for Ideal Standard, espresso machines for La Pavoni, lamps for Arredoluce and Reggiani, glass objects for **Venini** and ceramics and silver cutlery.

406

1 *Vecchia Dama*, *Elisir* and *Donna Campigliesca* bottles, 1956
2 *Pirellone* floor lamp, 1967
3 *Fato* lamp, 1969
4 *Bilia* lamp, 1931
5 Glass table, 1954
6 *Superleggera* chair, 1957
7 *Piatti in Smalto del Campo* plates, 1957

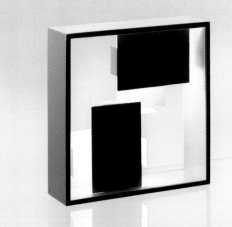

3

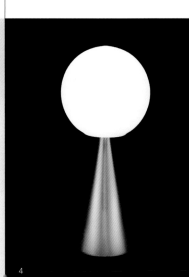

4

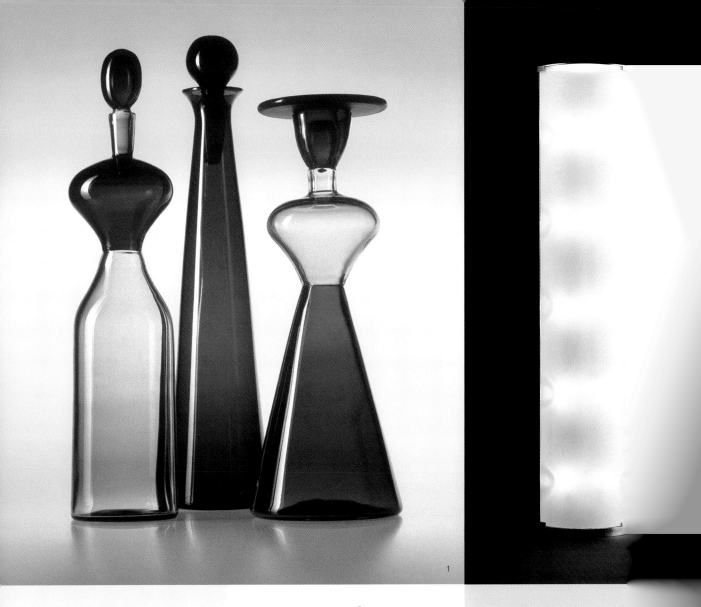

1

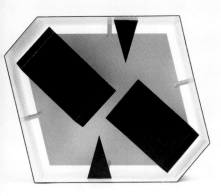

5

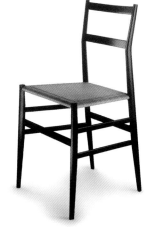

6

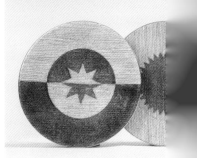

Porro

Italy | Porro Industria Mobili Srl, Montesolaro | Furniture manufacturer | **www.porro.com**

Porro is based near Como in Brianza, an area of northern Italy with a high concentration of high-quality furniture manufacturers. The company was founded in the mid-1920s by the Porro family, and initially produced furniture using traditional craft techniques. It first adopted a decisively design-orientated product philosophy in the design boom of the 1960s, a decision that was vindicated by the company's increased commercial success. Since the 1970s the family business has pursued an export-orientated policy. Today Porro represents the 'Made in Italy' label throughout the world. The appeal of its products lies in the combination of high-quality materials with a clear design philosophy. The collection is consistent in its lack of ornamentation and its extreme minimalism. Multifunctionality is an important theme: Porro is convinced that the room of the future will increasingly serve a vast range of needs.

Since the 1990s numerous designs by ▸**Piero Lissoni**, Porro's art director, have been outstandingly successful, including the *Cell* and *Aero* beds; the delicate *Spindle* chair; the *Camogli* chair, inspired by the craft traditions of fishing villages; the flexible *Modern* storage system; and *Mondrian*, the multifunctional bench/low table. All these designs reflect the essence of the Porro philosophy: they are linear and highly restrained. In this sense, the collaboration between Porro and Lissoni, who also designs exhibition stands and showrooms, is that of two kindred spirits. Apart from Lissoni, Porro works with various international designers, among them Wolfgang Tolk, who designed the *Load It* shelving, Adrian Peach, who created the *Cargo* storage unit, and **Werner Aisslinger**, whose simple but elegant *Endless Shelf* storage system can be extended by using cross-shaped aluminium joints to link together the self-supporting square panels.

1   Sideboard (*Modern* storage system), 1997

2   *Beam* table, *Spindle* chair, 2002, and *Load It* shelving, 1996

3   *Beamglass* table, 2003

4   *Endless Shelf* modular shelf system, 1994

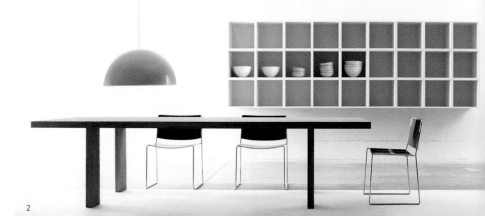

2

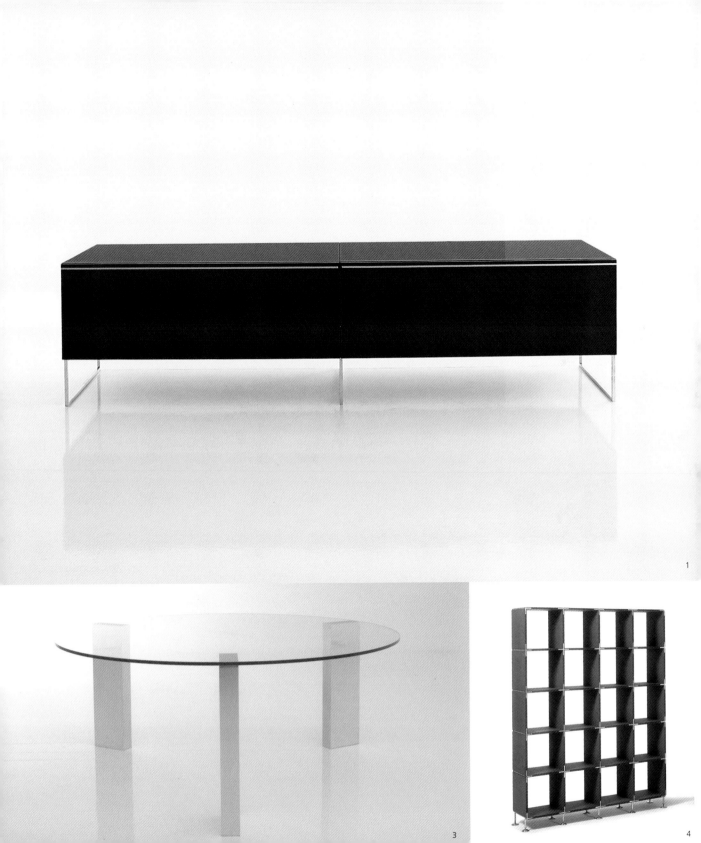

1

3

4

Porsche

Germany | Porsche AG, Stuttgart | Automobile manufacturer | **www.porsche.com**

After the Second World War the automobile engineer Ferdinand Porsche, together with his son Ferry, built the first car to bear the family name. The Porsche *356* was a sports car strongly reminiscent of the **Volkswagen** *Beetle* and, like the *Beetle*, had its four-cylinder boxer engine behind the rear axle. This model – first produced as a convertible and later as a hardtop – had a top speed of 140 kph (87 mph), and its engine produced only 40 bhp. It was therefore hardly the most powerful of sports cars, yet its bodywork was utterly convincing. The *356* came from the workshop of Erwin Komenda, who since the early 1930s had been in charge of body construction at Porsche and was a master of controlled streamlining. Komenda created the new style of closed coupé, the fastback roofline of which became the epitome of the sports car. Komenda and Ferdinand Alexander 'Butzi' Porsche, the grandson of the company's founder, continued this tradition with the the *911*, the follow-up model. The curved bonnet, with the characteristic 'frog-eye' headlights, and the arch extending from the top of the windscreen to the rear bumper, coupled with the ruler-straight waistline, made the *911* an archetype in which the stylistic features of the original Porsche were preserved. From a functional and technical point of view, however, the model had more in common with the ▸ **BMW** *1500* of the same period.

These developments laid the foundation for a brand identity characterized by design – something that was not always recognized as positive. Attempts in the 1970s and 1980s to escape from its own mythology brought the company to the brink of crisis. Neither the *914*, a very modern people's Porsche developed with Volkswagen, nor the *928* fulfilled expectations. What for two decades was often seen as a formal straightjacket, however, is now proving to be a decisive marketing advantage. The typical Porsche features appear to be timeless. The renowned company has once again become profitable. In recent years the forty or so employees in the design department have been kept busy presenting new versions of the successful *911*, such as the *Type 997*, which harks back to the lines of the original. With the *Boxster* and the *Cayenne* SUV, created under the aegis of chief designer Harm Lagaay, the company succeeded in establishing an independent series of models.

410

1 *911 Carrera* (detail), 2004
2 *Type 914*, 1969
3 *Boxster* convertible, 1996
4 *911 Carrera*, 2004
5 *911 coupé*, 1963
6 *356 coupé*, 1948
7 *911 Carrera* (interior), 2004

1930 Porsche Engineering Office established by Ferdinand Porsche in Stuttgart
1931 Erwin Komenda takes charge of body construction
1948 Ferdinand Porsche and son Ferry build *Type 356*
1950 Production begins at Stuttgart factory
1951 Ferdinand Porsche dies
1965 *Type 911* shown at *Good Form* design exhibition, London
1969 Begins collaboration with **Volkswagen**
1971 Opens Development Centre in Weissach
1972 Company goes public
1978 *Type 928* voted Car of the Year
1989 Harm Lagaay (from **BMW**) becomes chief designer
1997 Develops water-cooled boxer engine
1998 Ferry Porsche dies
2004 Michael Mauer becomes chief designer

Products
1948 *356* coupé
1963 *911* coupé (▸ p. 389) by F. A. Porsche (establishes **Porsche Design** in 1972)
1967 *911 Targa* 'Safety Convertible'
1969 *Type 914* 'People's Porsche' by Porsche and **Volkswagen**
1972 *911 Carrera RS* coupé
1975 *924* coupé
1977 *928* coupé
1989 *Panamericana* (concept)
1991 *968* coupé and convertible
1993 *911 Carrera* coupé (*Type 993*)
1996 *Boxster* convertible by Harm Lagaay
1997 *911 Carrera* coupé (*Type 996*) with water cooling
2002 *Cayenne* SUV by Harm Lagaay
2003 *Carrera GT* high-performance sports car
2004 *911 Carrera* coupé (*Type 997*); *Cayman* coupé

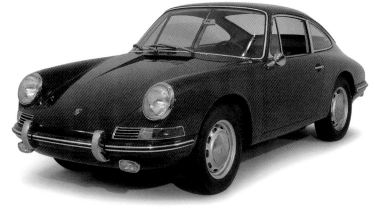

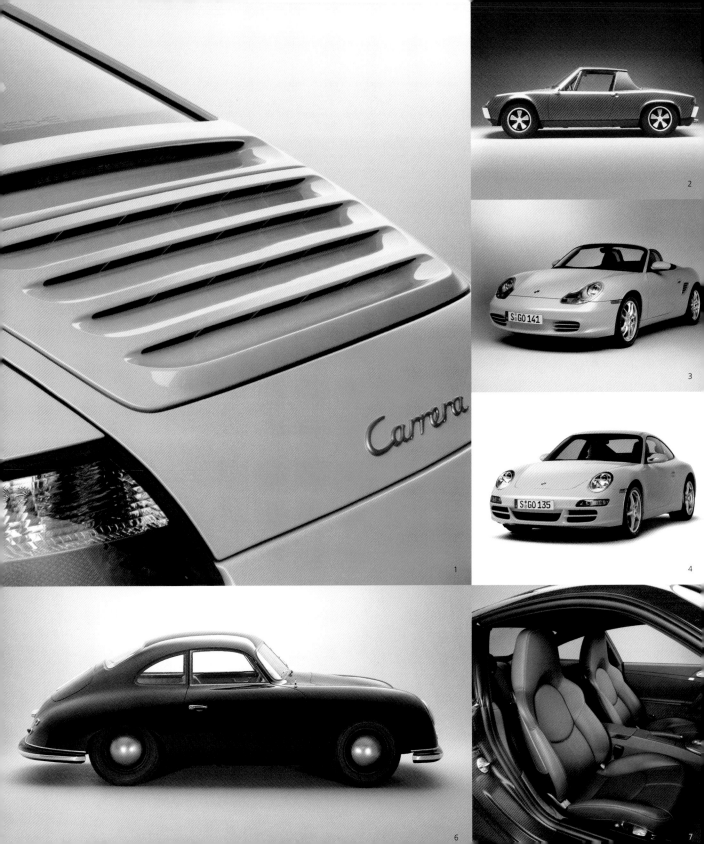

1

2

3

4

6

7

Porsche Design

Austria | Product design studio | www.porsche-design.com

When Porsche Design presented the *909* smoking pipe in the 1980s, a new type of luxury product was born. The idea came from Ferdinand Alexander Porsche, creator of the legendary *911* coupé (▶ p. 389). Grandson of the founder of the Porsche automobile company, he established his own design studio at the beginning of the 1970s. Unlike other studios, the majority of his designs are sold worldwide under his own (famous) name, and today amount to a considerable and exquisite collection that includes shoes, cigarette lighters and golf clubs. The designs are manufactured under licence by various prestigious companies: for example, spectacles by Rodenstock, watches by Eterna and writing utensils by Faber-Castell.

    Porsche's disciplined approach to design is reminiscent of work by **Jacob Jensen**. Porsche favours clear proportions, smoothly polished surfaces and precious materials. Among the numerous products the studio has designed for external clients are the *Premium* series of domestic appliances (for Siemens) in distinctive black and silver, the *Type 301* knife collection (for Chroma Cutlery) and the *FinePix 4800* (for Fujifilm), a successful attempt at a redefinition of the camera.

1 Kitchen knife (*Type 301* collection), 2002
2 *Premium* domestic appliance collection, 1997
3 Pipe, 1983 (here as redesign, 2002)
4 *Jazz* desk lamp, 1989
5 *FinePix 4800* digital camera, 2001

412

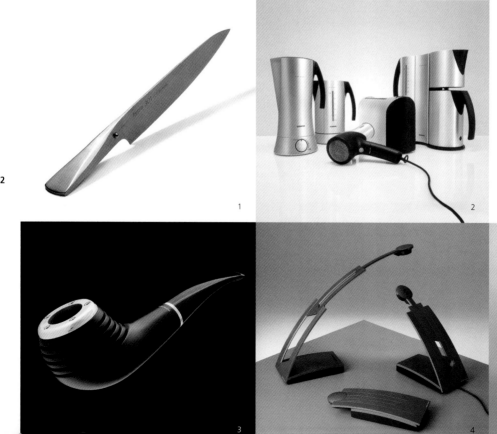
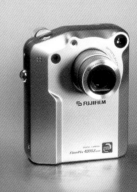

1

2

3

4

5

Pott

Germany | C. Hugo Pott GmbH & Co. KG, Solingen | Cutlery manufacturer | **www.pott-bestecke.de**

The family company Pott was founded in Solingen, a German town that, much like Sheffield in England, is associated with the manufacture of cutlery. When Carl Pott junior took over the business in the early 1930s, he pursued a new policy that was in complete contrast to a tradition of historical borrowings. One of his very first sets of cutlery, called simply *Model 2716*, attracted international attention. This was cutlery of Spartan simplicity. However, although the 1935 model was awarded a prize at the *Exposition Internationale des Arts et Techniques dans la Vie Moderne* in Paris in 1937, many dealers rejected Pott's products. He nevertheless stuck to his Bauhaus-inspired ideas. His reward came in the 1950s, when Modernist design gained popularity. During this period the company developed cutlery for Lufthansa, and designs by Hermann Gretsch and **Wilhelm Wagenfeld** were included in the collection.

The company often invested years of work into the development of new types of knives, forks and spoons. Carl Pott created many of the models himself and won a great number of design awards. The recent collection also includes work by contemporary designers. Even though a certain degree of design freedom is occasionally evident, as in the case of Ralph Krämer's prize-winning *Picado* Parmesan knife, Pott's purism ultimately serves as the benchmark for the entire product range.

413

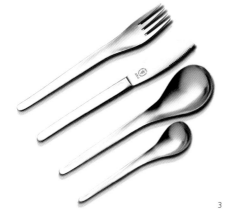

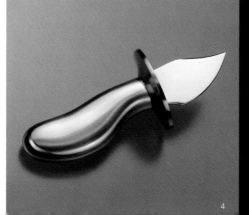

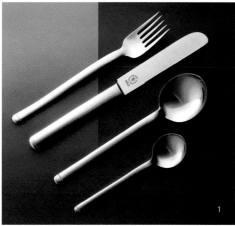

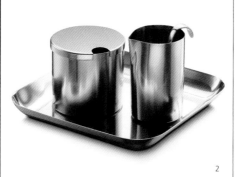

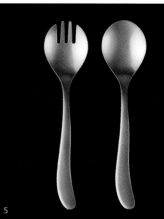

Jean **Prouvé**

France | Furniture designer

Jean Prouvé was a designer who enjoyed experimenting. In the first half of the twentieth century he created a sensation with his intentional violations of style. Prouvé came into contact with contemporary artistic currents at an early age. His father, Victor, had founded the Ecole de Nancy, a centre of Art Nouveau, with Emile Gallé. At the age of fifteen, Jean began an apprenticeship as a metalsmith, which he continued when he moved to Paris. In the early 1920s he founded his own workshop, producing ornamental doors, railings and grilles in Art Nouveau and Art Deco styles. He soon developed an interest in Modernism. A central issue in his work was the functionality of objects – in the materials used, industrial production and everyday use.

By the end of the 1920s Prouvé had discovered the material he had been searching for – thin sheet steel. From this he developed (for a time in conjunction with Charlotte Perriand) chairs, school furniture, desks and beds. His provocative and unconventional use of the material was equivalent to **Marcel Breuer**'s adoption of tubular steel. Prouvé's principle of using only the latest techniques, whether for a chair or a petrol station, made him a controversial but also progressive figure. He was involved in the founding of the pioneering Union des Artistes Modernes, a body of French Modernists, alongside **Le Corbusier**, and in the early 1970s he was chairman of a panel that selected the winning design in the competition to build the Centre Georges Pompidou in Paris.

For a long time Prouvé's furniture designs were familar only to experts and connoisseurs. It fell to two German companies to ensure that his work was saved from oblivion. The furniture manufacturer **Tecta** was responsible for the first re-editions of his designs, and, after a lengthy court case was decided in its favour, **Vitra** has also made numerous pieces available to a wider public, among them the *Cité* armchair and the *Trapèze* table.

1 *Cité* armchair, 1927
2 *Trapèze* table, 1954
3 *Chaise inclinable en tôle d'acier*, 1930
4 *Standard* chair, 1950
5 *Fauteuil de grand repos*, 1930
6 *Guéridon* table, 1950

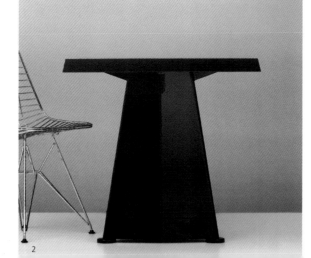

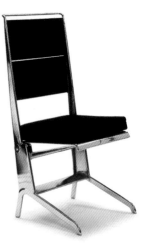

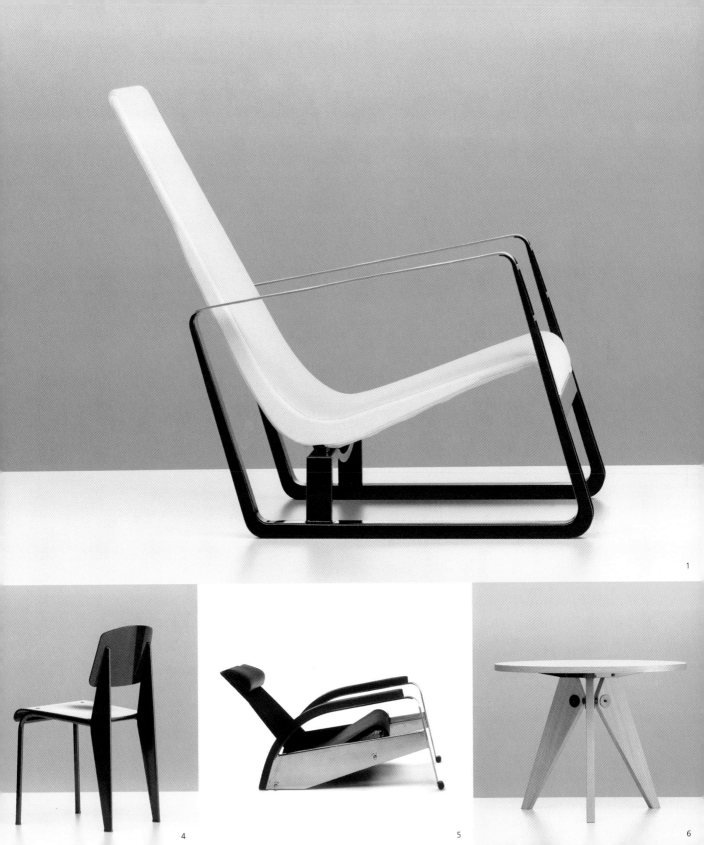

1

4

5

6

Dieter Rams, *T1000* world receiver, 1963

Never before had such a large amount of radio equipment been
squeezed into so small a space. The *T1000*, designed by Dieter Rams
for Braun, was the company's most complex project to date and
signalled a new approach to product design. The first 'all-wave'
portable radio with unlimited reception, it secured a place in the
world's great design collections.

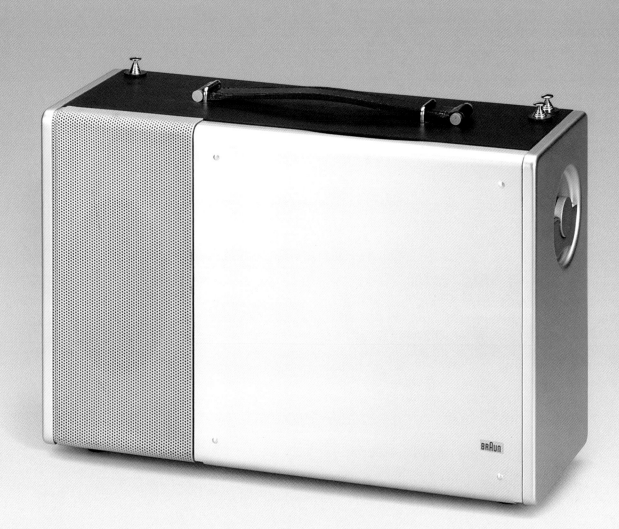

Ingegerd **Råman**

Sweden | Glass designer | www.orrefors.se

One of Ingegerd Råman's early designs is the *Samuraj* decanter. A simple yet ingenious silver-plated brass insert turns it into a candle holder. Råman is skilled at completely transforming objects with the absolute minimum of intervention. Her work is often based on the principle that items can be used in several different ways. For example, she has designed carafes with lids that also serve as glasses. She used the same idea for her *Undercover* whisky and water glasses.

At the end of the 1960s, when Råman started designing glass, there were still around fifty independent glassworks in Sweden. She first worked for Johansfors, then the Skruf glass factory, before going to **Orrefors** in the late 1990s. Råman swam against the tide for a long time. In the 1980s, when glass objects became increasingly large in size, she made small ones. And in those days there were, for example, no simple schnapps glasses. Her *Bellman* series closed this gap. It is "very easy to create grotesque things", she says. What is particularly enchanting about her work is the complete avoidance of the spectacular and the nonchalance with which she unites shape, function, proportion and decoration to form a cohesive whole.

By cautiously modifying her designs at regular intervals, Råman creates entire families of vases, bottles and carafes. As disarmingly simple as her objects appear, the details are often surprising. The spherical stopper used to close an oil bottle, for example, is slightly flattened so that it cannot roll off the table. This pragmatic designer is also good at creating subtle nuances, which is why she likes using patterns incorporating narrow glossy or matt stripes. The raw material of her designs is clear glass. Precisely because her objects are so elementary, Råman is dependent on perfect craftsmanship. Simplicity in design is particularly difficult, as even the smallest deviations disturb the overall impression. But when everything gels, her unpretentious forms emphasize to great effect the lightness, fragility and beauty of the material. The *Basket* glass collection, in which Råman combined strict basic forms with subtle decoration, introduced a new tension into her work.

418

1 *Mamsell* carafe, 1990

2 *Undercover* whisky and water glasses, 2001

3 *Zvizz* vases, 2004

4 Cognac glass, 1997

5 *Samuraj* decanter, 1989

6 *Basket* glass collection, 2004

7 *Gras* vase, 1995

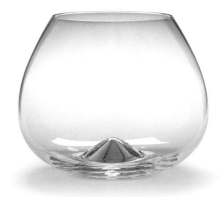

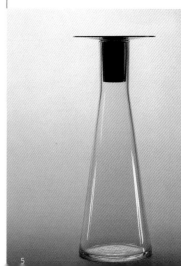

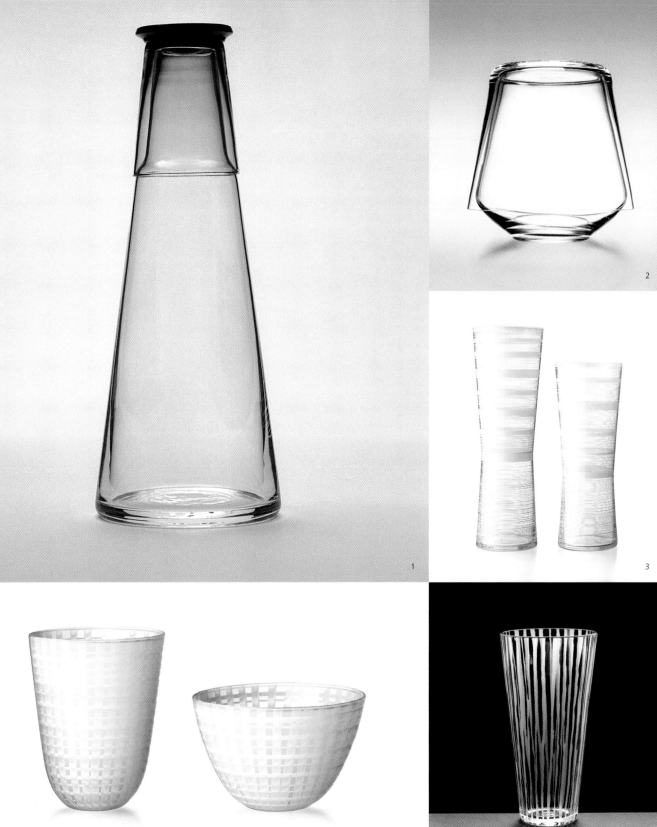

1

2

3

6

7

Dieter **Rams**

Germany | Product designer

In 1954 Dieter Rams, a young interior designer with black horn-rimmed spectacles, was employed by **Braun**. In the early 1960s he was appointed head of the product design department, even though it had been expected that either **Hans Gugelot** or Gerd Alfred Müller would get the job. Over the course of the next four decades Rams and his committed team were successful in applying the practical design principles associated with the Bauhaus and the Hochschule für Gestaltung in Ulm to completely new consumer products. Although Rams designed flashlights, pocket radios and lighters, it was his audio equipment and television sets that achieved particular fame, to the extent that he emerged as a symbol of the German design renaissance of the 1950s and 1960s.

Among Rams's most innovative designs are the *Phonosuper SK4* radio/record player combination (with ▶ Hans Gugelot), the *TP1* portable radio/record player and the *T1000* world receiver (▶ p. 417). The *Studio 2* system was also epoch-making and consisted of individual matching modules – record player, tuner and speakers. Matching receivers and tape recorders were added later to the range. This revolutionary idea – individual elements, all with a similar design, that could be used separately or together – was developed by the Ulm designers Gugelot and Herbert Lindinger and executed perfectly by Rams, who thereafter was recognized as the pioneer of the modern stereo system. In order to perfect the design of the *Studio 2* system, he also provided the matching *606* shelf system, a classic that is still in production today. The austere box-like architecture and the geometry of the knobs and control panels became almost legendary. Rams was influential in emancipating a generation of young designers. His work was the very epitome of functional aesthetics in their disciplined, German manifestation. Ironically enough, the next generation rebelled against the values that Rams espoused. Nevertheless, Rams has pursued his course doggedly. He has received countless international awards and remains one of the great names in industrial design.

1932   Born in Wiesbaden
1947   Studies architecture at Werkkunstschule Wiesbaden (until 1953)
1948   Begins apprenticeship as cabinetmaker (until 1951)
1954   Begins working for **Braun** (until 1997; chief designer from 1961)
1981   Appointed professor of industrial design at Hochschule für Bildende Künste, Hamburg
1987   Becomes president of Rat für Formgebung (German design council; until 1997)

Products

1956   *Phonosuper SK4* radio/record player (with ▶ **Hans Gugelot**)
1959   *Studio 2* hi-fi system; *H1* fan heater; *T3* pocket radio receiver; *TP1* portable radio/record player
         All for Braun
1960   *606* shelf system and *601/602* seating system for Vitsoe
1961   *RT20* table radio for Braun
1962   *RZ62* armchair for Vitsoe; *Audio 1* compact stereo system
1963   *T1000* world receiver (▶ p. 417)
1964   *FS80* TV set with base
1965   *TG60* tape recorder
1966   *F100* flash gun
1968   *TFG2* table-top cigarette lighter
1970   *Cockpit* compact stereo system
1973   *Regie 308* tuner
1976   *ET22* pocket calculator (with Dietrich Lubs)
1978   *A301* and *A501* amplifiers
         Last eleven for Braun
1984   *RHa* desk lamp for ▶ **Tecnolumen** (with Andreas Hackbarth)
1986   *1138* door handle for **FSB**

420

1   *TP1* portable radio/record player, 1959
2   *1138* door handle, 1986
3   *ET22* pocket calculator, 1976
4   *T1000* world receiver, 1963
5   *TFG2* cigarette lighter, 1968
6   *606* shelf system, 1960

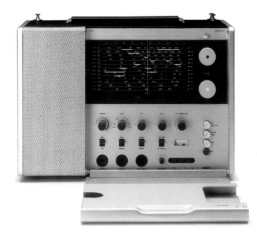

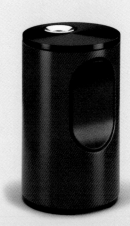

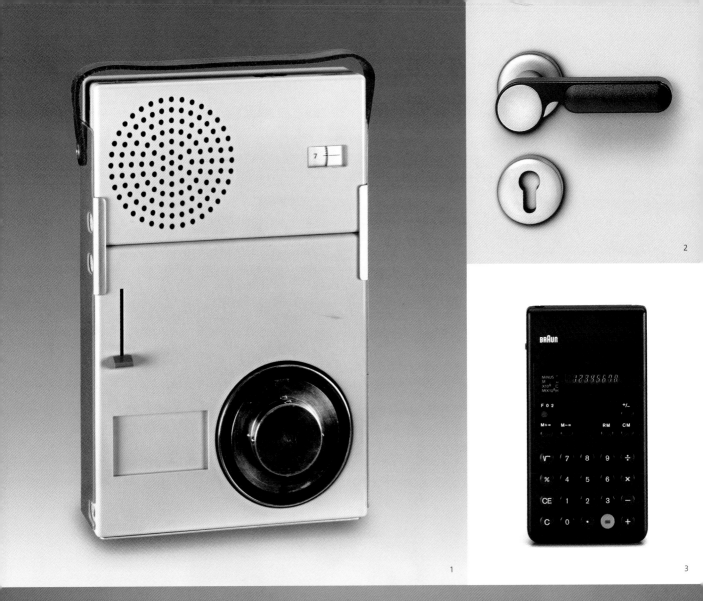

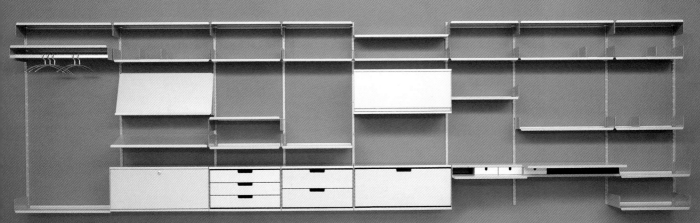

1

2

3

6

Karim **Rashid**

USA | Furniture and product designer | **www.karimrashid.com**

"The faster you work, the better the design", claims Karim Rashid. The furniture and product designer is always happy to make a provocative statement. His sales figures, however, carry even greater conviction: his *Garbo Can* waste bin and the *Oh Chair* (both for Umbra) sold by the millions and are sometimes credited with introducing design into everyday life in the United States.

Rashid was born in Egypt, grew up in Britain and Canada, went to university in Italy and is now based in Manhattan. His dazzling career is reminiscent of **Raymond Loewy's**: like Loewy, Rashid is a highly effective self-promoter and has made a huge success of his studio, where dozens of assistants and interns work. He is also extremely productive. According to Rashid's own figures, he has designed approximately one hundred products every year over the last ten years, including such diverse objects as attractive manhole covers, jars for ointments, shop fittings, suitcases, lamps (for **Artemide** and **Foscarini**), porcelain (for **Danese**) and a chess set made of coloured acrylic (for Bozart). Rashid earned worldwide fame for his retro furniture, including the lightweight *Superblob* (for **Edra**) and *Orgy* (for ▶ **Offecct**) sofas inspired by the 1960s.

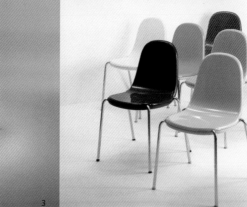

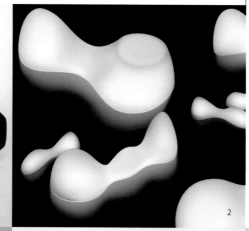

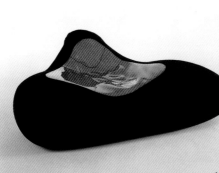

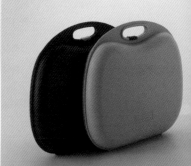

Renault

France | Renault SA, Boulogne-Billancourt | Automobile manufacturer | **www.renault.com**

The inventor Louis Renault developed a new gearbox around 1900. Within only seven years his company had risen to become the biggest car manufacturer in France. The Renault marque was ubiquitous in the country throughout the first half of the twentieth century. The company built taxis, lorries, buses, sports cars and even aeroplanes. Among the most beautiful cars of the 1940s and 1950s were the *4CV* and the popular, down-to-earth *Dauphine*. The *Dauphine*'s direct successor, the extremely practical *R4* small car, became one of the first mass-market models, along with the **Citroën** *2CV*, the **Volkswagen** *Beetle* and the Austin *Mini*. The *R4*'s vertical back and large hatch, features also applied to the *R16* family saloon, created a distinctive style. The super compact *R5* was a response to the oil crisis of the early 1970s and anticipated the Volkswagen *Golf*. The innovative plastic bumpers were particularly suited to the traffic conditions in Paris. The 1980s were an unremarkable decade for Renault, despite the introduction of the groundbreaking *Espace* MPV in 1984. Nevertheless, the company continued to build highly original cars, including the *R19* and, in 1990, the *Clio*, with its 'winking-eye' headlights. In 1993 the likeable *Twingo* microcar proved that Renault, like **Fiat**, was a specialist in the category of small cars. Patrick Le Quément, chief designer since the late 1980s, ensured the uniqueness of the brand with the introduction of distinctive lines and unusual backs, as in the *Mégane*, *Scénic* and *Vel Satis*. The *Kangoo* mini MPV has proved to be a natural successor to the *R4*.

1898 Established by Louis Renault in Paris
1944 Louis Renault dies in Paris
1945 Company nationalized
1979 Buys share of Mack Trucks; achieves first victory in Formula One racing
1988 Patrick Le Quément becomes chief designer
2002 Le Quément receives Lucky Strike Designer Award

Products
1898 *Voiturette* small car
1923 *Torpédo Sport 40CV*
1935 *Nervasport 28CV* convertible
1946 *4CV* small car
1951 *Frégatte* saloon
1955 *Dauphine* saloon
1961 *R4* small car (until 1986); *Estafette* minibus (until 1980); *Floride* convertible
1962 *R8* saloon
1965 *R16* saloon (until 1979)
1972 *R5* small car by Michel Boué
1978 *R18* saloon
1979 *R5 Turbo* sports car
1984 *Espace* MPV by Antoine Volanis
1988 *R19* small car
1990 *Clio* small car
1993 *Twingo* small car by Jean-Pierre Ploué
1994 *Laguna* saloon
2000 *Kangoo* mini-MPV
2001 *Avantime* van-coupé
2002 *Vel Satis* saloon; *Mégane* and *Scénic* compact cars
2004 *Mégane II* coupé/convertible; *Wind* roadster and *Fluence* coupé (concepts)

1 *Mégane* compact car, 2002
2 *Twingo* small car, 1993
3 *Kangoo* mini-MPV (detail), 2000
4 *Fluence* coupé (concept), 2004

423

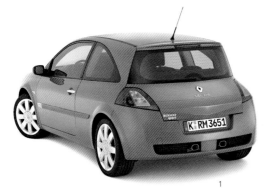

1

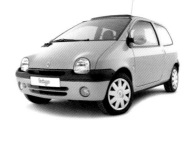

2

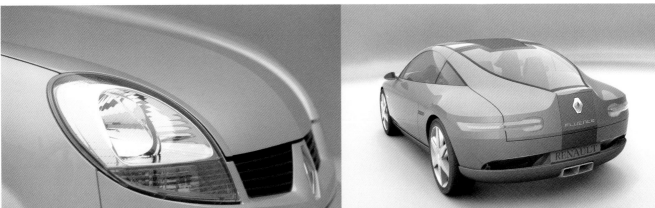

3   4

Rexite

Italy | Rexite SpA, Cusago | Manufacturer of office furniture and equipment | **www.rexite.it**

The Rexite world consists of innumerable useful small items for the home and the office: brightly coloured wastepaper baskets, height-adjustable side tables, ergonomically shaped barstools, practical trays for breakfasting in bed, bookends, wall clocks, tea trolleys and umbrella stands. Founded in 1968, the Italian company produces objects that, in the view of the founders of the firm, Rino Boschet and Rino Pirovano, should be simple but not banal, original without being bizarre. Raul Barbieri, who has been art director since 1978, and his team of internal and external designers, among them Giorgio Marianelli, Julian Brown, Gabriella Montaguti and Kuno Prey, work to implement this vision. New materials have been used in many of the company's designs. Rexite was, for example, one of the first firms that experimented extensively with new plastics. This innovate approach is reflected in designs by Giotto Stoppino, including his *Bilbio* cassette holder, and in *Multiplor*, Pirovano's attractively rounded plastic swivel storage container. Barbieri has also contributed functional and aesthetically pleasing products to the collection, including, for example, his *Fumo* ashtray, with a steel insert for easy cleaning, which is regarded as a design classic.

424

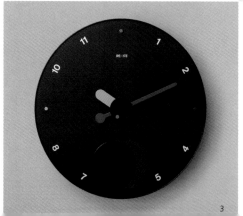

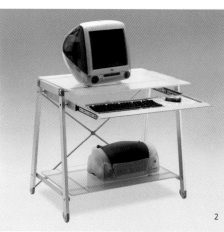

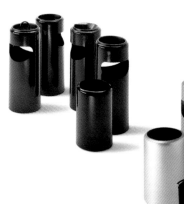

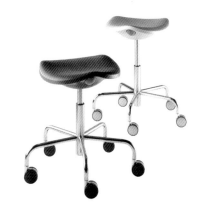

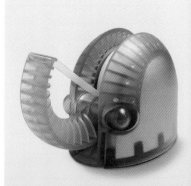

Gerrit **Rietveld**

The Netherlands | Architect and furniture designer

From the age of eleven Gerrit Rietveld trained as a cabinetmaker in his father's workshop and then worked as a draughtsman for a jeweller. In 1917 he opened his own furniture workshop. The overriding aim of this socially committed designer – who during the Great Depression created a 'recession chair' made of wood from a packing crate – was to produce furniture that everyone could afford. Following this principle, he created his *Red Blue* chair (now at **Cassina**), the first truly modern piece of furniture. It was initially produced without the primary colours inspired by the painter Piet Mondrian. After the First World War Rietveld joined the avant-garde De Stijl group of artists. He subsequently created other important pieces of furniture, including a child's high chair, a piano stool and the *Military* chair, designed for the Catholic Military Home in Utrecht. These were simple, skeletal constructions made of wooden bars and boards; they gave the effect of being spatial experiments. They inspired numerous other Modernist designers, not least **Marcel Breuer** at the Bauhaus. Other designs, such as the *L40* lamp or the *Schröder* occasional table, were also products of Rietveld's architectural projects. Later, in his *Beugel* chair, he turned to tubular steel. *Zig-Zag*, a z-shaped cantilever chair, is among the most radical furniture designs ever created. After the Second World War, Rietveld worked mainly as an architect.

425

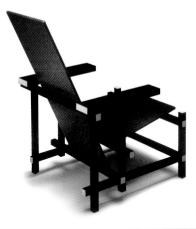

1

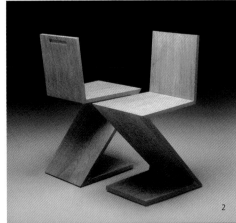

2

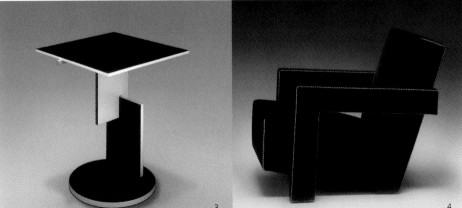

3

4

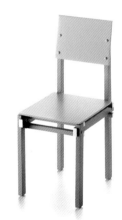

5

Rosenthal

Germany | Rosenthal AG, Selb | Porcelain manufacturer | **www.rosenthal.de**

Rosenthal's first studio shop opened in Nuremberg in 1960. Alongside its own porcelain, it displayed products by its competitors. Even today, the chain of stores continues to sell a range of well-designed products selected by the company's design advisory panel. The *Studio-Line* collection, introduced in the early 1960s, is only available at the studio shops. Rosenthal was one of the first companies to collaborate with a range of international designers, a practice that did not become generally established until the 1980s. It also sought alliances with other design-orientated companies, including **Braun**. Rosenthal's collection ranges from Modernist design, as represented by **Walter Gropius**, to work by contemporary American, Scandinavian and Italian designers. The company has long recognized that design products have tremendous value and longevity from an aesthetic point of view.

Rosenthal was founded in 1879 and had expanded considerably by the beginning of the Second World War. Although an art department had been established before the First World War, it was not until Philip Rosenthal Jr, a non-conformist, democrat and visionary, took over the management of the company in the 1950s that a particular emphasis was placed on design. The *Form 2000* service from 1954, by the Americans Richard Latham and **Raymond Loewy**, set the ball rolling. It was followed by the *Berlin* service, an exemplary piece of post-war functionalism. The Finnish glass designer **Tapio Wirkkala**, who represented the union of art and design, started working for the company towards the end of the 1950s. In the 1970s another Finnish designer, ▶ **Timo Sarpaneva**, created the *Suomi* range. It was a supreme example of the 'artist's service', a Rosenthal project for which renowned artists design the decoration for some of the company's products. The artists H.A.P. Grieshaber and Eduardo Paolozzi, for example, decorated items from the *Suomi* service. Rosenthal gradually extended its collection to include glass, cutlery and furniture, but it still offers an extremely wide range of high-quality porcelain – from the *Sanssouci* Rococo service and Versace's luxurious *Russian Dream* to the simple yet elegant *Moon* service by the English designer ▶ **Jasper Morrison**.

1 *Form 2000* service, 1954
2 *Pollo* vases, 1970
3 *Drop* service, 1972
4 *Self-Cooling Glass*, 2000
5 *TC 2000* tableware, 1960
6 *Berlin* service, 1959
7 *Fuga* glasses, 1969
8 *Century* service, 1979
9 *Russian Dream* service, 1998

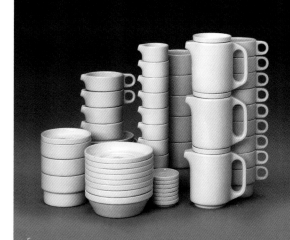

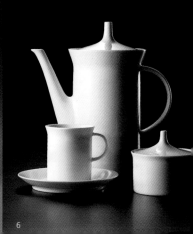

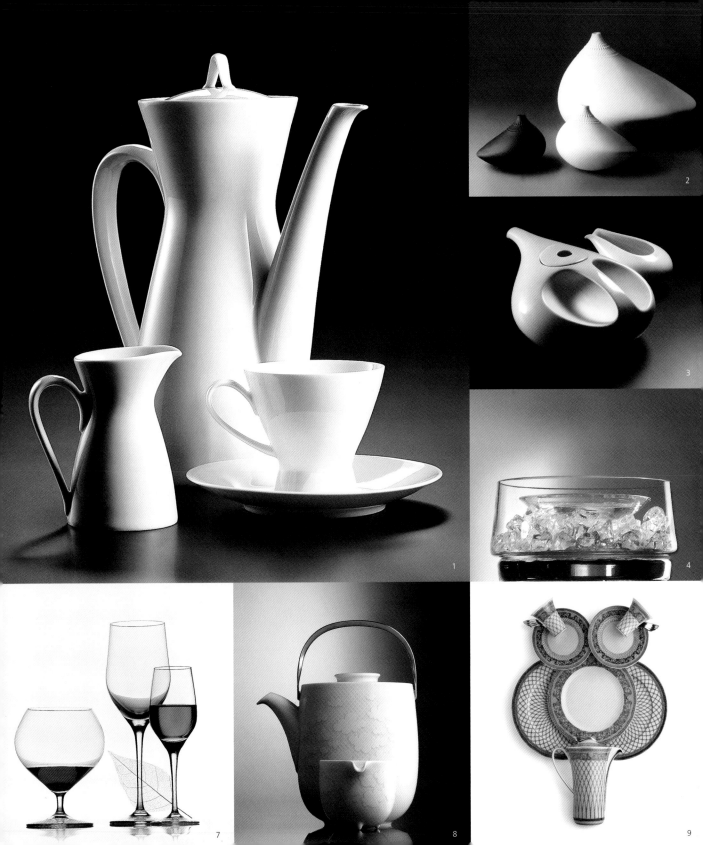

Aldo **Rossi**

Italy | Architect and furniture and product designer

Cylinders, cones, spheres, cuboids – the Italian architect Aldo Rossi designed his products as pieces of miniature architecture and, as in the creation of his actual buildings, consistently restricted himself to basic, geometric forms. The *La Conica* espresso maker, a cylinder with a conical lid, designed for **Alessi** in the mid-1980s, guards the table like a watchtower. It was followed by the *Il Conico* kettle and the *La Cupola* espresso maker, both equally purist.

Rossi's *Capitolo* seating system (for **Molteni & C**) and the *Parigi* armchair (for Unifor) were both timeless classics. His *Cartesio* cupboard (also for Unifor) from the 1990s resembles a high-rise building with a symmetrical arrangement of windows on the façade. Rossi's rigorous restriction to a limited design vocabulary was based on theoretical principles. In his seminal work *L'architettura della città* (Urban architecture), Rossi contrasted the model of reduced architecture with organic or functional architecture and in so doing made an important contribution to the debate on Post-modern architecture. Among his architectural works are the town hall square and the memorial fountain in Segrate, near Milan, and the Bonnefanten Museum in Maastricht, The Netherlands.

1931 Born in Milan
1955 Works at *Casabella* magazine (editor 1961–44)
1959 Graduates in architecture from Politecnico, Milan
1966 Publishes book *L'architettura della città*
1971 San Cataldo Cemetery, Modena
1979 Il Teatro del Mondo at Venice Biennale
1987 Hotel Il Palazzo, Fukuoka, Japan
1994 Bonnefanten Museum, Maastricht, The Netherlands
1997 Dies in Milan

Products

1984 *La Conica* espresso maker
1986 *Il Conico* kettle
1988 *La Cupola* espresso maker
1993 *Momento* wall clock
All for **Alessi**
1994 *Il Faro* service for **Rosenthal**
1995 *Pressofilter* coffee machine for Alessi
1996 *Consiglio* table, *Parigi* armchair and *Cartesio* cupboard for Unifor

1   *Il Faro* service, 1994
2   *Pressofilter* coffee machine, 1995
3   *Cartesio* cupboard, 1996
4   *La Cupola* espresso maker, 1988
5   *La Conica* espresso maker, 1984

428

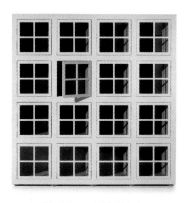

1

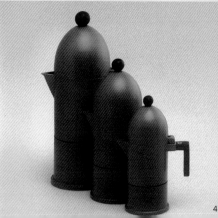

2

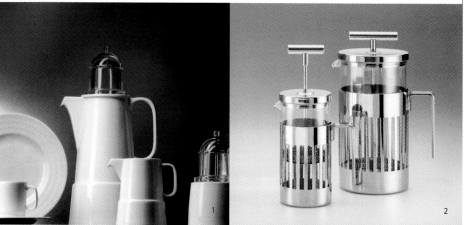

3

4

5

Rowenta

France | Groupe SEB, Ecully | Manufacturer of electrical appliances | **www.rowenta.com**

With the introduction of *Morrison* – named after the British designer ▸ **Jasper Morrison** – Rowenta redefined the coffee machine. Instead of simply following the construction principles outlined by **Braun** in the 1980s, Morrison, a purist, integrated all the elements in a casing that encloses the jug like a triumphal arch. Only the ground coffee need be kept separately. The development of this appliance was part of the general repositioning of the Rowenta brand. With this in mind, Morrison also designed a kettle and a toaster; although similarly austere, they were somewhat less exciting conceptually. Rowenta's interest in design began with the colourful *Brunch* and *Neo* ranges by the French studio Elium. The simple, clean lines of these series ushered in a new era of minimalist kitchen appliances.

Based originally in Hesse, central Germany, Rowenta began producing electrical domestic appliances in the 1920s, and in the 1950s and 1960s was successful with designs that reflected the new German functionalism. The *Men* cigarette lighter, from 1967, attracted particular attention. After having been integrated into the French company SEB in the late 1980s, Rowenta is now to poised to reposition itself – alongside Krups and Tefal – as a brand that appeals to consumers with aesthetic awareness. As part of Rowenta's repositioning, SEB collaborated with **Konstantin Grcic**, whose designs included a sandwich-maker.

1884 Weintraud & Co. established by Robert Weintraud
1909 Registers Rowenta brand name
1945 Redevelops main works in Offenbach
1948 Begins producing cigarette lighters
1963 Sunbeam Corp. of Chicago, USA, takes over company
1988 French SEB Group takes over company
2002 Brand is repositioned; launches new Rowenta logo

Products
1926 Professional coffee machines
1949 First iron with thermostat
1953 *Featherlight* ironing machine
1957 First steam iron; *Gas-Snip* gas cigarette lighter
1967 *Men* cigarette lighter
1984 *Toast-Star* toaster
1999 *Balloon* vacuum cleaner by **Seymour Powell**
2001 *Infinium* and *Dumbo* vacuum cleaners by ▸ Seymour Powell
2003 *Neo* domestic appliance collection and *Soft* iron by Elium; *Access Body+care* epilator
2004 *Morrison* domestic appliance collection by ▸ **Jasper Morrison**

1 Coffee machine (*Morrison* collection), 2004
2 *Soft* iron, 2003
3 Kettle (*Morrison* collection), 2004
4 Juicer (*Neo* collection), 2003
5 *Access Body+care* epilator, 2003

429

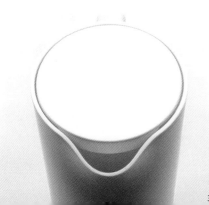

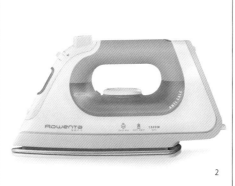

1

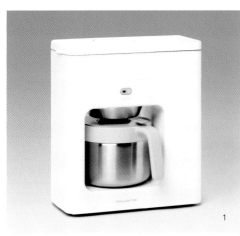

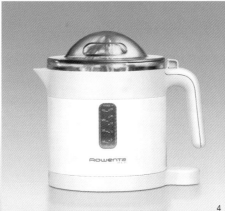

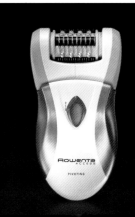

2

3

4

5

Royal Copenhagen

Denmark | Royal Copenhagen A/S, Glostrup | Porcelain manufacturer | **www.royalcopenhagen.com**

Founded in the eighteenth century, the Royal Copenhagen Porcelain Manufactory struggled to survive its early years. It nevertheless entered a golden era at the end of the nineteenth century, when the painter and architect Arnold Krog became artistic director and revised the company's product range. The introduction of an underglaze decoration technique and of a range of new colours met with international approval. While in Paris, Krog met the art dealer Siegfried Bing, who later became responsible for the inclusion of Japanese-inspired products in the collection. Experiments conducted under the guidance of the Swedish ceramicist Patrick Nordström also gave the firm a high profile throughout the world in the field of stoneware. Among the company's most successful potters were Axel Salto, Jais Nielsen and Jean-René Gauguin, son of the famous painter.

After the Second World War, tableware that had once been popular soon became obsolete, largely as a consequence of the impact of Modernism. In the late 1950s, in a bold attempt at change, Royal Copenhagen manufactured a range of heat-resistant dishes and plates designed by Magnus Stephensen. The series transformed the entire Danish porcelain industry. In the 1960s Grethe Meyer, an architect, became a leading figure at Royal Copenhagen. Meyer worked in glass and ceramics and was responsible for introducing the much-lauded *Blue Line* series, which she has since redesigned as the multicoloured *4 All Seasons*. From the 1960s onwards, a number of companies were taken over by or merged with Royal Copenhagen, including **Georg Jensen** and **Orrefors**. Today the company boasts a wide range of products and offers a unique mix of individual artistic pieces, services and household accessories in contemporary style. There are also selected items available from the historic series, including the famous *Blue Fluted* tableware, the company's very first product. This range is now also manufactured in a modern version, *Blue Fluted Mega*, designed by Karen Kjældgård-Larsen. Among well-known contemporary designers are Ursula Munch-Petersen, with her prize-winning *Ursula* crockery, and Jørgen Møller, with his *Minimum* service. Royal Copenhagen also works continuously with young creative talents such as Ole Jensen, a ceramics designer who casts functional objects in biomorphic forms.

1755 First Danish porcelain factory opens (closes 1766)

1775 Royal Copenhagen Porcelain Manufactory established (almost destroyed by British warships 1807)

1884 Arnold Krog becomes artistic director

1911 Patrick Nordstöm becomes technical director; establishes design studio

1923 Opens joint foreign retail outlets with Holmegaard Glassworks

1969 Acquires A. Michelsen metalsmiths (1972 **Georg Jensen**, 1987 Bing & Grøndahl)

1985 Merges with Holmegaard Glassworks; becomes Royal Copenhagen A/S

1997 Merges with **Orrefors** Kosta Boda; group becomes known as Royal Scandinavia (porcelain division retains the name Royal Copenhagen)

Products

1775 *Blue Fluted* tableware

1802 *Flora Danica* tableware

1887 *Fishing Net* vase by Arnold Krog

1911 Clay vase by Patrick Nordström

1957 Oven-proof tableware by Magnus Stephensen

1960 *Gemina* service by Gertrud Vasegaard

1965 *Blue Line* service by Grethe Meyer

1971 *White Pot* service by Grethe Meyer (based on *Blue Line*)

1993 *Ursula* faience dinnerware by Ursula Munch-Petersen

1997 *Ole* service and kitchen accessories by Ole Jensen

2000 *4 All Seasons* service by Grethe Meyer (redesign of *Blue Line*); *Blue Fluted Mega* service by Karen Kjældgård-Larsen (redesign of *Blue Fluted*)

2001 *Fish* serving dishes and *Minimum* service by Jørgen Møller

430

1 *White Pot* coffee pot, 1971 (based on *Blue Line* service)

2 Citrus squeezer (*Ole* kitchen accessories), 1997

3 *Fish* serving dish, 2001

4 *Minimum* teapot, 2001

5 *4 All Seasons* service, 2000 (redesign of *Blue Line* service)

6 *4 All Seasons* set of bowls, 2000

7 Plate (*Ole* service), 1997

8 Jug (*Ursula* faience dinnerware), 1993

9 *Ole* thermos jug, 1997

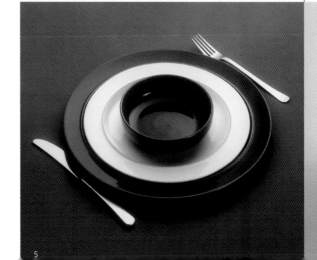

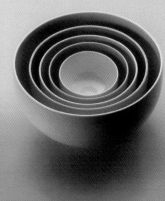

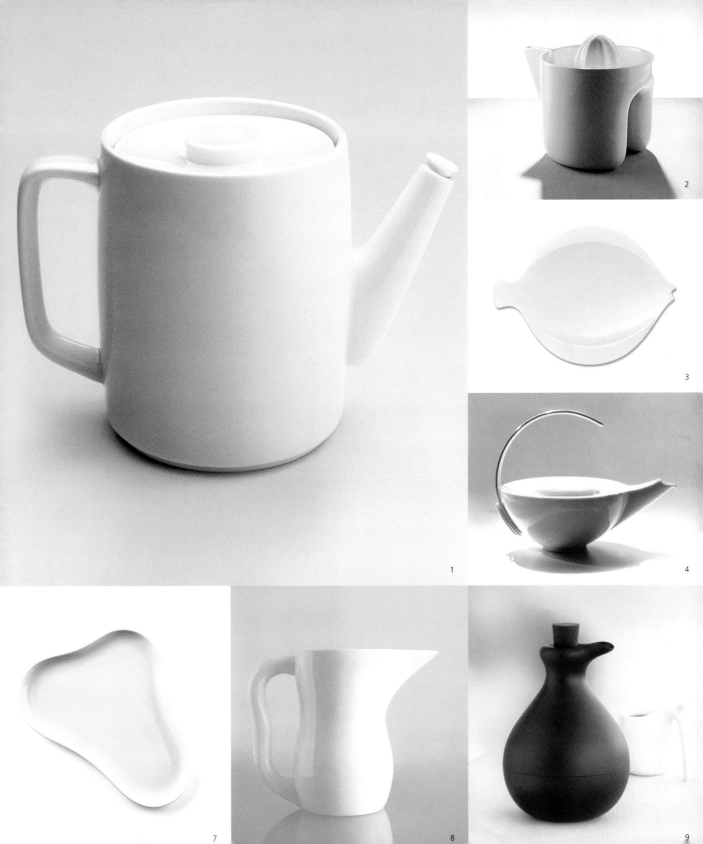

1

2

3

4

7

8

9

Sony, *TR-610* transistor radio, 1958

The *TR-610* pocket transistor radio was smaller than all its predecessors, had rounded edges and could be operated with one hand. Combining the latest technology with a compact, functional design, it represented a breakthrough for Sony on the world market and put the manufacturer's name – derived from the Latin *sonus* (sound) and the American word 'sonny' (little boy) – on the map.

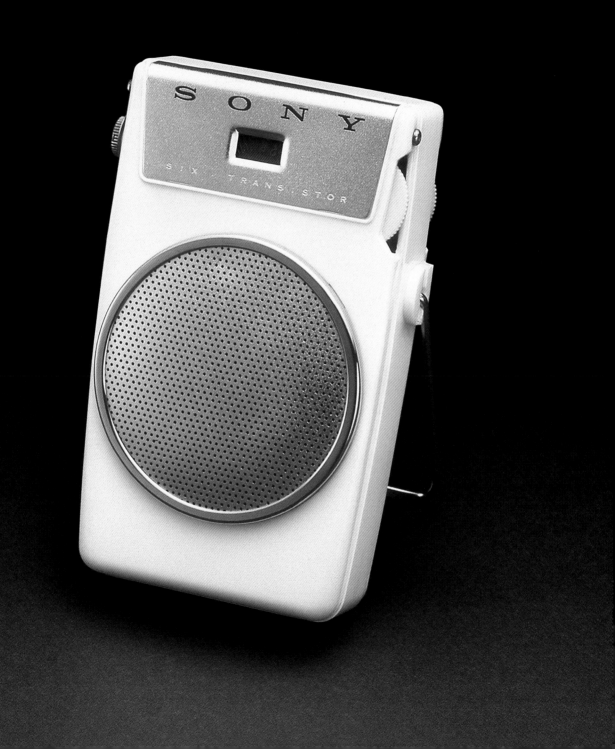

Eero **Saarinen**

Finland | Furniture designer

The vastly enhanced technical potential of what were considered 'new' materials – steel and concrete in architecture, plywood and plastic in the design of furniture – contributed to the expressiveness of Eero Saarinen's works. With his good friend **Charles Eames**, Saarinen created moulded-plywood seating for the *Organic Design in Home Furnishings* competition organized by the Museum of Modern Art (MoMA) in New York in 1940. Their ground-breaking design won first prize.

Saarinen emigrated with his parents to the United States from Finland in 1923, when he was thirteen years old. He initially studied sculpture, but then, following in the footsteps of his father, Eliel, he turned to architecture. Saarinen's work epitomizes the Scandinavian version of the International Style. Although he produced relatively few furniture designs, they were almost always iconic. This is certainly true of his innovative *Womb* chair, the first mass-produced item of furniture made of a fibreglass shell (covered with foam). The *Tulip* flower-bud chair was perhaps even more revolutionary. This one-legged piece of furniture was the first in which the base and the seat formed a unified whole. With the support of the **Knoll** company, Saarinen worked on this construction of plastic-coated aluminium and fibreglass for more than five years.

1910 Born in Kirkkonummi
1923 Emigrates to USA
1930 Studies sculpture in Paris
1934 Graduates in fine arts from Yale University, Connecticut
1935 Collaborates with Norman Bel Geddes
1936 Joins father's architecture practice
1940 Collaborates with **Charles Eames** for *Organic Design in Home Furnishings* competition, organized by MoMA, New York
1942 Produces first designs for **Knoll**
1948 **General Motors** Technical Center, Warren, Michigan (until 1956)
1950 Opens own architecture practice in Ann Arbor, Michigan
1956 US Embassy, London
1961 TWA Terminal, Idlewild (now John F. Kennedy) Airport, New York; dies in Ann Arbor

Products
1946 *Grasshopper* chair
1948 *Womb* chair
1956 *Tulip* furniture series
1957 Office furniture collection (incl. *Visitor* armchair)
All for Knoll

1   *Visitor* armchair, 1957
2   *Womb* chair, 1948
3   *Tulip* armchair, 1956
4   *Tulip* tables, 1956

434

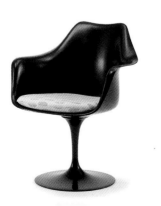
1

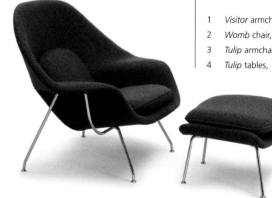
2

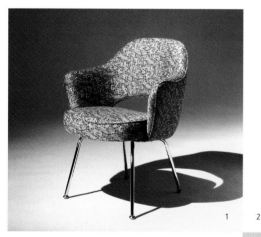
3   4

Roberto **Sambonet**

Italy | Product designer

Robert Sambonet's elegant household articles are precise structures; with their clear contours and perfect proportions they have an almost graphic effect. His prize-winning *Pesciera* fish poacher from the 1950s, *Center Line* set of bowls from the 1960s and stackable crystal glasses (for Baccarat) from the 1970s are characterized by harmony and a sensitive use of materials. A close friend of the Finnish architect and designer **Alvar Aalto** and an admirer of the works of **Frank Lloyd Wright**, Sambonet looked to the world of art for inspiration. He himself had already had considerable success in Europe and Brazil as a painter and illustrator before turning his attention to product design.

In the early 1950s Sambonet opened his own studio in Milan and began working for the family business, which had been founded in the mid-nineteenth century. Known originally for producing silverware, the company was eventually transformed into a manufacturer of high-quality stainless steel goods, many of which were designed by Sambonet himself. He also worked as a graphic artist and collaborated with Bruno Monguzzi, Max Huber and Bob Noorda. Such companies as Pirelli and **Alfa Romeo**, as well as La Rinascente, the department store chain, and *Zodiac,* the architectural journal, made use of Sambonet's artistic talents.

1924 Born in Vercelli
1945 Graduates in architecture from Politecnico, Milan
1956 Becomes art director of *Zodiac* journal (until 1960); receives Compasso d'Oro (also 1970, 1979, 1995)
1960 Acts as consultant to La Rinascente department store
1974 Designs logo for region of Lombardy (with Bob Noorda and Pino Tovaglia)
1995 Dies in Milan

Products
1957 *Pesciera* fish poacher
1959 Cutlery packaging for Sambonet
1960 *Posate Metron* cutlery
1961 *Vassoio Domus Inox* metal cutlery for Sambonet
1965 *Center Line* set of bowls for Sambonet
1971 *Empilage* and *Tir* glasses
1975 *Prehistoire* set of four crystal vases
1978 *Vasi ad Angolo* set of four crystal vases
     Last three for Baccarat
1993 *Apollo* fitting for Kleis Collection

1 *Pesciera* fish poacher, 1957
2 *Center Line* bowls, 1965
3 *Prehistoire* vases, 1975
4 *Posate Metron* cutlery, 1960

435

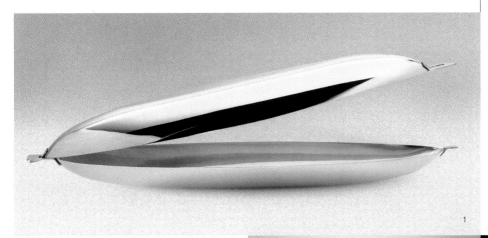

1

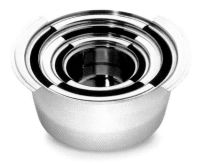

2

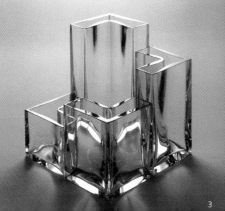

3

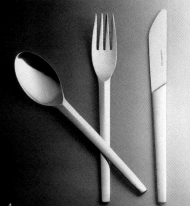

4

Samsonite

USA | Samsonite Corporation, Warren, Rhode Island | Luggage manufacturer | **www.samsonite.com**

The biblical hero Samson, famous for his legendary strength, is the inspiration behind the name of this brand, which, as the Shwayder Trunk Manufacturing Company, first set out to conquer the luggage market in the early twentieth century. Advertising campaigns emphasized the unique stability and durability of its products: in one well-known commercial, a company executive uses his case as a sleigh before going calmly about his daily business. The introduction of the *Silhouette* range of luggage, which incorporated hard-wearing locks and fittings into its design, was a turning point for the company in the late 1950s. The appearance of the *Attaché Case* at the beginning of the 1960s ushered in a new era in briefcase design. Made of a tough injection-moulded plastic rather than the traditional leather, the case was highly resistant to wear and tear and was tailored perfectly to meet the needs of the new breed of jet-setting businessmen. Its tremendous popularity made the company synonymous with robust, hard-shell cases. Samsonite succeeded in bridging the gap between a mass-market product and the image of an upmarket quality brand. This image was soon extended to the *Black Label* clothing collection and the Trunk & Co. backpack brand. In recent years the company has collaborated with **Philippe Starck**, whose brief was to introduce a note of "pure elegance" into the product range.

1908 Shwayder Trunk Manufacturing Co. established by Jesse Shwayder in Denver, Colorado
1965 Company name changes to Samsonite Corporation
1969 Introduces polypropylene as a product material
1997 Receives iF Design Award for *Epsilon* collection
2001 Receives Red Dot Design Award for *Gaoua* suitcase
2002 Receives iF Design Award for *T-Plus Hisize* laptop case

Products
1958 *Silhouette* luggage
1962 *Attaché Case*
1969 *Saturn* briefcase in polypropylene
1996 *Epsilon* collection
1998 *Genesis* laptop case
1999 *Black Label* clothing
2000 *Samsonite by Starck* product collection (incl. *Aua* handbag, *Gaoua* suitcase and *Oô* toilet bag) by **Philippe Starck**
2002 *Hardlite* case collection
2003 *900 Series Hommage* luggage; *F'Lite* case collection

1 *Hardlite* case collection, 2002
2 *Florid* case (*F'Lite* collection), 2003
3 *Aua* handbag, 2000
4 *Aua* handbag (detail), 2000
5 *Soyuz* trolley (*F'Lite* collection), 2003

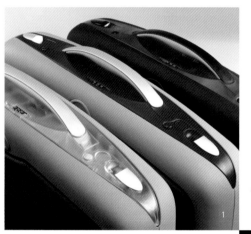
1

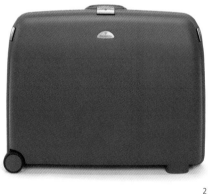
2

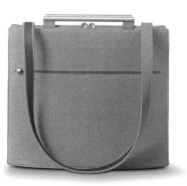
3

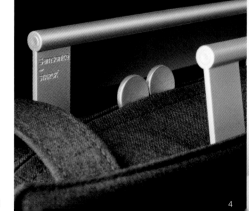
4

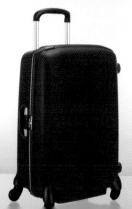
5

Thomas **Sandell**

Sweden | Furniture and product designer | **www.sandellsandberg.se**

No one in Sweden was surprised when, at the beginning of the 1990s, Thomas Sandell was invited to join **Cappellini**'s illustrious circle of designers. Among his contributions to the collection of the Italian furniture manufacturer was a steel cupboard for storing keys. A highly gifted interior designer and architect, Sandell is repeatedly successful in competing for public commissions. In the 1990s he established his own studio and collaborated with the advertising specialist Ulf Sandberg. His restaurants, including the Shaker-inspired Rolf's Kök in Stockholm (designed with **Jonas Bohlin**), have attracted considerable attention. The fact that he has been associated with the design of the new football stadium in Stockholm gives some indication of his tremendous standing in the country.

Sandell's furniture exudes luxurious restraint. He plays on traditional Swedish aesthetics, which he combines with references to designs of the 1950s and 1960s. His *Vågö* plastic chair (for **Ikea**) is a homage to **Sergio Mazza**. What this successful designer creates is occasionally nostalgic, but always light and rarely ironic. He has frequently collaborated with such well-known Scandinavian companies as Artek, **Asplund**, **Offecct** and **Källemo**. In the mid-1990s Sandell was one of the initiators of Ikea's *PS* series, which formed part of the Swedish furniture giant's attempt to overhaul its image.

1959 Born in Jakobstad, Finland
1985 Graduates in architecture from Royal Institute of Technology, Stockholm
1990 Opens own office
1995 Establishes Sandellsandberg design office with Ulf Sandberg
1997 Interior design of Moderna Museet, Stockholm

Products

1992 *Sandra* table, *Air* bench and *Wedding Stool* for ▸ **Asplund**
1995 *Snow* collection of cupboards and chests for Asplund (with **Jonas Bohlin**); *PS* product collection for **Ikea**
1996 *T.S.* chair for Asplund
1998 *Miami* table for **B&B Italia**
2001 *Annino* easy chair for **Swedese**
2003 *Vågö* plastic chair for Ikea; *Annino* table for Swedese
2004 Door handle collection for **FSB**; *Metro* chair for **Offecct**

1 *Metro* chair, 2004
2 *PS* mobile chest, 1995
3 *Snow* cupboard, 1995
4 *Vågö* plastic chair, 2003
5 Door handle, 2004

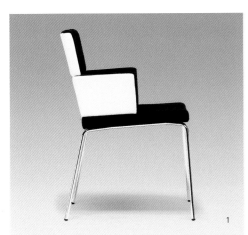

1

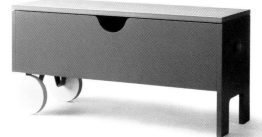

2

437

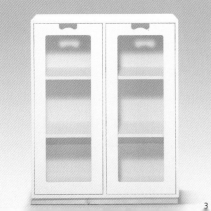

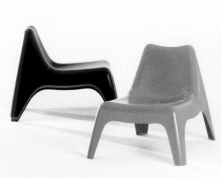

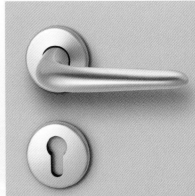

3

4

5

Denis **Santachiara**

Italy | Furniture and product designer | www.denisantachiara.it

Babà, for De Padova, is a typical Denis Santachiara product. The attractive pouffe, equipped with a gas-piston mechanism, rises to a maximum of 50 centimetres (20 in.) in height. It is a fun product and gives some indication of Santachiara's interests, one of which is undoubtedly the interaction between objects and their users.

Self-taught, Santachiara opened his own automobile design studio at the age of just sixteen. He finds small inventions more important than superficially beautiful forms. His products, which take advantage of new technologies, sometimes assume lives of their own and often have quite unique and unexpected features. The *Notturno Italiano* bedside table lamp, for example, is designed to project sheep on to the wall in an attempt to encourage sleep. The *Pisolò* pouffe transforms itself into a guest bed and bedside table in a matter of seconds, thanks to the addition of an integrated motor. Santachiara's designs have also included a hairdryer with a controllable airstream, to which different fragrances can be added. His products are particularly appealing and innovative as a result of their playfulness. The user is encouraged to interact with the product and, almost subconsciously, becomes involved in a process of reflection on the nature and function of objects.

1950 Born in Campagnola

1966 Opens own studio, working on automobile design

1975 Develops 'soft technology', between art and design

1986 *Epsylon* discotheque, Reggio Emilia

1990 Establishes Domodinamica with Cesare Castelli, for production of experimental designs

2000 Receives Good Design Award, Chicago

Products

1986 *Work Station* prototype for Italtel Telematica (with Franco Raggi and **Alberto Meda**)

1987 *Mistral* room ventilation unit for Dilmos; *Sister Chairs* prototype for **Vitra**

1988 *On/Off* table lamp for **Luceplan** (with Alberto Meda and Franco Raggi)

1989 *Oxalis* chair for Cidue; *Astro* waiting-room furniture for Campeggi; plastic bicycle for Stil Resine

1990 *Domodinamica Oggetti Animari per la Casa* collection

1993 *Notturno Italiano* bedside table lamp for Domodinamica

1995 *Mama* rocking armchair for **Baleri Italia**

1997 *Pisolò* pouffe/table/bed for Campeggi

1999 *Babà* pouffe for De Padova; *Elfo* table lamp for **Foscarini**

2002 *Pankassa* bench for **Magis**

2003 *Giubbe Rosse* and *Bongo* sofas for Bonaldo

1 *Elfo* table lamp, 1999

2 *Giubbe Rosse* sofa, 2003

3 *Pisolò* pouffe/table/bed, 1997

4 *Mama* rocking armchair, 1995

5 *Babà* pouffe, 1999

438

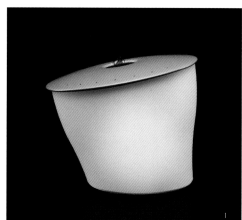

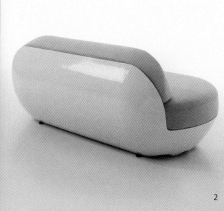

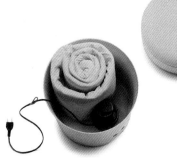

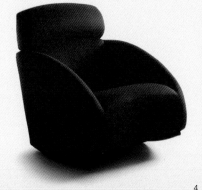

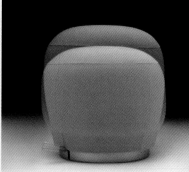

Marco Sousa **Santos**

Portugal | Furniture and product designer | marcosousasantos.com

Along with the renowned architect Álvaro Siza, Marco Sousa Santos is one of the few designers from Portugal who are known outside their own country. Santos's talent has taken him from the geographical periphery of Europe to the very centre of the European design scene. He has earned his fame not only through the objects he has designed (furniture, lamps and accessories), but also through the commitment he displays as a publicist and supporter of the contemporary debate on design.

After completing his studies at the School of Fine Arts in Lisbon, Santos became one of the founding members of the Ex-Machina group. He also established Proto Design, a company manufacturing glassware and ceramics. In the course of his career he has developed a restrained style, avoiding even the merest hint of excess. Clear, sometimes flowing, lines predominate and convey a distinctive warmth and dynamism, despite the fact that the materials used are often those that are considered to be cool: aluminium, glass and porcelain, as, for example, in his *Metamax T* table, made of sheet aluminium, the *Farol* table lamp for Tronconi and the *Terra* hanging lamp for Proto Design. Santos's work represents Portugal's extremely vibrant design scene, the true quality of which is rarely appreciated.

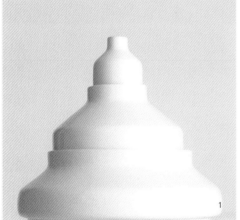

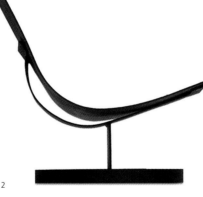

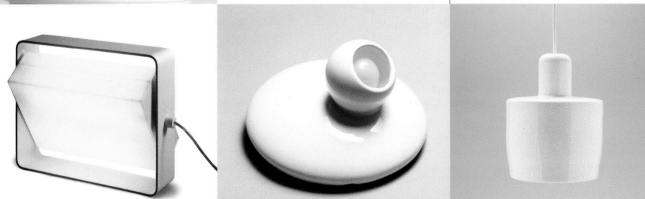

1
2
3
4
5

Richard **Sapper**

Germany/Italy | Furniture and product designer

Richard Sapper is without doubt one of the world's most successful designers, and in the last few decades he has had a decisive influence on Italian design. Sapper's products are precise, functional, innovative and highly complex. One of his main concerns is to "give form meaning", an aim that he often achieves with overwhelming success. According to **Ettore Sottsass**, Sapper has never produced a bad design.

Since the 1980s Sapper has had a major impact on the design of **IBM** computers. The black *ThinkPad 700C* triggered a laptop revolution. Furniture, watches, bathroom fittings, espresso makers, bicycles – there are few things that he has not designed. In the early 1960s, with his mentor, **Marco Zanuso**, the young Sapper developed his first wholly plastic chair, the *K 4999* child's chair (for ▶ **Kartell**), which soon became the model for numerous 'adult' chairs. Again with Zanuso, he also designed novel and exciting audio-visual equipment for ▶ **Brionvega**, including the *Black ST 201*, *Algol 11* and *Doney 14* television sets and the *TS 502* portable folding radio. Sapper developed the *Tizio* desk lamp for **Artemide** in the early 1970s – a product that fully justifies its reputation as a design classic. This bestselling lamp combines a characteristic skeletal form with technical innovation and functionalism. It was also intended as a type of manifesto, a public statement devised to counter the widespread belief that design is mere decorative frivolity.

Sapper's collaboration with **Alessi** has continued uninterrupted since the late 1970s. Among his many products for the company are the *9090* stove-top espresso maker, an electric kettle with a melodic whistle and *La Cintura di Orione,* a set of professional cooking pots, for which he took advice from leading chefs. In the mid-1990s Sapper designed the aluminium *Zoombike* for Elettromontaggi, which is almost as easy to fold up as an umbrella. In recent years he has designed a triangular high-tech ballpoint pen for the German manufacturer ▶ **Lamy**.

440

1   *Tizio* desk lamp, 1972

2   *Cobán* espresso machine, 1997

3   *Leapfrog* computer, 1992

4   *9091* kettle, 1982

5   *TS 502* radio, 1964

6   *Static* table clock, 1960

7   *Aida* chair, 2002

8   *Sapper* office chair, 1979

9   *9090* espresso maker, 1978

1932	Born in Munich
1955	Graduates in economics from Technische Universität, Munich
1956	Works in design department at **Mercedes-Benz** (until 1958)
1958	Works for **Gio Ponti** and La Rinascente; collaborates with **Marco Zanuso** (until 1977)
1960	Receives Compasso d'Oro (eight times by 1998)
1970	Works as consultant to **Fiat** (until 1976)
1972	Participates in *Italy: The New Domestic Landscape* exhibition at MoMA, New York
1986	Appointed professor at Staatliche Akademie der Bildenden Künste, Stuttgart (until 1998)
1993	Solo exhibition held at MoMA, New York

Products

1954	Wing mirror for Mercedes *300 SL*
1959	*Transmaster* radio for La Rinascente
1960	*Static* table clock for Lorenz
1962	*Doney 14* TV set for ▶ **Brionvega**
1963	*Lambda* chair for Gavina
1964	*K 4999* child's chair for ▶ **Kartell**; *Algol 11* TV set and *TS 502* radio for ▶ Brionvega
1965	*Grillo* telephone handset for Siemens
1969	*Black ST 201* TV set
	From 1962, all with ▶ Marco Zanuso
1972	*Tizio* desk lamp for **Artemide**
1978	*9090* espresso maker for **Alessi**
1979	*Sapper* office chair for **Knoll**
1982	*9091* kettle for Alessi
1992	*ThinkPad 700C* laptop computer and *Leapfrog* computer for ▶ **IBM**
1995	*Zoombike* folding bicycle for Elettromontaggi
1997	*Cobán* espresso machine for Alessi
2002	*Aida* chair and table for ▶ **Magis**
2003	*La Cintura di Orione* cookware for Alessi; *Dialog 1* ballpoint pen for ▶ **Lamy**

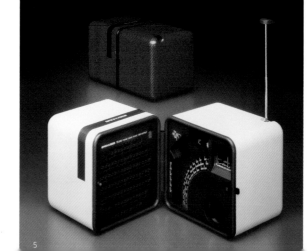

5

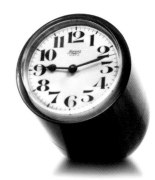

6

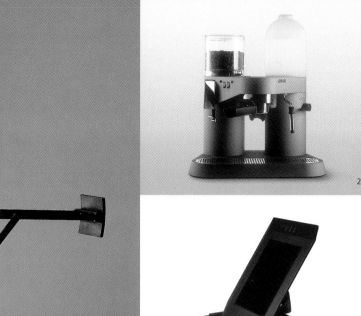

2

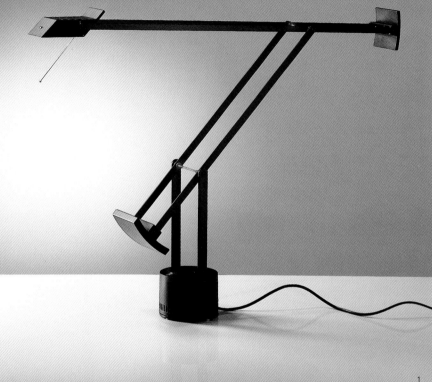

3

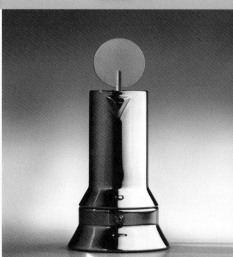

4

7

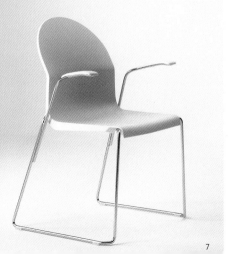

8

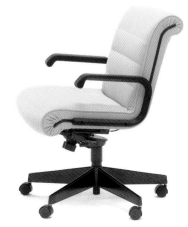

9

Gino **Sarfatti**

Italy l Lamp designer

Gino Sarfatti was greatly inspired by light as a design feature. The former aeronautical engineer became a pioneer in the field of lighting design and production, concentrating all his energies on the lamp manufacturer Arteluce, which he established near Como in the late 1930s. A self-taught designer, he more or less created the company's entire early collection; in total, he developed around 4000 lamps. Sarfatti was highly enthusiastic about the design ethic in post-war Italy. Under his leadership, Arteluce was not only an exemplary promoter of modern lighting design, but also a pillar of the new Italian design scene in general. In the golden years of the post-war period, the company was responsible for lighting in schools, offices, luxury liners, airports and museums. Sarfatti's ideas were simple and modern and sought to create the greatest possible effect in order to accentuate a building's architecture. He developed light-mobiles and functional wall, table and standard lamps for private living-rooms in the typical style of the 1950s, but he never descended into the realms of kitsch. In the early 1970s Arteluce encountered financial difficulties and was finally taken over by **Flos**. Sarfatti withdrew, unable to accept a subordinate role in what had been his own company. Arteluce continues to exist as a separate brand at Flos. A large number of lamps by Sarfatti are still in production.

1912 Born in Venice; studies aeronautical engineering in Genoa
1939 Establishes Arteluce
1951 Develops first use of Plexiglas
1954 Receives Compasso d'Oro for *559* table lamp
1971 Develops first halogen lamp
1973 Sells Arteluce to **Flos**
1984 Dies in Gravedona

Products
1948 *1045* standard lamp
1950 *Suspension* hanging lamp
1952 *187* wall lamp
1953 *559* table lamp
1954 *1063* and *1064* standard lamps
1957 *2097* lamp
1958 *SP 13* ceiling lamp, *584 P* table lamp and *2097* chandelier
1966 *600* table lamp
1969 *604* table lamp
1970 Clip-on table light
1971 *607* halogen low-voltage table lamp
1976 *2133* hanging lamp
All for Arteluce

1 *2097* chandelier, 1958
2 Clip-on table light, 1970
3 *SP 13* ceiling lamp, 1958
4 *2133* hanging lamp, 1976
5 *600* table lamp, 1966

442

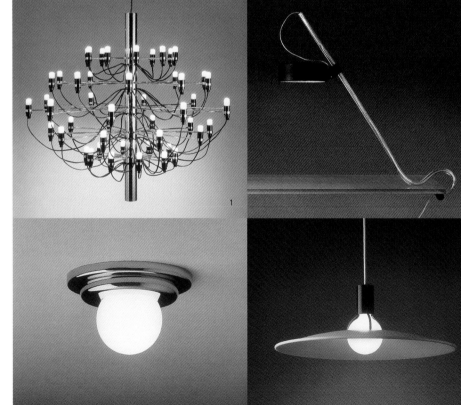

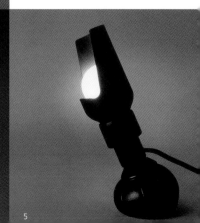

Timo **Sarpaneva**

Finland | Glass designer

Timo Sarpaneva is one of the grand masters of Finnish glass design. He has also had considerable success in the related fields of sculpture, painting and graphic design; in addition, he is able to work in a wide variety of materials, including porcelain, iron and plastic. Two of his designs from the 1970s are famous: the *Suomi* tableware service (for **Rosenthal**) and a cast-iron cooking pot with a lid that is removed with a wooden lever (today available at **littala**). Despite Sarpaneva's versatility, however, glass remains his favoured medium.

In the early 1950s Sarpaneva created a series of art-glass objects for littala by means of the steam-blowing process, a method used for the first time in an artistic context. One of his best-known pieces, the *Orkidea* (Orchid) vase, has been described as the most beautiful in the world. The *I-line* collection was similarly innovative. With this set of bottles, glasses and plates, Sarpaneva bridged the gap between luxurious art-glass and inexpensive, mass-produced items. The *Finlandia* art-glass collection, which was manufactured using the new wood-burning process famous for creating an ice-like effect on the surface of the glass, was followed in the 1980s by the *Claritas* vase series, in which drop shapes and irregular air bubbles unite the poetry of ice and water.

1926 Born in Helsinki
1948 Graduates from Central School of Arts and Crafts, Helsinki
1950 Opens design studio; works for **littala**
1954 Receives gold medal at Milan Triennale
1963 Elected Honorary Royal Designer for Industry
1967 Granted honorary doctorate from Royal College of Art, London
1993 Granted honorary doctorate from University of Art and Design, Helsinki

Products
1951 *Hiidenkirnu* (Devil's head) art-glass collection
1952 *Lansetti* glass sculptures
1954 *Kajakki* and *Maailmankaunein* glass sculptures; *Orkidea* (Orchid) vase
1956 *I-line* glass collection
All for littala
1963 Cast-iron cooking pot for Rosenlew (re-edition at littala)
1964 *Finlandia* art-glass collection for littala
1967 *Ambiente* fabrics for Tampella
1968 *Bolero* cotton fabrics
1974 *Suomi* service for **Rosenthal**
1984 *Kolibri* glass series and *Claritas* vase collection for ▶ littala; *Suomi* cutlery for Rosenthal
1990 *Marcel* vase collection for littala
1992 Silver service for Finland's head of state for Kultakeskus; *Black Brother* glass sculpture

1 *Marcel* vase collection, 1990
2 Vase (*Claritas* collection), 1984
3 Cast-iron cooking pot, 1963
4 *Suomi* service, 1974
5 *I-line* glass collection, 1956

443

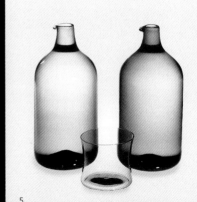

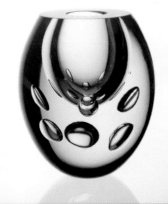

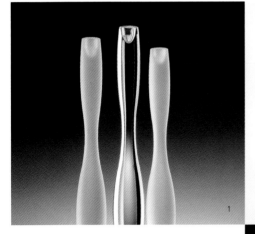

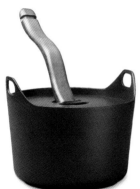

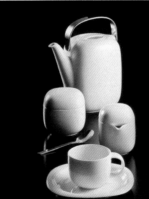

Sixten **Sason**

Sweden | Automobile and product designer

During the Second World War the Swedish camera manufacturer Hasselblad developed the *1600-F* (reissued as the *501CM*), a civilian version of its reconnaissance camera. A few years later the camera was presented in New York and set the international standard for medium-format studio photography. Sixten Sason, a Swedish industrial designer, had been involved in the development of the product from the outset, a collaboration that was unprecedented at that time. A silversmith by training, Sason already boasted references from two giants of Swedish industry – Electrolux, the manufacturer of domestic appliances, and Saab, the automobile company. He was one of the first modern product designers in Europe to move between different branches of industry. The Hasselblad camera, initially entitled *Rossex*, was designed to be as compact as possible. Sason reduced the casing to a block form and simplified the operating buttons. The result was an easy-to-handle, user-friendly masterpiece, acclaimed by professional photographers for several decades. The casing, just like the **Leica** *M3* camera, was in elegant black and silver and was given a mere suggestion of streamlining; it was a true classic of industrial design.

Sason was a rather eccentric character. His real name was Anderson, but he chose to give himself an interesting and exotic-sounding pseudonym. He was fascinated by technology. The products he designed throughout the course of his career – whether a vacuum cleaner (for Electrolux) or sewing machines (for Husqvarna) – were all highly innovative and frequently had lasting success. This is particularly true of his best-known designs, the models that he developed as chief designer for Saab. Until well into the 1960s, all the cars had the wing-shaped profile that Sason had first introduced in the Saab *92* at the end of the 1940s. In this bold design he adapted the 1930s ideas of streamlining to accommodate post-war realities. The futuristic car was designed on aerodynamic principles that even included a streamlined underside. Sason's last car, the model *99*, had an unmistakable silhouette that was retained for almost two decades. It is impossible to overestimate the impact Sason had on the international success of the Saab marque, and his influence lingers to this day.

444

1 *501CM* camera (reissue of *600-F*), 1948
2 *92001* prototype of *92* saloon, 1947
3 *Sonnett II* coupé, 1966
4 *99* saloon, 1967

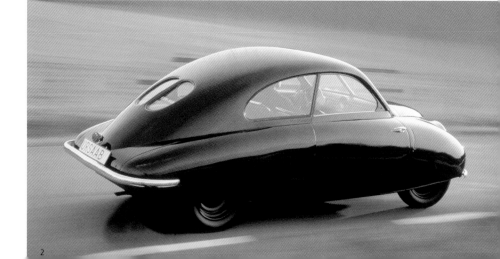

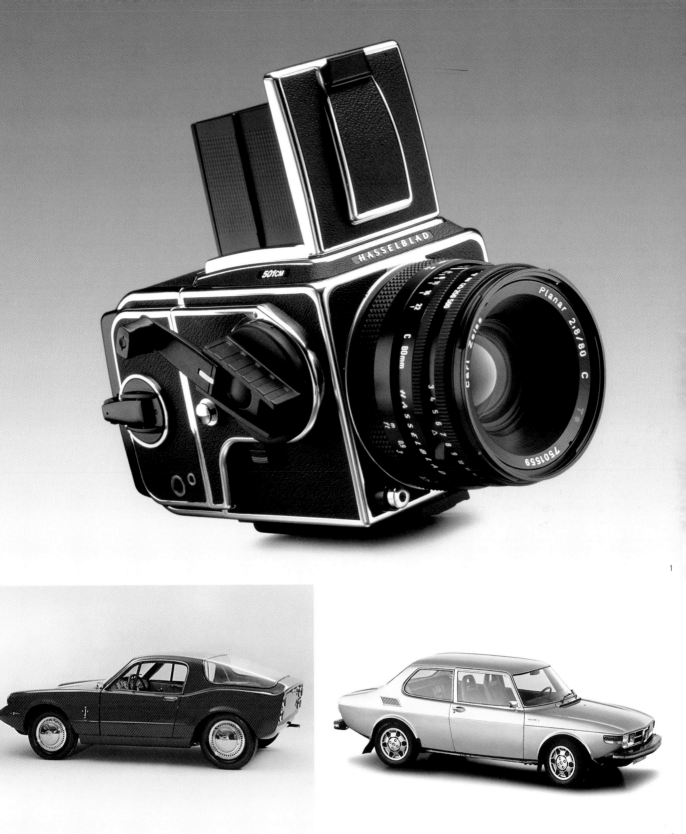

1

3

4

Sawaya & Moroni

Italy | Sawaya & Moroni SpA, Milan | Furniture and silverware manufacturer | **www.sawayamoroni.it**

In the mid-1980s Beirut-born William Sawaya and the Italian Paolo Moroni invited a group of renowned international architects – among them **Michael Graves**, Charles Jencks, Oswald Mathias Ungers, Zaha Hadid, **Jean Nouvel** – to design furniture and silverware for their newly founded design company in Milan. Their programme steered away from minimalism and focused instead on stylistic diversity. At Sawaya & Moroni, whose showrooms are on the prestigious Via Manzoni in Milan, great value is placed on designers who have the courage to make an individual, visually convincing statement. While Jean Nouvel created a purist design with his *TBL Inox* table, Toni Cordero made an ironic allusion to nostalgia for the 'good old days' with his velvet-covered *Faia* armchair. Marcello Morandini decorated his *Bine* chair with striking black-and-white stripes; Zaha Hadid's *Glacier* sofa is an expressive sculptural form. The *Three* bookcase, by Jakob & MacFarlane, is too spectacular to be referred to simply as 'shelving'. The semi-transparent object is made of a special resin and could be more accurately described as a sculpture for the living-room. It radiates both exuberance and eccentricity.

For a number of years now Sawaya & Moroni has also produced the *Spring Furniture* and *Spring Accessories* collections, a complementary programme offering furniture and furnishings with more simple lines. The *Spring Furniture* collection includes the *MY 068* wooden chair by **Michael Young**, which is utterly convincing in its originality and clear design. Handmade silverware, including designs by **Matthew Hilton**, **Toshiyuki Kita**, William Sawaya and Zaha Hadid, also forms part of the company's product range. Hadid contributed a tea and coffee service, the individual elements of which are reminiscent of a collection of coarsely worked crystals. Exquisite glassware by Sawaya likewise has a special place in the company's programme. The vase series *Dialetti Impossibili*, made from precious Murano glass, and the *Fleurs du Mal* are superb creations in which the possibilities of the delicate material are pushed to extremes to create a magnificent overall form.

446

1 *Three* bookcase, 2002
2 Tea and coffee service by Toshiyuki Kita, 1997
3 *Gravity* easy chair, 2002
4 *01* table, 2001
5 *Moraine* sofa, 2000
6 *MY 068* chair, 1998
7 *Bine* chair, 1991
8 *TBL Inox* table, 1995

1984 Established by William Sawaya and Paolo Moroni in Milan

Products

1984 *MG3* armchair and *MG4* sofa by **Michael Graves**

1986 *Suspiral* chair by Luigi Serafini; *Editto* sofa by William Sawaya

1988 *Crust* armchair by **Ron Arad**

1990 *Santa* chair by Luigi Serafini

1991 *Bine* chair by Marcello Morandini; *Drum* occasional table by Marco Mencacci

1992 *Wienerin* chair and *Acqua di Fuoco* bar by William Sawaya; *Antiopa* armchair and sofa by Toni Cordero

1993 *Patty Diffusa* chair by William Sawaya; *Faia* armchair by Toni Cordero

1995 *Dialetti Impossibili* glass vase series and *Le Diable en Tête* jug by William Sawaya; *TBL Inox* table and *Milana* armchair by **Jean Nouvel**

1997 *Ex Libris* shelf by William Sawaya; tea and coffee services by Zaha Hadid and **Toshiyuki Kita**

1998 *Spring Furniture* collection, incl. *MY 068* chair by **Michael Young**, *Povera* armchair by William Sawaya and *Lintaro* side table by Makoto Kawamoto

1999 *Darwish* sofa by William Sawaya; *MY 072* sofa by Michael Young; *Superstore* shelf by Platt & Young

2000 *Moraine* sofa by Zaha Hadid

2001 *Glacier* sofa by Zaha Hadid; *01* table by John Maeda; *Beppu* table lamp by Toshiyuki Kita

2002 *Gravity* easy chair and *Maxima* chair by William Sawaya; *Z-Play* sofa by Zaha Hadid; *Fergus Table* by Matt Sindall; *Three* bookcase by Jakob & MacFarlane

2003 *Iceberg* sofa by Zaha Hadid; *Aya* table lamp by Toshiyuki Kita

2005 *Vortexx* chandelier by Zaha Hadid and Patrik Schumacher (in partnership with **Zumtobel**)

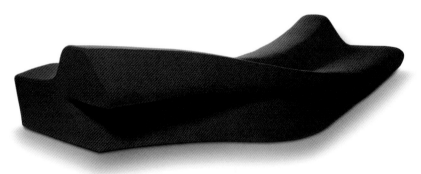

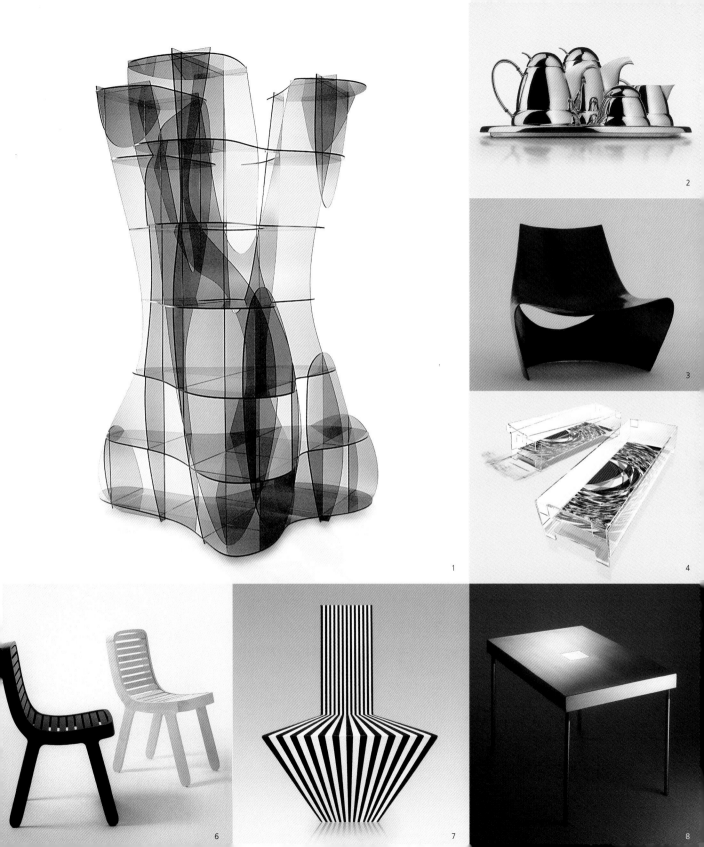

Carlo **Scarpa**

Italy | Architect and furniture and product designer

Carlo Scarpa was a progressive architect and designer whose works were for many years misunderstood in academic circles. His exhibition designs, including the Paul Klee retrospective at the Venice Biennale in 1948, and his architectural commissions, including a showroom for **Olivetti** in Venice in the 1950s, are regarded as conceptual milestones. Scarpa's furniture and product designs are also distinctive, not least for their simplicity and the magical qualities of the materials used.

Scarpa was an uncompromising aesthete who always gave precedence to craftsmanship over mass production. The bowls and vases in Murano glass that he designed in the 1930s and 1940s for ▶ **Venini**, although often simple in their basic shape, display a meticulous attention to detail that reflects a clear awareness of tradition and a cautious interpretation of familiar forms. Scarpa's occasionally monumental tables, such as *Orseolo*, in wood, *Doge*, in steel and crystal, and *Delfi*, in marble (designed in collaboration with **Marcel Breuer**), were often created in the context of specific architectural commissions and seemed designed to last forever. In the 1970s Scarpa developed mass-produced furniture for Bernini, including the elegant and commodious *Zibaldone* shelves.

1906 Born in Venice
1926 Graduates in architecture from Accademia di Belle Arte, Venice
1931 Casa Asta, Venice, with painter Mario Deluigi
1948 Designs Paul Klee exhibition at Venice Biennale
1951 Becomes acquainted with **Frank Lloyd Wright** in Venice
1956 Receives **Olivetti** Architecture Prize
1957 Showroom for Olivetti in Venice
1960 Designs Frank Lloyd Wright exhibition at Milan Triennale
1978 Dies in Sendai, Japan

Products
1927 Glass objects for **Cappellini**
1933 Glass objects for ▶ **Venini** (until 1947)
1940 *Murrine Opache* glass collection and *Battuto Bicolore* vase for Venini
1969 *Doge* and *Delfi* tables for Simon (*Delfi* with **Marcel Breuer**)
1971 *Valmarana* table for Gavina
1972 *Orseolo* table for Simon
1974 *Zibaldone* shelving for Bernini
1976 *Gritti* table for Simon; *1934* furniture collection for Bernini

1 *Orseolo* table, 1972
2 *Battuto Bicolore* vase, 1940
3 *Murrine Opache* bowl, 1940
4 Chair (*1934* collection), 1976

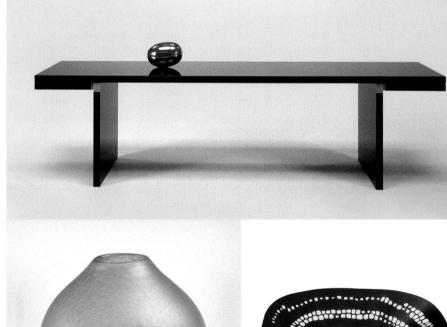

1

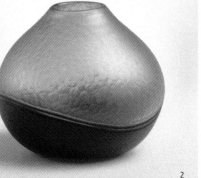

2

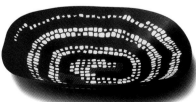

3

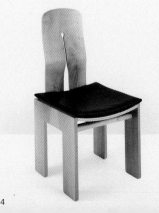

4

Herbert H. **Schultes**

Germany | Furniture and product designer

From the end of the 1960s and for almost three decades, Herbert H. Schultes, together with Norbert Schlagheck, ran one of the most successful German design studios of the time. Schlagheck Schultes Design created sophisticated designs for computers, cameras, watches and medical appliances as well as for such everyday items as rubber boots. The studio was regarded as an exemplary representative of post-war functionalism. Among its loyal clients was Agfa, for which the studio designed a compact super-8 camera in 1970 and later the *Agfamatic* pocket camera, which has a lens that is protected by an innovative sliding mechanism when not in use. In the mid-1980s Schultes became design director at Siemens. In the mid-1990s he developed the third generation of high-speed *ICE* trains for Deutsche Bahn. Schultes has been championing the importance of design for several decades. After having resigned as director of **Designafairs** (formerly Siemens Design), he again set up his own company, Ritz Schultes Design (with Regina Ritz). Such designs as the super-light *Elephant Chair* (for **Lensvelt**) and the *System 20* kitchen system (for ▶ **Bulthaup**), consisting of individual pieces of furniture, clearly reflect his considerable potential.

449

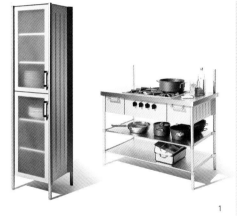

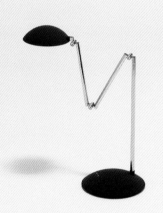

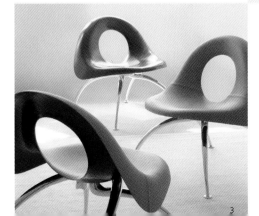

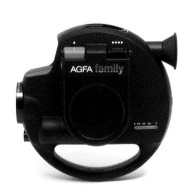

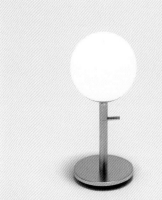

SCP

England I SCP Ltd, London I Furniture manufacturer I **www.scp.co.uk**

SCP stands for Sheridan Coakley Products. Coakley is a former antiques dealer who developed a passion for Bauhaus furniture. In the mid-1980s he opened a showroom in the East End of London. The first display was devoted to **Philippe Starck**, whose designs Coakley imported to Britain. Coakley played an unprecedented role in the London design scene largely on account of his unerring ability to spot talent. He discovered many young cabinet-makers who were capable of creating modern classics, including such pieces as the *Woodgate* sofa by Terence Woodgate, the zoomorphic *Balzac* armchair by **Matthew Hilton** and the simple *Hoop* chaise longue by **Tom Dixon**. Coakley pursued his purist line uncompromisingly.

SCP was responsible for launching the career of **Jasper Morrison**, the grand master of new British design. Coakley's aim was to create a circle of eminent designers – among them **Konstantin Grcic, Michael Marriott** and **Michael Sodeau** – whose works reflect such qualities as understatement and durability. In this way, Coakley put his stamp on a minimalist line that ushered in the 'New Simplicity', initially in British design and later across the international design scene. SCP has always favoured a long-term strategy that relies on an extremely strong network of personal contacts. This network includes not only the élite of the London design community but also selected suppliers. Bute Fabrics, for example, is a traditional old wool factory in the Hebrides with an excellent reputation; it regularly supplies upholstery materials to SCP. Since a large number of pieces in the SCP product range are still based on tubular steel constructions, there is also lively collaboration with small workshops, so-called 'metal bashers'. British supremacy in Formula One engineering is relevant here because it is responsible for numerous small high-tech firms having sprung up in the back streets of London – firms that often help in solving SCP's technical problems. In one particular case, for example, a manufacturer that usually produces exhaust systems for racing cars came up with a perfect solution to a complex problem involving the attachment of the seat and legs to a piece of furniture.

1985	Established by Sheridan Coakley in London; shows first presentation at International Furniture Fair, Milan
1992	Wins first public contracts
1998	Expands showroom in east London

Products

1984	*Side Table* by **Jasper Morrison**
1986	*Bow* shelf by **Matthew Hilton**
1988	Sofa by Jasper Morrison
1989	*Flipper* table by Matthew Hilton
1991	*Club* armchair, *Balzac* armchair with footstool and *Auberon* folding table by Matthew Hilton
1993	*Unit* shelves by **Konstantin Grcic**
1995	*Rook* table and *Analogue* wall clock by Konstantin Grcic; *Reading Chair* by ► Matthew Hilton
1997	*Woodgate* furniture collection by Terence Woodgate
1998	*Missed* chaise longue by **Michael Marriott**; *JM 510* sofa by Jasper Morrsion; *Hoop* chaise longue by **Tom Dixon**
1999	*Stafford* armchair by Andrew Stafford
2001	*Converse* furniture collection by Matthew Hilton; *Mono* furniture collection by ► **Michael Sodeau**
2002	*Sax* upholstered furniture collection by Terence Woodgate; *X* sofa and *A* table by Michael Sodeau; *Buffalo* armchair by ► Matthew Hilton
2003	*Orford* sofa collection by ► Matthew Hilton; *Plus* sofa system by Michael Sodeau

450

1 *Balzac* armchair, 1991

2 Table (*Woodgate* collection), 1997

3 *Unit* shelves, 1993

4 *Missed* chaise longue, 1998

5 *Hoop* chaise longue, 1998

6 *Auberon* folding table, 1991

7 *Side Table*, 1984

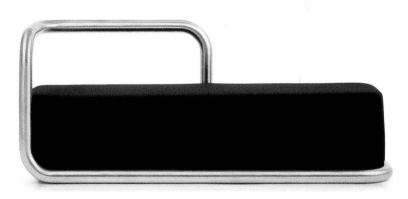

5

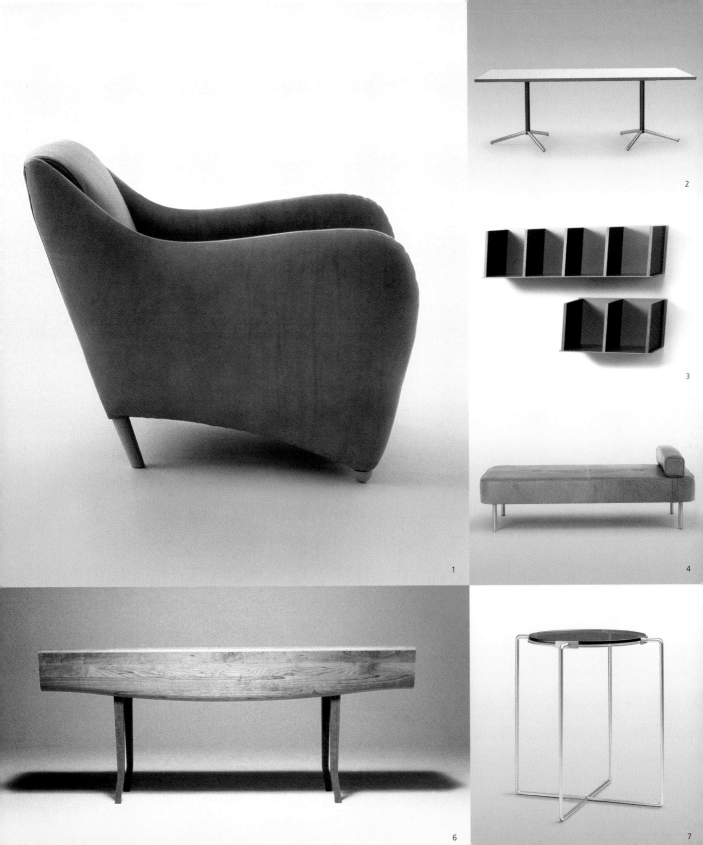

1

2

3

4

6

7

Serien Lighting

Germany | Serien Raumleuchten GmbH, Rodgau | Lamp manufacturer | **www.serien.com**

The lamp collection of the German manufacturer Serien still betrays its origins in the experimental and sometimes playful 1980s. The prize-winning *Zoom* hanging lamp, by Floyd Paxton, is an ingenious design. The lamp's diameter can easily be adjusted depending on whether the user requires a compact lamp to light a small table or an imposing chandelier to illuminate a much larger area; the variation in diameter (anything up to 260 cm/102 in.) creates dramatically different lighting effects. ▶ **Uwe Fischer** and Achim Heine's *Take Five* hanging lamp is also adjustable, and can be arranged either as a compact square of parallel light tubes or a long, straight row.

Serien has made a name for itself with a range of original, carefully thought-out lamp designs. Some of its products, such as the *Basis* ceiling light, an aluminium construction that is striking for its clean lines, delicate dimensions and efficient use of energy, were designed by Jean-Marc da Costa and Manfred Wolf, the firm's founders. The *SML T5* series, a flat glass rectangle (available as a wall, ceiling or hanging lamp) that directs its light both upwards and downwards, is even more minimalist. The name of the series reflects product availability: all versions are available in small, medium and large size.

1983 Leuchten und Mobiliar established by Manfred Wolf and Jean-Marc da Costa in Rodgau

1986 Company name changes to Serien Raumleuchten, today Serien Lighting

1995 Receives Red Dot Design Award for *Take Five* hanging lamp

1999 Receives Red Dot Design Award for *Jones* standard lamp

2003 Receives International Design Award of State of Baden-Württemberg for *Zoom* hanging lamp

Products

1977 *Seventy Seven* hanging lamp by Bruno Ninaber van Eyben

1982 *Ventilator* ceiling lamp by Manfred Wolf

1983 *Lift* hanging lamp and desk lamp

1984 *Basis* lamp collection; *Reflex* ceiling lamp

1992 *Cosy* lamp collection

Last four by Jean-Marc da Costa

1993 *Take Five* hanging lamp by ▶ **Uwe Fischer** and Achim Heine

1995 Exterior lighting series by Manfred Wolf

1996 *Club* lamp collection by Jean-Marc da Costa

1999 *Jones* standard lamp by ▶ Uwe Fischer

2001 *Zoom* hanging lamp by Floyd Paxton; *Reef* lamp collection by Nextspace

2003 *Pan Am* lamp collection by Hopf & Wortmann; *SML T5* lamp collection by Jean-Marc da Costa

2004 *One Eighty* lamp collection by Yaacov Kaufman

1 Standard lamp (*Basis* collection), 1984
2 Wall lamp (*SML T5* lamp collection), 2003
3 *Zoom* hanging lamp, 2001
4 *Zoom* hanging lamp, 2001
5 *Lift* hanging lamp, 1983

452

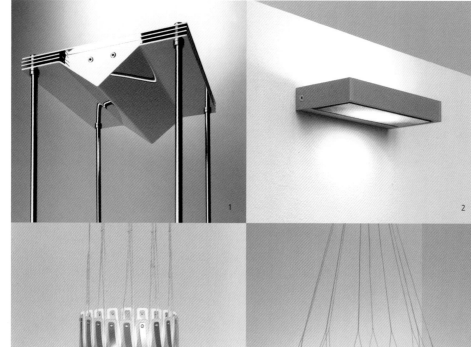

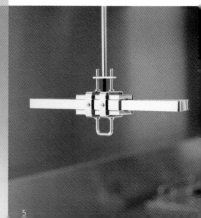

Maarten van **Severen**

Belgium | Furniture designer

Even though Maarten van Severen called one of his trestle desks *Schraag*, or 'Crooked', he himself was a supreme representative of intellectual straight-thinking. The Belgian furniture designer had no time for frivolity and was driven by the belief that design should be reduced to the simplest possible forms. There are few pieces of furniture from the last decade that are as simple as his *Blue Bench* sofa (for **Edra**), which consists of a low, upholstered block and a bar-shaped backrest. Despite the formal rigour, Van Severen took the needs of the user into consideration: the backrest is made of polyurethane foam and can be removed so that the sofa can be used either for sitting or for sleeping on.

The clarity of his designs earned Van Severen a reputation as a designer who was faithful to his principles. He designed chairs for **Vitra**, including the highly acclaimed *.03*, the *LCP* loop-shaped plastic chair for **Kartell** and interiors for the renowned architect Rem Koolhaas. Van Severen was the son of the abstract painter Dan van Severen, but his own work epitomized the very opposite of figurative and organic design, and managed to combine formality with functionality. His *Schraag* desk, for example, is easy to dismantle and transport.

453

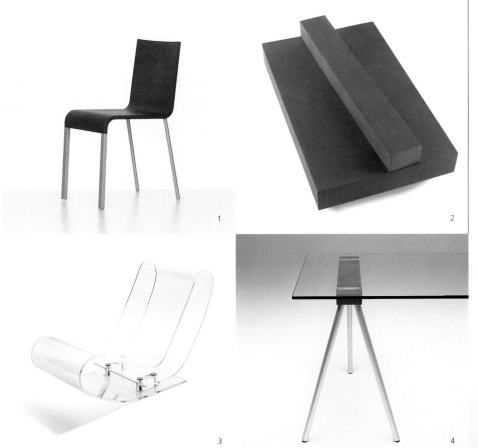

1

2

3

4

5

Seymour Powell

England | Product design studio | www.seymourpowell.com

Richard Seymour, who began his career in the advertising industry, and Dick Powell, an industrial designer, have together created a vast number of everyday products, including hairdryers, kettles, guitars, radios, lawnmowers, cameras and motorbikes. The Seymour Powell studio has around two dozen staff and, like Minale Tattersfield and Pentagram, is an example of a typically British, all-round design consultancy. Since the partnership was founded in west London in 1984, Seymour Powell has helped to change the image of British product design abroad. Successful designs include the *Freeline* cableless kettle for the French firm Tefal, radios for **Philips** in The Netherlands, a lawnmower for the Japanese company **Yamaha** and the *GX* camera series for Minolta. The products are innovative, imaginative and sometimes unconventional in appearance. **Rowenta**'s response to the high-tech vacuum cleaner from **Dyson**, for example, is the *Infinium* model. Stylishly designed by Seymour Powell, it looks like a gleaming metallic robot with a pointed snout. As well as working on commercial design commissions, Seymour Powell has also committed itself more generally to enhancing the profile of British design culture.

1984 Established by Richard Seymour and Dick Powell
1991 Receives D&AD Silver Award for *Technophone* telephone handset
1994 Receives BBC Design Award for *Skorpion* motorbike
1998 Seymour becomes president of D&AD (charity promoting good design)

Products

1984 *Durabeam* electric torch for Duracell
1986 Cableless kettle for Tefal
1987 Hairdryer for Clairol; *Freeline* kettle for Tefal
1988 Deep-fat fryer for SEB
1990 *Zero* knife collection; *Mower* lawnmower for **Yamaha**
1991 *G-Shock Thermo* wristwatch for Casio
1992 Hairdryer for Clairol; *Trichrono* watch collection for Casio; bathroom scales for Tefal; *Classic* toaster for SEB; *Skorpion* motorbike for MZ
1993 *Adventure* watch collection for Casio; *Vantage* secateurs
1994 *Bantam* motorbike for BSA
1996 *GX* camera series for Minolta
1997 *Avanti* toaster for Tefal; aeroplane interior for Cathay Pacific
1998 *Esterna* wristwatch for Casio; *Academy* bathroom taps for Ideal Standard
1999 *Balloon* vacuum cleaner for **Rowenta**
2000 *Avantis* iron for Calor
2001 *Infinium* and *Dumbo* vacuum cleaners for Rowenta

1 *Classic* toaster, 1992
2 *Vectis* camera (*GX* series), 1996
3 *Academy* bathroom tap, 1998
4 *Infinium* vacuum cleaner, 2001
5 *Vantage* secateurs, 1993

454

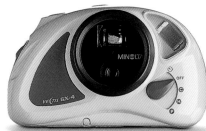

1

2

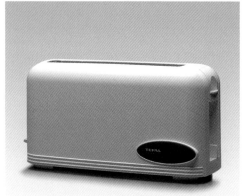

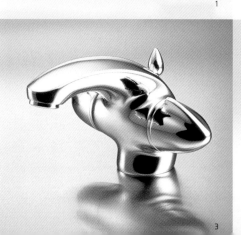

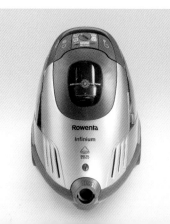

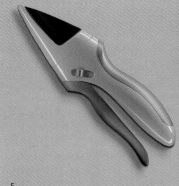

3

4

5

Sieger Design

Germany | Product design studio | **www.sieger-design.com**

Dieter Sieger has designed washstands, baths, soap holders, electric water-heaters and entire bathrooms. His company's rise has been meteoric, and it may soon be difficult to imagine any bathroom without a Sieger design in it. Initially, there was no indication that Sieger's products would become quite so ubiquitous. Following his schooling, Sieger completed an apprenticeship as a stonemason and then studied architecture. He has built numerous houses and has also constructed and fitted out luxury yachts. Sieger runs the family business with his two sons and lives in a moated Baroque castle – a distinct contrast to the frequently cool aesthetic of his own buildings. His third career began in the early 1980s, when he started designing sometimes severely modern, sometimes wildly luxurious bathroom series. His first product design, the modular *Lavarset*, was followed by the prize-winning *Domani* and *Tara* fittings (for ▶ **Dornbracht**). Sieger Design has gradually moved from the bathroom into the living-room with such products as glasses (for Ritzenhoff), china (for Arzberg) and even a television set (for **Sony**). As the in-house designer for Dornbracht and with designs for Alape, another bathroom specialist, however, Sieger Design has remained faithful to its origins.

1983 Dieter Sieger produces first product designs
1988 Moves studio to Schloss Harkotten, Sassenberg; Sieger Design established
1992 Manages design for glassmaker Ritzenhoff

Products
1983 *Lavarset* bathroom series for Alape
1985 *Domani* bathroom fittings for **Dornbracht**
1986 *Lavarlo* washbasin for Alape
1992 *Tara* bathroom fittings for ▶ Dornbracht; milk glasses for Ritzenhoff
1994 *Cult* service for Arzberg
1996 *4 x 9* furniture collection for **Duravit**
1997 *Materia* cutlery for **WMF**; *Tric* service for Arzberg
1998 *Happy D* bathroom series for ▶ Duravit; fireplace accessories for Commoto; TV set for **Sony**
2000 *Archetyp* fireplace stoves for Skantherm
2001 *Meta Plasma* bathroom furnishings and *e-Mote* and *Meta* bathroom fittings for▶ Dornbracht; *In the Mood* bathroom furniture for ▶ Duravit; external hard drive for X Mem
2003 *Betty Blue* washstand for Alape; *E-Pool* bathtub for Kaldewei; *Light Modules* modular light system and *MEM* and *Haute Cuisine* fittings for ▶ Dornbracht; *Components* washbasin series for Alape

1 *Betty Blue* washstand, 2003
2 *Meta Plasma* bathroom furnishings, 2001
3 *Tric* service, 1997
4 *Haute Cuisine* kitchen tap, 2003
5 *Domani* bathroom tap, 1985

455

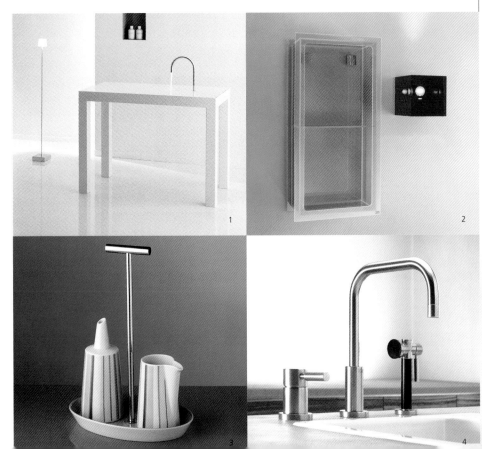

Snowcrash

Sweden | Furniture design studio and manufacturer

In the late 1990s several young Finnish designers working at the Valvomo architecture and design studio in Helsinki presented a bold exhibition at the Milan International Furniture Fair. They chose the name Snowcrash for this venture. The critics enthused about "**Aalto**'s heirs" and their "visionary articles for the networking age". The *Glowblow* standard lamp (today at ▸ **David Design**), which automatically inflates itself when switched on and deflates when switched off, pointed the way. Among the group's products that aroused most interest was the *Netsurfer*, a computer seat/desk that allows users to surf the Internet in comfort, and the rocking *Chip* plywood lounger (similar to the seat from the *Netsurfer*), both by Ilkka Terho and Teppo Asikainen. The takeover of Snowcrash by the Swedish Proventus group, which also acquired the furniture manufacturer Artek, was followed by relocation to Stockholm. Snowcrash was envisaged as a centre of innovation for Scandinavian design, and the range was expanded to include such unusual products as Monica Förster's *Cloud* tent, an inflatable enclave for those in need of relaxation, and Asikainen's *Soundwave*, a series of relief-like sound absorbers that can be used to transform a room optically and acoustically. Following the closure of Snowcrash in 2004, both products are now distributed by **Offecct**.

1 *Netsurfer* computer seat/desk, 1995
2 *Infinite Light* virtual lamp, 1999
3 *Cloud* tent, 2003
4 *Airbag* armchair, 1997
5 *Scrunch* wall panelling, 2000

456

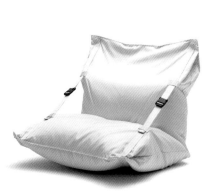

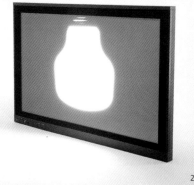

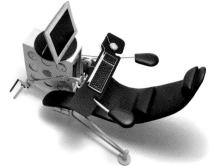

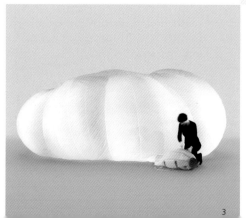

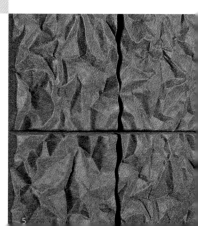

1

2

3

4

5

Michael **Sodeau**

England | Furniture and product designer

Michael Sodeau has had one of the most astounding careers in the recent history of British design, which is not lacking in modern fairytales. Directly after completing his degree in product design, Sodeau co-founded the **Inflate** studio, a company based on the concept of inflatable products. After two years, he left Inflate to establish his own design studio with Lisa Giuliani. The studio's first collection, which was greeted with enthusiasm, had the faintly ironic title *Comfortable Living* and consisted of wicker lamps, ceramics, tables, carpets and a living-room chair. Sodeau's approach is dictated by the materials with which he works; organic forms and natural colours predominate in his designs. His *Bolla* series of wicker lamps (for Gervasoni) established a design trend.

The rugs and ceramic objects produced by Sodeau all exhibit recurrent motifs, an indication of his holistic approach. His minimalist *Mono* furniture series for **SCP**, and also the more exciting designs for the *Wing* series of sideboards for **Isokon Plus**, reveal him to be a designer who follows a clear line that is independent of short-term fashion fads.

1969 Born in London
1994 Graduates from Central Saint Martins College of Art and Design, London
1995 Establishes **Inflate** with Nick Crosbie and Mark Sodeau
1997 Leaves Inflate to establish Michael Sodeau Partnership with Lisa Giuliani
1999 Receives Best Design Award at *100% Design* exhibition, London

Products

1994 Inflatable postcard
1995 Inflatable eggcup
1996 *Lily* lamp
All for **Inflate**
1997 *Duo* shelf, *Molar* vase and *Satellite* table for MSP; *Charlie* carpet for **Asplund**
1999 *Bolla* standard lamps for Gervasoni; *Wing* sideboard collection for **Isokon Plus**
2001 *Mono* furniture collection for **SCP**; *Corallo* coat stand for Gervasoni
2002 *X* sofa and *A* table for SCP
2003 *Box* lamp for Tronconi; *Float* sofa collection and *Multi* chair for Modus; *Oscar* folding table for Gordon Russell

1 *Multi* chair, 2003
2 *Mono* chaise longue, 2001
3 Inflatable eggcup, 1995
4 *Wing* sideboard, 1999
5 *Bolla* standard lamp, 1999

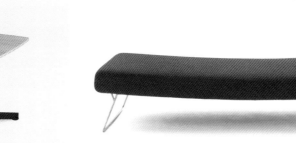

457

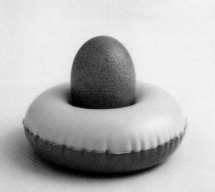

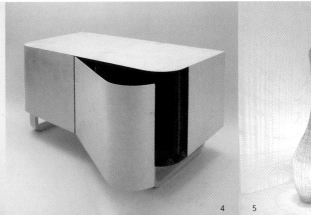

1   2

3   4   5

Sony

Japan | Sony Corporation, Tokyo | Manufacturer of electronic products | **www.sony.com**

The Japanese electronics giant Sony is one of the biggest media concerns in the world and has made technology a part of everyday life. In the case of *AIBO*, the robotic dog, it has even created appliances that interact with humans. The miniaturization of electronic appliances continues to be of decisive importance to the company. In the late 1950s it introduced the *TR-610* transistor radio (▶ p. 433), which became a symbol of its time. It was soon followed by the *TV8-301* portable television set, with a smooth outer casing and strongly rounded edges that gave it both a futuristic and timeless form. Whether it was the introduction of the *Walkman* personal stereo, which took the streets by storm in the early 1980s, the camcorder or the *Discman* portable CD player, Sony was a pioneer in equipping people with audio-visual appliances for everyday life. The company introduced numerous technical innovations, including the video cassette, the *Watchman*, the *MiniDisc* and such long-forgotten products as an electronic timepiece for dictation machines.

Sony's range of products has expanded enormously in more recent years, and today ranges from hi-fi systems to PCs and laptop computers, digital cameras and mobile phones. The company's design department employed no fewer than seventeen designers by the beginning of the 1960s (among them Shuhei Taniguchi, who developed the black-and-silver corporate colour scheme, still in use today). This focus on design highlighted Sony's affinity with the German manufacturer **Braun**, as did the fact that it took over the design-orientated WEGA Radio company and also adopted the practical box as its dominant motif. This motif is represented not only by the famous *Walkman* but also by such legendary products as the *Captain 55* world receiver and the *TC-55* compact dictation machine. Design became an increasingly integral part of market strategy and was reflected in new product segments such as the *VAIO* laptop, designed by Teiyo Goto, and the *PlayStation*, which, despite its often garish content, was given a clean and well-designed form. In collaboration with **Ericsson**, Sony succeeded in setting distinctive design accents on the hotly contested mobile phone market. The *T 610* is reminiscent – and not in name alone – of the appliance that started the ball rolling in the late 1950s.

458

1 *TV8-301* portable TV set, 1960
2 *PlayStation SCPH-1000*, 1994
3 *Cybershot DSC-F1* digital camera, 1996
4 *DCR-IP 220* digital camcorder, 2002
5 *AIBO* entertainment robot, 1999
6 *Walkman II* personal stereo, 1981
7 *KV-27* colour TV set, 1980
8 *WEGA* plasma TV set, 2002

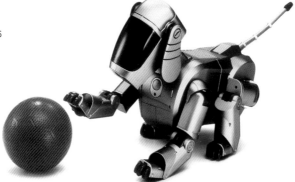

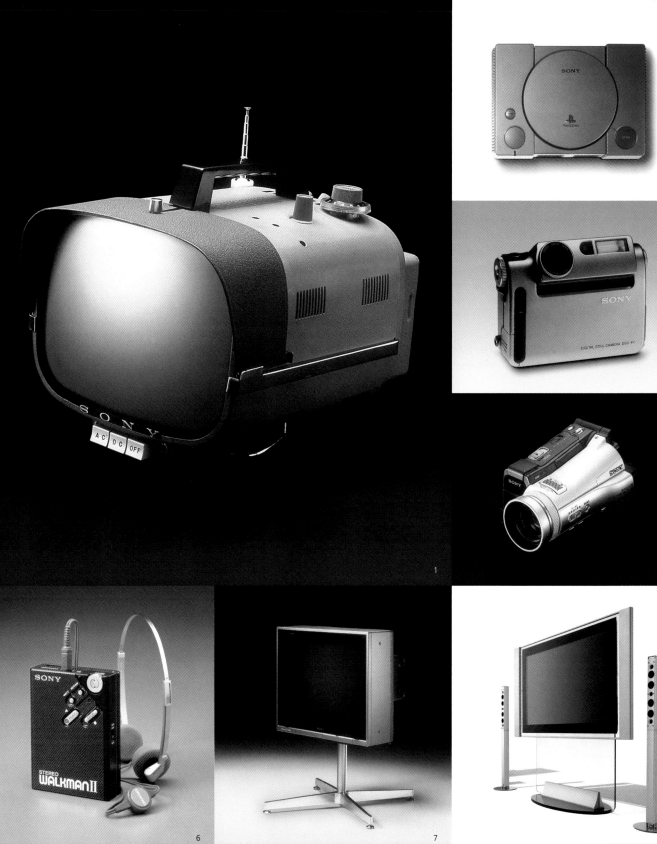

Ettore **Sottsass**

Italy | Architect and furniture and product designer | **www.sottsass.it**

Ettore Sottsass has a special place among the great designers of the twentieth century. The career of the Austrian-born architect began in Milan in the late 1940s. There was little indication that one day he would work for such renowned companies as **Alessi**, **Artemide**, Abet Laminati, **Vitra**, **Zumtobel** and Siemens. In the late 1950s he became famous almost overnight – not as an architect, but as a designer. *Elea 9003*, a design for **Olivetti**, was the first Italian-made mainframe computer, and Sottsass made its user 'interface', to use a modern expression, a model of user-friendliness. As chief design consultant for Olivetti, he created such successful products as the *Valentine*, *Tekne 3* and *Praxis 48* typewriters. During this period, the 1960s, Sottsass frequently travelled to India and brought back expressive ceramics and other objects that bear the imprint of a different culture and a different perception of form. His dual existence as an artist and an industrial designer, which was already quite pronounced in the 1960s, has remained a prominent feature of his life and work. Sottsass distanced himself from purely functional design that appealed largely to the design industry itself rather than to the ordinary person. When the Radical Design movement caught on in Italy, he designed a number of provocative anti-bourgeois objects such as beds and mirrors illuminated with neon lighting (for ▶**Poltronova**). In the early 1970s his furniture designs were featured in the legendary exhibition *Italy: The New Domestic Landscape* at the Museum of Modern Art (MoMA) in New York. In the same decade he co-founded the alternative design school Global Tools and, as a member of Studio Alchimia, became involved in the Anti-Design movement.

A turning point came in 1981. Sottsass co-founded the avant-garde Memphis design group, for which he created the colourful, laminated *Carlton* room divider that has since become a design icon. His brightly coloured Post-modern collage-like works were an ironic comment on industrial mainstream products and turned conventional aesthetic perceptions upside down – at least for a brief, yet historic moment. Memphis cleared the way for an 'anything-goes' approach and thus for new forms of kitsch. During that exciting period, Sottsass also founded Sottsass Associati, a design studio in which he and his partners have created consumer goods of all kinds, ranging from electronic appliances to lamps, office furniture and pens. Ceramics continue to play an important role in Sottsass's career. They are a perfect medium for revealing the designer's talents.

460

1   *Casablanca* cabinet, 1981
2   *Valentine* portable typewriter, 1969
3   *Tekne 3* typewriter, 1964
4   *Angel Note* electronic phonebook, 1990
5   Glass object for Memphis, 1981
6   *Mandarin* chair, 1986
7   Wine cooler (*Boston* collection), 1979
8   *Lipari* table, 1992
9   *Carlton* room divider, 1981

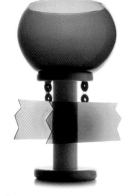

5

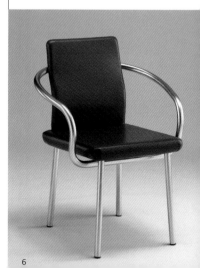

6

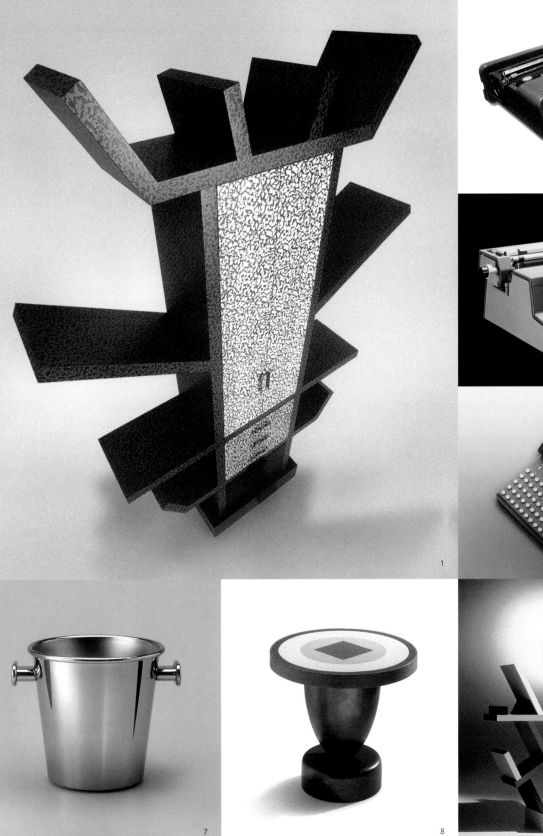

1

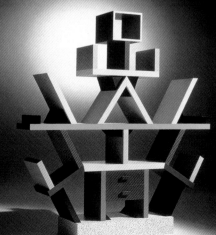

2

3

4

7

8

9

George J. **Sowden**

England/Italy | Product designer | **www.sowdendesign.com**

George J. Sowden studied design in the traditional way, at the drawing board, before moving to Milan in the 1970s to work for **Olivetti**. He was one of the founders of the Memphis design co-operative, an avant-garde group that was to have a profound influence on his career. Sowden regards himself as a poetic designer: his electrical and electronic appliances, which form the major focus of his work, not only include useful ergonomic details but are also imbued with subliminal meaning. Curved lines, broad diameters and unusual proportions play an important role in his designs. Sowden even succeeds in breathing life into the keyboards of pocket calculators. His domestic appliances, such as the toaster for Guzzini, adopt the same approach: the chrome-topped cover, unlike that of other toasters, has not been set into the casing, but curves outwards and has an ornamental as well as a protective function. The top section, with its ergonomic handles (somewhat reminiscent of umbrella handles), unifies the design. But Sowden's design team can also keep a low profile if need be, as demonstrated in the designs for stackable plastic containers with castors (for ▸Steelcase) and the lightweight *Pacific* chair made from polypropylene (for Segis). The *Pacific* is a quintessential interpretation of the immortal topic of 'the chair'.

462

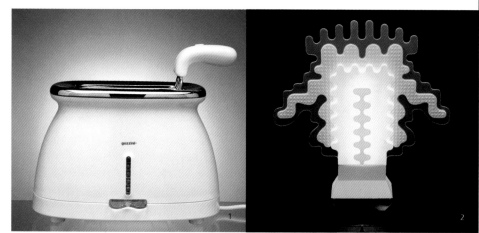

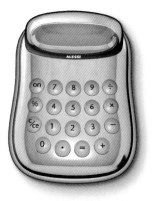

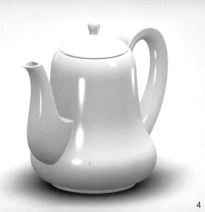

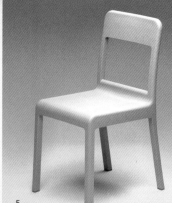

Henk **Stallinga**

The Netherlands | Product designer | www.stallinga.nl

Henk Stallinga offers a solution for all those who watch the swift passage of time with some trepidation. His wall clocks are an ironic comment on our difficult relationship with time. One such design is entitled *Paniki* and looks like a clock in a railway station – except for the misalignment of the six o'clock mark, which generates a strange sense of panic. Stallinga markets his products under his own name and enjoys playing with conventional forms. He uses *objets trouvés* and puts them to new use. *The Taste of Talking* salt and pepper shakers, for instance, are reminiscent of the earpieces of old-fashioned telephones.

Stallinga, who is also active as an interior designer, creates somewhat mundane objects such as ashtrays, candlesticks and holders for toilet paper, but he is devoted to one particular classic design discipline – the art of lamp design, which he enlivens with his unusual ideas. His *Lumalasch* double hanging lamp was inspired by gym rings, perhaps in an attempt to entice people to swing across the table. The *Watt* plug-in table lamp – a light bulb on the end of a lead – is a simple and functional archetype, and illustrates how the electric current feeds the bulb directly from the socket.

463

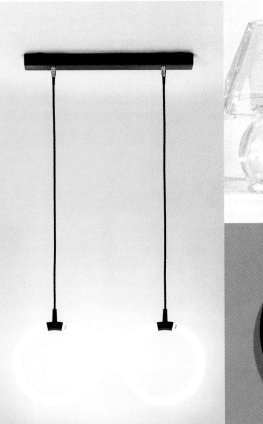

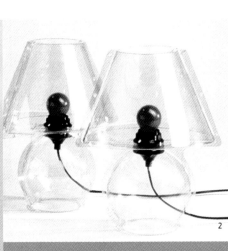

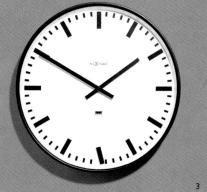

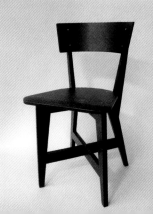

Mart **Stam**

The Netherlands | Architect and furniture and product designer

Experts disagree about who actually invented the famous cantilever chair: some argue that it was Mart Stam, and others insist that it was **Marcel Breuer**. Yet Stam's *S 43* model (for **Thonet**) has remained the epitome of this type of chair to the present day. After completing his training as a draughtsman in Amsterdam, Stam embarked on an international career as an architect. He worked in Berlin, Switzerland, Paris and Rotterdam and came into contact with such Modernists as Max Taut and El Lissitzky. In the late 1920s his designs for high-quality, yet affordable housing were hugely successful. Stam had a guest lectureship at the Bauhaus and was involved in the famous Weissenhofsiedlung housing project in Stuttgart. It was during that period that he started experimenting with tubular steel chairs. Some of his designs have been manufactured and copiously plagiarized to the present day. In the early 1930s he joined his wife, Lotte, in becoming a member of the 'May Brigade' (a group of architects and planners led by the architect Ernst May), developing designs for the new Soviet towns of Magnitogorsk, Makiyivka and Orsk. Back in The Netherlands, Stam was appointed director of the Institute of the Applied Arts in Amsterdam. From 1948 he taught in the German Democratic Republic. He returned to The Netherlands in 1953 and worked on housing and commercial building projects until his retirement in 1966.

1899 Born in Purmerend
1922 Travels to Germany, later Switerland, collaborating with various architects
1926 Returns to The Netherlands; works as draughtsman in Rotterdam
1927 Develops plans for Weissenhofsiedlung, Stuttgart
1928 Nursing home of Henry and Emma Budge Foundation, Frankfurt am Main
1930 Develops plans for Soviet cities of Magnitogorsk, Makiyivka and Orsk; Van Nelle factory, Rotterdam
1932 Hellerhof housing estate, Frankfurt am Main; Villa Palicka, Baba Werkbundsiedlung, Prague
1939 Becomes director of Institute of the Applied Arts, Amsterdam
1948 Teaches in German Democratic Republic (until 1952)
1953 Returns to The Netherlands; works with Merkelbach & Elling, architecture practice
1959 *De Geillustreerde Pers* office building, Amsterdam
1966 Retires and moves to Switzerland
1986 Dies in Goldbach, Switzerland

Products
1926 *S 33* chair (re-edition at **Thonet**)
1927 *MSW 27* wall lamp (re-edition at **Tecnolumen**)
1931 *S 43* chair (re-edition at **Thonet**)

1   *S 43 F* chair, 1931
2   *S 43* chair, 1931
3   *S 33* chair, 1926
4   *MSW 27* wall lamp, 1927

464

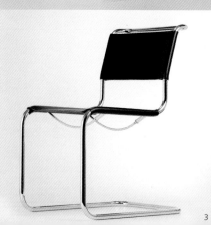

1

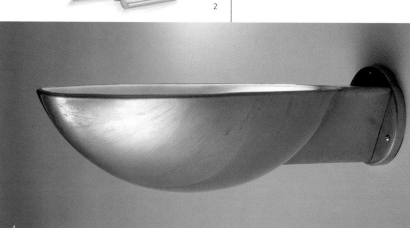

2

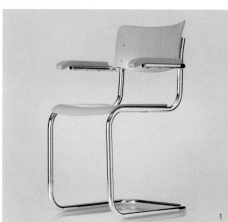

3

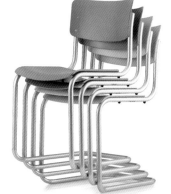

4

The **Stanley Works**

USA | The Stanley Works Corporation, New Britain, Connecticut | Tool manufacturer | **www.stanleyworks.com**

For more than one hundred and fifty years The Stanley Works had been synonymous with robust, professional tools, but in the late 1990s the management decided to follow new paths in product design. One of the reasons for this change may have been the success of the company's major competitor, Black & Decker, with its award-winning *Kitchen Tools* series. An independent department for industrial design was established at The Stanley Works, and Gary Van Deursen was poached from Black & Decker and appointed chief designer. He embarked on a series of reforms, including the introduction of the 'Innovation Team System' that enabled the company to test and implement new ideas developed by the team without delay. The management soon reaped the benefits of the new pioneering spirit. The arch-shaped *Composite* saw is easier to use than similar products by competitors. The X-shaped *100" Long Tape* measure is a new and intelligent revision of a well-known tool: the tape roll is placed between the upper 'legs' and the handle between the lower 'legs' of the X, thus giving the tool great stability. Like **Oxo**, The Stanley Works combines innovation with the American tradition of manufacturing specialist, high-quality tools.

1843 Stanley Bolt Manufactory established by Frederick T. Stanley
1852 Company is incorporated and name changes to The Stanley Works
1920 Establishes hand tools division
1937 Acquires J.A. Chapman Ltd, England
1980 Acquires Mac & Proto Mechanics Tools and Bostitch Fastening Systems
1997 Establishes industrial design department
2000 Receives Golden Hammer Award for product innovation

Products
1936 Utility knife
1997 *MaxGrip* pliers
1998 *High Tension* hacksaw; *100" Long Tape*
1999 *Composite* hacksaw; *Box Miter* hacksaw; *Anti-Vibe 3* hammer
2000 *IntelliSensor DigiScan* sensor device; *FatMax* tool series
2002 *Lighted High Impact Torpedo Level*

1 *100" Long Tape*, 1998
2 *MaxGrip* pliers, 1997
3 *IntelliSensor DigiScan* sensor device, 2000
4 *Composite* hacksaw, 1999
5 Cutter (*FatMax* tool series), 2000

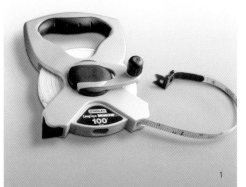

1

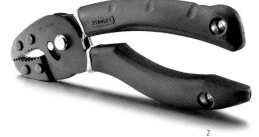

2

465

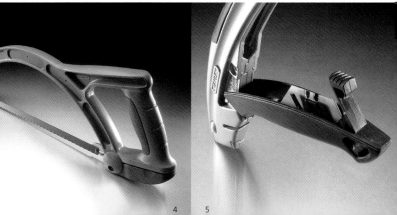

3

4

5

Philippe **Starck**

France I Furniture and product designer I **www.philippe-starck.com**

Philippe Starck's products are on display in millions of homes around the world. His staggering range of designs includes a dynamically shaped toothbrush, a television set that rocks (for Thomson), a lemon squeezer on spider's legs (for **Alessi**), an equally theatrical toilet brush, and chairs and lamps of all shapes and sizes. Almost everyone will have come across one of his designs at some time or another in their lives. One of Starck's most surprising statements is that he is not interested in the external form of his designs, despite the fact that they often appeal directly to the senses. Perhaps as a result of his assertiveness in his dealings with the various companies with which he is associated, he has been successful in producing affordable mass-market products.

The son of an aeronautical engineer, Starck studied architecture and design in Neuilly and Paris and subsequently worked as a designer for Pierre Cardin. His first successes were as an interior designer, and at the beginning of the 1980s he was commissioned by President François Mitterrand to design furnishings for the Elysée Palace. His *Costes* tripod chair, for the café of the same name in Paris, was another spectacular success. Starck exerted a strong influence on the Post-modern 1980s and the slightly more sober 1990s and became a truly international designer. Designs from that period include the innovative *Dr Glob* chair (for **Kartell**), with its unique combination of metal and plastic, an almost archetypal motorcycle for Aprilia, spectacles for Alain Mikli, mixer taps for **Hansgrohe** and **Duravit**, toys, clocks, domestic appliances and lamps, including the *Romeo Moon* for **Flos**. Starck also made a name for himself as a designer of such cool interiors as in the Delano Hotel in Miami and the Peninsula Restaurant in Hong Kong, and he has long been in demand as a design consultant (for example, for the Eurostar lounges in London and Paris). A highly self-promoting designer, he has undoubtedly contributed to the erroneous perception of design as 'expensive rubbish', but he has also worked hard to refute this view, as, for example, in his design of the *Cozy Chair* (for the American company Target), which costs just a few dollars. He has also argued that plastic is more ecological than wood, and on the occasion of an exhibition of his work at the Centre Georges Pompidou in Paris he gave a fascinating lecture on life, economics and design, but refrained from referring to his own work.

466

1 *Romeo Moon* hanging lamp, 1995
2 *Louis XX* chair, 1992
3 *Hula Hoop* office chair, 2001
4 *Dr No* chair, 1996
5 *Miss Sissi* table lamp, 1991
6 Washstand with cupboard (*Starck 1* bathroom series), 1994
7 Mixer tap (*Starck 1* bathroom series), 1994
8 *Time & Weather* weather station, 2003

1949 Born in Paris
1968 Studies at Ecole Nissim de Camondo, Paris
1976 Interior design of La Main Bleue nightclub, Paris
1979 Establishes Starck Product company
1982 Furnishes private suite of President Mitterrand in Elysée Palace, Paris
1984 Interior design of Café Costes, Paris
1989 Asahi Beer Hall, Tokyo

Products
1983 *Dr Sonderbar* armchair for XO
1984 *Costes* chair for ▶ **Driade**
1985 *Richard III* chair for ▶ **Baleri**
1988 *Ará* table lamp for ▶ **Flos**
1989 *Dr Glob* chair for **Kartell**
1990 *Hot Bertaa* kettle and *Juicy Salif* lemon squeezer for **Alessi**; *1191* door handle for **FSB**
1991 *Miss Sissi* table lamp for Flos
1992 *Hi-Glob* stool for Kartell; *Lord Yo* chair for Driade; *Louis XX* chair for **Vitra**
1993 *Dadada* stool for XO; *Excalibur* toilet brush for ▶ **Heller**
1994 *Starck 1* bathroom series for ▶ **Duravit**
1995 *Romeo Moon* hanging lamp for Flos; *Ici Pari* radio for Thomson/Telefunken (with ▶ **Matali Crasset**)
1996 *Dr No* and *Miss Trip* chairs for Kartell
1998 *Ero(S)* chair for ▶ **Kartell**; *LWS* furniture series for ▶ **Cassina**; *Archimoon* lamp collection for ▶ **Flos**
1999 *La Marie* chair and *Napoleon* and *Attila* stools for Kartell
2001 *Bubble* furniture collection for ▶ **Kartell**; *Hula Hoop* office chair for Vitra
2002 *Louis Ghost* chair for Kartell
2003 *Time & Weather* weather station for Oregon Scientific

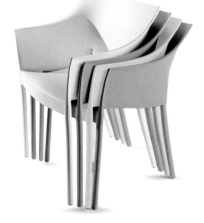

4

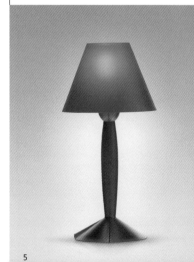

5

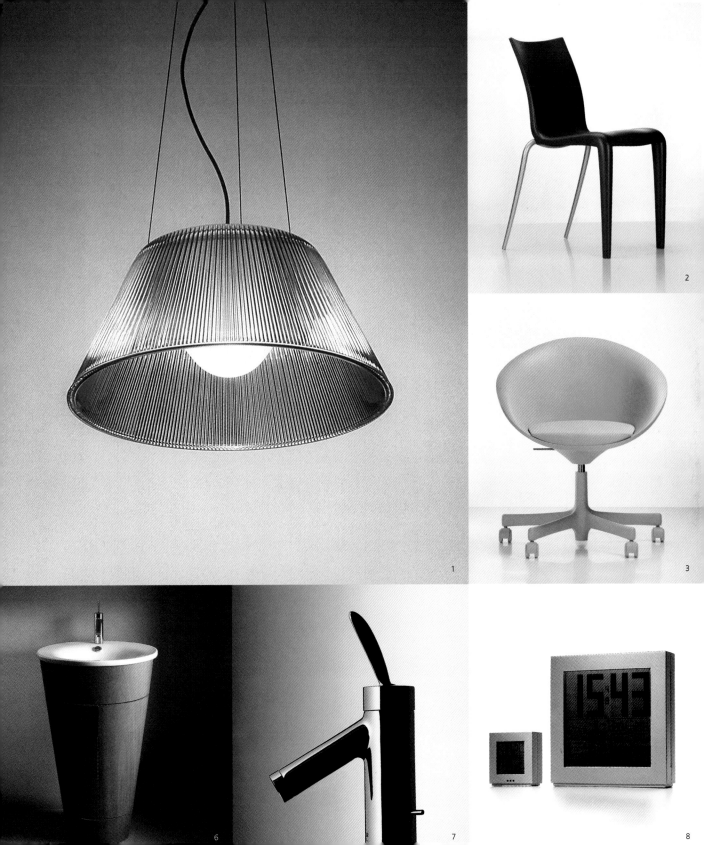

1

2

3

6

7

8

Steelcase

USA | Steelcase, Inc., Grand Rapids, Michigan | Manufacturer of office furniture | www.steelcase.com

A study conducted over a period of more than one year and involving two hundred office workers who had used (and had been instructed to use correctly) the *Leap* office chair, manufactured by Steelcase, revealed an increase in productivity of almost 18 per cent. This increase was attributed, above all, to a decline in problems involving the back muscles; the back of the *Leap* chair is flexible and thus supports the spinal column. In addition, the individual elements of *Leap* can be adjusted and the firmness of the seat modified, thereby further improving the ergonomic benefits of the chair. Scientific field studies resulting in state-of-the-art products have made Steelcase, along with **Herman Miller** and **Knoll**, one of the leading manufacturers of office furniture in the United States. Established in the early twentieth century, the Michigan-based company specialized originally in metal waste-paper baskets and desks. The first really remarkable product series were the oval-shaped desks designed by ▶ **Frank Lloyd Wright** in the 1930s for the open-plan office in the Johnson Wax Administration Building in Racine, Wisconsin. These were among the first examples of ergonomically designed office furniture. The document outlining Japan's unconditional surrender at the end of the Second World War was signed at a Steelcase desk, an act of symbolic significance insofar as it emphasized the furniture's robust reliability.

Since the 1950s Steelcase has enjoyed rapid expansion, initially in the United States, but later throughout the world. In the late 1960s the company launched *Mobiles*, the first series to introduce the concept of systems furniture. It was followed a few years later by *Movable Walls*, the first complete line of systems furniture. In the mid-1980s Steelcase opened its own development centre, the biggest in the entire furniture industry. Around the same time, *Sensor*, the first office chair to respond to movements of the body, was launched, and Steelcase Design Partnership was founded, a consortium of design-orientated companies that included Vecta, Metropolitan Furniture and Brayton International, later joined by the New York-based company Details. At the end of the 1980s Steelcase received an award from the Industrial Designers Society of America for its *Context* systems furniture. Today it is recognized as one of the best-managed companies in the United States. It offers the most comprehensive range of sophisticated office furniture and furniture systems, ranging from simple desk–chair combinations to furniture for waiting areas and built-in furniture.

468

1 *Leap* office chair, 1999
2 *Lightlounge* easy chair, 2003
3 *Freestanding* table lamp, 2003
4 *Pathways* partition system (detail), 2003
5 *Bix* lounge furniture system, 2000
6 Office trolley, 2001
7 *Happening* furniture system, 2004
8 *Cachet* office chair, 2000

1912	Metal Office Furniture Company established by Peter M. Wege and Walter Idema in Grand Rapids, Michigan
1914	Receives first patent: waste bin in steel
1954	Company name changes to Steelcase
1983	Opens new headquarters building in Grand Rapids
1987	Establishes Steelcase Design Partnership, group of companies specializing in high-end design
1989	Acquires four furniture companies: A.F. Sistemas (Spain), Eurosteel (Portugal), Gordon Russell (UK), Sannash (Morocco)
1998	Listed on New York Stock Exchange
2000	Opens Steelcase University Learning Center in Grand Rapids

Products

1915	Fireproof steel desks for Customs House Tower, Boston
1937	Desks for Johnson Wax Administration Building, Racine, Wisconsin, by ▶ **Frank Lloyd Wright**
1953	*Sunshine Styling*, first coloured office furniture
1968	*Mobiles* furniture system
1971	*Movable Walls* furniture system
1973	*Series 9000* furniture system
1986	*Sensor* office chair
1989	*Context* furniture system
1999	*Leap* office chair by **Ideo**; *Canopy* desk lamp
2000	*Cachet* office chair by Peter Jon Pearce; *Bix* lounge furniture system
2001	Office trolley by **George J. Sowden**
2003	*Pathways* partition system; *Lightlounge* easy chair; *Freestanding* table lamp
2004	*Happening* furniture system by **Christophe Marchand**; *Please 2* office chair by **NPK**

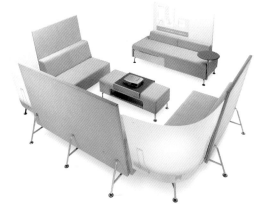

5

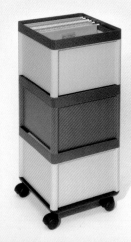

6

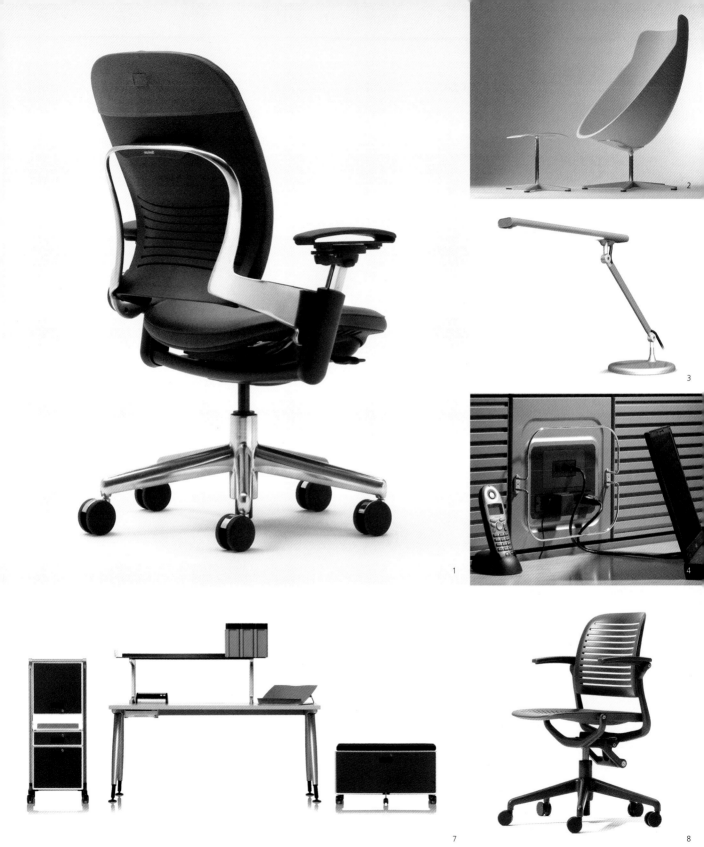

1

2

3

4

7

8

Stelton

Denmark I Stelton A/S, Copenhagen I Tableware manufacturer I **www.stelton.com**

In the early 1960s Peter Holmblad, founder of the Stelton company, came up with the idea of using the cylinder as the basic form for a collection of household goods. He succeeded in persuading ▶ **Arne Jacobsen** to take on the project. The process of developing the idea into the first product took three years. The *Cylinda Line* was eventually introduced in 1967. It included as many as seventeen different items. Placed next to each other, they formed a miniature 'skyline' of high-rise buildings. The series was a commercial success, first in Denmark, then internationally (the company's export quota is roughly 50 per cent).

After Jacobsen's death, ▶ **Erik Magnussen** became his successor. His first design for Stelton, a sleek thermos jug with a novel tilting lid, surpassed all expectations. The jug – today also offered in plastic and in various different colours – is the company's unchallenged bestseller. It is thanks to the successful team of Holmblad and Magnussen and to a long-term rigorous design strategy that this small company has managed to establish itself as the equivalent of **Bang & Olufsen** in the production of bowls, pepper mills and cutlery. The *2000* model, a thermos jug in which a considerable amount of research has been invested, will undoubtedly help Stelton continue its successful course. The flask combines maximum insulation with optimum user-friendliness.

470

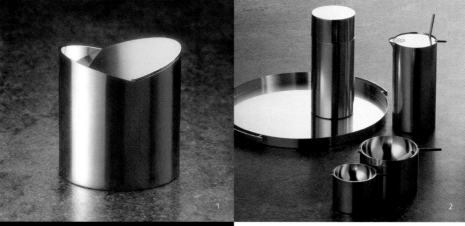

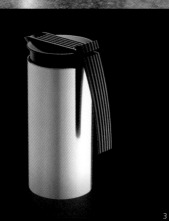

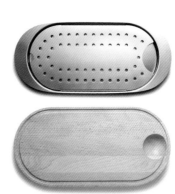

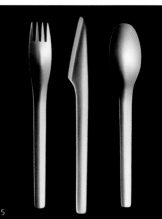

Stokke

Norway | Stokke Fabrikker A/S, Skodje | Furniture manufacturer | **www.stokke.com**

Peter Opsvik, the chief designer at Stokke, works on the basic premise that people who sit on chairs keep moving all the time. Stokke chairs are therefore designed to enable users to move without any physical strain. The result is a range of chairs that, when it was first introduced, was completely different from anything that had been produced before, both in concept and in appearance. Not only have these chairs been ergonomically designed, but they are also unique objects. Apart from Opsvik's designs, the Stokke range famously also includes Terje Ekstrøm's *Ekstrem*, a chair for relaxing in, and *Hippo*, Wolfgang Rebentisch's abstract rocking chair. The biggest chair in the programme is the *Gravity* recliner, with a length of 1.5 metres (5 ft) and a height of 1.25 metres (4.1 ft). It can be adjusted to four different sitting positions by a slight shift of weight, enabling the user to determine his or her individual point of balance. As for choice of material, the company has followed **Alvar Aalto**'s example, and uses plywood, which is robust without looking bulky. Parts that are subject to wear and tear, such as seats, can be replaced easily. The range of furniture for children includes *Tripp Trapp*, an ingenious chair that can be adjusted to suit the child's height as he or she grows older. The product has become an international bestseller since its launch in 1972.

471

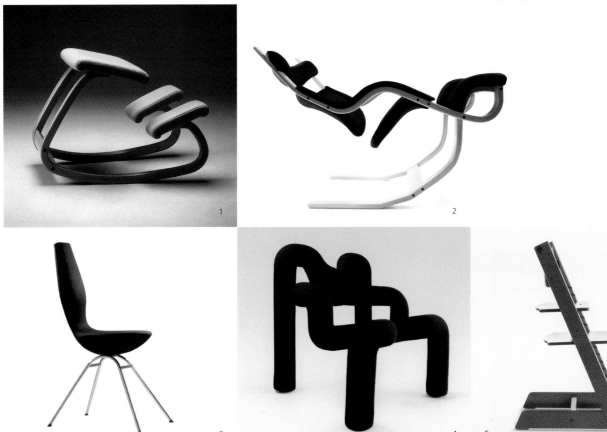

Swedese

Sweden | Swedese Möbler A/B, Vaggeryd | Furniture manufacturer | **www.swedese.se**

The *Tree* coat stand by **Michael Young** and Katrin Petursdottir for Swedese resembles a bare, leafless tree from a wintry forest in Scandinavia. It has become an icon of the Swedish company's furniture programme. The *Twister* seat was created by the young Japanese designer Yuriko Takahashi. Several individual seats can be lined up to form a bench with a surface that is evocative of a gently rolling landscape. The British designer **James Irvine** contributed his simple *Sonia* chair, an understated piece of furniture with distinct echoes of modern Scandinavian design. Michael Young's *Lemonade* chair, by contrast, is an allusion to the cool and stylish early 1960s, when 'good design' was most definitely the order of the day. The *Sascha* suite, designed by **Jeffrey Bernett** from the United States, also takes up this design philosophy, and consists of an easy chair, footstool and daybed. Along with these international designers, Swedese, the family-owned company from the southern Swedish town of Vaggeryd, has recently also commissioned such young Swedish designers as **Thomas Sandell**, whose subtle *Annino* easy chair is available with or without armrests. The Swedish design trio Mårten Claesson, Eero Koivisto and Ola Rune (**Claesson Koivisto Rune**) are also well represented; included in their range is the *Berliner* sofa, created for the residence of the Swedish ambassador to Germany.

Swedese became successful thanks to the designs of the company founder Yngve Ekström, a representative of the golden era of the 1950s and 1960s, when the design ideas of **Bruno Mathsson** and **Alvar Aalto** conquered the world. Such product names as *Lamino*, *Laminett* and *Lamello* speak for themselves. Ekström used laminated wood for his curved designs, a material that was very popular during that period. Its aesthetic appeal continues to this day. A large number of Ekström's designs are still produced, including his *Rondino* swivel armchair, which is comfortable, aesthetically pleasing and has a circular outline that signals its function. Yet even in Scandinavia Ekström's work is rarely associated with his name; his designs blend effortlessly with those of the new generation, which often draw on the iconographic reservoir of modern Scandinavian design. One example is the *Flower* table by Christine Schwarzer – a retro-style object reminiscent of the amoeba-like design forms of the 1950s.

472

1 *Tree* coat stand, 2000
2 *Lemonade* chair, 2002
3 *Rondino* swivel armchair, 1964
4 *X3* table, 2002
5 *Berliner* sofa, 1999
6 *Bend* chair, 1999
7 *Twister* seat, 2002
8 *Sonia* chair, 2001

1945	Established by Yngve and Jerker Ekström
2003	Receives Interior Innovation Award at International Furniture Fair, Cologne

Products

1956	*Lamino* armchair, footstool and table; *Laminett* armchair; *Lamello* armchair and footstool
1964	*Rondino* swivel armchair
1982	*Melano* armchair
	All by Yngve Ekström
1997	*Zao* chair by Komplot Design
1999	*Berliner* armchair and sofa by **Claesson Koivisto Rune**; *Bend* furniture collection by Marten Claesson
2000	*Tree* coat stand by **Michael Young** and Katrin Petursdottir
2001	*Sonia* chair by **James Irvine**; *Annino* easy chair by **Thomas Sandell**
2002	*Lemonade* chair by Michael Young; *Twister* seat by Yuriko Takahashi; *Bilbao* armchair by Joel Karlsson; *X3* and *X4* tables by James Irvine; *Brasilia* table, *Beat* chair and *Cloud* furniture collection by Claesson Koivisto Rune
2003	*Gran Turismo* armchair and *Rodrigo* stackable chair by Claesson Koivisto Rune; *Sascha* easy chair, footstool and daybed by **Jeffrey Bernett**
2004	*Gran Turismo* furniture collection; *Gemini* armchair and sofa by Claesson Koivisto Rune; *Flower* table by Christine Schwarzer

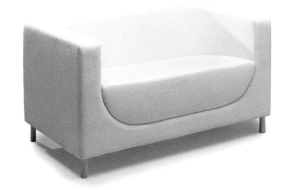

5

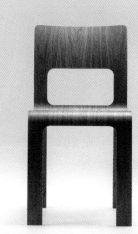

6

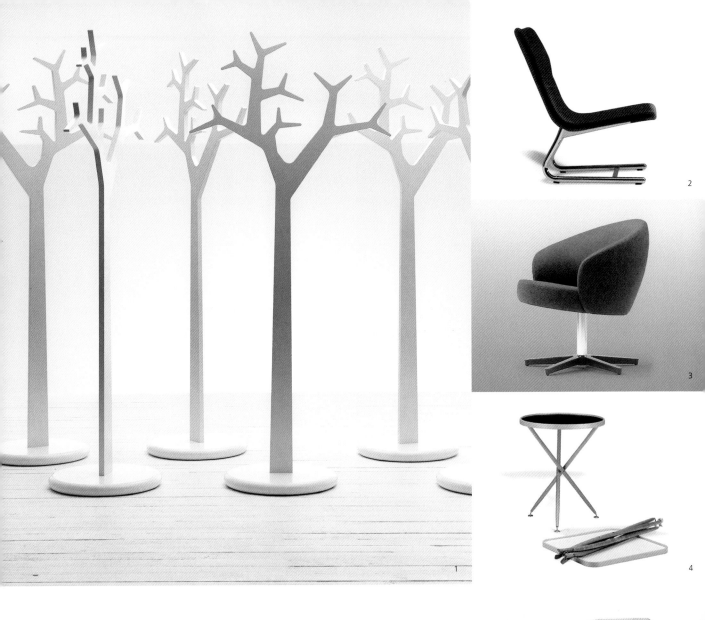

1

2

3

4

7

8

Thut Möbel, *No. 385 Foil Cupboard*, 1994

Kurt Thut's design for a wardrobe made from corrugated aluminium was modelled on an aeroplane, the Junkers *Ju-52*. The construction proved to be too heavy and expensive, however, so Thut replaced the metal with a lighter material that was usually used to make sails, and then edged this material with aluminium. The lightweight wardrobe has no hinges, and its even weight distribution allows the wooden elements to be reduced to an absolute minimum.

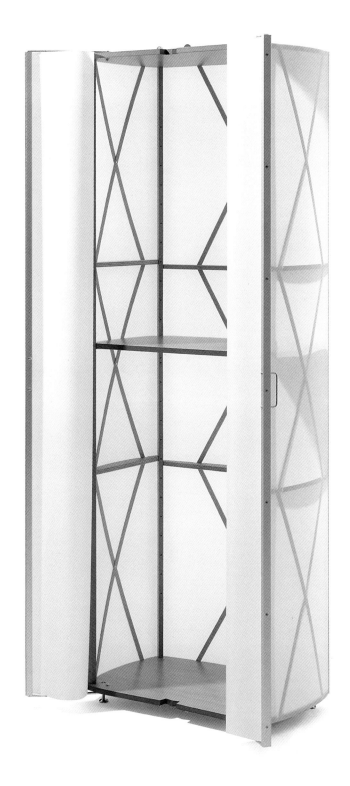

Walter Dorwin **Teague**

USA | Product designer

Walter Dorwin Teague studied art, was passionate about the cultures of ancient Greece and Rome and, like almost all American design pioneers, started out in the advertising industry. He was one of the first to take design to a professional level, and he made a significant contribution to the 'American Way of Life', as demonstrated by, for example, his interior design for Boeing aeroplanes. A trip to Europe in the 1920s marked a turning point in his career. He was strongly influenced by French design, and his subsequent design concepts bore the unmistakable hallmark of **Le Corbusier**. Teague was one of the first industrial designers to open his own studio and work independently. One of his first commissions came from the camera manufacturer **Kodak**, where he later worked as an in-house designer. His box-shaped *Baby Brownie* was available with various geometric patterns on its plastic casing. In the 1930s Teague was commissioned by the oil giant Texaco and redesigned its petrol stations as simple cubes, with large glass fronts and white façades. More than 10,000 were built, and the style copiously plagiarized. For the *New York World's Fair* in 1939, Teague designed the pavilion for National Cash Register (NCR) and succeeded in creating the ultimate icon of the consumer society – a gigantic cash register. In later life he tried his hand at writing and left designing largely to his son, Walter Dorwin Teague Jr.

1883 Born in Decatur, Indiana

1903 Moves to New York; studies at Art Students League

1911 Opens graphic design studio

1926 Travels to Paris; dedicates himself to product design

1928 Works for **Kodak** (until 1960)

1932 Works for glass manufacturer Corning Glass Works; designs *Design for the Machine* exhibition at Philadelphia Museum of Art

1935 Corporate image for Texaco petrol stations

1937 Showroom for **Ford** in New York

1939 Heads design committee of *New York World's Fair*; pavilions for National Cash Register (NCR), Ford and DuPont

1940 Publishes book *Design This Day: The Technique of Order in the Machine Age*

1944 Becomes president of Society of Industrial Designers

1954 Interior design of Boeing *707* jet airliner

1960 Dies in Flemington, New Jersey

Products

1930 *Model 16* automobile for Marmon; *Beau Brownie 2* and *2A* cameras for Kodak

1932 Glass products for Steuben

1934 *Baby Brownie* camera for ▸ Kodak

1935 *Blue Moon* radio for Sparton

1936 *Bantam Special* camera for Kodak; *Modell 517* radio for Sparton

1939 Metal table lamp

1952 *Scripto* pen for Parker

1 *Blue Moon* radio, 1935
2 Metal table lamp, 1939
3 *Bantam Special* camera, 1936
4 *Beau Brownie 2* and *2A* cameras, 1930

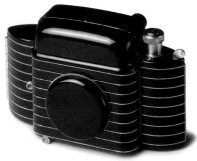

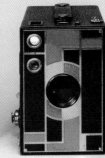

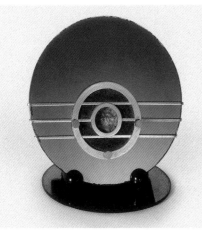

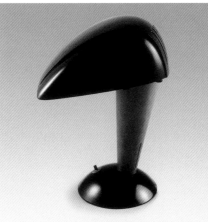

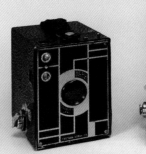

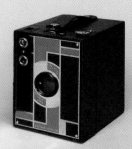

Teams Design

Germany | Product design studio | www.teamsdesign.com

Teams Design's founder, Hans Erich Slany, was awarded numerous design prizes during his career and was himself a member of many award juries. He was a central figure in German post-war design and, defying stylish trends, turned his hand to creating practical, everyday objects. At the *Good Design* exhibition in London in 1965, which was a platform for modern German post-war design, he was represented by a number of products. His Slany Design studio, which today is continued under the name of Teams Design by his former employees Reinhard Renner and Klaus Schön, was one of the first design studios in Germany. Its clients include such well-known names as Bosch, Leitz and Leifheit, the household goods manufacturer with which Teams Design has worked for many years. The studio boasts some spectacular success stories. A good example is the *2000* series of pans (for Silit), with glass lids that allow users to monitor the cooking process while at the same time saving energy. For Kärcher, a major client, Teams Design developed *Robocleaner*, a futuristic robotic vacuum cleaner. As well as everyday items, the company has also designed industrial products, including a fork-lift truck for Still that is visually pleasing and has an oval cabin that gives the driver a panoramic view.

1956 Slany Design established by Hans Erich Slany
1959 Slany co-founds Verband Deutscher Industriedesigner (VDID)
1990 Receives Design Team of the Year title, Design Zentrum Nordrhein Westfalen
1997 Studio name changes to Teams Design
2002 Studio wins its 1000th design award

Products

1958 *Starlet* mechanical carpet cleaner for Leifheit
1965 *Combi E1* hand drill for Bosch
1983 TV camera for Bosch
1990 *2000* pan collection for Silit
1993 *GEX 150 AC* sander for Bosch
1994 *Columbus* thermos jug for Leifheit
1996 Battery-powered hammer drill for Bosch
1997 *GST 100 BCE* jigsaw for Bosch; *R 60* fork-lift truck for Still
1999 *Color Clip* folder for Leitz
2000 *Quickfix* quick-action clamp for Wolfcraft
2001 *GSH 5 E* hammer for Bosch; pressure cooker for Silit; *RXX* fork-lift truck (concept) for Still
2003 Kitchen scales for Söhnle; *IXO* battery-powered screwdriver for Bosch
2004 *Robocleaner* vacuum cleaner for Kärcher; *Pico* wiper and spray wiper for Leifheit

1 *RXX* fork-lift truck (concept), 2001
2 *IXO* battery-powered screwdriver, 2003
3 *Robocleaner* vacuum cleaner, 2004
4 *Pico* wiper, 2004
5 Kitchen scales, 2003

477

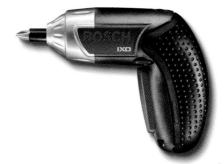

1

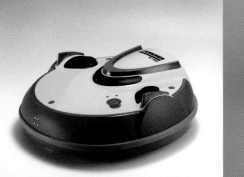

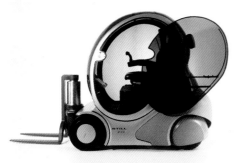

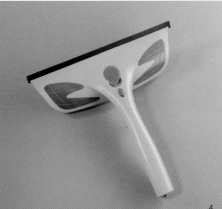

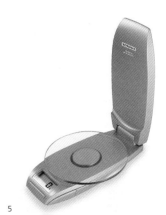

3
4
5

Tecnolumen

Germany | Tecnolumen GmbH & Co. KG, Bremen | Lamp manufacturer | **www.tecnolumen.com**

When Tecnolumen was founded in 1980, it produced only one lamp – the *WA 24* table lamp, designed originally by **Wilhelm Wagenfeld** in 1924. This lamp, also known as the Wagenfeld or Bauhaus lamp, has become a design classic. Today Tecnolumen is still the only authorized manufacturer of Wagenfeld's lamps. While re-editions of original Bauhaus designs remain at the centre of the company's range, it has expanded to include Bauhaus-style lights by contemporary designers. Among the company's 'anonymous' designs that cannot be attributed to any particular Bauhaus designer is the unconventional *BH 23* standard lamp from 1923, which is stabilized by a counterweight. This design feature is reminiscent of work by ▶ **Marianne Brandt**, who used similar construction principles in, for example, the *HMB 25/500* hanging lamp, which she designed in 1925 with Hans Przyrembel. Tecnolumen has also included one of Brandt's teapots in its range: the *MBTK 24*, a design that introduced basic geometric forms into tea rooms and parlours. The Frankfurt Neue Bauen movement, which was also associated with the Bauhaus, is represented by a door handle designed by Ferdinand Kramer, who introduced modern furnishings into the newly built working-class housing estates. Another avant-garde designer from the same period was Eduard-Wilfried Buquet, who patented the flexible connecting elements of his desk lamp. Tecnolumen today equips the lamp with a halogen bulb and houses the lamp's transformer in its stand.

The company has also re-edited a number of designs created after the Second World War in the spirit of the Bauhaus tradition, including the sleek *ES 57* ceiling reflector, which the architect **Egon Eiermann** designed originally for the German Pavilion at *Expo '58* in Brussels. The most appealing feature of this design is the symmetry of its cone-shaped reflector and stand. The *RHa* desk lamp by Andreas Hackbarth and **Dieter Rams** from the 1980s is unsurpassable in its simplicity. The precision achieved in the lamp is equivalent to such accomplished works as ▶ **Richard Sapper**'s *Tizio* and ▶ **Michele de Lucchi**'s *Tolomeo*.

1980 Established by Walter Schnepel in Bremen; initially produces only re-edition of *WA 24* table lamp by **Wilhelm Wagenfeld**

2002 Divides into three specialist firms: Tecnolumen for lamps and accessories; Tecnoline for door and window fittings; Tecnovo for chairs, tables and other furniture

Products

1923 *BST 23* standard lamp by Gyula Pap; *BH 23* standard lamp with counterweight (designer unknown)

1924 *WA 24* table lamp by ▶ Wilhelm Wagenfeld; *MBTK 24* teapot by **Marianne Brandt**; *JA 24* fruit bowl by Josef Albers

1925 Door handle by Ferdinand Kramer; *HMB 25/500* hanging lamp by ▶ Marianne Brandt and Hans Przyrembel

1927 *EB 27* desk lamp by Eduard-Wilfried Buquet; *MSW 27* wall lamp by ▶ **Mart Stam**

1928 *WG 28* table lamp by Wilhelm Wagenfeld; *HP 28* hanging lamp by Hans Przyrembel

1930 *WNL 30* multi-purpose lamp by Wilhelm Wagenfeld; *AD 32* table lamp (designer unknown, France); *WAD 37* wall lamp by Eckart Muthesius

1957 *ES 57* ceiling reflector by **Egon Eiermann** for German Pavilion at *Expo '58*, Brussels

1961 *EE 61* occasional table by Egon Eiermann

1980 *HAM T80* table by Richard Hamilton

1984 *RHa* desk lamp by **Dieter Rams** and Andreas Hackbarth

1988 *Kit TC 88* clock by **Toshiyuki Kita**

1998 *Helios WLZ 98* wall lamp by Zeno

2001 *ES 01* chair by Jürgen Lange

478

1 *WNL 30* muti-purpose lamp, 1930
2 *ES 57* ceiling reflector, 1957
3 *EB 27* desk lamp, 1927
4 *BH 23* standard lamp, 1923
5 *AD 32* table lamp, 1930
6 Door handle, 1925
7 *RHa* desk lamp, 1984

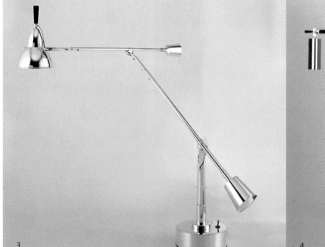

3

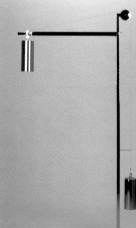

4

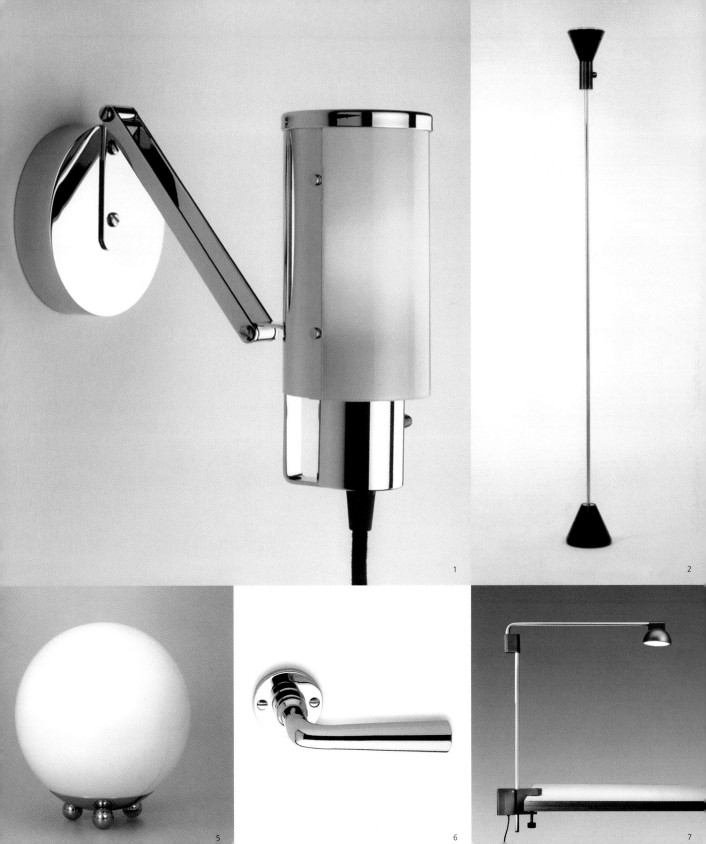

Tecta

Germany | Axel und Werner Bruchhäuser OHG, Lauenförde | Furniture and lamp manufacturer | **www.tecta.de**

When Axel Bruchhäuser travelled from the German Democratic Republic to the West in the early 1970s, he made contact with the grand masters of functionalism: he tracked down **Mart Stam** in Switzerland, visited **Marcel Breuer** in New York and discovered El Lissitzky's family in exile in Siberia. From these people he acquired the reproduction licences that enabled him to form the basis of the Tecta product range. The pioneers of Modernism had waited a long time for their work to reach a wider public. Suddenly, with Tecta, everything changed. Numerous designs, such as Breuer's nest of tables and the 'Fagus' armchair (D 51) by **Walter Gropius**, were produced in larger series than ever before. Bauhaus furniture still accounts for a considerable share of the company's sales. Among the lesser-known Bauhaus pieces are a tea table by Erich Brendel and a cradle by Peter Keler. Other classic Modernist designs, such as elegant metal chairs by **Jean Prouvé** and the innovative *L 10 Anglepoise* lamp by George Carwardine, have long been included. The product range also includes more recent designs, such as the *B 5* single-tube cantilever chair by the artist Stefan Wewerka. Tecta, like **Thonet**, has taken on a similar role in Germany to that of **Cassina** in Italy, **Knoll** in the United States and **Källemo** in Sweden, in that avant-garde design from the inter-war period is combined with contemporary styles.

1956 Established by Hans Könecke

1972 Axel Bruchhäuser leaves German Democratic Republic and takes over company

1982 Establishes chair museum at medieval castle of Burg Beverungen

2003 Opens Kragstuhlmuseum (cantilever chair museum), designed by architect Peter Smithson

Products

1956 *D 49* executive chair by Hans Könecke

1979 *B 1* three-legged chair by Stefan Wewerka

1982 *B 5* single-tube cantilever chair by Stefan Wewerka

1983 *Sammlertisch* (Collector's table) by Alison and Peter Smithson

1984 *Küchenbaum* (Kitchen tree) by Stefan Wewerka

1985 *M 5-1* dining table by Stefan Wewerka; *K 10* tea table by Erich Brendel (re-edition of 1924 design)

1993 *D 23-1 Kragstuhl* cantilever armchair

1995 *M 2* and *W 2* tables

1997 *B 20 Kragstuhl* cantilever chair; *D 24* cantilever armchair; *D 36* 'hover' easy chair

1998 *F 46-1E* armchair and *K 46E* occasional table by Alison and Peter Smithson; *D 14* office chair

1999 *F 42-1E* cantilever lounger

2002 *M 23* and *M 24* cantilever tables; *K 23* occasional table; *M 4R* trolley

2003 *D 82* reclining armchair; *D 35-1* cantilever armchair; *B 33* and *D 33* barstools

1 *M 4R* trolley, 2002
2 *B 20 Kragstuhl* cantilever chair, 1997
3 *B 9* set of occasional tables, 1927
4 *B 5* single-tube cantilever chair, 1982
5 *L 10 Anglepoise* lamp, 1932

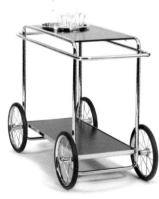

1

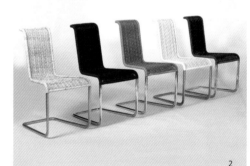

2

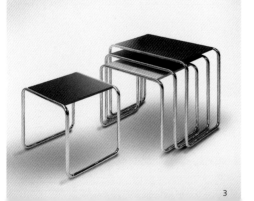

3

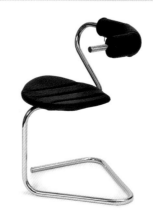

4

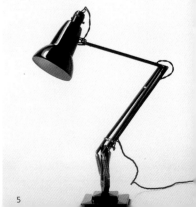

5

Mats **Theselius**

Sweden I Furniture designer

Mats Theselius was brought up in a family of artists. Apart from being a much sought-after interior designer, he is also a passionate collector of everyday design objects and an enthusiastic supporter of Russian products. However, he sometimes tends to make himself unpopular, as was the case when he staged an exhibition that focused on Sweden's dreary satellite towns. Whereas other Swedish designers draw inspiration either from international trends or from specifically Swedish traditions, Theselius is renowned for his playful combinations of the global and the local. His yellow wooden bookcase, custom-built for the *National Geographic* magazine, is famous. The comfortable *Theselius* armchair, which combines leather with unworked iron and which has a shape that was inspired by old Swedish farmhouse chairs, has almost achieved the status of a classic.

One of Theselius's specialities is his use of traditional materials in new and surprising contexts. He moves constantly on the boundary between design and art. His astounding eclecticism has made him not only one of the most highly regarded but also one of the most controversial designers in Sweden. It therefore comes as no surprise to learn that it was the enterprising Swedish manufacturer **Källemo** that first took up his designs.

1956 Born in Stockholm
1984 Graduates in interior design from Konstfack, University College of Arts, Crafts and Design, Stockholm
1992 Participates in *Exposición Universal*, Seville, Spain
1993 Publishes book *Miljonprogrammet* (Housing programme for millions)
1994 Publishes book *Kamrad Mats* (Comrade Mats) for an exhibition in Moscow
1995 Appointed professor of industrial design at University of Gothenburg; participates in *Good Design* exhibition at Athenaeum, Chicago
1998 Develops *Swap your Life* project for Stockholm 'Capital of Culture'
2003 Establishes Design Film Pool agency

Products
1990 *Theselius* armchair; *National Geographic* bookcase
1991 *Hermit's Cabin* for Arvesund; *Canapé* couch in steel and leather
1992 *Chaise Longue*; *Elk-leather* armchair
1994 *Järn/mocca* sheet-steel armchair; *The Ritz* armchair
1995 *Rex* armchair
1996 *Ceramic Carrot Stand*; *Onkel Vanja* armchair
1999 *Ambassad* armchair; *El Rey* chair
2001 *Elektra* armchair
2002 *El Dorado* armchair
2003 *Herbarium* desk
2004 *Sheriff* office chair; *X-Ray* coffee table
All for ▶ **Källemo**, unless otherwise stated

1 *National Geographic* bookcase, 1990
2 *Theselius* armchair, 1990
3 *Onkel Vanja* armchair, 1996
4 *Ambassad* armchair, 1999

481

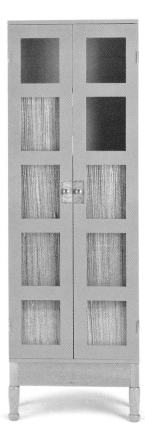

1

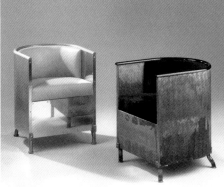

2

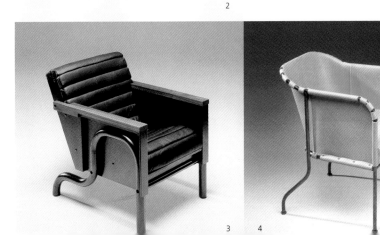

3   4

Thonet

Germany I Gebr. Thonet GmbH, Frankenberg I Furniture manufacturer I **www.thonet.de**

Two achievements in the history of design are associated with the German manufacturer Thonet: one is the development of the bentwood technique of production in the early 1830s, which meant that furniture could be mass-produced for the first time; the other is the production of Bauhaus designs and the first tubular steel furniture, including the cantilever chair, on a large scale. This was a result of the company's collaboration in the 1920s and 1930s with such Bauhaus designers as **Mart Stam**, **Marcel Breuer** and **Ludwig Mies van der Rohe**.

Thonet has always been a family enterprise. The company is currently managed by the fifth generation of the family in Frankenberg, Hesse. It all began with master carpenter Michael Thonet, who set up his own firm in Boppard am Rhein in 1819. In 1842 Prince Metternich invited Thonet to Vienna, where he began manufacturing his *No. 14* chair (designed for the famous Café Daum) using his newly developed bentwood technique of production. This simple, functional chair was easy to dismantle and transport. Michael Thonet and his sons subsequently developed numerous successful models. By 1930 more than thirty million models of the *No. 14* chair alone had been sold.

The principle of 'less is more' is characteristic of Thonet's tubular steel designs of the 1920s and 1930s. The very first cantilever chairs, the *S 43* by ▶ Stam, the *S 32* by Breuer and the *S 533* by Mies van der Rohe, along with many other tubular steel classics, are still produced today. The factories and real estate belonging to the family in Eastern Europe were expropriated during the Second World War, and the Thonet factory in Frankenberg was destroyed. It was rebuilt after the conflict, when Georg Thonet, the great-grandson of the firm's founder, took charge of continuing the family business. Tubular steel remained the company's material of choice. Each decade has produced classics, and from the 1950s to the present day Thonet has collaborated with some of the best-known designers of the time, from Eddie Harlis to **Verner Panton** and from Wulf Schneider and Ulrich Böhme to **Foster and Partners**, Glen Oliver Löw and **James Irvine**. In recent years Irvine has designed the *A 660* chair, which is a contemporary fusion of the bentwood technique with aluminium and gauze.

482

1 *S 64* chair, 1929
2 *S 3001* armchair, 1990
3 *A 660* chair, 2003
4 *214* chair, 1859, and *210* chair, 1910
5 *S 411* armchair, 1932
6 *S 664* chair, 1954
7 *S 1080* folding table, 1996

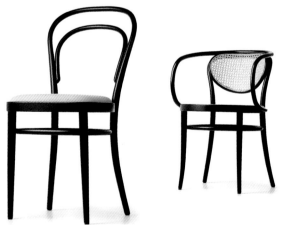

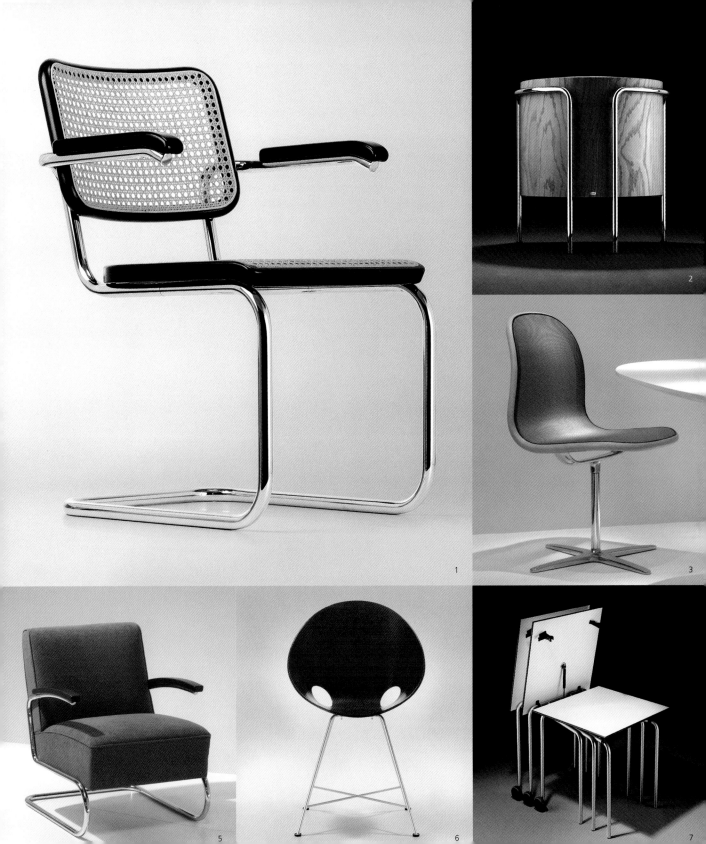

1

2

3

5

6

7

Matteo **Thun**

Italy | Architect and furniture and product designer | www.matteothun.com

In the 1980s, a time when Post-modernism dominated the industry, the Italian designer Matteo Thun advocated diversity and called on his fellow designers to take different historical styles into consideration in their work. A co-founder of the avant-garde Memphis design group in 1981, Thun relied on ornamentation and a mixture of forms in his ceramics. For a long time his often exuberant accessories steered far away from elegant restraint. It was precisely as a result of this approach that he was appointed art director at Swatch in 1990. Thun has also designed bathroom fittings and shower systems for Rapsel, chairs for Brunner and door handles for Valli & Valli.

In recent years Thun has returned to more restrained tones and clearer forms, as in the simple *S. Vigilio* hanging lamp developed for **Fontana Arte** or the porcelain *Dune* series for Villeroy & Boch. Ceramic products and accessories are still an important focus of his work. He collaborates with such manufacturers as **Rosenthal**, **WMF** and Illy. He has also been commissioned to design cups and packaging for **Koziol** and Lavazza.

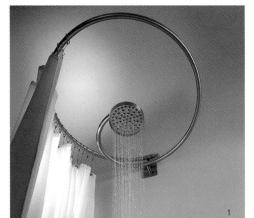

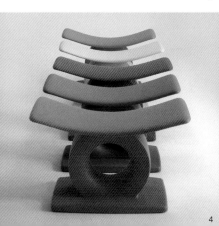

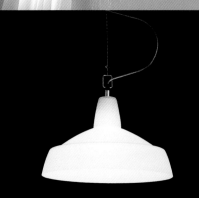

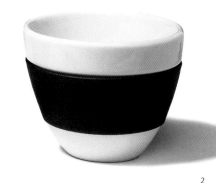

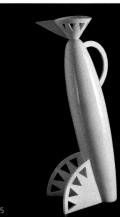

Thut Möbel

Switzerland | Thut Möbel AG, Möriken | Furniture manufacturer | **www.thut.ch**

Unusually for a manufacturer, Kurt Thut designs his own products. When asked about the principles behind his design concepts, he expresses the importance of creativity and open-mindedness: "Whatever sells is allowed", he explains. In 1958 Thut, Robert and Trix Haussmann and Hans Eichenberger founded the design group Swiss Design. It was around this time that furniture from Switzerland began to achieve international fame. Thut drew inspiration for his collection from the Bauhaus and was able to meet the constantly changing requirements of the design industry with an approach that emphasized continuity, imagination and functionality. This is true both of his early work, such as his strictly rational folding swivel tables, ascetic sofas and chair and table combinations, and also of Thut Möbel's designs from the 1980s and 1990s. Some of these designs are by his son Benjamin and include square tables with a single support, adjustable folding lattice beds that adapt to any size of mattress, concertina tables and lightweight cupboards with a frame made of aeronautical plywood concealed beneath canvas. Whatever the stylistic tendencies of his products – whether Post-modernist, Deconstructivist or Functionalist – Kurt Thut continues to offer an innovative and eclectic range of furniture.

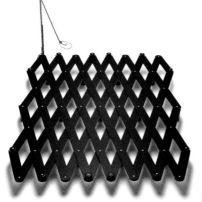

1

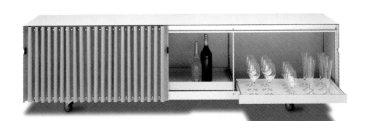

2

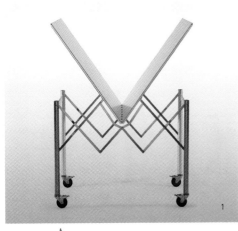

3

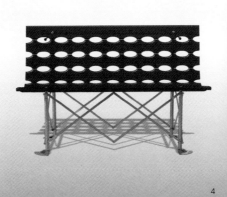

4

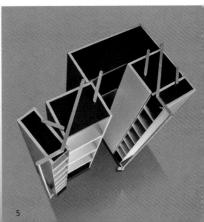

5

TKO

England | Product design studio | **www.tkodesign.co.uk**

Although small, TKO is one of Britain's leading design studios. The fact that the company specializes in high-tech products and in services – two areas with a promising future – may have contributed to its success. In 1996 TKO won the BBC Design Award for *Freeplay*, a clockwork radio that does not require batteries. The product was created for use in developing countries by Trevor Baylis. He gave the radio a form that was neither particularly fashionable nor amateurish and succeeded in creating a robust set that looks as though it will work even in extreme conditions.

The *TKOti* urban hybrid bicycle, with its clean outline, and the *Titan* washing machine (for Monotub Industries), with a capacity that does justice to its name, are also impressive designs. Some of the studio's products have won prizes in Japan, including, for example, *Crystal Mu*, the LCD computer display (for NEC Design), an original design that is reminiscent of a music stand with a touch screen. TKO has established a prestigious clientele in the Far East, including **Sony**, Sanyo, Daiko and Seiko. By contrast, collaboration with British manufacturers is less well developed.

1990 Established by Anne Gardiner and Andy Davey

Products

1991 *Submarine* portable CD player for **Sony**

1992 *Comet* low-voltage lamp and *Slaphead* child's bedside lamp for Daiko Electric Company

1995 *Freeplay* clockwork radio for BayGen Power; *New Wave* microwave oven for Sanyo; writing utensils for Hasbro

1996 *Crystal Mu* LCD computer display for NEC Design

1998 *Inca Microanalysis* computer for Oxford Instruments Analysis

1999 *Millennium Diamond* jewellery case for De Beers

2000 *Titan* washing machine for Monotub Industries

2002 *TKOti* urban hybrid bicycle; *FM800* foetal monitor for Oxford Instruments Medical

2003 *T1 Racer* toy car for Tomy; *Sonicaid One* foetal monitor for Oxford Instruments Medical

1 *Titan* washing machine, 2000
2 *TKOti* urban hybrid bicycle, 2002
3 *Sonicaid One* foetal monitor, 2003
4 *Freeplay* clockwork radio, 1995
5 *Crystal Mu* LCD computer display, 1996

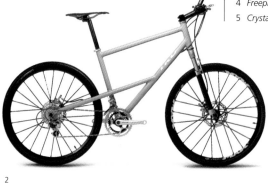

1

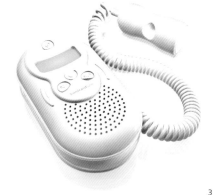

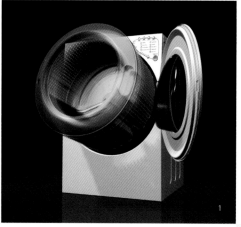

3

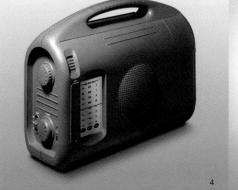

4   5

Tupperware

USA | Tupperware Corporation, Orlando, Florida | Kitchenware manufacturer | **www.tupperware.com**

Tupperware food containers can be found in almost every kitchen. They are hygienic, easy to clean, unassumingly simple in form and, above all, extremely useful. Earl S. Tupper, the company's founder, was fascinated by the possibilities offered by the development of new plastics in the mid-twentieth century. He was one of the first to use the newly developed polyethylene. He proved that plastic was not just a cheap substitute for other materials but was also, in some contexts, far superior. Shortly after the Second World War he launched the *Wonderlier* bowl on the market. Its most impressive feature was its airtight lid, which meant that food could be kept fresh for longer periods.

Tupperware's opaque plastic boxes are light and unbreakable and, although rigid, retain some flexiblility. In recent years the company has introduced dishes and containers suitable for microwave cooking and a range of products made from recycled granulate. New products also include the *TupperChef* knife series and a garlic press. In the late 1940s, in order to ensure that its products reached the right customers – at that time, suburban housewives – Tupper introduced the Tupperware party, a unique and much-admired sales concept that involves demonstrating and selling goods directly to customers in their own homes.

1938	Tupper Plastics established by Earl S. Tupper
1946	Develops use of polyethylene in products; develops airtight seals
1948	Introduces Tupperware home parties
1951	Begins selling products exclusively through home sales demonstrations
1958	Rexall buys company
1983	Tupper dies in Costa Rica
1990	Redesigns classic products

Products

1946	*Wonderlier* bowl; milk jug
1956	Handmixer
1991	*Double Colander*
1994	*TupperCare* product line
1998	*Cereal Storer; Kolumbus* egg storer
1999	*UltraPlus* casserole dish
2000	*FridgeSmart* container series; *Beauty Oyster* cosmetic purse
2001	Baking tins in silicon; *Sharp Star* knife sharpener
2002	*TupperChef* kitchen knife series; *CombiPlus* mixing bowl; *TupperCare* product line for children; *Garlic Wonder* garlic press
2004	*Mini-Max* container series

1 *Garlic Wonder* garlic press, 2002

2 *UltraPlus* casserole dish, 1999

3 Milk jug, 1946

4 *CombiPlus* mixing bowl, 2002

5 *FridgeSmart* containers, 2000

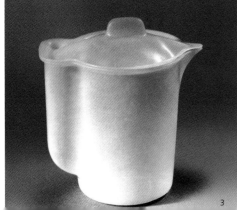

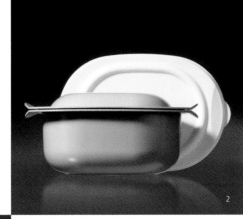

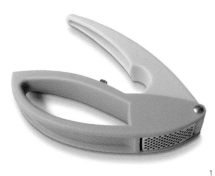

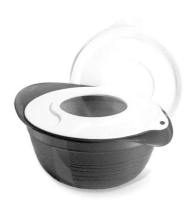

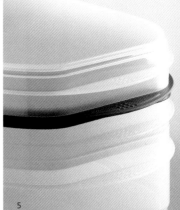

1

2

3

4

5

Óscar **Tusquets Blanca**

Spain | Architect and furniture designer | **www.tusquets.com**

In the late 1970s the architect, painter, furniture and product designer Óscar Tusquets Blanca took on the role of co-editor of the Spanish edition of Robert Venturi, Denise Scott Brown and Steven Izenour's book *Learning from Las Vegas*, a landmark of Post-modernism. Tusquets Blanca was also one of the founders of Studio PER in the 1960s, and in the early 1970s he co-founded the furniture manufacturer **BD Ediciones**. His work displays an unashamed exuberance that is enriched with Dalí-esque ideas, a style that for many years proved too risky for Spanish manufacturers. Yet when impressive designs are required for international projects (such as, for example, the *Milk* glass series by Ritzenhoff, which sold worldwide), this rebellious designer is always in demand.

Tusquets Blanca has created some unusual products for well-known brands, including the complex *Oronda* tea service for **Alessi** and the *Columnata* book shelf, inspired by ancient Greek temples, for **Driade**. His furniture demonstrates a freedom from formal constraints as well as a close affinity with forms characteristic of his native Catalonia, as in the *Metalástica* chair or the *Bib Luz Doble* lamp (both for BD Ediciones). He thus creates a new architecture for living; this is particularly evident in his irregular, sometimes unrefined-looking shelf constructions.

488

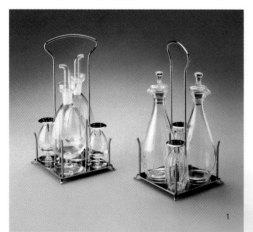

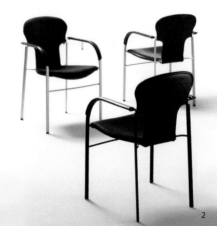

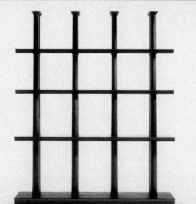

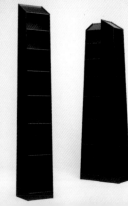

Masanori **Umeda**

Japan | Furniture and product designer

Among Masanori Umeda's most memorable designs, and one that has emerged as an icon of Post-modernism, is the *Ginza Robot* cabinet – a stiff, stylized and somewhat comic figure that alludes to the robots that appear in Japanese science fiction. Equally extraordinary is his famous *Tawaraya* 'boxing-ring' bed, which, aside from its obvious function, can be used as a playpen or a place for conversation. Umeda's designs often made reference to everyday culture with a humour and non-conformism typical of the avant-garde Memphis design group, for which he worked in the 1980s. He was one of the young Japanese designers who, from the 1960s onwards, were attracted to Europe. While in Italy he worked for **Achille Castiglioni** and later acted as a consultant to the office equipment manufacturer **Olivetti**.

In the mid-1980s Umeda returned to Japan and founded the studio U-Metadesign. He also expanded his range of activities to include industrial design. Among his products from this period were street lamps and bathroom fittings (for Iwasaki and Inax) and more traditional items such as *Be-Byobu* (for Ishika Waseishi), an illuminated wall screen made of steel and Japanese paper. Umeda's most successful designs include the *Rose* and *Getsuen* chairs (for ► **Edra**), which take up floral forms and have an almost erotic appeal.

1941 Born in Kanagawa
1962 Graduates from Kuwasawa Design Institute, Tokyo
1967 Works in studio of Pier Giacomo and **Achille Castiglioni** in Milan (until 1969)
1968 Receives Braun Prize for Technical Design
1970 Becomes design consultant at **Olivetti** (until 1979)
1981 Works at Memphis design group
1986 Establishes U-Metadesign in Tokyo
1996 Designs Swatch Art Clock Tower for Olympic Summer Games in Atlanta

Products
1970 *Gemini* bowl collection for **Arflex**
1981 *Tawaraya* bed
1982 *Ginza Robot* cabinet
1983 *Orinoco* vase
     Last three for Memphis
1985 *Star Tray* for Nichinan
1986 *Umeda Stand* lamp for Yamagiwa
1987 *Standard* lamp for Memphis
1989 Bathroom collections for Inax
1990 *Soshun* stool, *Anthurium* occasional table and *Rose* and *Getsuen* armchairs for ► **Edra**
1993 *Baseball* table for Kumax
1994 *Toppo* chair for Kumax
1996 *Be-Byobu* illuminated wall screen for Ishika Waseishi; *Be-Andon* lamp for Yamagiwa
1997 *Yantra-C* vase and *Ombra* vase collection for Marutomi
1999 *Shell* monitor for Marutomi

1 *Getsuen* armchair, 1990
2 *Star Tray*, 1985
3 *Tawaraya* bed, 1981
4 *Ginza Robot* cabinet, 1982
5 *Orchid* armchair, 1991

489

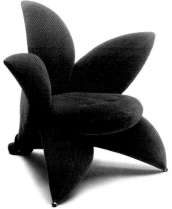

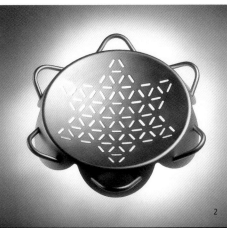

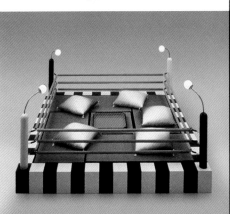

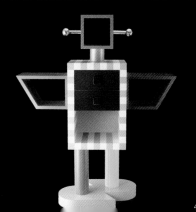

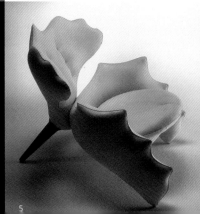

Patricia **Urquiola**

Spain | Furniture designer

Although Spanish by birth, Patricia Urquiola has been based for around twenty years in Milan, where she works for some of the most prestigious furniture manufacturers. She is one of the few successful female furniture designers in Italy. Apart from her mentor, **Achille Castiglioni**, she cites two women furniture producers – Maddalena De Padova and Patrizia **Moroso** – as having had a decisive influence on her career. In the early 1990s Urquiola gained considerable experience as a project manager in De Padova's studio. There she learned from the grand master **Vico Magistretti**, who directed the studio for a long time. During this period she worked with Magistretti mainly on the *Flower* armchair, the *Loom* sofa and *Chaise* and *Chaiselongue*. In the mid-1990s Urquiola became head of Lissoni Associati (the studio of **Piero Lissoni**), and in 1998 she established her own studio. Since around 2002, when she started to work increasingly with Moroso and **B&B Italia**, virtually all her designs have been greeted with enthusiasm by the press as well as by the general public, and she is today regarded as one of the leading lights of the contemporary interior design scene.

Urquiola's designs are fresh, modern and elegant. Although always functional and with a clearly defined conceptual profile, they nevertheless possess a distinctive sensuality. Urquiola prefers gentle forms to hard, sharp edges, as reflected in her striking *Lowseat* easy chair and chaise longue for ▶Moroso and in her ingenious *Fat-Fat* pouffes for B&B Italia, which can also be used as storage boxes. The *Fjord* chair and armchair series for Moroso demonstrates her ability to create unusual yet highly practical designs. The chairs have armrests that appear to grow out of the basic structure, and the strangely divided amorphous shape of the backrests encourages the user to relax. For Moroso, Urquiola has also developed the *Bloomy* armchair series, made of a special polyurethane foam covering a steel frame. The chairs in the series are designed to look like the bud of a flowering plant opening out into full bloom. Another eye-catching design is Urquiola's *Lens* table series (for B&B Italia); its spectacular kaleidoscopic effect is produced by laying a sheet of film between two surfaces.

490

1 *Fjord* armchair, 2002
2 *One* shelf system, 1999
3 *Bague* table lamp, 2002
4 *Highlands* seating system, 2000
5 *Lazy* armchair, 2003
6 *Fjord* chair, 2002
7 *Lens* table, 2004

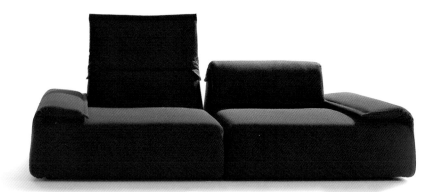

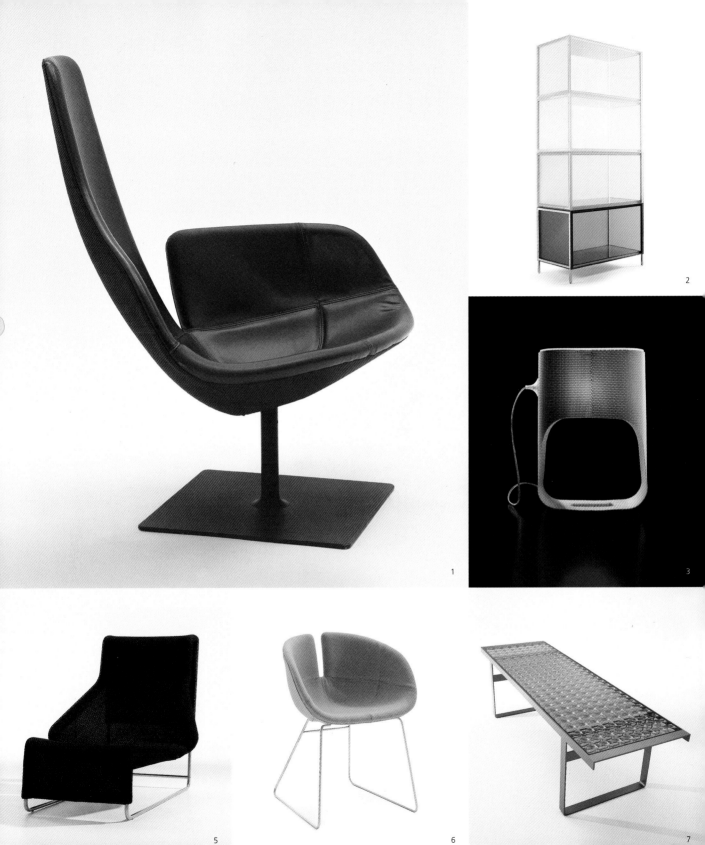

1

2

3

5

6

7

Volkswagen, *Karmann Ghia* coupé, 1955

Wilhelm Karmann was keen to develop a sports car based on the VW *Beetle* – an idea that was rejected by Volkswagen's CEO, Heinrich Nordhoff. Karmann nevertheless commissioned Luigi Segre of Carrozzeria Ghia in Turin to design a car based on this concept. Not long after this, the *Karmann Ghia* coupé was presented to Volkswagen. Segre and Karmann immediately received a commission to start production.

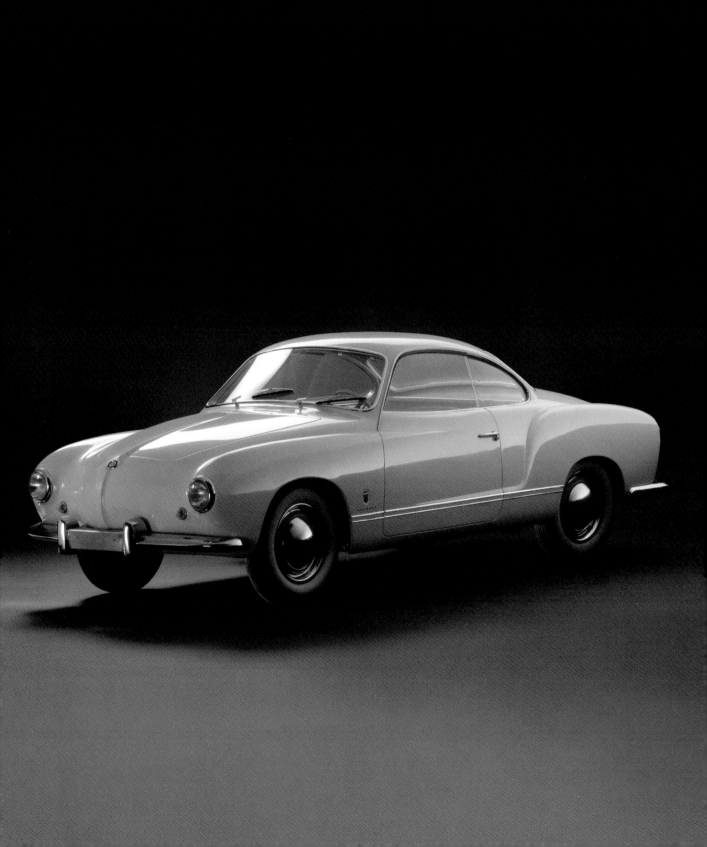

Venini

Italy I Venini SpA, Venice I Glassware and ceramics manufacturer I **www.venini.it**

When the Milan-born lawyer Paolo Venini opened a glassworks with his partner Giacomo Cappellin on the Venetian island of Murano in the early 1920s, he immediately placed himself at the forefront of the artistic glass-blowing avant garde. The company's vases, mosaics, sculptures and lamps were often more restrained, rigorous and innovative than the characteristically exuberant Venetian designs.

Success was not long in coming, in terms of both sales and involvement in major exhibitions of the 1920s. Venini's designs were represented at such venues as the 1923 Monza Biennale and the highly acclaimed *Exposition Internationale des Arts Décoratifs et Industriels Modernes* in Paris in 1925. Venini was always keen to engage leading artists, and their collaboration with his master glass-blowers resulted in the production of genuine innovations. In the company's early years, the painter Vittorio Zecchin contributed highly creative designs; later, the artistic director, Napoleone Martinuzzi, developed several new techniques, including the famous *pulegoso* glass (glass with thousands of tiny air bubbles). The work of the well-known Venetian architect **Carlo Scarpa** was also important. In the 1930s Scarpa found himself under attack from Italy's Fascists. He became friends with Venini and withdrew to the safety of his glassworks. In this quite lonely period, Scarpa developed a heavy, opaque glass as well as a particularly lightweight one that could be worked in two layers. In the 1940s and 1950s **Gio Ponti**'s resplendent chandeliers and shining coloured ornaments also contributed to Venini's fame.

In the early 1950s Fulvio Bianconi had great success with his *Pezzati* vases, a mosaic of coloured squares fused together, and also with the vases in the *Fazzoletto* series, the legendary 'handkerchief' vases. The glass for this series is processed in such a way that the corners of the vases point upwards in neatly folded tips. When Paolo Venini died in 1959, his son-in-law, Ludovico Diaz de Santillana, continued his design strategy. In the last few decades Venini has collaborated with the great figures of Italian design, including **Ettore Sottsass**, **Alessandro Mendini**, Marco Zanini, **Rodolfo Dordoni**, Masimo Vignelli (**Vignelli Associates**), **Pininfarina** and Versace.

494

1 *Yemen* vase, 1994
2 *Ego* vase, 2003
3 *Ebano* bowl, 2003
4 *Pezzati* vases, 1952
5 *Murrine Opache* bowls, 1940
6 *A Fasce Orizzontali* bottles, 1951
7 *Decoro a Fili* vase, 1942
8 *Gotico* and *Orbital* vases, 2003
9 *Fazzoletto* vases, 1949

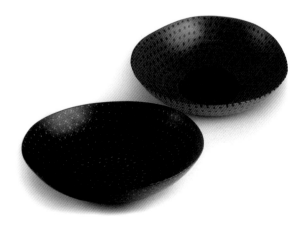

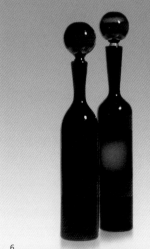

5

6

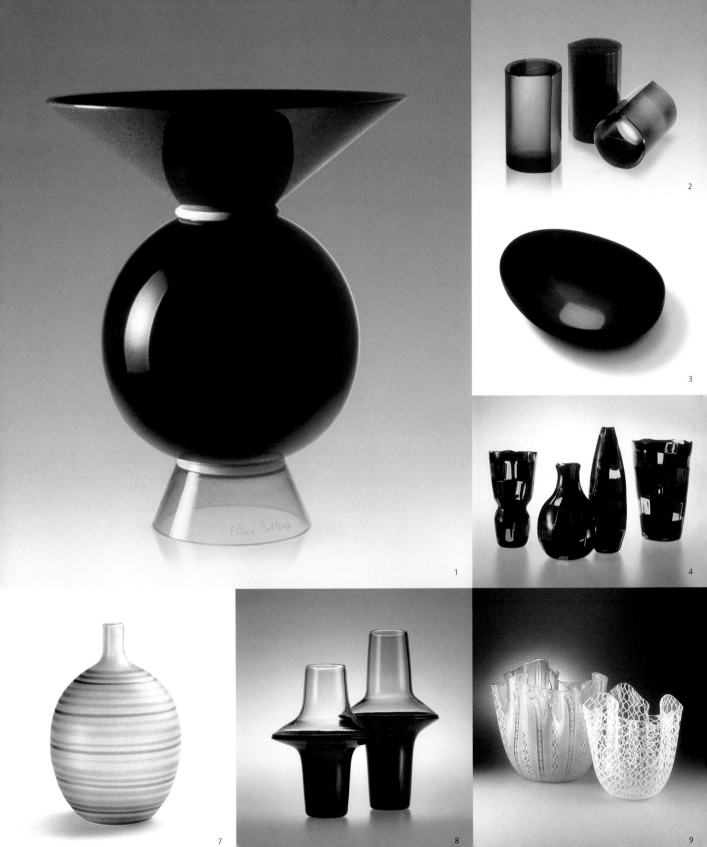

1

2

3

4

7

8

9

Vignelli Associates

USA/Italy | Product and communications design studio | **www.vignelli.com**

Since the mid-1960s the two Italian designers Lella and Massimo Vignelli have been making their mark on New York. They have not only designed the sign systems and map for the city's subway system, but have also created the distinctive logo for Bloomingdale's, one of the world's leading department stores. Throughout this period they have maintained their strong contacts in Europe, particularly in Italy. Among their designs for European clients are *Saratoga*, the minimalist furniture series, based on squares, for **Poltronova** (1964); the solid *Serenissimo* table for Acerbis (1985); and the lightweight stackable *Handkerchief* chair, with a curved seat reminiscent of billowing cloth, for **Knoll** (1985).

Vignelli Associates has also designed exhibition stands and showrooms (for **Artemide** and Poltrona Frau), as well as lamps and a number of other products. The corporate identities the studio created for Knoll International in New York and Cinzano in Turin were milestones in the history of design. Throughout the design process, the studio always takes into consideration the specific resources of the clients concerned and seeks ultimately to provide them with the elegance that has come to be associated with Vignelli products. The common features of many of the designs are a clear structure combined with a confident yet sparing use of colour.

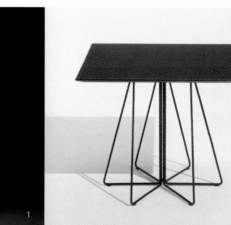

1

2

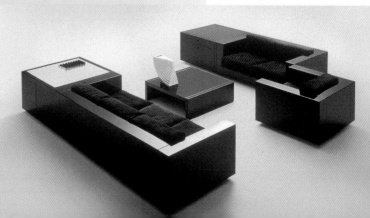

3   4

Arnout **Visser**

The Netherlands | Product designer | **www.arnoutvisser.com**

A healthy mistrust of the way things normally function is the point of departure for much of Arnout Visser's work. His designs therefore often contain an element of surprise. He is a specialist in the creation of mutifunctional objects for everyday use, as in the tiles designed in collaboration with Erik Jan Kwakkel, which are equipped with built-in writing slates or towel holders. Visser loves to experiment with physical properties. In his *Salad Sunrise* dispenser, for example, the oil and the vinegar separate, with the vinegar, being the heavier substance, settling at the bottom. A letter is weighed on the *Archimedes* scales by being placed on top of a graduated cylinder of Pyrex glass (slotted inside another cylinder) that is floating in liquid: the weight of the letter pushes down the upper cylinder, causing the liquid to rise in between the two cylinders. Such ingenious constructions, with instructive overtones, are part of Visser's repertoire. A leading light at **Droog Design**, Visser, with **Hella Jongerius**, **Henk Stallinga** and **Marcel Wanders**, is one of the major figures of the new Dutch design scene. The fact that he has brought some Italian levity from Milan (where he studied design) to northern Europe adds to the appeal of his work. From drinking glasses that look like melting ice cubes, to a fruit bowl on wheels, and bird-like sugar and milk glasses, Vissier has frequently demonstrated his ability to combine intellect and humour in equal measure.

497

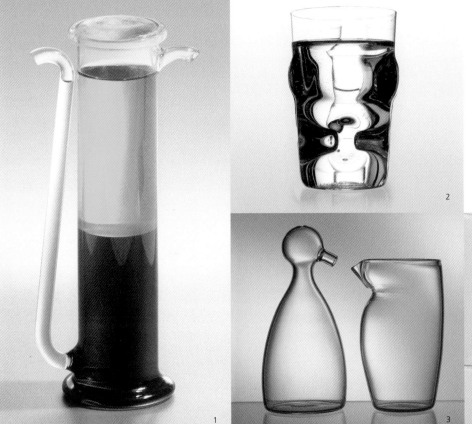

1   2   3   4

Vitra

Germany I Vitra GmbH, Weil am Rhein I Furniture manufacturer I **www.vitra.com**

In the mid-1980s Vitra attracted attention with its *Vitra Edition* series of experimental chairs. Among the most convincing designs were ▶ **Shiro Kuramata**'s *How High the Moon* armchair made of metal mesh, ▶ **Ron Arad**'s *Well Tempered Chair* in folded sheet steel and **Frank O. Gehry**'s *Grandpa Chair*, which has the shape of a traditional armchair but consists of glued layers of card. In the same decade, Gehry also designed the building for the Vitra Design Museum in Weil am Rhein, which houses a large collection of innovative chair designs. An impressive series of exhibitions was staged under the direction of Alexander von Vegesack. Gehry's exuberant museum is part of a long-term programme that since the early 1980s has involved half a dozen prominent architects designing distinctive buildings on the company's site, among them such diverse representatives of the profession as Nicholas Grimshaw (manufacturing hall, 1981), the Deconstructivist Zaha Hadid (fire station, 1993) and the minimalist Tadao Ando (conference pavilion, 1993). Even though Vitra's image is very different from that of most manufacturers, the one thing it has in common with such companies as **Erco** or **FSB** is the presence of an ambitious, open-minded businessman who drives the company's design programme and corporate-identity strategy: Rolf Fehlbaum is one of the industry's most inspired entrepreneurs and has been a major factor in establishing Vitra's pre-eminent position among Europe's furniture manufacturers, particularly as far as offices and public spaces are concerned.

Leading designers who have been collaborating with Vitra over the last couple of decades include the Italians **Mario Bellini** and **Antonio Citterio**, the Englishmen **Jasper Morrison** and Norman Foster (of **Foster and Partners**) and the French brothers **Ronan and Erwan Bouroullec**. The company has been attracting such creative talent since the 1950s, when it obtained a licence from **Herman Miller** in the United States to manufacture and distribute in Europe furniture designed by **Charles and Ray Eames** and **George Nelson**. ▶ **Verner Panton**'s *Panton Chair* from 1967 was a significant contribution to the range. Throughout the 1980s and 1990s Vitra continued to produce design icons – whether Morrison's understated *Plychair* or ▶ **Philippe Starck**'s anthropomorphic *Louis XX* chair.

498

1934	Willi Fehlbaum takes over shop-fitting business in Basel, Switzerland
1950	Establishes Vitra in Weil am Rhein, Germany; starts producing chairs
1976	Rolf Fehlbaum takes over management
1989	Opens Vitra Design Museum, Weil am Rhein (architect: **Frank O. Gehry**)

Products

1957	Obtains production and distribution rights in Europe from **Herman Miller** for Eames and Nelson funiture, incl. *DKR* wire chair (▶ p. 9), lounge chair and *Elliptical Table* (*ETR*) by ▶ **Charles and Ray Eames**; *Coconut Chair* and *Marshmallow* sofa by ▶ **George Nelson**
1967	*Panton Chair* by ▶ **Verner Panton** (reissued 1999)
1987	*Vitra Edition* (incl. *Well Tempered Chair* by ▶ **Ron Arad**; *How High the Moon* armchair by ▶ **Shiro Kuramata**)
1988	*Plychair* by Jasper Morrison
1992	*WW Stool* and *Louis XX* chair by ▶ **Philippe Starck**; *Wiggle Side Chair* by ▶ Frank O. Gehry (re-edition)
1994	*Ad Hoc* office furniture system (with Glen Oliver Löw) and *T-Chair* office chair by ▶ **Antonio Citterio**
1996	*Axion* office chair by Antonio Citterio and Glen Oliver Löw
1997	*Meda* office chair for ▶ **Alberto Meda**
1998	*.03* chair by ▶ **Maarten van Severen**
1999	*Ypsilon* office chair by ▶ **Mario Bellini**
2000	*Transphere* shelf system by Antonio Citterio
2002	*Joyn* office system and table by ▶ **Ronan and Erwan Bouroullec**; re-edition of furniture by ▶ **Jean Prouvé** (incl. *Trapèze* and *Guéridon* tables)
2005	*Level 34* office furniture system by **Werner Aisslinger**

1 *DKR* chair (*Wire Collection*), 1957 (1951 design)

2 *Guéridon* table, 1950 (re-edition 2002)

3 *Ad Hoc Office* office furniture system, 1994

4 *Transphere* shelf system, 2000

5 *Plychair*, 1988

6 *Axion* office chair, 1996

7 *Elliptical Table* (*ETR*), 1957 (1951 design)

8 *WW Stool*, 1992

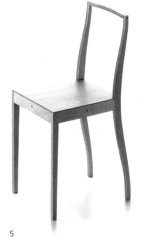

5

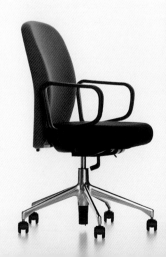

6

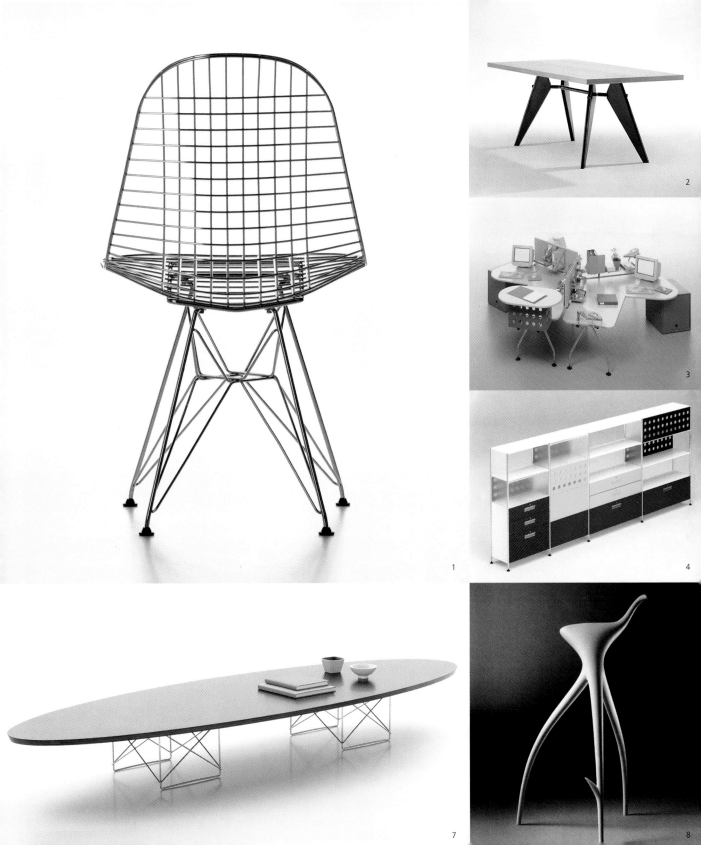

1

2

3

4

7

8

Vogt & Weizenegger

Germany | Furniture and product design studio | **www.vogtweizenegger.de**

Oliver Vogt and Hermann Weizenegger´s basic philosophy is that a product design does not necessarily have to be completely new. Their *Pure Glass* series of glassware for **Authentics** was a novelty for a company that specializes in plastic objects, but heatproof industrial glass had already been used by **Wilhelm Wagenfeld** in the 1930s. The *Imaginäre Manufaktur* (Imaginary factory) project, initiated in the late 1990s, was another example of the designers' interest in experimentation. Vogt & Weizenegger invited design students to create products that could be manufactured by the Institute for the Blind in Berlin and then sold in the adjacent shop. The project was a huge success and has now been running for several years.

Vogt & Weizenegger's completely new concept for a door (for the Dutch furniture manufacturer Svedex) is cutting-edge design. The door is not permanently connected to a frame, but wedged into an opening in the wall using a bolted clamp. Another spectacular design is the *Sinterchair*, a biomorphic honeycomb structure created by a sinter machine, a a special laser developed for use in the automobile and aeronautical industries. This sintering technique makes it possible to manufacture 'made-to-measure' chairs according to the preferences of the individual customer. Each *Sinterchair* is an original.

500

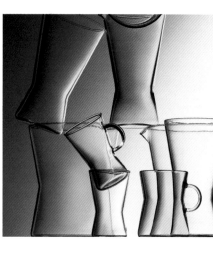

1

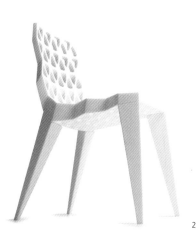

2

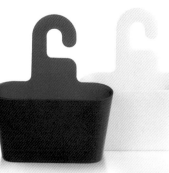

3

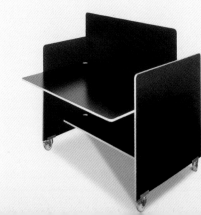

4

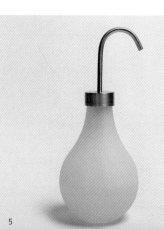

5

Burkhard **Vogtherr**

Germany | Furniture designer | **www.vogtherrdesign.com**

In 1969 Burkhard Vogtherr (with Hartmut Esslinger) was the very first recipient of the Bundespreis Gute Form (Federal Prize for Good Form), Germany's most prestigious design award. The design he submitted was an audio system with plastic spheres that housed the individual elements. This product immediately drew the industry's attention to the young designer. Vogtherr's first furniture designs were for **Rosenthal**, and included a futuristic bedsit unit that came with a wardrobe, a bed and built-in hi-fi system.

Following his apprenticeship as a cabinetmaker, Vogtherr studied industrial design, which opened up new perspectives for him. He has always been fascinated by the design challenges posed by chairs, and today he is very much in demand the world over as a specialist in seating of all kinds. Vogtherr's list of clients includes such leading international furniture manufacturers as Bushy, **Cappellini**, **Cor**, Dietiker, **Fritz Hansen** and **Wittmann**. In the mid-1980s he achieved a breakthrough in Italy. **Arflex** bought his striking *T-Line* armchair, the clear, precise lines of which made it a particular favourite with television talk-show hosts. Vogtherr's thoughtful approach to design has undoubtedly contributed to his commercial success.

501

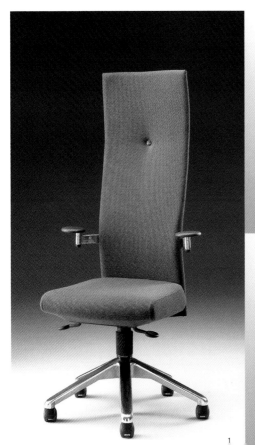

1

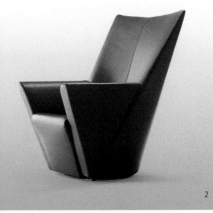

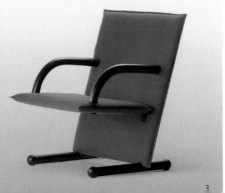

2

3   4

Volkswagen

Germany | Volkswagen AG, Wolfsburg | Automobile manufacturer | **www.volkswagen.com**

The development of car design at Volkswagen (VW) can be traced by looking at the different versions of the *Passat* and the five generations of the *Golf* that have been produced by the company over the last three or so decades. Volkswagen is more closely associated with another model, however: the hugely famous and successful *Beetle*, which came to symbolize the German post-war economic miracle that catapulted the company to the pinnacle of commercial success. Although designed during the Third Reich by Ferdinand Porsche, the *Beetle* went into mass production only after the end of the Second World War. The convertible model was launched a few years later. Its styling and soft top were created by the coachbuilder Karmann. This early example of a recreational car became VW's first cult car. Within a short period of time the company launched the *Transporter*, the *Microbus* and the *Karmann Ghia* coupé (▶ p. 493). The coupé had been commissioned by Karmann from the Turin-based coachbuilder Ghia. The VW management board, although initially sceptical about the project, was eventually won over.

The 1960s saw a number of unsuccessful attempts at combining the technical principles of the *Beetle* with designs for follow-up models and more upmarket cars. It was only when ▶ **Giorgetto Giugiaro** designed the *Golf* and *Scirocco* in the mid-1970s that the company's fortunes took a turn for the better. VW set up its own design department, and its chief designer, Herbert Schäfer, developed a new stylistic approach. The **Audi 50** was added to the VW range and became the *Polo*. The cars that were produced in the 1970s and 1980s had, above all, to fulfil one specific criterium – to radiate an aura of German solidity. Some of the cars from that period, such as the *Golf Cabrio*, achieved cult status. By the early 1990s VW, already Europe's leading car manufacturer, had become a global operator, having taken over Seat in the early 1980s and later Skoda. The company adopted another new approach, making design one of its main priorities (also for VW's subsidiary Audi). Design studios in Barcelona and California steered a new course, turning away from the tried-and-tested, although sometimes pedestrian, stylistic concepts of previous models. New designs, such as the *New Beetle*, were created under J. Mays. With the *Touareg* SUV and the *Phaeton* executive saloon, VW sought to establish itself as a luxury car manufacturer for the twenty-first century.

502

1 *New Beetle* (detail), 1998
2 *Phaeton* executive saloon, 2002
3 *New Beetle Convertible*, 2002
4 *Phaeton* executive saloon (detail), 2002
5 *Transporter* van, 1950
6 *Beetle* compact car, 1938 (1969 model shown)
7 *Golf* compact car, 1974
8 *Lupo* small car, 1998

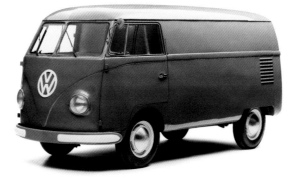

1935 Ferdinand **Porsche** develops prototype of KdF-Wagen (*Volkswagen,* or 'People's car')
1938 Work begins on new factory and new town, Kraft-durch-Freude-Stadt (today Wolfsburg)
1945 Volkswagen automobile production begins in earnest under auspices of British military government in Germany
1953 Opens subsidiary in Brazil
1955 Opens subsidiary in USA
1966 Acquires Auto Union (later **Audi**)
1969 Acquires NSU
1974 Establishes design department
1982 Acquires Seat
1990 Acquires Skoda
1993 Hartmut Warkuss becomes chief designer
1995 Opens Seat Design Centre in Sitges, near Barcelona
1998 Takes over Bentley
1999 Begins constructing futuristic factory in Dresden for *Phaeton* saloon
2002 Peter Schreyer (formerly Audi) becomes VW's chief designer
2003 Production of VW *Beetle* finally ceases; Murat Günak becomes the group's chief designer

Products
1938 *Volkswagen Type 1 (Beetle)* by Ferdinand Porsche
1949 *Beetle Cabriolet*
1950 *Transporter* van; *Microbus*
1955 *Karmann Ghia* coupé (▶ p. 493)
1961 *1500* saloon
1968 *411* saloon
1969 *914* sports car (with ▶ Porsche)
1973 *Passat* estate by **Giorgetto Giugiaro** (later models in 1980, 1988, 1993, 1996)
1974 *Golf* compact car (later models in 1982, 1991, 1997, 2003) and *Scirocco* coupé by ▶ Giorgetto Giugiaro
1976 *Polo* small car by **Bertone** (later models in 1981, 1989, 1994, 2002)
1979 *Golf Cabrio*
1997 *W 12* sports car (concept) by ▶ Giorgetto Giugiaro
1998 *New Beetle* compact car by J. Mays; *Lupo* small car
1999 *Bora* saloon
2000 *Sharan* minivan
2002 *Touran* van; *Touareg* SUV; *New Beetle Convertible*; *Phaeton* executive saloon
2004 *Concept T* off-road coupé (▶ p. 11) and *Concept C* convertible (both concepts)

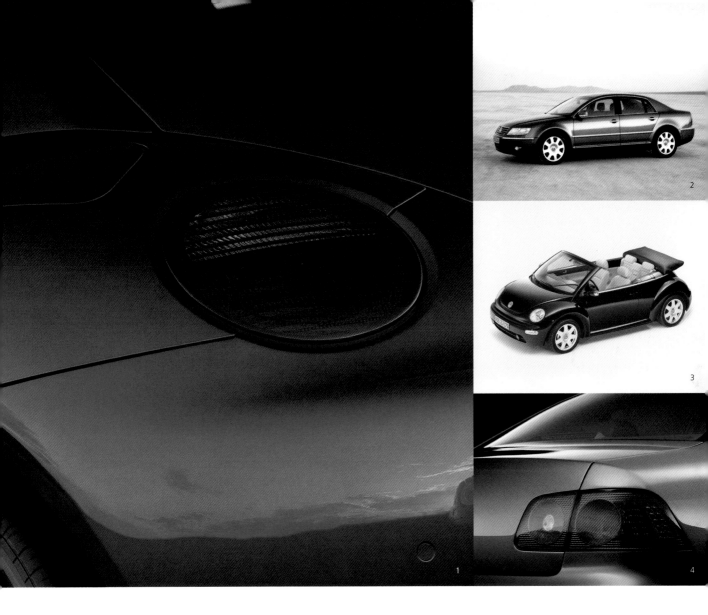

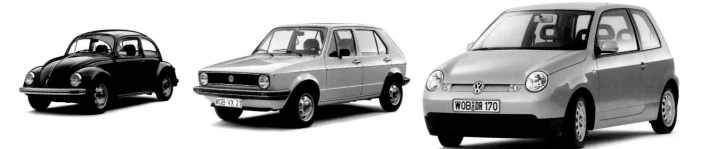

Volvo

Sweden | Volvo Personvagnar A/B, Gothenburg | Automobile manufacturer | **www.volvocars.com**

In the early 1930s Volvo unveiled the *Venus Bilo* concept car, a highly streamlined vehicle. The *PV36* (*Carioca*) saloon, based on the *Venus Bilo*, was launched a couple of years later and also followed the American streamlining principle; in fact, designers from the United States were specially commissioned to create the bodywork. The follow-up models were likewise reminiscent, in size and styling, of American saloons. The *PV444*, presented in 1944, was Volvo's first successful export model. The harsh Swedish climate, rough terrain and long distances prompted the development of cars that would have the ability to withstand adverse conditions. For this reason, Volvo placed great emphasis on designs with a high degree of passive safety. The utility principle also dominated the design of the *445* estate, a new type of car that was launched under the name of *Duett* and became a Swedish automobile icon. In the 1950s Volvo engaged its first in-house designer, Jan Wilsgaard. He established Volvo's image as a producer of reliable 'workhorses', but occasionally ventured into the sports car territory, as with the *P1800*. The most attractive, although unfortunately short-lived, example of the Volvo sports car was the sleek *P1800 ES* estate coupé, with its strikingly large rear window. It was therefore sometimes referred to as 'Snow White's coffin'. The estate version of the *240/260* range became the epitome of the ideal family car. Its massive front was modelled on the *VESC* (Volvo Experimental Safety Car) of the early 1970s; this stylistic feature was to dominate Volvo design for many years.

In the mid-1970s Volvo won a design competition organized by the Museum of Modern Art (MoMA) in New York for a new taxicab. This design was never put into production, however, much to the regret of everyone involved in the competition. A few years later, the *700* series, the company's first luxury estate, designed by Wilsgaard, was launched. Volvo's name came to be associated with very high standards of comfort and safety. In the 1990s the new chief designer, Peter Horbury, changed the company's approach to design. Volvo sought to target new customer groups by emphasizing softer lines. The curving lines of the tail lights of the *V70* estate, for example, are reminiscent of designs by **Alvar Aalto**. The coupé and convertible versions of the same model – created by the Design Center in California – focused on the fun aspect of driving. In 1999 Volvo was bought by Ford. Experimental studies for a car designed for women drivers and for a fully glazed estate were regarded as investments in Volvo's future.

504

1926	Established by Assar Gabrielsson and Gustav Larson in Gothenburg
1935	Company goes public
1959	Introduces first three-point safety belt
1974	Replaces assembly-line production with team production
1977	Introduces first catalytic converter with Lambda sensor
1979	Participates in Ariane space programme
1991	Peter Horbury becomes chief designer
1994	Opens Design Center in California
1999	**Ford** takes over company

Products

1927	*ÖV4* (*Jakob*) small car
1935	*PV36* (*Carioca*) saloon
1944	*PV444* saloon
1950	*Duett* estate
1956	*P120 Amazon* saloon
1960	*P1800* coupé
1962	*P22* estate
1966	*144* saloon
1970	*P1800 ES* estate coupé
1972	*VESC* (Volvo Experimental Safety Car)
1974	*244* saloon (until 1993)
1982	*760* saloon
1985	*760* estate; *480* coupé
1990	*940* saloon
1991	*850* saloon
1995	*S40* saloon
1996	*V70* estate (later model in 2000)
1997	*C70* coupé by Peter Horbury
1998	*S80* saloon
2000	*SCC* (Safety Concept Car)
2002	*XC90* SUV; *ACC2* (Adventure Concept Car 2)
2003	*YCC* (Your Concept Car); *VCC* (Versatility Concept Car)
2004	*S40* saloon; *V50* estate
2005	*C70* convertible

1 *VCC* (Versatility Concept Car), 2003
2 *SCC* (Safety Concept Car), 2000
3 *ACC2* (Adventure Concept Car 2; interior), 2002
4 *S80* saloon, 1998
5 *V70* estate, 2000
6 *P120 Amazon* saloon, 1956
7 *P1800 ES* estate coupé, 1970

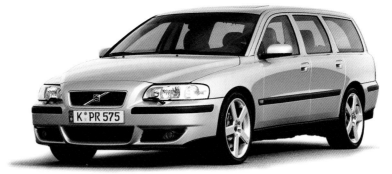

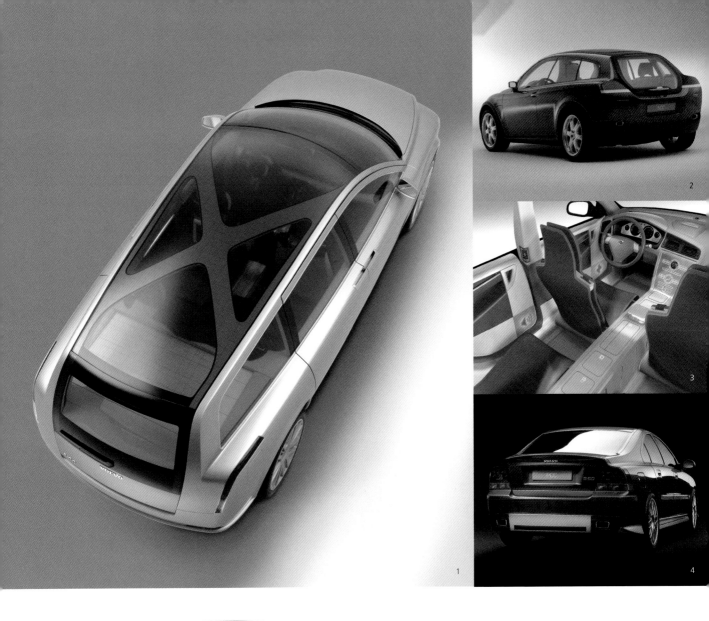

1

2

3

4

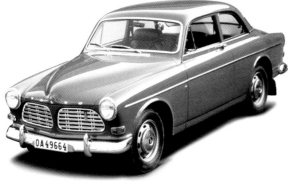

6

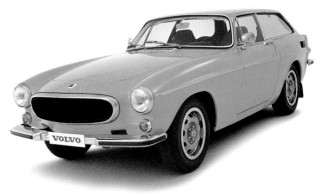

7

Marcel Wanders, *Foam Bowl*, 1997

The Dutch designer Marcel Wanders achieves unusual effects by using traditional techniques in an unconventional way. For his *Foam Bowl* he immersed a natural sponge in liquid porcelain. During the firing process, the sponge dissolves, but its irregular biomorphic structure is still clearly visible in the finished bowl.

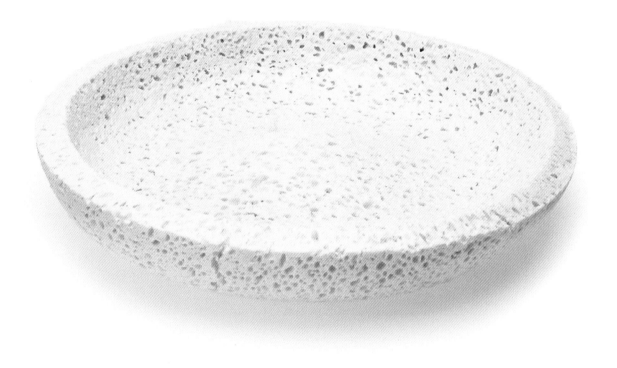

Wilhelm **Wagenfeld**

Germany | Product designer

Wilhelm Wagenfeld was one of the first German product designers. His most famous object, designed in collaboration with Carl J. Jucker at the Bauhaus in the mid-1920s, is a table lamp with a glass base and a shade of white opaque glass. The small, delicate lamp (today available as model *WG 24* at **Tecnolumen**) is as simple and straightforward as a street lamp and has come to symbolize the minimalist style of design that evolved in Germany. It is virtually synonymous with classic Bauhaus and is a designer product *par excellence*. Wagenfeld claimed that unassuming modesty was the most important characteristic of everyday objects; in other words, they should be practical, inexpensive and aesthetically pleasing. He created a number of objects of such sophisticated modesty in glass, plastic and metal (he was a silversmith by training). All his products are of the very highest design standards, as is evident in such pieces as a zigzag-shaped ink bottle (for Pelikan), the *83* cutlery series (for **Pott**) and *Form 3600* cutlery (for **WMF**).

Wagenfeld began studying at the Bauhaus metal workshop under László Moholy-Nagy in the early 1920s. He worked with **Marianne Brandt**. When the Bauhaus moved to Dessau in 1926, he became head of its workshop there. While many Bauhaus designers were forced to leave Germany after Adolf Hitler came to power in 1933, Wagenfeld was allowed to continue his work. During the early 1930s he taught at the Berlin Staatliche Kunsthochschule. He experimented with pressed glass – a material with a negative, 'cheap' image – and used it in designs for Jenaer Glaswerk. The heat-proof covered bowls that he designed in the late 1930s have become kitchen icons, as have his stackable *Kubus* storage containers. After the Second World War Wagenfeld resumed his successful career in design and worked for **Rosenthal** and **Braun**, among other companies. In the mid-1950s he designed a record player for Braun that was used in the company's famous *Phonosuper SK4* radio/record player. It was also used in his own portable *Combi* radio/record player, which had softly rounded edges and oblique lines. The design of the *Combi* still looks amazingly modern to this day. Some of Wagenfeld's most successful designs were for tableware, and include a butter dish and the *Max und Moritz* salt and pepper shakers (for WMF).

508

1 *WG 24* table lamp, 1924

2 *Form 3600* cutlery, 1952

3 *Max und Moritz* salt and pepper shakers, 1952

4 Tea service, 1932

5 *Combi* radio/record player, 1955

6 *Kubus* storage containers, 1938

7 *Model 83* cutlery, 1950

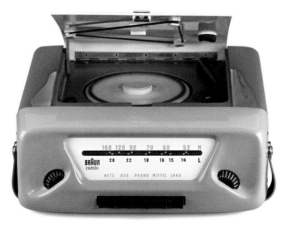

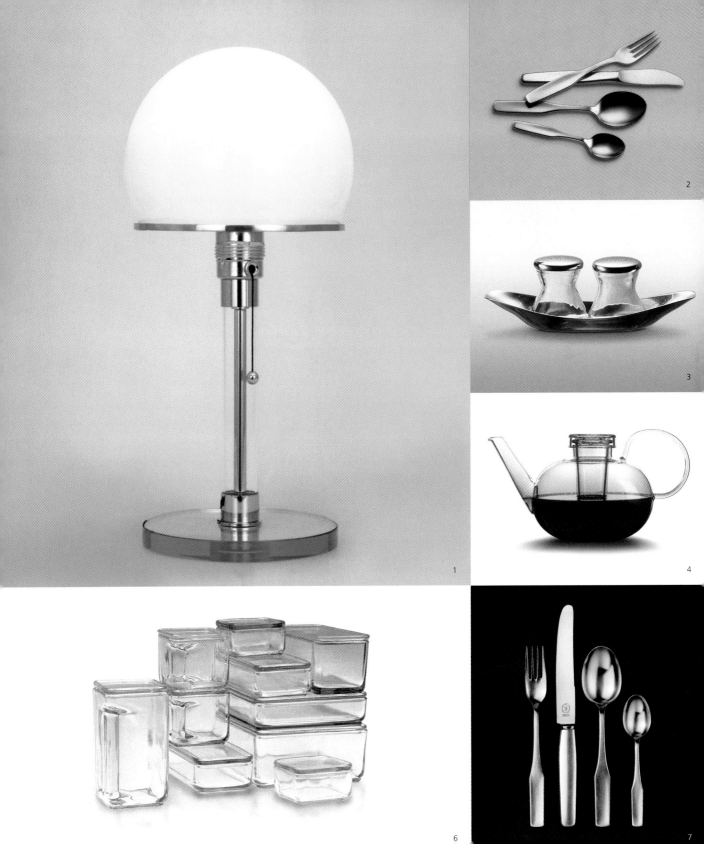

1

2

3

4

6

7

Marcel **Wanders**

The Netherlands | Furniture and product designer | www.marcelwanders.com

"I'm inspired by things that already exist", says Marcel Wanders in a matter-of-fact way, knowing full well that he will not be branded a plagiarist. The Dutch designer believes that there is no respect for tradition in modern society. He is convinced, however, that it is precisely such tradition that gives people a feeling of security and warmth. Wanders studied product design at four different design academies in The Netherlands and Belgium and is among the best-known representatives of contemporary design in the region. Consistent with his belief in the importance of tradition, he creates tried-and-tested objects that have an unexpected twist to them. His *Knotted Chair*, for example, combines a traditional form and the ancient technique of knotting with space-age material – carbon fibre coated with an epoxy resin. The source material for his *Foam Bowl* (▶ p. 507) is a natural sponge that has been immersed in a liquid porcelain mixture. The sponge itself dissolves during the firing process, leaving behind the imprint of its delicate structure.

Wanders won international acclaim with his designs for **Droog Design**. In the mid-1990s he founded his own company, Wanders Wonders. He sold the firm in 2001 (today known as **Moooi**; Wanders is its art director) and established the Marcel Wanders Studio. He is adept at creating products of poetic simplicity, a skill he shares with other representatives of avant-garde Dutch design. The plain, unassuming forms of his works are a unique mixture of traditional and unconventional elements. His *V.I.P. Chair*, for example, conveys lightness, despite having somewhat bulky legs reminiscent of flared trousers. Other Wanders designs that create such visual contrasts include *Birdhouse*, which consists of a pitched roof with a suspended tray.

The *Big Shadow* standard lamp series (for **Cappellini**) is another playful treatment of visual perceptions and expectations. The lamps resemble traditional table lamps in form, but their size is that of standard lamps. The visual anomaly has a slightly unsettling but nevertheless appealing effect. Wanders has a superb command of a wide variety of styles, yet all his designs bear his unmistakable hallmark. He shuns pure functionality and is not interested in the mass market. He claims that he simply wants to be the best designer that his abilities permit.

510

1   *Big Shadow* standard lamps, 1998

2   *Flower Chair*, 2001

3   *Knotted Chair*, 1996

4   *V.I.P. Chair*, 2000

5   *Set Up Shades* standard lamp, 1989

6   *Flare* table, 2003

7   *Egg* vase, 1997

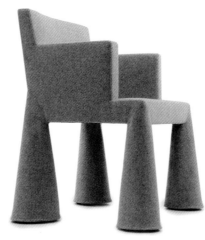

4

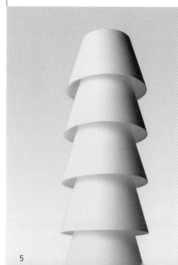

5

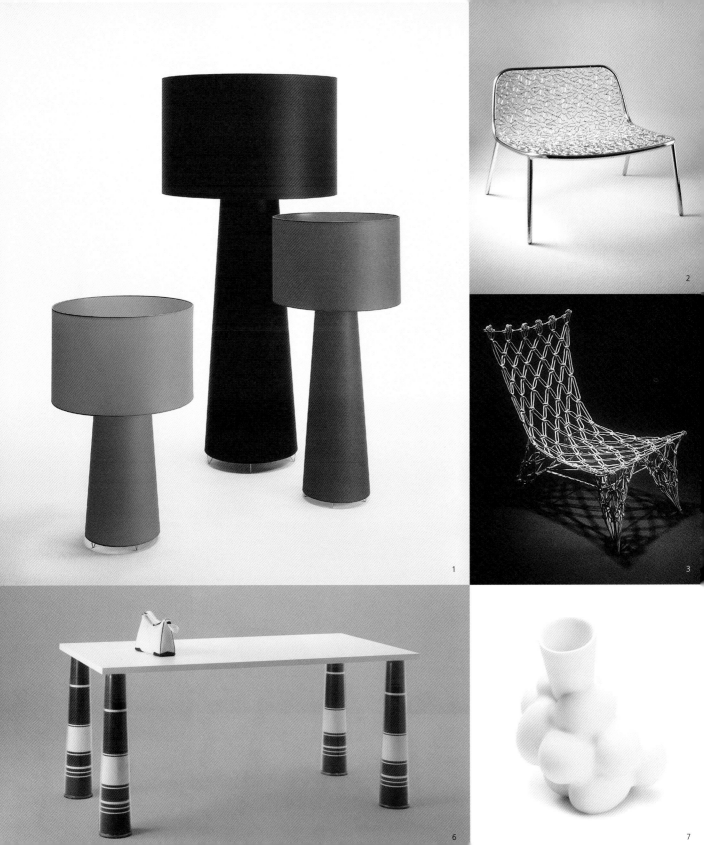

1

2

3

6

7

Hans J. **Wegner**

Denmark I Furniture designer

One of Hans Jørgen Wegner's design principles was that a piece of furniture should still be interesting even when viewed from the back. In the mid-1930s, aged twenty-two, Wegner began his studies at the Copenhagen School of Applied Arts. During the Second World War he worked for **Arne Jacobsen** and Erik Møller, before opening his own studio in 1943. Immediately after the war he held an exhibition with Børge Mogensen, a lifelong friend. Wegner's career is closely associated with the Copenhagen Cabinetmakers' Guild annual exhibition, where he was frequently awarded design prizes. Mogensen and Wegner represented a new type of cabinetmaker, referred to as a 'form-giver'. In order to execute their design ideas, they recruited the very best craftsmen. Wegner's principle was to reduce old chairs to their basic framework, which he then used in his experiments. His unconventional interpretation of the English Windsor chair, for example, caused quite a sensation in the mid-1940s. It was manufactured by PP Møbler under the name of *Peacock* chair. Wegner himself did not give names to his designs. The *Round* chair was his greatest success. Modelled on Chinese chairs, the design is characterized by graceful lines, such as the crescent formed by the merging back and armrests. Despite its elegance, it was possible to mass-produce the chair. When *Interior* magazine in the United States featured Wegner's *pièce de résistance* on its title page in 1950, one customer alone ordered four hundred copies of the *Round* chair. Wegner's success story had begun. By the mid-1950s his furniture was manufactured by **Fritz Hansen** and no fewer than five other companies, all of which set up a joint distribution company to keep abreast of the soaring export demand.

Today, numerous Wegner designs are sold by Danish firms, including PP Møbler and Carl Hansen. Wegner's work comprises around five hundred chairs (he reworked some models many times). He created numerous innovative designs, among them the *Valet* chair, which has a backrest in the shape of a coat hanger, the *CH 07* three-legged shell chair and the *Circle* armchair, which has castors on its back legs, enabling it to be moved easily using the front legs like the handles of a wheelbarrow. Wegner's tubular steel, plywood and upholstered furniture was less successful, although his *Ox* armchair from the late 1950s is an attractive combination of comfort and expressiveness.

512

1 *Ox* armchair, 1958
2 *Valet* chair, 1953
3 *Flagline* armchair, 1950
4 Three-legged shell chair (*CH 07*), 1963
5 *Cowhorn* chair (*CH 29*), 1952
6 *Y* chair (*CH 25*), 1950
7 *Circle* armchair, 1986
8 *Round* chair, 1949

1914 Born in Tønder, Jutland
1927 Begins apprenticeship as cabinetmaker
1936 Studies furniture design at School of Applied Arts, Copenhagen
1938 Participates in exhibition of Copenhagen Cabinetmakers' Guild, (winning 27 prizes by 1968)
1940 Works for **Arne Jacobsen** and Erik Møller; interior of Århus Town Hall
1943 Opens own studio in Gentofte
1946 Teaches design at School of Applied Arts, Copenhagen
1994 Retrospective held at Danish Design Centre

Products
1944 Rocking chair for Tarm; *China Chair* for **Fritz Hansen**
1947 *Peacock* chair for PP Møbler
1949 *Round* chair for Johannes Hansen (re-edition at PP Møbler, 1992); folding easy chair for hanging up and *512* chaise longue for PP Møbler
1950 *Flagline* armchair for Getama; *Y* chair for Carl Hansen (today *CH 25*)
1952 *Cowhorn* chair (re-edition as *CH 29* at Carl Hansen)
1953 *Valet* chair for Johannes Hansen (re-edition at PP Møbler, 1992)
1955 Swivel office chair for Johannes Hansen (re-edition at PP Møbler, 1991)
1958 *Ox* armchair for Johannes Hansen (re-edition at Eric Jørgensen)
1963 Three-legged shell chair for Johannes Hansen (re-edition as *CH 07* at Carl Hansen)
1965 Easy chair for PP Møbler
1976 *Wegner* lamp for **Louis Poulsen**
1986 *Circle* armchair for PP Møbler
1988 Rocking chair for PP Møbler

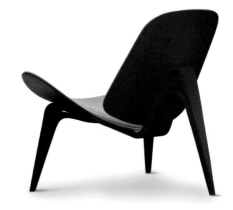

4

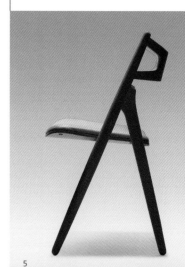

5

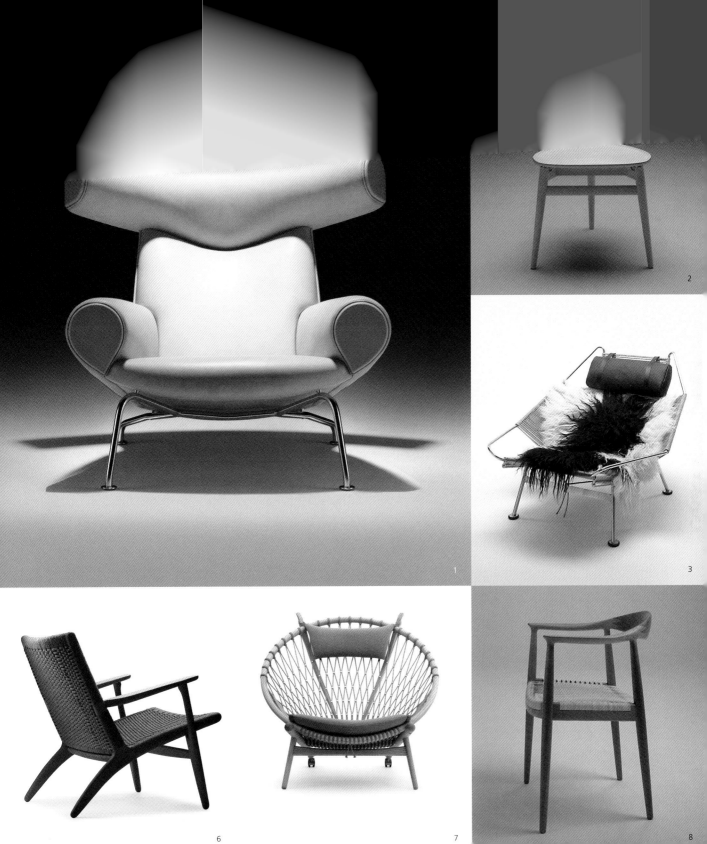

1

2

3

6

7

8

Wellis

Switzerland | Wellis AG, Willisau | Furniture manufacturer | **www.teambywellis.com**

For Egon Babst, managing director of the Swiss furniture manufacturer Wellis, an essential precondition for good design is to be courageous enough to work with designers who are prepared to push boundaries and challenge ideas. The entire product range of the prestigious Team by Wellis brand reflects this spirit of risk-taking, but it is perhaps best exemplified by the highly successful *Volare* system of office and living-room furniture by Kurt Erni. The system consists of numerous modules, including shelves, sideboards and partitions, that can be used flexibly to suit individual requirements. The elements are made of such high-quality materials as light maple wood, cool aluminium and shimmering glass. The series has received numerous design prizes. Wellis places great emphasis on innovation, as demonstrated again by Erni's products, including his *Container* storage system, in which he uses clear and frosted glass and walnut. The delicate *ErRo* chair, a moulded seat mounted on a graceful metal frame, combines formal restraint and innovative technology. This combination of elegant simplicity and practical detail makes the furniture appear aesthetically timeless.

Founded in the early 1930s by Albert Babst, Wellis initially produced country-style furniture. In the late 1980s Albert's sons, Kurt and Egon, transformed the company into a high-tech manufactory, but with an emphasis on such traditional Swiss qualities as durability and accuracy. The firm began to be showered with design awards. Wellis has collaborated increasingly with such respected designers as Daniel Kübler, **Christophe Marchand**, **Hannes Wettstein**, Hanspeter Wirth and Ulf Moritz. Erni, chief designer since 1986, has mastered the art of reductionism, a skill he passes on to his team. Stylish frivolity and gadgetry are taboo, with the result that the range can sometimes appear somewhat austere. The overall impression, however, is elegant, distinctive and highly unified.

1931 Established in Willisau
1936 Starts producing furniture for the home
1964 Establishes design office Team Möbel
1988 Launches Team by Wellis label
1990 Team Möbel moves to Wellis's base at Willisau
1995 Introduces upholstered furniture line by Team by Wellis
1998 Launches Room by Wellis collection
2002 Extends collection to include office furniture

Products
1986 *Triangolo* product line
1988 *Scaletta* product line
1989 *Girotondo* bed by Leo Laube and Kurt Erni
1990 *Ripiano* furniture system
1995 *Ilion* sofa by Beck & Rosenburg
1997 *Vetrina* glass cabinet series; *Campus* upholstered furniture
1999 *Dea* armchair by Hanspeter Wirth; *Container* storage system by Kurt Erni
2001 *MaRe* chaise longue by **Christophe Marchand**; *Libero* bed and *Arioso* and *Spazio* cupboards by Kurt Erni
2002 *LiDa* sofa by Daniel Kübler; *ErRo* chair and *ErQu* table by Kurt Erni
2003 *UiMo* sofa by Ulf Moritz; *Chillout* sofa by **Hannes Wettstein**; *KuFo* chair, *Volare* furniture system, *SaMo* occasional table, *VaRe* shelf system, *ArEs* work table and *ErOf* container trolley by Kurt Erni

1 *Container Cuboid* and *Container Round*, 1999
2 *MaRe* chaise longue, 2001
3 *Chillout* sofa, 2003
4 *ErRo* chair, 2002
5 *ErQu* table, 2002
6 *UiMo* sofa, 2003
7 *Arioso* cupboard, 2001

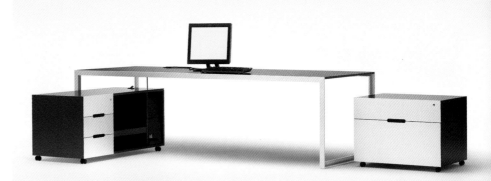

5

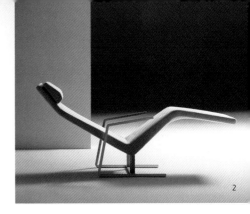

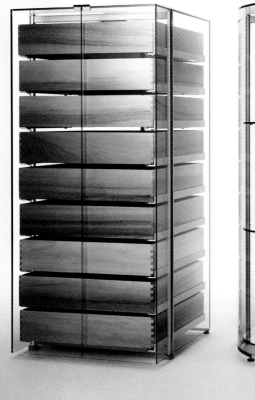

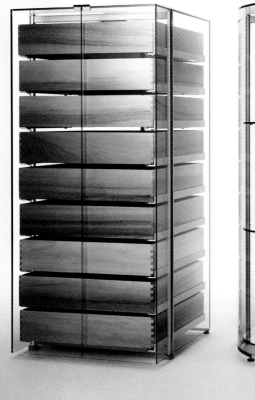

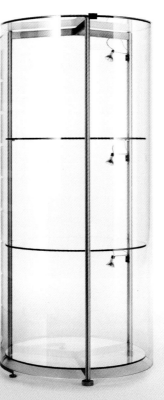

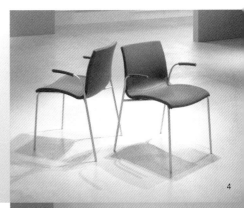

3

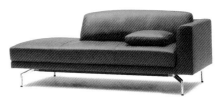

4

1

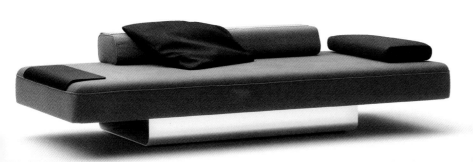

6

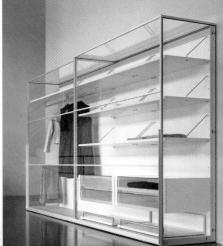

Hannes **Wettstein**

Switzerland | Interior, furniture and product designer | **www.zednetwork.com**

Hannes Wettstein initially attracted attention in the early 1980s, when he created the first low-voltage cable-track lighting systems for the lamp manufacturer **Belux**. His *Metro* lighting system was not only a commercial success for the company, but also kick-started the career of the young Swiss designer. In the following years Wettstein created numerous other designs for the ambitious and technologically innovative firm. Lamps and lighting systems remained his major focus. He also designed lamps for **Artemide** and in the 1990s worked as art director for **O Luce**.

Wettstein has also created a number of sophisticated and successful furniture designs, such as the comfortable *Capri* armchair, the *Ludwig* table and the delicate *Juliette* chair (all for ▶ **Baleri Italia**). For the Italian firm ▶ **Molteni & C** he designed elegant living-room furniture, including the *Alfa* and *Zeta* chairs and *Joseph*, a set of occasional tables. For the Belgian office furniture manufacturer ▶ **Bulo** he created the sophisticated *Double You* desk. The simple plastic storage box he developed for the Swiss firm Wogg is typical of Wettstein's conceptual approach. It has a sheet metal lid and can be used either as a mini-cupboard or to transport goods. The box appears almost spectacularly undesigned, but its surface has small indentations and ridges to aid stacking; several boxes can be stacked on top of each other to create an entire storage system without any additional mounts or support.

Wettstein also specializes in classic product design, including such everyday objects as pens for **Lamy**, watches for Ventura, glassware for Ritzenhoff and binoculars for Zeiss. A large number of his designs are distinctive for their tremendous intellectual rigour, often with ironic overtones. He is also much in demand as an interior designer. For the Hyatt hotel in Berlin and the Swiss embassy in Washington, DC, his studio created interiors that are both modern and lavishly sumptuous. Wettstein's projects are not predominantly about style, but rather about ways of living. He is convinced that objects can create or prevent opportunities; his own objects are definitely on the creative side.

1958 Born in Ascona
1982 Opens studio in Zurich (until 1988)
1991 Establishes Zed design network
1992 Becomes art director of **O Luce**
1993 Co-founds 9D Design in Zurich
1994 Teaches at Hochschule für Gestaltung, Karlsruhe
2000 Receives Good Design Award, Chicago, for *Scribble* pen and pencil
2002 Opens Zed studio in Zurich; works as design consultant for **Brionvega**

Products
1980 *Snodo* standard lamp and table lamp for **Belux**
1982 *Metro* low-voltage cable-track lighting system for Belux
1987 *Juliette* stackable chair
1989 *Ludwig* table
1991 *Capri* armchair
Last three for ▶ **Baleri Italia**
1992 *Intro* and *Soirée* lamps for O Luce
1995 *CYOS* lighting system for Belux
1996 *Duke* armchair for **Wittmann**; *Xen* bed system for **Cassina**; *Spy* lamp collection and *Antinoo* standard lamp for **Artemide**
1998 *Wogg 40* stackable container for Wogg
1999 *Minta* chair and *Thea* table for Cassina
2000 *Alfa*, *Delta*, *Zeta* chairs and *Sigma* chaise longue for ▶ **Molteni & C**; *Scribble* mechanical pencil and ballpoint pen for **Lamy**; *Globe* sofa, *Ariane* chair and *Units* shelf and container system for Cassina; *Allround* energy-saving standard lamp for ▶ **Belux**; *Master* furniture collection for ▶ **Arflex**
2002 Telescope for Zeiss; *Double You* desk for ▶ **Bulo**
2003 *Murphy* armchair for ▶ **Wittmann**; *Chillout* sofa for ▶ **Wellis**

1 *Alfa* chair, 2000
2 Telescope, 2002
3 *Scribble* mechanical pencil and ballpoint pen, 2000
4 *Sigma* chaise longue, 2000
5 *Wogg 40* container, 1998
6 *Metro* lighting system, 1982
7 *Globe* sofa, 2000
8 *CYOS* hanging lamp, 1995

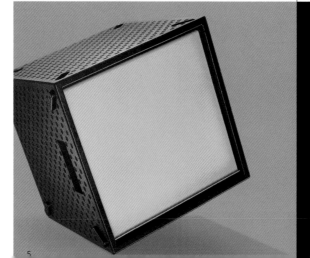

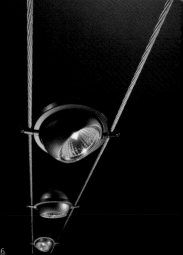

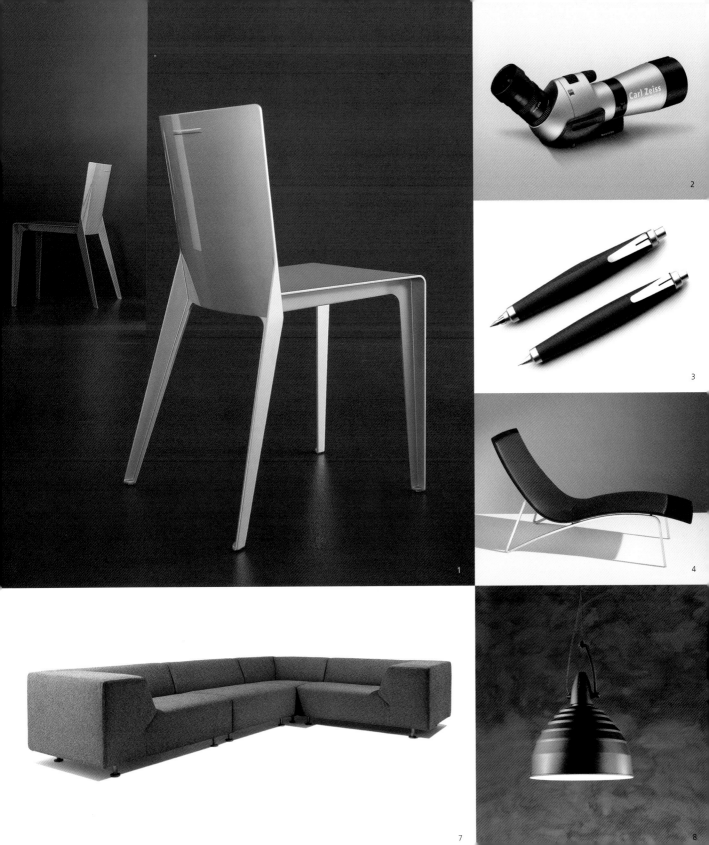

1

2

3

4

7

8

Wilkhahn

Germany I Wilkhahn Wilkening & Hahne GmbH & Co. KG, Bad Münder I Furniture manufacturer I **www.wilkhahn.com**

When the *FS* office chair was presented by Wilkhahn in the early 1980s, it caused quite a sensation. This swivel/rocking-chair hybrid had a highly flexible seat that adjusted automatically to the user's seating position. It was perfect from an ergonomic point of view and had the advantage of looking less like a machine than some of the products of Wilkhahn's competitors. The company started out in the early twentieth century in much the same way as the other one hundred or so other firms in the same area of northern Germany that were producing chairs using wood from the local beech forests. In the 1950s Wilkhahn began to focus on modern design and thus secured its economic survival. Salvation had come in the form of Fritz Hahne, the son of one of the firm's founders. An ambitious entrepreneur, Hahne sought to reposition the company by developing new products in close collaboration with the Hochschule für Gestaltung in Ulm. One of the designers of the *FS* chair, Klaus Franck, graduated from Ulm, as did Hans Roericht and Herbert Ohl, both of whom were committed to reinterpreting the hitherto neglected office chair.

One unusual design to have come from Wilkhahn is Roericht's *Stitz* stool, which – like **Stokke**'s designs in general – is intended to support our natural urge to be active. It encourages the user to change his or her posture, in the process stimulating the circulation and relieving physical strain. The Wiege studio, which emerged from Wilkhahn's own design department, has created the *Solis* chair, the backrest and seat of which adjust intuitively according to the movements and posture of the user. *Solis* consists of simple, geometric forms and homogeneous surfaces. Its moulded seat, back support, feet and frame all follow the design principles of simplicity and clarity. *Sito* is another Wiege creation, a very delicate and subtle reinterpretation of the classic cantilever chair.

With the *ConsulTable*, *InteracTable* and *InterWall*, Wilkhahn has introduced a completely new product segment: office furniture with integrated monitors. These products allow team members to share information on their computers more easily. Wilkhahn, like **Knoll**, **Lensvelt**, **Steelcase** and **Thonet**, is an upmarket supplier that has conquered the international market: anyone who flies from Hong Kong, Milan and Munich airports will appreciate its *Tubis* seating system.

518

1 *Solis* swivel chair, 2001
2 *Confair* desk, 1994
3 *Stitz* stool, 1991
4 *FS* office chair, 1980
5 *Picto* office chair, 1995
6 *Tubis* seating system, 1992
7 *Sito* cantilever chair, 2001

1907 Chair factory established by Friedrich Hahne and Christian Wilkening near Hanover
1946 Sons Fritz Hahne and Adolf Wilkening take over company
1965 Collaborates with Hochschule für Gestaltung, Ulm
1985 Wiege established as separate company, functions as design division
1988 Opens new production plant designed by Frei Otto
1993 Opens new production plant designed by Thomas Herzog
2004 Receives Bundespreis Produktdesign for *DinA* table collection

Products
1955 *224* chair by Georg Leowald
1957 *486* armchair by **Herbert Hirche**
1965 *120* bench system by Friso Kramer
1976 *190* swivel chair by Hans Roericht
1980 *FS* office chair by Klaus Franck and Werner Sauer
1982 *O-Line* seating series by Herbert Ohl
1991 *Stitz* stool by Hans Roericht
1992 *Tubis* seating system by Wiege
1994 *Modus* office chair by Klaus Franck and Werner Sauer; *Confair* desk by Wiege
1995 *Picto* office chair by Wiege
1996 *Logon* table system by Andreas Störiko
1998 *Senzo* chair by Thomas Starczewski; *Nuvola* armchair by Jutta and Herbert Ohl; *Avera* furniture system by Wiege
2000 *Timetable* table by Andreas Störiko
2001 *Solis* swivel chair and *Sito* cantilever chair by Wiege
2002 *DinA* table collection by Udo Schill and Timo Küchler
2005 *Neos* office chair by Wiege

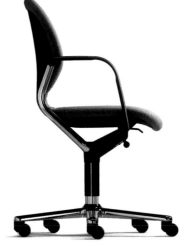

4

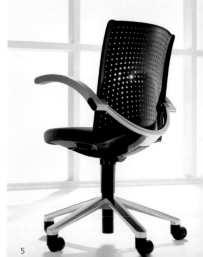

5

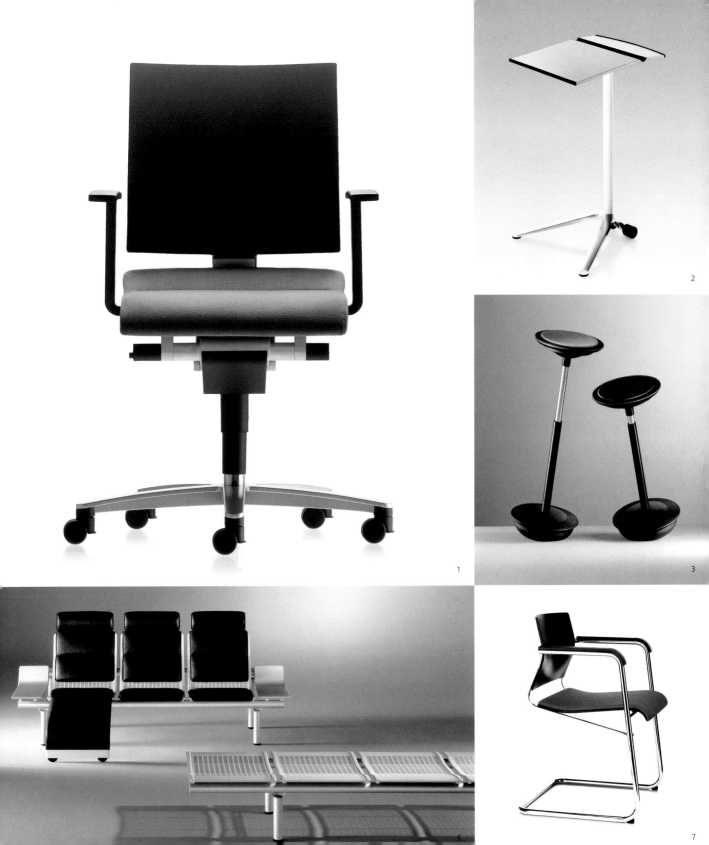

1

2

3

6

7

Tapio **Wirkkala**

Finland | Glass and product designer | www.scandinaviandesign.com/tapioWirkkala

Tapio Wirkkala was one of the most productive Finnish designers of the post-war period. He was also a national symbol, not only because he used the traditional methods and materials of Finnish craftsmen, but also because he represented Finland's recovery following the hardships of the Second World War. Wirkkala created a number of knives, among them *Puukko*. The Finnish word refers to a knife that is worn on the belt (the designer himself was a skilled user); it has been a symbol of freedom from time immemorial. The Italian designer **Gio Ponti** called his friend Wirkkala a "noble savage" who came straight from the woods, but in reality he grew up in Helsinki and was as much an intellectual as Ponti. Wirkkala studied sculpture at the Central School of Arts and Crafts in Helsinki and later became its director.

It was not until he won joint first prize (with **Kaj Franck**) in a competition organized by **Iittala** in 1946 that Wirkkala became a glass designer. He was taken on by the company after receiving the prize. Wirkkala did not follow the strictly functional tradition of **Alvar Aalto**, but defined himself – like **Timo Sarpaneva** – as an expressive artist–designer. He achieved international fame with his mushroom-shaped *Kantarelli* vase, which he created by cutting decorative lines into the paper-thin glass. The organic form of this vase turned it into an erotic object.

Natural materials used in an unusual way were typical of Wirkkala's approach. An example is plywood, from which he fashioned sculptures. "He composes his own wood", wrote the American critic Edgar Kaufmann. Wirkkala's graceful, finely veined plywood bowl from the early 1950s, with a leaf shape that became something of an emblem for Scandinavian design, was justly famous; the influential American magazine *House Beautiful* selected it as the "most beautiful object of the year" in 1951. In the same year the young Finn won three major awards at the Milan Triennale and designed the Finnish Pavilion. Later Wirkkala also worked for **Rosenthal**, the German company for which he designed ceramics, dinnerware and a number of cutlery services. In addition, he created designs for the **Venini** glass company.

1 *Kurve* cutlery, 1972

2 *Composition* service, 1963

3 *Gaissa* glasses, 1972

4 *Ultima Thule* glass series, 1968

5 *Kantarelli* vase, 1946

6 Plywood bowl, 1951

7 *Bolla* bottle collection, 1966

8 *Tapio* glasses, 1952

9 *Puukko* knife, 1961

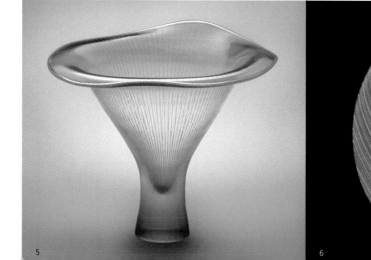

5

6

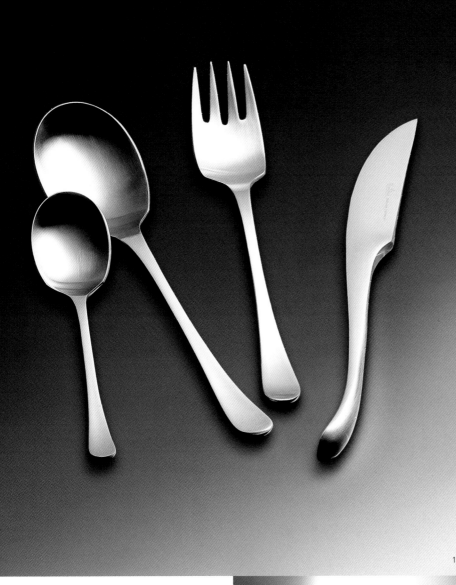

1

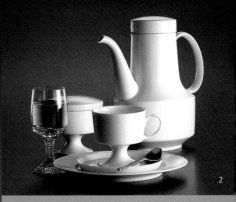

2

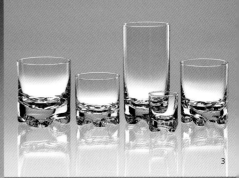

3

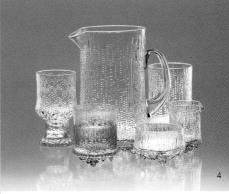

4

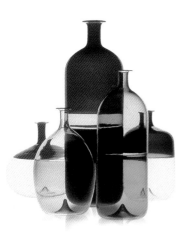

7

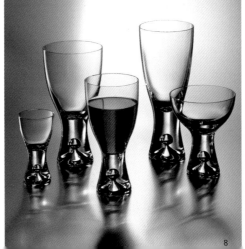

8

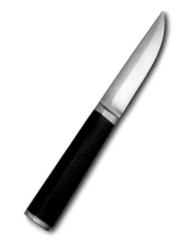

9

Wittmann

Austria | Franz Wittmann Möbelwerkstätten GmbH, Etsdorf am Kamp | Furniture manufacturer | **www.wittmann.at**

Two product lines define the Wittmann programme: contemporary furniture for the home and the office, and re-editions of Modernist design classics. Like such manufacturers as **Cassina**, **ClassiCon**, **Knoll** and **Källemo**, the Austrian company has a twofold strategy. Its programme of re-editions is determined largely by designs by ▸ **Josef Hoffmann**. Hoffmann was one of the leading figures of Modernism, but by the end of the Second World War his work had largely faded into obscurity. Wittmann has carefully reconstructed a large number of his designs. The Hoffmann Collection ranges from innovative nests of tables, the famous *Sitzmaschine* (Sitting machine) and the *Kunstschau 1908* bentwood armchair (which Hoffmann's friend **Charles Rennie Mackintosh** greatly admired) to the *Kubus* upholstered furniture series, from which such colleagues as **Walter Gropius** drew inspiration. The *Correalistic* furniture by Friedrich Kiesler – an Austrian who emigrated to the United States and pioneered organic design as early as the 1930s – also consists of highly interesting historic pieces. Among the contemporary designers who collaborate with Wittmann today are Jan Armgardt from Germany and Paolo Piva from Italy. One of the company's most striking designs is the *Murphy* easy chair by the Swiss designer **Hannes Wettstein**, which takes the form of a floating 'C' that cups the sitter as if in the palm of a hand.

1 *Kunstschau 1908* armchair, 1905 (re-edition 1972)

2 *Murphy* easy chair, 2003

3 *Correalistic* instrument and rocker, 1942

4 *Carré* armchair, 2002

5 *Hop* armchair, 1988

522

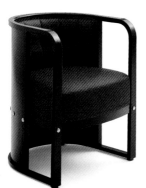

1

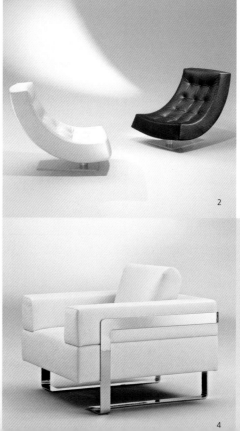

2

3

4

5

WMF

Germany | Württembergische Metallwarenfabrik AG, Geislingen an der Steige | Tableware manufacturer | **www.wmf.de**

In the 1920s the Württembergische Metallwarenfabrik (WMF) secured from Krupp the exclusive rights to use V2-A stainless steel, better known as Cromargan, for household goods. WMF became the first company to offer a range of Cromargan cookware and, later, Cromargan cutlery. After the Second World War, as WMF had hoped, there was a boom in the demand for stainless steel items. The designer ▶ **Wilhelm Wagenfeld** in particular is associated with this development. His products – which included salt and pepper shakers and egg cups – blended functionality with the distinctive 1950s style. By contrast, his *Form 3600* cutlery had a clear, angular shape. The unusually short blade of the knives in the series was especially striking. During the 1960s and 1970s WMF produced rather uninspiring products; it took until the mid-1980s for the company to rediscover the value of original design. Such well-known international designers as **Matteo Thun** and Dieter **Sieger**, as well as the fashion designer Pierre Cardin and the Danish product designer Ole Palsby (who designed no fewer than six sets of cutlery) contributed to the revamped collection. Today the WMF range includes glasses, candlesticks, ladles, cooking pots and gift items. WMF continues to collaborate with renowned designers, including **James Irvine**, who created the *Lounge* bar accessories, and **Sebastian Bergne**, who designed the *Kult* table accessories.

1853 Metallwarenfabrik Straub & Schweizer established

1880 Merges with Ritter to form Württembergische Metallwarenfabrik (WMF)

1924 Acquires licence for V2-A stainless steel, patented as Cromargan

1987 Acquires **Alfi** Zitzmann company

1989 Buys share in Hutschenreuther porcelain factory

Products

1927 Cromargan cookware

1932 Cromargan cutlery

1952 *Max und Moritz* salt and pepper shakers and *Form 3600* cutlery by ▶ **Wilhelm Wagenfeld**

1985 *Modern Classic No. 1* thermos jug by Ole Palsby

1992 *Cafemat* coffee machine by **Sieger Design**

1994 *Grand Gourmet* kitchen knives by Makio Hasuike

1998 *Candy* cutlery by **Matteo Thun**

1999 *Kult* table accessories by **Sebastian Bergne**

2002 *Lounge* bar accessories and *Il Meglio* kitchen utensils by ▶ **James Irvine**

2003 *Lyric* cutlery by Köhler & Wilms

2004 *Bar Basso* glass series

1 *Lounge* bar accessories, 2002

2 *Bar Basso* glass series, 2004

3 *Kult* table accessories, 1999

4 *Lyric* cutlery, 2003

5 *Grand Gourmet* kitchen knife, 1994

523

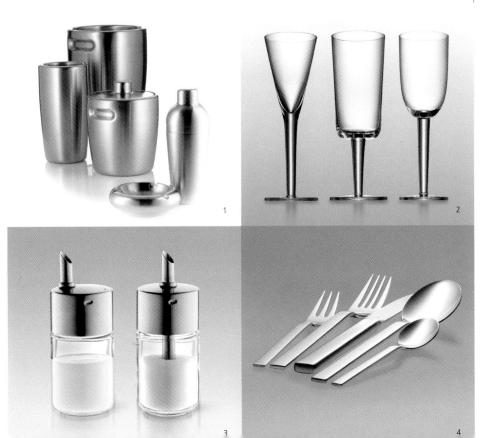

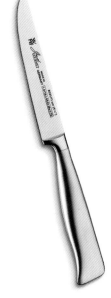

Frank Lloyd **Wright**

USA I Architect and furniture designer I **www.franklloydwright.org**

Frank Lloyd Wright was indisputably one of the most important American architects of the twentieth century. His work was characterized by its unity and coherence, and by the fact that even the smallest detail fell perfectly into place. Whenever possible, his furniture was integrated into his designs for buildings, and he sometimes commissioned small suppliers to produce free-standing pieces. Wright was always keen to retain complete control of his projects. Distinguished by its simplicity and the use of basic geometric forms, his furniture was in keeping with the machine aesthetic of the times, even though very few pieces were actually mass-produced.

Wright was groomed to be an architect from an early age. In the late 1880s, after having completed his studies, he joined the architectural office of Louis Sullivan in Chicago. He established his own practice in 1893. Many of Wright's furniture designs were created after the turn of the century, when he built a number of private houses, among them his own house, Taliesin, in Wisconsin. In the *Robie* sofa Wright extended the armrests to form practical surfaces. The *Midway* chair (re-edition at **Cassina**), a wire construction based on circles and triangles, softened the industrial effect of tubular steel. Wright's Imperial Hotel in Tokyo, completed in the early 1920s, was a total work of art that was full of his furniture, lamps, tableware and carpets. The hotel chairs were a skilful combination of squares, triangles and hexagons, a geometric repertoire that recurred in many of his other designs.

One of Wright's best-known projects was the range of office furniture he developed in the mid-1930s for the Johnson Wax Administration Building in Racine, Wisconsin. The range was among the first to be consciously tailored to fit the requirements of white-collar workers. The *Johnson Wax* chair, with castors and armrests to support the forearms, was greatly appreciated by shorthand typists. The accompanying desk had freely accessible storage and surfaces suspended one above the other; its aluminium frame was painted a warm shade of red that harmonized with the colour of the walnut. Although Wright was famed for his architecture, his work as a designer was relatively unknown until just before his death in the late 1950s, when he was 'discovered' by the magazine *House Beautiful*.

524

1 *Johnson Wax 2* desk chair, 1936
2 *Peacock* chair (Imperial Hotel), 1921
3 *Midway 2* chair, 1914
4 *Robie 3* sofa, 1906
5 *Johnson Wax 1* desk, 1936
6 *Lewis* coffee table, 1939

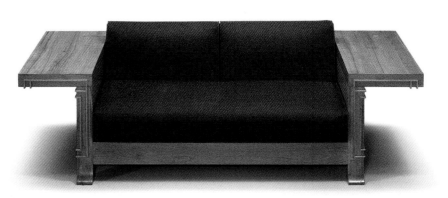

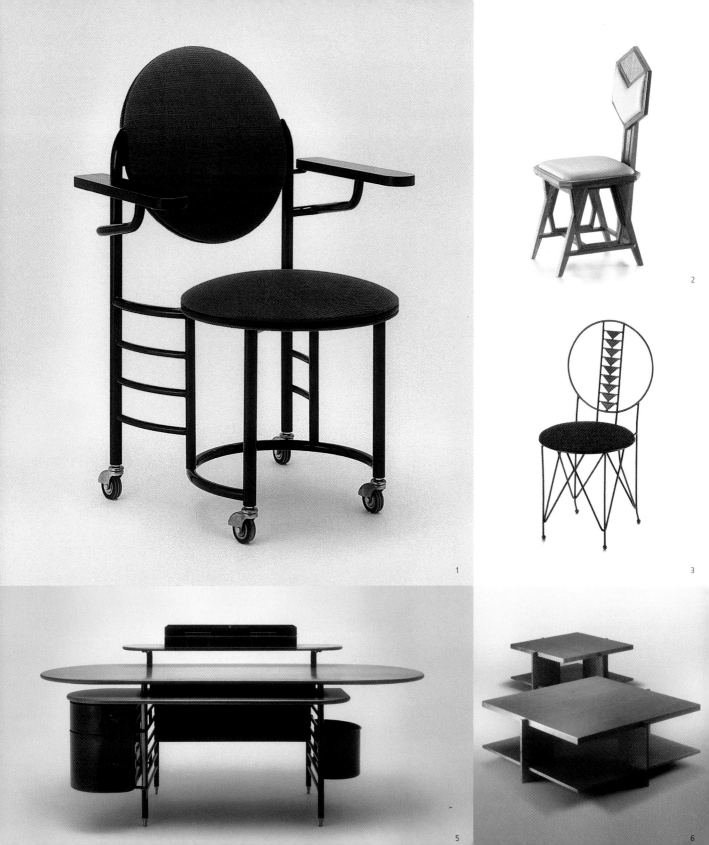

1

2

3

5

6

YZ

Yamaha, *YZF R-1* motorbike, 1997 (2002 model)

This 180-bhp racing bike attempts to contain a lot of power in a small frame. Oblique angles and complex surfaces predominate, creating a kind of futuristic geometry. Construction elements such as the tank, saddle and casing can be recognized as individual elements and form a jigsaw puzzle of overlapping edges.

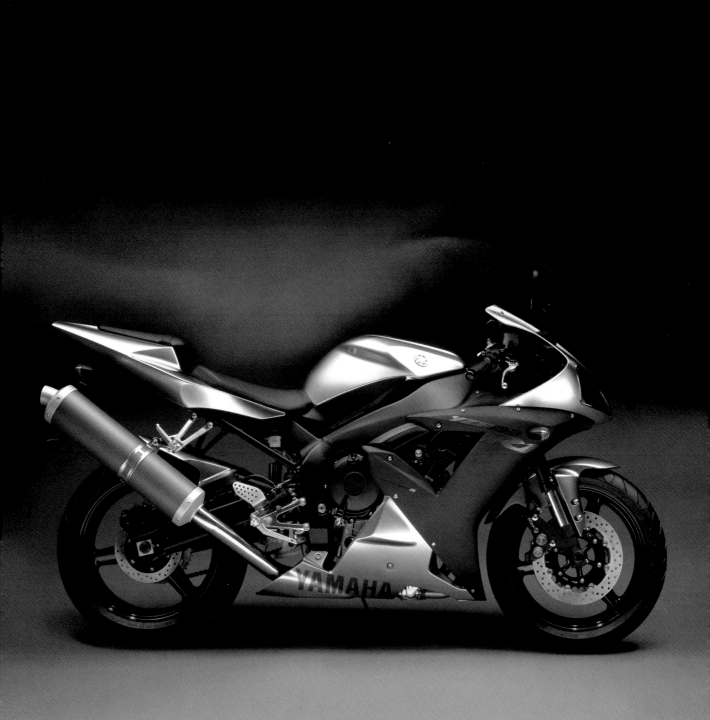

Yamaha

Japan I Yamaha Corporation, Hamamatsu I Manufacturer of musical instruments and motorbikes I **www.yamaha.com**

The history of Yamaha, one of the biggest consumer electronics and automotive companies of the modern age, begins with a single musical instrument. In 1887 Torakusa Yamaha built his first reed organ. Ten years later, the Nippon Gakki Company was founded, with Yamaha as president, and started exporting organs. In the years that followed, the company made a name for itself manufacturing a range of musical instruments. In the mid-1950s, as a result of its expertise in metallurgical technologies, it diversified into motorcycle production. The success of *YA-1*, its first motorbike, led to the establishment of the Yamaha Motor Company, which focused initially on the development of low-powered recreational vehicles.

As well as motorcycles, the Yamaha Motor Company has developed motor scooters, snowmobiles, golf carts, powerboats and industrial machinery. Typical of Yamaha motorbikes and scooters – whether the ergonomically sophisticated *Morpho II* concept from the early 1990s or the *YZF* model range designed by **GK Design** – is a dynamism reminiscent of **Ducati**, both visually and in terms of performance. The company favours a bold use of metal and racy lines in its designs.

The creation of the separate motor company did not mean that Yamaha's other product ranges stagnated. Since the 1950s Yamaha has focused increasingly on product development in the fields of leisure and entertainment. It has successfully produced equipment for such diverse sports as archery and skiing. It has also expanded its range of musical instruments. The *Silent* string instrument series (electrical string instruments that do not require a resonance chamber) won the prestigious Industrial Design Excellence Award (IDEA) in 2000. Although the *Silent* series retains the traditional colour scheme of wood instruments, the skeleton-like structure of these products is highly unconventional and can take some getting used to. The sheer immateriality of these instruments is nevertheless fascinating – and of course the highly restrained design also makes them easy to transport.

528

1 *Silent Bass* double bass and *Silent Violin*, 1997

2 *TC 800* cassette recorder, 1975

3 *DSP-Z9* home cinema system, 2003

4 *DPX-1100* video projector, 2004

5 *RX-1* snowmobile, 2003

6 *XP 500* scooter, 2002

7 V-Max motorbike, 1985

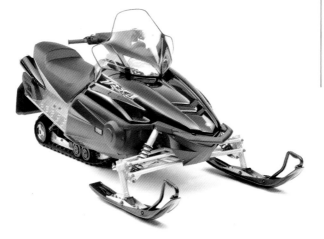

1887	Torakusu Yamaha builds his first reed organ
1897	Nippon Gakki Company established, with Yamaha as president
1900	Begins producing upright pianos
1914	Begins producing harmonicas and exports them worldwide
1922	Begins producing gramophones
1955	Establishes Yamaha Motor Company
1965	Begins producing wind instruments
1968	Begins producing hi-fi stereo equipment
1975	Begins producing tennis rackets
1976	Adds electronic pianos to range
1989	Introduces world's first CD recorder

Products

1942	Acoustic guitar
1954	Hi-fi player; *YA-1* motorcycle
1959	*Electone* electronic organ
1967	*CF* concert grand piano
1968	*Enduro DT-1* off-road motorbike; *ST 350* snowmobile
1970	*XS-1* motorbike
1971	*ST 433* snowmobile
1974	*CSY-1* synthesizer
1975	*TC 800* cassette recorder by **Mario Bellini**
1978	*SR 500* and *XS 1100* motorbikes
1979	*RD 250/400* two-stroke motorbike
1980	*Trimoto YT125* off-road car
1981	*Virago 750* motorbike
1982	Carbon-composite golf clubs; *CD-1* CD player
1985	*V-Max* motorbike by **GK Design**
1987	*WaveRunner* and *WaveJammer* jet skis
1993	Golf clubs in titanium
1997	*Silent* string instrument series; *SRX 700S* snowmobile; *YZF R-1* (▶ p. 527) and *YZ 400 F* motorbikes; *Grizzly* off-roader by ▶ GK Design
2002	*YZF 600R* motorbike; *XP 500* scooter; *FX 140 WaveRunner* jet ski
2003	*DSP-Z9* home cinema system; *BT1100* motorbike; *RX-1* snowmobile
2004	*MT* motorbike (concept); *DPX-1100* video projector

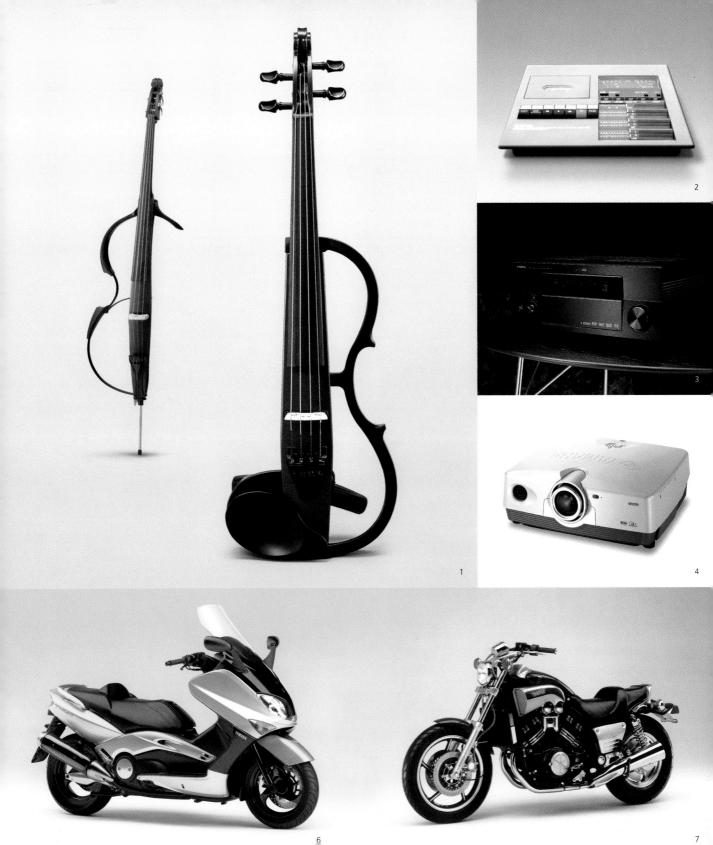

1

2

3

4

6

7

Sori **Yanagi**

Japan | Furniture and product designer | **www.japon.net/yanagi**

The *Butterfly* stool from the 1950s is Sori Yanagi's best-known design and can be regarded as Japan's response to post-war functionalism, with its essential requirement of 'good design'. Yanagi, an architect and immensely influential pioneer of product design in his home country, was a co-founder of the Japan Industrial Designers Association in 1952 and in the 1970s became director of the Japan Folk Crafts Museum. He had always been drawn to the idea of combining old and new in his work, and established the Japanese design tradition of developing a creative dialogue between East and West. This approach is evident in his choice of materials: bamboo, wood and ceramics are combined with plastic, aluminium and steel. The *Butterfly* stool unites a traditional form with plywood, a modern material. In the mid-1950s such a chair would have been quite a novelty in Japan. Yanagi, who had worked as an assistant to Charlotte Perriand when she lived in Japan during the early 1940s, was extremely versatile and innovative. In addition to chairs and tableware, he designed electrical appliances and tractors. He also designed the torches for the 1964 Olympic Summer Games in Tokyo and the 1972 Olympic Winter Games in Sapporo. He viewed these commissions as a great patriotic honour.

1915 Born in Tokyo

1940 Graduates in painting from Tokyo University of Fine Arts and Music; works in office of architect Junzo Sakakura

1942 Collaborates with Charlotte Perriand in design consultancy for Japanese companies

1947 Studies industrial design

1952 Opens own design studio in Tokyo; co-founds Japan Industrial Designers Association

1957 Receives gold medal at Milan Triennale for *Butterfly* stool

1964 Torch for Olympic Summer Games in Tokyo

1972 Torch for Olympic Winter Games in Sapporo

1977 Appointed director of Japan Folk Crafts Museum, Tokyo

1981 Receives Medal of Honour for services to Japanese culture

Products

1952 Record player with radio for Nihon-Columbia

1953 Kettle for Nikkei Aluminium

1954 *Elephant* plastic stackable stool for Kotobuki; *Butterfly* stool for Tendo Mokko

1956 Teapot and soy sauce bottle for Tajimi Porcelain Institute

1958 Watering can for Uehan Shoji; teapot for Kyoto Gojazaka Kiln

1974 *1250* cutlery for Sato Shoji

1 *Butterfly* stool, 1954
2 Kettle, 1953
3 *1250* cutlery, 1974
4 *Elephant* plastic stackable stool, 1954

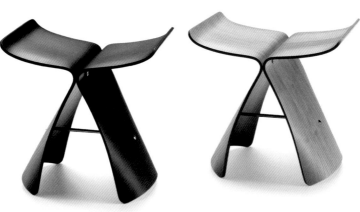

1

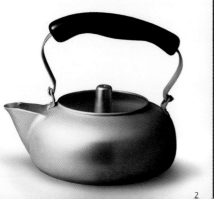

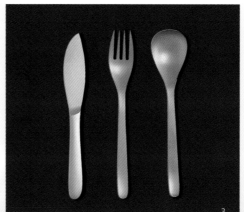

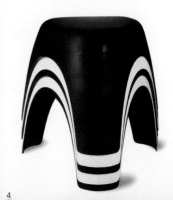

2   3   4

Tokujin **Yoshioka**

Japan | Architect and furniture and product designer | www.tokujin.com

Tokujin Yoshioka has mastered the design of folds and lines as expertly as his teacher, the fashion designer Issey Miyake. Yoshioka epitomizes all the positive qualities that for decades have been associated with Japanese design. One of his great talents is to create an ambience infused with poetic and transcendental overtones. His skilful combination of traditional craftsmanship, modern materials and innovative techniques is further proof of his ingenuity.

After graduating from the Kuwasawa Design Institute in Tokyo in the mid-1980s, Yoshioka worked as an apprentice to **Shiro Kuramata**, the designer of bold and striking furniture. This period had a tremendous influence on Yoshioka's career and his work, as is evident in his playful treatment of transparency, which characterizes much of his interior design. Another important feature of Yoshioka's work is his ingenious use of lighting: his *ToFu* table lamp, for example, establishes the light, rather than the object itself, as the focus of attention. Such designs as the poetic *Honey Pop* paper armchair and, above all, the *Tokyo Pop* seating range, which includes a boldly curved chaise longue vaguely reminiscent of **Ray Eames**'s *La Chaise* (▶ p. 147), confirm that Yoshioka is among the most interesting designers of his generation.

1967 Born in Japan

1986 Graduates from Kuwasawa Design Institute, Tokyo

1987 Works in office of **Shiro Kuramata** (until 1988)

1988 Works for Issey Miyake, in charge of shop design

1992 Works as freelance designer

2000 Establishes Tokujin Yoshioka Design, Tokyo

2001 Receives A&W Award, Coming Designer of the Future

Products

2000 *ToFu* table lamp for Yamagiwa; *Honey Pop* folding paper armchair

2002 *Tokyo Pop* chaise longue for **Driade**

2003 *Nami* table collection; *Sen* and *En* tables and *Tokyo Pop* and *Tokyo Soft* furniture collections for ▶ Driade

1 *Tokyo Soft* armchair, 2003
2 *Tokyo Pop* chaise longue, 2002
3 *En* table, 2003
4 *Tokyo Pop* stool and table, 2003
5 *Nami* table, 2003

531

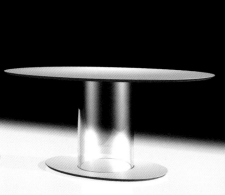

1

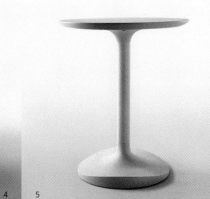

2

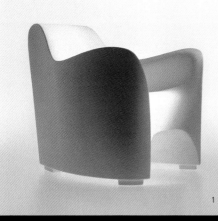

3

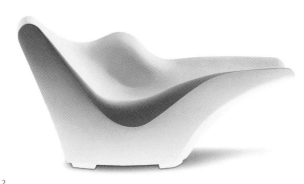

4   5

Michael **Young**

England I Furniture and product designer I www.michael-young.com

There are few areas in which the British designer Michael Young has not been active. His designs include a dog kennel and a series of garden furniture, the vivid colour scheme and naïve forms of which are reminiscent of illustrations in children's books. Humour always plays an important role in Young's designs, as in the computer game in which he combines baseball and a traditional Icelandic ball game. When he relocated his studio from trendy London to remote Reykjavik in the late 1990s, it caused quite a stir in the design world – but Young has always enjoyed creating a sensation.

Even before graduating from Kingston University, Young found himself a job in the early 1990s in **Tom Dixon**'s studio; he also secured a manufacturer – the Japanese company E&Y – for *Magazine*, his first furniture series. This series was bulkier than his later designs for the prestigious Italian companies **Cappellini** and **Sawaya & Moroni**. His style became noticably more restrained, with more flowing lines, as evident in his *Sticklight* lamp from the late 1990s. In recent years Young has opened an office in Brussels and designed a store for **Mandarina Duck** in Berlin.

1 Dog kennel, 2001
2 Wine cooler, 1999
3 *Sticklight* lamp, 1999
4 *Smartie* seat, 1998
5 *Flatlight* table lamp, 2002

532

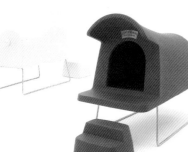

1

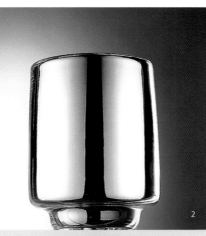

2

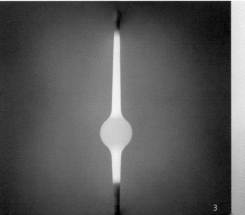

3

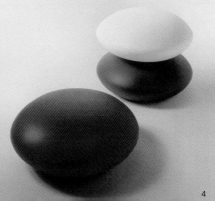

4

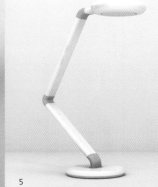

5

Zani & Zani

Italy I Zani industria dell'acciaio SpA, Toscolano I Kitchenware manufacturer

Zani & Zani is a typical example of a small, traditional Italian firm that specializes in the production of high-quality household goods. A number of renowned designers have worked for the company, among them Lino Sabattini and **Bruno Munari**, who contributed an ice bucket made from aluminium and fibreglass.

The company was founded in the 1920s and initially made hunting accessories. Today Franco and Luigi Zani manufacture cutlery, pots and pans and kitchen utensils from stainless steel and aluminium. A few years ago they introduced high-quality textiles (such as tablecloths, aprons and dressing gowns made from natural materials) into the range, as well as PVC vases designed by Claudio La Viola. A large proportion of the product range has been designed by **Enzo Mari**, who appreciates the fact that the company's experience and technical expertise allow him to produce even the most complex designs. Among his contributions is the versatile *Smith e Smith* range of kitchen utensils, the individual items of which, such as chopping knives and graters, can be hung from a rail. Mari's *Piuma* cutlery has holes punched in the handles, enabling each item to be hung on a stand.

533

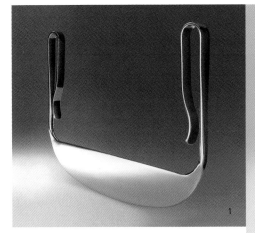

3

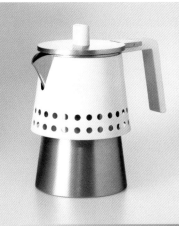

2

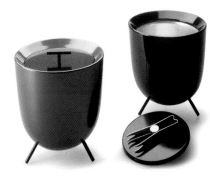

1

Zanotta

Italy | Zanotta SpA, Nova Milanese | Furniture manufacturer | **www.zanotta.it**

The architect Emilio Ambasz stated that it would be impossible to write a history of Italian design without referring to the work produced by Zanotta. The company has a rich history of brilliant designs that have turned the rules of the traditional home decoration upside down. Its products are often both ironic and innovative, as in, for example, *Mezzadro*, a recycled tractor seat; *Sacco*, the amorphous beanbag seat; the inflatable *Blow* armchair and the *Sciangai* coat stand, which is reminiscent of giant Mikado sticks. Aurelio Zanotta, the company's founder, discovered avant-garde design in London in the 1960s, and ever since that time, the company has valued products that reflect the character of each designer. When Zanotta saw the prototype of an unusual, frameless armchair by Willie Landels, he decided spontaneously to have it produced under the name of *Throw Away*. This marked the beginning of a corporate policy that has led to the production of a large number of unconventional objects. Many renowned designers have worked for the company, among them Pier Giacomo and **Achille Castiglioni, Ettore Sottsass, Joe Colombo, Marco Zanuso, Enzo Mari, Alessandro Mendini** and Gae Aulenti.

Zanotta has always been prepared to take risks. In the late 1960s, for example, the company was courageous enough to produce the *Sacco* beanbag seat by Piero Gatti, Cesare Paolini and Franco Teodoro, which redefined the act of sitting. ▸ Achille Castiglioni contributed a number of playfully elegant designs to the range, including the *Cumano* bistro table from the late 1970s, which can be folded flat and hung on the wall as decoration. Among the younger generation of designers who have collaborated with Zanotta are the German **Werner Aisslinger**, who used innovative materials to create his gel furniture, the British designer ▸ **Ross Lovegrove**, who created the expressive *Brasilia* easy chair, coated with a scratch-proof lacquer varnish, and the Swiss designer **Alfredo Häberli**, who designed elegant upholstered office swivel chairs. Zanotta also focuses on the reproduction of classic designs, including tubular steel furniture from the 1930s by Giuseppe Terragni, Gino Levi Montalcini, Giuseppe Pagano and Gabriele Mucchi, the *Ulm Stool* from the 1950s by the Swiss architect ▸ **Max Bill** (with **Hans Gugelot** and Paul Hilbinger) and some of **Carlo Mollino**'s plywood designs.

534

1 *Sacco* beanbag seat, 1968
2 *Poker* table, 1968
3 *Servento* screen, 1986
4 *Throw Away* armchair, 1965
5 *Mezzadro* stool, 1970 (1957 design)
6 *Chair for Very Brief Visits*, 1991 (1945 design)
7 *Ambo* table, 1987
8 *Sciangai* coat stand, 1973
9 *Soft* chaise longue, 2000

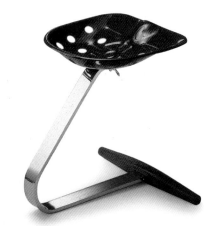

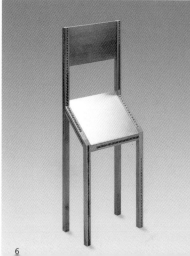

5

6